NOBEL LECTURES

ECONOMIC SCIENCES

2001–2005

Nobel Lectures

Including Presentation Speeches and Laureates' Biographies

Physics

Chemistry

Physiology or Medicine

Literature

Peace

Economic Sciences

NOBEL LECTURES

INCLUDING PRESENTATION SPEECHES AND LAUREATES' BIOGRAPHIES

ECONOMIC SCIENCES

2001–2005

EDITOR

Peter Englund

Department of Finance
Stockholm School of Economics

World Scientific

NEW JERSEY • LONDON • SINGAPORE • BEIJING • SHANGHAI • HONG KONG • TAIPEI • CHENNAI

Published by

World Scientific Publishing Co. Pte. Ltd.
5 Toh Tuck Link, Singapore 596224
USA office: 27 Warren Street, Suite 401-402, Hackensack, NJ 07601
UK office: 57 Shelton Street, Covent Garden, London WC2H 9HE

NOBEL LECTURES IN ECONOMIC SCIENCES (2001–2005)

Published with permission from Nobel Media AB in 2008 by World Scientific Publishing Co. Pte. Ltd.

ISBN-13 978-981-279-438-3
ISBN-10 981-279-438-7
ISBN-13 978-981-279-439-0 (pbk)
ISBN-10 981-279-439-5 (pbk)

Printed in Singapore by Mainland Press Pte Ltd

PRIZE IN ECONOMIC SCIENCES IN MEMORY OF ALFRED NOBEL

Sveriges Riksbank (Central Bank of Sweden) at their tercentenary in 1968 instituted an Alfred Nobel Memorial Prize in Economic Sciences and placed an annual amount at the disposal of the Nobel Foundation as basis for a prize to be awarded by the Royal Swedish Academy of Sciences. Nobel Prize rules will, mutatis mutandis, be followed regarding nomination of candidates, prize adjudication, prize award and prize presentation. The latter takes place on Nobel Day, December 10, each year. The prize amount will equal that of a Nobel Prize for the same year. Special Statutes and Regulations (valid from January 1, 1969) have been issued for this Alfred Nobel Memorial Prize in Economic Sciences.

FOREWORD

Since 1901 the Nobel Foundation has published annually *Les Prix Nobel* with reports from the Nobel award ceremonies in Stockholm and Oslo as well as the biographies and Nobel lectures of the Nobel laureates. In order to make the lectures available for people with special interests in the different fields the Nobel Foundation gave Elsevier Publishing Company the right to publish in English the lectures for 1901–1970, which were published in 1964–1972 through the following volumes:

Physics 1901–1970	4 vols.
Chemistry 1901–1970	4 vols.
Physiology or Medicine 1901–1970	4 vols.
Literature 1901–1967	1 vol.
Peace 1901–1970	3 vols.

Thereafter, and until the year 2000, the Nobel Foundation has given World Scientific Publishing Company the right to bring the series up to date and also publish the Prize Lectures in Economics from the year 1969. Between the years 2001–2005, the Nobel Foundation has given World Scientific Publishing Company a publishing right through an agreement between Nobel Media AB and World Scientific Publishing Company.

The Nobel Foundation is very pleased that the intellectual and spiritual message to the world laid down in the laureates' lectures, thanks to the efforts of World Scientific, will reach new readers all over the world.

Michael Sohlman
Executive Director
Stockholm, April 2008

PREFACE

According to the statutes, "The Sveriges Riksbank Prize in Economic Sciences in Memory of Alfred Nobel" is awarded according to the same principles as the Nobel Prizes in Physics and Chemistry. Thus, the Royal Swedish Academy of Sciences is responsible for the entire process in selecting the laureates.

In December of each year, in the days prior to the Prize Award ceremony in Stockholm, the laureates give special *lectures* presenting their work and reflecting on their contributions. At the award ceremony, a member of the Prize Committee gives a brief *presentation speech*, summarizing, in a popular fashion, the prize-winning contribution. This volume collects, for the years 2001–2005, these lectures and presentation speeches along with the laureates own *autobiographies*. Earlier volumes have covered the years 1969–1980, 1981–1990, 1991–1995, and 1996–2000, respectively.

George Akerlof, Michael Spence and Joseph Stiglitz were awarded the 2001 prize "for their analyses of markets with asymmetric information". They had developed theories for markets, where actors on one side of the market are better informed than other actors. Borrowers, as an example, know more than lenders about their repayment prospects, and managers often know more than shareholders about the firm's profitability. Applications of the laureates' theories have been abundant, ranging from traditional agricultural markets to modern financial markets.

In 2002 the prize was shared between two researchers: Daniel Kahneman "for having integrated insights from psychological research into economic science, especially concerning human judgment and decision-making under uncertainty" and Vernon Smith "for having established laboratory experiments as a tool in empirical economic analysis, especially in the study of alternative market mechanisms". They have pioneered rapidly growing research areas devoted to modifying and testing basic economic assumptions about human behavior. Kahneman's work (in collaboration with the late Amos Tversky) has inspired a new generation of researchers in economics and finance to enrich economic theory using insights from cognitive psychology. Smith has been instrumental in establishing experiments as an essential tool in empirical economic analysis.

The 2003 prize recognized two scholars for the development of new methods of analyzing economic time series: Robert Engle "for methods of analyzing economic time series with time-varying volatility (ARCH)" and Clive Granger "for methods of analyzing economic time series with common trends (cointegration)". Engle's ARCH models have become indispensable tools not only for researchers, but also for analysts on financial markets, who use them in asset pricing and in evaluating portfolio risk. Granger has developed methods that allow researchers to better analyze data that, like GDP and other macroeconomic time series, follow a stochastic trend, so that temporary disturbances have long-lasting effects.

In 2004, Finn Kydland and Edward Prescott were honored "for their contributions to dynamic macroeconomics: the time consistency of economic policy and the driving forces behind business cycles". Their work has helped us to better understand the driving forces behind business cycle fluctuations and the design of economic policy, both key areas in macroeconomic research. Their contributions are of great significance for macroeconomic theory, but have also affected the practice of monetary and fiscal policy in many countries.

Robert Aumann and Thomas Schelling received the 2005 prize "for having enhanced our understanding of conflict and cooperation through game-theory analysis". Their work has established game theory — or interactive decision theory — as the dominant approach to the age-old questions of conflict and cooperation. Schelling's analysis of strategic commitments has explained a wide range of phenomena, from the competitive strategies of firms to the delegation of political decision power. Aumann has analyzed how cooperation may be easier to sustain in a long-term relationship than in a single encounter.

Peter Englund

CONTENTS

Economic Sciences 2001

GEORGE A. AKERLOF, A. MICHAEL SPENCE and JOSEPH E. STIGLITZ

"for their analyses of markets with asymmetric information"

THE SVERIGES RIKSBANK (BANK OF SWEDEN) PRIZE IN ECONOMIC SCIENCES IN MEMORY OF ALFRED NOBEL

Speech by Professor Jörgen W. Weibull of the Royal Swedish Academy of Sciences.
Translation of the Swedish text.

Your Majesties, Your Royal Highnesses, Honoured Nobel Laureates, Ladies and Gentlemen,

A well-functioning economy is of utmost importance for society, not only for the material well-being of its citizens, but also for the social and cultural development of society as a whole. Economists strive to improve our understanding of how economies work in the hope of helping society find ways to improve the human condition.

A key ingredient for the effective functioning of an economy is information. Economic agents, such as firms and households, need a great deal of information about available goods, services and trading possibilities. This year's Laureates analyzed problems that may arise in markets where information is asymmetric, that is, where sellers know something buyers don't, or *vice versa.*

Asymmetric information is a common feature of market interactions. The seller of a good often knows more about its quality than the prospective buyer does. The job applicant will typically know more about his own ability than the potential employer does. The buyer of an insurance policy usually knows more about her individual risk than the insurance company does. What happens to prices and traded quantities if agents on one side of the market are better informed than those on the other? What can better-informed agents do to improve their individual market outcome? What can less informed agents do?

This year's Laureates addressed precisely these questions. The methods of analysis they suggested have become indispensable instruments in the economist's toolbox, being nowadays taught in universities all over the world. Applications abound, and range from traditional agricultural markets to modern financial markets. Questions as diverse as the following can, and have been, analyzed: Why is private health insurance so expensive? Why are interest rates so high in many local credit markets in developing countries? Why do some firms pay dividends even when these are taxed more heavily than capital gains? Why do rich landowners not bear the entire harvest risk in contracts with poor tenants? These questions exemplify familiar – but seemingly very different – phenomena. However, they share a common feature: one side of the market is better informed than the other is.

George Akerlof initiated the research on such markets. He pointed out the importance and implications of the fact that sellers in many markets are better informed about product quality than buyers. At any given price, a seller of high-quality units is less willing to sell than is the seller of low-quality units. Rational buyers anticipate this, suspecting that the item they face is of low quality. This rational suspicion depresses prices, which further discourages sellers of high-quality units, who continue to leave the market until only low-quality items remain for sale. Such a downward quality bias is called adverse selection. Adverse selection may thus hinder mutually beneficial transactions. In other words: Adam Smith's "invisible hand" does not always work as effectively as traditional economics had us believe. Akerlof suggested that many observed market institutions may have arisen precisely to cope with the problem of adverse selection, an insight that has spawned a rich body of subsequent research.

Michael Spence asked under what conditions the better informed agents in the market can truthfully and credibly transmit, or "signal", their information to the less informed. For such "signaling" to function, sellers of high quality items must take observable measures that are too costly for low quality sellers to undertake. In Spence's own example, the "sellers" are job applicants in a market where employers cannot observe the job candidates' ability directly, only indirectly via their educational record. If the less able need to spend more effort and time than the more able to obtain any given level of education, then the latter can signal their ability by undertaking an education which the less able do not find worthwhile, given the prevailing wage difference. Under such circumstances, signaling removes the curse of adverse selection, albeit at a cost – the more able have to educate themselves beyond the less able, even if education has no effect on their productivity. Spence pointed out the existence of a variety of equilibria and how these may entail different returns to education for men and women or blacks and whites, even in the absence of innate productivity differences between these groups. Other examples of market signals are costly advertisements, guarantees, highly taxed dividends paid to shareholders, and a range of other observed phenomena.

Together with Michael Rothschild, Joseph Stiglitz provided a natural complement to Akerlof's and Spence's analyses. Rothschild and Stiglitz asked what less informed agents can do to improve their lot. They showed how and when less informed economic agents can extract information from better informed agents on the other side of the market by offering a whole menu of contracts. Like market signaling, such screening by self-selection promotes mutually beneficial transactions otherwise rendered unfeasible by adverse selection. A prime example can be found in insurance, where companies usually offer alternative contracts, where higher deductibles may be traded off against lower premiums. In this way, their clients are, by their own choice of contract, effectively divided into distinct risk classes. Low-risk clients typically pay a lower premium, but have to accept a relatively high deductible, which is needed for high-risk clients not to choose this option. Stiglitz has also studied the consequences and economic policy implications of asymmetric information in a host of other markets. In particular, he has analyzed credit markets, financial markets, and labor markets, and, along with Akerlof, pioneered much of modern development economics.

Dear Professors Akerlof, Spence and Stiglitz,

Your combined work forms the core of modern information economics.

Professor Akerlof, you have shown how and when informational asymmetries in markets can give rise to adverse selection, and you have demonstrated the importance and prevalence of this phenomenon.

Professor Spence, you have shown how and when informed economic agents in such a market can improve their outcome by way of signaling their private information to the less informed agents.

Professor Stiglitz, among your many contributions you have shown how and when less informed economic agents can improve their outcome by way of screening the informed agents in the market. The work by the three of you has changed the way economists think about markets.

On behalf of the Royal Swedish Academy of Sciences, I wish to convey our warmest congratulations for your achievements, and ask you to step forward to receive the Prize from the hands of His Majesty the King.

GEORGE A. AKERLOF

FAMILY BACKGROUND

I was born on June 17, 1940 in New Haven, Connecticut. My father was a chemist on the Yale faculty, my mother a housewife. They had met ten years earlier at a departmental picnic when my mother had been a chemistry graduate student at Yale. My brother, Carl, was two years older. My father, who was born in Sweden in 1898, had come to the United States on a fellowship to obtain a Ph.D. at the University of Pennsylvania. When his thesis adviser received an appointment at Yale in 1928, my father followed, and continued up the career path as instructor, assistant professor, and associate professor. His own roots were partly in Dalarna, which was the ancestral home of his mother's family, and partly in Stockholm, which was his father's home. My Swedish grandmother was the daughter of a dairy farmer who lived near Hedemora. My Swedish grandfather worked as a clerk for the Swedish railways in the Stockholm station. His avocation was painting, which absorbed more of his psychic energy than his career. At least some of the murals in the Stockholm station are a remnant of his handiwork. Beyond this my knowledge of my Swedish heritage is not expansive. Partly this reflects my father's move to America in an age when travel was both time-consuming and expensive and therefore I lack first-hand knowledge. But it also reflects his taciturnity and also his scorn for history in all forms, even at the family level. He considered himself to be beyond all else a scientist.

On my mother's side of the family, I know a great deal more, partly because my grandmother and some of her relatives were present in America at the time of my birth, but also because my mother made up for my father's taciturnity by her loquacity. She also believed in family history as a lesson to her children. Thus her accounts included the good parts, but omitted the bad parts. For example, I only heard late in life that in the late 19th century her grandmother's father had gone from San Francisco to Sacramento for a day trip on a steamboat, and never returned, his disappearance always a mystery. My mother came from an academic family. Her father and mother were of German Jewish descent. The practical implications of this ancestry for my grandfather was that he was denied tenure at Johns Hopkins, where he had established the first clinic in cardiology in the United States. A man of wide interests, he changed fields. He had a deep interest in the applications of chemistry to medicine and so he accepted the chairmanship of the department of pharmacology at the University of Minnesota medical school. My grandfather's German Jewish ancestry also had cultural implications. My great-grandfather had been born in Oakland, California. He graduated from

Berkeley in 1873, then returned to Germany for his medical education; he became a pharmacological chemist and was professor of medicine at Cooper Medical College in San Francisco, later the Stanford Medical School. The tradition of chemistry established by my great-grandfather was maintained for three generations. Like his father, my grandfather also attended Berkeley, graduating at age 18, and went on to Germany for his medical education. As I already mentioned he became a pharmacologist, as well as a cardiologist. In turn he passed the chemistry tradition on to his children. My mother, whose interest in chemistry was rather minimal, nevertheless went to graduate school in the subject, and married my father, for whom it was as important as life itself. My mother's brother became professor at the University of Wisconsin and was one of the best-known physical chemists of his day, having been the lead author of a massive green tome entitled: *The Molecular Theory of Gases.* Being a chemist or, at least some form of physical scientist, was thus a family ideal, for my brother and for myself. My brother Carl became a physicist; I became an economist.

My US grandmother is more peripheral to the story. She came from a previously wealthy family which had fallen into hard times. Her grandfather had advanced from peddler with a horse cart to being one of the richest men in the state of Maryland, a fortune which was divided among his 12 children and then lost by my great-grandfather. He died not in penury, but in debt, perhaps to the tune of $500,000. He had loaned considerable sums to brewers who went bankrupt with the innovation of pasturized beer. The appearance of my grandfather as suitor to my grandmother in such circumstances was thus particularly welcome.

EARLY YEARS

Although the early pictures of my youth show me as happy and smiling, my mother assures me otherwise. I was considered to be a sickly child. Perhaps it was true. School began in Pittsburgh, Pennsylvania. My father had not received tenure at Yale; during the war he worked on the Manhattan Project in Dayton, Ohio; afterwards he transferred to the Mellon Institute in Pittsburgh where he was supported by the Koppers Corporation. Thus my first years of schooling were in Pittsburgh at the Shady Side Academy, a fine private school. I was, however, dismissed from kindergarten, not for misbehavior, or for academic failure, but rather for throwing up in school. My brother was an exceptional student, and I think that this may have caused the school to take some pity on me, since they allowed me to return to first grade, only with a special place at lunch away from the other students, a precaution which was unnecessary since by this time my stomach problems had subsided. I was not only the physical runt of the litter, but also the intellectual inferior of my brother. I always knew this from experience, and it was scientifically affirmed for me when I was 7 by an IQ score that was three points higher. In Pittsburgh, my father made a habit of taking my brother to his laboratory in the Mellon Institute on Saturdays. I remember going there a few times, but the last time

I went there I burned myself blowing glass. I did not want to confess my foolishness, but I also did not want to return. To the best of my knowledge I never returned to his laboratory as a participant; only as the outside child observer. But my brother and father continued their weekly visits, and as time passed my brother became the scientist. Relative to this two-some I was an outsider who failed to understand the mysteries of the world; no doubt they were right. This left for me the task of finding an identity for myself. I thought about things that did not interest them. I was interested in social things: history and, if children can have such interests, economics. My family, not knowing what such people could do for a living decided that I was going to be a lawyer. Yes, I would go to Law School. That was their view of what a non-scientist might do that would permit some modicum of self-respect. I also found another way to establish a niche for myself. My brother did well in school, but I found that I could do better. After I was re-admitted to Shady Side I discovered that I could be first in my class, which gave me an identity in school as well as at home. These early years then were partly defining, but they were comfortable and happy. I liked my school, and also my mother would migrate from Pittsburgh to New Hampshire to escape the heat of the summer taking along me and my brother and my grandmother (my grandfather having died in 1942). For the first six years we rented cottages on Squam Lake in New Hampshire; then my family built one of our own. There were very few other children, so I had my brother as a sole companion. We did the types of things that brothers tend to do when they spend the summer at a lake: use of the motor boat, swimming, some badminton, and following along in the rounds of my mother and grandmother as from farm to farm they searched for the best tomato in the state of New Hampshire. I remember enjoying reading books about animals that talk, such as the Freddy books about Freddy the Pig, and Thornton Burgess' animal stories. I also remember being terminally bored when there was no such book available and my brother was engaged in his multifarious projects. I participated as the person who would look for the hammer when it was needed (and also who invariably would not find it, so he had to go for it anyway).

The Pittsburgh part of this life ended when I was ten. Koppers Chemical had decided to terminate my father's contract at the Mellon Institute, and so he was sent packing. With the support of the Office of Naval Research, he relocated to the Naval Powder Factory at Indian Head, Maryland, about 40 miles south of Washington. My mother felt that the schools in Indian Head were not of sufficient quality for her boys, and therefore a compromise was reached. My father would work at Indian Head during the week, and the rest of the family would live in a rented house north of Washington. My brother and I were sent to Sidwell Friends School in Washington. This sojourn did not last long. In the spring of 1950, my father showed us some titanium rings that he had produced by his own method of electro-discharge chemistry. And Princeton University, which was opening up the Forrestal Research Laboratories, hired him.

And so my family moved again, this time to Princeton. The University gave us one half of a huge colonial house. My brother and I went to a small private school, about a mile away, the Princeton Country Day School. The school was old fashioned: it was all male, even the teachers, and had an emphasis on classical education. Since my brother would have been quite behind in Latin, it was imperative that he be absolved of this requirement. My mother and father thus entertained the principal at dinner, with unusually strong martinis, and afterwards successfully pleaded my brother's case. My father felt no regret that Carl would not be learning the language of Roman Civilization. Science was not emphasized in the school. When it was introduced, partly at my family's urging, for eighth graders, the math teacher, who had majored in French at Princeton, made the students memorize stars in constellations. The conflict between my brother and this math teacher regarding what one considered astrology and the other considered astronomy had some fallout even on me, as I learned when he told me that he had been reading books of handwriting analysis and he was certain that I had the handwriting of a murderer, a prediction which has so far proven incorrect. Aside from that I had relatively little conflict with teachers. I belonged to a small group of students, who in today's terminology would be called nerds. Bikes gave us a great deal of freedom, not only as transport back and forth to school, but also to get together with friends who lived at considerable distance from home, and also for such entertainment as touch football and the movies. I formed a close friendship with Robert Fernholz, who later received his Ph.D. in math. School was out early on Wednesday afternoons and we would often rent a canoe to explore Lake Carnegie. We had our own games of touch football, our own movie group, and went out for tennis rather than baseball in the spring. We were differentiated, for the most part, from those who were richer and also more athletically inclined.

The idyllic life in Princeton in the large colonial house was, however, broken after one and a half years. My family would continue to live in Princeton, but in at least subtly different circumstances. At Indian Head, and after coming to Princeton, my father had never been able to reproduce his previous feat of the titanium rings. After the initial success the equipment had broken, and Humpty Dumpty could never be put back together again. So my family had to move. They decided to stay in Princeton, where a consortium of Princeton scientists set him up in his own research laboratory. It was supported by government research grants. It was at this time, when I was 11 or 12, that I remember one of my first significant thoughts about economics. If my father lost his job, and my family stopped spending their money, then another father (it was typically fathers rather than mothers who worked at the time) would lose his job, and so on. The economy would spiral downward. Well, as I have told it my father got re-employed, so the system was not put to a test. Although slightly wrong, I had understood the foundation of Keynesian economics. The exploration of the reasons for unemployment and the defense of Keynesian macroeconomics have dominated my work as an economist. It is thus no coincidence, perhaps, either that I had made this observation, or that I now remember it.

The Princeton Country Day School ended at grade nine. At that point most of my classmates dispersed among different New England prep schools. Both for financial reasons and also because they preferred that I stay at home, my family sent me down the road to the Lawrenceville School. Indeed the house my parents built after my father left Princeton was on the Princeton-Lawrenceville Road, so that my brother and I could hitch hike easily to school and back. Again this was an excellent school. Almost all classes were in sections of 10 to 15; sometimes advanced sections with low demand were smaller. Students and faculty arrayed themselves around large oval tables. By skipping a year of math and a year of French, I entered college with advanced standing in English, history, math, Latin and French. This advanced standing was very useful in my college career, especially the advanced standing in math. The teaching was of the highest caliber. My French teacher in tenth and twelfth grades had won awards for his excellence in teaching. One of my English teachers was a leading scholar renowned for his work on Emily Dickinson. Socially, I was a misfit. I failed to understand why my classmates spent the typical free afternoon watching *American Bandstand*, a TV program of teenagers dancing. Nor did it help that I was the lone day-boy from the Princeton area. As a scholarship boy, I delivered the intercampus mail half the afternoons thereby avoiding the PT (physical training) program that was the athletic dumping ground for those who were on neither varsity nor junior varsity teams. The other afternoons I looked for other ways out: such as visits to the infirmary, use of *cum laude* privileges to skip class or athletics, etc. I also knew that in a short period of time I would be off to college.

COLLEGE AND GRADUATE SCHOOL

Regarding college, I had no choice. My brother had gone to Yale. Even if my brother's choice were not over-riding for my decision, I would probably have heeded the assistant principal of Lawrenceville, who admonished me that I should not wreck my life by even thinking about going to Harvard instead. My first two years at Yale were mainly spent in taking liberal arts courses and working on *The Yale Daily News*. My last two years were spent learning economics, and then math. When I went to Yale, I was convinced that I wanted to be either an economist or an historian. Really, for me it was a distinction without a difference. If I was going to be an historian, then I would be an economic historian. And if I was to be an economist I would consider history as the basis for my economics. This interest in history informed my academic program. In my Freshman year I signed up for a rather fuzzy course called Directed Studies, which was said to cover Western Civilization from many different aspects: history, philosophy, art, literature, etc. I also separately signed up for math and economics. The concern with history led to another decision regarding extracurricular activities. If I were going to be an historian I thought that it would also be useful to see how the news is made: the user of documents should also be aware of how the truth is distorted in the making. And so I decided to "heel," to go out for, *The News*. I may also have lied to myself. I may also have gone out for *The News* because I knew that I would enjoy it. Until Thanksgiving of junior year *The News* dominated my life. I wanted to do two things with the newspaper. First, I found it too much of an official organ. A typical prime assignment was for a leading reporter to interview the President (of Yale University) and to report his views. I wanted the newspaper to do something different. I wanted it to have more stories about student issues, and also more features of human interest. I wanted it to be less solemn and more serious. Surprisingly, just one individual reporter could make a difference. For example, I wrote a story protesting Yale's policy of keeping students in Directed Studies for sophomore year if they wanted to get out at the end of freshman year (I myself had been denied). I also wrote many articles which tabulated a questionnaire on the feelings of scholarship students who were forced to work in the dining halls in freshman year. Regarding stories of more general interest, in my sophomore year a friend of mine and a photographer went South at the time of the first sit-ins and covered that for *The News*. We talked to Black and White leaders throughout the South. I also covered the Nixon and Kennedy campaigns. Despite this record, in the beginning of junior year I was denied election to the news board. This was probably the best thing that ever happened to me. I would never have been a good reporter because I am not accurate regarding facts (probably the reporter's worst sin and the probable reason for my denial). Also the time I would have spent in junior and senior year at *The News* would have seriously impaired my education in economics. In some sense my career in economics has paralleled my vision for *The News*. Relative both to the economics of the 1960s and perhaps also to the dominant strand of economics today, I have sought to develop a theory that is similarly more serious and less solemn. I want a theory that is more closely linked to substantial policy issues and less tied to the official (competitive general equilibrium) model and its assumptions.

At the time of this decision at the *News* I was taking my first course in abstract mathematics, as well as four courses in economics. Because I had gotten a jump ahead in math at prep school, I had somehow avoided any course in which proof was required. I thus found myself failing to understand, and literally flunking, my course in *Modern Algebra*. It was only through the intervention of my family that I survived. My mother's best friend's husband was a leading mathematician at Princeton. He gave me an hour's tutoring; he diagnosed my problem and showed me where my thinking was lacking. After that I was able to make headway in the course, and later got a perfect score on the final. In the first two years at Yale I mainly worked on *The News*; in my last two years I was entirely a student. In junior year I took almost all economics, except for modern algebra; in my last year almost all my courses were in math. This school work would then be the background for the next phase of my career, which was graduate school.

I entered MIT in the fall of 1962, and I was surprised that my background in both math and economics was better than that of almost everyone else in my class. I was surprised because previously I had not been impressed by the economics that I learned at Yale. Indeed my all-math senior year had been as much determined by the pull of the math courses as the push of the economics courses. My good undergraduate background then left me time to pursue interests outside economics. I spent most of my intellectual and psychic energy in my first year of graduate school on a course in algebraic topology taught by Raoul Bott at Harvard. Bott not only taught the details of algebraic topology, but also, much more deeply, how mathematicians truly think. He taught how to divide the meat of a proof from the detail. In this course I learned to respect the variety of mathematical structure that can be used to describe a problem. It bolstered my suspicion that many of the results of the economic theory of the time were due to economists' lack of (mathematical) knowledge rather than to the truth of their arguments. As a crude example, consider the cartoonist Edward Koren's furry animals. In contrast to the traditional clear-lined cartoon, Koren's characters are like fibre bundles, characterized by hairs everywhere. This distinction is relevant to economic theory: the standard economic model is mathematically represented by simple clear surfaces, but alternative models in the spirit of Koren's cartoons are also possible. Solow demonstrated two models of this sort in the course he taught us in growth theory. In the first model the output of labor depends upon the vintage of capital with which it is combined; in the second, capital is substitutable for labor before the capital is produced, but is no longer substitutable thereafter. Solow's models converged with what I was learning in algebraic topology. Together they suggested that standard economic theory was based on mathematics that failed to capture a good portion of economic reality. Richer structure would give a more realistic picture.

Socially, MIT was also a great deal of fun. I made many friends there, including Joe Stiglitz, Bill Nordhaus, Giorgio La Malfa, Joe Mooney, Eva Colorni, Mrinal Datta Chaudhuri, Vahid Nowshirvani, Tom Weisskopf, Steve Marglin, Marcelle Arak, Karl Shell, Mike Rothschild, Dick Auster, Les Aspin, Eytan Sheshinski, and many others.

At MIT at the time everyone learned growth theory. That was the core and center of the curriculum. I learned growth theory not because I had any intrinsic interest in the subject, but because it was there. The best of it, like Solow's models, and Arrow's "learning by doing" model were very interesting; after that most papers were rather mediocre and there were rapidly diminishing returns. Growth theory was useful because we learned from it how to model issues that were much closer to the heart of economics, which is how markets worked. But that comes later in the story. The leading chapter in my thesis demonstrated the stability of a putty-clay model without technical change, which I had been told was one of the burning topics in economic growth. I used the techniques derived there for the "Market for 'Lemons.'" Another chapter made a very preliminary attempt at deriving a theory of unemployment; a third represented the leads and lags resulting from changes in monetary policy. These last two papers were only marginally publishable, but they were the beginnings of an attempt to base Keynesian economics on sound microeconomic foundations.

BERKELEY AND INDIA

I graduated from MIT in 1966, which was one of the years of highest demand ever for graduating PhD's in economics. I was lucky enough to obtain an assistant professorship at Berkeley. In my first year at Berkeley I wrote the "Market for 'Lemons;" which is the work for which I have been cited for the Nobel Prize. I was helped considerably both in choice of topic and in execution by Tom Rothenberg, who also came to Berkeley in the fall of 1966. Tom and I had dinner together most nights that first year. On one such occasion I listed the possible topics on which I might work. "Lemons" was on the list, and Tom guided me not only in choice of topic, but also in turning it into a paper. I shall always to be grateful to him for his help and kindness. At the same time I was continuing my work on Keynesian macroeconomics. In that first year after graduate school I also turned out the first model of staggered wage and price setting. This is the basis both for the Fischer and Taylor models, which have more complex monetary rules than my original model, and also rational, rather than adaptive, expectations.

In 1967–68 I took leave from Berkeley to spend a year at the Indian Statistical Institute in New Delhi, where Steve Marglin headed a group that was seeking to develop a program to allocate the waters of the Bhakra-Nangal dam in northern Punjab. He wanted to produce a timetable for the release of the water so that peasants planting the new varieties of wheat could be assured that they would get the water they needed to make such an investment worthwhile. I was brought into the project as an extra. By joining it, I thought that I would gain a first-hand view why India was so poor. My role in the project very quickly came to an end, when I discovered problems with the basic assumption needed to make the project feasible. Because of unseasonal rain and glacial melt I was unable to predict winter in flow into the reservoir from the rainfall of the previous monsoon. Instead, I wrote a paper on Federal-State fiscal policy in India. Planning had been temporarily suspended in India because of the bad monsoons, and my paper gave principles for planning if it should be revived. I also revised "The Market for 'Lemons'" which had been rejected two or three times in the course of the year by editors who felt that the issues in the paper were too trivial to merit publication in a serious academic journal. I included examples of incomplete markets from my readings of Indian economic history.

The trip to India was important for my intellectual development. Especially, it confirmed for me that nonstandard analyses were needed to understand many economic transactions. As I have hinted earlier, the fundamental problem I wished to explore in economics, was the reason for unemployment. Unemployment involves, above all, a gap between supply and demand. In India, the caste system for centuries has interposed itself between supply and demand. The gaps between supply and demand in the Indian caste system were then potentially informative as to how similar gaps might exist in labor markets in Western countries. What I learned in India became the keystone for my later contributions to the development of an efficiency wage theory of unemployment in Western countries. This theory unfolded over the next twenty years. Curiously, Joe Stiglitz visited Kenya at about the same time and developed models embodying alternative efficiency wage theory based on his similar observations of the underdeveloped world.

I returned from India in September 1968. In the fall of 1969 I was voted tenure by the department of economics at Berkeley, which was uncontroversial because the one person opposed was away on sabbatical at the time. In 1973–74 I served as Senior Economist at the Council of Economic Advisers. I was an extraordinarily poor staff member (partly because I had never been a research assistant in graduate school and partly because I am very bad at writing good bureaucratese.) Nor did it help that I had no loyalty to the Republican incumbents, Richard Nixon, and, in the beginning of my tenure there, Spiro Agnew. My tenure at the Council may have had little payoff for the government, but I personally learned a great deal, largely from June O'Neil and Barry Chiswick, the senior staffers in charge of labor economics. From them I learned how to do empirical economics. Also, of yet more importance, a former graduate student from Berkeley, Judy Graves introduced me to Kay Leong, who was a friend of hers from undergraduate days at Cornell and, coincidentally also a native of Berkeley. Kay and I got married at the end of the year.

After returning to Berkeley, it was time to be promoted to full professor, but the department did not think I had published enough. This lack of productivity had several different causes. First, after returning from India I suffered from colitis. A doctor at UCSF had cured the colitis, but by the use of drugs whose side effect was severe depression. Second, I spent a year studying Hindi-Urdu. Third, I had spent a year at the Council of Economic Advisers. Also, I spent two years on a paper which might have been considered interesting before the introduction of the accelerationist Phillips Curve into macroeconomics, but which was obsolete afterwards.[1] The consequence of my failure to receive this promotion was that Kay discovered a new facet of my personality, a trait she had not previously seen. This was the extreme concentration I am able to devote to a problem, in this instance the erasure of the department's implicit censure. She disliked my monomaniacal focus on this issue. This propensity to perseverate is sometimes self-destructive, as when I am unable to stop practicing a single piece on the piano or to quit solitaire, but I also consider it a major asset as an economist. For example, before the computer made the notion of "draft" obsolete because of continual revision, I wrote at least 50 drafts of papers on the effects of target-threshold monitoring of bank accounts on the efficacy of monetary policy. Gradually from the crude ideas in my thesis, these drafts developed into papers that in my opinion are a significant precursor to the modern work on this topic by

[1] In the accelerationist view there is only one unemployment rate which would give constant inflation. In the pre-accelerationist view at any given rate of unemployment relative prices and wages would converge to particular steady-state values; lower unemployment caused higher steady-state inflation. This paper showed that in such a "quasi-equilibrium," standard cost-benefit analysis would apply: the amount of inflation resulting from any given expenditure would be proportional to the dollar expenditure on it. In consequence standard cost benefit analysis worked.

Ricardo Caballero. I began working on this idea in 1963; I stopped working on it twenty years later in 1983. Similarly, in some sense I began work on unemployment theory when I was 12. 50 years later I am still mulling over the same subject. When Kay married me she had not appreciated either my persistence or its side effects, which were greatly magnified in the promotion crisis. The result was twofold. Kay went off with another man and I, after not being promoted, and with little personal reason to remain in Berkeley, accepted a professorship at the London School of Economics.

THE LSE AND RETURN TO BERKELEY

In between Berkeley and the LSE I spent a year at the Federal Reserve Board in Washington, D.C., where I met Janet Yellen. We liked each other immediately and decided to get married. Not only did our personalities mesh perfectly, but we have also always been in all but perfect agreement about macroeconomics. Our lone disagreement is that she is a bit more supportive of free trade than I. We decided to get married hastily, not only because we had so little doubt about each other, but also for practical reasons. I had already accepted a professorship at the LSE for the coming year and if we were to avoid being separated, Janet would also need to get a job in England too. Luckily, she also was given a tenure-track lectureship at the LSE. There seemed to be no question about her tenure since she had already published several distinguished articles on the economics of bundling and advertising. After a year in Washington, we left for England. We very much liked both the LSE and London, but both of us had problems of identity: we were American, not English. Luckily, Berkeley had never accepted my proffer of resignation when I left for the LSE, so I was still nominally on the faculty. And Janet got a tenure–track job in the business school with a promise of early review for tenure. We had met at the Fed in the Fall of 1977, married in June 1978, and left for the LSE in September of that year. We came back to Berkeley in August 1980. Shortly thereafter, in June 1981, our son Robert was born.

Meanwhile the focus of my research had changed in a subtle way. Previously the main focus of my research had been to discern the consequences for macroeconomics of different microeconomic structures, such as staggered contracts, target-threshold monitoring, asymmetric information, and also the existence of "jobs." Now, increasingly, my research concerned the effects of different assumptions regarding fairness and social customs on unemployment. In my view, there were two leading problems in macroeconomics. The first was whether there could be such a thing as involuntary unemployment: why couldn't an unemployed person obtain a job by being willing to accept a less advantageous job? The second was whether with complete information monetary policy could have real economic impact. In my early papers I posited a wage established by social custom, in turn resulting in unemployment. The theory was based on my understanding of the institution of caste in India. But it somehow did not have the ring of truth. When I presented this anthropology–based paper at Yale, Tjalling Koopmans asked whether I had read any sociology. It turns out that I had not, and so in my first year in England I made amends, reading the sociology classics. I then wrote a paper on efficiency wages in which non–market clearing results from the lower morale and productivity of workers whose sense of fairness has been violated. This was a sociologically-based efficiency wage theory of unemployment. Other authors at the time were developing, or had developed, similar theories of unemployment which were variously based on training costs and on information. These theories answered the first key question regarding how involuntary unemployment could occur, but the second question remained. Subsequently, Janet and I, in response to probing by James Tobin, who was a visitor to Berkeley in 1982–83, devised a theory to explain the second phenomena: sticky wages and prices in an economy with monopolistic competition and efficiency wages would be near-rational. Firms that followed rules of thumb, causing them to change prices and wages slowly, would lose something, but not much. Such sticky prices and wages would explain why monetary policy would be effective: if the money supply increased, real balances, which determine real demand, would rise. Thus rules of thumb, whose individual losses were economically insignificant, could have a significant effect on the economy. Janet and I worked together on many papers for the ten years from 1984 to 1994. For the first part of that decade we focused on macroeconomic theory: near-rationality and efficiency wages. We later turned to working on poverty and policy issues, such as the economic strategy for East Germany after German unification and the causes of rising out-of-wedlock childbearing in the United States.

WASHINGTON AND RETURN TO BERKELEY

Our work together was interrupted when in 1994 Janet was named to the Board of Governors of the Federal Reserve System. Janet, Robby and I moved from Berkeley to Washington. The Brookings Institution named me a Senior Fellow and generously supported about one third of my salary for the next five years. For the first three years, while Janet was at the Fed, I commuted back to Berkeley in the Spring term to teach. When Janet later became Chair of the Council of Economic Advisers in 1997, Berkeley gave me full-time leave. When Janet was at the Fed, I supported her as much as possible by taking over household duties; later when she was at the White House my role in providing psychological support in the daily political storms was yet more important. I also continued to work on both macroeconomics and poverty. With Bill Dickens and George Perry, I wrote on the economics of low inflation. This work challenges the natural rate, accelerationist theory of the Phillips Curve. It shows that at low inflation there is likely to be a significant long run trade-off between inflation and unemployment. This result has potentially important implications for monetary policy. With Rachel Kranton of the University of Maryland I also wrote papers that incorporate the concept of identity into economics. This work yields a theory of minority poverty in the United States and new views on the economics of gender and discrimination and the economics of education. The initial impetus for this work came from Rachel's understanding of the importance of identity in Middle Eastern Studies.

This takes us almost to the present. In 1999 Robby graduated from St. Albans School, the high school he attended in Washington, D.C., and he set off for college, at Yale. At the same time Janet left the Council of Economic Advisers, and we returned to Berkeley. Rachel Kranton and I are still working on identity, whose introduction into economic analysis, we believe, will help unify economic, with sociological, anthropological and psychological theory. We are excited about the range of economic analysis and policy implications for this approach.

CONCLUSION

In conclusion, I am very honored to have been named co-recipient of the Prize in Economic Sciences in Memory of Alfred Nobel. Economics is a far richer field with more interesting, realistic, and detailed models than when I first entered the profession. Asymmetric information is a good example of this evolution. In addition, there is now an increased willingness to base economics on findings in the other social sciences. Over the last thirty years we have been gradually evolving an economics that relies more on careful empirical observation, and less on questionable assumption regarding how rational people must behave. It has been a great pleasure to have been a contributor to this development. I hope, with the help of my co-authors, to continue to do so as long as time permits.

BEHAVIORAL MACROECONOMICS AND MACROECONOMIC BEHAVIOR

Prize Lecture, December 8, 2001

by

George A. Akerlof*

Department of Economics, University of California, Berkeley, CA 94720-3880, USA.

Think about Richard Scarry's *Cars and Trucks and Things That Go.*[1] Think about what that book would have looked like in sequential decades of the last century had Richard Scarry been alive in each of them to delight and amuse children and parents. Each subsequent decade has seen the development of ever more specialized vehicles. We started with the model-T Ford. We now have more models of backhoe loaders than even the most precocious four-year old can identify.

What relevance does this have for economics? In the late 1960s there was a shift in the job description of economic theorists. Prior to that time microeconomic theory was mainly concerned with analyzing the purely competitive, general equilibrium model based upon profit maximization by firms and utility maximization by consumers. The macroeconomics of the day, the so-called neoclassical synthesis, appended a fixed money wage to such a general equilibrium system. "Sticky money wages" explained departures from full employment and business cycle fluctuations. Since that time, both micro and macroeconomics have developed a Scarry-ful book of models designed to incorporate into economic theory a whole variety of realistic behaviors. For example, "The Market for 'Lemons'" explored how markets with asymmetric information operate. Buyers and sellers commonly possess different, not identical information. My paper examined the pathologies that may develop under these more realistic conditions.

For me, the study of asymmetric information was a very first step toward the realization of a dream. That dream was the development of a behavioral macroeconomics in the original spirit of Keynes' *General Theory.* Macroeconomics would then no longer suffer from the *ad hockery* of the neoclassical synthesis, which had over-ridden the emphasis in *The General Theory* on the role of psychological and sociological factors, such as cognitive bias, recipro-

* The author would like to thank Janet Yellen for extraordinarily helpful discussions and editorial assistance. He would also like to thank Henry Aaron, William Dickens, Ernst Fehr, William Gale, and Robert Shiller for invaluable comments and the Canadian Institute for Advanced Research for generous financial support.

[1] See Richard Scarry (1974).

city, fairness, herding, and social status. My dream was to strengthen macroeconomic theory by incorporating assumptions honed to the observation of such behavior. A team of people have participated in the realization of this dream. Kurt Vonnegut would call this team a *kerass*, "a group of people who are unknowingly working together toward some common goal fostered by a larger cosmic influence."[2] In this lecture I shall describe some of the behavioral models developed by this *kerass* to provide plausible explanations for macroeconomic phenomena that are central to Keynesian economics.

For the sake of background, let me take you back a bit in time to review some history of macroeconomic thought. In the late 1960s the New Classical economists saw the same weaknesses in the microfoundations of macroeconomics that have motivated me. They hated its lack of rigor. And they sacked it. They then held a celebratory bonfire, with an article entitled "After Keynesian Macroeconomics."[3] The new version of macroeconomics that they produced became standard in the 1970s. Following its neoclassical synthesis predecessor, New Classical macroeconomics was based on the competitive, general equilibrium model. But it differed in being much more zealous in insisting that all decisions – consumption and labor supply by households, output, employment and pricing decisions by producers, and the wage bargains between both workers and firms – be consistent with maximizing behavior.[4] New Classical macroeconomics therefore gave up the assumption of sticky money wages. To account for unemployment and economic fluctuations, New Classical economists relied first on imperfect information and later on technology shocks.

The new theory was a step forward in at least one respect: price and wage decisions were now based upon explicit microfoundations. But the behavioral assumptions were so primitive that the model faced extreme difficulty in accounting for at least six macroeconomic phenomena. In some cases, logical inconsistency with key assumptions of the new classical model led to outright denials of the phenomena in question; in other cases, the explanations offered were merely tortuous. The six phenomena are:

- *The existence of involuntary unemployment*: In the new classical model, an unemployed worker can easily obtain a job by offering to work for just a smidgeon less than the market-clearing salary or wage; so involuntary unemployment cannot exist.
- *The impact of monetary policy on output and employment*: In the new classical model, monetary policy is all but ineffective in changing output and employment. Once changes in the money supply are fully foreseen, prices and wa-

[2] See http://www.gibbsonline.com/gibbsbooks.html.

[3] See Lucas and Sargent (1979).

[4] Most of these puzzles were dormant at the time; they were inherent in the literature, but there was no active discussion of them. Probably the most active research program in macroeconomics during the late1960s was the development of large scale macroeconometric models. The models of search unemployment by Phelps *et al* (1970) appeared in the late 1960s to answer the question: what is the meaning of unemployment? But they adopted a framework of search unemployment, which was, by nature, voluntary.

ges change proportionately; real wages and relative prices are constant; and there is no impact on the real economy whatsoever.

- *The failure of deflation to accelerate when unemployment is high*: The New Classical model produces an accelerationist Phillips Curve with a unique natural rate of unemployment. If unemployment falls below this natural rate, inflation accelerates. With unemployment above the natural rate, inflation continually decelerates.
- *The prevalence of undersaving for retirement*: In the New Classical model individuals decide how much to consume and to save to maximize an intertemporal utility function. The consequence is that privately determined saving should be just about optimal. But individuals commonly report disappointment with their saving behavior and, absent social insurance programs, it is widely believed that most people would undersave. "Forced saving" programs are extremely popular.
- *The excessive volatility of stock prices relative to their fundamentals*: New Classical theory assumes that stock prices reflect fundamentals, the discounted value of future income streams.
- *The stubborn persistence of a self-destructive underclass:* My list of macroeconomic questions to be explained includes the reasons for poverty because I view income distribution as a topic in macroeconomics. Neoclassical theory suggests that poverty is the reflection of low initial endowments of human and nonhuman capital. The theory cannot account for persistent and extreme poverty coupled with high incidence of drug and alcohol abuse, out-of-wedlock births, single-headed households, high welfare dependency, and crime.[5]

In what follows I shall describe how behavioral macroeconomists, incorporating realistic assumptions grounded in psychological and sociological observation, have produced models that comfortably account for each of these macroeconomic phenomena. In the spirit of Keynes' *General Theory*, behavioral macroeconomists are rebuilding the microfoundations that were sacked

[5] I have left out two important questions whose microfoundations have been developed since the late 1960s. First, why might credit be rationed? Donald Hodgman (1960, p. 258) makes clear that the economic theory of the early 1960s found credit rationing to be an unexplained puzzle: "Economists of a more analytical persuasion have been reluctant to accept [credit rationing] at face value because of their difficulty in providing a theoretical explanation for the phenomenon which is consistent with the tenets of rational economic behavior. Why should lenders allocate by non-price means and thus deny themselves the advantage of higher interest income?" He attributes such views to Paul Samuelson as revealed in Congressional testimony. Asymmetric information provides an excellent reason for credit rationing. (See especially Jaffee and Russell (1976) and Stiglitz and Weiss (1981)). A second question relating to microfoundations concerns the reasons for leads and lags in macroeconomic variables, such as durable consumption, money demand, and prices. S-s models with lumpy costs to making changes can explain such leads and lags (unless the variable in question is either always decreasing or always increasing). Pioneering work on the effects of S-s pricing has been done especially by Iwai (1981) and Barro (1972). Caballero (see, for example, 1993) has compared the leads and lags in such models with a situation with no costs of adjustment. Caplin and Spulber (1987) and Caplin and Leahy (1991) have also looked at the implications of S-s policy for the relation between the shifts in the ideal price and the actual price being charged. See Akerlof (1973, 1979) for analysis of the effects of target-threshold monitoring on the short-run income and interest elasticity of the demand for money.

by the New Classical economics. I shall begin my review by describing one of my earliest attempts in this field, which led to the discovery of the role of asymmetric information in markets.

ASYMMETRIC INFORMATION

I first came upon the problems resulting from asymmetric information in an early investigation of a leading cause for fluctuations in output and employment – large variations in the sales of new cars.[6] I thought that illiquidity, due to the fact that sellers of used cars know more than the buyers of used cars, might explain the high volatility of automobile purchases.[7] In trying to make such a macroeconomic model, I got diverted. I discovered that the informational problems that exist in the used car market were potentially present to some degree in all markets. In some markets, asymmetric information is fairly easily soluble by repeat sale and by reputation. In other markets, such as insurance markets, credit markets, and the market for labor, asymmetric information between buyers and sellers is not easily soluble and results in serious market breakdowns. For example, the elderly have a hard time getting health insurance; small businesses are likely to be credit-rationed; and minorities are likely to experience statistical discrimination in the labor market because people are lumped together into categories of those with similar observable traits. The failure of credit markets is one of the major reasons for underdevelopment. Even where mechanisms such as reputation and repeat sales arise to overcome the problem of asymmetric information, such institutions become a major determinant of market structure.

To understand the origins of the economics of asymmetric information in markets, it is useful to reflect on the more general intellectual revolution that was occurring at the time. Prior to the early 1960s, economic theorists rarely constructed models customized to capture unique institutions or specific market characteristics. Chamberlin's monopolistic competition and Joan Robinson's equivalent[8] were taught in graduate and even a few undergraduate courses; but such "specific" models were the rare exception; they were presented not as central sights, but instead as excursions into the countryside, for the adventurous or those with an extra day to spare.[9] During the early 1960s, however, "special" models began to proliferate as growth theorists, working slightly outside the norms of standard price-theoretic economics, began to construct models with specialized technological features: putty-clay, vintage capital and learning by doing. The incorporation into models of such specialized technologies violated no established price-theoretic norm, but it sowed

[6] See Akerlof (1970).

[7] Mishkin (1976) later developed the ideas that set me on this course initially. He showed why the demand for automobiles is more volatile because cars are illiquid due to asymmetric information.

[8] See Chamberlin (1962), and Robinson (1942).

[9] For example, I could well imagine a graduate student being unaware of Hotelling's (1929) model of spatial competition. I cannot remember it in the graduate curriculum and remember finding it tucked away as an appendix to Chamberlin's *Monopolistic Competition*.

the seed for the revolution that was to come. During the summer of 1969, I first heard the word *model* used as a verb, and not just as a noun.[10] It is no coincidence that just a few months earlier "The Market for 'Lemons'" had been accepted for publication.[11] The 'modeling' of asymmetric information in markets was to price theory what the 'modeling' of putty-clay, vintage capital, and learning by doing had been to growth theory.[12] It was the first application of a new economic orientation in which models are constructed with careful attention to realistic microeconomic detail. This development has brought economic theory much closer to the fine grain of economic reality. Almost inevitably, the analysis of information asymmetries was the first fruit of this new modeling orientation. It was the ripest fruit for picking. In the remainder of this essay I shall discuss the payoffs of this new orientation for the new field of behavioral macroeconomics.

INVOLUNTARY UNEMPLOYMENT

I once had an economist friend who said that he *could not* sell his house, a complaint that I reiterated sympathetically to one of his colleagues. The colleague responded that there was only one problem: the house was unreasonably priced. At a lower price the house would sell, perhaps instantly.

New Classical economics views involuntary unemployment as a logical impossibility, like my friend's inability to sell his house. Could not an unemployed worker obtain a job if only she were willing to reduce her reservation wage? The New Classical answer is yes: unemployed workers are those searching for work (hence unemployed, rather than out of the labor force) but rejecting jobs that are available because they had expected better pay. The unemployed may be unhappy that they cannot sell their labor at the wage or salary that they would ideally like, but except for those affected by the minimum wage or union bargaining, they are voluntarily, not involuntarily, unemployed. Everyone can get a job at the market-clearing wage. In New Classical theory, periods of declining employment – business cycle downturns – may be caused by an unexpected decline in aggregate demand, which leaves workers mistakenly holding out for nominal wages that exceed the new market-clearing level.[13] Alternatively, declining employment may be due to negative supply shocks, which cause workers to withdraw from the labor force and eschew the jobs that are available. Any account of the business cycle based on voluntary variations in job-taking faces a significant empirical dif-

[10] Conversation with Michael Rothschild in Cambridge, Massachusetts, Summer of 1969. I remember the usage just as many people today may remember the first time they heard someone say they would "grow the economy."

[11] I do not have the exact date of the acceptance of this article, but I remember that it took slightly more than a year between acceptance and publication.

[12] See Solow (1959, 1962) and Arrow (1962).

[13] This theory suffers from a further theoretical difficulty. Since aggregate unemployment is readily observable with a short lag, workers should condition their expectations of prevailing wage distributions on the aggregate unemployment rate. Such conditioning would eliminate serial correlation in unemployment.

ficulty – to explain why quits decline in cyclical downturns. If higher unemployment results from workers' rejection of the poor returns from work, quits should rise along with unemployment. But there are fewer quits, not more, when unemployment rises. The procyclic behavior of quits is indisputable.[14]

Instead of denying the very existence of involuntary unemployment, behavioral macroeconomists have provided coherent explanations. Efficiency wage theories, which first appeared in the 1970s and 1980s, make the concept of involuntary unemployment meaningful.[15] These models posit that, for reasons such as morale, fairness, insider power, or asymmetric information, employers have strong motives to pay workers more than the minimum necessary to attract them.[16] Such "efficiency wages" are above market-clearing, so that jobs are rationed and some workers cannot obtain them. These workers are involuntarily unemployed. In the next section I will extend this reasoning to explain why involuntary unemployment varies cyclically.

The pervasive empirical finding of a wide spread of earnings for seemingly similar workers is strongly suggestive of the near ubiquity of efficiency wages. Long before the efficiency wage was a gleam in the eye of macroeconomists, labor economists had documented wide dispersion in earnings across seemingly similar jobs and among workers with apparently identical characteristics.[17] Analysis of panel data indicates that workers of the same quality receive different wages depending upon their place of work. Moreover, data show that workers who switch industries receive wage changes that are correlated with the respective wage differentials between the industries.[18] Industries with higher pay (conditional on characteristics) also have lower quit rates, suggesting that pay differences are not simply compensating differentials due to different working conditions or benefits.[19] It thus appears that there are "good jobs" and "bad jobs."

The existence of good jobs and bad jobs makes the concept of involuntary unemployment meaningful: unemployed workers are willing to accept, but cannot obtain, jobs identical to those currently held by workers with identical ability. At the same time, involuntarily unemployed workers may eschew the

[14] This question was raised by Tobin (1972). For some data on the countercyclical behavior of quits, see Akerlof, Rose and Yellen (1988). Kenneth McLaughlin (1991) has attempted to reconcile the procyclicality of quits with New Classical economics as follows: He defines quits as employee initiated separations, and layoffs as firm induced separations. In McLaughlin's model a positive productivity shock causes more workers to ask for wage increases. Since some requests are rejected, quits rise as unemployment declines. But why should firms' wage offers lag behind worker demands in the face of a positive productivity shock?

[15] An excellent concise summary of this literature is given by Yellen (1984).

[16] The inclusion here of insider-outsider models is taking an especially broad interpretation of the concept of efficiency wages.

[17] See Dunlop (1957).

[18] See Dickens and Katz (1987) and Krueger and Summers (1988). Note that these studies are for the United States in a period when unionization was quite weak; it is thus unlikely to be the major factor in such wage differentials. In contrast, Dunlop's wage differentials, may have been mainly the result of differentials in union power.

[19] See Krueger and Summers (1988).

lower-paying or lower-skilled jobs that are available. The definition of involuntary unemployment implicit in efficiency wage theory accords with the facts and agrees with commonly held perceptions. A meaningful concept of involuntary unemployment constitutes an important first step forward in rebuilding the foundations of Keynesian economics.

But why do firms pay wages above rock bottom? In my view, psychological and sociological explanations for efficiency wages are empirically most convincing.[20] Three important considerations are: reciprocity (gift exchange theory from anthropology), fairness (equity theory from psychology) and adherence to group norms (reference group theory in sociology and theory of group formation in psychology). In the earliest "sociological" version of efficiency wage theory based on gift exchange, firms give workers above market-clearing wages and workers reciprocate in their commitment to the firm.[21] The payment of above-market-clearing wages may also be motivated by considerations of fairness: in accordance with the psychological theory of equity, workers may exert less effort insofar as their wage falls short of what is considered fair.[22] Group norms typically determine the conceptions workers form about how gifts should be reciprocated and what constitutes a fair wage. In the laboratory, Fehr and his co-authors have established the importance both of reciprocal behavior and social norms for worker effort in experimental settings.[23] My favorite version of efficiency wages is the insider-outsider model, whereby insider workers prevent the firm from hiring outsiders at a market clearing wage lower than what the insiders are currently receiving.[24] This theory implicitly assumes that insiders have the ability to sabotage the inclusion of new workers into a firm. A detailed study by Donald Roy of an Illinois machine shop reveals the dynamics by which this may occur: In Roy's machine shop, insiders established group norms concerning effort and colluded to prevent the hiring of rate-busting outside workers. Workers who produced more than the level of output considered "fair" were ostracized by others.[25] Collusion by insiders against outsiders is a compelling motive for many firms to pay wages that are above market clearing.

An alternative version of efficiency wage theory, grounded in asymmetric information, views above-market clearing wages as a disciplinary device. In the Shapiro-Stiglitz model, firms pay "high" wages to reduce the incentive of workers to shirk. The attempt of all firms to pay "above average" wages, however, pushes the average level of wages above market-clearing, creating unemployment. Unemployment serves as a disciplinary device, because wor-

[20] See Katz (1986) and Blinder and Choi (1990). Blinder and Choi find strong evidence in favor of morale considerations for paying high wages as well as mixed evidence in favor of efficiency wages as a worker discipline device. Bewley (2000) concludes that morale is an important reason for failure to make wage cuts. Campbell and Kamlani (1997) report that morale is a major reason firms do not make money wage cuts, but so is concern over quits by the best workers.

[21] See Akerlof (1982) and Rabin (1993).

[22] See Akerlof and Yellen (1990) and Levine (1992).

[23] See, for example, Fehr, Kirchsteiger and Reidl (1993), Fehr and Falk (1999) and Fehr, Gachter and Kirchsteiger (1996).

[24] See Lindbeck and Snower (1988).

[25] See Roy (1952).

kers who are caught shirking and fired for lack of effort can become re-employed only after a period of unemployment.[26]

The worker discipline model fits the standard logic of economics more comfortably than approaches grounded in sociology and psychology. But sociological and psychological models, including the insider-outsider model, that rely on elements outside the standard economic box, probably yield a better over-all explanation for involuntary unemployment. These behavioral models capture Keynes' emphasis, in the initial chapters of the *General Theory,* on equity and relative wage comparisons.

EFFECTIVENESS OF MONETARY POLICY

A central proposition of the New Classical Economics is that monetary policy, as long as it is fully perceived, can have no effect on output or employment. Perfectly foreseen changes in the money supply induce rational wage and price setters to raise or lower nominal wages and prices in the identical proportion, leaving output and employment constant.[27] This New Classical hypothesis conflicts, however, with empirical evidence on the impact of monetary policy and the widespread popular belief in the power of central banks to affect economic performance.

A major contribution of behavioral macroeconomics is to demonstrate that, under sensible behavioral assumptions, monetary policy *does* affect real outcomes just as Keynesian economics long asserted. Cognitive psychology pictures decision-makers as "intuitive scientists" who summarize information and make choices based on simplified mental frames.[28] Reliance on rules of thumb that omit factors whose consideration have only a small effect on profit or utility is an implication of such cognitive parsimony. In the wage-price context, simple rules cause inertia in the response of aggregate wages (and prices) to shocks – the exact "sticky wage/price" behavior that New Classical economists had so scornfully derided. In the New Classical critique, the inertial wage behavior hypothesized in the "neoclassical synthesis" is irrational, costly for workers and firms, hence implausible. Behavioral economists have responded by demonstrating that rules of thumb involving "money illusion"

[26] See Shapiro and Stiglitz (1985) and also Bowles (1985), Foster and Wan (1984) and Stoft (1982). The worker-discipline model captures a slice of reality, but, as the whole explanation for involuntary unemployment, it suffers from both theoretical and empirical difficulties. Theoretically, in jobs where supervision is imperfect and workers can determine their own effort, firms with good reputations could demand that workers post bonds. These bonds would be forfeited in the event that a worker is caught shirking. As long as they remain employed by the firm, workers would receive wages augmented by the interest on the bond; the principal would be returned at retirement. This payment scheme solves the incentive problem facing the firm and is cheaper for the firm than above, market-clearing efficiency wages. Becker and Stigler (1974) make this precise suggestion. In their scheme the worker receives the bond back when he leaves the job in good standing. (Other ways to reduce wages to market-clearing in similar spirit have been pointed out by Carmichael (1985) and Murphy and Topel (1990).) Empirically, the discipline-device theory fails to explain why industry wage differentials are so highly correlated across occupations, so that some industries offer "good jobs" to workers in all occupations, including those where there is little scope to shirk. (See Dickens and Katz (1987).)

[27] This logic is clearly spelled out by Patinkin (1956).

are not only commonplace but also sensible – neither foolhardy nor implausible: the losses from reliance on such rules are extremely small.[28]

In joint work with Janet Yellen, I first demonstrated this result in the context of a model with efficiency wages and monopolistic competition. We assumed that some price setters follow the rule of thumb of keeping prices constant following a shock to demand (caused by a change in the money supply.) We showed that the losses to the "rule-of-thumb" firms from their failure to readjust prices following a change in the money supply are *second-order* (or *small*),[29] whereas the impact on output of a monetary shock in this economy is *first-order* (or *significant*) relative to the size of the shock.[30] We dubbed the rule-of-thumb strategies employed by firms with inertial price-setting "near-rational" since the losses they suffer from their departure from complete optimization are *second-order* (or *small*.)

The logic of the key result – that near-rational price stickiness is sufficient to impart significant power to monetary policy – is simple. With monopolistic competition, each firm's profit function is second-differentiable in its own price so that the profit function is flat in the neighborhood of the optimum own-price. In consequence, any deviation from the profit-maximizing price causes a loss in profits that is small – second-order with respect to the size of those deviations. But if the deviations from the optimum of a large number of firms are similar – for example, if they are all slow to adjust their prices following a change in the money supply – then real balances – the money supply deflated by the price level – change by a first-order amount relative to a situation with fully optimizing price-setting behavior. This first-order change in real balances, in turn, causes first-order changes in aggregate demand, output and employment. For example, suppose that the money supply increases by a fraction ε and a fraction of firms keep their prices unchanged. Each firm's losses, relative to fully optimizing behavior, are approximately proportional to the square of ε. If ε is .05, for example, its square is quite a small number, .0025, so the losses from price stickiness are apt to be small. However, assuming money demand is proportional to income, the change in real output is first-order – proportional to ε. (With fully maximizing behavior by all firms, the change in the money supply leaves output unchanged.) Thus small deviations from complete rationality – indeed small and *reasonable* deviations from complete rationality – reverse the conclusion that expected changes in the money supply have no effect on real income and output.[31]

Rule-of-thumb pricing behavior takes many forms. For example, staggered

[28] See Nisbett and Ross (1980).

[29] In this context *second-order* is the mathematical representation of the concept *small*. Correspondingly, *first-order* is the mathematical representation of the concept *significant in size*.

[30] See Akerlof and Yellen (1985a, b), Mankiw (1985), Parkin (1986) and Blanchard and Kiyotaki (1987).

[31] The same results hold in a number of alternative frameworks. For example, if firms set profit-maximizing efficiency wages, nominal wage stickiness is a form of rule-of-thumb behavior with similar consequences: the losses to the firm holding wages constant are second-order, but shocks to the money supply change real variables by a first-order amount. In Mankiw's formulation small "menu costs", which are fixed costs for making a price change, inhibit price changes with effects on equilibrium output that are an order larger than the menu cost.

price (wage) models, in which firms keep nominal prices (wages) fixed for a period of time, correspond closely to descriptions of price (wage) setting processes.[32] In the Taylor staggered contract model, during each period, half of all firms set a nominal price which they maintain for the succeeding two-period interval.[33] A variant of the staggered contract model, due to Calvo, assumes instead that a fixed nominal price is reset at randomly varying intervals.[34] New Classical economists object to both renditions of the model, on the grounds that such price setting is not maximizing.[35] Of course, they are right: instead of keeping nominal prices unchanged during a fixed interval, Taylor's and Calvo's firms would do better by establishing prices that vary within the interval in accordance with the firm's expectations of the money supply (aggregate demand.) Such profit-maximizing behavior would again render money supply changes neutral. However, price-setting (wage-setting) strategies of the Taylor/Calvo type are near-rational: the small amount of nominal rigidity that characterizes these models is sufficient to allow monetary policy to be stabilizing, yet the losses relative to a strategy that varies prices within the pricing interval are second-order.[36] There are many other forms of near-rational rule of thumb behavior that render monetary policy efficacious.[37]

[32] Especially see Carlton (1986).
[33] See Akerlof (1969), Fischer (1977) and Taylor (1979).
[34] See Calvo (1983).
[35] See Barro (1977) for this complaint about staggered contract models.
[36] See Akerlof and Yellen (1991). Technically, it turns out that the amplitude of the business cycle, as measured by the standard deviation of (log) income rises due to Taylor's staggered contracts by an amount that is proportional to the standard deviation of the pricing "error" made by Taylor's firms. Monetary policy can offset this price stickiness and reduce business cycle volatility. But the losses realized by firms from the use of Taylor-type staggered contracts are second-order: proportional to the variance of shocks to the system. In this sense, staggered pricing has a first-order effect on both the size of the business cycle and the stabilizing properties of monetary policy. But the nonmaximizing behavior which allows monetary policy to stabilize the economy results in losses that are second-order.
[37] For example, Gregory Mankiw and Ricardo Reis (2001) have recently suggested that the response of income to monetary shocks is better explained by a "near-rational" model in which prices (and/or wages) respond slowly to new information than by near-rational, staggered price models in the Taylor/Calvo style. Slow response to new information may result from the considerable managerial costs involved in gathering, processing, and sharing information involved in the price-setting process. (See Zbaracki *et al.* (2000), quoted in Mankiw and Reis.) The Mankiw-Reis formulation resolves three paradoxes present in rational expectations staggered price models. Sticky information yields the empirically-observed long lags of response of income to changes in monetary policy (Friedman (1948) and Romer and Romer (1989)); it is consistent with the surprisingly slow response of inflation to shocks found in estimates of Phillips Curves (Gordon (1997)); and it fails to yield the theoretical perversity in rational expectations staggered contract models of deflationary policies that lead to increases, not decreases in output (Ball (1994)).

Experimental evidence suggests that the coordination problems involved in reaching a new equilibrium may be external as well as internal to the firm. Fehr and Tyran (2001) conducted experiments in which price setters were given payoffs derived from a near-rational model with monopolistic competition. They found that negative changes in the money supply caused considerable output reductions when payoffs were denominated in nominal terms. Subjects acted as if other price setters suffered from money illusion, making them, in turn, reluctant to cut prices. (A new approach to the dependence of monetary policy on co-ordination failure is implicit in Howitt and Clower (2000).) This paper suggests that the reaction of prices to money supply changes involves the formation of expectations concerning the response of other price-setters to the same shock. Fehr and Tyran's (2001) experiment points to yet another form of near-rational behavior: price setters may fully maximize, but on the assumption that other firms follow sticky, rule-of-thumb pricing behavior. Again, monetary policy is effective in changing output and employment.

Near-rational, rule-of-thumb models solve the great puzzle posed by Robert Lucas regarding the effectiveness of monetary policy with rational expectations.[38] New Classical Economics finds it difficult to explain more than a fleeting relation between money and output. The new behavioral economics, with a variety of plausible near-rational behaviors, yields a robust relation between changes in the money supply and changes in output.

THE PHILLIPS CURVE AND THE NAIRU

Probably the single most important macroeconomic relationship is the Phillips Curve. The "price-price" Phillips Curve relates the rate of inflation to the level of unemployment, the expected rate of inflation, and variables affecting aggregate supply, such as the price of oil or food. The trade-offs between inflation and unemployment implicit in this relation define the "feasible set" for monetary policy and thus play a decisive role in its formulation. The Phillips Curve was first estimated for Britain,[39] then subsequently for the U.S.[40] and many other countries.[41]

The basis of the Phillips Curve is supply and demand. Phillips posited that when demand is high and unemployment low, workers can bargain for higher nominal wage increases than when demand is low and unemployment high. Firms' pricing policies translate wage inflation (adjusted for productivity) into price inflation. For policymakers, therefore, a durable tradeoff exists between inflation and unemployment.

In the late 1960s, Milton Friedman (1968) and Edmund Phelps (1968) added an important new wrinkle. They argued that workers care about and bargain for real, not nominal, wage gains: workers routinely expect and receive compensation for expected inflation, then bargain from there, demanding higher expected real wage gains at lower rates of unemployment. Again, pricing policies translate wage inflation into price inflation. The consequence of this small shift in assumption – that workers bargain for real, not nominal wage increases – is enormous: instead of a durable unemployment-inflation tradeoff, there is now just a unique "natural" unemployment rate consistent with stable inflation. With "real-wage" bargaining, the long-run Phillips curve – the unemployment/inflation combinations consistent with equality between actual and expected inflation – is vertical because there is one and only one unemployment rate – the "natural rate" – at which actual and expected inflation match.

To see why the long-run Phillips curve must be vertical, imagine that a central bank attempts via monetary policy to hold unemployment below the natural rate. With labor markets abnormally tight, workers demand nominal wage increases in excess of expected inflation (plus normal real wage cum

[38] See Lucas (1972).
[39] See Phillips (1958) and Lipsey (1960).
[40] See Gordon (1970) and Perry (1970) for some early estimates for the United States.
[41] To give just one example, Flanagan, Soskice and Ulman (1983) estimated the Phillips Curve for many different countries.

productivity gains.) Firms, in turn, pass the associated cost increases into prices, so that inflation exceeds what workers initially anticipated when they bargained. With unemployment below the natural rate, actual inflation therefore exceeds expected inflation. *Ex post*, workers have been fooled. So, over time, inflationary expectations, and inflation in turn, accelerates. With unemployment held below the natural rate, the consequence is ever accelerating *inflation*. Similarly, the Friedman-Phelps model predicts that a Central Bank attempting to hold unemployment above the natural rate indefinitely eventually causes accelerating *deflation*. Only the natural rate of unemployment yields steady inflation.

Economists accepted the natural rate hypothesis remarkably quickly after it was first proposed by Friedman and Phelps in the late 1960s. Three things conspired in its favor. First, it seemed to explain remarkably well the inflation-unemployment experience of the 1960s and 1970s. At the low unemployment rates of the late 1960s, inflation rose, which apparently drove up inflationary expectations, shifting the short-run unemployment inflation trade-off outward. Thus the 1970s began with a much less favorable unemployment inflation tradeoff than the 1960s. (Analysts ignored the equally plausible explanation that as inflation increased, as it did in the late 1960s, wage bargains and price setting began to take inflationary expectations, which had previously been ignored, into account.)[42] Second, empirical estimates of the Phillips Curve yielded coefficients on past inflation whose sum was not statistically different from unity. The inference was drawn that the lagged inflation terms in such estimates correspond to expected inflation, which is an autoregressive weighted average of past inflation, and that the coefficient on expected inflation in determining current inflation is one.[43] Finally, there is a bias for economists to accept rationally-based null hypotheses, even though accepted only by tests with relatively low power.[44]

Economists should not have accepted the natural rate hypothesis so readily. There are both theoretical and empirical reasons to be highly suspicious. Theoretically, the natural rate hypothesis reminds me of a common diet-book rule of thumb. According to that rule of thumb for every 3200 calories extra that we eat, we gain a pound. For every 3200 calories less we lose a pound. This always makes me imagine twin brothers. One of these twin brothers eats just enough to keep his weight even. The other twin eats one more 100-calorie cookie per day. If the rule of thumb is right, after one year the cookie eater is 11 pounds heavier than his brother. After a decade he is 110 pounds heavier. Fifty years later, should he live so long, he would be 550 pounds

[42] This alternative explanation was given by Eckstein and Brinner (1972), but did not make it into the mainstream.

[43] We should here note Sargent's (1971) criticism that the coefficient on lagged inflation will not equal one in an accelerationist model if the process generating inflation is stable, without a unit root.

[44] We shall see an example of such bias below when we review Summers' criticism of the acceptance of the random walk hypothesis based on failure to reject by tests with very low power against alternative hypotheses.

heavier. Just as expected, the rule of thumb does break down when extrapolated over long time periods: more accurate renditions of the relationship between weight and calories show that the maintenance of higher weight requires extra caloric intake. Happily the twins' weights will not diverge forever. Similarly my guess is that for at least some band of unemployment rates, inflation would asymptote to a constant value rather than accelerate or decelerate indefinitely. Such *a priori* reasoning could be wrong, but the error from over-extrapolation of the diet book rule of thumb warns us that the natural rate hypothesis is rather odd. At very low unemployment rates, the Friedman/Phelps prediction of accelerating inflation seems quite possibly reasonable and empirically relevant.[45] But I am suspicious about the theory's applicability when unemployment is high.

My suspicions regarding the natural rate hypothesis are supported by an empirical fact, which reveals that its applicability is not *universal.* Unemployment in the U.S. for the whole of the 1930s was indisputably in excess – surely *greatly* in excess – of any plausible natural rate. According to the natural rate hypothesis, price deflation should have accelerated for the whole decade. That did not happen. Prices fell for a time, but deflation stopped after 1932; there was no significant deflation for the next ten years, despite extremely high unemployment. This evidence suggests that, at least after some time, at high levels of unemployment and low inflation rates, the natural rate hypothesis breaks down. Such a failure would not be terribly serious for a theory derived from empirical observation, but it constitutes a serious flaw for a relationship derived from *a priori* principles, principles that are accepted because they are supposed to be always and everywhere true.

The evidence of the 1930s is not unique. Modern economies display similar characteristics. For example, Pierre Fortin estimates that from 1992 to 2000, the Canadian economy experienced almost 12 points of unemployment in excess of a very conservative 8% estimate of NAIRU.[46] During that same period, inflation averaged a very low 1 1/2 percent per year. According to natural rate theory, core inflation should have declined by roughly 6 percentage points, since a typical estimate of the Phillips curve slope is 1/2. Instead, inflation declined over that period by only .1 percent.

Econometric evidence further suggests that the natural rate theory rests on shifty sand rather than bedrock. Time-varying estimates of the natural rate show that it changes over time; but, even with allowance for such shifts, estimates of the natural rate possess high standard errors. Staiger, Stock, and Watson (1997) compute a 95% confidence interval for the US natural rate which exceeds 5 percentage points; this is more than three times the standard deviation of the US monthly unemployment rate over the last 50 years.

[45] The occurrence of hyperinflation with low unemployment maintained sufficiently long is one prediction of the theory. The frequent occurrence of hyperinflation seems to support the theory. But these hyperinflations have occurred when governments have lost fiscal credibility (and could only pay their deficits by seigniorage). It may be the loss of fiscal credibility, not the maintenance of low unemployment, which is the cause of the hyperinflation.

[46] Observation due to Pierre Fortin in Fortin, Akerlof, Dickens and Perry (2001).

In recent papers, William Dickens, George Perry and I have explored two behavioral hypotheses that, contrary to the natural rate model, produce a stable tradeoff between unemployment and inflation at sufficiently high unemployment and low inflation rates. The first hypothesis is "pure Keynes": workers resist, and firms rarely impose, cuts in nominal pay. The second hypothesis concerns the role of inflationary expectations in wage bargains: we argue that, at very low inflation, a significant number of workers do not consider inflation sufficiently salient to be factored into their decisions. However, as inflation increases, the losses from ignoring it also rise, and therefore an increasing number of firms and workers take it into account in bargaining.

Keynes' assumption that workers resist nominal wage cuts was consistent with his intuitive understanding of psychology. The assumption also coincides with psychological theory and evidence. Prospect theory posits that individuals evaluate changes in their circumstances according to the gains or losses they entail relative to some reference point. The evidence suggests that individuals place much greater weight on avoiding losses than on incurring gains. Kahneman and Tversky have demonstrated that many experimental results which are inconsistent with expected utility maximization can be rationalized by prospect theory. Downward wage rigidity is a natural implication of prospect theory if the current money wage is taken as a reference point by workers in measuring gains and losses. In support of this view, Shafir, Diamond and Tversky (1997) found in a questionnaire study that individuals' mental frames are defined not just in the real terms hypothesized by classical economists but also exhibit some money illusion.

Numerous empirical studies document that money wages are, in fact, downward sticky. Using panel data, Card and Hyslop (1997) and Kahn (1997) found that distributions of nominal wage changes are asymmetric around zero. Fortin found a remarkable pile-up of wage changes at zero in Canadian data. From 1992 to 1994, when Canadian inflation was 1.2 percent and the unemployment rate averaged 11.0 percent, only 5.7 percent of non-COLA union agreements had first-year wage cuts, whereas 47 percent had wage freezes.[47] In detailed interviews in Connecticut, Bewley found that managers are willing to cut nominal wages only as a last resort.[48] To investigate whether firms cut total compensation through benefit cuts as opposed to money wage cuts, Lebow, Saks and Wilson examined the individual industries covered by the Employment Cost Index: they found that benefit cuts are only a minor substitute for nominal wage cuts.[49] Using Swiss data Fehr and Goette found that even a seven-year period of low inflation and low productivity growth did not increase the frequency of money wage cuts.[50]

At low inflation there is a long-run trade-off between output and inflation if there is aversion to nominal pay cuts. Unlike the Friedman-Phelps model, in which such a trade-off is transitory, long-term increases in inflation (if it is close

[47] See Fortin (1995, 1996).
[48] See Bewley (1999).
[49] See Lebow, Saks and Wilson (1999).
[50] See Fehr and Goette (2000).

to zero) result in significantly less unemployment and more output.[51] The logic goes as follows. In both good times and bad, some firms and industries do better than others. Wages need to adjust to accommodate these differences in economic fortunes. In times of moderate inflation and productivity growth, relative wages can easily adjust. Unlucky firms can raise the wages they pay by less than the average, while the lucky firms can give above-average increases. However, if productivity growth is low (as it was from the early 1970s through the mid 1990s in the United States) and there is no inflation, firms that need to cut their real wages can do so only by cutting the money wages of their employees. Under realistic assumptions about the variability and serial correlation of demand shocks across firms, the needed frequency of nominal cuts rises rapidly as inflation declines. An aversion on the part of firms to impose nominal wage cuts results in higher permanent rates of unemployment. Because the real wages at which labor is supplied are higher at every level of employment when inflation is low, the unemployment rate consistent with stable inflation rises as inflation falls to low levels. Spillovers produce an aggregate employment impact which exceeds the employment changes in those firms that are constrained by their inability to cut wages. Thus, a benefit of a little inflation is that it "greases the wheels of the labor market."

Simulations of a model with intersectoral shocks and aversion on the part of firms to nominal wage cuts suggests that, with realistically chosen parameters, the tradeoff between inflation and unemployment is severe at very low rates of inflation, when productivity growth is low. For example, a permanent reduction in inflation from two percent per year to zero results in a permanent increase in unemployment of approximately two percentage points.[52] Estimation of a Phillips curve for the United States after World War II, corresponding to the simulation model just described, gives similar results. When the Phillips curve thus estimated is used to simulate the inflation experience of the 1930s, the fit is shockingly close to actual U.S. inflation experience during the depression.[53] A comparable simulation of the standard natural rate model, in contrast, counterfactually, shows accelerating deflation throughout the 1930s.

An alternative behavioral theory also generates a permanent tradeoff between inflation and unemployment at low inflation. This theory is based on the idea that because inflation is not salient when it is low, anticipated future changes in the price level are ignored in wage bargaining.[54] With monopolistic competition and efficiency wages such ignorance of inflation when it is low is near-rational.[55] The psychology of just noticeable differences and cog-

[51] See Tobin (1972).

[52] See Akerlof, Dickens and Perry (1996).

[53] This is done by sequentially feeding in the simulated inflation of the previous period to derive adaptively the next period's inflationary expectations. The fit is so excellent that there must be a component of luck.

[54] Past inflation is incorporated indirectly because wage bargains take into account the wages paid by competitors.

[55] See Akerlof, Dickens and Perry (2000).

nitive psychology both suggest that people tend to ignore variables that are unimportant to their decisions.[56] Econometric estimates of the Phillips curve which allow for the possibility that past inflation has a different impact on current inflation when inflation is high than when it is low are consistent with this hypothesis: at high inflation, the sum of coefficients on past inflation is close to one.[57] At low inflation, this sum of coefficients is much closer to zero. Similarly, regressions using survey measures of expected inflation as an independent variable yield much higher coefficients on the expected inflation term at high inflation than at low inflation.[58] Not surprisingly then, when periods of low and high inflation are combined to estimate a non-linear model of the influence of inflationary expectations we find that their impact depends on the recent history of inflation.

The demonstration by behavioral macroeconomics that very low inflation has the cost of permanently high unemployment and low output, has important implications for monetary policy. Most of us think of central bankers as cautious, conservative, and safe. But I consider many to be dangerous drivers: to avoid the oncoming traffic of inflation, they drive on the far edge of the road, keeping inflation too low and unemployment too high. During the 1990s, Canada had very low inflation and an unprecedented unemployment gap – close to four percentage points – with the United States.[59] Europe has also had high unemployment and very low inflation. Japan has gone much further, allowing deflation. Central bankers who accept the textbook version of the natural rate hypothesis should follow the advice of Oliver Cromwell to the General Assembly of the Church of Scotland: "I beseech you in the bowels of Christ, think it possible you may be mistaken." It is no coincidence that the leading survey of cognitive psychology uses this citation to demonstrate a common perceptual error: overconfidence.[60]

UNDERSAVING

It is common wisdom that people save too little. To compensate for this failure, most developed country governments heavily support the elderly in retirement. In addition, a very large number of employers require and subsidize

[56] This formulation is also influenced by the public's mental frame regarding inflation. Shiller (1997a, 1997b) has elicited the differences in mental frame between the public and economists by questionnaire responses.

[57] One is not, however, necessarily the magic number for the reasons noted earlier by Sargent (1971).

[58] Such regressions address the problem suggested by Sargent that the natural rate model should produce coefficients on expected inflation that correspond to the money supply rule, and those coefficients need not be equal to unity. If expectations are observed without error, the coefficient on expected inflation with natural rate theory should be unity. Error in the expectations data should bias its coefficient downward, but it should not, as observed, result in changes in the coefficient, unless there are also changes in the error of observation between periods of high and low inflation.

[59] 3.8 percent from 1990 to 1999, according to *Economic Report of the President,* 2000, Table B-107.

[60] See Nisbett and Ross (1980). This book is one of the leading primers for the psychology of behavioral macroeconomics. Curiously, cognitive psychologists have a much more empirical basis for their theories than economists.

pension contributions of their employees. Many forms of saving receive tax advantage. Even with these legs up, the common wisdom is that financial assets of most households still fall considerably short of what they need to maintain their consumption in retirement.[61]

For New Classical economics, saving too little or too much, like involuntary unemployment, is an impossibility, a straightforward contradiction of the assumptions of the model. Since saving is the result of individual utility maximization, it must, absent externalities, be just right. Behavioral macroeconomics, in contrast, has developed theoretical tools and empirical strategies to advance understanding of such time-inconsistent behavior.

A key theoretical innovation permitting systematic analysis of time-inconsistent behavior is the recognition that individuals may maximize a utility function that is divorced from that representing "true welfare." Once this distinction is accepted, "saving too little" becomes a meaningful concept. The idea can be illustrated by the ancient myth of the lemmings, who every few years are said to converge in a death march, which ends with their final plunge into the sea.[62] The alleged behavior of those lemmings reveals a distinction common among psychologists, but rare for economists. Unless the lemmings experience an unusual epiphany in that final plunge, their utility or welfare is given by one function; yet they maximize another.

Think about it: the popular view of saving, that people undersave, is similarly described. Determining whether people save too much or too little involves asking whether people, like the lemmings, have one (intertemporal) utility function which describes their welfare, but maximize another.[63] Such evidence as there is suggests potentially large difference between the two concepts. High negative rates of time discount are necessary to explain actual wealth-earnings ratios.[64] Yet, questionnaire responses on the consumption-saving tradeoffs that people think they *ought to make* reveals an intertemporal discount rate that is on average slightly positive.[65]

The hyperbolic discount function, which has been used to study intertem-

[61] Engen, Gale, and Uccello (1999, p. 97) reach the opposite conclusion. They compare the actual wealth with that derived in a calibrated optimization model. Their preferred calibration has a rate of time preference of three percent. With data from the U.S. Health and Retirement Survey with a broad definition of wealth to include all home equity, 60.5 percent of households have more than the median optimal wealth in the calibrated model. But I would focus on an alternative result from their simulations. If we exclude home equity investment in spendable financial capital, and assume a zero rate of intertemporal time discount, only 29.9 percent of households reach the pre-retirement age of 60 or 61 with more than the optimal median wealth for someone of their age (p. 99, Table 5). Like the discussants, both for empirical and *a priori* reasons, I view a zero rate of discount as more correct. This conforms to people's stated preference for non-declining consumption at a zero rate of interest (see below) and it weights utility at different ages on a one-for-one basis. My choice to exclude home equity capital assumes that retirees should not have to leave their homes for financial reasons, or to reverse-mortgage them, as they get older.

[62] My 1946 version of *The Encyclopedia Britannica* describes as fact the march of the lemmings, which "never ceases until they reach the sea, into which they plunge and are drowned."

[63] This difference is made explicit in Laibson (1999).

[64] See Engen, Gale, and Uccello (1999, pp. 157–8).

[65] See Barsky, Kimball, Juster, and Shapiro (1997, p. 34).

poral savings choices, can be used to formalize the distinction between the utility function that describes actual saving behavior and the utility function that measures the welfare resulting from that behavior. The hyperbolic function captures the difficulty people have in exercising self-control. In contrast to the exponentially declining discount rates that are standard in neoclassical theory, the hyperbolic function assumes that the discount rates used to evaluate tradeoffs between adjacent periods decline as the time horizon lengthens: individuals use high discount rates to evaluate options that require an immediate sacrifice for a future reward and lower discount rates when the same sacrifice is deferred into the future. Thus, they are patient in making choices requiring gratification delays when those sacrifices are deferred; but impatient in delaying gratification in the short run. Because present consumption is more salient than future consumption, individuals procrastinate about saving. The hyperbolic function accords closely with experimental findings: Human and animal subjects are far less willing to delay gratification immediately than to commit to such delays in the future.[66]

Two forms of procrastination may result from hyperbolic discounting. "Naive procrastination" occurs when an individual assumes incorrectly that her utility function will be different in the future. She mistakenly projects that, although today is salient, tomorrow will be different. She fails to see that tomorrow's self will be different from today's self, so that tomorrow will be just as salient as today once it has moved one step closer. The naive procrastinator mistakenly believes that she will save (diet, exercise, quit smoking...) tomorrow, although she has not done so today, and is surprised that the sacrifices deferred today are also deferred again tomorrow. More sophisticated procrastination takes the form of preproperation, according to the terminology of O'Donoghue and Rabin (1999). The preproperator has fully rational expectations about who her future self will be. She says to herself: there is no reason to save today if tomorrow is going to be especially salient. If tomorrow is especially salient then I will spend whatever savings I have laid aside today when it was also especially salient. So I should not make the sacrifice today.

Laibson has used hyperbolic discounting as the basis of a research program on saving behavior and policy. With co-authors Repetto and Tobacman (1998) he has simulated the effects of different tax incentive programs in a world in which consumers preproperate. They estimate that large positive welfare effects result from small changes in incentives to save which reduce the amount of preproperation. Because of this work the regulations regarding tax advantaged 401(k) savings plans have been changed. If firms so choose, workers may now be automatically enrolled with an automatic default contribution. Adoption of such plans significantly increases plan participa-

[66] See Laibson (1997), Laibson, Repetto and Tobacman (1998), Strotz (1956), Phelps and Pollak (1968), Loewenstein and Prelec (1992), and Ainslie (1992). In Akerlof (1991) I was regrettably unaware of earlier work on intertemporal inconsistency. In economics this includes Strotz (1956), Phelps and Pollak (1968), Thaler (1981), and Loewenstein (1987). Loewenstein and Thaler (1989) give an excellent early review of the previous literature on dynamic inconsistency including the psychological experiments and theory. See also Ainslie (1992).

tion and many workers maintain their contributions at the level of the default.[67]

Besides the popularity of social security and other programs that "force" consumers to save, the best evidence of undersaving is probably the observation that, upon retirement, individuals, on average, reduce consumption substantially.[68] In fact, consumption at retirement declines discontinuously.[69] Those with more wealth and higher income replacement reduce their consumption by much less. This finding is difficult to explain with the standard life cycle, exponential discounting model.[70]

Thaler and Benartzi (2000) have devised a savings plan to overcome workers' tendency to procrastinate and have tested it on an experimental basis at a mid-size manufacturing firm: employees were invited to join a savings plan allowing them to elect, in advance, the fraction of wage or salary increases to be set aside for savings. Consistent with hyperbolic discounting, but not with the standard exponential model, workers chose relatively modest saving out of current income but committed to save large fractions of future wage and salary increases. Within a short period of time, the average savings rate had doubled.[71]

ASSET MARKETS

Keynes' *General Theory* was the progenitor of the modern behavioral finance view of asset markets. In Keynes' metaphor "professional investment may be likened to those newspaper competitions in which competitors have to pick out the six prettiest faces from a hundred photographs, the prize being awarded to the competitor whose choice most nearly corresponds to the average preferences of the competitors as a whole."[72] Thus stock markets are too volatile and also too responsive to news. This view of the stock market contrasts with the efficient markets model in which stock prices measure the present value of future returns adjusted for risk.

In the early 1980s Robert Shiller conducted a direct test of the Keynesian excess volatility hypothesis. He reasoned that if stock prices really are the predicted value of expected future returns, they should vary less than the discounted returns themselves. Shiller's insight was a direct application of a

[67] See Madrian and Shea (2001).

[68] See Bernheim, Skinner and Weinberg (2001) and Banks, Blundell, and Tanner (1998).

[69] Such declines might occur if retirement is associated with negative income shocks. Bernheim, Skinner, and Weinberg (2001, p, 854) suggest that such an adjustment is relatively minor.

[70] Retirees, of course, obtain greater leisure, and thus one might expect a reduction in consumption as leisure is substituted for consumption. It is difficult, but not impossible, to explain, in addition, why such substitution varies systematically both with the level of wealth and with the income replacement ratio. This could occur if those with a particular taste for leisure in retirement have by choice high income replacement ratios and have accumulated high levels of savings.

[71] From 4.4 percent to 8.7 percent. This behavior is also explained by prospect theory by Kahneman and Tversky (1979). According to prospect theory the framing of decision-making is important and people resist taking losses. In this context these employees do not want to take losses in their consumption.

[72] Keynes (1936, p. 156).

simple statistical principle: a good forecast should have lower variance than the variable being forecast. If the weather forecast has greater variance than the actual weather, the weather forecaster should be fired.[73] Using 100 years of U.S. data on stock prices and dividends, Shiller (1981) compared the variance of detrended stock prices to the variance of the detrended present discounted values of dividends.[74] He found just what Keynes would have expected: the standard deviation of (detrended) stock prices is five times larger than the standard deviation of (detrended) discounted dividends. These results have been confirmed in more sophisticated tests that properly allow for the nonstationarity of both stock prices and the present discounted values of dividends.[75]

The results of variance-bounds tests notwithstanding, belief in efficient markets was sustained by empirical results such as the finding of insignificant serial correlation in returns in monthly data.[76] Rejection of the hypothesis that returns are serially correlated suggests that the stock market follows something close to a random walk. In response, Summers (1986) showed in a model of "fads" – with serially correlated deviations from perfect markets – that serial correlation tests have very low power: the power of such tests is so low as to require 5,000 years worth of data before it could discriminate 50 percent of the time between the random walk hypothesis and a fad that would drive stock prices more than 30 percent away from fundamentals 35 percent of the time.[77]

Beyond establishing the existence of excess volatility, Shiller has also examined its possible causes. In *Irrational Exuberance* (1999), he reviews the news coverage of the stock market bubble of the 1990s and explains how the idea of a "new era" both in financial markets and the real economy was propagated. As stock prices rose, the "new economy" mantra was transmitted from person to person; individual investors acted on the opinions of the media,

[73] For example, drawing from a normal distribution, the forecast that yields the smallest squared deviation between the actual draw and the forecast is the mean of the distribution, which is a constant with no variance at all.

[74] He extrapolated future dividends for times beyond his period of observation. For a similar test also see LeRoy and Porter (1981).

[75] See Campbell and Shiller (1987). Although Shiller's *tour de force* initially seemed to clinch the case, two technical problems cast a shadow of doubt. The first problem is that detrending potentially introduces a serious bias into Shiller's procedure: neither stock price series nor dividends are stationary and a nonstationary series does not even possess a variance. The second problem relates to the shortness of Shiller's sample and his extrapolation of future dividends beyond the present. Allen Kleidon (1986) showed in simulated data that the difference between the variance of Shiller's detrended stock price and of his dividend series is not large enough to confidently reject the efficient market null hypothesis when returns follow a random walk. The Campbell-Shiller test allows for the nonstationarity of stock prices and dividends, provided the two series are cointegrated. This test is also valid even if firms smooth dividends.
The high volatility of stock prices could also be explained by a high frequency cycle in the expected real rate of return on stocks. But such a cycle is inconsistent with most standard classical models of the economy, where real returns are mainly determined by the state of technology, and the capital-labor ratio. In the standard classical model both technology and the capital labor ratio change slowly.

[76] Where not insignificant in the statistical sense, such correlation seemed insignificant in magnitude.

[77] West (1988) similarly demonstrated the low power of Kleidon's efficient markets test using Shiller's detrended data.

which exaggerated the effects of economic fundamentals such as the internet on productivity. Such stock market bubbles are common; they have occurred in many other countries and frequently over the course of history. Indeed, Kindleberger's accounts of manias and panics and Galbraith's history of the *Great Crash* of 1929 are distinguished predecessors to *Irrational Exuberance.*

A second major empirical finding that casts doubt on the rationality of the stock market is the equity premium puzzle. Over the last two hundred years, the return on equity has been significantly higher than the return on bonds. For example, from 1802 to 1998 the real return on a value-weighted market equity index was 7.0 percent per annum compared to 2.9 percent for a relatively riskless security.[78] Over the last 75 years, 1926-2000, the real returns were 8.7 percent on equity versus 0.7 percent on bonds, a gap of 8.0 percent. A gap of this size is huge: Siegel and Thaler (1998) calculate that a $1,000 investment made 75 years ago would have yielded $12,400 in bonds and $884,000 in stocks. This gap is so large that rejection of rationality is duck soup: With intertemporal maximization of utility, the marginal utility of consumption today should equal the expected extra utility tomorrow from foregoing one unit of consumption today. With a constant relative risk aversion utility function, this condition implies that the expected equity premium should equal the product of the coefficient of risk aversion and the covariance between the growth of consumption and the return on stock prices. For reasonable values of the coefficient of risk aversion, however, this product is much smaller than the equity premium, thus rejecting rational consumption behavior. This rejection is known as the equity premium puzzle.[79]

Further evidence of the irrationality of stock prices comes from cross section data. Similar to Shiller's time-series finding of excess volatility coupled with reversion to the mean in price/dividends ratios, De Bondt and Thaler (1987) find reversion to the mean of stock returns in a cross section: successive portfolios formed by the previous five years' 50 most extreme winners considerably underperform the market average, while portfolios of the previous five years' 50 worst losers perform better than the market average. Other stock market anomalies, such as a 20% one-day decline in stock prices in October 1987 in the absence of any significant news also cast doubt on the efficient markets hypothesis.[80]

Asset markets are not only important for their own sake, they are also important because they affect the macroeconomy, through at least three channels. First, the value of assets affects wealth and, in turn, consumption. Second, the price of existing assets relative to the price of new capital –

[78] See Mehra (2001, p.1).

[79] It is remarkable that even this weak test leads to rejection, since most theories of consumption, whether maximizing or not, would suggest considerable correlation between the rate of return on stocks and the rate of growth of consumption. For example, such a correlation occurs if consumers have a consumption function which naively depends on their wealth, or, alternatively, if the same optimism that leads to high returns in the stock market also leads to consumption binges. Parker (2001) suggests a possible resolution of the equity premium puzzle.

[80] See Romer (1993, p. 1112).

Tobin's q ratio – affects investment since investment can be viewed as an arbitrage between new capital stock and claims to similar existing assets.[81] Finally, asset values affect the chances that firms will go bankrupt. Firms close to bankruptcy find it difficult, if not impossible, to borrow, and thus commonly forego profitable investment opportunities.[82]

POVERTY AND IDENTITY

If income distribution is a topic in macroeconomics, as many have professed, then behavioral economics also offers insight on the most enduring macroeconomic problem facing the United States: the disparity in income and social condition between the majority white population and the African-American minority. As a legacy both of slavery and the Jim Crow discrimination that followed it, poverty weighs especially heavily on African-Americans. The black poverty rate of 23.6 percent in 2000 was roughly triple the white rate of 7.7.[83] Despite comprising only about 1/8 of the population, African-Americans have almost 1/4 of all U.S. poverty.[84] The reality is yet more disparate than these statistics indicate because the problems of the poorest African-Americans go beyond mere poverty. They include extraordinarily high rates of crime, drug and alcohol addiction, out-of-wedlock births, female-headed households and welfare dependency. Statistics on incarceration indicate that even the worst of these problems affect a significant fraction of African-Americans. Thus, for example, about 4.5 percent of black males are either in jail or in prison.[85] The black male incarceration rate exceeds the white male rate by a factor of eight to one.[86] And the life-time chances of a black male youth entering prison exceeds 1/4.[87]

Because standard economic theory, in our view, is incapable of explaining such self-destructive behavior, Rachel Kranton and I have developed models, based upon sociological and psychological observation, to understand the persistence of African-American disadvantage. Our theory stresses the role of identity and the decisions that individuals make about who they want to be. In our theory of minority poverty, dispossessed races and classes face a

[81] See the literature on q theory, especially including Tobin (1969), Abel (1982), Hayashi (1982) and Summers (1981).

[82] See Myers (1974), Jensen and Meckling (1976). Lamont (1995) shows how dual equilibria may occur because of such dependence.

[83] Hispanics have a similar but less extreme history of discrimination.

[84] See http://www.census.gov/Press-Release/www/2000/cb00-158.html.

[85] In 1996 there were 530,140 Black male prisoners and 213,100 Black Non-Hispanic and 80,900 Hispanic jail inmates of both sexes. There were 462,500 male and 55,800 female inhabitants of jails. Extrapolating the Black Hispanic rate at .3 and the male/female rate for Black as the same as White yields 211814 black males in jail in 1996. The Black male population was about 1/2 * (30 + .6 * 4.7) million = 32.82/2 = 16.14 million. The net result is about 4.5 percent the the African male population in prison or jail. Source of incarceration rates: Correctional populations of the US 1996, US Department of Justice, Table 5.7, p. 82. Source: http://www.census.gov/statab/www/part1a.html.

[86] See www.hrw.org/reports/2000/usa/Table3.pdf.

[87] This is an estimate based on incarceration rates in 1993.

Hobbesian choice. One possibility is to choose an identity that adapts to the dominant culture. But such an identity is adopted with the knowledge that full acceptance by members of the dominant culture is unlikely. Such a choice is also likely to be psychologically costly to oneself since it involves being someone "different"; family and friends, who are also outside the dominant culture are likely also to have negative attitudes toward a maverick who has adopted it. Thus individuals are likely to feel that they can never fully "pass." A second possibility is to adopt the historically-determined alternative identity, which, for many minorities, is an oppositional culture. Each identity is associated with prescriptions for ideal behavior. In the case of the oppositional identity, these prescriptions are commonly defined in terms of what the dominant culture is *not.* Since the prescriptions of the dominant culture endorse "self-fulfillment," those of the oppositional culture are self-destructive. The identity of the oppositional culture may be easier on the ego, but it is also likely to be economically and physically debilitating.

This identity-based theory of disadvantage is consistent with a considerable body of evidence. For example, it captures the central findings of studies by authors such as Anderson (1990), Clark (1965), Du Bois (1965), Frazier (1957), Hannerz (1969), Rainwater (1970), and Wilson (1987, 1996). Read any African-American biography: the uncomfortable dance between acceptance and rejection invariably takes center stage.

The identity theory of minority poverty has social policy implications that depart from those derived from standard neoclassical theory. For example, the standard economic theory of crime and punishment implicitly argues for combating crime by deterrence: raise the stakes high enough, as California did with its "three strikes and you're out" law, and the potential criminal will think twice. But the prisons are full and crime has not stopped. An identity-based theory suggests, in contrast, that large negative externalities from incarceration may offset the short-run gains from deterring criminal activity through tougher incarceration policies.[88] Prison itself is a school for countercultural identity, and thus the breeding ground for future crime. Moreover, externalities in identity formation argue for programs to allay crime before it has occurred. These include, for example, effective, easily accessed drug treatment and rehabilitation programs and public jobs for inner-city youth. Identity theory suggests that the benefits of increased expenditures for schools in African-American neighborhoods with high poverty rates are likely to be substantial: African-American children have been found to be particularly responsive to differences in teacher quality and class size.[89] It may take the extraordinary teacher and close personal attention to sort through student issues concerning identity in addition to covering the standard curriculum.[90] Finally, the externalities involved in identity formation argue for af-

[88] See Levitt (1996).
[89] See Ferguson (1998) on the effect of teacher quality and Krueger and Whitmore (1999) on the effect of class size.
[90] See Delpit (1995).

firmative action, because it is a symbol of welcome for African-Americans into the white society that has rejected them for so long.[91]

CONCLUSION

It is now thirty years since the revolution that began in growth theory and then swept through microeconomics. The new microeconomics is standard in all graduate programs, half of a two-course sequence. Adoption of the new macroeconomics has been slower, but the revolution is coming here as well. If there is any subject in economics which should be behavioral, it is macroeconomics. I have argued in this lecture that reciprocity, fairness, identity, money illusion, loss aversion, herding, and procrastination help explain the significant departures of real-world economies from the competitive, general-equilibrium model. The implication, to my mind, is that macroeconomics *must* be based on such behavioral considerations.

Keynes' *General Theory* was the greatest contribution to behavioral economics before the present era. Almost everywhere Keynes blamed market failures on psychological propensities (as in consumption) and irrationalities (as in stock market speculation). Immediately after its publication, the economics profession tamed Keynesian economics. They domesticated it as they translated it into the "smooth" mathematics of classical economics.[92] But economies, like lions, are wild and dangerous. Modern behavioral economics has rediscovered the wild side of macroeconomic behavior. Behavioral economists are becoming lion tamers. The task is as intellectually exciting as it is difficult.

REFERENCES

Abel, Andrew B., "Dynamic Effects of Permanent and Temporary Tax Policies in a *q* Model of Investment," *Journal of Monetary Economics* (May 1982), pp. 353–73.

Ainslie, George, *Picoeconomics.* Cambridge: Cambridge University Press 1992.

Akerlof, George A., "Relative Wages and the Rate of Inflation," *Quarterly Journal of Economics,* 83 (August 1969), pp. 353–74.

–, "The Market for 'Lemons': Quality Uncertainty and the Market Mechanism," *Quarterly Journal of Economics*; 84 (August 1970), pp. 488–500.

–, "The Demand for Money: A General-Equilibrium Inventory-Theoretic Approach," *Review of Economic Studies,* 40 (January 1973), pp. 115–30.

–, "The Economics of 'Tagging" as Applied to the Optimal Income Tax, Welfare Programs, and Manpower Planning," *American Economic Review* 68, (March 1978), pp. 8–19.

–, " Irving Fisher on His Head: The Consequences of Constant Threshold-Target Monitoring of Money Holdings" *Quarterly Journal of Economics,* 93 (May 1979), pp. 169–87.

–, " Labor Contracts as Partial Gift Exchange," *Quarterly Journal of Economics,* 97 (November 1982), pp. 543–69.

[91] Glenn Loury (1995) has suggested that affirmative action may also have the opposite effect: it may exacerbate blacks' sense of exclusion and make them feel that they are viewed as not belonging even when they do achieve.

[92] See Hicks (1937) and Patinkin (1956).

–, "Procrastination and Obedience," *American Economic Review, Papers and Proceedings* 81 (May 1991), pp. 1–19.
–, William T. Dickens and George L. Perry, "The Macroeconomics of Low Inflation," *Brookings Papers on Economic Activity*, 1996:1, pp. 1–59.
–, and –, "Near-Rational Wage and Price Setting and the Long-Run Phillips Curve," *Brookings Papers on Economic Activity*; 2000:1, pp. 1–44.
–, and Rachel E. Kranton, "Economics and Identity," *Quarterly Journal of Economics*, 115 (August 2000), pp. 715–53.
–, Andrew K. Rose and Janet L. Yellen, "Job Switching and Job Satisfaction in the U.S. Labor Market," *Brookings Papers on Economic Activity*, 1988:2, pp. 495–582.
–, and Janet L. Yellen, "A Near-rational Model of the Business Cycle, with Wage and Price Inertia," *Quarterly Journal of Economics*, 100 (Supp. 1985a), pp. 823–38.
–, and Janet L. Yellen, "Can Small Deviations from Rationality Make Significant Differences to Economic Equilibria?" *American Economic Review*, 75 (September 1985b), pp. 708–20.
–, and –, "The Fair Wage-Effort Hypothesis and Unemployment," *Quarterly Journal of Economics*, 105, (May 1990), pp. 255–83.
–, and –, "How Large are the Losses from Rule-of-Thumb Behavior in Models of the Business Cycle?" William C. Brainard, William D. Nordhaus and Harold W. Watts, eds., *Money, Macroeconomics, and Economic Policy: Essays in Honor of James Tobin*. Cambridge and London: MIT Press, 1991, pp. 59–78.
Anderson, Elijah, *StreetWise: Race, Class, and Change in an Urban Community*. Chicago: University of Chicago Press, 1990.
Arrow, Kenneth J. "The Economic Implications of Learning by Doing," *Review of Economic Studies*, 29, (June 1962), pp. 155–173.
Ball, Lawrence, "Credible Disinflation with Staggered Price-Setting," *American Economic Review*, 84 (March 1994), pp.282–89.
Banks, James, Richard Blundell, and Sarah Tanner, "Is There a Retirement-Savings Puzzle?" *American Economic Review*, 88 (September 1998), pp. 769–88.
Barro, Robert J., "A Theory of Monopolistic Price Adjustment," *The Review of Economic Studies*, 39 (January 1972), pp. 17–26.
–, "Long-Term Contracting, Sticky Prices, and Monetary Policy," *Journal of Monetary Economics*, 3 (July 1977), pp. 305–16.
Barsky, Robert S., Miles S. Kimball, F. Thomas Juster, and Matthew Shapiro, "Preference Parameters and Behavioral Heterogeneity: An Experimental Approach in the Health and Retirement Survey," Working Paper 5213, National Bureau of Economic Research, Cambridge, MA, August, 1995.
Becker, Gary S. and George J. Stigler, "Law Enforcement, Malfeasance, and the Compensation of Enforcers," *Journal of Legal Studies*, 3 (1974), pp. 1–18.
Bernheim, B. Douglas, Jonathan Skinner, and Steven Weinberg, "What Accounts for the Variation in Retirement Wealth Among U.S. Households?" *American Economic Review* 91 (September 2001), pp. 832–55.
Bewley, Truman, *Why Wages Don't Fall During a Recession;* Cambridge, MA: Harvard University Press, 1999.
Blanchard, Olivier and Nobihiro Kiyotaki, "Monopolistic Competition and the Effects of Aggregate Demand," *American Economic Review*; 77 (September 1987), pp. 647–66.
Blinder, Alan S. and Don H. Choi, "A Shred of Evidence on Theories of Wage Stickiness," *Quarterly Journal of Economics*, 105 (November 1990), pp. 1003–1015.
Bowles, Samuel, "The Production Process in a Competitive Economy: Walrasian, Neo-Hobbesian, and Marxian Models," *American Economic Review* 75 (March 1985), pp. 16–36.
Caballero, Ricardo, "Durable Goods: An Explanation for Their Slow Adjustment, *Journal of Political Economy*, 101 (April 1993), pp. 351–384.
Calvo, Guillermo A., "Staggered Prices in a Utility-Maximizing Framework," *Journal of Monetary Economics*; 12 (September 1983), pp. 383–98.
Campbell, Carl M., III and Kunal S. Kamlani, "The Reasons for Wage Rigidity: Evidence from a Survey of Firms," *Quarterly Journal of Economics*; 112(August 1997), pp. 759–89.

Campbell, John Y., and Robert J. Shiller, "Cointegration and Tests of Present Value Models," *Journal of Political Economy*, 97 (October 1987), pp. 1062–1088.

Caplin, Andrew F., and Daniel F. Spulber, "Menu Costs and the Neutrality of Money," *Quarterly Journal of Economics*, 102 (November 1987), pp. 703–25.

–, and John Leahy, "State-Dependent Pricing and the Dynamics of Money and Output," *Quarterly Journal of Economics*, 106 (August 1991), pp. 683–708.

Card, David, and Dean Hyslop, "Does Inflation 'Grease the Wheels' of the Labor Market?'" in Christina D. Romer and David H. Romer, eds., *Reducing Inflation: Motivation and Strategy*. NBER Studies in Business Cycles, vol. 30. Chicago and London: University of Chicago Press, 1997, p. 195–242.

Carmichael, Lorne, "Can Unemployment Be Involuntary? Comment on 'Equilibrium Unemployment as a Worker Discipline Device,'" *American Economic Review* 75 (December 1985), pp. 1213–14.

Chamberlin, Edward, *The Theory of Monopolistic Competition: A Re-orientation of the Theory of Value*. Cambridge: Harvard University Press, 1962.

Clark, Kenneth, *Dark Ghetto*. New York: Harper & Row, 1965.

De Bondt, Werner F. M., and Richard H. Thaler, "Does the Stock Market Overreact?" *Journal of Finance Papers and Proceedings*, 40 (July 1985), pp. 793–805.

Delpit, Lisa, *Other People's Children: Cultural Conflict in the Classroom*. New York: The New Press, 1995.

Dickens, William T. and Lawrence F. Katz, "Inter-industry Wage Differences and Industry Characteristics," in Kevin Lang and Jonathan S. Leonard, eds. *Unemployment and the Structure of Labor Markets*, pp. 48–89. New York and Oxford: Blackwell, 1987.

Du Bois, William E., *The Souls of Black Folk*. Greenwich, Conn.: Fawcett Publications, 1965.

Dunlop, John T., "The Task of Contemporary Wage Theory," in John T. Dunlop, *ed.*, *The Theory of Wage Determination*, pp. 3–27. New York: St. Martin's Press, 1957.

Eckstein, Otto and Roger Brinner, "The Inflation Process in the United States," Joint Economic Committee of the Congress of the United States. Washington: Government Printing Office, 1972.

Engen, Eric M., William G. Gale, and Cori E. Uccello, "The Adequacy of Household Saving," *Brookings Papers on Economic Activity*, 1999:2, pp. 65–187.

Fehr, Ernst, Georg Kirchsteiger, and Arno Riedl, "Does Fairness Prevent Market Clearing? An Experimental Investigation," *Quarterly Journal of Economics*, 108 (May 1993), pp. 437–59.

– and Armin Falk, "Wage Rigidity in a Competitive Incomplete Contract Market," *Journal of Political Economy*, 107 (February 1999), pp. 106–34.

–, Simon Gachter, and Georg Kirchsteiger, "Reciprocal Fairness and Noncompensating Wage Differentials," *Journal of Institutional and Theoretical Economics*, 152 (December 1996) pp. 608–40.

–, and Lorenz Goette, "Robustness and Real Consequences of Nominal Wage Rigidity," Working Paper # 44, Institute for Empirical Research in Economics, University of Zurich, May 2000.

–, and Jean-Robert Tyran, "Does Money Illusion Matter?" *American Economic Review*, 91 (December 2001), pp. 1239–62.

Ferguson, Ronald F., "Can Schools Narrow the Test Score Gap?" pp. 318–374 in Christopher Jencks and Meredith Phillips, *The Black-White Test Score Gap*, eds. Washington: The Brookings Institution, 1998.

Fischer, Stanley, "Long-Term Contracts, Rational Expectations, and the Optimal Money Supply Rule," *Journal of Political Economy* 85 (February 1977), pp. 191–205.

Flanagan, Robert J., David W. Soskice and Lloyd Ulman, *Unionism, Economic Stabilization and Incomes Policies: European Experience*. Washington, D.C.: The Brookings Institution, 1983.

Fortin, Pierre, "Canadian Wage Settlement Data," memo, Université de Québec à Montréal, April, 1995.

–, "The Great Canadian Slump," *Canadian Journal of Economics*, 29 (November 1996), pp. 761–787.

–, George A. Akerlof, William T. Dickens and George L. Perry, "Inflation, Unemployment, and Macroeconomic Policy in the United States and Canada: A Common Framework," mimeo, June, 2001.

Foster, James E. and Henry Y. Wan, Jr., "Involuntary Unemployment as a Principal-Agent Equilibrium," *American Economic Review*, 74 (June 1984), pp. 476–84.

Frazier, Franklin, *The Black Bourgeoisie: The Rise of the New Middle Class in the United States*. New York: The Free Press, 1957.

Friedman, Milton, "The Lag in Effect of Monetary Policy," *Journal of Political Economy*, 69 (October 1961), pp. 447–66.

–, "The Role of Monetary Policy," *The American Economic Review*, 58 (March 1968), pp. 1–17.

Gordon, Robert J., "The Recent Acceleration in Inflation and Its Lessons for the Future," *Brookings Papers on Economic Activity*, 1970:1, pp. 8–41.

–, "The Time-Varying NAIRU and Its Implications for Economic Policy," *Journal of Economic Perspectives*, 11 (Winter 1997), pp. 11–32.

Hannerz, Ulf, *Soulside: Inquiries into Ghetto Culture and Community*. New York: Columbia University Press, 1969.

Hayashi, Fumio, "Tobin's Marginal *q* and Average *q*: A Neoclassical Interpretation," *Econometrica* 50 (January 1982), pp. 213–224.

Hicks, John R., "Mr. Keynes and the 'Classics': A Suggested Interpretation," *Econometrica*, 5 (April 1937), pp. 147–159.

Hodgman, Donald R., "Credit Risk and Credit Rationing," *Quarterly Journal of Economics*, 74 (May 1960), pp. 258–278.

Hotelling, Harold, "Stability in Competition," *Economic Journal*, 39 (March 1929), pp. 41–57.

Howitt, Peter and Robert Clower, "The Emergence of Economic Organization," *Journal of Economic Behavior and Organization*, 41 (January 2000), pp. 55–84.

Iwai, Katsuhito, *Disequilibrium Dynamics: A Theoretical Analysis of Inflation and Unemployment*. New Haven: Yale University Press, 1981.

Jaffee, Dwight and Thomas Russell, "Imperfect Information and Credit Rationing," *Quarterly Journal of Economics*, 90 (November 1976), pp. 651–66.

Jensen, Michael C. and William H. Meckling, "Theory of the Firm; Managerial Behavior, Agency Costs and Ownership Structure," *Journal of Financial Economics* 3 (October 1976), pp. 305–60.

Kahn, Shulamit, "Evidence of Nominal Wage Stickiness from Microdata," *American Economic Review*, 87 (December 1997), pp. 993–1008.

Kahneman, Daniel and Amos Tversky, "Prospect Theory: An Analysis of Decision under Risk," *Econometrica*, 47 (March 1979), pp. 263–292.

Katz, Lawrence F., "Efficiency Wage Theories: A Partial Evaluation," *NBER Macroeconomics Annual* 1986, *1*, 235–76.

Keynes, John Maynard, *The General Theory of Employment, Interest and Money*. New York: Macmillan, 1936.

Kleidon, Allan W., "Variance Bounds Tests and Stock Price Valuation Models," *The Journal of Political Economy*, 94 (October 1986), pp. 953–1001.

Krueger, Alan B. and Lawrence H. Summers, "Efficiency Wages and the Inter-Industry Wage Structure," *Econometrica*, 56 (March 1988), pp. 259–293.

–,and Diane M. Whitmore, "The Effect of Attending a Small Class in the Early Grades on College-Test Taking and Middle School Test Results: Evidence from Project STAR," mimeo, Industrial Relations Section, Princeton University, September 28, 1999.

Laibson, David I., "Comment on 'The Adequacy of Household Saving,'by Eric M. Engen, William G. Gale, and Cori E. Uccello, *Brookings Papers on Economic Activity*, 1999:2, pp. 65–165.

–, Andrea Repetto, and Jeremy Tobacman, "Self-Control and Saving for Retirement," *Brookings Papers on Economic Activity*, 1998:1, pp. 91–172.

Lamont, Owen, "Corporate-Debt Overhang and Macroeconomic Expectations," *American Economic Review*, 85 (December 1995), pp. 1106–1117.

Lebow, David E., Raven E. Saks, and Beth Anne Wilson, "Downward Nominal Wage Rigidity: Evidence from the Employment Cost Index," Board of Governors of the Federal Reserve System, Finance and Economics Discussion Series: 99/31, July 1999.

LeRoy, Stephen F. and Richard Porter, "The Present Value Relation: Test Based on Implied Variance Bounds," *Econometrica,* 49 (May 1981), pp. 555–74.

Levine, David I., "Cohesiveness, Productivity, and Wage Dispersion," *Journal of Economic Behavior and Organization,* 15 (March 1991), pp. 237–55.

Levitt, Steven D., "The Effect of Prison Population Size on Crime Rates: Evidence from Prison Overcrowding Litigation," *Quarterly Journal of Economics*; 111 (May 1996), pp. 319–51.

Lindbeck, Assar and Dennis J. Snower,, *The Insider-Outsider Theory of Employment and Unemployment.* Cambridge, MA: MIT Press, 1988.

Lipsey, Richard G., "The Relation between Unemployment and the Rate of Change of Money Wage Rates in the United Kingdom, 1862–1957: A Further Analysis," *Economica,* New Series, 27 (February 1960), pp. 1–31.

Loewenstein, George, "Anticipation and the Valuation of Delayed Consumption," *The Economic Journal,* 97 (September 1987), pp. 666–684.

–, and Drazen Prelec, "Anomalies in Intertemporal Choice: Evidence and an Interpretation," *Quarterly Journal of Economics,* 107 (May 1992), pp. 573–597.

–, and Richard H. Thaler, "Anomalies: Intertemporal Choice," *The Journal of Economic Perspectives,* 3 (Autumn 1989), pp. 181–193.

Loury, Glenn C., *One By One From the Inside Out.* New York: The Free Press, 1995.

Lucas, Robert E., Jr. and Thomas J. Sargent, "After Keynesian Macroeconomics," in Federal Reserve Bank of Boston, *After the Phillips Curve: Persistence of High Inflation and High Unemployment,* Conference Series No. 19, 1979, pp. 49–72.

Madrian, Brigitte C., and Dennis F. Shea, "The Power of Suggestion: Inertia in 401(k) Participation and Savings Behavior," *Quarterly Journal of Economics,* 116 (November 2001), pp. 1149–87.

Mankiw, N. Gregory, " Small Menu Costs and Large Business Cycles: A Macroeconomic Model," *Quarterly Journal of Economics,* 10 (May 1985), pp. 529–38.

–, and Ricardo Reis, "Sticky Information versus Sticky Prices: A Proposal to Replace the New Keynesian Phillips Curve," unpublished paper, Harvard University, February 2002.

McLaughlin, Kenneth J., "A Theory of Quits and Layoffs with Efficient Turnover," *Journal of Political Economy,* 99 (February 1991), pp. 1–29.

Mehra, Rajnish, "The Equity Premium Puzzle: Why Is It a Puzzle;" mimeo, University of Chicago, May 6, 2001.

Mishkin, Frederic S., "Illiquidity, Consumer Durable Expenditure, and Monetary Policy," *American Economic Review,* 66 (September 1976), pp. 642–654.

Murphy, Kevin M., and Robert J. Topel, "Efficiency Wages Reconsidered: Theory and Evidence," in Yoram Weiss and Gideon Fishelson, eds., *Advances in the Theory and Measurement of Unemployment,* pp. 204–240. New York: MacMillan, 1990.

Myers, Stewart C., "Interactions of Corporate Financing and Investment Decisions: Implications for Capital Budgeting," *Journal of Finance,* 29 (March 1974), pp. 1–25.

Nisbett, Richard and Lee Ross, *Human Inference: Strategies and Shortcomings of Social Judgment.* Englewood Cliffs, NJ: Prentice-Hall, 1980.

O'Donoghue, Ted and Rabin, Matthew, "Doing It Now or Later," *American Economic Review,* 89 (March 1999), pp. 103–24.

Parker, Jonathan A., "The Consumption Risk of the Stock Market," *Brookings Papers on Economic Activity,* 2001:2, pp. 279–348.

Parkin, Michael, "The Output-Inflation Trade-off When Prices Are Costly to Change," *Journal of Political Economy,* 94 (February 1986), pp. 200–224.

Patinkin, Donald, *Money, Interest, and Prices: An Integration of Monetary and Value Theory.* Evanston, Illinois: Row, Peterson, 1956.

Perry, George L., "Changing Labor Markets and Inflation," *Brookings Papers on Economic Activity,* 1970: 3, pp. 411–441.

Phelps, Edmund S. *et al., Microeconomic Foundations of Employment and Inflation Theory.* New York: W. W. Norton, 1970.

–, The New Microeconomics in Inflation and Employment Theory," *American Economic Review,* Papers and Proceedings of the Eighty-first Annual Meeting of the American Economic Association, 59 (May 1969), pp. 147–160.

–, "Money-Wage Dynamics and Labor-Market Equilibrium, *The Journal of Political Economy,* 76 (July/August, Part 2, 1968), pp. 678–711.

–, and Robert A. Pollak, "On Second-Best National Saving and Game-Equilibrium Growth," *Review of Economic Studies,* 35 (April 1968), pp. 185–199.

Phillips, A. W., "The Relationship between Unemployment and the Rate of Change of Money Wages in the United Kingdom, 1861–1957," *Economica* 25 (November 1958), pp. 283–99.

Rabin, Matthew, "Incorporating Fairness into Game Theory and Economics," *American Economic Review,* 83 (December 1993), pp. 1281-1302.

Rainwater, Lee, *Behind Ghetto Walls: Black Families in a Federal Slum.* Chicago: Aldine, 1970.

Robinson, Joan, *The Economics of Imperfect Competition.* London : Macmillan, 1942.

Romer, Christina D. and David H. Romer, "Does Monetary Policy Matter? A New Test in the Spirit of Friedman and Schwartz," in Olivier J. Blanchard, and Stanley Fischer, eds. *NBER Macroeconomics Annual: 1989,* pp. 121–70. Cambridge, Mass. and London: MIT Press, 1989.

Romer, David H., "Rational Asset-Price Movements Without News," *The American Economic Review* 83 (December 1993), pp. 1112–1130.

Roy, Donald, "Quota Restriction and Goldbricking in a Machine Shop," *American Journal of Sociology,* 57 (March 1952), pp. 427–442.

Sargent, Thomas J. 1971. "A Note on the 'Accelerationist' Controversy," *Journal of Money Credit and Banking,* 3 (August), 721–5.

Scarry, Richard, *Richard Scarry's Trucks and Cars and Things That Go.* New York: Golden Books, 1974.

Shafir, Eldar, Peter Diamond, and Amos Tversky, "Money Illusion," *Quarterly Journal of Economics,* 112 (May 1997) pp. 341–74.

Shapiro, Carl and Joseph E. Stiglitz, "Equilibrium Unemployment as a Worker Discipline Device," *American Economic Review,* 74 (June 1984), pp. 433–444.

Shiller, Robert J., "Do Stock Prices Move Too Much to be Justified by Subsequent Changes in Dividends?" *The American Economic Review,* 71 (June 1981), pp. 421–436.

–, "Why Do People Dislike Inflation?", in *Reducing Inflation: Motivation and Strategy,* edited by Christina D. Romer and David H. Romer. Chicago: University of Chicago Press: 1997a.

–, "Public Resistance to Indexation: A Puzzle," *Brookings Papers on Economic Activity,* 1997: 1, pp.159–211.

–, *Irrational Exuberance.* Princeton, NJ: Princeton University Press, 2000.

Siegel, Jeremy J. and Richard H. Thaler, "Anomalies: The Equity Premium Puzzle," *The Journal of Economic Perspectives,* 11 (Winter, 1997), pp. 191–200.

Solow, Robert M., "Substitution and Fixed Proportions in the Theory of Capital," *Review of Economic Studies,* 29 (June 1962), pp. 207–218.

–,"Investment and Technical Progress, " in Kenneth J. Arrow, Samuel Korbin and Patrick Suppes, eds. *Mathematical Methods in the Social Sciences,* pp. 89–104. Stanford, Stanford University Press, 1959.

Staiger, Douglas, James H. Stock, and Mark W. Watson, "How Precise Are Estimates of the Natural Rate of Unemployment?" in Christina D. Romer and David H. Romer, eds., *Reducing Inflation: Motivation and Strategy.* NBER Studies in Business Cycles, vol. 30. Chicago and London: University of Chicago Press, 1997, pages 195–242.

Stiglitz, Joseph E. and Andrew Weiss, "Credit Rationing in Markets with Imperfect Information," *American Economic Review,* 71(June 1981), pp. 393–410.

Stoft, Steven, "Cheat-Threat Theory: An Explanation of Involuntary Unemployment," mimeo, Boston University, May 1982.

Strotz, Robert H., "Myopia and Inconsistency in Dynamic Utility Maximization," *The Review of Economic Studies*, 23 (January 1956), pp. 165–180.

Summers, Lawrence H., "Taxation and Corporate Investment: A q-Theory Approach" *Brookings Papers on Economic Activity*, 1981: 1, pp. 67–127.

–, "Does the Stock Market Rationally Reflect Fundamental Values?" *Journal of Finance*, Papers and Proceedings of the Forty-Fourth Annual Meeting of the America Finance Association, 41 (July 1986), pp. 591–601.

Taylor, John, "Staggered Wage Setting in a Macro Model," *American Economic Review Papers and Proceedings*, 69 (May 1979), pp. 108–113.

Thaler, Richard H., and Shlomo Benartzi, "Save More Tomorrow: Using Behavioral Economics to Increase Employee Saving," mimeo, University of Chicago, November, 2000.

Tobin, James, "Inflation and Unemployment," *American Economic Review*, 62 (March 1972), pp. 1–18.

–, "A General Equilibrium Approach To Monetary Theory," *Journal of Money, Credit and Banking*, 1 (February 1969), pp. 15–29.

Kenneth D. West, "Bubbles, Fads and Stock Price Volatility Tests: A Partial Evaluation," *Journal of Finance*, Papers and Proceedings of the Forty-Seventh Annual Meeting of the American Finance Association, 43 (July 1988), pp. 639–656.

Wilson, William J., *The Truly Disadvantaged.* Chicago: University of Chicago Press, 1987.

–, *When Work Disappears: The World of the New Urban Poor.* New York: Knopf, 1996.

Yellen, Janet L., "Efficiency Wage Models of Unemployment," *American Economic Review*, Papers and Proceedings of the Ninety-Sixth Annual Meeting of the American Economic Association, 74 (May 1984), pp. 200–205.

Zbaracki, Mark J., Mark Ritson, Daniel Levy, Shantanu Dutta, and Mark Bergen, "The Managerial and Customer Costs of Price Adjustment: Direct Evidence from Industrial Markets," unpublished paper, Emory University.

A. Michael Spence

A. MICHAEL SPENCE

GETTING STARTED

I was born during the second World War in Montclair New Jersey. This was more or less an accident (the location that is). My father was based in Ottawa as a member of the War Time Prices and Trades Board, the Canadian version of wartime price controls. That work entailed frequent trips to Washington to coordinate with their American counterparts. New Jersey is more or less half way between the two capitals and my mother was visiting friends. So although I grew up in Canada during and after the war until leaving for college in the United States, I managed to also be an American by birth.

My father once said about being a parent that it is the only thing you do that requires a very long period of learning and at about the time that you are becoming competent, you don't need the skills anymore. Notwithstanding this modest assessment of their parenting skills, they were wonderful parents. My father was the son of the registrar of the University of Manitoba. He was an intellectual by instinct (he had a PhD from Northwestern University in Commerce and Finance) and in another time, might very well have chosen a career in academic life. I learned from him to love precision in thought, the power of abstraction and the use of symbols to capture structures and relationships. He was also a very good athlete and we spent a lot of time playing basketball, football, hockey, just about anything.

My mother was the only child of my grandparents, who lived in Minnesota at the time of her birth and later moved to Winnipeg. My grandfather was an engineer with the Canadian Pacific Railway. [For the younger generation, an engineer in those days was the person who drove the train.] My mother was strong-willed, demanding and very supportive all at the same time. I think I inherited from her a kind of tenacity (sometimes referred to as stubbornness) that served me well. It partially filled gaps when sheer intellectual horsepower (of which others had much more than I) proved insufficient.

The overall effect of my parents upbringing was to provide a great sense of security, being surrounded by love and affection, a great (perhaps too great) sense of self-confidence (there really weren't any challenges that were deemed beyond reach for any reason), and an equally great sense of intellectual adventure, a world populated by opportunities and challenges rather than obstacles and roadblocks. I don't have the professional expertise to know whether and how important these general frames of reference that one's parents impart, are. An amateur's guess based on my own experience is that they are important and I believe the sense of freedom and the confidence to try to use it were among our parents' greatest gifts to us.

I have included a time line that places events in my life and in my family's life generally in the right place and the right order. I hope that this has the advantage from the reader's point of view, that it is fairly easy to skim without using up much time, and also easy just to skip.

EDUCATION

Next to my family, it seems clear to me that the educational institutions and the teachers from whom I had the privilege of learning, were especially important. They were (i) excellent and (ii) a liberating force. In looking back, what is surprising is how uniformly true this was. My middle and high school in Canada, UTS, attached to the College of Education at the University of Toronto, was for my American friends, not dissimilar to the Lab School at the University of Chicago. It was then and it still is excellent in two respects. The teaching achieved a very high average quality and topped out in the superlative range, and the students were without question in the same league. This combination that I have now seen (and even presided over in academic administration) several times strikes me as particularly potent.

I would also add that all of the schools and universities I attended seemed to me to be excellent at the time and in measurable ways they are even better now. This is really very encouraging. The combination of a workable basic formula and the capacity to improve over time is what one hopes for in any aspect of society: business, government, the non-profit sector. Thus the pattern of excellence was repeated at Princeton, Oxford and Harvard. There are probably many reasons for the high standards and the continuous improvement. One is the healthy synergy between teaching and research – the excitement of the research is transmitted to the learning process, and the energy and curiosity of the students produces new ideas in research. A second is competition. All of these institutions have very successful competitors who, with the help of vigilant alumnae and alumni, keep them constantly on their toes.

TEACHERS, COLLEAGUES AND STUDENTS

Education is in the end about individual interactions and about learning. As someone who aspired to become a teacher and a scholar, it is hard for me now to imagine a better group of teachers and mentors and colleagues than those with whom I worked and learned.

The research side of academic life is often viewed from the outside as a solo and at times lonely activity. In fact it is quite the opposite, a communal activity in significant part where interaction and interchange generate ideas and critiques of them. The research for which we were recognized this year was part of an exciting time in which many helped build the applied microeconomic foundations of several applied fields. I personally owe a great debt to my colleagues and former students who were part of that effort. While it is not possible to acknowledge all those debts, there are many whose help was

Bruce Owen.

Jim Rosse.

both generous and invaluable. Jim Rosse and Bruce Owen at Stanford in the 1970's helped me make the link between theory and industrial organization. Many of the problems that I had the opportunity to work on were the result of teaching and working side by side with them.

My thesis advisors are very different and very gifted. Kenneth Arrow taught me (and many others) mathematical economics and general equilibrium theory. When I took his course in general equilibrium theory, the take-home exam that I produced was lost. After a frightening phone call and a successful search for a copy, I rushed it in and waited while Ken read it, which he did (all twelve pages) at a rate of about 2 seconds a page. Now I have to say that there was a lot of mathematics on those pages. I just assumed that he wasn't really reading it, until he finished and then started asking me some detailed questions about the assumptions and analysis on page five. Describing Ken Arrow's contributions to economics in the second half of the 20th century would come quite close to just describing the evolution of economics during that period.

Tom Schelling, as all who studied with him knew, had an extraordinarily

Kenneth Arrow.

Tomas Schelling.

original mind. Unique in our experience was his capacity to analyze using carefully constructed analogies, with just the right number of similarities and differences. Many of my younger colleagues were motivated in the best possible way by normative and policy questions. I think I tended more to being just fascinated by how markets and mechanisms like them worked. A great deal of that interest and motivation came from hours spent with Tom Schelling. It could be tipping points, focal points, sorting out congestion on a beach with surfers and swimmers, deterrence. Schelling's curiosity seemed endless and his capacity to shed light remarkable.

Richard Zeckhauser saved me from exiting from academia prematurely, after perhaps too many years in classes and libraries. He started me teaching and tolerated with grace the first few embarrassing outings. I wrote my first paper with him on insurance markets, moral hazard and adverse selection. Richard's lightning quick mind was and is matched by the tremendous breadth of his interests and his intuitive grasp of complex phenomena. More than once I had the experience of having him tell me the answer to some complex market problem, my not completely understanding the answer, going away for a couple of weeks to try to capture it in a model, and deciding after that effort that he was right in the first place.

It is not uncommon for graduate students to be encouraged to pick something relatively safe or at least manageable as a thesis topic. Honestly, it is not bad advice. But I have to say that I never received advice like that, or if I did, I didn't hear it. In addition to their time and insight, I owe to my advisors their encouragement and support for grappling with the informational structure of markets, however risky that might have been.

I should like to acknowledge and thank Gilbert Harmon, Richard Ludwig and Robert Kuenne at Princeton University. They are largely responsible for my interest in philosophy and economics and for the interest I developed in trying scholarship and teaching as a career.

Richard Zeckhauser.

Mark Wolfson.

Derek Bok.

At UTS, Don Fawcett taught several generations of us about hard work, competing, winning and losing gracefully, and about the importance of trying to do something that makes a difference.

As one can tell from a glance at the autobiographical timeline, I have had two careers (first as teacher and scholar and then in academic administration) and with luck I am embarking on a third, though the last will in part be a return to the first. My colleagues and friends, Edward Lazear and Mark Wolfson have shared the excitement and the challenges in all three, and enriched the whole experience in ways that are hard to describe accurately.

As an administrator, I had the privilege of working with two associate deans, Phyllis Keller at Harvard and Paul Johnson at Stanford. These two served with and trained several deans, and had a lot to do with the sustained excellence in their respective faculties and schools.

Derek Bok, the President of Harvard for over 20 years, gave me the chance to be a dean and then used his legendary skills as a leader and educator to help me become competent at my job. Whether he succeeded in this is for others to judge, but with his patience and wisdom, he taught me much that I value greatly.

OUR FAMILY

It has always struck me as ironic and wonderful that the most important parts of life, one's family, the unconditional love for one's spouse and children and the joy of seeing children learn and grow to wonderful human beings, are exactly those things that one shares with all the rest of humanity. Monica and I have had a wonderful ten years together. Our children (Monica's step children) Graham, Catherine and Marya have thrived with the continued support of their mother, Ann Bennett Spence. We all hope that as they enter adulthood, that the world that they will live and work in has as much freedom and opportunity as the one we enjoyed.

THE NOBEL PRIZE

It is a wonderful and unexpected honor to receive the Bank of Sweden Prize in Economic Sciences in Memory of Alfred Nobel. Receiving this prize with Joseph Stiglitz and George Akerlof, whose work I have learned from and admired makes it even more gratifying. It was also very nice to see that Michael Rothschild's important contributions were recognized during Nobel week in December. And perhaps most importantly, it is a source of great satisfaction that the work on the informational structure of markets seems to have taken hold in microeconomics and that it has had some influence in other disciplines. The three of us, and many others, contributed to the development of this sub-field and all share in the recognition that goes with this extraordinary prize.

Ernie Spence.

Michael and Monica.

Mary Jane Spence.

Ed Lazear, Mike Spence and BMW.

Brother Alan.

Brother Randy.

Marya Graham Catherine.

MICHAEL SPENCE BRIEF AUTOBIOGRAPHY

Year		
1943	Born Montclair New Jersey	
1944	Brother Randy born in Ottawa	
1945		
1946	Family moved to Winnipeg	
1947		
1948		
1949		
1950	Moved to farm outside of Toronto – attended school in two room school house	
1951		
1952	Moved to Toronto – attended John Ross Robertson elementary school	Flunked first test in grammar in grade 4
1953	Brother Allan born	
1954		Built houses on our island in Georgian Bay (north of Toronto) in summers with Father and brothers
1955	Attended University of Toronto Schools (part of U of Toronto) in grade 7	
1956		Played Pee Wee hockey for Ted's Pal's – 96 games – school suffered – chose school over hockey – never looked back
1957		
1958		
1959		
1960		
1961		Went to Europe for the first time – later took young people to Europe in the summers
1962	School Captain in last year in High School – Graduated from High School (UTS): went to Princeton University as a freshman – liberal arts not prevalent in Canada at the time	Met Cook family – roomate Steve, father Peter (portrait painter and freshman hockey coach) and mother Joan – became family friends
1963		Randy comes to Princeton – family dog David (a female springer spaniel – don't ask) dies
1964		Played ice hockey for Princeton for 4 years
1965	Brother Allan goes to UTS	
1966	Graduated from Princeton	Majored in philosophy – met Ann Bennett in last year – received Canadian Rhodes Scholarship – went

		to Magdalen College Oxford – decided to try an academic career with encouragement from parents
1967	Majored in Mathematics at Oxford	Randy graduated from Princeton – went on to a PhD at University of Toronto focussing on Economic Development
1968	Graduated from Oxford – entered PhD program in Economica at Harvard in the fall – supported by Danforth Fellowship	Married Ann Bennett – recovered from mononucleosis – spend summer in Georgian Bay
1969		The Vietnam War dominated the environment for all of the time I spent in the PhD
1970	Rapporteur in Faculty Seminar in Kennedy School – included my thesis advisors, Thomas Schelling, Richard Zeckhauser and Kenneth Arrow	Wonderful teachers and mentors – owe a particular debt also to Martin Feldstein for his mentorship at that time
1971	Began teaching analytic methods at the Kennedy School of Government at Havard – it was one year old at the time	Summer spent at Berkeley in mathematical economics seminar – realized Andreu MasCollel knew more math than I
1972	Received PhD – received David A Wells prize for doctoral thesis	Wrote thesis call "Market Signaling" – seemed qutie well received
1973	Moved to Stanford in the Economics Dept as Associate Professor – taught and did research in applied microeconomic theory and Industrial Organization –	Ann enrolled in MBA at Stanford Business School – exciting group of young people in Economics – wonderful support from Bruce Owen and Jim Rosse getting into Industrial Organization – visited Brother Randy in East Africa in the summer
1974		
1975	Returned to Harvard Economics as Professor – began to teach graduate economic theory and undergraduate industrial organization using Michael Porter strategy cases –	Met Mike Porter
1976		Had two undergraduates in graduate theory course – Bill Gates and Steve Ballmer – both got A's
1977		
1978		
1979	Became a joint appointment in Economics and the Harvard Business School at Harvard – received Galbraith prize for teaching at Harvard	Son Graham born in the spring

1980		
1981		
1982	Received the John Bate's Clark medal from American Economic Association (given every two years to an economist under age 40)	Daughter Catherine born in January
1983	Became chairman of the Department of Economics at Harvard	
1984	President Derek Bok asked me to succeed Henry Rosovsky as Dean of the Faculty of Arts and Sciences – accepted – learned a lot from President Bok	Phyllis Keller as associate dean taught me how to be a dean – wonderful colleague and friend
1985		Daughter Marya born in March – I am learning how to be a dean in my first year
1986	Joined board of directors of Polaroid Corporation – Harvard celebrated its 350th anniversary –	My father died in the summer after a difficult struggle with dementia – I missed him a lot
1987		
1988		
1989		
1990	Stepped down as dean of FAS – Became Dean of the Graduate School of Business at Stanford University – succeeded Bob Jaedicke –	Family moved to California – joined by Mark Wolfson in dean's office – became very good friends
1991		Separated from Ann and later divorced in 1995
1992	Stanford gets into altercation with Government over Overhead cost recovery	Paul Johnson as associate dean for many years in the business school – wonderful colleague and later good friend – Took up windsurfing with good friend Ed Lazear who was nice enough to watch out for me
1993		Met Monica Cappuccini – later married in 1997
1994		Graham takes up golf – achieves handicap of 4 after 18 months
1995		Met Tom Siebel and joined board of Siebel Systems – his new company
1996		
1997		Monica and I are married in the summer – Graham graduates from Menlo School and heads for Princeton as a freshman – Monica and I take trip to Himalaya's in the fall
1998		
1999	Stepped down as dean of the business school at Stanford after 9 years – rejoined Mark Wolfson	Catherine graduated from Menlo School and headed for Columbia University as a freshman – visited

	and his colleagues at Oak Hill Capital Partners –	Singapore as Lee Kwan Yew distiguished visitor
2000		Our mother made it to the new millenium and passed away peacefully on January 5. – developed and taught a new course in electronic commerce with colleague Garth Saloner – acquired a small condo on Maui in Hawaii
2001	Received word of receipt of Nobel Prize in October – family together for the award in December – a wonderful shared moment	Graham graduated from Princeton and I had my 35th reunion in June – almost a definition of aging. – brief bout with melanoma – successfully caught early thanks to a very alert dermatologist – Recia Blumenkranz

SIGNALING IN RETROSPECT AND THE INFORMATIONAL STRUCTURE OF MARKETS

Prize Lecture, December 8, 2001

by

A. MICHAEL SPENCE[1]

Stanford Business School, Stanford University, 518 Memorial Way, Stanford, CA 94305-5015, USA.

INTRODUCTION

When I was a graduate student in economics at Harvard, I had the privilege of serving as rapporteur for a faculty seminar in the then-new Kennedy School of Government. Among other distinguished scholars, it included all of my thesis advisers, Kenneth Arrow, Thomas Schelling, and Richard Zeckhauser. In the course of that seminar there were discussions of statistical discrimination and many other subjects that relate to the incompleteness of information in markets. One of my advisers came in one day with the strong suggestion that I read a paper he had just read called "The Market for Lemons" by George Akerlof.[2] I always did what my advisers told me to do and hence followed up immediately. It was quite electrifying. There we all found a wonderfully clear and plausible analysis of the performance characteristics of a market with incomplete and asymmetrically located information. That, combined with my puzzlement about several aspects of the discussion of the consequences of incomplete information in job markets, pretty much launched me on a search for things that I came to call signals, that would carry information persistently in equilibrium from sellers to buyers, or more generally from those with more to those with less information.[3] The issue, of course, was that signals are not terribly complicated things in games where the parties have the same incentives, i.e. where there is a commonly under-

[1] This paper is based on a lecture delivered by the author in Stockholm on the occasion of the 100th anniversary of the founding of the Nobel Prize. I would like to thank my fellow recipients of the Nobel Prize in Economics this year, Professor George Akerlof and Professor Joseph Stiglitz, for their work and their inspiration, and my thesis advisers, Professors Kenneth Arrow, Thomas Schelling and Richard Zeckhauser whose ideas and guidance got me launched on the study of market structure (particularly informational structure) and performance. My colleagues Professors Edward Lazear and Mark Wolfson gave me a great deal of constructive input. I also owe a great debt to Professors James Rosse and Bruce Owen, with whom I learned and taught industrial organization and applied microeconomic theory at Stanford. It was a great group of young people and a wonderful time to be in that part of the field.

[2] George Akerlof, "The Market for Lemons: Qualitative Uncertainty and the Market Mechanism, *Quarterly Journal of Economics.*

[3] I believe is was Robert Jervis who introduced the terms "indices" and "signals." Indices are attributes over which one has no control, like gender, race, etc. Think of them as unalterable attributes of something, not necessarily a person. Signals are things one does that are visible and that are in part designed to communicate. In a sense they are alterable attributes. I thought it was a useful set of distinctions and terminology and I still do.

stood desire to communicate accurate information to each other. Even in that case (sometimes called the pure coordination case) however, there are potential problems of choosing among equilibria as illustrated in Schelling's brilliant analysis of the use of focal points and contextual information to solve communication/coordination problems when the parties have been deprived of the ability to communicate directly.[4] In markets where the issue is often undetectable or imperfectly detectable quality differentials, the alignment of incentives is typically imperfect and the incentive of the high-quality product owners to distinguish themselves and the incentive of the low-quality owners to imitate the signal so as to obscure the distinction is fairly clear. Of course there is more to it, as one needs to know such things as who is in the market persistently and hence who has an incentive to establish a reputation through repeated plays of the game. I am going to devote a good portion of this lecture to these issues, in a sense to revisit signaling, and then turn to some other aspects of the informational structure of markets that are raised by the parameter shifts caused by the proliferation of the internet as a communication medium in the past few years.[5]

I was asked recently by a somewhat incredulous questioner (actually a journalist) whether it was true that you could be awarded the Nobel Prize in Economics for simply noticing that there are markets in which certain participants don't know certain things that others in the market do know. I thought it was pretty funny. It was as if this had somehow been a closely guarded secret up until about 1970, at least in economics. I clearly cannot speak for those who make the decisions about the Nobel Prize, but I suspect that the correct answer to that question is no. What did blossom at that time was a serious attempt by many talented economists to capture in applied microeconomic theory a whole variety of aspects of market structure and performance. That work produced a partial melding of theory, industrial organization, labor economics, finance and other fields. An important early part of that effort was the attempt to capture *informational* aspects of market structure to study the ways in which markets adapt, and the consequences of informational gaps for market performance.

Therefore, in answer to the question, we noticed that there are many markets with informational gaps. These include most consumer durables, virtually all job markets, many financial markets, markets for various types of food and pharmaceuticals, and many more. These informational gaps were widely acknowledged and those of us who taught applied microeconomic theory, freely admitted that these gaps might change some of the performance characteristics, not to mention the institutional structure, of markets in which

[4] Thomas Schelling, *The Strategy of Conflict.*

[5] In economics and other social sciences, models abstract from reality and focus on structural features of organizations or markets that drive outcomes. There are embedded and usually unstated parameters that are not the focus of attention, as they do not normally change. When I refer to parameter shifts caused by the internet, I mean changes in structural elements that formerly did not change. For example, most markets have geographic dimensions and boundaries that are implicitly understood and are not the focus of attention. The internet however, has moved those boundaries by collapsing time and distance in the information/communication dimensions of markets.

they appear. But I think it is fair to say that we did not have much systematic knowledge based on theory of what those changes might be. And so we thought that applied microeconomic theory deserved an attempt to build these informational characteristics into models that capture the structure and performance of these markets with reasonably accurate assumptions about the ex ante informational conditions. It was a very exciting time for all of us who were involved. One of the wonderful aspects of receiving this award is that it has triggered in me, and I think others, fond memories of the sense of discovery and excitement. And in that context, I would like to take this opportunity to express my admiration and deep gratitude to the many extant young colleagues with whom I worked and shared these ideas. They should, and certainly in my mind, do share in the recognition triggered by awarding of the distinguished Nobel Prize for what was accomplished during those years.

The plan for this lecture is as follows. The overriding goal is not to look too stupid to the next generation of students and scholars. More seriously, following the advice that my advisers once gave me, I will first discuss the simplest model that I can devise that illustrates in reasonably general form the definitions and properties of signaling equilibria.[6] Next, we will allow the signal (in this case education in the job market context), to contribute directly to the productivity of the individual as well as functioning as a signal. Following that, the paper examines a market in which there is signaling and both separating and pooling in the equilibrium.

The section after that examines a fairly general partial equilibrium model of signaling and discusses competitive equilibria and certain kinds of "optimal" responses to signals.[7] Those who are more interested in the general idea and less in the general case can skip over this section without risk of missing any impor-

[6] John von Neumann, who deserves to be on a short list of the greatest minds of the 20th century, is reported to have said that you don't understand a theory or an abstract structure until you have seen and worked through hundreds of examples of it. Even if he didn't say that (and I think he did), I agree with it. Few people can say that they had the idea that calculating machines didn't have to be hard-wired, that you could store instructions in memory and then execute them in order: that is, you could build a programmable computer.

[7] These optimal responses problems are selection problems. In insurance markets, they can be moral hazard or adverse selection problems, and in other contexts they are agency problems or optimal taxation problems. You want to confront people with schedules that cause them to make appropriate choices and in so doing to reveal themselves and the information that they privately hold ex ante. Generally the results are below what is achievable with perfect information, because with perfect information, you don't have to worry about the revelation problem. These problems have the economic and mathematical properties of second-best taxation problems, of which perhaps the first to be analyzed was the "optimal" income tax problem, by the Reverend Ramsey, though the analysis seemed to have largely escaped notice until Jim Mirrlees, Tony Atkinson, and then others rediscovered it. The idea is that the taxing authority cannot directly observe an individual's earning power (think of it as maximum potential hourly wage) so they tax what they can see and monitor, which is income. This produces a disincentive with respect to work that could have been avoided if the tax were based on earning potential rather than actual earnings. The second best optimizing calculation then trades off in the most efficient way disincentives for work and the need to meet a revenue goal for the taxing authority. The mathematics of these problems are sometimes referred to as optimal control problems and sometimes the calculus of variations. In later work, Holmström applies these models to a labor setting, incorporating Wilson's work on syndicates (optimal risk-sharing). Here the second-best optimizing calculation sacrifices optimal risk- sharing employees and owners to provide incentives for employees to work diligently.

tant properties. However, this is the section in which the formal relationship between signaling models and models of self-selection and optimal taxation with imperfect information is examined, and that may be of interest to some readers. I also want to introduce in that context a new possibility that I discovered only recently and that is that one can have a signaling equilibrium in which the costs of the signal appear to vary with the unseen ability characteristics in the wrong way. That is to say the costs of education (absolutely and at the margin) rise with ability, or more generally, with the unobserved attribute that contributes positively to productivity. For the most part, I will use the job market case for expositional purposes and comment on some other signaling situations more briefly later in the essay. There is a risk in using job markets to illustrate signaling. In order to illustrate the fundamental properties of signaling models, I have stripped away other features of the market, particularly in the simpler models. But I have noticed in the past that there is a tendency for the simpler models set in the job market context, to convey unintended messages such as (1) education does not contribute to productivity, or (2) the information contained in the signal does not increase efficiency. This essay is mainly about the theory of signaling and information transfer in markets, and not mainly about human capital and labor markets. There are many who are more knowledgeable about the latter than I.

The paper concludes with two sections. The first of these discusses the ubiquitous use of time and the allocation of time as a signal and as a screening device. The second focuses on the potentially rather large information parameter shifts that the internet may have caused and speculates a little on how applied models of markets, organizations, and boundaries between them may have changed and on what is needed to capture the effects of these parameter shifts in models of markets and the economy.

THE SIMPLEST JOB MARKET SIGNALING MODEL

The idea behind the job market signaling model is that is there are attributes of potential employees that the employer cannot observe and that affect the individual's subsequent productivity and hence value to the employer on the job. Let us suppose that there are just two groups of people. Group 1 has productivity or value to any employer of 1, and Group 2 has productivity of 2. In this example, these productivity values do not depend on the level of investment in the signal. If there were no way to distinguish between people in these two groups then if both groups stay in the market, the average wage would be $2 - \alpha$, where α is the fraction of the population in group 1, and everyone would get that wage. If the higher productivity group through dissatisfaction or for any other reason, exits this labor market, the average productivity and the wage drop to 1. This phenomenon when it occurs is sometimes called the adverse selection problem, a label most commonly applied to insurance markets. It is structurally the same problem that Akerlof described in his famous paper on used cars (lemons).[8]

[8] George Akerlof, "The Market for Lemons: Qualitative Uncertainty and the Market Mechanism," *Quarterly Journal of Economics*, 1971.

Now suppose that there is something called education, which we will denote by E, that can be acquired or invested in. It is assumed to be visible, and its acquisition costs differ for the two types. Let us suppose that the cost of E years of education for group 1 is E, and the cost for group 2 individuals is E/2. For this example I am going to assume that education does not affect the individual's productivity. I do this purely to keep it simple and not to suggest that human capital, including that acquired through education, is somehow not relevant. In later sections, the assumption will be relaxed.

Equilibrium in a situation like this, and in general, has two components. First, given the returns to and the costs of investing in education, individuals make rational investment choices with respect to education. Second, employers have beliefs about the relation between the signal and the individual's underlying productivity. These beliefs are based on incoming data from the marketplace. In equilibrium, the beliefs must be consistent, that is, they *must not be disconfirmed* by the incoming data and the subsequent experience. Therefore, one could say that the beliefs must be *accurate*. But one should also notice that employers' beliefs/expectations determine the wage offers that are made at various levels of education. These wage offers in turn determine the returns to individuals from investments in education, and finally, those returns determine the investment decisions that individuals make with respect to education, and hence the actual relationship between productivity and education that is observed by employers in the marketplace. This is a complete circle. Therefore it is probably more accurate to a say that in equilibrium, the employers' beliefs are *self-confirming*. This may sound like a minor restatement but it is important. It is the self-confirming nature of the beliefs that gives rise to the potential presence of *multiple equilibria* in the market.

In the example at hand, suppose that group 1 individuals set $E_1 = 0$ and individuals in group 2 set $E_2 = E^*$. Suppose further that employers, none of whom individually influence investment decisions by individuals[9], believe that if $E < E^*$ then productivity is 1 and if $E \geq E^*$, then productivity is 2. With these assumptions, individuals in group 1 will rationally set $E = 0$ provided that

$$2 - E^* < 1$$

Members of group 2 will rationally set $E = E^*$ provided that

$$2 - \frac{E^*}{2} > 1 \ .$$

Therefore the choices will be rational and the expectations confirmed in the market if

$$1 < E^* < 2.$$

Though it is a highly stylized example it has many of the general properties of

[9] Investment decisions are made by individuals in advance of knowing with whom they will work and employers are such that none of them individually influences materially the perceived offers in the market place.

signaling equilibria. There is a continuum of equilibria, in each of which there is more investment in the signal than there would be in a world of full information. Because investment in the signal dissipates resources without improving productivity, the result is inefficient. Moreover the equilibria are orderable by the Pareto criterion, that is, as you move from one equilibrium to another, everyone is either worse off or no better off. The signal actually does distinguish low- and high-productivity people and the reason it is able to do so is that the cost of the signal is negatively correlated with the unseen characteristic that is valuable to employers, in this case productivity itself. The equilibrium is characterized by a schedule that gives the returns to education, that is a wage for each level of education, and optimizing choices given that schedule by individuals in the two groups.

The equilibrium is depicted in Figure 1. The wage schedule is the dark line and jumps from a wage level of 1 to a wage level of 2 at e*. E* is between 1 and 2 so that group 1 chooses the education level 0 and group 2 chooses E*. It is not essential that net income for group 1 at e* is negative as it is in this example. We could make the productivity levels for the two groups 3 and 4. The same signaling result would occur with suitable adjustments in the level of the wage schedule.

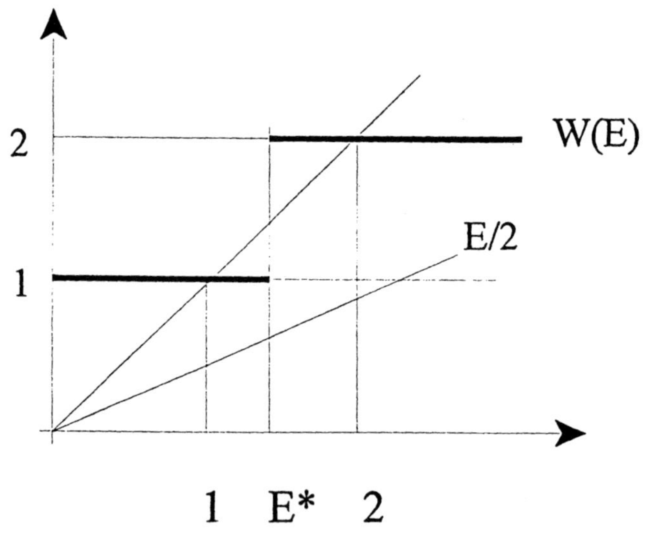

Figure 1

There are in fact other signaling equilibria. For example, there could be a minimal level of education that group 1 invests in. But unless it is a productive investment, there is no reason to think that over time the market would not discover this and eliminate it as an inefficiency that can be removed costlessly. In the spectrum of equilibria described above, probably the most interesting is the most efficient one. That equilibrium is the one in which $E^* = 1 + \delta$, where δ is to be thought of as a small positive number. In this equilibrium,

$$w_1 = N_1 = 1, \text{ and}$$

$$w_2 = 2, \text{ and } N_2 = 1.5 - \delta/2,$$

where N_i is income net of signaling costs for group i.

On the assumption that the market will find equilibria that are Pareto-efficient, one can ask whether there is a better equilibrium in the Pareto sense (everyone is better off) than the one described above. The answer is sometimes yes. It involves pooling and it depends on the relative sizes of the two groups. What is really going on here is that the market is, in a sense, acting as if it is trying to maximize the net income of the higher productivity group. In some cases that is accomplished by recognizing that it is too expensive for that group to distinguish itself. The alternative is to appear undifferentiated in a pool. That clearly benefits group 1 as they are mistaken for the average productivity, which is above 1. As a reminder, α is the fraction of the population in group 1. In a pooling situation the average productivity is $2 - \alpha > 1$. Group 1 would clearly prefer it. Group 2 prefers it as well if

$$2 - \alpha > 1.5 - \delta/2, \text{ or}$$

$$\alpha < .5(1 - \delta)$$

Since δ can be made as small as we want, there is a preferred pooling equilibrium (in the Pareto sense) if in this example, group 1 is less than half the population. In general with discrete groups, pooling with lower level groups becomes attractive if they are relatively small, because the higher level groups don't give up too much by being mistaken for the average and they avoid the signaling costs. In a later section I will describe briefly a case in which one can observe pooling and separating in the same equilibrium.

If you wanted to make the result in this market more efficient than the equilibria described above, you would tax education (assuming that such a tax is not costly to impose and administer), making it more expensive for group 2, and thereby make it possible to lower the level of education without losing the informational content of the signal. The revenues generated could be distributed equally to all participants in both groups independent of their education choice. The lump-sum component of the tax will therefore not affect their signaling behavior.

Let t be the tax rate on investment in education and let k be the lump-sum distribution from the tax revenues. This distribution goes to everyone. Let the signaling level of education be E*. Group one individuals will rationally choose not to send the signal if

$$2 - (1 + t)E^* + k < 1 + k$$

and group 2 will rationally send the signal if

$$2 - (.5 + t)E^* + k > 1 + k.$$

We have an equilibrium then if

$$\frac{1}{5+t} > E^* > \frac{1}{1+t}.$$

We will pick the efficient end of the signling spectrum by setting

$$E^* = \frac{1+\delta}{1+t}.$$

The lump sum distribution is equal to the tax revenues so that $k = \frac{t(1+\delta)(1-\alpha)}{1+t}$. Thus the equilibrium net incomes are

$$N_1 = 1 + k, \text{ and}$$

$$N_2 = 2 - \frac{(.5+t)(1+\delta)}{1+t} + k.$$

As δ becomes small and t becomes very large, k approaches $(1 - \alpha)$, and hence both net incomes approach $(2 - \alpha)$. This, the reader will recall, is the pooling equilibrium outcome in terms of net income. Here however, there is no upper limit on the size of group 1, namely α. Signaling costs (socially) are negligible as E* approaches zero, though the private marginal costs of signaling (including the tax) approach 1.

To summarize, one can get rid of the inefficiency and keep the signaling and the informational content of the signals with an appropriate tax on the signaling activity. The effect is to redistribute income in such a way as to reproduce the results of the pooling equilibrium. It could be that the information the signal carries is itself productive. In that case it is important that the equilibrium actually be a separating one.[10] That is the case here. Separating is retained in this equilibrium. Groups are correctly identified. The use of a tax on the signaling activity reduces the level of the signal required to distinguish the groups, and hence reduces the inefficiency of the untaxed signaling equilibrium.

THE TWO-GROUP MODEL WHEN EDUCATION ENHANCES HUMAN CAPITAL AND ALSO SERVES AS A POTENTIAL SIGNAL

It will naturally occur to the reader to ask what is the effect on the market signaling that we have just examined, at least in the context of labor markets, when the signal also contributes directly to productivity for the individual worker.[11] This section addresses the subject by modifying the two-group model of the preceding section to allow education to be productive. I will make

[10] Information is directly productive, for example, if there is a job allocation or training decision that is made more efficiently with accurate knowledge of the type. In that case the pooling equilibrium would be inefficient.

[11] Actually this issue does not just arise in labor markets. Generally signals can change the value of the product. For example, in the used car case, a warrantee changes the value of the bundle, the car and the warrantee in addition to carrying information about the product itself.

the model slightly more general in terms of functional forms. Let $s_i(E)$ be the value of a worker of type I with education E to an employer. Here I = 1,2 and we assume that $s_2(E) > s_1(E)$, and $s_2'(E) > s_1'(E)$. Let $c_i(E)$ be the cost of investing in E units of education for group I and assume that $c_1(e) > c_2(e)$, and that $c_1'(E) > c_2'(E)$. These assumptions simply capture the idea that the group with the higher productivity also has the lower costs of signaling. As before, the individual's type is not directly observable. We will also assume that $S_i(E)$ is concave, that $C_i(E)$ is convex and hence that the net income function $N_i(E) = S_i(E) - C_i(E)$ is concave.

There are three qualitatively different kinds of equilibria in this market. The first is a fully efficient separating equilibrium. It is easiest to see the types of equilibrium pictorially. In Figure 2, we have various forms of net income plotted as a function of E. Let $V_1(E) = S_2(E) - C_1(E)$. Our interest in the function V clearly relates to the question of whether group 1 will adopt the group 2 signal and hence create a problem with the separating equilibrium.

In Figure 2, you will see the functions N_1, N_2, and V. The points E_1* and E_2* are the points that maximize N_1 and N_2. The point $\bar{E}$ is the largest value of E such that V is larger than N_1*, the maximum value of N_1. In Figure 1, you can see that E_2* is to the right of $\bar{E}$. This means that as long as the wage offer schedule jumps up from $s_1(E)$ to $s_2(E)$ to the right of $\bar{E}$, individuals in group 1 will have no incentive to imitate the signaling behavior of group 2.

This is the fully efficient separating equilibrium. The signal carries accurate

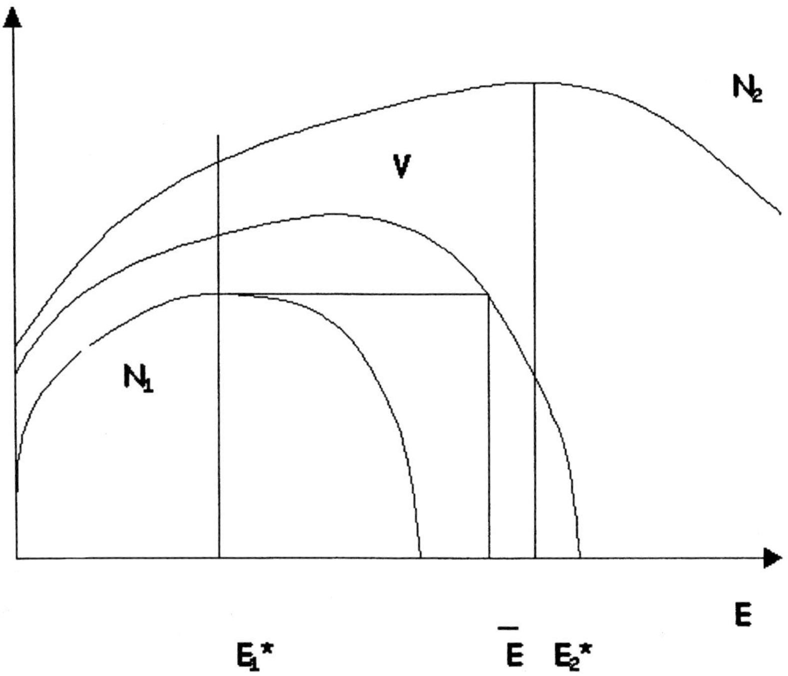

Figure 2

information, and the investments in education are the efficient ones. The outcome is as if there was perfect information in the market place. In essence, the two groups are sufficiently different in terms of some combination of the productivity of education as human capital and the costs of education that the fully efficient outcome survives as an equilibrium. Note however, that the negative relation between productivity and costs really matters. If signaling costs were the same, then the functions N_2 and V would be the same and we could not have this market outcome. When signaling costs are the same one can never prevent group 1 from imitating group 2 behavior when it is to their advantage to do so.

Now turn to Figure 3. It is essentially the same picture as Figure 2 except that E_2^* is to the left of $\bar{E}$. This means that if the wage schedule jumps to $s_2(E)$ before E_2^*, the group 1 will imitate group 2 behavior and dismantle the separating equilibrium. To prevent this we will specify that the wage schedule jumps up to $s_2(E)$ at $\bar{E} + \delta$. Subject to a qualification that I will come to in a minute, this is a separating equilibrium. To achieve the separation, the group 2 investment in education is pushed up above the efficient level, in order for the individuals in that group to achieve the signaling effect and avoid imitation by group 1. So here we have the same kind of result that we had in the no-human-capital case. Here the return to investing in education has a signaling component and a human capital component. The former can push the levels of investment above the full information optimum. In the first model the human-capital effect was zero, leaving only the signaling effect, an as-

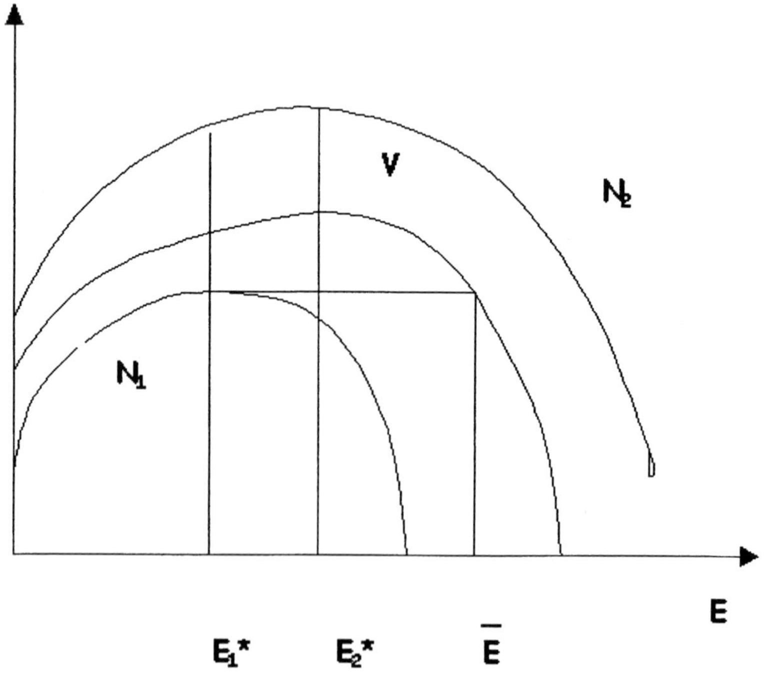

Figure 3

sumption that ensures that overinvestment will occur in any separating equilibrium in which signaling occurs.

There remain two issues. One is whether and under what circumstances, pooling will destroy the hypothesized separating equilibrium and the second is, "Can one tax the signal in such a way as to improve market performance?" Pooling first. Let α be the fraction of the total population in group 1. In a pooling equilibrium, the wage for all will be $\alpha s_1(E) + (1 - \alpha) s_2(E)$ for any level of E that emerges. This cannot break a fully efficient separating equilibrium because group 2 cannot be better off. Thus if pooling breaks a separating equilibrium it can only be in the case where the more productive group has been forced, for signaling purposes, above its optimal level of E from the standpoint of investment in human capital. Let $W(E) = \alpha s_1(E) + (1 - \alpha) s_2(E)$. By making α arbitrarily small we can make W as close to $s_2(E)$ as we want. Now let us look again at Figure 2. If you start at $\bar{E}$ and reduce E and move to the left and up the curves N_2 and V, it is clear that both groups are better off. For small α, the net income functions W-c_1 and W-c_2 are close to V and N_2. Hence for a range of α at the low end, pooling will break the separating outcome. For these cases, the natural choices of equilibrium levels of E are those that lie between the education levels that maximize W-c_1 and W-c_2.

As α rises, eventually the function W-c_2 will fall below the level of group 2 net income at the separating point $\bar{E}$, at which point the pooling outcome is not capable of breaking the separating equilibrium. To summarize, in the case of an inefficient separating equilibrium, there exist pooling equilibria that are Pareto-superior to the separating equilibrium provided the size of the lower productivity group is below some threshold level. If the market has a way of finding the pooling equilibria, they will break the separating one.

We turn now to the problem of improving the efficiency of the market. We saw in the preceding section that in the case where there is no human capital component of productivity, one can in principal come arbitrarily close to the efficient outcome through appropriate taxes. The same is true when the signal adds to the individual's productivity as well as functioning as a signal. We have already seen that in some cases the market equilibrium itself is efficient in the sense of maximizing total net income as part of a separating equilibrium. We now want to show that one can achieve the same result in the case where the higher productivity group has been forced by signaling considerations to move above its efficient level of investment in human capital.

To achieve an efficient outcome, we want to maximize total net income. To do that we need to have $s_i' = c_i'$ for i = 1,2. To accomplish that if it is possible, we need a wage function that induces these choices. The wage function can be thought of as a schedule of taxes on education superimposed on a wage function that sets wages equal to productivity. Since each individual in each group considers all possible levels of E in making its education investment decision, it turns out to be easier to solve this problem indirectly rather than directly. Let us suppose therefore that counter to fact, there is a continuum of types specified by the parameter z, where productivity for type z is $zs_1+(1\text{-}z)s_2$ and costs for type z are $zc_1+(1\text{-}z)c_2$. Let E(z) maximize

$$z(s_1 - c_1) + (1 - z)(s_2 - c_2).$$

Note that E(z) declines as a function of z. Invert E(z) to get Z(E). If the wage schedule we are looking for is w(e), then individuals will have maximized by setting

$$w' = zc_1' + (1 - z)c_2'.$$

Substitute Z(E) into the differential equation above and integrate with respect to E, setting the constant so that total wages equal total output. This wage schedule and/or the implied tax schedule will induce the efficient choices of E.[12]

The reader notices that the optimal wage schedule above does not depend on the distribution of z in the population.[13] Therefore let us assume that almost all the weight in the distribution is at either z = 0 or z = 1. This is the two group case we are studying.

To summarize, with two groups and education as productive human capital, one can have a signaling equilibrium with full efficiency or overinvestment in education by the more productive group. You can also have a pooling equilibrium that dominates the separating equilibrium provided that the less-productive group is not too large. And finally there exists a tax/subsidy scheme that produces a fully efficient separating outcome as an equilibrium.

A MODEL WITH SIGNALING, SELECTION AND POOLING[14]

The model we are going to look at briefly in this section is of interest for two reasons. First it illustrates a case in which there is both pooling and separating components of the equilibrium, and second, it shows that the critical criterion for having a separating component in an equilibrium is that the net benefits of issuing the signal are positively correlated with an unseen attribute that contributes positively to productivity. This positive correlation can result as in preceding examples, from signaling costs that are negatively correlated with the valued attribute. That is a sufficient but not a necessary condition for a separating equilibrium. In this very nice example the information is acquired at a fixed cost and the positive correlation comes from subsequent discovery of the attribute post-employment.

The idea behind the model is that the value of individuals to firms is not directly observed, at least at the time of hiring. The value which we will denote by q is distributed on the interval $[q_{min}, q_{max}]$. Let the distribution of q in the

[12] Note that $w'' - [zc_1'' + (1 - z)c_2] = z'(E)[c_1' - c_2'] < 0$, so that the second order condition for a maximum is satisfied. The optimal tax schedule will actually consist of a rising tax on education at all levels of education combined with a lump sum distribution to everyone so that net tax revenues are zero. In this example, group 1 will receive a net subsidy and group 2 will pay a net tax.

[13] This is a general property of the continuous case, when the objective is, as it is here, to maximize net income by inducing the efficient levels of investment in human capital.

[14] This example was developed by Professor Edward Lazear. It illustrates nicely the coexistence of pooling and separating in equilibrium and also a different structural condition that permits the signaling and selection to occur. It can be found in his book, Edward Lazear, *Personnel Economics*.

population be f(q). Individuals have a choice. They can work for firms that do not distinguish among them and hence pay everyone the same amount. Or they can work for firms that incur an expense, denoted by e, as a result of which, the firm eventually learns the value of q for the individual and pays the person accordingly. In equilibrium this cost, which is the same for everyone, is passed on to the individual in the form of a reduction in compensation. Labor markets are assumed to be competitive. For those individuals who choose the firms where they are distinguished, the wage is q-e. If the individual chooses a firm that does not incur the cost and does not distinguish among workers, then the compensation is the average value of the individuals who work for that firm.

Let us suppose that the average value of the workers in the pooling firms is $\bar{q}$. If we consider the optimizing decisions of individuals, it is clear that if

$$q - e > \bar{q}$$

then the individual will choose to work for the separating firm and conversely. Let $q^* = \bar{q} + e$. In equilibrium, $\bar{q}$ is the actual average value of those who work in the pooling firms, so that

$$q^* - e = \frac{\int_{q\min}^{q^*} qf(q)dq}{F(q^*)} = E(q|q \le q^*)$$

where F(q) is the cumulative distribution function for the attribute q. The equilibrium is illustrated in Figure 4.

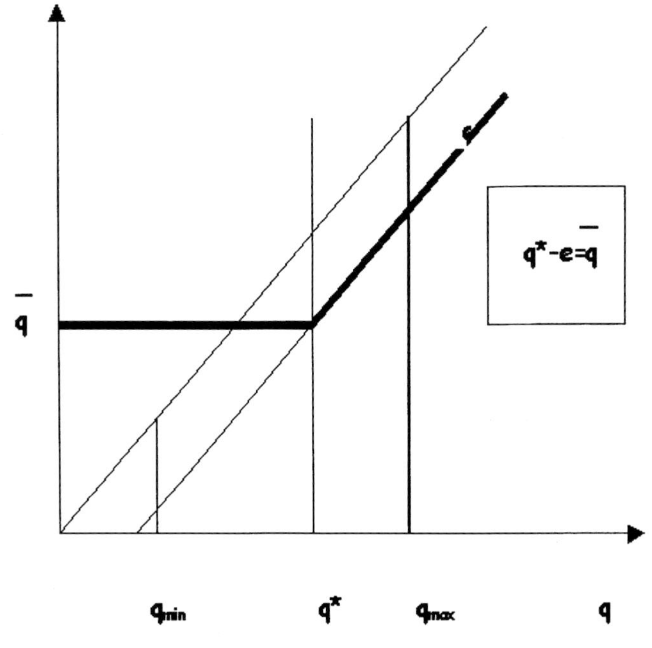

Figure 4

Those with $q \leq q^*$ receive $\bar{q}$ and are pooled, while those with $q > q^*$ receive $q - e$ and are identified and are in the separating part of the equilibrium. It is possible that everyone will be pooled. This occurs when e, the cost of discovery, is large enough that $q_{max} - e$ is less than the unconditional mean of the whole distribution. Another view of the equilibrium is provided in Figure 5.

Here we plot the functions q^*, and $E(q \mid q \leq q^*) + e$, as a function of q^*. The second function is upward-sloping and will cross the 45-degree line, unless e is large enough to keep the second function above the 45-degree line for all q^*. The crossover point is the equilibrium level of q^*.[15]

The signal is the choice of which type of firm to go to and it is partially, but not completely, informative about the individual's value to the firm. I noted in the first model that the signal retains its informational content in equilibrium if the cost of the signal is negatively correlated with the (hard-to-observe) valued attribute. In this case, the cost of the signal is a constant across people but because of the subsequent discovery and adjustment, the net benefit to the individual of issuing the signal is positively correlated with the valued attribute.

It is possible that the information carried by the signal increases efficiency. That circumstance increases the return to going into the separating side of

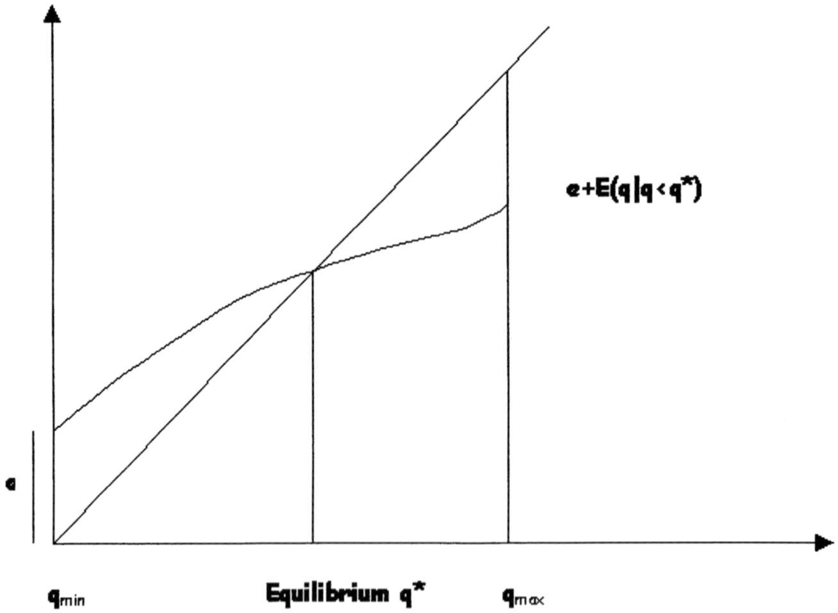

Figure 5

[15] While the conditional expected value function is upward-sloping, its slope is not necessarily less than one, and depends on f(q). It is therefore in principal possible to have an odd number of multiple crossovers. If there are three, the middle one will be unstable and the ones at the outside will cross over with a slope of less than one and be stable. To see this, note that if at some point of time, $q^* - e > \bar{q}$, then q^* will rise, and conversely.

the market and has the overall effect of increasing the size of the group that sends the signal. I should also note that it has been implicitly assumed here that the information about productivity, once it is acquired, is public. That would force the employer to pay the employee his or her productivity minus the discovery cost. If, on the other hand, the discovery is private, there will be a negotiation between the employer and the employee over the net income, and that will have the effect of lowering the net income of the employee relative to the case in which the information is public. Thus one should expect the size of the pooling component of the market equilibrium to rise when the discovery is private.

THE GENERAL CONTINUOUS MODEL[16]

I would now like to establish some reasonably general properties of signaling models.[17] Following that we will look at improving the equilibrium performance of the market through taxes and subsidies, using the approach of optimal taxation with imperfect information. The variables are n, standing for some attribute that is (a) not directly observable, and (b) valuable to employers, and y, which is years of education. The latter is observable and may be valuable to employers. The functions with need are S(n,y) which specifies an individual's productivity or value to an employer as a function of education and n, which I will hence forth refer to as ability. The remaining functions are c(y,n) which specifies the cost of education as a function of the same two variables and w(y) which is the wage offered to an individual who presents him or herself in the market with education of y. Since this is quite familiar territory, I will proceed fairly quickly. The equilibrium is defined by two conditions. First, given w(y), individuals maximize income net of education costs with respect to y. Thus they maximize w(y) – c(y,n) by setting

$$w'(y) = c_y(y, n).$$

This holds for all n. The second order condition, $w''(y) - c_{yy}(y, n) < 0$ must hold.

The second condition is that employers' experience in the market over time must be consistent with the offers they are making, so that for all n

$$\omega(y) = s(y, n).$$

Ignore the second-order conditions for the moment. Since by assumption

[16] This section is somewhat technical. It is not difficult mathematics but does require a general knowledge of differential equations and the calculus of variations. It is not essential for those interested in learning the basic properties of signaling equilibria and can be skipped by readers who are willing to accept that the properties cited in the earlier examples survive in the general case. The second best optimizing calculations are of some interest in interpreting what is going on in the market.

[17] Much of the material in this section is taken from parts of the the paper, "Competitive and Optimal Responses to Signals: An Analysis of Efficiency and Distribution," by Michael Spence, *Journal of Economic Theory*, 1974.

$s_n > 0$, one can in principle solve the equation above for n in terms of w and y, say n=N(w,y). Substituting in the first order conditions, we have

$$\omega'(y) = c_y(y, N(\omega, y)). \tag{1}$$

This is a first-order, ordinary differential equation. It has a one-parameter family of solutions that do not cross each other. In principle each member of this one-parameter family can be part of a market-signaling equilibrium.[18]

If c(0,n) = 0 for all n and if $c_{yn} < 0$, then assuming $c_y > 0$, c(y,n) will be declining in n and that combined with an upward sloping w(y) (without which no one would invest in education), ensures that y is an increasing or at least a non-decreasing function of n. Let the net income function be

$$N(y, n) = w(y) - c(y, n).$$

This function has the property that N_y is an increasing function of n, which ensures that if $N_y = 0$ for a particular value of n, then if you raise n, N_y will be greater than zero and the maximum will occur at a higher value of y.

Differentiating (1) with respect to y we have

$$w'' - c_{yy} = c_{yn}\frac{dn}{dy} < 0 ,$$

which means that the second order condition is in fact satisfied.

Without being too formal about it, education or any potential signal transmits information in equilibrium if its costs absolutely and at the margin decline as the unseen valued attribute increases. This is a sufficient condition. In a later section I will show by example that it is not a necessary condition.

Since for every level of n, in equilibrium $w(y) \equiv s(n, y)$, differentiating we have

$$w'(y) = s_y + s_n\frac{dn}{dy} > s_y$$

because $s_n > 0$ and $\frac{dn}{dy} > 0$. This implies that in equilibrium, the private return to education is higher than its direct contribution to productivity, because of the second term in the equation above. This second term is the signaling effect. It is the part of the private return to the investment in education that is tied to the unobserved level of n. Since $w' = c_y$, the above inequality implies that $s_y - c_y < 0$, so that in equilibrium for all n, the investment in education is higher than it would be with perfect information. If n were observable, then individuals would be paid s(n,y), and they would select education to maximize s – c by setting $s_y = c_y$. Note that if $s_n \equiv 0$ for all n, then the signaling effect goes away. The attribute n is still unobservable to employers but individuals make efficient education investment decisions as they have the infor-

[18] The solutions cannot cross because if they did, then the derivative at a given point in (w,y) space would have two values, which contradicts the statement that w' has a well-defined value F(w,y) at every point. As a consequence, let us assume that the family of solutions is w(y,K) where K is a parameter. If $w_K > 0$ anywhere, then it is true everywhere, since to assume the opposite would mean that the solutions cross.

mation they need to make the investment decision optimally, and they are the only ones who need that information.

As noted earlier, there is a one-parameter family of equilibrium wage schedules that do not cross. Let the parameter be k and denote the schedules by w(y,k). As the solutions do not cross, without loss of generality we can assume that $w_k > 0$. Net income to the individual is N = w − c. Differentiating partially with respect to k, with n held constant, we have

$$N_k = w_k + (w_y - c_y)(\partial y / \partial k) = w_k > 0. \tag{2}$$

Thus a shift from one equilibrium to another makes everyone better or worse off together. The equilibria are orderable by the Pareto criterion. What happens as one moves from one equilibrium to another is that the extent of overinvestment in the signal is increasing or declining for everyone. I have to confess that at the time, even after discovering that there might be multiple equilibria, I did not expect that there would be such a simple relationship among them in terms of market performance.

We can use (2) above and the fact that $w \equiv s$ to derive the effect of a shift in the equilibrium on the levels of investment in education. N = w − c = s − c. Differentiating with respect to k, holding n constant and using (2) we have

$$\frac{\partial y}{\partial k} = \frac{w_k}{(s_y - c_y)} < 0 .$$

Finally, from the equilibrium condition $w' = cy$, differentiating with respect to k with n fixed, we have

$$w_{yk} = -\left[\frac{\partial y}{\partial k}\right](w_{yy} - c_{yy}) < 0 .$$

This gives us a pretty complete picture of what happens when the equilibrium wage schedule shifts up. It becomes flatter, inducing lower levels of investment in education. Average wages decline and average education costs decline more, so that net incomes rise and everyone is better off. Figure 6 represents the family of equilibrium wage schedules. As they rise they become flatter and the range of investment in education shifts to the left. Figure 6 shows the range of investment in education for each of the schedules.

As the schedules rise and become flatter, the ranges of investment in education move to the left, that is they fall.

While it is perhaps interesting to note that the signaling effect causes overinvestment in the signal by the standard of a world in which there is perfect information, that isn't the world we live in. Thus it may be more interesting to examine the equilibrium outcomes in comparison to various second-best outcomes that acknowledge that there is an informational gap and asymmetry that cannot simply be removed by a wave of the pen.

I will begin by looking at the maximization of total net income. Here as we shall see, one can achieve the efficient levels of investment in education for all n. The required tax in effect undoes the signaling effect. The reason that this is a clean case is because a dollar of net income is of equal value regard-

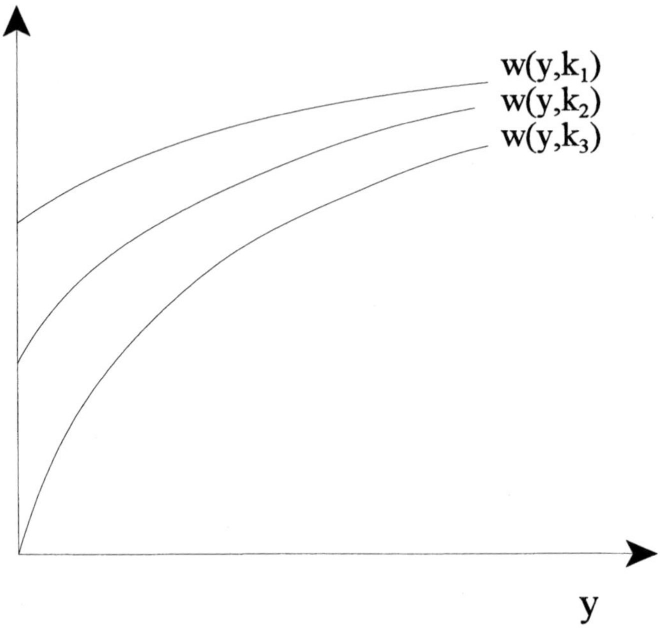

Figure 6

less of the recipient, we do not get into the business of trading off income distribution against the objective of efficiency. Following this brief analysis, we will look at social welfare functions that are not linear in net income. For these, there will be a tradeoff between efficiency and distribution. I will show that the market outcome is more akin to the outcome of maximizing a convex (that is to say anti-egalitarian) social welfare function. This is not a surprising result since the function of signaling is to distinguish low- from higher- productivity individuals, which results in a move away from egalitarian outcomes. I do also want to emphasize at the outset that the purpose of this analysis is not to propose or promote taxing or subsidizing signals but rather to help shed additional light on the properties of the competitive equilibrium.

MAXIMIZING TOTAL NET INCOME

We will assume that the unobservable attribute n is distributed in the population according to the density function f(n), and the cumulative distribution will be represented by F(n). The total net income then is

(3) $$\int_{\underline{n}}^{\bar{n}} N(y,n)f(n)dn\,.$$

Here $N(y, n) = w(y) - c(y, n)$ as before. The constraints are two. Individuals choose rationally so that $w' = c_y$ and total gross wages have to equal total productivity or value generated to employers:

(4) $$\int_{\underline{n}}^{\bar{n}} w(y)f(n)dn = \int_{\underline{n}}^{\bar{n}} s(y,n)f(n)dn\ .$$

Our goal here is to select a schedule w(y) that causes education choices y(n) for each n, that maximize total net income, net that is of education costs. This is actually pretty straightforward. Using (4), we can replace w(y) in (3) and choose y(n) to maximize

$$\int_{\underline{n}}^{\bar{n}} ((s(y,n) - c(y,n))f(n)dn\ .$$

This is the simplest form of a calculus of variations problem.[19] The solution is a schedule y(n) that causes $s_y = c_y$, for all levels of n. The reader will note that the implied levels of investment in education are those which would occur if n were observable, that is in the hypothetical world of perfect information. They are therefore also as a result the efficient levels of investment in education for each n: education is invested in up to the point where at the margin its direct contribution to productivity (the human capital effect) is equal to the marginal cost. That is to say, to maximize net income, the wage schedule is set so as to remove the signaling effect, though education still carries the information and acts as a signaling. The private part of the return to the signal (which has to do with distinguishing one individual from another and hence falls into the zero-sum/redistribution aspect of the market mechanism) is simply removed by the optimal tax or wage schedule. To find the required wage schedule, you invert the optimal schedule y(n) to r(y), substitute that in the optimizing condition $w'(y) = c_y(y, r(y))$, and integrate to get

(5) $$w(y) = w(0) + \int_0^y c_y(v, r(v))dv\ .$$

The parameter w(0) is then set to cause the breakeven condition (4) to be met. Individuals are likely being paid their productivity in the market place, s(y,r(y)). Therefore one can get to the desired result by imposing a tax/subsidy on education of t(y) = s(y,r(y)) - w(y) where w(y) is defined by (5) above. If you differentiate t(y) with respect to y you have

$$t'(y) = s_y + s_n r' - w' = s_y - c_y + s_n r' = s_n r'.$$

The last term in the equation is the signaling effect at the margin of a change in education. This then says that the optimal tax at the margin is equal to the signaling effect. It takes that part of the private return to education away, leaving only the human capital effect or the direct contribution to productivity.

One can also achieve the same result with an income tax. Let income be I. Its relation to education is given by I = s(y,r(y)). Invert that function to get

[19] A good treatment of the calculus of variations can be found in Courant. You displace y by $\delta\theta(n)$, differentiate with respect to δ and insist that the result be equal to zero for all $\theta(n)$. This gives us us $\int_{\underline{n}}^{\bar{n}} (s_y - c_y)\theta(n)f(n)dn = 0$. That in turn implies that $s_y = c_y$ for all n.

y=Y(I) and then set the income tax T(I) equal to I – w(Y(I)), where again w(y) is defined by (5). Individuals will select income so as to maximize I– T(I) – c(Y(I),n) = w(Y(I) – c(Y(I),n), by setting $w' = c_y$ which is the desired result.[20]

It is interesting for those of us who live in the United States that to a first crude approximation, our education costs are roughly similar in form to the efficiency-inducing tax schedule. Lower levels of education are subsidized and these subsidies decline at college and university levels because of the existence of a large private sector in higher education.

SECOND-BEST OPTIMA WITH ASYMMETRIC INFORMATION

We turn now to a brief examination of the effects of investment in education and on net incomes of maximizing some social welfare function. As before, N = w(y) – c(y,n) is net income and n is distributed in the population according to f(n). Let V(N) be the social value of net income of N to any individual. For the moment, we will place no restrictions on V(N) other than that it is upward-sloping – more net income is better. We will adopt an additive social welfare function

$$Z = \int_{\underline{n}}^{\bar{n}} V(N(n))f(n)dn \ .$$

For the moment, we will make no assumptions about the shape of V(N) except that it is upward-sloping. The objective is to maximize Z subject to two constraints. One is that individuals make a rational choice of education

$$w'(y) = c_y(y,\ n).$$

The second constraint is that gross wages add up to total output or productivity.

$$\int_{\underline{n}}^{\bar{n}} (w - s)f(n)dn = 0 \ . \tag{6}$$

Let us suppose that the particular function w(y) that is chosen induces a choice of y = r(n) for each level of the unobserved characteristic. Differentiating N(y,n) totally with respect to n gives

$$\frac{dN}{dn} = (w' - c_y)r' - c_n = -c_n > 0 \ . \tag{7}$$

Let $N(\underline{n}) = K$. Integrating (7) with respect to n we have

$$N(n) = K - \int_{\underline{n}}^{n} c_n(r(u),u)du \ . \tag{8}$$

Noting that w = N + c, and substituting in (6), the condition that total wages equal total productivity across the whole population, we have

[20] This analysis assumes that there are no adverse incentive effects of an income tax in terms of the choice between work and leisure. If there are such effects, then taxing income and taxing the signal are not equivalent in terms of the outcome.

(9) $$K = \int_{\underline{n}}^{\bar{n}} [(s - c + \int_{\underline{n}}^{n} c_n(r(u),u)du] f(n)dn \, .$$

The point of all this is simply to get rid of the function w(y). Thus we imagine selecting an upward-sloping function y = r(n) to maximize Z. By using (8) and (9) we are assured that both constraints in the problem are satisfied, and the wage or tax schedule is nowhere in sight. We can calculate it later using the optimal schedule r(n) by inverting that schedule to n = h(y), substituting for n in $w' = c_y$ and integrating to get the w(y) that induce the signal choices that solve the optimizing problem.

The solution to the problem is[21]

(10) $$(s_y - c_y)f = c_{yn} \times \left[F(n) - 1 + \frac{\int_{n}^{\bar{n}} V' f c du}{\int_{\underline{n}}^{\bar{n}} V' f c du} \right] .$$

If $V'(N)$ is a constant so that V(N) is linear, then the right side of (10) is zero. This is the case we have just looked at, where total net income is maximized by inducing the efficient choices of investment in education. It is just a special case of the more general problem and in that case, the optimal schedule is defined by $s_y = c_y$, for all n.

If V(N) is very concave so that the first derivative falls rapidly, then at the limit the only thing that matters is the net income of the people with the lowest net income. This case is normally called the maximin case. In this case (10) becomes

(11) $$(s_y - c_y)f = -\, c_{yn}(1 - F).$$

The right side of (11) is positive, which means that investment in education is below the efficient and full information level. At the top of the range of n, (1–F)/f approaches zero and the investment in education is efficient.[22]

The maximin outcome in terms of investment in the signal is also the result that would obtain if there were a monopsonist purchaser of labor services. The reason is that the monopsonist wants to maximize the difference between productivity and gross wages, subject to the constraint that the net income of the individuals with the lowest net income not fall below some prespecified level. Thus the solution to the monopsonist's problem is to maximize the net income of the lowest level and then take it all away by lowering w(y) uniformly across all education levels. Mathematically you are just reversing the objective function and one of the constraints.

[21] The derivation of this is a another application of the calculus of variations. You displace the function r(n) by $\delta\theta(n)$, differentiate the whole thing with respect to δ, and set the result equal to zero. After some reversing of orders of integration, you end up with an equation of the form $\int_{\underline{n}}^{\bar{n}} Q(r(n),n)\theta(n)dn = 0$. Since this must hold for all functions $\alpha(n)$, the optimizing condition is Q(r(n),n) = 0. The application of all that to this case yields condition (10).

[22] This follows from the fact that (1-F)/f is the reciprocal of the derivative of -log(1-F).

The opposite extreme occurs when the welfare function is extremely convex so that its slope rises rapidly. In the limit that would mean valuing only the net incomes of those with the highest net incomes, the maximax case. In this case, the optimizing condition (10) becomes

$$(s_y - c_y)f = c_{yn}F. \tag{12}$$

In this case, the right side of (12) is negative, implying that like the market equilibrium with imperfect information, the investment in education goes beyond the point at which the direction contribution to productivity is reached. At the bottom end of the range of n, F/f approaches 0 and thus at the lowest levels the investment in education is efficient.[23]

For the cases where v(N) is not approaching an extreme (very convex or concave), one can see from (10) that the right side approaches zero when n approaches its minimum and its maximum values. Provided that f(n) does not go to zero at the extremes, this would mean that at the end values of n, investment in education is efficient, that is $s_y - c_y = 0$. This is generally not a feature of the competitive equilibrium, and thus we may conclude that the competitive equilibrium is generally not the solution to some optimizing problem with this form of social welfare function. It is possible to rewrite the optimizing condition (10) in the following form.

$$(s_y - c_y)f = -c_{yn}[1 - F] \times \left[1 - \frac{E(V'|u > n)}{E(V')}\right]$$

where E(*|–) is the conditional expected value. For concave functions the term in the large square brackets on the right is always positive and thus investment in education is below the efficient level for all n except possibly at the end points. For convex welfare functions, the derivative is rising and thus the term in square brackets is negative. The levels of investment in education exceed the efficient ones.[24]

If you stand back from all this, the general pattern is fairly clear. The market equilibrium produces overinvestment in the signal because of the signaling effect, which is a private benefit to the investor, but yields no social benefit as its function is purely redistributive. The redistribution occurs in the

[23] This follows from the fact that F/f is the reciprocal of the derivative of log(F).

[24] Those familiar with optimal tax problems will recognize the form of this optimizing condition. In the income tax problem, individual welfare measured in dollars is $u(w,l) = wl - t(wl) - h(\bar{l} - l)$, where w is income per hour worked, l is working hours and t(wl) is a tax on income, and $\bar{l}$ is a constant- one can think of it as the total time available. Individuals maximize u with respect to l by setting $w - t'w - h' = 0$. The government has a revenue constraint so that $\int_{\underline{w}}^{\bar{w}} tf(w)dw = K$. If v(u) is the welfare function then we want to maximize $\int_{\underline{w}}^{\bar{w}} v(u)f(w)dw$. Here you change the optimizing schedule to y(w), get rid of tax function t(y) by noting that $\frac{du}{dw} = \frac{h'y}{w^2}$, impose the revenue constraint to determine u(0), and the displace the function y(w) to find the optimum. The optimum is achieved when $f\left[1 - \frac{h'}{w}\right] = \left[1 - \frac{yh''}{h'}\right]\frac{h'}{w^2} \times (1 - F)\left(1 - \frac{E(v'|u > w)}{E(v')}\right)$. Note that if v(u) is linear, then the right side of this equation is zero. Work leisure choices are efficient and the government revenue is raised by a lump sum tax, which does not distort the work-leisure choice.

direction of increasing the gross and net incomes of those with higher levels of education and productivity and hence income, the market equilibria tend to look more like the solutions to a second-best optimizing problem with a convex social welfare function. These, not surprisingly, are the welfare functions that weight higher net incomes more highly than lower net incomes.

THE CASE OF EDUCATION COSTS RISING WITH THE UNSEEN ATTRIBUTE: SIGNALING COSTS VARY THE WRONG WAY WITH RESPECT TO PRODUCTIVITY

The standard case of signaling in which the signal has the capacity to survive and retain its informational content occurs when there is an unobservable attribute that is valuable to buyers (in the examples we are looking at, employers), and the costs of undertaking some activity that is observable are negatively correlated with the valued attribute. The labor market examples, however, are slightly more complicated in that in that the unobserved attribute contributes to the individual's productivity and so does the signal. Thus, whatever the unobservable attribute is, it has two sources of value. One is the direct effect on productivity and the other is that lowering the costs of acquiring human capital also has value. Up to this point we have assumed that all of this works in the same direction. But it is possible that attributes that lower the cost of acquiring education might not be those that enhance productivity or might even be attributes that have a negative effect on productivity. We know that if $S_n = 0$, then you can get a signaling equilibrium, though in that case the signal isn't needed: it simply identifies ex post those with lower education costs and hence higher levels of education.

The question I pose now is, can you get a signaling equilibrium when $c_{yn} > 0$, assuming that $s_n > 0$? From the analysis of equilibria, we know that the second order condition for the individual's choice of education is satisfied only if $w'' - c_{yy} = c_{yn}\dfrac{dn}{dy} < 0$. This means that if $c_{yn} > 0$ one can have an equilibrium with signaling only if $\frac{dn}{dy} < 0$. So the question is, can that happen? The only way it could happen is if the human capital effect is large in the sense that it overrides the negative signaling effect. Thus if $s_y \equiv 0$, it certainly cannot happen. The signal makes no direct contribution to productivity and sends the wrong message about the unobserved attribute. Everyone will set $y = 0$. But the answer to the question posed above is yes, provided that the human capital effect is large enough to override the negative signaling effect. There can be signaling equilibria in which signaling costs rise with the level of the unobserved attribute that contributes to productivity. I will demonstrate this by example in a moment. Intuitively this should make sense if the human capital effect is big enough, because then the attribute that is of real value to the individual and to the employer is the one that drives education costs down. The key is that the wage schedule has to be upward-sloping in the signal, and this can happen if s_y is big enough even if $s_n > 0$. In this context, the correct statement about the condition that allows for a signaling equilibrium is that the net benefit of acquiring the signal has to be positively correlated with the gross effect on productivity. This could happen in segments of the population if very talented people face high opportunity costs associated with spending time on education.

This case may or may not be interesting from an empirical point of view, but it does illustrate that the more general formulation of the conditions for signaling are in terms of gross and net benefits and not just signaling costs. I did not realize this when I first worked on signaling equilibria. I thought then that the absence of the intuitively plausible negative cost correlation condition would destroy a signaling equilibrium. It is also of potential interest because the signaling effect is reversed. If $c_{yn} > 0$, then in equilibrium if there is signaling, dn/dy < 0, and thus

$$w' = s_y + s_n \frac{dn}{dy} < s_y .$$

Therefore the negative signaling effect causes the private return to education to fall short of the social return and hence causes under-investment in education.[25] It remains to show by a constructive example that this can happen at least in the theory, and perhaps also in the world.

We will show that this can happen with an example. Let $s(n, y) = ny^{\theta}$, and let $c(n, y) = n^{\alpha}y^{\beta}$, where $\alpha < 1$. Following the standard equilibrium analysis, we have

$$w = c_y = \beta n^{\alpha} y^{\beta-1}. \tag{13}$$

In addition $w = ny^{\theta}$, or $n = wy^{\theta}$. Substituting in (13), we have the differential equation in w(y) that defines the equilibrium wage schedules

$$w^{-\alpha}\, w' = \beta y^{(\beta-1-\alpha\theta)}.$$

One of the solutions to this differential equation is[26]

$$w(y) = Ky^{\frac{\beta-\alpha\theta}{1-\alpha}}$$

where K is a constant. If you then proceed to determine equilibrium choices of education, they are given by

$$y(n) = Tn^{\frac{1-\alpha}{\beta-\theta}}$$

where T is another constant. The second order condition is satisfied and this all works if dy/dn < 0 and this will in fact be the case provided that $\alpha < 1$, and $\beta < \theta$. That is to say, signaling occurs and there is a separating equilibrium, if the elasticity of productivity with respect to education is larger than the elasticity of education costs with respect to education. Or in simple ordinary lan-

[25] I thought Professor Gary Becker whose pioneering work in human capital, household production functions and much more, might appreciate this result.

[26] As this is simply an illustrative example, there is not much point in studying all the equilibria in the example.

guage, education is productive enough to justify its costs and override the negative signaling effect.

Another way to think about these relationships and this case is to change the unobserved variable from n to $t = \bar{n} - n$, where $\bar{n}$ is the highest level of n. In effect this defines the unobserved characteristic to be that which lowers education costs. Now investment in education will rise with t, provided there is a separating equilibrium, because $c_{yt} < 0$. But the effect of t on productivity is now negative, and if that effect is strong enough relative to the human capital effect, then that will prevent a separating version of the signaling equilibrium. The reason is that unless the human capital effect is large enough, the signaling effect will cause the wage function to be downward-sloping in y. There will be a pooling equilibrium at y = 0 and that of course entails in the hypothetical example, reasonably dramatic under-investment in the potential signal even though it is productive human capital.

THE INFORMATION CONTAINED IN THE SIGNAL CAN IMPROVE PRODUCTIVITY

It should be noted that the information carried by the signal can be productive itself. This will occur if there is a decision that is made better or with greater efficiency, with better information. In the job market context, one could build this in as follows. Let productivity be v(n,y,d) where d is a decision that the employer makes. It could be a decision about what type of job to assign to someone or a decision about required training. One can interpret the preceding analysis then, at least for equilibria in which the signal carries information in equilibrium, as s(n,y) being the maximum of v(n,y,d) with respect to d for each level of n and y. Note that this component of value is different from the human capital effect. Unlike the human capital effect, this element of value only exists if the signal is carrying information in equilibrium. You would lose it in a partial or complete pooling equilibrium even if that equilibrium included investment in education.

In situations like the Lazear model that we examined earlier, in which there is both pooling and separating components of the equilibrium, the addition of a decision that is made better with information will cause the value of the signal to rise, or more accurately the net benefits to rise. Those net benefits are passed on to individuals by virtue of competition on the employer side. Thus the relative sizes of the separating and pooling components of the equilibrium will shift in favor of the separating part. More people will opt to go to the firms that incur the expense of monitoring and learning productivity over time.

TIME AND THE ALLOCATION OF TIME AS A SIGNAL AND A SCREENING DEVICE[27]

The principles that govern the survival of signals in markets can be applied to other contexts. The kind of mixed or imperfectly aligned incentive structure that characterizes markets is common in many situations. In particular, situations in which individuals have an unknown or imperfectly perceived level of interest in someone or something are ubiquitous. In these situations, one frequently observes that time spent by the individual is taken as a signal of interest. Literature and everyday experience suggest that the allocation of time is a ubiquitous and persistent signal sometimes used deliberately as a screening device.

The persistence of spending time as a signal of interest in something is a reflection of the fact that time is in short supply and everyone knows it. There is a non- zero shadow price on time, and hence the use of it in pursuit of some person, goal or interest must mean that some implicit net benefit test has been passed for those who spent the time and failed for others who did not.

The use and interpretation of time as a signal is complicated and enriched by the accurate observation that there are both perceived and actual differences across people in the shadow price on time. These differences are used to interpret the signal. The allocation of a small amount of time by an individual with a high perceived shadow price on time has the same weight as a larger allocation of time by an individual with a lower perceived shadow price. As an example, those who have had visible leadership positions in virtually any organization know that the events they attend are taken as signals of interest and support, and conversely, when they do not show up, they deliberately and sometimes inadvertently signal a lack of interest, support or enthusiasm. It is noteworthy that the informational content of these common signals is not necessarily related to whether the individual (the signaler) is actually needed or has a role at the event. In fact, having a role at the event can dilute the signal because it complicates the interpretation of the reason for the leader's presence.

Time is also routinely used as a screening device or as part of the price of admission to events at which the number of places is in short supply. For entertainment and sporting events it is common to find that a mixed system that involves both price and time is used to allocate the limited number of places at the event. The question that I address briefly in this section is why the mixed system would be used in preference to the pure price system. The intuitive answer is that willingness or ability to pay may be a poor signal of real interest in the event, not withstanding the fact that failure to use the price system is inefficient for two reasons.[28] The mixed system allocates places or ac-

[27] Part of this section is based on a nearly unknown (probably for good reason) paper by the author, "Time and Communication in Economic and Social Interaction," *Quarterly Journal of Economics*.

[28] There are performers who want people with a genuine interest, and not just those with an interest and high incomes at the events, and who feel that the quality of the event is affected by interaction between the performer and among members of the audience.

cess to those who would (and often do if there is a secondary market) sell the place to someone with a higher willingness to pay – when that happens both parties are better off. Second, the time that is used to acquire the places is a dead-weight loss under most circumstances. Notwithstanding the clear problems with the failure to use the price system, the use of the mixed system is very common, and must mean that some objective is being pursued that is not respectful of the current distribution of income. For if the distribution of income is viewed as optimal, it is hard to conjure up a rationale for incurring the costs of the mixed system mentioned above.

I am going to use a simple example to look at the effects of using a mixed system for this class of resource allocation problems. It is not meant to be a general model, but rather to suggest what parameters are important in determining the performance characteristics of the outcome.

Let the value attached to an event by an individual be θ. One can think of this as a dollar valuation based on a roughly equal distribution of income, or you can think of it as a measure of value in a pure time system. What it is not is a current willingness to pay for access to the event. It is uniformly distributed in the population, on the interval [0,1]. The value of money is λ. It also is distributed uniformly in the population on the interval [0,1]. The assumption about the value of time at the margin is that it is equal to $G - \alpha\lambda$. If the parameter a is zero, then it is a constant, if a > 0, then the marginal value of time is negatively correlated with the marginal value of income, and the converse is also true. The fraction of the population that can have access to the even is N, and we will assume that N < 0.5. Finally let p be the monetary price for access to the event and let T be the time price.

The set of people who attend the event is the people with combinations of(θ, λ) that satisfy the inequality

$$\theta - \lambda p - (G - \alpha\lambda)T = \theta - (p - \alpha T)\lambda - GT \geq 0.$$

Let S = GT and $R = p - aT$. Then the inequality above becomes

$$\theta - R\lambda - S \geq 0.$$

Let A = $\{(\theta,\lambda)):\theta - R\lambda -$ S $\geq 0\}$. Then because of the fixed supply, the area of the region associated with A has to be N.

Figure 7 is useful in analyzing the choices. Each of the lines inside the unit square represent combinations of R and S, so that the area above the line is N. The line through the origin represents the pure price system. As the time price T is raised, S rises and R falls. It is easy to see without a complicated proof that as T rises, the average value of θ is rising while the total numbers stay the same, so that the total gross value to consumers is rising. This continues until the line goes flat, at which point R = 0. It is also clear that the increases are largest for low levels of T or S, because initially one is trading low levels of θ for much higher levels.

It is possible that the mixed time and price system is commonly used simply to achieve this result, namely allocating the spots to those who attach the highest value to them, and that whoever makes these decisions doesn't think

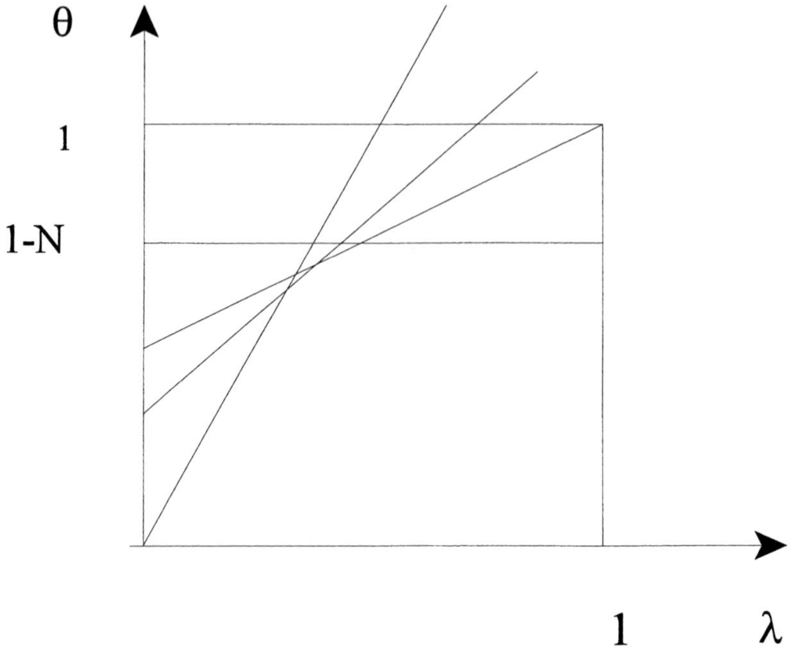

Figure 7

about or care about the dead weight cost of the time component of the price. But perhaps a more interesting question is whether the use of the mixed system ever increases the net benefits. We will assume that the dollar revenue is distributed in a neutral way so that price component of the access charge generates neither net benefits or costs. The time component of the access charge however generates a dead weight cost.

The net benefits are

$$Z = \int_A \theta - SN + \frac{aS}{G} \int_A \lambda \quad .$$

The second two terms are the dead-weight cost of the time component of the access charge. We have already observed that the first term, the gross benefits, are a rising function of S = GT, reflecting the use of time as part of the allocation mechanism. This is true independent of the sign or size of the parameter "a". Moreover, one can see from Figure 7 that starting at S = 0, the gains from increasing S, or T, are largest at the start (that is near S = 0) because as the lines rise and rotate right, low average levels of the valuation parameter θ are being knocked out and high ones are being brought in. The difference between the exits and the entries steadily declines as S increases, and the lines become flatter.

This brings us to the question of whether the net benefits also increase at least over some range as s increases. It is somewhat tedious but not difficult to show that in this example that the slope of gross benefits at S = 0 is

$$\frac{d\int_A \theta}{dS}\Big|_{s=0} = \frac{1}{3}N.$$

The derivative of net benefits at S = 0 is[29]

$$\frac{dZ}{dS}\Big|_{S=0} = \frac{2}{3}N\left[N\frac{a}{G} - 1\right].$$

If the parameter a is zero, then one can see that in this example, the dead-weight costs outweigh the gain in gross benefits. However if "a" is positive and large enough, then the net benefits rise at least over some range. Why should this occur intuitively? Here price is a badly flawed signal of value. Time, if its marginal cost is uncorrelated with price, is a better signal of value, but not good enough to overcome the dead-weight cost. But if the marginal cost of time is negatively related to the marginal value of income, then the combination of price and time is a much better signal of value. And if marginal time costs fall quite rapidly as the marginal value of income increases, then the cost of the time that is need to *screen out* the high income-low value purchasers is relatively low.

To illustrate, Figure 8 shows the value of net benefits as a function of S, for a case in which G = 2, N = .25 and a = 14. Here the reader should ignore the higher levels of S, as they are associated with negative prices. Above a certain level of S, or time cost, the model starts redistributing income, which is counter to the spirit of the analysis.[30]

To summarize, while this simple example hardly disposes of the issue of how markets go about trying to solve complex allocation problems in a world of imperfect information, it does, I hope, suggest that the kinds of mixed systems that we observe in reality may be quite innovative solutions to these problems and probably should not be dismissed in all cases as mistakes made by people who don't understand the virtues of the price system. There may even be more interesting and less wasteful alternative currencies, such as hours spent in public service work, that could be used in conjunction with the price system to allocate highly valued access to important events. While such alternatives might not be as effective as time in undoing the effect of the price system, they may also have considerably less dead weight cost associated with them.

[29] These results follow from the following facts. For R + S > 1, $R = \frac{(1-S)^2}{2N}$, gross benefits are $\frac{1}{R}\left[(1/3)(1-S^3) - (S/2)(1-S^2)\right]$, and the dead weight time cost is $\frac{2}{3}N^2\left[\frac{aS}{G(1-S)}\right] - SN$. Similarly, when R + S < 1, which occurs as S becomes larger, $R = 2(1 - S - N)$, gross benefits are (1/2) [(1 – $S2$) – RS – ($R^2/3$], and the dead weight cost of the use of time is $\frac{(1-s)}{2} - \frac{R}{3}$. When R + S = 1, the line that separates those who are admitted from those who are not goes through the point (1,1) which is why the formulae shift at that point.

[30] The existence of secondary market will to some extent reduce the benefit of the mixed system because it will draw into to primary allocation system entrepreneurs who are there to use their relatively low valuation on time to make an arbitrage profit. They will bid up the price required to clear the primary market and hence drive some of those with high gross valuations of the event from that market.

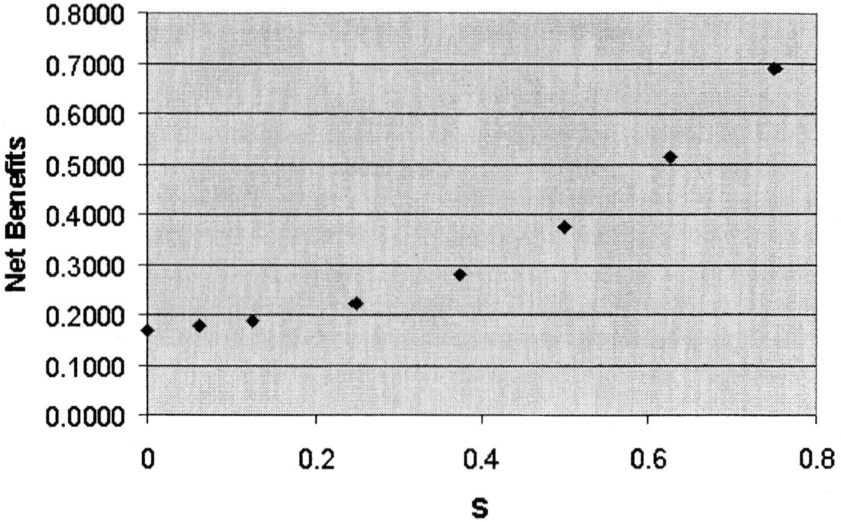

Figure 8

THE INTERNET AND THE CHANGING INFORMATIONAL STRUCTURE OF MARKETS

The proposition that the internet, or more accurately its relatively recent accessibility to a broad spectrum of users, has changed the informational structure of many markets, industries and economies, is probably not controversial. One could argue about how rapid the change has been from quite sudden on the one hand to a gradual evolution from the telegraph (which was the first time that communication over distance did not require the physical movement of something and hence became in a certain sense nearly instantaneous) through radio, the telephone, television, fax etc. on the other. It has also been easy for some to dismiss all of this as a fad, relying on the boom-and-bust cycle that we have just observed. But in my judgment that would be a mistake. We know from the economics of information that there are periods in which enough has changed so that we operate in a data-free environment, that is, one in which there is temporarily little or no relevant data to constrain expectation. The data trickle in and the beliefs and expectations start to line up with reality again.

The more fundamental point is that investors and others were probably not wrong about the ultimate effect of this technology on markets and the economy, but almost everyone overestimated the speed with which individuals and organizations change their behavior, and we also underestimated the amount of difficult technical infrastructure that needed to be built in order to have the foreseen outcomes become a reality. We would undoubtedly have been better off if we had reminded ourselves of the important work of the late Zvi Griliches on the diffusion of innovation, as that would have caused some questioning of the assumption that what very intelligent people can foresee will come about quickly. I wanted also to recognize Zvi's work as an early and very important example of behavioral economics.

Nevertheless there are powerful forces driving the outcomes and changing the informational structure of markets. Three of the most important are Moore's law, Metcalfe's law and the dramatic reduction of the noise to signal ration in fiber optic cable resulting in very large expansions in the throughput capacity of these pipes measured in signal processing terms. Moore's law is well-known. It is an empirical observation that the number of transistors on a chip doubles every eighteen months to twenty-four months. To a first approximation this has produced roughly a 10-billion-times cost reduction in the first fifty years of the computer age, dated from about 1950. Or to put it another way, things that were imaginable but unimaginably expensive in 1950 are essentially costless today. Economic historians will be better able than I to say whether there were comparable periods of change in the past with respect to costs of doing something important.

Metcalfe's law states that the value of a network to the entities attached to it is proportional to the square of the number of connected entities.[31] In economic terms this probably means that the value and hence the speed of connecting accelerates as the numbers increase. This is sometimes referred to as the network effect.

From signal processing theory we know that the capacity of a channel is proportional to the log of one plus the ratio of signal to noise. Through scientific and technical advances (in addition to being able to use lasers with multiple wavelengths), the noise generated when the light reflects off the side of the fiberoptic cable is being reduced dramatically, causing very large increases in data rates on existing fiber. In economic terms this translates into large cost reductions in providing bandwidth.

These three effects interact with each other over time to produce accelerating economic effects. Much of the recent economic impact of the internet is associated with reducing transaction costs of a variety of kinds. I will return to this subject in a moment. For most of these effects, one needs not just computing power, but also a reasonably ubiquitous reliable network that has standardized protocols, is more or less always on. After all, transactions involve, almost by definition, more than one party, though increasingly one or more of the parties are machines. It is interesting and not surprising therefore, that for the first forty years of the proliferation of computers, not much measurable productivity increase was detectible in macroeconomic data. In the past ten years, the period in which the expansion of the network occurred, there are noticeable measurable productivity gains. It seems very likely that the pro-

[31] This should be thought of as an empirical regularity as well. It can be derived as follows. Suppose that the value a person to each other person on a network is x. If there are n people on the network and we add another person, the n people experience added value of nx and the new person experiences value of nx. If $V(n)$ is the value of a network, being the sum of its value to all connected people, then $V(n + 1) = V(n) + 2nx$. Therefore $V(n) = 2x[1 + 2 + ... + (n-1)]$. Using Gauss's formula for the sum of the integers from one to n, we have $V(n) = 2xn(n-1)$, which is the quadratic relationship that Metcalfe's law asserts.

ductivity gains (the ones we can detect) are associated with reduced transaction costs, improved performance of markets, the ability to create new markets that were too expensive to create without the technology, and the important ability to take time and cost out of the coordination of economic activity, inside the firm and in the supply or value-added chain. That is what the network, with high and reliable capacity, with growing numbers connected to it and with enough computing power to run the endpoints and the nodes has permitted. It is a cumulative effect that we are just beginning to see.

Building models in economics is an art and a science. The science part consists of determining analytically the consequences of the assumption that create the structure of the model. The art consists in deciding what to put into the structure and what to leave out. Putting in too much makes the models intractable and of little use in illuminating the determinants of market performance. Putting in either too little or the wrong structural features makes the results, though tractable, uninteresting. A natural consequence of this is that parameters that don't change much from market to market or over time tend to be suppressed, as a matter of good practice in applied microeconomic theory. I mention all of this because it is possible and even likely that some parameters related to search costs, transaction costs, acquiring information, and geography have shifted reasonably rapidly in the past few years (or are in the process of shifting), as a result of the increasing speed, ubiquity and connectivity of the internet. This potential shift in parameters creates the opportunity to revisit aspects of the informational structure of markets and organizations, and in a sense, reintroduce the suppressed parameters as they have become interesting again. I would like to conclude this essay by suggesting a few areas in which such an inquiry might yield some interesting results.

One might have the impression from a first course in economic theory that markets combine supply and demand curves to produce prices, quantities and to determine who buys the good. There is nothing wrong with that view. But in addition, a market economy performs lots of other functions. Potential buyers and sellers need to find each other. Often buyers and sellers need to acquire information about each other and about the product. If the buyers, sellers, and products are differentiated, then there is a matching problem that in one form or another needs to be resolved in the marketplace. If sellers are charging different prices, then buyers need to consider engaging in some sort of reasonable search for the lower prices. These functions are not performed costlessly, and the costs of performing them are frequently lumped together under the heading of transaction costs. Broadly these costs are being changed and lowered by the internet.

BUYERS AND SELLERS FINDING EACH OTHER

Probably the most obvious example of reduced transaction costs is that associated with the rapid expansion of the markets for collectibles and used products of all kinds. In this arena the overwhelmingly largest market making entity is eBay. There are on average 750,000 transactions or each day with an average total daily dollar volume of 30 million.[32] Most of these markets simply did not exist previously, and those that did exist were more costly to create, less efficient, and less liquid. It is worth noting that the drop in the cost of buyers and sellers finding each other is largely independent of physical geography (recall that both distance and time are simultaneously compressed with the internet technology). This partial removal of the geographic bounds of markets makes them more liquid and in a certain sense more competitive. However, there are elements of natural monopoly in the market-making function. As the number of bidders increases the expected winning bid rises in these auctions. Hence the marketplace that is in the lead will attract the sellers, and the variety of products will attract the buyers.[33] Figure 9 shows the relationship between the number of bidders and the expected selling price in an ordinary auction.

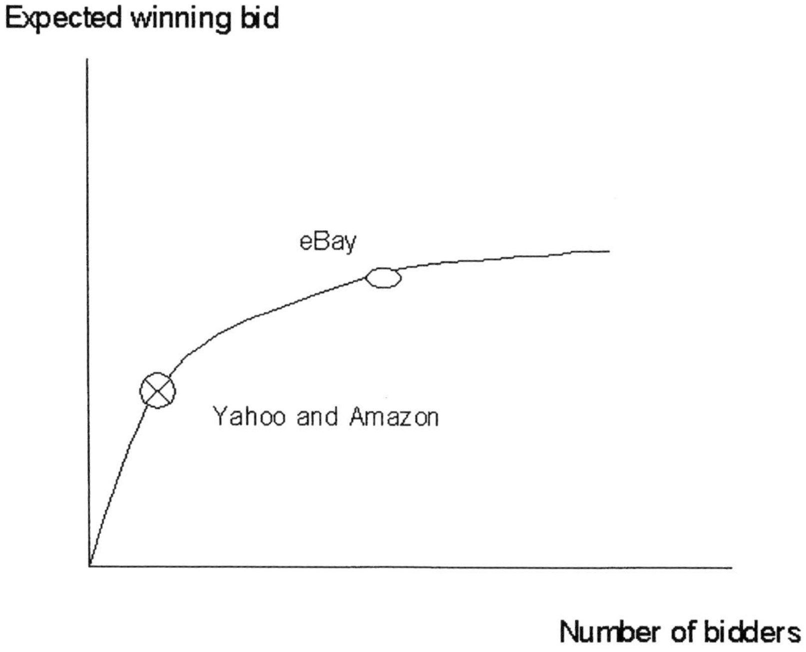

Figure 9

[32] Figures from Jeff Skoll, cofounder of eBay. There are of course more markets open in any given day than there are transactions.

[33] There is a potential qualification to this tendency. Intelligent software agents are in principle capable of searching for low prices across marketplaces. If individuals were prepared to use these agents, that would eliminate the liquidity advantage of the larger market-makers. However, this does not appear to have happened, at least not to the extent that it significantly diminishes eBay's advantage. The making of online markets is pretty clearly a potential area for research.

SEARCHING FOR THE LOWEST PRICE

The late George Stigler recognized that finding the lowest price was an activity that required resources and that there was a tradeoff between incurring costs of further search and the expected benefits of finding even lower prices. For prices that are posted in an internet environment, the cost of finding the lowest price is pretty close to zero. In principle, this should eliminate price dispersion by eliminating one side of the tradeoff. There was a kind of natural partial protection from price competition, the magnitude of which is a function of the search costs. The reduction or elimination of these search costs in the first instance increases competition. However there is probably more to this story. The decision to post a price is a strategic decision and in the face of negligible search costs, it is possible that sellers' willingness to post prices will decline and that there will be more negotiated prices or prices that are tailored to the individual buyer.

THE BOUNDARIES OF THE FIRM

There is a well-known and important literature in economics associated with Ronald Coase and Oliver Williamson and others. It deals in part with the fundamental question of the question of what economic processes are contained within a firm and which are mediated by markets, that is, transaction between firms. One aspect of this general set of questions has to do with outsourcing: the decision to conduct a certain set of activities in-house or to contract with another entity to have them conducted for the firm. Generally on the side of outsourcing is the likelihood that certain functions can be performed better by specialists who have the advantages of economies of focus and scale. Countering that are the contracting, monitoring and implementation costs of having a second party provide the service. Some of these countervailing costs are just transaction costs associated with complexity in communication. It is becoming reasonably clear that the internet platform is reducing some of these transaction costs and hence tipping the balance in a number of areas in the direction of outsourcing. Many, if not most, informationally based services are efficiently deliverable and monitorable on the platform.

We have in a sense, for the period of transition, a natural laboratory in which transaction cost parameters are being shifted, resulting in new experimental behavior on the part of firms. In general, the range of economic activity that can be effectively coordinated across a complex multifirm supply chain is just starting to be explored by companies and those who do research on these subjects. The boundaries of the firm, transaction costs, supply chain architecture and coordination, and outsourcing are all facets of a large mosaic in which incentives, communication and coordination, and the boundaries of the firm are worked out. The outsourcing extends to the employment relationship, where again the relative costs of in-house and the outsourced resources may have shifted. I hasten to add that these issues are far from being settled in the world of practice and in the world of economic research.

BIBLIOGRAPHY

Akerlof, George. "The Economics of Caste and of the Rat Race and Other Woeful Tales," *Quarterly Journal of Economics* 90 (November 1976): 599–617.
– "Gift Exchange and Efficiency Wage Theory: Four Views," *American Economic Review* 74 (May 1984): 79–83.
– "Labor Contracts as Partial Gift Exchange," *Quarterly Journal of Economics* 97 (November 1982): 543–69.
– "The Market for 'Lemons': Quality Uncertainty and the Market Mechanism," *Quarterly Journal of Economics* 84 (August 1970): 488–500.
Alchian, Armen A., and Demsetz, Harold. "Production, Information Costs, and Economic Organization," *American Economic Review* 62 (December 1972): 777–95.
Arnott, Richard J., and Stiglitz, Joseph E. "Moral Hazard and Nonmarket Institutions: Dysfunctional Crowding Out or Peer Monitoring?" *American Economic Review* 81 (March 1991): 179–90.
Arrow, Kenneth J. *Essays in the Theory of Risk Bearing.* Chicago: Markham, 1971.
– "Higher Education as a Filter," *Journal of Public Economics* 2 (July 1973): 193–216.
– "Models of Job Discrimination," in *Racial Discrimination in Economic Life,* A. Pascal, ed. Lexington, Mass.: Lexington Books, 1972.
– "The Role of Securities in the Optimal Allocation of Risk Bearing," *Review of Economic Studies* 31 (1964): 91–96.
– "The Organization of Economic Activity," in The Analaysis and Evaluation of Public Expenditures: The PPB System, 1, Joint Economic Committee, 91st Congress, Washington, DC, 1969.
Atkinson, Anthony, "Maximin and Optimal Income Taxation," Working Paper, circa 1971.
Baker, George, Michael Gibbs and Bengt Holmström. "The Internal Economics of the Firm: Evidence from Personnel Data," *Quarterly Journal of Economics,* November, 1994: 881–919.
Becker, Gary S. *The Economic Approach to Human Behavior.* University of Chicago Press, 1976.
Becker, Gary S. *The Economics of Discrimination.* Chicago: University of Chicago Press, 1957. HD 4903 .5 .U5B4.
– "Human Capital and the Personal Distribution of Income," W. S. Wotinsky Lecture #1, University of Michigan, 1967.
– *Human Capital: A Theoretical and Empirical Analysis, with Special Reference to Education,* 2d ed. New York: Columbia University Press for National Bureau of Economic Research, 1975.
– "Investment in Human Capital: A Theoretical Analysis," *Journal of Political Economy* 70 (October 1962): 9–49.
Bergmann, B. "The Effect on White Incomes of Discrimination in Employment," *Journal of Political Economy* 76 (March/April 1971): 294–313.
Bergmann, Barbara. "Occupational Segregation, Wages and Profits when Employers Discriminate by Sex," *Eastern Economic Journal* 2, pp. 103–110.
Bhattacharya, Sudipto; Partha Dasgupta, and Dilip Mookherjee, "Patents and Choice of Technique in Research and Development," *Journal of Political Economy* (March 1984).
Bhattacharya, Sudipto, and J. Luis Guasch, "Heterogeneity, Tournaments, and Hierarchies," *Journal of Political Economy* 96 (August 1988): 867–81.
Bowles, Samuel. "Schooling and Inequality from Generation to Generation," *Journal of Political Economy* 82 (May/June 1972):S219–S251.
Cain, Glen G. "The Economic Analysis of Labor Market Discrimination: A Survey," in *Handbook of Labor Economics,* O. Ashenfelter and R. Layard, eds. Amsterdam: North Holland, 1987.
Carlton, Dennis W. "Planning and Market Structure," in *The Economics of Information and Uncertainty,* ed. John J. McCall. Chicago: University of Chicago Press, 1982.
Coase, Ronald H. "The Nature of the Firm," *Economica* 4 (November 1937): 386–405.
– "The Problem of Social Cost," *Journal of Law and Economics* (October 1960): 1–44.

Cohen, K. J., and Cyert, R. M. *Theory of the Firm: Resource Allocation in a Market Economy*, 2d ed. Englewood Cliffs, NJ: Prentice–Hall, 1975.

Debreu, Gerard. *The Theory of Value*. Cowles Foundation Monograph No. 17. New Haven, CT: Yale University Press, 1959.

Diamond, Peter, and Michael Rothschild, *Uncertainty in Economics*. New York: Academic Press, 1978.

Doeringer, P., and M. Piore, *Internal Labor Markets and Manpower Analysis*. Lexington, Mass.: D.C. Heath, 1971.

Downs, Anthony. *An Economic Theory of Democracy*. New York: Harper & Row, 1957.

Ekern, S. and R. Wilson, "On the Theory of the Firm in an Economy with Incomplete Markets," *Bell Journal of Economics and Management Science*. 5 No. 1 (Spring 1974).

Fama, Eugene. "Agency Problems and the Theory of the Firm," *Journal of Political Economy* (April 1980): 288–307.

Fogel, Robert William, and Stanley L. Engerman, *Time on the Cross: The Economics of American Negro Slavery* (New York: W. W. Norton, 1989).

Gibbons, Robert. "Piece-Rate Incentive Schemes," *Journal of Labor Economics* 5 (October 1987): 413–29.

Gibbons, Robert, and Lawrence F. Katz, "Layoffs and Lemons," *Journal of Labor Economics* 9 (October 1991): 351–80.

Griliches, Zvi. "Estimating Returns to Schooling: Some Econometric Problems," *Econometrica* 45 (1977).

Grossman, Sanford, and Joseph Stiglitz, "On the Impossibility of Informationally Efficient Markets," *American Economic Review* 70 (1980): 393–408.

Hart, Oliver D. "Optimal Labour Contracts under Asymmetric Information: An Introduction," *Review of Economic Studies* 50 (1983): 3–35.

Hirshleifer, J. "The Private and Social Value of Information and the Reward to Inventive Activity," *American Economic Review* 51 (September 1961): 561–74.

Holmström, Bengt "Moral Hazard and Observability," *Bell Journal of Economics* 10 (Spring 1979): 74–91.

– "Moral Hazard in Teams," *Bell Journal of Economics* 13 (Autumn 1982): 324–40.

Jencks, Christopher, *et al. Inequality*. New York: Basic Books, 1972. LB 3062 .142.

Kreps, David M.; Paul Milgrom, John Roberts and Robert Wilson, "Rational Cooperation in the Finitely Repeated Prisoners' Dilemma," *Journal of Economic Theory* 27 (August 1982): 245–52.

Lazear, Edward *Personnel Economics for Managers*, Edward P. Lazear. New York: John Wiley & Sons, 1998.

– "Salaries and Piece Rates," *Journal of Business* 59 (July 1986): 405–31.

– "Educational Production," *Quarterly Journal of Economics*, August, 2001.

Leibenstein, Harvey. "Allocation Efficiency vs. 'X-Efficiency,'" *American Economic Review* 56 (June 1966): 392–415.

Levhari, D., and Yoram Weiss, "The Effect of Risk and Investment in Human Capital," *American Economic Review* 64 (December 1974): 950–63.

McCall, J. J. "Economics of Information and Job Search," *Quarterly Journal of Economics* 84 (197?): 113–26.

Mincer, Jacob. *Schooling, Experience, and Earnings*. New York: Columbia University Press for NBER, 1974.

Mirrlees, James A. "An Exploration in the Theory of Optimum Income Taxation," *Review of Economic Studies* 38 (1971): 175–208.

– "The Optimal Structure of Incentives with Authority within an Organization," *Bell Journal of Economics* 7 (Spring 1976): 105–31.

– "The Optimum Town," *Swedish Journal of Economics* 74 (1972): 114–35.

Modligiani, Franco, and Merton Miller, "The Cost of Capital, Corporation Finance and the Theory of Investment," *American Economic Review* (June 1958).

Nelson, Phillip. "Information and Consumer Behavior." *Journal of Political Economy* 78 (March/April 1970): 311–329.

Pencavel, John. "Work Effort, On-the-Job Screening, and Alternative Methods of Remuneration," in *Research in Labor Economics*, vol. 1, Ronald Ehrenberg, ed. Greenwich, Conn.: JAI Press, 1977.

Radner, Roy, and Michael Rothschild, "On the Allocation of Effort," *Journal of Economic Theory* 10 (June 1975): 358–76.

Ramsey, F.P. "A Contribution to the Theory of Taxation," *Economic Journal* 37 (1927) 47–61.

Riley, John G. "Competitive Signalling," *Journal of Economic Theory* 10 (April 1975): 174–86.

Rogerson, William. "Repeated Moral Hazard," *Econometrica* 53 (January 1985): 69–76.

Ross, Stephen A. "The Economic Theory of Agency: The Principal's Problem," *American Economic Review* 63 (May 1973): 134–39.

Rothschild, Michael, "Searching for the Lowest Price When the Distribution of Prices Is Unknown," *The Journal of Political Economy*, Vol. 82, No. 4. (Jul.–Aug., 1974): 689–711.

– "Models of Market Organization with Imperfect Information: A Survey." *Journal of Political Economy* 81 (November/December 1973): 1283–1308.

Rothschild, Michael, and Stiglitz, Joseph E. "Equilibrium in Competitive Insurance Markets: An Essay on the Economics of Imperfect Information," *Quarterly Journal of Economics* 90 (November 1976): 629–49.

– "Increasing Risk: I. A Definition," *Journal of Economic Theory* 2 (1970): 225–43.

Salop, Joanne, and Steven Salop, "Self-Selection and Turnover in the Labor Market," *Quarterly Journal of Economics* 90 (November 1976): 619–27.

Samuelson, Paul A. "Foundations of Economic Analysis." Harvard Economic Studies. HB 31. H33 v.80.

Schelling, Thomas. *The Strategy of Conflict.* Cambridge: Harvard University Press, 1960.

Simon, Herbert A. *Models of Man.* New York: John Wiley & Sons, 1957.

Solow, Robert M. "Investment and Technical Progress," in *Mathematical Models in the Social Sciences,* Kenneth J. Arrow, S. Karlin, and P. Suppes, eds. Stanford: Stanford University Press, 1960.

Spence, Michael, *Market Signaling: Informational Transfer in Hiring and Related Processes,* Cambridge: Harvard University Press, 1974.

– "Insurance, Information, and Individual Action," (with R. J. Zeckhauser), *American Economic Association, Papers and Proceedings,* May 1971.

Spence, Michael and Richard J Zeckhauser,"The Effect of the Timing of Consumption Decisions and the Resolution of Uncertainty on the Choice of Lotteries," *Econometrica,* March 1972.

Spence, Michael, "Job Market Signaling," *Quarterly Journal of Economics,* August 1973.

– "Time and Communication in Economic and Social Interaction," *Quarterly Journal of Economics,* November 1973.

– "Competitive and Optimal Responses to Signals: An Analysis of Efficiency and Distribution," *Journal of Economic Theory,* March 1974.

– "Consumer Misperceptions, Product Safety and Producer Liability," *Review of Economic Studies,* October 1977.

– "Competition in Salaries, Credentials, and Signaling Prerequisites for Jobs," *Quarterly Journal of Economics,* February 1976.

– "An Economist's View of Information," in *Annual Review of Information Science and Technology,* vol 9, 1974,Carlos Cuadra, ed. American Society for Information Science.

– "The Economics of Internal Organization: An Introduction," *Bell Journal of Economics,* Spring 1975.

– "Informational Aspects of Market Structures: An Introduction," *Quarterly Journal of Economics.* 1976.

– "Markets and Imperfect Information," *Portfolio,* vol 5, number 5.

– "Product Differentiation and Consumer Choice in Insurances Markets," *Journal of Public Economics,* 1979.

– "Signaling and Screening," in S. Rosen, ed. *Low Income Labor Markets,* National Bureau of Economics (forthcoming).

Stigler, George J. "The Economics of Information," *Journal of Political Economy* 69 (June 1961): 213–25.
– "Information in the Labor Market," *Journal of Political Economy* 70 (October 1962): S94–S104.
Stiglitz, Joseph E. "Approaches to the Economics of Discrimination," *American Economic Review* 63 (May 1973): 287–95.
– "Incentive and Risk Sharing in Sharecropping," *Review of Economic Studies* 41 (April 1974): 219–56.
– "Incentives, Risk, and Information: Notes Toward a Theory of Hierarchy," *Bell Journal of Economics and Management Science* 6 (August 1975): 552–79.
– "The Theory of `Screening', Education, and the Distribution of Income," *American Economic Review* 65 (June 1975): 283–300.
Stiglitz, Joseph E., and Andrew Weiss, "Incentive Effects of Terminations: Applications to the Credit and Labor Markets," *American Economic Review* 73 (December 1983): 912–27.
Thurow, Lester. "Education and Economic Equality," *Public Interest* 28 (Summer 1972): 66–81.
Tversky, Amos, and Daniel Kahneman, "The Framing of Decisions and the Psychology of Choice," *Science* 211 (1981): 453–58.
– "Judgment under Uncertainty: Heuristics and Biases," *Science* 185 (September 1974): 1124–31.
Waldman, Michael. "Job Assignments, Signalling, and Efficiency," *Rand Journal of Economics* 15 (Summer 1984): 255–67.
– "Up-or-Out Contracts: A Signalling Perspective," *Journal of Labor Economics* 8 (April 1990): 230–50.
Weiss, Andrew. *Efficiency Wages: Models of Unemployment, Layoffs, and Wage Dispersion.* Princeton: Princeton University Press, 1990.
– "Job Queues and Layoffs in Labor Markets with Flexible Wages," *Journal of Political Economy* 88 (June 1980): 526–38.
Wilson, Robert. "The Theory of Syndicates," *Econometrica* 68 (1968): 119–32.
Williamson, Oliver E. "The Vertical Integration of Production: Market Failure Considerations," *The American Economic Review*, Vol 61, No. 2 (May 1971).
– *Corporate Control and Business Behavior*, Englewood Cliffs: Prentice Hall, 1970.

JOSEPH E. STIGLITZ

I was born in Gary, Indiana, at the time, a major steel town on the southern shores of Lake Michigan, on February 9, 1943. Both of my parents were born within six miles of Gary, early in the century, and continued to live in the area until 1997. I sometimes thought that my perignations made up for their stability.

There must have been something in the air of Gary that led one into economics: the first Nobel Prize winner, Paul Samuelson, was also from Gary, as were several other distinguished economists. (Paul allegedly once wrote a letter of recommendation for me which summarized my accomplishments by saying that I was the best economist from Gary, Indiana.) Certainly, the poverty, the discrimination, the episodic unemployment could not but strike an inquiring youngster: why did these exist, and what could we do about them.

I grew up in a family in which political issues were often discussed, and debated intensely. My mother's family were New Deal Democrats – they worshipped FDR; and though my uncle was a highly successful lawyer and real estate entrepreneur, he was staunchly pro-labor. My father, on the other hand, was probably more aptly described as a Jeffersonian democrat; a small businessman (an independent insurance agent) himself, he repeatedly spoke of the virtues of self-employment, of being one's own boss, of self-reliance. He worried about big business, and valued our competition laws. I saw him, conservative by nature, buffeted by the marked changes in American society during the near-century of his life, and adapt to these changes. By the mid-seventies, he had become a strong advocate of civil rights. He had a deep sense of civic and moral responsibility. He was one of the few people I knew who insisted on paying social security contributions for household help – regardless of whether they wanted it or not; he knew they would need it when they were old. (This attitude served me well; in 1993, while many Clinton appointees faced problems in being vetted because of their failure to pay these taxes, I was spared these problems because I had followed his example.)

I went to public schools, and while Gary was, like most American cities, racially segregated, it was at least socially integrated – a cross section of children from families of all walks of life. The Gary public school system was designed to integrate the immigrants who constituted such a large fraction of its inhabitant; here, the melting pot rhetoric that is so important part of America's self-image was taken seriously. All of us had to learn, for instance, two trades (mine were printing and being an electrician). I had the good fortune of having dedicated teachers, who in spite of relatively large classes, provided a high level of individual attention. My teachers helped guide and motivate me; but the responsibility of learning was left with me, an approach to learning which was later reinforced by my experiences at Amherst.

The extra curricular activity in which I was most engaged – debating – helped shape my interests in public policy. Every year, a national debating topic is chosen. (One year, it was the reform of the agricultural support programs, an issue which I had to grapple with almost forty years later; some of my colleagues in the Clinton Administration too had been debaters, but they got taken up by the sport. I was attracted more by the ideas.) In debate, one randomly was assigned to one side or the other. This had at least one virtue – it made one see that there was more than one side to these complex issues.

The intellectually most formative experiences occurred during the three years 1960–1963 I spent at Amherst college, a small, new England college (at the time, a men's college with around 1000 students). I went to Amherst because my brother had gone there before me, and he went there because his guidance counselor thought that we would do better there than at a large university like Harvard Amherst is a liberal arts college, committed to providing students with a broad education. (Today, I serve on its board of trustees.) The notion that every well educated person would have a mastery of at least the basic elements of the humanities, sciences, and social sciences is a far cry from the specialized education that most students today receive, particularly in the research universities. But what distinguished Amherst was not only what was taught, but how it was taught, and the close relationships we had with our teachers. The best teachers still taught in a Socratic style, asking questions, responding to the answers with still another question. And in all of our courses, we were taught that what mattered most was asking the right question – having posed the question well, answering the question was often a relatively easy matter.

I thrived on the atmosphere; while until late in my third year, I majored in physics, and enjoyed immensely the camaraderie of the physics students as we strove to solve the hard problems that were assigned to us. I took a smattering of courses in mathematics, history, English, philosophy, and the standard fare of introductory biology and chemistry. I still remember well the courses, and have frequently drawn upon this learning. For instance, the discussions of the encounters between different civilizations that was a major theme in our Freshman history class helped shape my thinking about globalization more than three decades later; I felt I was in a better position to think about the current episode from an historical perspective, and see it more through the eyes of the *other* side.

But while I loved all of these courses, there was an irresistible attraction of economics. My three teachers at Amherst showed me the range of the subject: Arnold Collery, later to be Dean of Columbia College, was a thoughtful and erudite scholar, from whom I studied both micro-economics and macroeconomics. The style of teaching was exemplified by his choice of texts for the micro course. Rather than a standard textbook, he used Abba Lerner's *Economics of Control*, a book written as a theoretical contribution to our understanding of how markets work, an inquiry into whether planning provided an alternative. James Nelson, who taught me introductory economics, was a vivacious policy economist, who conveyed the sense of excitement that came from trying to shape economic policies. Finally, Ralph Beals was a young graduate of MIT, trained in mathematical techniques that were just then coming into vogue. It was not until late in the spring of my junior (third) year that I decided to major in economics; I thought it provided an opportunity for me to apply my interests and abilities in mathematics to important social problems, and somehow, I thought it would also enable me to combine my interest in history and in writing. I wanted it all, and economics seemed to have it all. When I advised my teachers of my decision, they advised me that I should go on to graduate school. What I would study during my senior year would be largely repeated in my first year of graduate school. They then arranged for me to go to MIT, and to receive the finance I required (I had been on full scholarship at Amherst; the modest last minute fellowship from MIT entailed my living on a dollar a day beyond my rent – the number that today is taken as the threshold for absolute poverty.) The flexibility of MIT, and Amherst, – the deadlines for application were well past, the money for fellowships had largely already been dispensed – is a tribute to America's higher educational system, and one of the reasons that it continues to excel. I left Amherst for MIT without a degree, or without any promise of one. It was before I had done my work on the economics of information, and I think I didn't grasp the information that might be conveyed by having a degree from Amherst. I simply wanted to learn as much as I could as quickly as I could – not from any sense of "getting ahead" but simply from an overwhelming sense that there was so much to learn, and one needed to get on with it. (Later, Amherst did give me a degree, and still later, in 1974, they gave me an honorary doctorate.) One of my teachers, and one of the world's greatest economists, Hirofumi Uzawa, when asked where he got his advanced degree, would say they he had no degree to speak of; in academic circles, there is a certain pride in simply having pursued one's studies on one's own, outside the confines of a regular program. If Amherst hadn't given me a degree, I could have given a similar response.

My love of politics first manifested itself in my days at Amherst. I served on the Student Council both in my freshman and sophomore years (there were three representatives from each class), and in junior year, got elected president of the student council. My conviction that if one attains positions of "power" one should view them as opportunities for social change also manifested itself. I began a campaign to abolish fraternities (to which 90% of the students belonged), because they were socially divisive, and contrary to the spirit of a liberal arts school and community. It was a campaign that was not welcomed by many of my classmates, and it took years to come to fruition, but it did, and I believe that Amherst is the better for it. This was only one of the many issues that I raised in my "activist" presidency. I, like many members of my generation, was concerned with segregation and the repeated violation of civil rights. We were impatient with those (like President Kennedy) who took a cautious approach. How could we continue to countenance these injustices that had gone on so long. (The fact that so many people in the *establishment* seemed to do so – as they had accepted colonialism, slavery, and other forms of oppression – left a life-long mark. It reinforced a distrust of authority which I had had from childhood.) I marched on Washington – the march where Martin Luther King gave his "I have a dream" speech remains an indelible memory. I organized an exchange program with a small, African-American, southern school; I believed it was important for us to understand, as much as we could, what they were confronting. These were the years where many civil rights activists from the North were killed; but in our enthusiasm for doing what was right, these risks never crossed our minds.

Not surprisingly, there was considerable opposition to some of my initiatives, so much so that a recall referendum was initiated. It was also my first encounter with the power of the press and personal rivalries; the editor of the student paper took on the cause of removing me. But my friends and allies beat back the initiative, and I continued to use the platform of the presidency of the student council to promote social change.

Amherst was pivotal in my broad intellectual development; MIT in my development as a professional economist. I spent but two years at MIT as a student (I did my generals in a year and a half, and then began writing my thesis.) It was the hey-day of MIT first-rate professors (I had at least four Nobel Prize winners as professor: Samuelson (Nobel Laureate in 1970), Solow (Nobel Laureate in 1987), Modigliani (Nobel Laureate in 1985), and Arrow (Nobel Laureate in 1972)) teaching first-rate students. My first paper presented at an academic meeting, to the econometric society, was jointly coauthored with George Akerlof, with whom I shared this year's prize. I had many other first rate classmates that were to make truly important contributions to economics.

The particular style of MIT economics suited me well – simple and concrete models, directed at answering important and relevant questions. I sometimes wonder what would have happened had I gone to one of the universities in which other styles of economics were taught, either the abstract general equilibrium models, for which Berkeley was then noted, or the simpler partial equilibrium models for which Chicago was famous. The politics of MIT also suited me well. My teachers were mostly establishment liberals, but there were a few that were more questioning. I wonder too how I would have fared had I gone to one of the schools, like Chicago, where there is a more conservative bent. Would I have changed? Or would I have just been unhappy?

But, as I comment in my Prize lecture, there was an incongruity between many of the models that we were taught and the policy positions that our teachers (and we) believed in. The models seemed more consonant with free market prescriptions, though they were presented more as benchmarks rather than full characterizations.

The students and faculty at MIT were highly interactive. There was a group of friends (mostly from the year ahead of me, including George), which included a few young economists from Harvard, with whom I spent much of my time. We lived economics and politics. We debated about what was wrong with the models that we were being taught. We thought about how we could or would go about changing the models, and occasionally about how we could or would go about changing the world. One of our group was from India (Mrinal Datta-Chaudhuri) and we learned from him a host of stories concerning the colonial experience.

After my first year as a graduate student, I was offered a wonderful opportunity, editing Paul Samuelson's collected papers. I often took Paul as a role model, the expansiveness of his learning, the breadth of his work, its originality and penetration. He wrote forcefully and beautifully. For many years after leaving MIT, I was best known as Samuelson's editor, to which I did not appreciate, since I wanted to be known for my own work.

The summer after my second year as a graduate student was one of the most exciting. Hirofumi Uzawa had moved from Stanford to Chicago, and had received an NSF grant to bring around a dozen graduate students form around the country to work together on theory. Eytan Sheshinki and his wife Ruthie, George Akerlof, Mrinal Datta-Chaudhuri, Georgio LaMalfa (later to be head of the Republican party of Italy and a minister in several of that country's governments) and his wife, Eva drove off to Chicago. We stopped on the way at my home in Gary for a night, where my parents were delighted to have a chance to meet my friends. At Chicago, we were joined by some of Hiro's Chicago students and by Frank Levy from Yale (who now teaches at MIT), among others. Growth theory was then all the rage, and we did growth theory, day in and day out. Many of us worked on technical change, on work which would be rediscovered, two decades later and popularized under the name of endogenous growth theory. (The fact that the work that was done in this period received so little attention in the subsequent revival of interest in growth theory two decades later has been a subject of some interest to me, as part of what may be thought of as the sociology of knowledge. Economists tend to move in particular circles, defined by their "school" and "subject." Endogenous growth theory in the 80s grew out of the Chicago school, while the earlier work on growth theory was part of the MIT school – treating Uzawa, though a professor at Chicago, as an honorary member of the MIT fraternity. I moved both across schools and subjects. This allowed me to learn from each, and the cross fertilization was highly productive. But it did pose problems. Not being a dues paying member of any particular school/sub discipline sometimes meant it was more difficult to get one's ideas accepted, or even widely discussed. This was particularly the case in macro-economics, where in the 70s and 80s, the reining paradigms were either rational expectations/representative agent models or fixed price new Keynesian models. The models that Greenwald and I formulated, focusing on imperfect capital markets, risk averse, credit constrained firms, in which concerns about bankruptcy often play an important role, only became widely accepted after similar ideas were picked up by the card carrying members of the macro-fraternity.)

While the group of us who went to Chicago to study under Uzawa was supposedly chosen for our prowess as students, we shared a broad weltanschauung. As the month of intensive work ended, leaving a lifelong impression on all of us, most of us went up to George's family place on Lake Squam. I was working as Bob Solow's research assistant, and so had to commute from Cambridge.

After two years at MIT (supported in the second year by the National Science Foundation), I received a Fulbright fellowship to Cambridge for 1965–1966. At the time, there were three High Churches in the economics profession: Chicago on the right and Cambridge, U.K. on the left, with MIT being in the center. Cambridge was still basking in the reflected glory of Keynes, who had revolutionized economics some thirty years earlier. Lord Kahn, of the Kahn multiplier (which explained how a dollar of government expenditure had a multiple effect in increasing GDP), Joan Robinson, Nicky Kaldor, James Meade, David Champernowne, Piero Sraffa, these were among the gods that populated the colleges of Cambridge. I wanted to see as many views as I could, and I worried about coming too much under the influence of Samuelson and Solow. Joan Robinson was assigned as my tutor. She had originally wanted me to redo my undergraduate degree – she thought it would take some time to undo the damage of my MIT education, but eventually she was prevailed upon instead to take on the responsibility of my reeducation. We had a tumultuous relationship. Evidently, she wasn't used to the kind of questioning stance of a brash American student, even a soft-spoken one from the mid-west, and after one term, I switched to Frank Hahn. He was flamboyant, and always intellectually provocative. Cambridge was in ferment. The quality of the students and the young lecturers matched that of the gray eminces: Jim Mirrlees (later to get the Nobel prize), Partha Dasgupta, Tony Atkinson; Geoff Heal, David Newbery and a host of others. There was a sense of excitement that was associated not just with the generation of new ideas, but with the belief that those ideas were important, and not just for economics, but for society more broadly. As Frank Hahn demonstrated the dynamic instability of the economy (a problem posed by the absence of futures markets going out infinitely far into the future; in technical terms, the absence of a transversality condition), he would excitedly exclaim that he had put another nail in the coffin of capitalism.

One evening I gave a seminar on a paper I was then completing, on the distribution of income among individuals (using the kinds of tools that had been used to describe the dynamics of growth to describe the dynamics of inequality). The discussion had been followed by a lively debate. The next morning, I received a twenty-page comment from James Meade (who received the Nobel Prize in 1977), suggesting elaborations and alternative interpretations. There was a sense of a community of scholars trying to understand some very important and complex problems.

My research in this period centered around growth, technical change, and income distribution, both how growth affected the distribution of income and how the distribution of income affected growth. The most important paper to emerge from my thesis, "The Distribution of Income and Wealth Among Individuals,"[1] received considerable attention at the time, but unfortunately, the topic has not been one which has received much attention from the economic profession, so that it has not generated as much follow-on research as I had hoped.

But the subject of the causes and consequences of inequality has remained one of my abiding concerns, one which I pursued as I began to delve into the economics of information.[2]

My early research project in this area illustrated one feature of my research style which, while it may have contributed to the overall success of some of my research program, was a source of unending frustration. Once I undertook the analysis of a problem, I often looked at it from a variety of perspectives. I approached the problem as a series of thought experiments – unlike many other sciences, we typically cannot do actual experiments. I would construct models changing one assumption or the other. Each would provide some insight into what drove the results. The whole was more than the sum of the parts; while each of the models was, by itself, of some interest, it was the collection of models, and how the results depended on the particular assumptions employed, which provided the greatest insight. My original work thus grew into a monograph of some hundred pages. Unfortunately, the preferred form of expression in the profession was narrowly defined articles, making a single point. I thus had to extract from the longer monograph a series of papers, a process which not only took a long time, but diminished (in my judgment) the insights provided. (This problem was even greater in the next two research projects, one exploring the behavior of the firm under uncertainty, and in particular, the consequences of risk with an incomplete set of risk markets; most (but not all) of that "paper" – an eight hour lecture I delivered in 1970 at Hakone, Japan, in another one of Hirofumi Uzawa's workshop – was published as a series of articles over the next decade.[3] The exploration of "Alternative theories of wage determination and unemployment in less developing countries," completed while I was at the Institute of Development Studies at the University of Nairobi in the summer of 1969, was similarly published in a series of articles – the more recent of which was not published until 1982).[4]

Another project that I began in Cambridge concerned the interaction between the distribution of income and short run macro economic behavior. At the time, most macro economic models simply assumed that wages and prices were fixed. But of course during the great depression wages and prices had fallen considerably. The problem was not that they were absolutely fixed, but with the dynamics of adjustment. With Robert Solow (Solow and Stiglitz, 1968), I explored these dynamics, to explain the persistence of unemploy-

[1] Stiglitz (1969a)

[2] See e.g. Stiglitz (1973a, 1975, 1976), Rothschild and Stiglitz (1973, 1982) and Braverman and Stiglitz (1989).

[3] Including Stiglitz (1972a, 1972b, 1974a, 1989a)

[4] See Stiglitz (1974b, 1982a). See also Stiglitz (1974c, 1992).

ment. With George Akerlof (see Akerlof and Stiglitz, 1969), I showed how such dynamics can give rise to cyclical behavior. Later work would attempt to provide stronger micro foundations for these adjustment dynamics.

I returned from Cambridge to take up a one-year appointment as an assistant professor at MIT, from which I went to Yale. My teaching at Yale seemingly warranted an indefinite deferment from the Vietnam War draft. During this period, I continued my work on economic dynamics, and began my research on the economics of uncertainty, which in turn, quickly led to the work on the economics of information.

The major concern in my research on dynamics was the stability of the market economy. The standard models assumed that there were future markets extending infinitely far into the future. Following work of Frank Hahn (1966), Karl Shell and I showed that a competitive economy with futures markets extending an arbitrarily large finite number of periods into the future would, in general, exhibit dynamic instabilities; that is, it would take off onto a path that *appeared* to be efficient and stable, with the inefficiency and instability only manifesting itself some distance into the future (Shell and Stiglitz, 1967). This theme was explored in a variety of different contexts. The subject was central to the on-going debate concerning the efficiency of the capitalist economy. If stability and efficiency required that there existed markets that extended infinitely far into the future – and these markets clearly did not exist – what assurance do we have of the stability and efficiency of the capitalist system? In one important variant on this theme, I assumed that there were rational expectations. Simplistic representative agent models living infinitely long had been constructed, and, not surprisingly, in these models, the problems of instability and inefficiency did not arise. I assumed, on the contrary, that individuals were finitely lived; there were overlapping generations. In that case, there were an infinite number of paths consistent with rational expectations extending infinitely far into the future. (Stiglitz, 1973b.)

This concern with *multiplicity* of equilibrium (both in the short run and the long) was to appear over and over again in my subsequent work, where under a wide variety of circumstances, the economy could be trapped in a "bad" equilibrium. In some cases, some individuals are better off in one equilibrium, some worse off, but in other cases, one equilibrium could Pareto dominate others.[5]

Much of my work in this period was concerned with exploring the *logic* of economic models, but also with attempting to reconcile the models with every day observation. Thus, in much of my earlier work I began by asking what would happen to the standard results if there were not the complete set of risk markets which Arrow and Debreu (Nobel Laureate in 1983) had postulated in their analysis of competitive equilibrium. This was a question

[5] For a more complete analysis of these multiple equilibria models, see Hoff and Stiglitz (2001). The first example of such multiplicity out of the growth context was my model on equilibrium in stock markets (Stiglitz, 1972a), where the riskiness of the projects chosen by one firm depends on those chosen by other firms. Other examples of multiple equilibria can be found in Stiglitz (1972b, 1974c, 1977, 1995).

which one could approach largely (though not entirely) deductively. (Stiglitz, 1972a, 1982b.) But my research in this area quickly posed problems for which there was no obvious answer: what should (or do) firms maximize? This early work exposed how sensitive not only were the *results* of the standard model to the (clearly unrealistic) assumptions posited, but even the reasonableness of the *assumed* behavior.[6] As my work progressed, the discrepancies between the kind of behavior *implied* by the standard model and actual behavior also became increasingly clear. In the standard model, the only risk that firms should worry about was the correlation of the outcomes (profits) with the "market"; in practice, businesses seem to pay less attention to that than they do to "own" risk, the chance the project will succeed or fail. In the standard model, everyone agrees about what the firm should do; in practice, there are often heated disagreements. It seemed to me that any persuasive theory of the firm had to be consistent with these, and other, aspects of widely observed firm behavior. (Stiglitz, 1982c, 1989b.)

Economists spend enormous energy providing refined testing to their models. Economists often seem to forget that some of the most important theories in physics are either verified or refuted by a single observation, or a limited number of observations (e.g. Einstein's theory of relativity, or the theory of black holes). Thus, models which suggested that there was no such thing as unemployment, or that it was at most short lived, to my mind were suspect. Economists often like startling theorems, results which seem to run counter to conventional wisdom. Perhaps the most important result in the economics of uncertainty in the 1950s was that of Modigliani and Miller (Nobel Laureate in 1990), who argued that corporate financial structure – whether firms finance themselves with debt or equity – made no difference (other than as a result of taxes). What was interesting about the theory was that it was based on assumptions of rational behavior, and yet if it were true, there was ample evidence of market irrationality – the thousands of people on Wall Street and other financial centers who seemed to be worrying about corporate finance – and for reasons that had noting to do with taxation. I began my analysis of corporate finance by demonstrating that the result was far more general than they had shown. (Stiglitz, 1969b.) But there were two assumptions that they had ignored, and these turned out to be crucial: they had assumed no bankruptcy and perfect (or at least symmetric) information. Over the succeeding years, I was to explore the consequences of these (related) assumptions, not only for the theories of corporate finance, but also for corporate governance (including takeovers) and macro-economics. As I note in my Prize lecture, the failure of the IMF to take on board fully the consequences of these assumptions played an important role in their policy failures almost three decades later.

My work on the economics of uncertainty led naturally to the work on information asymmetries, and more generally, imperfect information. In the work on the economics of uncertainty, I explored the consequences, *given be-*

[6] Sanford Grossman and I pursued these ideas further in Grossman and Stiglitz (1977, 1980).

liefs about probability distributions, say, of prices and outputs, of economic behavior. The standard theory not only had assumed that there was a complete set of markets for these risks, but that beliefs about these probability distributions were exogenous, unaffected by any actions. But individuals and firms spend an enormous amount of resources acquiring information, which affects their beliefs; and actions of others too affect their beliefs.

As I approach the problems that are today referred to as the economics of information, I was greatly helped by the breadth of my education at Amherst and MIT. The problem of how people form their *beliefs* is, of course, the central question of statistics: making inferences on the basis of limited data. The first course for which I served as a teaching assistant was statistics (with Harold Freeman), and it was concerned with using probability theory to make statistical inferences (rather than "classical" statistics). I am sure that I was, at least subconsciously, affected too by the work going on in Cambridge in statistical decision theory, by people, by Raiffa, and while I never took a course from him, he was active in the Harvard-MIT theory seminar, and was a presence at the dinners we often had afterwards.

Another set of central insights came from the work that I had been doing in public finance (as it was called at that time; with my 1984 textbook, I helped shift the sub discipline to focus more broadly on the *economics of the public sector.*) As I noted in my Nobel lecture, an early insight in my work on the economics of information concerned the problem of appropriability – the difficulty that those who pay for information have in getting returns. This is, of course, the central concern of *public goods,* one of the main subjects within the economics of the public sector. I recognized that information was, in many respects, like a public good, and it was this insight that made it clear to me that it was unlikely that the private market would provide efficient resource allocations whenever information was endogenous. (See, e.g. Stiglitz, 1987a.) Much of the subsequent work was trying to define more precisely the nature of the market failures.

As I explain in my Nobel lecture, the time I spent in Kenya was pivotal in the development of my ideas on the economics of information. I have often wondered why. I think in part the reason is that seeing an economy that is, in many ways, quite different from the one grows up in, helps crystallize issues: one takes too much for granted, without asking why things are the way they are. As I studied development, I was forced to think everything through from first principles. Had I grown up in a world in which everyone was a sharecropper, I probably would have accepted this as the way things are. As it was, sharecropping seemed like a peculiar institution, for it seemed to attenuate greatly the incentives workers had to work (since they typically had to give one out of two dollars that they earned to the landlord).

Similarly, growing up in Gary Indiana gave me, I think, a distinct advantage over many of my classmates who had grown up in affluent suburbs. They could read articles that argued that in competitive equilibrium, there could not be discrimination, so long as there are some non-discriminatory individuals or firms, since it would pay any such firm to hire the lower wage discriminated against individuals, and take them seriously. I *knew* that discrimination existed, even though there were many individuals who were not prejudicial. To me, the *theorem* simply proved that one or more of the assumptions that went into the theory was wrong; my task, as a theorist, was to figure out which assumptions were the critical ones.

A topic of abiding concern since I was in high school was *economic organization*. I grew up in the midst of the cold war. At the time, Communism *seemed* to be delivering faster economic growth, but at the expense of liberty. Much of the world seemed to be suffering under the yoke of colonialism, which neither delivered economic growth or democracy, and one which seemed to inconsistent with the principles in which I had been taught, and come to believe. The market economy seemed to be plagued by repeated periods of unemployment, and to leave large fractions of their populations in poverty. Yugoslavia's system of self-managed firms intrigued me. Economics seemed to provide the tools with which one could analyze these alternative economic systems. A central question was on how, and how well, alternative systems addressed the problems of gathering, analyzing, and disseminating information, and making decisions based on imperfect information. Understanding the limitations of the market – the so-called market failures – became one of the central foci of my research.

I recognized that the standard model was deficient not only in its assumptions about information, but also in ignoring technical change. The latter I thought particularly curious, given the importance that technical change clearly played in our economy. I joined the growing band of those who paid homage to Joseph Schumpeter because of his emphasis on technical change, a subject which was not even broached in the standard first year graduate economics course, let alone in undergraduate principles courses. (I tried to remedy the latter deficiency by introducing a chapter on the subject in my Principles book.) But while I thought that Schumpeter had asked the right question, I was not convinced he gave the right answer. The close links between the work that I had been doing on information and technical change allowed me to begin to formalize models of Schumpeterian competition, and I quickly realized that several of the "accepted" results of Schumpeterian competition were not valid, e.g. that there would necessarily be a succession of short lived monopolies. (See, e.g. Dasgupta and Stiglitz, 1980a, 1980b, 1981, 1988.) I showed that a monopoly, once established, could be persistent, that Schumpeterian competition was not, in general, "efficient," and that in particular the incumbent could/would take actions which deterred entry, that potential competition would not in general suffice to ensure a rapid (efficient) pace of innovation. – These ideas are, of course, of particular relevance in the "new economy," which centers around innovation.

There was a rather different strand of literature (often associated with Hayek) which praised the virtues of the market economy, not on the basis of the standard competitive (Arrow Debreu model), or on the basis of Schumpeterian competition, but rather on "evolutionary" grounds. In the early 70s, I had become fascinated with this alternative approach, and begun to subject it to scrutiny. At the time, there was little formal work on evolutionary modeling, and even later, most of the modeling focused around *describing* (often in simulation exercises) evolutionary processes. I was interested in *evaluating* evolutionary processes. What could one say about whether free markets, by themselves, led to "efficient" or "desirable" evolution? Were there interventions in the market which might "shape" evolution in ways which would lead to better outcomes? Hayek and his disciples had argued for free markets, but never really even addressed these questions. This remains a question that has still not been well investigated, but preliminary results (cited in my Prize lecture) suggest strongly the limitations of unfettered free market evolution. (Part, but only part, of the problem lies with imperfections of capital markets.)

Later, with the collapse of the Soviet system, and the recognition of the problems of socialism more broadly, I rethought the lessons that might be gleaned from the failed experiment. In *Whither Socialism?* (See Stiglitz, 1994) I came to the conclusion that the failure of the socialist economies reinforced my belief in the inadequacy of the competitive equilibrium model. If that model had been correct, market socialism probably could have succeeded. The standard competitive market equilibrium model had failed to recognize the complexity of the information problem facing the economy – just as the socialists had. Their view of decentralization was similarly oversimplified – a point which I had earlier emphasized in my work with Raj Sah, where we had compared hierarchical and polyarchical decision making structures[7]. Here, our concern was not with asymmetries of information or incentives, but with how different economic organizational structures in effect *aggregated* the disparate and limited information of different individuals.

As the former socialist economies decided to make the transition to a market economy, a host of fascinating problems was posed on how best to make that transition. China provided the first venue for looking at these questions, in a series of meetings in 1980 and 1981, and Russia and the other countries of the former Soviet Union and Eastern Europe provide a second. The debates were heated. Much was at stake. And underlying the debate were very different understandings of the fundamentals of a market economy – what was necessary to make it function. My views on the inadequacy of the standard model played a central role in my thinking. I emphasized the importance of competition, corporate governance, finance, and more broadly the institutional (including legal) infrastructure. I did not place much stress on privatization. I was part of a wider school, sometimes referred to as "gradualists," as opposed to the shock therapists that focused on rapid transitions, with quick privatization. The strategy for transition that I advocated was markedly different from that pushed by the IMF and the shock therapists. The failures of so many countries to make a successful transition back to a market economy has provided new insights into what makes market economies function, one which I had occasion to explore during my years as the Chief Economist of

[7] See e.g. Sah and Stiglitz (1985a, 1986).

the World Bank. There is now a wide consensus on the importance of the institutional infrastructure, and on the dangers of rapid privatization. (See the references cited in my Prize lecture.)

I referred earlier to my work in the economics of the public sector.[8] I was convinced that there was an important role for government to play. Given that, it was natural for me to turn to the question of how it could play that

[8] My work in the economics of the public sector has gone through four stages. It began with extensive collaborations with Tony Atkinson and Partha Dasgupta. Diamond and Mirrlees had helped revive interest in Ramsey's work in optimal taxation. They had extended Ramsey's analysis to a general equilibrium context, and *seemed* to incorporate distributional concerns. This work also seemed one of the few positive results in the theory of the second best: even though government could not impose lump sum taxes, one could say something meaningful about what the government should do. But the conclusions were unpersuasive. They suggested, for instance, that the government should not impose taxes on corporations and should not impose tariffs, and Ramsey's earlier analysis suggested that high tax rates ought to be imposed on commodities, like food, with low demand elasticities. Such taxes were regressive, and I could not believe that they were truly "optimal." Atkinson and I (1972) formally incorporated distributional concerns in the design of tax policy, with results that were more in accord with our intuition. Similarly, Dasgupta and I took into account limitations on the ability of the government to impose taxes, and within this broader, and we would argue more realistic framework, tariffs and corporate income taxes did make sense. (Dasgupta and Stiglitz, 1971, 1972, 1974). Later, I began to think of the problem of taxation as an information problem – limited information imposed restrictions on the set of taxes that could be imposed; and asked what were the set of *pareto efficient* tax structures, that is, given the limitations on information, what were the set of tax structures such that no one could be made better off without making anyone worse off. (Stiglitz, 1998b). Within this framework, it became clear that Ramsey's analysis of optimal commodity taxes made little sense; only if the government could not impose income taxes as well as commodity taxes (as was the case in some developing countries) was it of much relevance. (Atkinson and Stiglitz, 1976).

A second set of issues to which I turned was project evaluation, and in particular the determination of shadow wages and discount rates. I argued that one could not calculate shadow wages without a model of the labor market, one which including a theory of wage determination and migration. Once that was done, one obtained results that were markedly different from the "standard" wisdom; for instance, the shadow wage on labor in some central cases was the market wage, *even though there was a high level of unemployment.* (Stiglitz, 1982d and Sah and Stiglitz, 1985b). On the other hand, I argued against the use of market interest rates for project evaluation. (Stiglitz 1982e, Arrow *et al.*, 1996). When I went to the Council of Economic Advisers, many of these views on cost benefit analysis became incorporated in the guidelines issues by the Office of Management- and -Budget for project and regulatory evaluations.

A third quite distinct research project developed the theory of local public goods. Tiebout (1956) had put forward the conjecture that competition among local communities was like competition in markets, and would yield efficient outcomes. My doubts about market competition naturally led me to have doubts about competition in this arena, perspectives that were confirmed as our formalized the theory of local public goods. (Stiglitz, 1977). This project, in turn, led to a joint research project with Richard Arnott on the relationship between expenditures on public goods and land rents: was it possible to finance the optimal supply of public goods by a tax on land only (what I referred to as the Henry George theorem).

There was a quite different strand of work motivated in part by a request from the U.S. Treasury concerning capital gains taxation. I had done earlier work on the impact of capital gains taxation in the presence of uncertainty, which changed many of the long standing presumptions. (Stiglitz, 1969c). But more complicated issues were raised by the dynamics, and by the obvious use of capital gains as part of tax avoidance strategies. I showed that, were markets perfect, one could take advantage of the special treatment of capital gains taxes to avoid all taxation. (See Stiglitz, 1983a.) Though a variety of provisions of the tax code have been introduced to try to circumscribe such tax avoidance behavior, they are imperfect. At a theoretical level, this led me to consider the general principles of tax avoidance (Stiglitz, 1985b), and had a great deal of influence on my thinking about the problems of tax reform, reflected both in my writing and the advice I gave both while at the Council of Economic Advisers and the World Bank. (See Stiglitz, 1997b, 1998a).

role most effectively. (See, e.g. Stiglitz, 1991, 1997a.) One of the main questions with which I was concerned was how to redistribute income in a way as to minimize the loss in efficiency that are inevitably associated with tax distortions. Economics of information had provided a framework within which this question could, for the first time, be addressed in a meaningful way, as I explain in my Prize lecture.

Still another important strand of my research, only tangentially related to my work on the economics of information, concerned industrial organization. In one of my most cited papers, that with Avinash Dixit[9], we constructed a model in which there are so many firms that each can ignore its impact on others' economic actions, but still, firms face downward sloping demand curves – there is monopolistic competition. This seemed to describe many of the markets in the economy far better than either the models of pure competition, pure monopoly, or oligopoly. (Markets in which information are imperfect are also likely to be characterized by monopolist competition). Little progress on the theory of monopolistic competition had been made in the more than forty years since Edwin Chamberlain first broached the idea. In particular, he had only formulated a partial equilibrium model. We were interested in constructing a general equilibrium model, within which one could assess how well the market functioned, in particular in making the tradeoffs between economies of scale and product diversity. We showed that there was a single borderline case – of immense simplicity – in which the market made that trade-off perfectly; but more generally, it did not.[10]

While my work on industrial organization and imperfect information undermined the confidence in the ability of unfettered markets to allocate resources efficiently, there was another strand of research in the economics profession which was trying to argue the contrary. In particular, there were those who argued that even with natural monopoly markets could be efficient; competition for the market could replace competition in the market; all that one required was potential competition. On the face of it, this idea seemed suspect. If it were true, there would be no monopoly rents. And indeed, my suspicions turned out to be true: I showed that even if there were arbitrarily small sunk costs (which there always are) then potential competition would not suffice to limit the abuses of monopoly.[11]

The most important *systemic* failure associated with the market economy is the periodic episodes of underutilization of resources. Trying to understand why the labor market does not clear – why there is persistent unemployment – has been another abiding concern, one which I have tried to approach from a variety of angles. The work with Solow and with Akerlof cited above focused on the consequences of finite speeds of adjustment. Even if wages fall, if prices fall too, real wages may not adjust very quickly. Subsequent work with Greenwald tried to explain in a more coherent way these speeds of adjust-

[9] See Dixit and Stiglitz (1977).
[10] Subsequent work explored alternative versions of monopolistic competition. See Hoff and Stiglitz (1997), Salop and Stiglitz (1977) and Stiglitz (1979a,b, 1986, 1989a).
[11] Stiglitz, (1987b).

ment.[12] The efficiency wage theories (described in greater detail in my Prize lecture) explain why it may pay firms to pay a wage higher than the market clearing wage: the increase in productivity more than offsets the increase in wages. The theory of equity rationing[13] helped explain why more "flexible" contractual arrangements were not adopted; such arrangements (such as those where wages depend on firm profitability) in effect make the worker have an implied equity stake in the firm, and, given asymmetries of information, the value which workers are willing to assign to such contractual provisions is less than that which is acceptable to the firm.

The 1970s and 1980s represented decades during which the rational expectations/representative agent model was in ascendancy. This model suggested not only that, with rational expectations, government policy was ineffective, but that unemployment was not a serious problem. Neither of these conclusions made much sense to me; and with my former student, Peter Neary, we sought to show that the results depended not on the rational expectations assumption, but on the assumptions concerning wage and price flexibility. We constructed a fixed wage/price model with rational expectations, and showed contrary to the suggestion of the rational expectations school, not only could unemployment be persistent, but that government policy was even more effective with rational expectations that without it (i.e. multipliers associated with government expenditures were larger). The reason was simple: an increase in government expenditures today had some spill overs to future periods. Today's increased savings translated into tomorrow's increased income, and, with rational expectations, that increased income translated into higher consumption today. We also showed that there were *multiple rational expectations equilibria*: if everyone was pessimistic, then income would indeed be low today *and* tomorrow; but if everyone was optimistic, then both could be high.

Our work also emphasized that it was not just wage and price rigidities which could give rise to macro-economic problems. (This work could be thought of as a revival and formalization of Fisher's earlier work on debt deflation[14].) Incomplete contracts meant that unanticipated changes in wages and prices had large distributional effects, with correspondingly large consequences. While when we first put forward these ideas almost twenty years ago, they met with considerable resistance, they are now coming to be more widely accepted.

While I spent most of my time teaching and doing research, I learned a great deal from the limited amount of consulting I did, and I thought it important to engage in issues of public policy. My first major consulting project was a direct outgrowth of work on imperfect information; it was concerned with the information externalities that arose in the process of oil exploration, externalities which played an important role in a heated dispute between the

[12] Greenwald and Stiglitz (1989, 1995).
[13] Greenwald, Stiglitz, and Weiss (1984)
[14] See Fisher (1933).

federal government and the states (which was eventually settled out of court for $12 billion). A variety of other consultations, typically associated either with antitrust violations or issues of corporate governance, gave me insights both into how real markets work as well as the behavior of firms.

In the 1980s, I was involved in two major public interest litigations, one concerning the treatment of Native Americans, the other with the exploitation of our natural resources. The first, involving the Seneca Indians in upstate New York, gave me further insights into the nature of America's past – and ongoing – exploitation of Native Americans. An unfair lease that had been imposed on the tribe was about to expire, and it insisted that it would renew only on more equitable terms. I helped calculate the magnitude of the amount by which the previous lease had "cheated" them – magnitudes in excess of a billion dollars in present terms – and though the tribe was never compensated for these past injuries, the information I provided did, I think, contribute to a settlement which was far fairer than would otherwise have been the case.

The second suit was one against the federal government. In the 1980s, President Reagan tried to turn over as much of the offshore oil tracts to private companies as fast as he could – the fire sale was a give-away to the oil companies, depriving the American taxpayers of billions of dollars. Working with Jeffrey Leitzinger and a conservation minded NGO, -NRDC, we tried to estimate this cost, and, unsuccessfully, to bloc the fire sales.

I moved to Washington in March 1992 to join the Clinton Administration, first as a member, and then as Chairman of the Council of Economic Advisers, in which capacity I also served as a member of the cabinet. The Council helps formulate economic policies for the Administration, and serves as a consultant for all the agencies in the government. Our span of responsibilities included not only macro-economics, but policies in almost every sphere, from trade to anti-trust, from environment to agriculture, from energy to transportation, from welfare to health, from social security to taxation, from affirmative action, to tort reform. It was a wonderful experience – I had to draw upon all of my previous research, all my connections, and go beyond. I became deeply involved in environmental issues, which included serving on the International Panel for Climate Control, and helping draft a new law (including a new legal framework) for toxic wastes (which unfortunately never got passed). I was pleased to see how ideas that I had helped formulate only a few years earlier, like adverse selection and moral hazard, were now part of the every day language of the policy debate in health care.[15]

Perhaps our most important contribution in this period was helping define a new economic philosophy, a "third way," which recognized the important, but limited, role of government, that unfettered markets often did not work well, but that government was not always able to correct the limitations of

[15] See Stiglitz (1997b, 1998a) for brief descriptions of some of my views concerning these experiences.

markets. The research that I had been conducting over the preceding twenty five years provided the intellectual foundations for this "third way."

Being on the Council was particularly exciting for me as a student of the economics of the public sector. I was a fly on the wall – but at the same time – I could work to put into place some of the ideas that I had been devcloping.

I believe that institutions like the Council play an important role in our democracies. Work on information asymmetries emphasized the importance of incentives and the discrepancy between the incentives of government officials, and in particular professional politicians, and those who they are supposed to serve. As a citizen-bureaucrat, the members of the council, who are typically drawn from academia and return to academia, have markedly different incentives than those of a professional politician. Typically, though not always, the fact that our professional reputations as economists were at stake circumscribed what was said – we could not just be political hacks – and encouraged us to work for the adoption of economic policies that were consistent with economic principles.

When the President was re-elected, he asked me to continue to serve as Chairman of the Council of Economic Advisers for another term. But I had already been approached by the World Bank, to be its senior vice president for development policy and its chief economist. America's economic policy had been successfully redefined, and the economy was performing well. There were many problems yet to be addressed, such as pointing social security on a sound financial footing, but I was not optimistic about making progress on most of them in the coming years, given the Republican control of Congress. The challenges and the opportunities in the developing world seemed far greater. I had always wanted to return to the problems of development, and though I had had many visits to developing countries in the twenty five years since leaving Kenya, I had not really been immersed in their problems.

I had no strong agenda, other than doing what I could to promote the development of these countries, in ways which did as much as possible to eliminate poverty. But as I quickly became engrossed in the problems of development, a variety of issues surfaced, the most important of which was the intellectual framework with which development was to be pursued. In a recent article in *Atlantic Monthly*[16] I described a trip to Ethiopia, where I saw the IMF advocate policies of financial market liberalization which made no sense, in which it argued that the countries budget was out of balance – when in my estimate that was clearly not the case – and in which it had suspended its program, in spite of that country's first rate macro-economic performance. More broadly, the IMF was advocating a set of policies which is generally referred to alternative as the Washington consensus, the neo-liberal doctrines, or market fundamentalism, based on an incorrect understanding of economic theory and (what I viewed) as an inadequate interpretation of the historical data. The IMF was using models that failed to incorporate the advances in eco-

[16] See Stiglitz (2001a).

nomic theory of the past twenty five years, including the work on imperfect information and incomplete markets to which I had contributed. Most importantly, they had departed from the mission for which they had been founded, under the intellectual guidance of Keynes – they actually promoted contractionary fiscal policies for countries facing an economic downturn – and they advocated polices like capital market liberalization, for which there was little evidence that growth was promoted, while there was ample evidence that such policies generated instability.

As an academic I was scandalized; as a former adviser to the President who had helped design a "third way" for the United States – a view of the role of government that was markedly different from that envisioned by the Washington consensus – I was particularly disturbed by the role of the US government (or more accurately, the US Treasury) in pushing these views.

If the IMF had only *pushed* its views – misrepresenting them as the lessons of economic orthodoxy, describing them as if they were Pareto dominant (that is, they were policies which would make everyone better off, so that there were no trade-offs), rather than the policies which reflected the perspectives and interests of particular groups within society – that would have been bad enough. But all too often they used their economic power effectively to *force* countries to adopt these policies, undermining democratic processes. As some-one who had grown up in mid-America, strongly inculcated with democratic values, I found this hard to accept; and even more so because the IMF's own governance was so dissonant with democratic principles (a single country has an effective veto; countries like China were long underrepresented, the "governors" of the IMF, those responsible for its decisions, finance ministers and the heads of the central banks, are hardly representative, and the heads of the central banks themselves are typically not directly democratically accountable).

With the East Asia crisis, my disagreements with the Fund came to a head. The Fund's policies seemed neither to accord with an understanding of the crisis countries (several of which I had studied closely during my East Asia Miracle project) and what I viewed as basic economics, especially as it had come to incorporate concerns about asymmetries of information and bankruptcy, corporate governance and finance, with which I had long been concerned. I argued against their prescriptions, and those within the World Bank broadly agreed. But I made little headway with the Fund. There seemed to be no way out other than to bring the issues out into the public – and since as a democratic, I believed that there should be public discussion of such issues, I had few misgivings. I believe the public pressure that was generated did work; the counterproductive policies of excessive monetary and fiscal stringency were eased.

A third set of controversies was opened up as the World Bank began its ten year review of the transition of the former Communist countries to the market. The failures of the countries that had followed the IMF shock therapy policies – both in terms of the declines in GDP and increases in poverty – were even worse than the worst that most of its critics had envisioned at the onset of the transition. There were clear links between the dismal performances and the particular policies that the IMF had advocated, such as the voucher privatization schemes and excessive monetary stringency. Other failures were related to the inadequate attention given to issues of corporate governance (the importance of which had, for instance, been stressed in my earlier theoretical work (see Stiglitz, 1985a). Meanwhile, the success of a few countries that had followed quite different strategies suggested that there were alternatives that could have been followed. Again, while the IMF defended its previous policies, I believe that the clear lessons that were drawn from these experiences did have some impact on policy prescriptions going forward.

I left the World Bank in January 2000. The US Treasury had put enormous pressure on the World Bank to silence my criticisms of the policies which they and the IMF had pushed, and though the President of the World Bank agreed with the stances I took on most of the issues, he was, I think, less comfortable about open discourse of these issues. I had come to the World Bank under an agreement that I would be more than a corporate spokesperson, that I could speak out on the relevant issues, in a responsible way. I believed, in part, that the credence that would be given to what I said – and my ability to advance the development agenda – depended in part on the perception that I was expressing my views, not just repeating the institution's official views. Under Treasury pressure, it was impossible to maintain this kind of independence, which had been a hallmark of the World Bank's research division, at least from the time that it achieved international prominence under the leadership of Hollis Chenery. I was, in any case, ready to return to academia – when President Clinton had asked me to be his adviser, it had been my intention to come to Washington for only two years; I had stayed seven, and although I had managed in that period to carry out a moderate research program, I had had my fill of bureaucracy. Still, it was a great disappointment to me that my own government should have gone so much against the principles for which I believed it stood, including transparency and the importance of the role of government. (My conversations with the President convinced me that he himself supported both my stances and the values that underlay them, but that the US Treasury often did not adequately inform him about the policies they were advocating, let alone ask for his approval.)

The experiences during the seven years in Washington have helped shape my activities since then. I helped found the Initiative for Policy Dialogue, with support of the Ford, Rockefeller, McArthur, and Mott Foundations and the Canadian and Swedish government, to enhance democratic processes for decision making in developing countries, to ensure that a broader range of alternative are on the table and more stakeholders are at the table. This effort has enlisted the support of dozens of economists and other social scientists throughout the world, in a set of task forces that are intended to lay out alternative policy alternatives in a wide range of areas, and has conducted policy dialogues bringing together academics, government officials, NGO's, labor leaders, and the press in a number of countries, including Serbia, Nigeria,

Viet Nam, and the Philippines. Both through the Initiative for Policy Dialogue and independently, I have continued to take an active role advising governments on a broad range of issues, from the role of monetary policy under dollarization (Ecuador) to the reform of social security systems and second and third generation reforms in China, to the lessons that can be drawn from the past failures and successes for privatization, to the design of macro-economic responses to an economic slowdown.

I have also continued to work actively to change the international economic arrangements, including the international institutions, to make them more transparent, to ensure that the policies that they have been pushing reflect the interests and concerns of the developing countries, and especially the poor within those countries, as well as the advances in economic science of the past quarter century. I have been pleased with the progress that has occurred: perspectives, such as greater reliance on bankruptcy and standstills, that I had long advocated have now either been adopted or are at the center of the policy debate. But much remains to be done, and I anticipate that pushing this agenda will occupy much of my time in the years ahead.

My research agenda too has been greatly affected by these experiences. While I have continued the research program on the economics of information – I have recently completed a book with my long time collaborator Bruce Greenwald which explores more fully the implications of information economics for macro-economics, and monetary theory in particular[17] – I have turned more of my attention to an analysis of the role of information and incentives in political processes, as well as continuing my work on development more generally. (Stiglitz, 1999a.) Another major area of research involves the continuing analysis of the appropriate role of the state in the economy; in particular, how to design policies which combine concerns for economic efficiency, social justice, individual responsibility, and liberal values.

REFERENCES

Akerlof, George and Stiglitz, Joseph E. "Investment, Income and Wages." *Econometrica,* (abstract), 1966 *(Supplementary Issue), 34*(5), p.118. (Presented at December meetings of the Econometrica Society, New York.)

–."Capital, Wages and Structural Unemployment." *Economic Journal,* June 1969, *79*(314), pp. 269–281.

Arnott, Richard J. and Stiglitz, Joseph E. "Aggregate Land Rents, Expenditure on Public Goods and Optimal City Size." *Quarterly Journal of Economics,* November 1979, *93*(4), pp. 471–500.

–. "Aggregate Land Rents and Aggregate Transport Costs," *Economic Journal,* June 1981, *91*(362), pp. 331–347. (Also NBER Working Paper 523.)

Arrow, Kenneth J.; Cline, William R.; Mäler, Karl-Göran; Munasinghe, Moran; Squitieri R. and Stiglitz, Joseph E. "Intertemporal Equity, Discounting, and Economic Efficiency," in J. Bruce, H. Lee, and E. Haites, eds., *Climate Change 1995 – Economic and Social Dimensions of Climate Change.* Cambridge: Cambridge University Press, 1996, pp. 125–144. (Also in *Global Climate Change: Economic and Policy Issues,* M. Munasinghe (ed.), World Bank Environment Paper 12, Washington, D.C. 1995, pp. 1–32.)

[17] See Greenwald and Stiglitz (1999).

Atkinson, Anthony B. and Stiglitz, Joseph E. "The Structure of Indirect Taxation and Economic Efficiency." *Journal of Public Economics,* March 1972, *1,* pp. 97–119.

–. The Design of Tax Structure: Direct Versus Indirect Taxation." *Journal of Public Economics,* July–August 1976, *6*(1–2), pp.55–75.

Bevan, David L. and Stiglitz, Joseph E. "Intergenerational Transfers and Inequality," *The Greek Economic Review,* August 1979, *1*(1), pp. 8–26.

Braverman, Avishay and Stiglitz, Joseph E. "Credit Rationing, Tenancy, Productivity and the Dynamics of Inequality," in P. Bardhan, ed., *The Economic Theory of Agrarian Institutions.* Oxford: Clarendon Press, 1989, pp.185–201.

Cass, David and Stiglitz, Joseph E. "The Structure of Investor Preferences and Asset Returns, and Separability in Portfolio Allocation: A Contribution to the Pure Theory of Mutual Funds," *Journal of Economic Theory,* June 1970, *2*(2), pp. 122–160.

–. "Risk Aversion and Wealth Effects on Portfolios with Many Assets." *Review of Economic Studies,* July 1972, *39,* pp. 331–354.

Dasgupta, Partha and Stiglitz, Joseph E. "Differential Taxation, Public Goods, and Economic Efficiency." *Review of Economic Studies,* April 1971, *38*(114), pp. 151–174.

–. "On Optimal Taxation and Public Production." *Review of Economic Studies,* 39, January 1972, *39*(1), pp. 87–103.

–. "Benefit-Cost Analysis and Trade Policies." *Journal of Political Economy,* January–February 1974, *82*(1), pp. 1–33. (Presented to Conference on Project Evaluation, Nairobi, July, 1971.)

–. "Industrial Structure and the Nature of Innovative Activity," *Economic Journal,* June 1980a, *90*(358), pp. 266–293. (Reprinted in Edwin Mansfield and Elizabeth Mansfield, eds., *The Economics of Technical Change.* Aldershot, UK: Elgar, 1993, pp. 133–60.)

–. "Uncertainty, Market Structure and the Speed of R&D." *Bell Journal of Economics,* Spring 1980b, *11*(1), pp.1–28. (Also see Princeton University Econometric Research Program Research Memorandum 255.)

–. "Entry, Innovation, Exit: Toward a Dynamic Theory of Oligopolistic Industrial Structure." *European Economic Review,* February 1981, *15*(2), pp. 137–158.

–. "Potential Competition, Actual Competition and Economic Welfare." *European Economic Review,* March 1988, *32*(2–3), pp. 569–577.

Dasgupta, Partha; Blitzer, Charles and Stiglitz, Joseph E. "Project Appraisal and the Foreign Exchange Constraint," *Economic Journal,* March 1981, *91*(361), pp. 58–74. (Presented at the Econometric Society Meeting, August 1976, Helsinki.)

Diamond, Peter and Stiglitz, Joseph E. "Increases in Risk and in Risk Aversion." *Journal of Economic Theory,* July 1974, *8*(3), pp. 337–360. (Presented at a Conference on Decision Rules and Uncertainty, Iowa City, May 1972.)

Dixit, Avinash K. and Stiglitz, Joseph E. "Monopolistic Competition and Optimal Product Diversity." *American Economic Review,* June 1977, *67*(3), pp. 297–308.

Fisher, Irving. "The Debt Deflation Theory of Great Depressions." *Econometrica,* October 1933, *1*(4), pp: 337–357.

Grossman, Sanford and Stiglitz, Joseph E. "On Value Maximization and Alternative Objectives of the Firm." *Journal of Finance,* May 1977, *32*(2), pp. 389–402.

–."Stockholder Unanimity in the Making of Production and Financial Decisions," *Quarterly Journal of Economics,* May 1980, *94*(3), pp. 543–566.

Greenwald, Bruce C. and Stiglitz, Joseph E. "Toward a Theory of Rigidities," with B. Greenwald, *American Economic Review,* May 1989, *79*(2), pp. 364–69.

–"Labor Market Adjustments and the Persistence of Unemployment." *American Economic Review,* May 1995, *85*(2), pp. 219–25.

–. *Towards a New Paradigm for Monetary Economics,* Mattioli lectures presented at Milan, November 1999, Forthcoming London: Cambridge University Press.

Greenwald, Bruce C.; Stiglitz, Joseph E. and Weiss, Andrew. "Informational Imperfections in the Capital Markets and Macro-economic Fluctuations." *American Economic Review,* May 1984, *74*(2), pp. 194–199.

Hahn, Frank. "Equilibrium Dynamics with Heterogeneous Capital Goods." *Quarterly Journal of Economics,* November 1966, *80*(4), pp. 633–646.

Hoff, Karla and Stiglitz, Joseph E. "Moneylenders and Bankers: Price-increasing Subsidies in a Monopolistically Competitive Market." *Journal of Development Economics,* April 1997, *52*(2), pp. 429–462.

–. "Modern Economic Theory and Development," in G. Meier and J. E. Stiglitz, eds., *Frontiers of Development Economics: The Future in Perspective.* New York: Oxford University Press, March 2001, pp 389–485.

Leitzinger, Jeffrey J. and Stiglitz, Joseph E. "Information Externalities in Oil and Gas Leasing," *Contemporary Policy Issues,* March 1984, (5), pp. 44–57. (Paper presented at the Western Economic Association Meetings, July 1983.)

Newbery, David M. G. and Stiglitz, Joseph E. "Pareto Inferior Trade," *Review of Economic Studies,* January 1984, *51*(1), pp. 1–12.

Rothschild, Michael and Stiglitz, Joseph E. "Increasing Risk: I. A Definition," *Journal of Economic Theory,* September 1970, *2*(3), pp. 225–243. (Subsequently in *Foundations of Insurance Economics,* G. Dionne and S. Harrington (eds.), Kluwer Academic Publishers, 1992.)

–. "Increasing Risk: II. Its Economic Consequences," with M. Rothschild, *Journal of Economic Theory,* March 1971, *5*(1), pp. 66–84.

–. "Some Further Results in the Measurement of Inequality." *Journal of Economic Theory,* 1973, *6,* pp. 188–204.

–. "A Model of Employment Outcomes Illustrating the Effect of the Structure of Information on the Level and Distribution of Income." *Economic Letters,* 1982, *10,* pp. 231–236.

Sah, Raaj K. and Stiglitz, Joseph E. "Human Fallibility and Economic Organization." *American Economic Review,* May 1985a, *75*(2), pp. 292–296.

–. "The Social Cost of Labor, and Project Evaluation: A General Approach." *Journal of Public Economics,* 1985b, *28,* pp. 135–163. (Economic Growth Center Discussion Paper No. 470, Yale University, March 1985.)

–. "The Architecture of Economic Systems: Hierarchies and Polyarchies," *American Economic Review,* September 1986, *76*(4), pp. 716–727.

Salop, Steven and Stiglitz, Joseph E., "Bargains and Ripoffs: A Model of Monopolistically Competitive Price Dispersions." *Review of Economic Studies,* October 1977, *44*(3), pp. 493–510. (Reprinted in S.A. Lippman and D.K. Levine (eds.), *The Economics of Information,* Aldershot, U.K: Edward Elgar, 1995, pp. 198–215.)

Shell Karl and Stiglitz, Joseph E. "The Allocation of Investment in a Dynamic Economy." Quarterly Journal of Economics, November 1967, *81*(4), 592–609.

Solow, R. and Stiglitz, Joseph E. "Output, Employment and Wages in the Short Run." *Quarterly Journal of Economics,* 82, November 1968, pp. 537–560.

Stiglitz, Joseph E. "Distribution of Income and Wealth Among Individuals." *Econometrica,* July 1969a, *37*(3), pp. 382–397.

–. "A Re-Examination of the Modigliani-Miller Theorem." *American Economic Review,* December 1969b, *59*(5), pp. 784–793. (Presented at the 1967 meetings of the Econometric Society, Washington, D.C.)

–. "The Effects of Income, Wealth and Capital Gains Taxation on Risk-Taking," *Quarterly Journal of Economics,* May 1969c, *83*(2), pp. 263–283.

– "On the Optimality of the Stock Market Allocation of Investment," *Quarterly Journal of Economics, 86*(1), February 1972a, pp. 25–60.

–"Some Aspects of the Pure Theory of Corporate Finance: Bankruptcies and Take-Overs." *Bell Journal of Economics, 3*(2), Autumn 1972b, pp. 458–482.

–"Education and Inequality." *Annals of the American Academy of Political and Social Sciences,* 409, September 1973a, pp. 135–145.

–"The Badly Behaved Economy with the Well Behaved Production Function," in *Models of Economic Growth,* J. Mirrlees (ed.), MacMillan Publishing Company, 1973b, pp. 118–137. (Presented at the International Economic Association Conference on Growth Theory, Jerusalem, 1970.)

– "Taxation, Corporate Financial Policy and the Cost of Capital," *Journal of Public Economics*, February 1973c, *2*(1), pp. 1–34. (Subsequently published in Modern Public Finance, vol. 1, International Library of Critical Writings in Economics, no. 15. A. Atkinson (ed.), Elgar, 1991, pp. 96–129.)
–. "On the Irrelevance of Corporate Financial Policy," *American Economic Review, 64*(6), December 1974a, pp. 851–866.
– "Alternative Theories of Wage Determination and Unemployment in L.D.C.'s: The Labor Turnover Model," *Quarterly Journal of Economics, 88*(2), May 1974b, pp. 194–227.
–. "Theories of Discrimination and Economic Policy," In *Patterns of Racial Discrimination*, G. von Furstenberg, *et al.* (eds.), D.C. Heath and Company (Lexington Books), 1974c, pp. 5–26.
–. "Growth With Exhaustible Natural Resources: Efficient and Optimal Growth Paths," Review of Economic Studies, March 1974d (*Symposium*), pp. 132–137.
– "Growth With Exhaustible Resources: The Competitive Economy," *Review of Economic Studies*, March 1974e (*Symposium*), pp. 139–152.
– "The Theory of Screening, Education and the Distribution of Income." *American Economic Review*, June 1975, *65*(3), pp. 283–300.
–. "The Efficiency Wage Hypothesis, Surplus Labor and the Distribution of Income in L.D.C.'s," *Oxford Economic Papers*, July 1976, *28*(2), pp. 185–207.
–. "Theory of Local Public Goods," In *The Economics of Public Services*, M.S. Feldstein and R.P. Inman (eds.), MacMillan Publishing Company, 1977, pp. 274–333. (Paper presented to IEA Conference, Turin, 1974.)
– "Notes on Estate Taxes, Redistribution and the Concept of Balanced Growth Path Incidence," *Journal of Political Economy*, April 1978a (*Part 2: Research in Taxation*), *86*(2), pp. 137–150. (Paper presented at NBER Conference on Taxation, Stanford University, January 1976.)
– "Equity, Taxation and Inheritance," in W. Krelle and A.F. Shorrocks. eds., *Personal Income Distribution*, Amsterdam: North-Holland Publishing Company, 1978b, pp. 271–303. (Proceedings of IEA Conference, Noordwijk aan Zee, Netherlands, April 1977.)
–. "Equilibrium in Product Markets with Imperfect Information." *American Economic Review*, May 1979a, *69*(2), pp. 339–345.
–. "On Search and Equilibrium Price Distributions," in *Economics and Human Welfare: Essays in Honor of Tibor Scitovsky*, M. Boskin (ed.), York: Academic Press Inc., 1979b, pp. 203–236.
–. "Alternative Theories of Wage Determination and Unemployment: The Efficiency Wage Model," in M. Gersovitz, *et al.*, eds., *The Theory and Experience of Economic Development: Essays in Honor of Sir Arthur W. Lewis*, London: George Allen & Unwin, 1982a, pp. 78–106.
–. "The Inefficiency of the Stock Market Equilibrium." *Review of Economic Studies*, April 1982b, *49*(2), pp. 241–261. (Paper presented at a Conference on Uncertainty and Insurance in Economic Theory in Honor of Karl Borch, Bergen, April 1979).
–. "Ownership, Control and Efficient Markets: Some Paradoxes in the Theory of Capital Markets," In *Economic Regulation: Essays in Honor of James R. Nelson*, Kenneth D. Boyer and William G. Shepherd (eds.), Michigan State University Press, 1982c, pp. 311–341.
–. "The Structure of Labor Markets and Shadow Prices in L.D.C.'s," in R. Sabot, ed., *Migration and the Labor Market in Developing Countries*. Boulder: Westview, 1982d, pp. 13–64.
–. "The Rate of Discount for Cost-Benefit Analysis and the Theory of the Second Best," in R. Lind, ed., *Discounting for Time and Risk in Energy Policy*, Resources for the Future, 1982e, pp. 151–204.
–. "Some Aspects of the Taxation of Capital Gains," *Journal of Public Economics*, July 1983a, *21*(2), pp. 257–294.
–. "Public Goods in Open Economies with Heterogeneous Individuals," in J.F. Thisse and H.G. Zoller, eds., *Locational Analysis of Public Facilities*, Amsterdam: North-Holland Publishing Company, 1983b, pp. 55–78.
–. "The Theory of Local Public Goods Twenty-Five Years After Tiebout: A Perspective," in G.R. Zodrow, ed., *Local Provision of Public Services: The Tiebout Model After Twenty-Five Years*. New York: Academic Press, 1983c, pp. 17–53.

–. "Credit Markets and the Control of Capital," *Journal of Money, Banking, and Credit,* May 1985a, *17*(2), pp. 133–152.

–. "The General Theory of Tax Avoidance," *National Tax Journal,* September 1985b, *38*(3), pp. 325–338.

–. "Toward a More General Theory of Monopolistic Competition," in M. Peston and R. Quandt, eds., *Prices, Competition, & Equilibrium.* Oxford: Philip Allan/Barnes & Noble Books, 1986, pp. 22–69.

–. "On the Microeconomics of Technical Progress," in Jorge M. Katz. ed., *Technology Generation in Latin American Manufacturing Industries.* New York: Macmillan Press, 1987a, pp. 56–77. (Presented to IDB-Cepal Meetings, Buenos Aires, November 1978.)

–. "Technological Change, Sunk Costs, and Competition," *Brookings Papers on Economic Activity,* 1987b, *3,* pp. 883–947. (Special issue of *Microeconomics,* M.N. Baily and C. Winston, eds., 1988.)

–. "The Wage-Productivity Hypothesis: Its Economic Consequences and Policy Implications," in M.J. Boskin, ed., *Modern Developments in Public Finance.* Oxford: Basil Blackwell, 1987c, pp. 130–165.

–. "Monopolistic Competition and the Capital Market." in G. Feiwel, ed., *The Economics of Imperfect Competition and Employment – Joan Robinson and Beyond,* New York: New York University Press, 1989a, pp. 485–507.

–. "Mutual Funds, Capital Structure, and Economic Efficiency," in S. Bhattacharya and G. Constantinides, eds., *Theory of Valuation – Frontiers of Modern Financial Theory, Vol. 1,* Totowa, NJ: Rowman and Littlefield, 1989b, pp. 342–356.

–. "The Economic Role of the State: Efficiency and Effectiveness," in T.P. Hardiman and M. Mulreany, eds., *Efficiency and Effectiveness in the Public Domain, The Economic Role of the State.* Dublin: Institute of Public Administration, 1991, pp. 37–59.

–. "Prices and Queues as Screening Devices in Competitive Markets," in D. Gale and O. Hart, eds., *Economic Analysis of Markets and Games: Essays in Honor of Frank Hahn,* Cambridge, MA: MIT Press, 1992, pp. 128–166.

–. *Whither Socialism?* Cambridge: MIT Press, 1994.

–. "Social Absorption Capability and Innovation," in B. Ho Koo and D.H. Perkins, eds., *Social Capability and Long-Term Economic Growth.* New York: St. Martin's Press, 1995, pp. 48–81.

–. "The Role of Government in Economic Development," in M. Bruno and B. Pleskovic, eds., *Annual World Bank Conference on Development Economics 1996,* The World Bank, 1997a. pp. 11–23.

–. "Looking out for the National Interest: the Principles of the Council of Economic Advisers," American Economic Review, May 1997b, *(Papers and Proceedings of the Hundred and Fourth Annual Meeting of the American Economic Association), 87*(2), pp. 109–113.

–. "Distinguished Lecture on Economics in Government: The Private Uses of Public Interests: Incentives and Institutions" *Journal of Economic Perspectives,* Spring 1998a, *12*(2), pp. 3–22.

–. "Pareto Efficient Taxation and Expenditure Policies, With Applications to the Taxation of Capital, Public Investment, and Externalities." Unpublished paper (Presented at conference in honor of Agnar Sandmo), January 1998b.

–. "Introduction," in B. Pleskovic and J. E. Stiglitz, eds., *Proceedings from the Annual Bank Conference on Development Economics 1997.* Washington DC: World Bank, 1998c: pp 1–7.

–. "On Liberty, the Right to Know and Public Discourse: The Role of Transparency in Public Life." Unpublished paper (Paper presented at Oxford Amnesty Lecture), January 1999a.

–. "Lessons From East Asia" *Journal of Policy Modeling,* May 1999b, *21*(3), pp. 311–330.

–. "Corporate Governance Failures in the Transition" in *Governance, Equity and Global Markets (Proceedings of Annual Bank Conference for Development Economics in Europe June 1999).* Paris: La Documentation Francaise, 2000, pp 51–84.

–. "Thanks for Nothing." *The Atlantic Monthly,* October 2001a, *288*(3), pp.36–40.

–. "Quis Custodiet Ipsos Custodes? Corporate Governance Failures in the Transition," in J. E. Stiglitz and P-A. Muet, eds., *Governance, equity, and global markets: the Annual Bank Conference on Development Economics in Europe,* New York: Oxford University Press, 2001b: pp 22–54.
–. "New Perspectives on Public Finance: Recent Achievements and Future Challenges." *Journal of Public Economics,* forthcoming 2002.
Stiglitz, Joseph E. and Wallsten, Scott J. "Public-Private Technology Partnerships: Promises and Pitfalls," *American Behavioral Scientist,* September 1999, *43*(1), pp. 35–51. (Reprinted in P. Rosenau, ed., *Public Private Policy Partnerships.* Cambridge: MIT Press, 2000.)
Tiebout, Charles M. "A Pure Theory of Public Expenditures." *Journal of Political Economy,* 1956, *64*(5), pp. 416–424.

INFORMATION AND THE CHANGE IN THE PARADIGM IN ECONOMICS

Prize Lecture, December 8, 2001

by

JOSEPH E. STIGLITZ

Columbia Business School, Columbia University, 1022 International Affairs Building, 420 West 118th Street, New York, NY 10027, USA.

The research for which George Akerlof, Mike Spence, and I are being recognized is part of a larger research program which, today, embraces hundreds, perhaps thousands, of researchers around the world. In this lecture, I want to set the particular work which was cited within this broader agenda, and that agenda within the broader perspective of the history of economic thought. I hope to show that Information Economics represents a fundamental change in the prevailing paradigm within economics. Problems of information are central to understanding not only *market* economics but also *political economy,* and in the last section of this lecture, I explore some of the implications of information imperfections for political processes.

INTRODUCTION

Many years ago Keynes wrote:

> The ideas of economists and political philosophers, both when they are right and when they are wrong, are more powerful than is commonly understood. Indeed, the world is ruled by little else. Practical men, who believe themselves quite exempt from any intellectual influences, are usually the slaves of some defunct economist. Madmen in authority, who hear voices in the air, are distilling their frenzy from some academic scribbler of a few years back. Keynes [1936].

Information economics has already had a profound effect on how we think about economic policy, and are likely to have an even greater influence in the future. The world is, of course, more complicated than our simple – or even our more complicated models – would suggest. Many of the major political debates over the past two decades have centered around one key issue: the efficiency of the market economy, and the appropriate relationship between the market and the government. The argument of Adam Smith [1776], the founder of modern economics, that free markets led to efficient outcomes, "as if by an invisible hand" has played a central role in these debates: it suggested that we could, by and large, rely on markets *without government intervention.* There was, at best, a limited role for government. The set of ideas that

I will present here undermined Smith's theory and the view of government that rested on it. They have suggested that the reason that the hand may be invisible is that it is simply not there – or at least that if is there, it is palsied.

When I began the study of economics some forty one years ago, I was struck by the incongruity between the models that I was taught and the world that I had seen growing up, in Gary Indiana, a city whose rise and fall paralleled the rise and fall of the industrial economy. Founded in 1906 by U.S. Steel, and named after its Chairman of the Board, by the end of the century it had declined to but a shadow of its former self. But even in its heyday, it was marred by poverty, periodic unemployment, and massive racial discrimination. Yet the theories that we were taught paid little attention to poverty, said that all markets cleared – including the labor market, so unemployment must be nothing more than a phantasm, and that the profit motive ensured that there could not be economic discrimination.[1] If the central theorems that argued that the economy was Pareto efficient – that, in some sense, we were living in the best of all possible worlds – were true, it seemed to me that we should be striving to create a different world. As a graduate student, I set out to try to create models with assumptions – and conclusions – closer to those that accorded with the world I saw, with all of its imperfections.

My first visits to the developing world in 1967, and a more extensive stay in Kenya in 1969, made an indelible impression on me. Models of perfect markets, as badly flawed as they might seem for Europe or America, seemed truly inappropriate for these countries. But while many of the key assumptions that went into the competitive equilibrium model seemed not to fit these economies well, the ones that attracted my attention was the imperfection of information, the absence of markets, and the pervasiveness and persistence of seeming dysfunctional institutions, like sharecropping. With workers having to surrender 50% or more of their income to landlords, surely (if conventional economics were correct), incentives were greatly attenuated. Traditional economics said not only that institutions (like sharecropping)[2] did not matter, but neither did the distribution of wealth. But if workers owned their own land, then they would not face what amounted to a 50% tax. Surely, the distribution of wealth did matter.

I had seen cyclical unemployment – sometimes quite large – and the hardship it brought as I grew up, but I had not seen the massive unemployment that characterized African cities, unemployment that could not be explained either by unions or minimum wage laws (which, even when they existed, were regularly circumvented). Again, there was a massive discrepancy between the models we had been taught and what I saw.

[1] See, e.g. Becker [1971] The insight was simple: that so long as there were sufficient numbers of, for instance, unprejudiced employers, they would bid up the wage of the discriminated to their marginal productivity.

[2] There was one brilliant, valiant attempt to show that sharecropping did not matter, a thesis by Steven Cheung completed at the University of Chicago, see Cheung [1969]. The unreasonable assumptions, especially concerning information, helped convince me of the need for an alternative theory.

The new ideas and models were not only useful in addressing broad philosophical questions, such as the appropriate role of the state, but also in analyzing concrete policy issues. In the 70s, economists became increasingly critical of traditional Keynesian ideas, partly because of their assumed lack of micro-foundations. The attempts made to construct a new macro-economics based on *traditional* micro-economics, with its assumptions of well functioning markets, was doomed to failure. Recessions and depressions, accompanied by massive unemployment, were symptomatic of massive market failures. The market for labor was clearly not clearing. How could a theory that began with the assumption that all markets clear ever provide an explanation? If individuals could easily smooth their consumption by borrowing at safe rates of interest, then the relatively slight loss of lifetime income caused by an interruption of work of six months or a year would hardly be a problem; but the unemployed do not have access to capital markets, at least not at reasonable terms, and thus unemployment is a cause of enormous stress. If markets were perfect, individuals could buy private insurance against these risks; yet it is obvious that they cannot. Thus, one of the main developments to follow from this line of research into the consequences of information imperfections for the functioning of markets is the construction of *macro economic* models that help explain why the economy amplifies shocks and makes them persistent, and why there may be, even in competitive equilibrium, unemployment and credit rationing.

I believe that some of the huge mistakes which have been made in policy in the last decade, in for instance the management of the East Asia crisis or the transition of the former communist countries to a market, might have been avoided if there had been a better understanding of issues, like bankruptcy and corporate governance, to which the new information economics called attention. And the so-called Washington consensus policies[3], which have predominated in the policy advice of the international financial institutions over the past quarter century, have been based on market fundamentalist policies which ignored the information-theoretic concerns, and this explains at least in part their widespread failures.

Information affects decision making in every context – not just inside firms and households. More recently, I have turned my attention to some aspects of what might be called the *political economy* of information: the role of information in political processes, in collective decision making. For two hundred years, well before the economics of information became a subdiscipline within economics, Sweden had enacted legislation to increase transparency. There are asymmetries of information between those governing and those governed, and just as markets strive to overcome asymmetries of information, we need to look for ways by which the scope for asymmetries of information in political processes can be limited and their consequences mitigated.

[3] See Williamson [1990] for a description. For a critique, see Stiglitz [1998a].

THE HISTORICAL SETTING

I do not want here to review and described in detail the models that were constructed. In recent years, there have been a number of survey articles[5], even several books[6], and interpretative essays[7]. I do want to highlight some of the dramatic impacts that information economics has had on how economics is approached today, how it has provided explanations to phenomena that were previously unexplained, how it has altered our views about how the economy functions, and, perhaps most importantly, how it has led to a rethinking of the appropriate role for government in our society. In describing the ideas, I want to trace out some of their origins: to a large extent, they were responses to attempts to answer specific policy questions or to explain specific phenomena to which the standard theory provided an inadequate explanation. But any discipline has a life of its own, a prevailing paradigm, with assumptions and conventions. Much of the work was motivated by an attempt to explore the limits of that paradigm – to see how the standard models could embrace problems of information imperfections (which turned out not to be very well.)

For more than a hundred years, formal modeling in economics has focused on models in which information was perfect. Of course, everyone recognized that information was in fact imperfect, but the hope, following Marshall's dictum "Natura non facit saltum" was that economies in which information was not too imperfect would look very much like economies in which information was perfect. One of the main results of our research was to show that this was not true; that even a small amount of information imperfection could have a profound effect on the nature of the equilibrium.

The reining paradigm of the twentieth century, the neoclassical model, ignored the warnings of the nineteenth century and earlier masters on how information concerns might alter the analyses, perhaps because they could not see how to embrace them in their seemingly precise models, perhaps because doing so would have led to uncomfortable conclusions about the efficiency of markets. For instance, Smith, in anticipating later discussions of adverse selection, wrote that as firms raise interest rates, the best borrowers drop out of the market. *If* lenders know perfectly the risks associated with each borrower, this would matter little; each borrower would be charged an appropriate risk premium. It is because lenders do not know the default probabilities of borrowers perfectly that this process of adverse selection has such important consequences.[8]

[5] See, for instance, Stiglitz [1975b, 1985d, 1987a, 1988b and Riley [2001]. There have also been reviews of particular aspects, some of which are referenced below.

[6] See, for instance, Fudenberg, and Tirole [1991], Hirshleifer and Riley [1992], Hart [1995] and Mas-Colell, Whinston and Green [1995].

[7] See, in particular, Stiglitz [2000d].

[8] "If the legal rate …was fixed so high… the greater part of the money which was to be lent, would be lent to prodigals and profectors, who alone would be willing to give this higher interest. Sober people, who will give for the use of money no more than a part of what they are likely to make by the use of it, would not venture into the competition." Smith, 1776. See also Marshall [1890], Sismondi [1814] and Mill [1848], as cited in Stiglitz [1987a].

I have already noted in the introduction that *something* was wrong – seriously wrong – with the competitive equilibrium models which represented the prevailing paradigm when we went to graduate school. It seemed to say that unemployment didn't exist, that issues of efficiency and equity could be neatly separated, so that economists could neatly set aside problems of inequality and poverty as they went about their business of designing more efficient economic systems. But there were a host of other predictions, empirical puzzles, that were hard to reconcile with the standard theory: in micro-economics, there were tax paradoxes such as why did firms seemingly not take actions which minimized their tax liabilities, security market paradoxes, such as why did asset prices seem to exhibit such high volatility[9], and behavioral puzzles, such as why did firms respond to risks in ways which were markedly different from that predicted by the theory.[10] In macro-economics, the cyclical movements of many of the key aggregate variables, such as consumption,[11] inventories,[12] real product wages[13], real consumption wages[14], and interest rates[15] are hard to reconcile with the standard theory, and if the perfect market assumptions were even approximately satisfied, the distress caused by cyclical movements in the economy would be much less than seems to be the case.[16]

The problems that we saw with the models that we were taught was not only that they seemed wrong, but that they left a host phenomena and institutions unexplained – why were IPO's typically sold at a discount? Why did equities, which provided far better risk diversification than debt, play such a limited role in financing new investment?[17]

There were, to be sure, some Ptolemaic attempts to defend and elaborate

[9] There was so many of these that the *Journal of Economic Perspectives* ran a regular column with each issue highlighting these paradoxes. See Thaler [1987] and Thaler *et al.* [1989, 1990, 1991, 1995, 1997]. The problem of excess volatility of asset prices has recently been highlighted in the work of Shiller [2000].

[10] In the discussion below, I elaborate on several of these paradoxes, and show how the new paradigm helps explain them.

[11] According to Hall [1978], consumption should be a random walk, responding only to new news. The evidence does not support this conclusion.

[12] Inventories should be used to smooth the economy, so that they should move in a countercyclical manner. In fact, they move pro-cyclically. See for instance Blinder and Fisher [1981], Blinder (1986), Kahn [1987], Blinder and Maccini [1991] Bernanke and Gertler [1995] and Bils and Kahn [2000].

[13] If firms operated along their production functions, then when employment fell, the marginal product of labor, and hence the real product wage, should rise. Yet, in cyclical downturns, it often does not. For empirical evidence on these and other seeming quandaries, see Greenwald and Stiglitz [1988b].

[14] If workers operate along their labor supply curves, and if, as most empirical evidence suggests, labor supply curves, especially for primary workers, is highly inelastic, then when employment goes down, the real consumption wage should go down a great deal. Yet in many cyclical downturns, that does not happen. Though observed behavior can be reconciled with the theory simply by assuming that there is a simultaneous shift in the labor supply schedule, such an explanation is hardly satisfying.

[15] See, e.g. Stiglitz [1995a, 1999a].

[16] Remarkably, Lucas [1987] (won the Nobel prize in 1995) uses the perfect markets model with a representative agent to try to argue that these cyclical fluctuations in fact have a relatively small welfare costs.

[17] See, for instance, Mayer [1990].

on the old model. Some, like George Stigler[18], while recognizing the importance of information, argued that once the real costs of information were taken into account, even with imperfect information, the standard results of economics would still hold. Information was just a transactions cost. In the approach of many Chicago economists, information economics was like any other branch of applied economics; one simply analyzed the special factors determining the demand and supply for information, just as agricultural economics analyzed those factors affecting the market for wheat. For the more mathematically inclined, information could be incorporated into production functions of, say, goods by inserting an "I" for the input "information," and I itself could be produced by inputs, like labor. Our analysis showed that that this approach was wrong, as were the conclusions derived from it.

Practical economists who could not ignore the bouts of unemployment which had plagued capitalism since its inception talked of the neoclassical synthesis: using Keynesian interventions to ensure that the economy remained at full employment, and once that was done, the standard neoclassical propositions would once again be true. But while the neoclassical synthesis[19] had enormous intellectual influence, by the 1970s and 80s it came under attack from two sides. It was an assertion, not based on a coherent view of the economy. One side attacked the underpinnings of Keynesian economics, its micro-foundations; why would rational actors by out of equilibrium – with unemployment persisting – in the way that Keynes had suggested. This side effectively denied the phenomena which Keynes was attempting to explain.

Worse still, some saw unemployment as largely reflecting an interference (e.g. by government in setting minimum wages, or trade unions, in using their monopoly power to set too high wages) with the free workings of the market, with the obvious implication: unemployment would be eliminated if markets were made more *flexible,* that is unions and government interventions were eliminated. Even if wages fell a third in the Great Depression, they should have, in this view, fallen even more.

There was an alternative perspective (articulated more fully in Greenwald and Stiglitz, 1987a, 1988b): why shouldn't we believe that massive unemployment was just the tip of the iceberg, of more pervasive market efficiencies that are harder to detect. If markets seemed to function *so* badly some of the time, certainly they must be malperforming in more subtle ways much of the time. The economics of information bolstered the latter view.

Similarly, given the nature of the debt contracts, the falling wages and prices led to bankruptcy and economic disruptions, actually exacerbating the economic downturn. Had there been more wage and price flexibility, matters might have been even worse. Moreover, neither government nor unions imposed the limitations on wage and price dynamics in many sectors of the economy; at the very least, those who argued that the problem was wage and price rigidities had to look for other *market* imperfections, and any policy

[18] Stigler [1961], who won the Nobel Prize in 1982.
[19] See Samuelson [1947]). He won the Nobel Prize in 1970.

remedy (including a call for greater flexibility) had to take those factors into account.

In the next section, I shall explain how it was not just the discrepancies between the standard competitive model and its predictions which lead to its being questioned. The model was not robust – even slight departures from the underlying assumption of perfect information had large consequences.

But before turning to those issues, it may be useful to describe some of the concrete issues which underlay the beginnings of my research program in this area. Key in my thinking on these issues was the time between 1969 and 1971 I spent at the Institute for Development Studies at the University of Nairobi with the support of the Rockefeller Foundation.

Education as a screening device[20]

The newly independent Kenyan government was asking questions that have never seemingly been raised by their colonial masters, as it attempted to forge policies which would promote their growth and development. How much should it invest in education? It was clear that a better education got one better jobs – the credential put one at the head of the job queue. Gary Fields, a young scholar working at the Institute of Development Studies there, developed a simple model[21] suggesting that the private returns to education – the enhanced probability of getting a good job – differed from the social return; and that it was possible that as more people get educated, the private returns got higher (it was even more necessary to get the credential) even though the social return might decline. Here, education was performing a markedly different function than it did in traditional economics literature, where it simply added to human capital and improved productivity.[22, 23] The analysis had important implications for Kenya's decision about how much to invest in higher education. The problem with Fields' work was that it did not provide a full *equilibrium* analysis: wages were fixed, rather than competitively determined.

This led me to ask, what would the market equilibrium look if wages were set equal to mean marginal products *conditional on the information that was available.* And this in turn forced me to ask: what were the *incentives* and *mechanisms* for employers and employees to acquire or transmit information. Within a group of otherwise similar job applicants (who therefore face the same wage), the employer has an incentive to identify who is the most able, to find some way of *sorting* or *screening* among them, *if he could keep that information private.* But he often can't, and if others find out about the true ability, the wage will be bid up, and he will be unable to *appropriate* the return to the information. At the very beginning of this research program we had thus iden-

[20] Stiglitz [1975c]
[21] Subsequently published as Fields [1972].
[22] See, e.g. Schultz [1960], who won the Nobel Prize in 1979, and Mincer [1974].
[23] At the time, there was other on-going work criticizing the human capital formulation, focusing on the role of education in socialization and credentialization. See, for instance, Bowles and Gintis [1976].

tified one of the key issues in information economics, the difficulty of *appropriating* the returns.

On the other hand, the employee, *if he knew his ability* (that is, if there were *asymmetries of information between the employee and the employer)* and he knew that his abilities were above the average of those in the market, had an incentive to convince the employer of his ability. But someone at the bottom of the ability distribution had an incentive not have the information revealed. Here was a second principle that was to be explored in subsequent years: there are incentives on the part of individuals for information not to be revealed, for secrecy, or, in modern parlance, for a lack of transparency. This raised a question: how did the forces for secrecy and for information disclosure get balanced? What was the equilibrium that emerged? I will postpone until the next section a description of that equilibrium.

Efficiency wage theory

That summer in Kenya I began three other research projects related to information imperfections. At the time I was working in Kenya, there was heavy urban unemployment. My colleagues at the Institute for Development Studies, Michael Todaro and John Harris had formulated a simple model of labor migration from the rural to the urban sector which accounted for the unemployment. High urban wages attracted workers, and they were willing to risk unemployment for the chance of those higher wages.[24] Here was a simple, general equilibrium model of unemployment, but again there was one missing piece: how could you explain the high wages, which were well in excess of the minimum wage. It did not seem as if either government or unions were *forcing* these high wages. One needed an equilibrium theory of wage determination. I recalled, during an earlier stint at Cambridge, discussions with Harvey Leibenstein who had postulated that in very poor countries, higher wages lead to higher productivity[25]. It might not pay firms to cut wages, if productivity was cut more than proportionately, even if there was an excess supply of labor. The key insight was to recognize that there were a variety of other reasons why, when information and contracting were imperfect, productivity might depend on wages.[26] In that case, it might pay firms to pay a higher wage than the minimum necessary to hire labor; such wages I referred to as *efficiency wages*. With efficiency wages, there could exist an equilibrium level of unemployment. I explored four explanations for why productity might depend on wages (besides through nutrition). The simplest was that

[24] See Harris and Todaro [1970], Todaro [1969]. I developed these ideas further in Stiglitz [1969b].

[25] See Leibenstein [1967]. There were, of course, historical antecedents to this idea (as to many of the other ideas discussed below), see, e.g. Marshall in Marshall [1920] wrote: ...highly paid labour is generally efficient and therefore not dear labour; a fact which though it is more full of hope for the future of the human race than any other that is known us, will be found to exercise a very complicating influence on the theory of distribution.

[26] Others were independently coming to the same insight, in particular Ned Phelps in Phelps [1968]. Phelps and Winter also realized that the same issues applied to product markets, in their theory of customer markets. See Phelps and Winter [1970].

lower wages lead to higher turnover, and therefore higher turnover costs which the firm bore.[27] It was not until some years later than we were able to explain more fully – based on limitations of information – why it was that firms had to bear these turnover costs.[28]

But there was another version of the efficiency wage related to the work I was beginning on asymmetric information. Any manager will tell you that you attract better workers by paying them higher wages. This was just an application of the general notion of adverse selection, which played a central role in earlier insurance literature, where firms had long recognized that as they charge a higher premium, the best risks stopped buying insurance.[29] Firms in a market do not passively have to accept the "market wage". Even in competitive markets, firms could, if they wanted, offered higher wages than others. Market clearing was not a constraint on firms. If all firms were paying the market-clearing wage, it might pay a firm to offer a higher wage, to attract more able workers. The efficiency wage theory meant that there could exist unemployment *in equilibrium.*

It was thus clear that the notion that had underlay much of traditional competitive equilibrium analysis – that markets *had* to clear – was simply not true if information were imperfect.

The formulation of the efficiency wage theory that has received the most attention over the years, however, has been that which has focused on problems of *incentives.* Many firms claim that paying high wages induces their workers to work harder. The problem that Carl Shapiro and I [1984] faced was to try to make sense of this claim. If all workers are identical, and paid workers the same wage, then if it paid one firm to pay a high wage, it would pay all of them. But if a worker was then fired for shirking, and there was full employment, he could immediately get another job, at the same wage. The high wage would provide no incentive. But if there was unemployment, then there was a price for shirking. We showed that *in equilibrium* there *had* to be unemployment: unemployment was the discipline device that forced workers to work.[30] The model had strong policy implications, some of which I shall describe below. Our work illustrated the use of highly simplified models to help

[27] In Nairobi, in 1969, I wrote a long, comprehensive analysis of efficiency wages, entitled "Alternative Theories of Wage Determination and Unemployment in LDC's. Given the custom of writing relatively short papers, focusing on one issue at a time, rather than publishing the paper as a whole, I had to break the paper down into several parts. Each of these had a long gestation period. The labor turnover paper was published as Stiglitz [1974a]; the adverse selection model as Stiglitz [1982a , 1992h (a revision of a 1976 unpublished paper)]. I elaborated on the nutritional efficiency wage theory in Stiglitz [1976c]. Various versions of these ideas have subsequently been elaborated on in a large number of papers, including Weiss [1980], Nalebuff, Rodriguez and Stiglitz [1993], Rodriguez and Stiglitz [1991a, 1991b], Stiglitz [1982f, 1986b, 1987a, 1987i], Sah and Stiglitz [1992], Akerlof and Yellen [1986] and Rey and Stiglitz [1996].

[28] See Arnott and Stiglitz [1985] and Arnott, Hosios, and Stiglitz [1988].

[29] For an early recognition of the importance of this concept in the economics literature, see Arrow [1965].

[30] The idea was recast in a more standard principle agent problem, but embedded within a general equilibrium model of the economy, in unpublished work with Patrick Rey, see Rey and Stiglitz [1996].

clarify thinking about quite complicated matters. In practice, of course, workers are not identical, so problems of adverse selection become intertwined with those of incentives; being fired does convey information – there is typically a stigma.

(There was a fourth version of the efficiency wage, where productivity was related to *morale* effects, perceptions about how *fairly* they were being treated. While I briefly discussed this version in my earlier work[31], it was not until almost twenty years later that the idea was fully developed, in the important work of Akerlof and Yellen [1986].)

Sharecropping and the general theory of incentives

This work on the economics of incentives in labor markets was closely related to the third research project that I began in Kenya. In traditional economic theory, while considerable lip service was paid to incentives, there was no real incentive issue. With perfect information, individuals are paid to perform a particular service; if they perform it they receive the contracted for amount; if they do not, they do not. With imperfect information, firms have to motivate and monitor, rewarding them for observed good performance and punishing them for bad. My interest in the issues was first aroused by thinking about sharecropping, a common form of land tenancy in developing country, where the worker surrenders half (sometimes two thirds) of the produce to the landlord in return for the use of his land. At first blush, this seemed a highly inefficient arrangement; it was equivalent to a 50% tax on workers' labor. But what were the alternatives. The worker could rent the land, but that meant he had to bear all the risk of fluctuations in output; and beside, he often did not have the requisite capital. He could work as wage labor, but that meant that the landlord would have to monitor him, to ensure that he worked. Sharecropping represented a compromise, between risk bearing and incentives. The underlying *information* problem was that the input of the worker could not be observed, but only his output, and his output was not perfectly correlated with his input. The sharecropping contract could be thought of as a combination of a rental contract *plus* an insurance contract, in which the landlord "rebates" part of the rent if crops turn out badly. There is not full insurance (which would be equivalent to a wage contract) because such insurance would attenuate all incentives. The adverse effect of insurance on incentives to avoid the insured against contingency is referred to as *moral hazard.*[32] In Stiglitz [1974b] I analyzed the *equilibrium* sharecropping contract. In that paper, I recognized that the incentive problems I explored there were isomorphic to those facing modern corporations, e.g. in providing incentives

[31] In particular, in the context of the economics of discrimination Stiglitz [1974d].

[32] This term, like adverse selection, originates in the insurance literature. Insurance firms recognized that the greater the insurance coverage, the less incentive there was for the insured to take care; if a property was insured for more than 100% of its value, there was even an incentive to have an accident (a fire). Not taking appropriate care was thought to be "immoral"; hence the name. Arrow's work in moral hazard [1963, 1965] was among the most important precursors, as it was in the economics of adverse selection.

to their managers,[33] and there followed a large literature on optimal and equilibrium incentive schemes[34], in labor, capital, and insurance markets. Contracts had to be based on observables, like processes (or which crops were grown) and *observable* inputs (like fertilizers). Many of the results obtained earlier in the work on adverse selection had their parallel in this area of "adverse incentives."[35] For instance, with Richard Arnott I analyzed the equilibrium [1988a, 1988b], which entail partial insurance.

Equilibrium wage and price distributions

The fourth strand of research looked at the issue of wage differentials that I had observed from a different perspective. The work on labor turnover had suggested that firms that faced higher wages might pay higher wages. But one of the reasons that individuals quit was to obtain a higher paying job. The turnover rate depended on the wage distribution. The challenge was to formulate an *equilibrium* model, in which there was a wage distribution, which led firms to charge different wages – the distribution of wages that had originally been postulated.

More generally, efficiency wage theory said that it paid firms to pay a higher wage than necessary to obtain workers; but the level of the efficiency wage could vary across firms; for instance, firms with higher turnover costs, or where worker inefficiency could lead to large losses of capital, or where monitoring was more difficult, might find it desirable to pay higher wages. The implication was that similar labor might receive quite different compensation; wage discrepancies might not be explicable solely in terms of differences in abilities.

I was to return to these four themes repeatedly in my research over the following three decades.

FROM THE COMPETITIVE EQUILIBRIUM PARADIGM TO THE INFORMATION PARADIGM

In the previous section, I described how my experiences, especially in Kenya – the disparities between the models used and the world that I saw – had motivated a search for an alternative paradigm. But there was another motivation, driven more by the internal logic and structure of the competitive model itself, which was the dominant paradigm thirty years ago.

The model virtually made economics a branch of engineering (with no aspersions to that noble profession), and the participants in the economy better or worse engineers. Each was solving a maximization problem, with full information: households maximizing utility subject to budget constraints, firms maximizing profits (market value), and the two interacting in competitive product, labor, and capital markets. One of the peculiar implications was that

[33] A problem which came to be called the principal-agent problem. See Ross [1973].
[34] For a classic reference see Hart and Holmström (1987). In addition see Stiglitz [1975a], Murphy [1985], Jensen and Murphy [1990], Haubrisch [1994] and Hall and Liebman (1998).
[35] Arrow's lectures (See Arrow [1965]) were an important precursor in this area, as they were in the area of adverse selection. See also Arrow [1964].

there never were disagreements about what the firm should do: alternative management teams would presumably come up with the same solution to the maximization problems. Another peculiar implication was the meaning of risk: when a firm said that a project was risky, that (should have) meant that it was highly correlated with the business cycle, not that it had a high chance of failure.[36] I have already described some of the other peculiar implications of the model: the fact that there was no unemployment or credit rationing, that it focused on only a limited subset of the information problems facing society, that it seemed not to address key issues – like incentives and motivation.

But much of the research in the profession is directed not at these big lacunae, but at seemingly more technical issues – at the mathematical structures. The underlying *mathematics* required assumptions of convexity and continuity, and with these assumptions one could prove the *existence* of equilibrium and its (Pareto) efficiency. The standard proofs of these fundamental theorems of welfare economics did not even list in their enumerated assumptions those concerning information: the perfect information assumption was so ingrained it did not have to be explicitly stated. The *economic* assumptions to which the proofs of efficiency called attention concerned the absence of externalities and public goods. The market failures approach to the economics of the public sector[37] discussed alternative approaches by which these market failures could be corrected, but these market failures were highly circumscribed.

There was, moreover, a curious disjunction between the language economists used to explain markets and the models they constructed. They talked about the information efficiency of the market economy, though they focused on a single information problem, that of scarcity. But there are a myriad of other information problems faced by consumers and firms every day, concerning for instance the prices and qualities of the various objects that are for sale in the market, the quality and efforts of the workers they hire, the returns of investment projects. In the standard paradigm, the competitive general equilibrium model[38], there were no shocks, no unanticipated events: at the beginning of time, the full equilibrium was solved, and everything from then on was an unfolding over time of what had been planned in each of the contingencies. In the real world, the critical question was how, and how well, do markets handle these information problems?

There were other aspects of the standard paradigm which seemed hard to accept. It argued that institutions did not matter – markets could see through them, and equilibrium was simply determined by the laws of supply and demand. It said that the distribution of wealth did not matter.[39] And it said that

[36] See Stiglitz [1989g].

[37] See Bator [1958].

[38] For which Kenneth Arrow and Gerard Debreu got the Nobel Prizes in 1972 and 1983, respectively.

[39] A central proposition of standard neoclassical theory was that issues of distribution and efficiency could be separated (the second welfare theorem), and the efficiency of the market outcome did not depend on the distribution of wealth, so long as there were well defined property rights (see Coase [1960], who received the Nobel prize for his work in 1991).

(by and large) history did not matter – knowing preferences and technology and initial endowments, one could describe the time path of the economy.[40]

Work on the economics of information began by questioning each of the underlying premises, each of the central theorems. Consider, to begin with, the mathematical structures that had underlay some much of the formalization of economics of the latter half of the twentieth century, the convexity assumptions which corresponded to long standing principles of diminishing returns. With imperfect information (and the costs of acquiring it) these assumptions were no longer plausible. It was not just that the cost of acquiring information could be viewed as fixed costs.[41] Work with Roy Radner (Radner and Stiglitz [1984] showed that there was a *fundamental non-concavity in the value of information,* that is, under quite general conditions, it never paid to buy just a little bit of information. Work with Richard Arnott (Arnott and Stiglitz [1988a]) showed that such problems were pervasive in even the simplest of moral hazard problems (where individuals had a choice of alternative actions, e.g. the amount of risk taking to undertake.) While we had not repealed the law of diminishing returns, we had shown its domain to be more limited than had previously been realized.[42]

Michael Rothschild and I showed that under natural formulations of what might be meant by a competitive market with imperfect information, equilibrium often did not exist[43] – even when there was an arbitrarily small amount of information imperfection.[44] While subsequent research has looked for alternative definitions of equilibrium,[45] we remain unconvinced; most of

[40] Strictly speaking, this was not an *inevitable* consequence of the neo-classical assumptions (e.g. it would not hold with irreversible investments), but it was a characteristic of the more widely used models.

[41] In the natural, "spaces," indifference curves and iso profit curves were ill behaved. The non-convexities which naturally arose implied, in turn, for instance, that equilibrium might be characterized by randomization (Stiglitz, [1975b]), or that Pareto efficient tax and optimal tax policies might be characterized by randomization. See Arnott and Stiglitz [1988a], Brito, Hamilton, Slutsky and Stiglitz [1995] and Stiglitz [1982g].

Even small fixed costs (of search, of finding out about characteristics of different investments, of obtaining information about relevant technology) imply that markets will not be *perfectly* competitive; they will be better described by models of *monopolistic competition* (see Dixit and Stiglitz 1977, Salop, 1987, Stiglitz, 1979a, 1979b, 1989f), though the basis of imperfect competition was markedly different from that originally envisioned by Chamberlain (1933).

[42] To be sure, critics of modern capitalism had argued that in many of its central industries, returns to scale were sufficiently large that many industries would be characterized by either monopolies or oligopolies.

[43] Non-convexities naturally give rise to discontinuities, and discontinuities to problems of existence, but the non-existence problem that Rothschild and I had uncovered was of a different, and more fundamental nature. The problem was in part that a single action of an individual – a choice of one insurance policy over another – discretely changed beliefs, e.g. about his type; and that a slight change in the actions of, say an insurance firm – making available a new insurance policy – could lead to discrete changes in actions, and thereby beliefs. Dasgupta and Maskin [1986] have explored mixed strategy equilibria in game theoretic formulations, but these seem less convincing than the imperfect competition resolutions of the existence problems described below. Other problems of non-existence were explored in the context of moral hazard problems in work with Richard Arnott [1987, 1991b].

[44] This had a particularly inconvenient implication: when there was a continuum of types, such as in the Spence [1973, 1974] -models, a full equilibrium never existed.

[45] See for instance Riley [1979].

them violate the natural meaning of competition, i.e. where each participant in the market is so small that he believes that he will have no effect on the behavior of others. (Rothschild and Stiglitz [1997]).

The new information paradigm went further in undermining the foundations of competitive equilibrium analysis, the basic "laws" of economics, which include: the law of demand and supply (holding that market equilibrium was characterized by market clearing), the law of the single price, holding that the same good sold for a single price throughout the market, the law of the competitive price, holding that in equilibrium price equaled marginal cost, the efficient markets hypothesis, holding that in stock markets prices convey all the relevant information from the informed to the uninformed. Each of these cornerstones was rejected, or was shown to hold under much more restrictive conditions.

- We have shown how, when prices affect "quality" – either because of incentive or selection effects – equilibrium may be characterized by demand not equaling supply; firms will not pay lower wages to workers, even when they can obtain such workers, because doing so will raise their labor costs; firms will not charge higher interest rates, even when they can do so, because of an excess demand for credit, because doing so will increase the average default rate, and thus lower expected returns.
- We have shown that the market will be characterized by wage and price distributions, even when there is no exogenous source of "noise" in the economy, even when all firms and workers are (otherwise) identical.
- We have shown that in equilibrium, firms will charge a price in excess of the marginal costs, or workers are paid a wage in excess of their reservation wage. The "surplus" is required to provide the *incentive* for maintaining a reputation.[46] Even in situations where reputation rents were not required, information imperfections gave rise to market power – there is *imperfect competition* –, which resulted in firms charging prices in excess of marginal cost.[47]
- The efficient markets hypothesis[48] held that prices in the stock market fully reflected all information. But if that were the case, then there would be no incentive for anyone to expend money to collect information. Work with Sanford Grossman [1976, 1980] showed that the price system both imperfectly aggregated information and that there was an equilibrium amount of "disequilibrium."

The most fundamental reason why markets with imperfect information differ from those in which it does is that *actions (including choices) convey information, market participants know this, and this affects their behavior.*

A decision by a firm to provide a guarantee is not just a matter that the firm is better able to absorb the risk of a product failure; his willingness to provide

[46] See also Shapiro [1983] and Klein and Leffler [1981].

[47] As I noted earlier, the models of imperfect competition were more akin to Chamberlinian monopolistic competition models than other versions of imperfect competition. See, e.g. Stiglitz [1979b].

[48] See, e.g. Fama [1970, 1991].

a guarantee conveys information about his confidence in the product. An insured is willing to take a policy with a large deductible not because he is not risk averse, but because this action conveys information to the insurance company, that he is willing to bear the risk because he thinks the likelihood of an accident is low. A firm may, at the same time, not assign an employee to a highly visible job, because it knows that the assignment will be interpreted as an indication that the employee is good, making it more likely that a rival will try to hire the person away. Even if he fails, the current employer will have to pay a higher salary.

One of the early insights (Akerlof, 1971) was that markets may be thin or absent. One of the standard assumptions of the old paradigm was that there was a complete set of markets – including intertemporal markets (capital markets) and risk markets. The absence of particular markets, e.g. for risk, has profound implications for how *other* markets function. The fact that workers and firms cannot by insurance against many of the risks which they face affects labor and capital markets; it leads, for instance, to labor contracts in which the employer provides *some* insurance. But the design of these more complicated, but still imperfect and incomplete, contracts, affects the efficiency, and overall performance, of the economy.

Perhaps most importantly, under the standard paradigm, markets are Pareto efficient, except when there one of a limited number of market failures occurs. Under the imperfect information paradigm, markets are almost never Pareto efficient.

While information economics thus undermined these long standing principles of economics, it also provided explanations for many phenomena that had long been unexplained. Earlier, I mentioned the seemingly inefficient institution of sharecropping, for which information economics provided an explanation. Before turning to these *applications*, I want to present a somewhat a more systematic account of the *principles* of the economics of information.

Some problems in constructing an alternative paradigm

The fact that information was imperfect was, of course, well recognized by all economists. While they may have *hoped* that economies with imperfect information behaved much like economies with perfect information, they real reason that models with imperfect information were not developed was that it was not obvious how do to so. There were several problems that had to be overcome: while there was a single way in which information is perfect, there are an infinite number of ways in which information can be imperfect. One of the keys to success was formulating simple models in which the set of relevant information could be fully specified – and so the precise ways in which information was imperfect could also be fully specified. But there was a danger in this methodology, as useful as it was: in these over simplistic models, there were sometimes ways in which there could be full information revelation; the information problems could be fully resolved. In the real world, of course, this never happens, which is why in some of the later work (e.g.

Grossman and Stiglitz [1976, 1980a], we worked with models with an infinite number of states.[49]

Perhaps the hardest problem was modeling equilibrium. It was important to think about both sides of the market – employers and employees, insurance company and the insured, lender and borrower. Each had to be modeled as "rational," in some sense, making inferences on the basis of available information. Each side's behavior too had to be rational, based on beliefs about the consequences of their actions; and those consequences in turn depended on what inferences others would draw from those actions. I wanted to model *competitive* behavior, where each actor in the economy was small, and believed he was small – and so his actions could not or would not affect the equilibrium (though others' inferences about himself might be affected). Finally, one had to think carefully about what was the feasible set of actions: what might each side do to extract or convey information to others.

As we shall see, the variety of results obtained (and much of the confusion in the early literature) arose partly from a failure to be as clear as one might about the assumptions. For instance, the standard adverse selection model had the quality of the good offered in the market (say of used cars, or riskiness of the insured) depending on price. The car buyer (the seller of insurance) knows the *statistical* relationship between price and quality, and this affects his demand. The market equilibrium is the price at which demand equals supply. But that is an equilibrium if and only if there is no way by which the seller of a good car can convey that information to the buyer – so that he can earn a quality premium – and if there is no way by which the buyer can sort out good cars from bad cars. Typically, there are such ways, and it is the attempt to elicit that information which has profound effects on how markets function. To develop a new paradigm, we had to break out from long established premises, to ask what should be taken as *assumptions* and what should be derived from the analysis. Market clearing could not be taken as an assumption; neither could the premise that a firm sells a good at a particular price to all comers. One could not *begin* the analysis even by assuming that in competitive equilibrium there would be zero profits. In the standard theory, if there were positive profits, a firm might enter, bidding away existing customers. In the new theory, the attempt to bid away new customers by slightly lowering prices might lead to marked changes in their behavior or in the mix of customers, in such a way that the profits of the new entrant actually became negative. One had to rethink all the conclusions from first premises.

We made progress in our analyses because we began with highly simplified

[49] Similarly, in many of the incentive models, there may be ways of resolving the problem *in the highly simplified models*, but these resolutions will not work in more complex models. Below, for instance, we describe a model in which higher interest rates lead individuals to take more risks, and so the expected return to the lender may actually decrease. As a result, the optimal interest rate may be lower than that at which markets clear; they can be credit rationing. In the simplified models, the problem could be resolved by requiring collateral (Bester [1985]); but in models in which there are both adverse selection *and* incentive problems, this is no longer true, since those most willing to provide collateral may be wealthy individuals, more willing to undertake risky projects. See Stiglitz and Weiss [1985].

models of *particular* markets, that allowed us to think through carefully each of the assumptions and conclusions. From the analysis of particular markets (whether the insurance market, as in Rothschild Stiglitz, the education market, the labor market, or the land tenancy/sharecropping market), we attempted to identify general principles, to explore how these principles operated in each of the other markets. In doing so, we identified particular features, particular *informational assumptions,* which seemed to be more relevant in one market or another. The nature of competition in the labor market is different than that in the insurance market or the capital market, though they have much in common. This interplay, between looking at the ways in which such markets are similar and dissimilar, proved to be a fruitful research strategy.[50]

SOURCES OF ASYMMETRIES OF INFORMATION

Information imperfections are pervasive in the economy: indeed, it is hard to imagine what a world with perfect information would be like. Much of the research I will describe below focuses on *asymmetries* of information, that fact that different people know different things: workers know more about their ability than does the firm; the person buying insurance knows more about his health, whether he smokes and drinks immoderately, than the insurance firm; the owner of a car knows more about the car than potential buyers; the owner of a firm knows more about the firm that a potential investor; the borrower knows more about his risk and risk taking than the lender.

The essential feature of a decentralized market economy is that different people know different things; in this sense, economists had long been thinking of markets with information asymmetries. But the earlier literature had neither thought about how they were created, or what their consequences might be. Moreover, while much of the earlier literature focused on simple situations of information asymmetry – such as those described in the previous paragraphs, the problems of information *imperfections* run deeper, and the research described below discusses some of these more general results. The individual may know little about his true health condition; the insurance company, through a simple examination, might even become more informed (at least concerning relevant aspects, e.g. implications for life expectancy).

Some of these information asymmetries are inherent: the individual naturally knows more about himself than does anyone else. Some of the asymmetries arise naturally out of economic processes. The current employer knows more about the employee than other potential employers; a firm knows may

[50] Some earlier work, especially in general equilibrium theory, by Radner [1972], Hurwicz [1972], and Marschak [1972], among others had recognized the importance of problems of information, and had even identified some of the ways that limited information affected the nature of the market equilibrium (e.g. one could only have contracts that were contingent on states of nature that were observable by both sides to the contract.) But the attempt to modify the abstract theory of general equilibrium to incorporate problems of information imperfects proved, in the end, less fruitful than the alternative approach of beginning with highly simplified, quite concrete models.

find out a great deal of information in the process of dealing with his supplier that others may not know; the owner of a car naturally knows the faults of the car better than others – and in particular, he knows whether or not he has a lemon. While such information asymmetries inevitably arise, the extent to which they do so and their consequences depend on how the market is structured, and the recognition that they will arise affects market behavior. For instance, one of the important insights of work in this area is to show how information asymmetries lead to thin or non-existent markets (Akerlof [1970]). But this means that even if an individual has no more information about his ability than potential employers, the moment he goes to work for an employer, an information asymmetry has been created – the employer may know more about the individual's ability than others. The consequence is that the "used labor" market does not work well. Others will be more tame in bidding for his services, knowing that they will succeed in luring him away from his current employer only if they bid too much. If they bid less than his productivity, his current employer will match. Labor mobility is impeded. But that gives market power to the first employer, which he will be tempted to exercise. The recognition of this naturally affects even the "new labor" market. Because an individual is locked into a job, he will be more risk averse in accepting an offer. The terms of the initial contract have to be designed to reflect the diminution of the workers' bargaining power and his reduced labor mobility that occurs immediately after signing.[51, 52]

To take another example, it is natural that in the process of oil exploration, a company finds out information that is relevant for the likelihood that there will be oil in a neighboring tract. There is an informational externality.[53] The existence of this asymmetric information affects the nature of the bidding for oil rights on the neighboring tract. Bidding where there is known to be asymmetries of information will be markedly different from that where such asymmetries do not exist.[54] Those who are uninformed will presume that they will win only if they bid too much – information asymmetries exacerbate the problem of the winners' curse.[55] The government (or other owners of large

[51] There are other incentives for the creation of information asymmetries. Individuals might originally not know their abilities, but if the market pays higher wages to an individual who is more able, it may pay an individual to ascertain whether he is or is not more able. See Stiglitz [1984a].

[52] If individual's productivity were the same on all jobs, and there were not other reasons for changing jobs (e.g. non-pecuniary preferences), there would be no labor mobility. The fact that there is *some* labor productivity does not undermine the central result: information asymmetries *reduce* the extent of mobility.

[53] See Stiglitz [1975d], and Leitzinger and Stiglitz [1984]. Of course, in the bidding for the initial leases, bidders know that should they win the lease, they will be able to win auctions on neighboring tracts at more favorable terms, and this will affect the size of the initial bids.

[54] Wilson [1977].

[55] The winners' curse is a manifestation of imperfect information. If different individual's get independent estimates of the amount of oil in a tract, the one with the most positive estimate will bid the highest. He knows that if he wins, others' information is less positive, and he takes this into account in forming his bid. See Cappen, Clapp and Campbell (1971) for the first empirical and very influential study of the winner's Curse and Wilson [1969] for a theoretical treatment. In the case of asymmetric information, an uninformed bidder knows that he is more likely to outbid the informed bidder if he bids more than it is worth, and this decreases his willingness to make a bid even further.

tracts to be developed) should take this into account in its leasing strategy. And the bidders in the initial leases too will take this into account: part of the value of winning in the initial auction is the information rent that will accrue in later rounds.

Creating asymmetries and imperfections of information

While early work in the economics of information dealt with how markets overcame problems of information asymmetries, and information imperfections more generally, later worked turned to how markets *create* information problems, partly in an attempt to exploit market power. Managers of firms attempt to *entrench* themselves, increasing their bargaining power, e.g. vis a vis alternative management teams[56], and one of the ways that they do this is to take actions which *increase* information asymmetries. (Edlin and Stiglitz [1995]). Doing so effectively reduces competition in the market for management. This is an example of the general problem of corporate governance, to which I alluded earlier, and to which I will return later.

Similarly, the presence of information imperfections give rise to market power; and firms can exploit this market power through "sales" and other ways of differentiating among individuals who have different search costs. (Salop, 1977, Salop and Stiglitz, 1976, 1982, Stiglitz 1979a). The price dispersions which exist in the market are *created* by the market – they are not just the failure of markets to arbitrage fully price differences *caused* by shocks that affect different markets differently.

OVERCOMING INFORMATION ASYMMETRIES

I now want to discuss briefly the ways by which information asymmetries are dealt with, how they can be (partially) overcome.

Incentives for gathering and disclosing information

There are two key issues: what are the *incentives* for obtaining information, and what are the *mechanisms*. My brief discussion of the analysis of education as a screening device suggested the fundamental incentives: more able individuals (lower risk individuals, firms with better products) will receive a higher wage (will have to pay a lower premium, will receive a higher price for their products) if they can establish that they are more productive (lower risk, higher quality).

We noted earlier that while some individuals have an incentive to disclose information, those who are less able have an incentive not to have the information disclosed. Was it possible that in market equilibrium, only *some* of the information would be revealed? One of the early important results was that, if the more able are able (costlessly) to establish that they are more able, then the market will be fully revealing, even though all of those who are below average would prefer that no information be revealed. In the simplest mo-

[56] See Shleifer and Vishny [1989].

dels, I described a process of unraveling: if the most able could establish his ability, he would; but then all but the most able would be grouped together, receiving the mean marginal product of that group; and the most able of that group would have an incentive to reveal his ability. And so on down the line, until there was full revelation.[57]

What happens if those who are more able cannot credibly convince potential employers of their ability (or if those who are low risk cannot convince potential insurance companies)? The other side of the market has an incentive too to gather information: an employer that can find a worker that is better than is recognized by others will have found a bargain; his wage will be determined by what others think of him. The problem, as we noted, is that if what he knows becomes known to others, the wage will be bid up, and he will be unable to appropriate the returns on his investment in information acquisition.

The fact that if there was competition, it would be difficult for the *screener* to appropriate the returns had an important implication: in markets where, for one reason or another, the more able (the firms with the better investment projects, the more able workers) cannot (fully) convey their attributes, *if* there is to be investment in screening *there must be imperfect competition in screening*. The economy, in effect, has to choose between two different imperfections: imperfections of information or imperfections of competition. Of course, in the end, there will be both forms of imperfection.[58, 59]

This is but one of many examples of the *interplay* between market imperfections. Earlier, for instance, we discussed the incentive problems associated with sharecropping, which arise when workers do not own the land that they till. This problem could be overcome if individuals could borrow money, to buy their land. But capital market imperfections – limiations on the ability to borrow, which themselves arise from information imperfections – explain why this "solution" does not work.

There is another important consequence: if markets were fully informationally efficient – that is, if information disseminated instantaneously and perfectly throughout the economy – then no one would have any incentive to gather information, so long as there was any cost of doing so. That is why markets cannot be fully informationally efficient. (See Grossman and Stiglitz, 1976, 1980a.)

Mechanisms for elimination of reducing information asymmetries

In simple models where individuals know their own ability, or the insured knows his own risk, or the borrower knows his own likelihood of repaying, there might seem an easy way to resolve the problem of information asym-

[57] I jokingly referred to this as "Walras' Law of Sorting" – if all but one group sorts itself out from the others, then the last group is also identified.

[58] And there is no reason to believe that the market "balances" these two forms of imperfection optimally.

[59] See Stiglitz [1975b], Jaffee and Stiglitz [1990]. – This perhaps helps explain why competition in banking – which is essentially concerned with screening among borrowers – is so imperfect.

metry: let each person tell his true characteristic. The underlying problem arose from the fact that individuals did not necessarily have the incentive to tell the truth. Assume employees knew their abilities. An employer might ask, what is your ability? The more able might answer honestly. As we have seen, the least able would have an incentive to lie, to say that he was more able than he was. Talk was cheap. There had to be some other ways by which information could be credibly conveyed.

Screening by examination

The simplest way by which that could be done was an exam. As I constructed a simple competitive equilibrium model[60], two further general principles became apparent: *the gains of the more able were largely at the expense of the less able*; by establishing that an individual is of higher ability, thereby leading, in equilibrium, to higher wages, he simultaneously establishes that others are of lower ability. The private returns to expenditures on education exceed the social returns. It was clear that there were important *externalities* associated with information, a theme which was to recur in later work.

But a more striking result emerged: there could exist multiple equilibria, one in which information was fully revealed (the market identified the high and low ability people) and the other of which it was not (called a pooling equilibrium). The pooling equilibrium Pareto dominated the equilibrium with full revelation. This work, done some thirty years ago, established two results of important policy import, which remarkably have not been fully absorbed into policy discussions even today. First, markets do not provide appropriate incentives for information disclosure. There is, in principle a role for government. And secondly, expenditures on information may be too great.[61]

The simplest adverse selection model

But much of the information firms glean about their employees, banks about their borrowers, insurance companies about their insured comes not from examinations but from making *inferences* based on their behavior. This was a commonplace in life – but not in our economic models. As I have already noted, the early discussions of adverse selection in insurance markets recognized that as an insurance company raised its premiums, those who were least likely to have an accident decided not to purchase the insurance; the willingness to purchase insurance at a particular price conveyed information to the insurance company.[62] George Akerlof recognized that this phenomenon was far more general: the willingness to sell a used car, for instance, conveyed information about whether the car was or was not a lemon.

Bruce Greenwald [1979, 1986] took the idea one important step further,

[60] Stiglitz [1974a]. Arrow [1973] simultaneously developed a theory of education which looked at it from much of the same perspective.

[61] This point was independently arrived at by Hirshliefer [1971] and is elaborated on in more detail below.

[62] Arrow [1965].

showing how adverse selection applied to labor and capital markets[63]: the willingness of an employer not to match the bid of a competitor conveyed information about the current employer's judgment of that individual's ability; the willingness of insiders in a firm to sell stock at a particular price conveyed information about the insider's view of the price relative to the expected return. Akerlof's insight that the result of these information asymmetries was that markets would be thin or absent helped explain why labor and capital markets often did not function well. It provided part of the explanation for why firms raised so little of their funds through equity (Mayer, 1990). Stigler was wrong: imperfect information was not just like a transactions costs.

The consequences go well beyond just an absent or missing market. Weak equity markets meant that risks could not be divested, leading firms to act in a risk averse manner, explaining some of what would otherwise seem to be anomalous aspects of firm behavior[64]. These capital market imperfections, in turn, played a central role in the macro-economic theories to be described below. We have already described how the labor market imperfections – the limited mobility of labor and the firm's market power that results – affects the labor market, both *before* the asymmetry of information is created in the process of hiring and after.

The simplest adverse incentive model

In the adverse selection model, individuals differed. There was a single action which conveyed information: they either entered or did not enter the particular market. But information imperfections also relate to *what people do.* A worker can work harder, a borrower can undertake greater risk and the insured can undertake greater care. The employer would like to know how hard his worker is working; if he could, he would specify that in the contract; the lender would like to know the actions which borrower will undertake; if he could, we would specify that in the contract. These asymmetries of information about *actions* are as important as the earlier discussed asymmetries. Just as in the adverse selection model, the seller of insurance may try to overcome the problems posed by information asymmetries by *examination,* so too in the adverse incentive model, he may try to *monitor* the actions of the insured. But examinations and monitoring are costly, and while they yield some information, typically there remains a high level of residual information imperfection. Just as in the adverse selection model, the seller of insurance recognizes that the average riskiness of the insurance applicants is affected by the terms of the insurance contract, so too the level of risk taking can be affected. And similar results hold in other markets. Borrowers' risk taking is affected by the interest rate charged. (Stiglitz and Weiss [1981]).

[63] See also Greenwald, Stiglitz, and Weiss [1984] and Myers and Majluf [1984].
[64] See discussion in subsection The Theory of Corporate Finance.

Efficiency wage theory, credit rationing

While the early work in adverse selection explored the equilibrium in markets where the seller of insurance (the employer, the buyer of used cars, the lender) was rational enough to recognize the dependence of quality on price, he was not rational enough to exploit as fully as he could the information. While the law of supply and demand had been assumed to be a law of economics, there is in fact no law that require the insurance firm to sell to all who apply at the premium he announces, the lender to lend to all who apply at the interest rate he announces, the employer to employ all those who apply at the wage he announces. So ingrained was the competitive equilibrium model in the mindset of economists that they simply assumed price-taking behavior. With perfect information and perfect competition, any firm that charged a price higher than the others would lose all of his customers; and at the going price, one faced a perfectly elastic supply of customers. In adverse selection and incentive models, what mattered was not just the supply of customers or employees or borrowers, but their "quality" – the riskiness of the insured or the borrower, the returns on the investment, the productivity of the worker.

Since "quality" may increase with price, it may pay to pay a higher wage than the market clearing wage, for the lender to lend at an interest rate which exceeds the market clearing interest rate. This is true whether the dependence on quality arises from adverse selection or adverse incentive effects (or, in the labor market, because of morale or nutritional effects). And what matters is that there be imperfect information, not asymmetries of information. The healthy who decide not to buy insurance at a high premium do not need to *know* that they are healthy; they could be as uninformed as the insurance company, but simply – perhaps because of their health – have different preferences, e.g. they prefer to spend more of their money on recreational sports.

The consequence, as we have noted, is that market equilibrium may be characterized by demand not equaling supply: in equilibrium, the interest rate is lower than that at which the demand for loans equals the supply – there is credit rationing (Stiglitz and Weiss [1981], Keeton [1979]); the wage rate is higher than that at which the demand for labor equals the supply – there is unemployment.[65]

Conveying information through actions

There is a much richer set of actions which convey information beyond those on which traditional adverse selection models have focused. An insurance company wants to attract healthy applicants. It might realize that by locating

[65] This is the efficiency wage theory discussed earlier. Constructing *equilibrium models is* more difficult than might seem to be the case at first, since each agents' behavior depends on opportunities elsewhere, i.e. the behavior of others. The workers that I attract at a particular wage depend on the wage offers of other firms. Rey and Stiglitz [1996], Shapiro and Stiglitz [1984], and Rodriguez and Stiglitz [1991a, 1991b] represent attempts to come to terms with these general equilibrium problems.

itself on the fifth floor of a walk up building, only those with a strong heart would apply. The willingness or ability to walk up five floors conveys information. More subtly, it might recognize that how far up it needs to locate itself, if it only wants to get healthy applicants, depends both on the premium charged and how high it locates itself. Or it may decide to throw in for free a membership in a health club, but charge a higher premium. Those who value a health club – because they will use it – willingly pay the higher premium. But these individuals are likely to be healthier.

There are a host of other actions which convey information. The quality of the guarantee offered by a firm can convey information about the quality of the product; only firms that believe that their product is reliable will be willing to offer a good guarantee. The guarantee is desirable not just because it reduces risk, but because it conveys information. The number of years of schooling may convey information about the ability of an individual. More able individuals may go to school longer, in which case the increase in wages associated with an increase in schooling may not be a consequence of the human capital that has been added, but rather simply be a result of the sorting that occurs.[66] The size of the deductible that an individual chooses in an insurance policy may convey information about his view about the likelihood of an accident or the size of the accidents he anticipates – *on average*, those who are less likely to have an accident may be more willing to accept high deductibles. The willingness of an entrepreneur to hold large fractions of his wealth in a firm (or to retain large fractions of the shares of the firm) conveys information about his beliefs in the firm's future performance. If a firm promotes an individual to a particular job, it may convey information about the firm's assessment of his ability.

The fact that these actions may convey information affects behavior. In some cases, the action will be designed to obfuscate, to limit information disclosure. The firm that knows that others are looking at who it promotes, and that it will compete more vigorously for those, may affect the willingness of the firm to promote some individuals or assign them to particular jobs. (Waldman, 1984.) In others, the action will be designed to convey information in a credible way, to alter beliefs. The fact that customers will treat a firm that issues a better guarantee as if its product is better – and therefore be willing to pay a higher price – may affect the guarantee that the firm is willing to issue. Knowing that his selling his shares will convey a negative signal concerning his views of the future prospects of his firm, an entrepreneur may retain more of the shares of the firm; he will be less diversified than he otherwise would have been (and accordingly, he may act in a more risk averse manner).

A simple lesson emerges: some individuals wish to convey information;

[66] Sorting out empirically the relative importance of human capital and sorting effects turns out to be quite difficult. In arguing that education sorts, I did not argue that it does not, at the same time, enhance productivity. See Weiss [1995]. There are a number of aspects of the education market which are consistent with the "sorting" hypothesis: for instance, wages go up markedly upon graduation. It could be that the knowledge just jells in the final days before graduation, but the more likely hypothesis is that the completion of four years, and the successful passing of all the relevant examinations, conveys a considerable amount of information.

some individuals wish not to have information conveyed (either because such information might lead others to think less well of them, or because conveying information may interfere with their ability to appropriate rents). In either case, the fact that actions convey information leads people to alter their behavior, and changes how markets function. This is why information imperfections have such profound effects.

Once one recognizes that actions convey information, two results follow. First, in making decisions about what to do, individuals will not only think about what they like (as in traditional economics) but how it will affect others' beliefs about them. If I choose to go to school longer, it may lead others to believe that I am more able, and I will therefore decide to stay in school longer, not because I value what is being taught, but because I value how it changes others' beliefs concerning my ability. This means, of course, that we have to rethink completely firm and household decision making.

Secondly, we noted earlier that individuals have an incentive to "lie" – the less able to say that they are more able. Similarly, if it becomes recognized that those who walk up to the fifth floor to apply for insurance are more healthy, then I might be willing to do so even if I am not so healthy, simply to fool the insurance company. If it becomes recognized that those who stay in school longer are more able, then I might be willing to do so, even if I am less able, simply to fool the employers. Recognizing this, one needs to look for ways by which information is conveyed *in equilibrium*. The critical insight in how that could occur was provided in a paper with Michael Rothschild [1976]. If those who were more able, less risk prone, more credit worthy *acted* in some observable way (had different preferences) than those who were less able, less risk prone, less credit worthy, then it might be possible to design a set of *choices*, which would result in those with different characteristics in effect *identifying* themselves through their *self-selection*. One of the reasons that they might behave differently is that they *know* they are more able, less risk prone, more creditworthy – that is there is asymmetric information. But it is only one of the bases for self-selection.

The particular mechanism which we explored in our insurance model illustrates how self-selection mechanisms work. People who know they are less likely to have an accident will be more willing to accept an insurance policy with a high deductible, so that an insurance company that offered two policies, one at a high premium and no deductible, one with a low premium and high deductible, would be able to sort out who were high risk and who low. It is an easy matter to construct choices which thus *separate*.

Monopoly and self-selection

Analyzing the choices which arise in *full* equilibrium behavior turned out, however, to be a difficult task. The easiest situation to analyze was that of a monopolist.[67] He could construct a set of choices that would *differentiate* among different types of individuals, and analyzed whether it was profit max-

[67] Stiglitz [1977a].

imizing for him to do so fully, or to (partially) "pool" – that is, offer a set of contracts such that several types might choose the same one. This work laid the foundations of a *general theory of price discrimination*. Under standard theories of monopoly, *with perfect information,* firms would have an incentive to price discriminate perfectly (extracting the full consumer surplus from each). If they did this, then monopoly would in fact be non-distortionary. Yet most models assumed no price discrimination (that is, the monopolist offered the same price to all customers), without explaining why they did not do so, and argued that monopoly was distortionary. This work showed how, given limited information, firms could price discriminate, but could do so only imperfectly. Subsequent work by a variety of authors (such as Salop [1977] and Adams and Yellen [1976]) explored a variety of ways by which a monopolist might find out relevant characteristics of his customers – the extent of discrimination limited by his ability to identify each person's "surplus", the maximum they would be willing to pay. (For an insurance company, the relevant characteristics are not only the likelihood of having an accident, but also the degree of risk averse, the premium that an individual would be willing to pay to divest himself of risk.) The economics of information thus provided the first coherent theory of monopoly.

Self-selection and competitive equilibrium

The reason that analyzing monopoly was easy is that the monopolist could structure the entire choice set facing his customers. The hard question is to describe the full competitive equilibrium, that is a set of insurance contracts such that no one can offer an alternative set which would be profitable. Each firm could control the choices that he offered, but not the choices offered by others; and the decisions made by customers depended on the entire set of choices available. In our 1976 paper, Rothschild and I succeeded in analyzing this case.

Three striking results emerged from this analysis. The first I have already mentioned: under plausible conditions, given the natural definition of equilibrium, equilibrium might not exist. There were two possible forms of equilibria, pooling equilibria, in which the market is not able to distinguish among the types, and separating equilibria, in which it is. The different groups "separate out" by taking different actions. We showed that there never could be a pooling equilibrium – if there were a single contract that everyone bought, there was another contract that another firm could offer which would "break" the pooling equilibrium. On the other hand, there might not exist a separating equilibrium. The cost of separation was too great. Any putative separating equilibrium could be broken by a profitable pooling contract, a contract which would be bought by both low risk and high risk types.

Second, even small amounts of imperfections of information can change the standard results, concerning the existence and characterization of equilibrium. Equilibrium, for instance, never exists when the two types are very near each other. As we have seen, the competitive equilibrium model is simply not robust.

Thirdly, and relatedly, we now can see how the fact that actions convey information affects the *equilibrium*. In particular, our analysis here reinforced the earlier analysis of adverse selection about markets not functioning well. In perfect information models, individuals would fully divest themselves of the risks which they face, and accordingly would act in a risk neutral manner. We explained why insurance markets would not work well – why most risk averse individuals would buy only partial insurance. There were numerous subsequent applications to other markets, reinforcing, for instance, the earlier conclusions concerning the limitations on equity markets. (The reason that the original owners of a firm might want to sell his shares was to "insure" himself against the risk of a bad outcome; an owner that believed that there was a smaller probability of a bad outcome would be willing to buy less insurance, i.e. to divest himself of fewer of his shares. Retention of shares can thus be thought of as a market sorting mechanism, the willingness to keep these shares a "signal" of the owners' confidence.[68])

The result was important not only for the insights it provided in the workings of an important set of markets in the economy, but because there are important elements of insurance in many transactions and the general principle that actions convey information, and that market transactions are greatly affected by this fact, has implications in a still wider variety of contexts. The relationship between the landlord and his tenant, or the employer and his employee, can be viewed as containing in it an insurance component; limitations on the ability to divest oneself of risk are important in explaining a host of contractual relationships.

Sorting, screening, and signaling

In equilibrium, both buyers and sellers, employers and employees, insurance company and insured, lender and creditor are aware of the informational consequences of their actions. Each side of the market needs to consider the consequences, e.g. of acting in a different way, or of confronting the other side of the market with different choices. In the case where say, the insurance company or employer or employee takes the initiative for sorting out applicants, self-selection is an alternative to examinations as a sorting device. In the case where the insured, or employee, or borrower, takes the initiative for identifying himself as a better risk, a better employee, a borrower more likely to repay, then we say he is *signaling*.[69] But of course, in equilibrium both sides are aware of the consequences of alternative actions, and the differences between signaling and self-selection screening models lie in the technicalities of game theory, and in particular whether the informed or uninformed (employee or employer, insured or insurance company) moves first.[70]

Still, some of the seeming differences between signaling and screeing

[68] See Stiglitz [1983], Ross [1973] and Leland and Pyle [1977].

[69] Spence [1973].

[70] See, in particular, Stiglitz and Weiss [1983a, 1994] and Yabushita [1983]. As we point out, in the real world, who moves first ought to be viewed as an endogenous variable. In such a context, it appears that the screening equilibria are more robust than the signaling equilibirum. Assume, for instance, that there were some signaling equilibrium that differed from the screening equilibrium, e.g. there were a pooling equilibrium, sustained because of the out-of-equilibrium beliefs of firms. Then such an equilibrium could be broken by a prior or later move of firms.

models arise because of a failure to specify a *full* equilibrium We noted earlier that there were many separating contracts, but a unique separating equilibrium. We argued that if one considered any other separating set of contracts, then, say, in the insurance market, a firm could come in and offer an alternative set of contracts and make a profit; the original set of separating contracts could not have been an equilibrium The same is true in, say, the education signaling model. There are many educational systems which "separate" – that is, the more able choose to go to school longer, and the wages at each level of education correspond to the productivity of those who go to school for that length of time. But all except one are not *full equilibrium.* Assume, for instance, there were two types of individuals, a low ability and a high ability. Then if the low ability goes to 12 years of schooling, then any education system in which the high ability went *sufficiently* long – say more than 14 years – might separate. But the low ability would recognize that if it went to school for 11 years, it would still be treated as low ability. The unique equilibrium level of education for the low ability is that which maximizes his net income (taking into account the productivity gains and costs of education); and the unique equilibrium level of education for the high ability is the lowest level of education such that, if his wage corresponds to his productivity at that level of education, the low ability will still prefer to remain at his low level of education rather than pretend to be more able by staying in school longer.[71]

The education system, of course, was particularly infelicitous for studying *market* equilibrium. The structure of the education system is largely a matter of public choice, not of market processes. Different countries have chosen markedly different systems. The minimum level of education is typically not a matter of choice, but set by the government. Within educational systems, examinations play as important a role as self-selection or signaling, though *given* a certain standard of testing, there is a process of self-selection involved in deciding whether to stay in school, to try to pass the examination.[72] For the same reason, the problems of existence which arise in the insurance market are not relevant in the education market – the "competitive" supply side of the market is simply absent. But when the signaling concepts are translated into contexts in which there is a robust competitive market, the problems of existence cannot be so easily ignored.[73]

[71] More accurately, the level of education of the more able is the minimum of that and the level of education which maximizes the individual's net income (discounted income minus expenditures on education).

[72] Moreover, even were the educational system not dominated by the government, there would be a coordination problem: a single firm cannot propose an alternative set of "contracts" – different wages corresponding to different levels of education – to "break" an inefficient separating equilibrium, because the employee does not know that he will necessarily remain with the firm for his entire working life.

[73] In particular, when there is a continuum of types (as in the Spence (1973)) model, there never exists a screening equilibrium. The intuition is provided by Rothschild and Stiglitz, who showed then when the types were "close" to each other, then the equilibrium, would not exist; the costs of separating exceed the benefits; a pooling equilibrium could always "break" the separating equilibrium. With a continuum of types, there are always types that are arbitrarily close to each other. At the "bottom" (the highest risk individuals), it is always possible to find a contract which made a profit and attracted the worst types.

Existence of equilibrium in the insurance market

What are we to make of the problem of that problem? Clearly, insurance markets *exist,* even if they are far from complete. To some extent, the market does exhibit instability. Rates vacillate enormously; as rates sometimes skyrocket and coverage is curtailed, the public clamors for reforms, Such periods are often followed by periods of relative stability, to be followed by another "crisis" in the market. Most states regulate rate setting, though at least partly for prudential reasons and this may help stabilize the market.

Moreover, though there is considerable evidence for the kinds of selection processes discussed above, there is also considerable evidence that the market is far from as rational as the theory would suggest. Most health insurance policies do not base premia on the number of children, though that is an easily observable variable which clearly affects the risk exposure. Many insurance companies do not use past experience as heavily as one would have expected in setting premia, i.e. there is less experience rating.

My own suspicion, however, is that the major limitation of Rothschild-Stiglitz is its assumption of perfect competition; competition is far more limited than we postulated; there are, for instance, significant search costs, and considerable uncertainty about how easiy it is to get the insurance firm to pay on a claim. Self-selection is still relevant, but the model of monopoly, or some version of monopolistic competition, may be more relevant than the model of perfect competition.

Theory of contracts and incentives

The work with Rothschild was, related to the earlier work that I had done on incentives (sharecropping), besides in the obvious way that both were concerned with problems of limited information. One focusing on selection effects, one on incentives. Both entailed an equilibrium in "contracts." The contracts that had characterized economic relations in the standard competitive model were extraordinarily simple: I will pay you a certain amount if you do such and such. If you did not perform as promised, the pay was not given. But with perfect information, individuals simply didn't sign contracts that they did not intend to fulfill. Insurance contracts were similarly simple: a payment occurred if and only if particular specified events occurred.

The work on sharecropping and on equilibrium with competitive insurance markets showed that with imperfect information, a far richer set of contracts would be employed, and thus began a large literature on the theory of contracting.[74]

In the simple sharecropping contracts of Stiglitz [1974b], the contracts involved shares, fixed payments, and plot sizes, and[75] more generally, optimal

[74] See, for instance, Stiglitz and Weiss [1983b, 1986, 1987]. Even with these additional instruments there could still be non-market clearing equilibria. Bester [1985] concludes that by increasing collateral requirements one can eliminate credit ratioining is wrong, simply because he ignores the interaction between selection and incentive effects.

[75] Though even here, there were subtleties, e.g. whether individuals exerted their efforts before they knew the realization of the state of nature, and whether there were bounds on the penalties that could be imposed, in the event of bad outcomes.

payment structures related payments to *observables*, inputs, processes, outputs.[76, 77, 78]. Because what went on in one market affect others, the credit, labor, and land markets were *interlinked;* one could not decentralize in the way hypothesized by the standard perfect information model. The theory thus served as the basis of the *rural organization*[79] in developing countries.

The basic principles were subsequently applied in a variety of other market contexts. The most obvious was the design of labor contracts. (Stiglitz 1975a).

Payments can depend too on *relative* performance; relative performance may convey more relevant information than absolute performance. If a particular company's stock goes up when all other companies' stock goes up, it may say very little about the performance of the manager. In Nalebuff and Stiglitz [1983a, 1983b] we analyzed the design of these relative performance compensation schemes (contests). One of the strong arguments for competitive, decentralized structures is that they provide information on the basis of which one can design better incentive pay structures than those which rely on the performance of a single individual only.

Credit markets too are characterized by complicated contracts. Lenders would specify not only an interest rate, but also impose other conditions (collateral requirements, equity requirements) which would have both incentive and selection effects.[80] Indeed, the simultaneous presence of both selection and incentive effects was important: in the absence of the former, it might be possible to increase the collateral requirement *and* raise interest rates, still ensuring that the borrower undertook the safe project.[81, 82]

[76] There was, in this sense, a close relationship between the equilibrium analysis of Rothschild and Stiglitz [1976] and Stiglitz [1974b]. Both explored equilibria in the space of contracts, where contracts imposed stipulations on actions and payments that were based on observables.

[77] In Stiglitz [1974b] the contracts were highly linear. In principle, generalizing payment structures to non-linear functions was simple. Though even here, there were subtleties, e.g. whether individuals exerted their efforts before they knew the realization of the state of nature, and whether there were bounds on the penalties that could be imposed, in the event of bad outcomes (Stiglitz, 1975a, Mirrlees [1975b], Mirrlees [1976]). The literature has not fully resolved the reason that contracts are often much simpler than the theory would have predicted (e.g. payments are linear functions of output), and do not adjust to changes in circumstances. See, e.g. Allen [1985] and Gale [1991].

[78] In work with Avi Braverman [1982, 1986a, 1986b, 1989], we explored, for instance, stipulations concerning what was to be grown and the use of inputs like fertilizers, and the interlinkages between credit, land, and labor contracts. For an earlier survey of sharecropping, see Stiglitz [1987g]. For a more recent survey see Chuma, Hayami and Otsuka [1992].

[79] See, in particular, Braverman, Hoff, and Stiglitz [1993].

[80] See, for instance, Stiglitz and Weiss [1983b, 1986, 1987]. Even with these additional instruments there could still be non-market clearing equilibria.

[81] Venture capital firms represent an interlinkage of capital and "management" markets. See Hellmann [1998].

[82] As another application, "contracting" – including provisions for risk sharing – came to play an important role in explaining macro-economic rigidities. See, for instance, Werin, and Wijkander (1992), the papers of the symposium in Quarterly Journal of Economics [1983], and the survey article by Rosen [1985], Azariadis and Stiglitz [1983], and Arnott, Hosios, and Stiglitz [1988].

Incentives and reputation in market equilibrium

Incentives are based on rewards and punishments. In modern economies, the most severe punishment that one can impose is to fire an individual.[83] But if the individual could get a job just like his current one, then there would be no cost. Good behavior is driven by earning a surplus over what one could get elsewhere. Thus, in labor markets, the wage must be higher than what the worker could get elsewhere (which may be zero, if there is unemployment); in the goods market, firms must feel a loss when they lose a customer because of a shoddy product, so the price must exceed the marginal cost of production. Thus, the long standing presumption that in competitive equilibrium price equals marginal cost *cannot* be true in markets with imperfect information. (See Shapiro and Stiglitz [1984], Shapiro [1983] and Klein and Leffler [1981].)

Equilibrium wage and price distributions

One of the most obvious differences between the predictions of the model with perfect information and what we see in every day life is the conclusion that the same good sell for the same price everywhere. We all spend a considerable amount of time shopping for good buys. The differences in prices represent more than just differences in quality (service). There are *real* price differences. Since Stigler's classic paper [1961], there has been a large literature exploring optimal search behavior. Stigler, and most of the search literature, took, however, the price or wage distribution as given. They did not ask how did it arise. Given the search costs, could it be sustained? For instance, if search costs are relatively low, one might have thought (if one bought the older theories) that markets would look very much like they would with zero search costs, in which case there would be no price or wage distribution. It is not surprising that given that information is costly, if there are shocks to the economy – the demand for a good goes up in some locale, so price there rises – that prices are not fully arbitraged instantaneously. But much of the wage and price dispersion cannot be related to such "shocks."

Our analysis of efficiency wage theory provided an alternative explanation. We showed that it paid firms to pay more than they had to, e.g. to reduce labor turnover costs. But it might pay some firms to pay higher wages than others.

As I began to analyze these models, an important insight occurred: there could be a wage distribution even if all firms were identical, e.g. faced the same search costs. It was clear that even small search costs could make a large difference to the behavior of product and labor markets. This was a point that Diamond [1971] had independently made in a highly influential paper, which serves to illustrate powerfully the lack of robustness of the competitive equilibrium theory. Assume, as in the standard theory, all firms were charging the

[83] This is not quite accurate: if individuals can post a bond, then they can be forced to forfeit the bond. But individuals may not have the wealth to post a bond, and there may be "moral hazard" issues – with a good bond, the firm may have an incentive to say the worker shirked when he did not.

competitive price, but there were an epsilon cost of searching, of going to another store. Then any firm which charged epsilon/2 greater would lose no customers. It would thus pay him to increase his price. And it would similarly pay all other firms to increase their prices. But at the higher price, it would again pay each to increase his price. And price increases until the price charged is the monopoly price. Even small search costs thus lead even a market with many firms to charge monopoly prices. Work with Salop (Salop and Stiglitz [1977, 1982, 1987], Stiglitz [1979b, 1989c]), showed that in situations where there were even small search costs, markets would be characterized by a price distribution. If everyone were charging the same price, it would pay some firm either to raise his price, to exploit the high search costs customers who he would not lose, or to lower his price, to steal customers away from his rivals. The standard wisdom that said that not everyone had to be informed to ensure that the market acted perfectly competitive was simply not in general true.[84]

EFFICIENCY OF THE MARKET EQUILIBRIUM AND THE ROLE OF THE STATE

Perhaps the most important single idea in economics is that competitive economies lead, as if by an invisible hand, to a (Pareto) efficient allocation of resources, and that every Pareto efficient resource allocation can be achieved through a competitive mechanism, provided only that the appropriate lump sum redistributions are undertaken. It is these (fundamental theorems) of welfare economics which provide both the rationale for the reliance on free markets, and the belief that issues of distribution can be separated from issues of efficiency, allowing the economist the freedom to push for reforms which increase efficiency, regardless of their seeming impact on distribution; if society does not like the distributional consequences, it should simply redistribute income.

The economics of information showed that neither of these results was, in general, true. To be sure, economists over the preceding three decades had identified important market failures – such as the externalities associated with pollution – which required government intervention.[85] But the scope for market failures was limited, and thus the arenas in which government intervention was required were limited.

Early work, already referred to, had laid the foundations for the idea that economies with information imperfections would not be Pareto efficient, *even taking into account the costs of obtaining information.* There were interventions in the market that could make all parties better off. We had shown, for instance, that incentives for the disclosure and acquisition of information were far from perfect; imperfect appropriability meant that there might be insufficient incentives, but the fact that much of the gains were "rents," gains by

[84] For a survey, see Stiglitz [1989c].

[85] Though even here, some economists suggested that in the absence of transactions costs, the market could handle the problem efficiently. See Coase [1960]. But this analysis too depended on assumptions of perfect information, as Farrell [1987] forcefully showed.

some at the expense of others, suggested that there might be excessive expenditures on information. One of the arguments for unfettered capital markets was that there were strong incentives to gather information; if one discovered that some stock was more valuable than others thought, if you bought it before they discovered the information, then you would make a capital gain. This price discovery function of capital markets was often advertised as one of its strengths. But the issue was, while the individual who discovered the information a nano-second before any one else might be better off, was society as a whole better off: if having the information a nano-second earlier did not lead to a change in real decisions (e.g. concerning investment), then it was largely redistributive, with the gains of those obtaining the information occurring at the expense of others. Another example illustrates what is at issue. Assume hundred dollar bills were to fall, one each at the left foot of each student in my class. They could wait to the end of the lecture, then pick up the money; but that is not a Nash equilibrium. If all students were to do that, it would pay any one to bend down and quickly scoop up what he could. Each realizing that immediately picks up the dollar bill at his foot. The equilibrium leaves each no better off than if he had waited – and there was a great social cost, the interruption of the lecture.[86]

There are potentially other inefficiencies associated with information acquisition. Information can have adverse effects on volatility[87]. And information can lead to the destruction of markets, in ways which lead to adverse effects on welfare. We described earlier how the existence of asymmetries of information can destroy markets. Individuals sometimes have incentives to obtain information (creating an asymmetry of information), which then leads to the destruction of insurance markets, and an overall lowering of welfare. Welfare might be increased if the acquisition of this kind of information could be proscribed. Recently, such issues have become sources of real policy concern, in the arena of genetic testing. Even when information is available, there are issues concerning its use, with the use of certain kinds of information having either a discriminatory intent or effect, in circumstances in which such direct discrimination itself would be prohibited.[88]

Moreover, asymmetries of information were shown to be related to absent or imperfect markets. They help explain why the market for lemons, or the credit or labor or equity markets worked imperfectly. The fact that markets with imperfect information worked differently – and less well – that markets with perfect information was not, by itself, a damning criticism of markets. After all, information is costly, and taking into account the costs of information, markets might be fully efficient. Stigler had essentially argued for this perspective, but without proof. Our research showed that this assertion – or hope – was simply not correct. Earlier work had established that when mar-

[86] See Stiglitz [1989k].
[87] For a discussion in the context of the East Asia crisis, see Furman and Stiglitz [1998].
[88] See, e.g. Rothschild and Stiglitz [1982, 1997]. For models of statistical discrimination and some of their implications, see Stiglitz [1973a, 1974d], Arrow [1972], and Phelps [1972].

kets are absent or imperfect, market equilibrium might be *constrained* Pareto inefficient, that is, taking into account the absence of the market, everyone could be made better off.[89] Moreover, since asymmetries of information give rise to market power, and *perfect* competition is required if markets are to be efficient, it is perhaps not surprising that markets with information asymmetries and other information imperfections are far from efficient.

But while it was thus not surprising that markets might not provide appropriate incentives for the acquisition and dissemination of information, the market failures associated with imperfect information are far more profound. The intuition can be seen most simply in the case of models with moral hazard. There, the premium charged is associated with the *average* risk, and therefore, the average care, taken by seemingly similar individuals. The moral hazard problem arises because the level of care cannot be observed. Each individual ignores the effect of his actions on the premium; but when they all take less care, the premium increases. The lack of care by each exerts a negative externality on others.

The essential insight of Greenwald and Stiglitz [1986][90] was to recognize that such externality-like effects are pervasive whenever information is imperfect or markets incomplete – that is always – and as a result, markets are essentially never constrained Pareto efficient.[91] In short, market failures are pervasive.

There were two other implications. The first was the non-decentralizability of efficient market solutions. The notion that one could decentralize decision making to obtain (Pareto) efficient resource allocation is one of the fundamental ideas in economics. Greenwald and Stiglitz showed that that was not in general possible. Again, a simple example illustrates what is at issue. An insurance company cannot monitor the extent of smoking, which has an adverse effect on health. The government cannot monitor smoking any better than the insurance company, but it can impose taxes, not only on cigarettes, but also on other commodities which are complements to smoking (and subsidies on substitutes which have less adverse effects.)[92] Earlier work with Braverman [1982] had shown the consequences of this decentralizability, the

[89] At first blush, the result might seem obvious, but interestingly, a number of economists had tried to show that the Arrow-Debreu results on the efficiency of the market were more robust than they seemed, that is even if there were not a complete set of securities markets, the market was constrained Pareto efficiency. See, e.g. Diamond [1967]. But these results were shown to depend on the overly simplistic nature of the models, e.g. involving a single commodity. See Stiglitz [1972a, 1982b], Newbery and Stiglitz [1982, 1984], Grossman and Stiglitz [1977, 1980b].

[90] Greenwald and Stiglitz [1986] focus on models with adverse selection and incentive problems. Greenwald and Stiglitz [1988a] showed that similar results hold in the context of search and other models with imperfect information. Earlier work, with Shapiro [1984] had shown, in the context of a specific model, that quilibria in an economy with an agency or principal agent problem was not (constrained) Pareto efficient. Later work, with Arnott [1990] explored in more detail the market failures that arise with moral hazard.

[91] Arnott, Greenwald, and Stiglitz [1994] provide a simple exposition using the standard self-selection and incentive compatibility constraints.

[92] These ideas are extended and generalized in Arnott and Stiglitz [1991b]. In Stiglitz [1998c]. I explore the role of corrective taxation (correcting for externalities) in the presence of imperfect information.

interlinkage of land, labor, and credit markets in agrarian markets of developing countries.

Markets are also interlinked over time. *Intertemporal linkages* impair the efficacy of competitive processes, as we have already noted. Standard theory has it that if an employer does not treat an employee well, he simply moves to another firm. But informational asymmetries impair labor mobility, partially locking the employee into his employer, or the borrower into his creditor[93]. While with perfect information and perfect markets, some of the consequences of this reduction in ex post competition could be corrected by the intensity of ex ante competition, there is little reason to believe that is in fact the case.[94]

One of the sources of the market failures is *agency problems*, such as those which arise when the owner of land is different from the person working the land. The extent of agency problems – and therefore of market failures – thus depends on the distribution of wealth, as we noted earlier in our discussion of sharecropping. It is simply not the case that one can separate out issues of equity and efficiency.[95]

Moreover, the notion that one could separate out issues of equity and efficiency also rested on the ability to engage in lump sum redistributions. But as Mirrlees [1971] had earlier pointed out, with imperfect information, this was not possible; all redistributive taxation was distortionary. But this had important implications for a wider range of policies beyond simply the design of tax structures. It meant that interventions in the market which changed the before tax distribution of income could be desirable, because they lessened the burden on redistributive taxation.[96] Again, the conclusion: the second welfare theorem, effectively asserting the ability to separate issues of distribution and efficiency, was not true.[97]

In effect, the Arrow-Debreu model had identified the single set of assumptions under which markets were (Pareto) efficient. There had to be perfect information, or, more accurately, information (beliefs) could not be *endogenous*, they could not change either as a result of the actions of any individual or firm, including investments in information. But in an information economy, a model which assumes that information is *fixed* seems increasingly irrelevant.

Dysfunction institutions

As the theoretical case that markets in which information was imperfect were not efficient became increasingly clear, several arguments were put forward against government intervention. One we have already dealt with: the gov-

[93] See Stiglitz and Weiss [1983b].

[94] See, for instance, Stiglitz [1987h]

[95] A point that had also been made earlier in Shapiro and Stiglitz [1984].

[96] See Stiglitz [1998c].

[97] The second welfare theorem also requires other mathematical assumptions, e.g. concerning convexity, which typically may not be satisfied in models with imperfect and endogenous information. Other problems with decentralizability were raised in Arnott and Stiglitz [1991b].

ernment too faces informational imperfections. For our analysis had shown that the incentives and constraints facing government differed from those facing the private sector, so that even when government faced exactly the same *informational* constraints, welfare could be improved upon.[98]

There was another argument, which held up no better. The existence of market failures – absent or imperfect markets – does give rise to non-market institutions. The absence of death insurance gave rise to burial societies. Families provide insurance to their members against a host of risks for which they either cannot buy insurance, or for which the insurance premium is viewed to be too high. But in what I call the *functionalist fallacy*, it is easy to go from the observation that an institution arises to fulfill a function to the conclusion that actually, *in equilibrium*, it serves that function. Those who succumbed to this fallacy seemed to argue that there was no need for government intervention because these nonmarket institutions would "solve" the market failure, or at least do as well as any government. Richard Arnott and I [1991] showed that, to the contrary, non-market institutions could actually make matters worse. Insurance provided by the family could crowd out market insurance; insurance companies would recognize that the insured would take less risk because they had obtained insurance from others, and accordingly cut back on the amount of insurance that they offered. But since the non-market (family) institutions did a poor job of divesting risk, welfare was decreased.[99]

The Arnott-Stiglitz analysis reemphasized the basic point made at the end of the last subsection: it was only under very special circumstances that markets could be shown to be efficient. Why then should we expect an equilibrium involving non-market institutions and markets to be efficient?

APPLICATIONS OF THE NEW PARADIGM

The new theory of the firm and the foundations of modern macro-economics

Of all the market failures, the extended periods of underutilization of resources – especially human resources – is of the greatest moment, the consequences of which in turn are exacerbated by capital market imperfections, which means that even if future prospects of an unemployed individual are good, he cannot borrow to sustain his standard of living.

We referred earlier to the dissatisfaction with traditional Keynesian explanations, in particular, the lack of micro-foundations. This gave rise to two schools of thought. One sought to use the old perfect market paradigm, relying heavily on representative agent models. While information was not perfect, expectations were rational. But the representative agent model, by construction, ruled out the information asymmetries which are at the heart of

[98] For a more extensive discussion of the economic role of the state, see Stiglitz [1989a].

[99] Whether non-market insurance increased or decreased welfare depended on what was observable (monitorable) by other members of the family. If they had no more information than did the insurance company, then the non-market insurance lowered welfare; if they had access to more information, then, in effect, the insurance company could free ride on this information, and welfare could actually be enhanced.

macro-economic problems. Only if an individual has a severe case of schizophrenia is it possible for such problems to arise. If one begins with a model that *assumes* that markets clear, it is hard to see how one can get much insight into unemployment (the failure of the labor market to clear).

The construction of a macro-economic model which embraces the consequences of imperfections of information in labor, product, and capital markets has become one of my major preoccupations over the past fifteen years. Given the complexity of *each* of these markets, creating a general equilibrium model – simple enough to be taught to graduate students or used by policy makers – has not proven to be an easy task. At the heart of that model lies a new theory of the firm, for which the theory of asymmetric information provides the foundations. The modern theory of the firm in turn rests on three pillars, the theory of corporate finance, the theory of corporate governance, and the theory of organizational design.

The theory of corporate finance

Under the older, perfect information theory, it made no difference whether firms raised capital by debt or equity, in the absence of tax distortions.[100] This was the central insight of the Modigliani-Miller theorem.[101] We have noted how the willingness to hold (or to sell) shares conveys information, so that how firms raise capital does make a difference.[102] Firms rely heavily on debt finance, and bankruptcy, resulting from the failure to meet debt obligations, matters. Both because of the cost of bankruptcies and limitations in the design of managerial incentive schemes,[103] firms act in a risk averse manner[104] – with risk being more than just correlation with the business cycle.[105]

[100] For early explorations of the implications of taxes for corporate finance, see Stiglitz [1973b, 1976a].

[101] See Modigliani and Miller [1958]. They won the Nobel Prize in 1985 and 1990, respectively. In Stiglitz [1969a], I showed that there result was, in some respects, considerably more general than their proof would have led one to believe (it did not require, for instance, risk classes and held in general equilibrium), but there was one critical assumption: bankruptcy, which they had ignored.

[102] The term "equity rationing" is used loosely to refer to the fact that firms do not rely on the issuance of equity to divest themselves of the risks which they face, in the way that perfect information theories predict; the issuance of equity, as we have noted, sends a signal that the owners/managers of the firm think the market has overvalued the shares, and the market responds by lowering price. Thus, the cost of raising funds through equity is extremely high. For empirical evidence showing that relatively little new investment is financed by equity, see Mayer [1990]; for empirical evidence concerning the adverse price effects of share issuance, see Asquith and Mullins [1986]; for the general theory, see Greenwald, Stiglitz, and Weiss [1984] and Myers and Maljuf [1984]. Other information based theories that help explain the limited use of equity markets, in spite of their advantages in risk sharing, are derived from signaling/self-selection models referred to earlier, and on models of "costly state verification." (Townsend [1979]). Equity markets give each shareholder a pro-rata share of the profits, but this requires that profits be observable. There are a variety of ways by which profits can be diverted to managers and dominant shareholders. Legal structures and accounting practices are designed to circumscribe such behavior (Greenwald and Stiglitz [1992]), and only where these have become well developed have strong equity markets with diversified share ownership developed. (Shleifer and Vishny [1997]).

[103] That is, we noted earlier that optimal incentive schemes typically involve the worker/manager bearing some risk. In some cases, incentive schemes can actually lead managers to act in a risk-loving way.

[104] See, in particular, Greenwald and Stiglitz [1991].

[105] For an elaboration of this point, see Stiglitz [1987c, 1989g].

Moreover, with credit rationing (or the potential of credit rationing) not only does the firm's net worth (the market value of its assets) matter, but so does its asset structure, including its liquidity.[106] While there are many implications of the theory of the risk averse firm facing credit rationing, some of which are elaborated upon in the next section, one example should suffice to highlight the importance of these ideas. In traditional neoclassical investment theory, investment depends on the real interest rate, and the firm's perception of expected returns. The firm's cash flow or its net worth should make no difference. The earliest econometric studies of investment, by Kuh and Meyer [1957], suggested that that was not the case. But under the strength of the theoretical strictures that these variables could not matter, they were excluded from econometric analysis for two decades following the work of Hall and Jorgenson [1967]. It was not until work on asymmetric information had restored theoretical respectability to introducing such variables in investment regressions that it was acceptable to do so; and when that was done, it was shown that, especially for small and medium sized enterprises, these variables were crucial.[107]

Moreover, in the traditional theory, there is no corporate veil; individuals can see perfectly what is going on inside the firm; it makes no difference whether the firm distributes or retains its profits (other than for taxes).[108] But if there is imperfect information about what is going on inside the firm, then there is a corporate veil, which cannot be easily pierced.

Corporate governance

In the traditional theory, firms simply maximized the expected present discounted value of profits (which equaled market value)[109] and with perfect information, how that was to be done was simply an engineering problem. Disagreements about what the firm should do were of little moment. In that context, corporate governance – how firm decisions were made – mattered little as well. But again, in reality, corporate governance matters a great deal. There *are* disagreements about what the firm should do[110] – partly motivated by differences in judgments, partly motivated by differences in objectives. Managers can take actions which advance their interests at the expense of that of shareholders, and majority shareholders can advance their interests at

[106] The very concept of liquidity – and the distinction between lack of liquidity and insolvency – rests on information asymmetries. If there were perfect information, any firm that was liquid would be able to obtain finance, and thus would not face a liquidity problem.

[107] There is now a vast literature in this area. See, for instance, Blanchard, Lopez-de-Silanes and Schliefer [1994], Hubbard [1990], Calomiris and Hubbard [1990] and Fazzari, Hubbard and Peterson [1988]. For a survey of this literature see Hubbard [1998].

[108] In Stiglitz [1974c], I again showed that the result was, in some respects, far more general than their analysis suggested, but that it was, in fact, undermined by the capital market imperfections which arose from imperfect information.

[109] It was also assumed that firm value maximization would lead to efficient outcomes. When there are not a complete set of Arrow-Debreu securities, this is in general not the case. See Stiglitz [1972a, 1982b], Newbery and Stiglitz [1982], Grossman and Stiglitz [1977, 1980b].

[110] For an early analysis of these issues, see Stiglitz [1972b]. For a general theorem, see Grossman and Stiglitz [1977].

the expense of minority shareholders. The owners (who, in the language of Steve Ross [1973] came to be called the principal) not only could not monitor their workers and managers (the agents), because of asymmetries of information, they typically did not even know what these people who were supposed to be acting on their behalf *should* do. That there were important consequences for the theory of the firm of the separation of ownership and control had earlier been noted by Berle and Means [1932][111], but it was not until information economics that we had a coherent way of thinking about the implications.

The problem of corporate governance, of course, arises both from the problems of information imperfections *and* the public good nature of management/oversight: if a shareholder engages in expenditures on oversight, and succeeds in improving the firm's performance, all shareholders benefit equally (similarly with creditors.) (See Stiglitz [1985b]).

Some who still held to the view that firms would maximize their market value argued that take-overs (and the threat of takeovers) would ensure that competition in the market for managers would ensure stock market value maximization. (If the firm were not maximizing its stock market value, then it would pay someone to buy the firm, and change its actions so that its value would increase.) Early on in this debate, I raised questions on theoretical grounds about the efficacy of the take-over mechanism (See Stiglitz [1972b]). The most forceful set of arguments were subsequently put forward by Grossman and Hart [1980], who observed that any small shareholder who believed that the takeover would subsequently increase the market value would not be willing to sell his shares. Only take-overs that were expected to be value decreasing would be successful.[112] The subsequent work by Edlin and Stiglitz [1995], referred to earlier, showed how existing managers could take actions to reduce the effectiveness of competition for management, i.e. the threat of take-overs, by increasing asymmetries of information.

[111] That the standard model of the theory of the firm – where there was a single owner concerned with maximizing the firm's value – did not fit well the modern theory of the corporation had been noted even earlier by Alfred Marshall [1897]. There was a large subsequent literature on the managerial theory of the firm. See, e.g. Marris [1964], Baumol [1959], and March and Simon [1958]. Even earlier, Adam Smith [1776] had noted the problem of corporate governance:

"The directors of such companies, however, being the managers rather of other people's money than their own, it cannot well be expected that they should watch over it with the same anxious vigilance with which the partners in a private copartnery frequently watch over their own. Like the stewards of a rich man, they are apt to consider attention to small matters as not for their master's honour, and very easily give themselves a dispensation from having it. Negligence and profusion, therefore, must always prevail, more or less, in the management of the affairs of such a company."pp. 264–265.

Marshall [1897], in his review of the advances of economics in the nineteenth century, and the challenges facing the discipline, cited the problems of (in modern parlance) corporate governance, of what motivates a manager to act in the interests of the owners of the firm.

[112] There has subsequently developed a large theoretical and empirical literature on take-overs. See, for instance, Manne [1965], Jensen and Rubac [1983], Stulz [1988] and Singh [1998]. For a surveys of the literature on takeover, see Hirshleifer [1995]. For a survey of the broader literature on corporate governance, see Shleifer and Vishny [1997].

(Proving that a firm does not maximize their stock market value is, of course, difficult, since it is hard to ascertain its opportunity set and the consequences of alternative actions. However, there are a large number of instances in which it is clear that firms do not maximize market value. For instance, closed end mutual funds regularly sell at a discount; there would be a simple action – dissolution of the firm – which would increase market value. There are a large number of tax paradoxes[113] – actions which firms could take which would reduce the total tax bill (corporate plus individual), though there remains some dispute about the extent to which such paradoxes are due to irrationality on the part of investors or non-value maximizing behavior on the part of managers.)

Organization design

So far, we have discussed two of the three pillars of the modern theory of the firm: corporate finance and corporate governance. The third is organizational design. In a world with perfect information, organizational design too is of little moment. In practice, it is of central concern to businesses. We have already extensively discussed the issue of incentives, how, on the one hand, information imperfections limit the extent of efficient decentralizability and how, on the other, organizational design – by having alternative units perform comparable tasks – can enable a firm to glean information on the basis of which better incentive systems can be based. (Nalebuff and Stiglitz [1983a, b]).

But there is another important aspect of organization design. Even if individuals are well intentioned, with limited information, mistakes get made. To err is human. Raj Sah and I, in a series of papers [1985, 1986, 1988a, 1988b, 1991] explored the consequences of alternative organizational design and decision making structures for organizational mistakes, for instance, where good projects get rejected or bad projects get accepted. We suggested that in a variety of circumstances, especially when there is a scarcity of good projects, decentralized polyarchical organizational structures have distinct advantages.[114]

Macro-economics

The central macro-economic issue is that of unemployment. The models I described earlier explained why there could exist unemployment *in equilibrium.* But much of macro-economics is concerned with *dynamics,* with *fluctuations,* with explaining why sometimes the economy, rather than absorbing shocks, seems to amplify them, and why their effects often persist. In joint work with Bruce Greenwald and Andy Weiss, we have shown how the theories of asymmetric information can help provide explanations of these macro-economic phenomena. The imperfections of capital markets – the phenomena of

[113] See, e.g. Stiglitz [1973b, 1982d].

[114] In addition, see Sah [1991]. These papers are just beginning to spawn a body of research. See, for instance, Bhidé [2001], Viser [1998] and Christensen and Knudsen [2002].

credit and equity rationing which arise because of information asymmetries – are key. They lead to risk averse behavior of firms and to households and firms being affected by cash flow constraints.

Standard interpretations of Keynesian economics emphasized the importance of wage and price rigidities, but without a convincing explanation of those rigidities. For instance, some theories had shown stressed the importance of costs of adjustment of prices[115], but what was at issue was why markets seemed to adjust quantities rather than prices, and the relative costs of adjustment of quantities seemed greater than those of prices. The Greenwald-Stiglitz theory of adjustment [1989b] provided an explanation based on capital market[116] imperfections arising from information imperfections: it argued that, at least for commodities for which inventory costs were reasonably low, the risks arising from informational imperfections were greater for price and wage adjustments than from quantity adjustments. Risk averse firms would make smaller adjustments where to variables, the consequences of which were more uncertain.

But even though wages and prices were not perfectly flexible, neither were they perfectly rigid, and indeed in the Great Depression, they fell by a considerable amount. There had been large fluctuations in earlier periods, and in other countries, in which there had been a high degree of wage and price flexibility. Greenwald and I [1987a, 1987b, 1988b, 1988c, 1988d, 1988e, 1989b, 1990b, 1993a, 1993b, 1995] argued that it was other market failures, in particular, the imperfections of capital markets and the incomplete contracting which provided part of the explanation of key observed macro-economic phenomena. In debt contracts, tipically not indexed for changes in prices, whenever prices fell below the level expected (or in variable interest rate contracts, when real interest rates rose above the level expected) there were transfers from debtors to creditors. In these circumstances, excessive downward price flexibility (not just price rigidities) could give rise to problems [117]. These (and other) redistributive changes had large real effects, and could not be insured against because of imperfections in capital markets. Large shocks could lead to bankruptcy, and with bankruptcy (especially when it results in firm liquidation) there was a loss of organizational and informational capi-

[115] Mankiw [1985], Akerlof and Yellen [1985].

[116] Our theories did not provide a complete explanation for such incomplete contracting. While part of the explanation may lie in the lack of observability (verifiability) of the relevant variables on which contracts should be contingent, still it seems that there should be more indexing than is observed. Theories of asymmetric information did, however, provide part of the explanation for why inefficient contractual arrangements might persist. In a complex economy, if one party proposes a change to a standard contract, the other party might reasonably infer that the alteration benefits the party proposing the change; in a world which is close to zero sum, the gains for that party are at the expense of the other, and so he will be reluctant to concur with the change, unless he can be persuaded that there is scope for a Pareto improvement. Because of limitations on information (knowledge), this may be hard to do. See Stiglitz [1992c].

[117] The importance of these phenomena had been emphasized earlier by Irving Fisher [1933]. Stiglitz [1999d] emphasizes the consequences of *differences* in the speeds of adjustments of different prices.

tal.[118] Even if such large changes could be forestalled, until there was a resolution, the firm's access to credit would be impaired, and for good reason; moreover, without "clear owners" those in control would in general not have incentives to maximize the firm's value.

Even when the shocks were large enough to lead to bankruptcy, they had impacts on firms' ability and willingness to take risks. Since all production is risky, shocks affect aggregate supply, as well as the demand for investment. Because firm net worth would only be restored over time, the effects of a shock persisted. By the same token, there were hysteresis effects associated with policy: an increase in interest rates which depleted firm net worth had impacts even after the interest rates were reduced. If firms were credit rationed, then reductions in liquidity could have particularly marked effects.[119] Every aspect of macro-economic behavior was affected: the theories helped explain, for instance, the seemingly anomalous behavior of inventories_(rather than using inventories to smooth production, which would result in countercyclical changes in inventories, inventories moved pro-cyclically, because of the importance of cash constraints, leading to a high shadow price of money, in recessions) and pricing with the "shadow price" of capital being high in a recession, firms did not invest as much in acquiring new customers and were less concerned about losing workers, so that mark-ups increased, so that real product wages could fall, even though the marginal productivity of labor was rising.

In short, our analysis emphasized the supply side effects of shocks, the interrelationships between supply and demand side effects, and the importance of *finance* in propagating fluctuations.

Theory of money[120]

A particularly important aspect of our reformulation of macro-economics focused on monetary economics. Traditionally, it was postulated that the interest rate was set to equate the demand and supply for money, with money being largely required for transactions purposes, and the with interest rate representing the opportunity cost of money. In modern economies, however, credit, not money, is required (and used) for most transactions, and most transactions are simply exchanges of assets, and therefore not directly related to GDP. Moreover, today, most money is interest bearing, with the difference between the interest rate paid, say on a money market account and T bill rates having little to do with monetary policy, and related solely to transactions costs. What is important is the availability of credit (and the terms at which it is available); this in turn is related to the certification of credit worthiness by banks and other institutions. In short, *information* is at the heart of

[118] In traditional economic theories bankruptcy played little role, partly because control (who made decisions) did not matter, and so the change in control that was consequent to bankruptcy was of little moment, partly because with perfect information, there would be little reason for lenders to lend to someone, rather than extending funds through equity (especially if there were significant probabilities of, and costs to, bankruptcy). For an insightful discussion about control rights see Hart [1995].

[119] For discussions of credit rationing and macro-economic activity, see Stiglitz and Weiss [1992].

[120] The ideas set forth in this section are developed at greater length in Greenwald and Stiglitz [1990b, 1991, 1999].

monetary economics. But banks are like other risk averse firms: their ability and willingness to bear the risks associated with making loans depends on their net worth.[121] Because of equity rationing, shocks to their net worth cannot be instantaneously undone, and the theory thus explains why such shocks can have large adverse macro-economic consequences. The theory shows how not only traditional monetary instruments (like reserve requirements) but regulatory instruments (like risk adjusted capital adequacy requirements) can be used to affect the supply of credit, interest rates charged, and the bank's risk portfolio. The analysis also showed how excessive reliance on capital adequacy requirements could be counterproductive.[122]

The theory has important policy implications. It provides a new basis for a "liquidity trap," explaining why in severe economic downturns, monetary policy may be relatively ineffective. It explains some of the recent policy failures, both in the inability of the Fed to forestall the 1991 recession and the failures of the IMF in East Asia in 1997. It shifts emphasis from looking at the Fed Funds rate, or the money supply, to variables of more direct relevance to economic activity, the level of credit,[123] and the interest rates charged to firms (and it explains the movement in the spread between that rate and the Federal Funds rate). The theory predicts that there is scope for monetary policy even in the presence of dollarization.[124]

We also analyzed the importance of credit interlinkages. Many firms receive credit from other firms, at the same time that they provide credit to still others (violating Polonius' injunction "neither a lender nor a borrower be" by being both.) The disperse nature of information in the economy provides an explanation of this phenomena, which has important consequences. As a result of these general interlinkages (in some ways, every bit as important as the commodity interlinkages stressed in standard general equilibrium analysis) a shock to one firm gets transmitted to others, and when there is a large enough shock, there can be a cascade of bankruptcies.

Growth[125] and development[126]

While most of the macro-economic analysis focused on exploring the implications of imperfections of credit markets arising out of information prob-

[121] The special nature of information also helps explain the link between the acquisition and processing of information and the provision of funds. If information were like any other good, "information" firms could sell their information to providers of funds, so that shocks which adversely affect the net worth of the information processors would have minimal effects on credit supply. While there is some sale of information, in most lending markets, such information constitutes only a small part of the information that affects lending decisions.

[122] See also Hellman, Murdoch, and Stiglitz [2000].

[123] There is now a large literature arguing that these are the crucial variables of concern. For an early discussion, see Blinder and Stiglitz [1983].

[124] See Stiglitz [2001d].

[125] This section is based in part on Greenwald, Kohn, and Stiglitz [1990] and Stiglitz [1992e, 1994a, 1994b].

[126] This section is based on Stiglitz [1986a, 1987d, 1988a, 1988e, 1989, 1990b, 1993b, 1995b, 1996a, 1997a, 1997b, 1998a, 1999b, 2001a, b], Hoff and Stiglitz [1997, 2000], Stern and Stiglitz [1997], and Stiglitz and Yusuf [2000] in addition to the work on the theory of rural organization (with Braverman and Hoff cited earlier).

lems for cyclical variations, another strand of our research program focused on growth. The importance of capital markets for growth had long been recognized; without capital markets firms have to rely on retained earnings. But how firms raise capital is important for their growth. In particular, "equity rationing" – especially important in developing countries, where informational problems are even greater – impedes firms' willingness to invest and undertake risks, and thus slows down growth. Changes in economic policy which enable firms to bear more risk (e.g. by reducing the size of macro-economic fluctuations, or which enhance firms' equity base, by suppressing interest rates, which result in firm's having larger profits) enhance economic growth. Conversely, policies, such as associated with IMF interventions, in which interest rates are raised to very high levels, discourage the use of debt, forcing firms to rely more heavily on retained earnings.

The most challenging problems for growth lie in economic development. Typically, market failures are more prevalent in less developed countries, and these market failures are often associated with information problems – the very problems that inspired much of the research described in this paper. While these perspectives help explain the failures of policies based on *assuming* perfect or well functioning markets, they also direct attention to policies which might remedy or reduce the consequences of informational imperfections.[127]

Research

One of the most important determinants of the pace of growth is, for developed countries, the investment in research, and for less developed countries, efforts at closing the knowledge gap between themselves and more developed countries. Knowledge is, of course, a particular *form* of information, and many of the issues that are central to the economics of information are also key to understanding research – such as the problems of appropriability, the fixed costs associated with investments in research, which give rise to imperfections in competition, and the public good nature of information. It was thus natural that I turned to explore the implications in a series of papers that looked at both industry equilibrium and the consequences for economic growth.[128] While it is not possible to summarize briefly the results, one conclusion does stand out: that market economies in which research and innovation play an important role are not well described by the standard competitive model, and that the market equilibrium, without government intervention, is not in general efficient.

[127] See, in particular, the discussion in the World Bank [1999].

[128] There were, of course, several precursors to what has come to be called endogenous growth theory. See in particular, the collection of essays in Shell [1967], and Atkinson and Stiglitz [1969]. For later work, see, in particular, Dasgupta and Stiglitz [1980a, 1980b, 1981, 1988], Dasgupta, Gilbert, and Stiglitz, [1982], Stiglitz, [1987e, 1990a].

POLICY FRAMEWORKS

The fact that when there are asymmetries of information, markets are not, in general, constrained Pareto efficient implies there is a potentially important role for government. The new paradigm has important implications for policy, going well beyond addressing how to prevent the creation of and overcome asymmetries of information. As we have seen, asymmetries of information give rise to a host of other market failures – such as missing markets, and especially capital market imperfections, leading to firms that are risk averse and cash constrained – and policy has to deal with these indirect consequences as well. An analysis, for instance, of the incidence of taxation which is predicated on perfectly competitive markets with perfectly informed consumers and risk neutral firms, is likely to go astray.

But beyond this, the new information paradigm helps us to think about policy from a new perspective, one which recognizes the pervasiveness of imperfections of information.

Pareto efficient taxation[129]

Information asymmetries, of course, arise among all participants in society – including between citizens and their government. In the final section of this paper, I wish to explore one side: the difficulties citizens have of controlling their government. Here, I want to briefly note the other side: the problems posed to government in the conduct of its "business" that arise from information asymmetries, in three key areas, taxation, regulation, and production.

One of the functions of government is to redistribute income; even if it did not wish to redistribute actively, it has to raise revenues to finance public goods, and there is a concern that the revenue be raised in an equitable manner, e.g. that those who are more able to contribute (or who benefit more) do so. But government has a problem of identifying these individuals. Just as those who a monopolist would like to charge more do not readily disclose that they might be willing to pay more for the product, and just as those who are less able, less likely to pay back a loan, or more likely to have an accident do not readily disclose that information to those with whom they deal, so too in the public sector. And the self-selection mechanisms for information revelation that Rothschild and I had explored in our competitive insurance model or that I had explored in my paper on discriminating monopoly can be used here. (The problem of the government, maximizing social "profit" (welfare) subject to the information constraints, is closely analogous to that of the monopolist, maximizing private profit subject to information constraints. This is why Mirrlees' [1971] paper on optimal taxation, though not couched in information-theoretic terms, was an important precursor to the work described here.)

The critical question for the design of a tax system thus becomes *what is observable.* In older theories, in which information was perfect, lump sum taxes

[129] The discussion of this section draws upon Atkinson and Stiglitz [1976], Stiglitz [1982e, 1987f], and Mirrlees [1975a], and Brito *et al.* [1990, 1991, 1995].

and redistributions made sense. If ability is not directly observable, the government had to rely on other observables – like income – to make inferences; but, as in all such models, market participants, as they recognize that inferences are being made, alter their behavior. In Mirrlees [1971] only income was observable. But in different circumstances, either more or less information might be available. It might be possible to observe hours worked, in which case wages would be observable. It might be possible to observe the quantity of each good purchased by *any particular individual* or it might be possible to observe only the aggregate quantity of goods produced.

For each information structure, there is a *Pareto efficient tax structure*, that is, a tax structure such that no one (group) can be made better off without making some other group worse off. The choice among such tax structures depends on the social welfare function (attitudes towards inequality.)[130] While this is not the occasion to provide a complete description of the results, two are worth noting: What had been thought of as optimal commodity tax structures (Ramsey [1927]) were shown to be part of a Pareto efficient tax system only under highly restricted conditions, e.g. that there was no income tax (see Sah and Stiglitz [1992]). On the other hand, it was shown that in a central benchmark case, it was not optimal to tax interest income.

Theory of regulation and privatization

The government faced the same problem posed by information asymmetries in regulation that it faced in taxation. Over the past quarter century, a huge literature has developed making use of self-selection mechanisms,[131] allowing far better and more effective systems of regulation than had existed in the past.[132]

In the 1980s, there was a strong movement towards privatizing state enterprises, even in areas in which there was a natural monopoly, in which case government ownership would be replaced with government regulation. While it was apparent that there were frequently problems with government ownership, the theories of imperfect information also made it clear that even the best designed regulatory systems would work imperfectly. This raised naturally the question of under what circumstances could we be sure that privatization would enhance economic welfare. As Herbert Simon [1991] the 1978 Nobel Laureate had earlier emphasized, both public and private sectors

[130] In that sense, Mirrlees' work confounded the two stages of the analysis. He described the point along the Pareto frontier that would be chosen by a government with a utilitarian social welfare function. Some of the critical properties, e.g. the zero marginal tax rate at the top, were, however, characteristics of *any* Pareto efficient tax structure, though that particular property was not *robust*, that is, it depended strongly on his assumption that relative wages between individuals of different abilities were fixed. See Stiglitz [2002] and the papers cited there.

[131] See, e.g. Laffont and Tirole [1993] and Sappington and Stiglitz [1987a].

[132] A sector in which government regulation was of particular importance is banking. We noted earlier that information problems are at the heart of financial markets, and it is thus not surprising that market failures be more pervasive, and the role of the government more important. See, e.g. Stiglitz [1993a]. Regulatory design needs to take into account explicitly the limitations in information. See, e.g. Stiglitz [2001c], Honahan and Stiglitz [2001], Greenwald and Stiglitz [1999] and Hellman, Murdock and Stiglitz [2000].

face information and incentive problems; there was no compelling theoretical argument for why large private organizations would solve these incentive problems better. In work with David Sappington [1987b] we showed that the conditions under which privatization would necessarily be welfare enhancing were extremely restrictive, and closely akin to those under which competitive markets would yield Pareto efficient outcomes. (See Stiglitz [1993d, 1994c] for an elaboration and applications.)

KEY POLICY DEBATES: APPLYING BASIC IDEAS

The perspectives provided by the new information paradigm not only shaped theoretical approaches to policy, but in innumerable concrete issues also led to markedly different policy stances from those wedded to the old paradigm.

Washington consensus

Perhaps most noted were the controversies concerning development strategies, where the Washington consensus policies, based on market fundamentalism – the simplistic view of competitive markets with perfect information, inappropriate even for developed countries, but particularly inappropriate for developing countries – had prevailed since the early 1980s within the international economic institutions. Elsewhere, I have documented the failures of these policies in development[133], as well as in managing the transition from Communism to a market economy[134] and in managing crises. Ideas matter, and it is not surprising that policies based on models that depart as far from reality as those underlying the Washington Consensus so often led to failure.

Bankruptcy, aggregate supply, and the East Asia crisis

This point was brought home perhaps most forcefully by the management of the East Asia crisis which began in Thailand on July 2, 1997. While I have written extensively on the many dimensions of the failed responses[135], here I want to note the close link between these failures and the theories put forward here. Our work had emphasized the importance of maintaining the credit supply and the risks of (especially poorly managed) bankruptcy. Poorly designed policies could lead to an unnecessarily large reduction in credit availability and unnecessary large increases in bankruptcy, both leading to large adverse effects on aggregate supply, exacerbating the economic downturn. But this is precisely what the IMF did: by raising interest rates to extremely high levels in countries where firms were already highly leveraged, it forced massive bankruptcy, and the economies were thus plunged into deep recession and depression; capital was not attracted to the country, but rather fled. Thus, the policies even failed in their stated purpose, which was to stabilize the exchange rate. There were strong hysteresis effects associated with these

[133] See, for instance, Stiglitz [1998a].
[134] See, for instance, Stiglitz [2001e, 2000a], Hussein, Stern, and Stiglitz[2000].
[135] See, in particular, Furman and Stiglitz [1998] and Stiglitz [1999e].

policies: when the interest rates were subsequently lowered, the firms that had been forced into bankruptcy did not become unbankrupt, and the firms that had seen their net worth depleted did not see an immediate restoration. There were alternative policies available, debt standstills followed by corporate financial restructurings, which, while they might not have avoided a downturn, would have resulted in the downturns being shallower and shorter. Malaysia, whose economic policies conformed much more closely to those that our theories would have suggested, not only recovered more quickly, but was left with less of a legacy of debt to impair its future growth, than did neighboring Thailand, which conformed more closely to the IMF's recommendation.

Corporate governance, open capital markets, and the transition to a market economy
The transition from communism to a market economy represents one of the most important economic experiments of all time, and the failure (so far) in Russia, and the successes in China, shed considerable light on many of the issues which I have been discussing. The full dimension of Russia's failure is hard to fathom. Communism, with its central planning (requiring more information gathering, processing, and dissemination capacity than could be managed with *any* technology), its lack of incentives, and its system rife with distortions, was viewed as highly inefficient. The movement to a market, it was assumed, would bring enormous increases in incomes. Instead, incomes plummeted, a decline confirmed not only by GDP statistics and household surveys, but also by social indicators. The numbers in poverty soared, from 2% to upwards of 50% (depending on the measure used.) While there were many dimensions to these failures, one stands out: the privatization strategy, which paid little attention to the issues of corporate governance which we stressed earlier. Empirical work confirms[136] that countries that privatized rapidly but lacked "good" corporate governance did not grow more rapidly. As Sappington and my paper warned, privatization might not lead to an increase in social welfare, rather than providing a basis for wealth creation, it led to asset stripping and wealth destruction[137].

BEYOND INFORMATION ECONOMICS

We have seen how the competitive paradigm that dominated economic thinking for two centuries, not only was not robust, not only did not explain key economic phenomena, but also led to misguided policy prescriptions.

My research over the past thirty years has focused, however, on only one aspect of my dissatisfaction with that paradigm. It is not easy to change views of the world, and it seemed to me the most effective way of attacking the paradigm was to keep within the standard framework as much as possible. I only

[136] See Stiglitz [2001e].
[137] For fuller discussions of these issues, see Hussein, Stern, and Stiglitz [2000] and Stiglitz [2000a].

varied one assumption – the assumption concerning perfect information – and in ways which seemed highly plausible. Early on, some objected that opening up the model to the possibilities of imperfect information was opening up a Pandora's box: there were so many ways in which information could be imperfect. But while there might be only one way in which information was perfect, surely it was better to understand the consequences of *different* forms of information imperfections that might exist in the real world. If the competitive model was not robust against all these different forms of information imperfections which existed in the world, surely it was not a model upon which we could rely. As time evolved, it became clear that imperfect information paradigm itself was highly robust; there were some quite general principles, while the workings out of the models in detail in different situations might well differ. We succeeded in showing not only that the standard theory was not robust – changing only one assumption in ways which were totally plausible had drastic consequences, but also that an alternative robust paradigm with great explanatory power could be constructed.

There were other deficiencies in the theory, some of which were closely connected. The standard theory assumed that technology and preferences were fixed. But changes in technology, R & D, are at the heart of capitalism. The new information economics – extended to incorporate changes in knowledge – at last began to address systematically these foundations of a market economy.

As I thought about the problems of development, I similarly became increasingly convinced of the inappropriateness of the assumption of fixed preferences.[138] I have criticized the Washington consensus development strategies partly on the grounds that they perceived of development as nothing more than increasing the stock of capital and reducing economic distortions. But development represents a far more fundamental transformation of society, including a change in "preferences" and attitudes, an acceptance of change and an abandonment of many traditional ways of thinking.[139]

Especially during the last few years, as I have become more deeply immersed in the problems of development, I have felt more strongly these and some of the other deficiencies of the standard paradigm, for instance, its attempt to separate out economics from broader social concerns. A major impediment to development in Africa has been the civil strife which has been endemic there, itself in part a consequence of the economic circumstances[140].

These perspectives have strong policy implications. For instance, some policies are more conducive to effecting a development transformation. Many of the policies of the IMF – including the manner in which in interacted with governments, basing loans on conditionality – were counterproductive. A fundamental change in development strategy occurred at the World Bank in the

[138] In addition, much of recent economic theory has assumed that *beliefs* are, in some sense, rational. As noted earlier, there are many aspects of economic behavior that seem hard to reconcile with this hypothesis.

[139] See, e.g. Stiglitz [1995b, 1998a].

[140] See Collier and Gunning [1999], Collier [1998] and Collier [2000].

years I was there, one which embraced this more comprehensive approach to development. By contrast, policies which have ignored social consequences have frequently been disastrous. The IMF policies in Indonesia, including the elimination of food and fuel subsidies for the very poor, just as the country was plunging into depression, with wages plummeting and unemployment soaring, predictably led to riots; the economic consequences are still being felt.

In some ways, as I pursued perspectives, I was returning to a theme I had raised thirty years ago, during my work on the efficiency wage theory in Kenya[141], where I had suggested how psychological factors – morale, reflecting a sense that one is receiving a fair wage – could affect efforts, an alternative, and in some cases more persuasive reason for the efficiency wage theory, that has subsequently been developed further by Akerlof and Yellen [1986]. It is curious how economists have almost studiously ignored factors, which are not only the center of day to day life, but even of business school education. Surely, if markets were efficient, such attention would not be given to such matters, to issues of corporate culture and extrinsic rewards, unless they were of some considerable importance.[142] And if such issues are of importance within a firm, they are equally important within a society.

Finally, I have become convinced that the dynamics of change may not be well described by equilibrium models that have long been at the center of economic analysis. Information economics has alerted us to the fact that history matters; there are important hysteresis effects. Random events – the black plague – have consequences that are irreversible. Dynamics may be better described by evolutionary processes and models, than by equilibrium processes. And while it may be difficult to describe fully these evolutionary processes, this much is already clear: there is no reason to believe that they are, in any general sense, "optimal."[143]

Many of the same themes that emerged from our simpler work in information economics applied here. For instance, repeatedly, in the information theoretic models discussed above we showed that multiple equilibria (some of which Pareto dominated others) could easily arise. So too here (Stiglitz, [1995b]). This in turn has several important consequences, beyond the observation already made that history matters. First, it means that one cannot simply predict where the economy will be by knowing preferences and technology (and initial endowments). There can a high level of indeterminacy. Secondly, as in Darwinian ecological models, the major determinant of one's environment is the behavior of others, and their behavior may in turn depend on their beliefs about others' behavior. (Hoff and Stiglitz [2000]). As Darwin noted after his visit to the Galapagos islands:

[141] Stiglitz [1973a, 1974d].

[142] For a discussion with references to the literature, see Stiglitz [2000d].

[143] There is a large and growing literature on evolutionary economics. See, for instance, Maynard Smith and Price [1973], Nelson and Winter [1982, 1990], Weibull [1996], Mailath [1992], Aoki and Feldman [1999], Stiglitz [1975b, 1992i] and Sah and Stiglitz [1991]. Some of this work emphasized the importance of capital constraints for evolutionary processes.

> The plants and animals of the Galapagos differ radically among islands that have the same geological nature, the same height, climate, etc... This long appeared to me a great difficulty, but it arises in chief part from the deeply seated error of considering the physical conditions of a country as the most important for its inhabitants; whereas it cannot, I think he disputed that the nature of the other inhabitants, with which each has to compete, is at least as important, and generally a far more important element of success. (Darwin [1959] 1993: 540)

Thirdly, government intervention can sometimes move the economy from one equilibrium to another; and having done that, continued intervention might not be required.

THE POLITICAL ECONOMY OF INFORMATION

Information imperfections, and asymmetries of information, are pervasive in every aspect of life and society. Here, I want to talk about three of the ways in which information affects political processes.

First, we have already noted the distributive consequences of information disclosures. Not surprisingly, then, the "information rules of the game," both for the economy and for political processes, can become a subject of intense political debate. The United States and the IMF argued strongly that lack of transparency was at the root of the 1997 financial crisis, and said that the East Asian countries had to become more transparent. The recognition that quantitative data concerning capital flows (outstanding loans) by the IMF and the US Treasury could have been taken as a concession of the inappropriateness of the competitive paradigm (in which *prices* convey all the relevant information); but the more appropriate way of viewing the debate was *political*, a point which became clear when it was noted that partial disclosures could be of only limited value, and could possibly be counterproductive, as capital would be induced to move through channels involving less disclosure, channels like off shore banking centers which were also less well regulated. When demands for transparency thus went beyond East Asia to Western hedge funds and off shore banking centers, suddenly the advocates of more transparency became less enthralled, and began praising the advantages of partial secrecy in enhancing incentives to gather information. The United States and US Treasury then opposed the OECD initiative to combat money laundering through greater transparency of off shore banking centers – these institutions served particular *political and economic* interests – until it became clear that terrorists might be using them to help finance their operations; at that point, the balance of American interests changed, and the US Treasury changed its position.

Political processes inevitably entail asymmetries of information: our political leaders are *supposed* to know more about threats to defense, about our economic situation, etc., than ordinary citizens. There has been a delegation of responsibility for day-to-day decision making, just as there is within a firm.

The problem is to provide incentives for those so entrusted to act on behalf of those who they are supposed to be serving – the standard principle agent problem. Democracy – contestability in political processes – provides a check on abuses of the powers that come from delegation just as it does in economic processes; but just as we recognize that the take-over mechanism provides an imperfect check, so too we should recognize that the electoral process provides an imperfect check. Just as we recognize that current management has an incentive to *increase* asymmetries of information in order to enhance its market power, increase its discretion, so to in public life. And just as we recognize that disclosure requirements – greater transparency – and specific rules of the game (e.g. related to corporate governance) can affect the effectiveness of the take-over mechanism and the overall quality of corporate governance, so too the same factors can affect political contestabilty and the quality of public governance.

In the context of political processes, where "exit" options are limited, one needs to be particularly concerned about abuses. If a firm is mismanaged – if the managers attempt to enrich themselves at the expense of shareholders and customers and entrench themselves against competition, the damage is limited: customers at least can switch. But in political processes, those who see the quality of public services deteriorate cannot do so as easily. If all individuals were as mean spirited and selfish as economists have traditionally modeled them, matters would indeed be bleak: as I have put it elsewhere, ensuring the public good (public management) is itself a public good. But there is a wealth of evidence that the economists' traditional model of the individual is too narrow – and that indeed intrinsic rewards, e.g. of public service, can be even more effective than extrinsic rewards, e.g. monetary compensation (which is not to say that compensation is not of some importance). This public spiritedness (even if blended with a modicum of self-interest) is manifested in a variety of civil society organizations, through which *voluntarily* individuals work *collectively* to advance their perception of the collective interests.

There are strong forces on the part of those in government to reduce transparency. More transparency reduces their scope for action – it not only exposes mistakes, but also corruption (as the expression goes, sunshine is the strongest antiseptic). Government officials may try to enhance their power, by trying to advance specious arguments for secrecy[144], and then saying, in effect, to justify their otherwise inexplicable or self-serving behavior, "trust me... if you only knew what I knew."

There is a further rationale for secrecy: secrecy is an artificially created scarcity of information, and like most artificially created scarcities, it gives rise to rents, rents which in some countries are appropriated through outright corruption (selling information), but in others are part of a "gift exchange" in which reporters not only provide puff pieces praising the government offi-

[144] Senator Patrick Moynihan, in his powerful book Moynihan [1998], shows how secrecy was abused during the Cold War, in ways which led to unnecessarily large military expenditures.

cial who has given the reporter privileged access to information, particularly in ways which are designed to enhance the officials influence and power, but distort news coverage. I was in the unfortunate position of watching closely this process work, and work quite effectively. Without unbiased information, the effectiveness of the check that can be provided by the citizenry is limited; without good information, the contestability of the political processes can be undermined.

One of the lessons of the economics of information is that these problems cannot be fully resolved, but there are laws and institutions which can decidedly improve matters. Right-to-know laws, demanding transparency, have been part of governance in Sweden for two hundred years; they have become an important if imperfect check on government abuses in the United States over the past quarter century. In the last five years, there has become a growing international movement, with some countries, such as Thailand, going so far as to include them in their new Constitution. Regrettably, these principles have yet to be endorsed by the international economic institutions.

CONCLUDING REMARKS

In this talk I have traced the replacement of one paradigm with another. The deficiencies in the neoclassical paradigm – both the predictions which seemed counter to what was observed, some so glaring that one hardly needed refined econometric testing, and the phenomena that were left unexplained – made it inevitable that it was simply a matter of time before it became challenged. One might ask, how can we explain the persistence of the paradigm for so long? Partly, it must be because, in spite of its deficiencies, it did provide insights into many economic phenomena. There are some markets in which the phenomena which we have discussed are not important – the market for wheat or corn – though even here, pervasive government interventions make the reining competitive paradigm of limited relevance. The underlying forces of demand and supply are still important, though in the new paradigm, they become only part of the analysis; they are not the whole analysis. But one cannot ignore the possibility that the survival of the paradigm was partly because the belief in that paradigm, and the policy prescriptions, has served certain interests.

As a social scientist, I have tried to follow the analysis, wherever it might lead. As any researcher, we know that our ideas can be used or abused – or ignored. Understanding the complex forces that shape our economy is of value in its own right; there is an innate curiosity about how this system works. But "All the world's a stage, and all the men and women merely players" Shakespeare [1599]. Each of us in our own way, if only as voters, is actor in this grand drama. And what we do is affected by our perceptions of how this complex system works.

I entered economics with the hope that it might enable me to do something about unemployment, poverty, and discrimination. As an economic researcher, I have been lucky enough to hit upon some ideas that I think do enhance our understanding of these phenomena. As an educator, I have been lucky enough to have had the opportunity to reduce some of the asymmetries of information, especially concerning what the new information paradigm and other developments in modern economic science have to say about these phenomena, and to have had some first rate students who themselves have pushed the research agenda forward.

As an individual, I have however not been content just to let others translate these ideas into practice. I have had the good fortune to be able to do so myself, as a public servant both in the American government and at the World Bank. We have the good fortune to live in democracies, in which individuals can fight for their perception of what a better world might be like. We as academics have the good fortune to be further protected by our academic freedom. With freedom comes responsibility: the responsibility to use that freedom to do what we can to ensure that the world of the future be one in which there is not only greater economic prosperity, but also more social justice.

REFERENCES

Adams, W. J. and J. L. Yellen "Commodity Bundling and the Burden of Monopoly", *Quarterly Journal of Economics* 90(3), August 1976: pp. 475–498.

Akerlof, G. A., "The Market for 'Lemons': Quality Uncertainty and the Market Mechanism," *Quarterly Journal of Economics* 84, 1970: pp. 488–500.

–, "The Economics of Caste and of the Rat Race and Other Woeful Tales", *Quarterly Journal of Economics* 90, November 1976: pp. 488–500.

Akerlof, G. A. and J. L. Yellen, "A Near-Rational Model of the Business Cycle with Wage and Price Inertia", *Quarterly Journal of Economics* 100, Supplement, 1985: pp. 823–38.

Akerlof, G. A. and J. L. Yellen (eds.), *Efficiency wages model of the Labor Market,* New York: Cambridge University Press, 1986.

Allen, F., "On the Fixed Nature of Sharecropping Contracts", *The Economic Journal* 95, March 1985: pp. 30–48.

Feldman, M. W., and Aoki, K. "Theoretical aspects of the evolution of human social behavior", in *World Social Science Report,* A. Kazancigil and D. Makinson (eds.), 1999: pp. 328–340.

Arnott, R., B. Greenwald, and J. E. Stiglitz, "Information and Economic Efficiency", *Information Economics and Policy* 6(1), March 1994: pp. 77–88. (Paper prepared for the New Orleans Meeting of the American Economic Association, 1992).

Arnott, R., A. Hosios, and J. E. Stiglitz, "Implicit Contracts, Labor Mobility and Unemployment", *American Economic Review* 78(5), December 1988, pp. 1046–1066.

Arnott, R. and J. E. Stiglitz, "Labor Turnover, Wage Structure & Moral Hazard: The Inefficiency of Competitive Markets", *Journal of Labor Economics* 3(4), October 1985: pp. 434–462.

–, "Moral Hazard and Optimal Commodity Taxation", *Journal of Public Economics* 29, 1986: pp. 1–24.

–, "Equilibrium in Competitive Insurance Markets with Moral Hazard", Princeton University Discussion Paper 4, 1987. (Also NBER Working Paper 3588, 1991.).

–, "Randomization with Asymmetric Information", *Rand Journal of Economics* 19(3), Autumn 1988a: pp. 344–362.

–, "The Basic Analytics of Moral Hazard", *Scandinavian Journal of Economics* 90(3), 1988b: pp. 383–413.

–, "The Welfare Economics of Moral Hazard", in *Risk Information and Insurance: Essays in the*

Memory of Karl H. Borch, H. Louberge (ed.), Norwell: Kluwer Academic Publishers, 1990: pp. 91–122.

–, "Moral Hazard and Non-Market Institutions: Dysfunctional Crowding Out or Peer Monitoring", *American Economic Review* 81(1), March 1991a: pp. 179–190.

–, "Price Equilibrium, Efficiency, and Decentralizability in Insurance Markets," NBER Working Paper 3642, 1991b.

Arrow, K. J., "Uncertainty and the Welfare Economics of Medical Care", *American Economic Review* 53(5), 1963: pp. 941–973.

–, "The Role of Securities in the Optimal Allocation of Risk-bearing", *The Review of Economic Studies* 31(2) April 1964: pp. 91–96.

–, *Aspects of the Theory of Risk-Bearing (Yrjo Jahnsson Lectures),* Helsinki, Finland: Yrjo Jahnssonin Saatio, 1965.

–, "Some Mathematical Models of Race in the Labor Market", in A.H. Pascal (ed.), *Racial Discrimination in Economic Life,* Lexington MA, Lexington Books, 1972: pp. 187–204.

–, "Higher Education as a Filter", *Journal of Public Economics* 3 (2), 1973, pp. 193–216.

–, "Limited Knowledge and Economic Analysis", *American Economic Review* 64(1), 1974: pp. 1–10.

–, "Risk Allocation and Information: Some Theoretical Development", *Geneva Papers on Risk and Insurance* 8, 1978.

Asquith, P. and D. Mullins, "Equity issues and offering dilution", *Journal of Financial Economics* 15, 1986: pp. 61–89.

Atkinson, A. B. and J. E. Stiglitz, "A New View of Technological Change", *Economic Journal* 79, September 1969, pp. 573–578.

–, "The Design of Tax Structure: Direct Versus Indirect Taxation", *Journal of Public Economics* 6, July-August 1976, pp. 55–75.

Azariadis, C. and J. E. Stiglitz, "Implicit Contracts and Fixed Price Equilibria", *Quarterly Journal of Economics* 98, Supplement, 1983: pp. 1–22.

Bator, F. M., "The Anatomy of Market Failure", *Quarterly Journal of Economics* 72(3), August 1958: pp. 351–379.

Baumol, W. J., *Business Behavior, Value and Growth,* New York: The MacMillan Co., 1959, (Revised Edition 1967).

Becker, G., *The Economics of Discrimination* (2nd Edition), University of Chicago Press, 1971.

Berle, A. A. and G. C. Means, *The Modern Corporation and Private Property,* New York: Harcourt Brace & World, 1932.

Bester, H., "Screening vs. Rationing in Credit Markets with Incomplete Information", *American Economic Review* 75, 1985, pp. 850–855.

Bernanke, B., "Credit in the Macro-economy", *Federal Reserve Bank of New York Quarterly Review* 18(1), Spring 1993: pp. 50–70.

Bernanke, B. and A. S. Blinder, "Credit, Money, and Aggregate Demand (in Is It Money or Credit, or Both, or Neither?)", *American Economic Review* 78(2), May 1988: pp. 435–439.

Bernanke, B. and M. Gertler, *"Agency Costs, Net Worth, and Business Fluctuations ", American Economic Review* 79(1), March 1989, pp. 14–31.

Bernanke, Ben and M. Gertler, *"Inside of Black Box- the Credit Channel of Monetary Policy Transmission," Journal of Economic Perspectives*, 9 (4), 1995: pp. 27–48.

Bhidé, A., "Taking Care: Ambiguity, Pooling and Error Control", Columbia Business School, Working Paper, November 2001.

Bils, M. and J. A. Kahn, "What Inventory Behavior Tells Us about Business Cycles", *American Economic Review* 90, June 2000: pp. 458–481.

Blanchard, O. J., F. Lopez-de-Silanes, and A. Schliefer, "What Do Firms Do with Cash Windfalls?", *Journal of Financial Economics* 36, 1994: pp. 337–360.

Blinder, A. S. and S. Fischer, "Inventories, Rational Expectations, and the Business Cycle", *Journal of Monetary Economics* 8, November 1981: pp. 277–304.

Blinder, A. S. and L. J. Maccini, "Taking Stock: A Critical Assessment of Recent Research on Inventories", *Journal of Economic Perspectives* 5(1), Winter 1991a: pp. 73–96.

Blinder, A., and J. E. Stiglitz, "Money, Credit Constraints and Economic Activity", *American Economic Review* 73(2), May 1983: pp. 297–302.
Blinder, A. S., "Can the Production Smoothing Model of Inventory Behavior Be Saved?", *Quarterly Journal of Economics* 101, August 1986: pp. 431–54.
Bowles, S. and H. Gintis, *Schooling in Capitalist America,* New York: Basic Books, 1976.
Braverman, A. and J. E. Stiglitz, "Sharecropping and the Interlinking of Agrarian Markets", *American Economic Review* 72(4), September 1982: pp. 695–715.
–, "Cost Sharing Arrangement Under Sharecropping: Moral Hazard, Incentive Flexibility and Risk", *Journal of Agricultural Economics* 68(3), August 1986a: pp. 642–652.
–, "Landlords, Tenants and Technological Innovations", *Journal of Development Economics* 23(2), October 1986b: pp. 313–332.
–, "Credit Rationing, Tenancy, Productivity and the Dynamics of Inequality" in *The Economic Theory of Agrarian Institutions,* Clarendon Press, Oxford, 1989: pp. 185–201.
Braverman, A., K. Hoff, and J. E. Stiglitz (eds.), *The Economics of Rural Organization: Theory, Practice, and Policy,* New York: Oxford University Press, 1993.
Brito, B., J.H. Hamilton, S.M. Slutsky and J. E. Stiglitz, "Pareto Efficient Tax Structures,", *Oxford Economic Papers* 42, 1990: pp. 61–77.
–, "Randomization in Optimal Income Tax Schedules", *Journal of Public Economics* 56(189), February 1995: p. 189–223.
–, "Dynamic Optimal Income Taxation With Government Commitment," *Journal of Public Economics* 44, 1991: pp. 15–35.
Calomiris, C.W. and R.G. Hubbard, "Firm Heterogeneity, Internal Finance, and Credit Rationing", *Economic Journal* 100, 1990: pp. 90–104.
Cappen, E., R. Clapp and W. Campbell, "Competitive Bidding in High Risk Situations", *Journal of Petroleum Technology* 23, 1971: pp 641–653.
Chamberlin, E., *"The Theory of Monopolistic Competition",* Harvard University Press, Cambridge, 1933.
Cheung, S., *The Theory of Share Tenancy* Chicago: University of Chicago Press, 1969.
Chuma, H., Y. Hayami, and Otsuka, K., "Land and Labor Contracts in Agrarian Economies: Theories and Facts", *Journal of Economic Literature* 30(4), December 1992: pp. 1965–2018.
Coase, R. H., "The Problem of Social Cost", *Journal of Law and Economics* 3, 1960: pp. 1 – 44.
Darwin C., *The Origin of Species by Means of Natural Selection,* Modern Library Edition, New York: Random House, 1993 (First Published 1859).
Collier, P. and J. W. Gunning, "Why has Africa Grown Slowly?" *Journal of Economic Perspectives,* 13(3) 1999: pp. 3–22.
Collier, P., "The Political Economy of Ethnicity", *Working Papers Series 98-8,* Centre for the Study of African Economies, University of Oxford, 1998.
–, "Economic Causes of Civil Conflict and Their Implications for Policy", in Chester, A. Crocker & Fen Osler Hampson with Pamela Aall (eds), *Managing Global Chaos,* Washington DC: US Institute of Peace, September 1986.
Christensen, M. and T. Knudsen, "The Architecture of Economic Organization: Toward a General Framework", Working Paper, University of Southern Denmark, January 2002.
Dasgupta, P. and Maskin, E., "The Existence of Equilibrium in Discontinuous Economic Games I: Theory", *Review of Economic Studies,* 53, 1986, pp. 1–26.
Dasgupta, P. and J. E. Stiglitz, "Industrial Structure and the Nature of Innovative Activity", *Economic Journal* 90, June 1980a: pp. 266–293.
–, "Uncertainty, Market Structure and the Speed of R&D", *Bell Journal of Economics* 11(1), Spring 1980b: pp.1–28, .
–, "Entry, Innovation, Exit: Toward a Dynamic Theory of Oligopolistic Industrial Structure", *European Economic Review* 15(2), Feb. 1981: pp. 137–158.
–, "Learning by Doing, Market Structure, and Industrial and Trade Policies", *Oxford Economic Papers* 40(2): 1988: pp. 246–268.
Dasgupta, P., R. Gilbert, and J. E. Stiglitz, "Invention and Innovation Under Alternative Market Structures: The Case of Natural Resources", *Review of Economic Studies* 49, 1982: pp. 567–582.

Diamond, P.A., "The Role of a Stock Market in a General Equilibrium Model with Technological Uncertainty", *American Economic Review* 57(4), September 1967: pp. 759–776.
–, "A model of price adjustment", *Journal of Economic Theory* 3, 1971: pp. 156–168.
Dixit, A., and J. E. Stiglitz, "Monopolistic Competition and Optimal Product Diversity", *American Economic Review* 67(3), June 1977: pp. 297–308.
Eaton, J., M. Gersovitz, and J. E. Stiglitz, "Pure Theory of Country Risk," *European Economic Review*, 30(3), June 1986, pp. 481–513.
Edlin, A. and J. E. Stiglitz, "Discouraging Rivals: Managerial Rent–Seeking and Economic Inefficiencies", *American Economic Review* 85(5), December 1995: pp. 1301–12.
Fama, E. F., "Efficient capital markets: a review and empirical work", *Journal of Finance* 25, 1970: pp. 383–417.
–, "Efficient capital markets: II", *Journal of Finance* 46(5), December 1991: pp. 1575 – 1617.
Farrell, J., "Information and the Coase Theorem", *Journal of Economic Perspectives* 1(2), Autumn 1987: pp. 113–129.
Fazzari, S.M., R.G. Hubbard and B.C. Petersen, "Financing constraints and corporate investment", *Brookings Papers on Economic Activity* 1, 1988: pp. 141–195.
Fields, G., "Private and Social Returns to Education to Labor Surplus Economies", *Eastern Africa Economic Review* 4 (1), June 1972: pp. 41–62.
Fisher, I., "The Debt Deflation Theory of Great Depressions." *Econometrica* 1(4), October 1933: pp: 337–357.
Fudenberg, D. and J. Tirole, *Game Theory*, Cambridge MA: MIT Press, 1991.
Furman, J. and J. E. Stiglitz, "Economic Crises: Evidence and Insights from East Asia", *Brookings Papers on Economic Activity* (2), 1998: pp. 1–114.
Gale, D., "Optimal Risk Sharing through Renegotiation of Simple Contracts", *Journal of Financial Intermediation* 1, 1991: pp. 283–306.
Gale, I. and J. E. Stiglitz, "The Informational Content of Initial Public Offerings", *Journal of Finance* 44(2), June 1989: pp. 469–478.
Greenwald, B., M. Kohn, and J. E. Stiglitz, "Financial Market Imperfections and Productivity Growth,", *Journal of Economic Behavior and Organization,* 13(3), June 1990: pp. 321–45.
Greenwald, B., J. E. Stiglitz, and A. Weiss, "Informational Imperfections in the Capital Markets and Macroeconomic Fluctuations," *American Economic Review* 74(2), May 1984: pp. 194–199.
Greenwald, B. and J. E. Stiglitz, "Externalities in Economies with Imperfect Information and Incomplete Markets," *Quarterly Journal of Economics* 101 (2), May 1986: pp. 229–264.
–, "Keynesian, New Keynesian and New Classical Economics," *Oxford Economic Papers* 39, March 1987a: pp. 119–133.
–, "Imperfect Information, Credit Markets and Unemployment", *European Economic Review* 31, 1987b: pp. 444–456.
–, "Pareto Inefficiency of Market Economies: Search and Efficiency Wage Models", *American Economic Review,* 78(2), May 1988a, pp. 351–355.
–, "Examining Alternative Macro-economic Theories," *Brookings Papers on Economic Activity,* No.1, 1988b, pp.207–270.
–, "Imperfect Information, Finance Constraints and Business Fluctuations," in *Finance Constraints, Expectations, and Macro-economics,* M. Kohn and S.C. Tsiang (eds.), Oxford: Oxford University Press, 1988c, pp. 103–140.
–, "Money, Imperfect Information and Economic Fluctuations," in *Finance Constraints, Expectations and Macroeconomics,* M. Kohn and S.C. Tsiang (eds.), Oxford: Oxford University Press, 1988d, pp.141–165.
–, "Information, Finance Constraints and Business Fluctuations," (Proceedings of Taipei) *Symposium on Monetary Theory,* Institute of Economics, Academia Sinica, 1988e, pp. 299–336.
–, "Impact of the Changing Tax Environment on Investments and Productivity", *The Journal of Accounting, Auditing and Finance,* 4(3), Summer 1989a, pp. 281–301.
–, "Toward a Theory of Rigidities," *American Economic Review,* 79(2), May 1989b, pp. 364–69.

–, "Asymmetric Information and the New Theory of the Firm: Financial Constraints and Risk Behavior", *American Economic Review,* 80(2), May 1990a, pp. 160–65. (NBER Working Paper No. 3359.)

–, "Macro-economic Models with Equity and Credit Rationing", In *Asymmetric Information, Corporate Finance, and Investment,* R. B. Hubbard (ed.), University of Chicago Press, 1990b, pp. 15–42.

–, "Toward a Reformulation of Monetary Theory: Competitive Banking", *Economic and Social Review* 23(1), October 1991, pp. 1–34.

–, "Information, Finance and Markets: The Architecture of Allocative Mechanisms," *Industrial and Corporate Change,* 1(1), 1992, pp. 37–63.

–, "Financial Market Imperfections and Business Cycles," *Quarterly Journal of Economics,* 108(1), February 1993a, pp. 77–114 .

–, "New and Old Keynesians," *Journal of Economic Perspectives,* 7(1) Winter 1993b, pp. 23–44.

–, "Labor Market Adjustments and the Persistence of Unemployment," *American Economic Review,* 85(2), May 1995, pp. 219–25.

–, *Towards a New Paradigm for Monetary Economics,* Mattioli lectures presented at Milan, November 1999, forthcoming Cambridge University Press.

Greenwald, B., *Adverse Selection in the Labor Market,* New York: Garland Press, 1979.

–, "Adverse Selection in the Labor Market", *Review of Economic Studies* 53(3), July 1986: pp. 325–347.

Grossman, S. and O. Hart, "Takeover Bids, the Free-Rider Problem, and the Theory of the Corporation", *Bell Journal of Economics* 11, 1980: pp. 42–64.

Grossman, S. and J. E. Stiglitz, "Information and Competitive Price Systems," *American Economic Review,* 66(2), May 1976, pp. 246–253.

–, "On Value Maximization and Alternative Objectives of the Firm," *Journal of Finance,* 32(2), May 1977, pp. 389–402.

–, "On the Impossibility of Informationally Efficient Markets," *American Economic Review,* 70(3), June 1980a, pp. 393–408.

–, "Stockholder Unanimity in the Making of Production and Financial Decisions", *Quarterly Journal of Economics* 94(3), May 1980b: pp. 543–566.

Hall, B. J. and J. B. Liebman "Are CEO's Really Paid like Bureaucrats?" *Quarterly Journal of Economics* 112, August 1998: pp 653–697.

Hall, R. E. and D. W. Jorgenson, "Tax Policy and Investment Behavior", *American Economic Review* 57(3), June 1967: pp. 391–414.

Hall, R. E., "Stochastic Implications of the Life Cycle-Permanent Income Hypothesis: Theory and Evidence", *Journal of Political Economy* 86(6), December 1978: pp. 971–987.

Harris, J. and Todaro, M., "Migration, Unemployment and Development: A Two-Sector Analysis", *American Economic Review* 60, 1970: pp. 126–142.

Hart, O. D., and B. Holmström "The Theory of Contracts", In *Advances of Economic Theory, Fifth World Congress,* ed. T. Bewley. Cambridge University Press, 1987.

Hart, O. D., *Firms, Contracts, and Financial Structure,* Oxford: Oxford University Press, 1995.

Haubrich, J., "Risk Aversion, Performance Pay and the Principal–Agent Problem", *Journal of Political Economy* 102, 1994: pp. 258–276.

Hellman, T., K. Murdock and J. E. Stiglitz, "Deposit Mobilization Through Financial Restraint," In *Financial Development and Economic Growth,* N. Hermes and R. Lensink (eds.), Routledge, 1996, pp. 219–46.

–, "Liberalization, Moral Hazard in Banking and Prudential Regulation: Are Capital Requirements Enough?", *American Economic Review* 90(1), 2000: pp. 147–165.

Hellman, T. and J. E. Stiglitz, Credit and Equity Rationing in Markets with Adverse Selection", in *European Economic Review* 44(2) February, pp. 281–304.

Hellmann, T. F., "The Allocation of Control Rights in Venture Capital Contracts" *The Rand Journal of Economics* 29(1) Spring 1998: pp. 57–76.

Hirshleifer, J., "Mergers and Acquisitions: Strategic and Informational Issues", in Jarrow, R. A., Makismovic, V. and Ziemba, W. T. (eds.), *Handbooks in Operations Research and Management Science* (Chapter 26 of Finance) North-Holland, Volume 9, 1995.

Hirshleifer, J. and J.G. Riley, *The Analytics of Uncertainty and Information,* Cambridge, UK: Cambridge University Press, 1992.
Hirshleifer, J., "The Private and Social Value of Information and the Reward to Inventive Activity", *American Economic Review* 61(4), September 1971: pp. 561–574.
Hoff, K. and J. E. Stiglitz, "Imperfect Information and Rural Credit Markets: Puzzles and Policy Perspectives," *World Bank Economic Review,* September 1990 4(3), pp. 235–250.
–, "Moneylenders and Bankers: Price-increasing Subsidies in a Monopolistically Competitive Market," *Journal of Development Economics* 52, 1997: pp. 429–462 .
–, "Modern Economic Theory and Development," in *Frontiers of Development Economics: The Future in Perspective.* Gerald Meier and Joseph E. Stiglitz (eds.) Oxford University Press, 2000, pp 389–485.
Honahan P. and J.E. Stiglitz "Robust Financial Restraint" in *Financial Liberalization: How Far, How Fast, ?* Caprio, G., Honohan, P. and Stiglitz, J. E. (eds.), Cambridge University Press, October 2001.
Hubbard, R.G. (ed.), *Asymmetric information, corporate finance, and investment,* Chicago. IL: University of Chicago Press, 1990.
–, "Capital-market imperfections and investment", *Journal of Economic Literature* 36(1) March 1998: pp. 193–225.
Hurwicz, L., "Optimality and Informational Efficiency in Resource Allocation Processes", in K.J. Arrow, S. Karlin, and P. Suppes, eds., *Mathematical Methods in the Social Sciences,* Stanford, CA: Stanford University Press, 1960.
–, "On Informationally Decentralized Systems" in *Decision and Organization,* ed., M.Mc Guire and R. Radner, North Holland, 1972.
Hussein, A., N. Stern, and J.E. Stiglitz, "Chinese Reforms from a Comparative Perspective" in *Incentives, Organization, and Public Economics: Papers in Honour of Sir James Mirrlees,* Peter J. Hammond and Gareth D. Myles (eds.) (Oxford UP: Oxford) 2000, pp. 243–277.
Jaffee, D. and J. E. Stiglitz, "Credit Rationing," in Friedman B. and F. Hahn (eds.), *Handbook of Monetary Economics,* Amsterdam: Elsevier Science Publishers, 1990, pp. 837–888.
Jensen, M.C., and Meckling, W., "Theory of the Firm: Managerial Behavior, Agency Costs and Ownership Structure", in J. Michael Brennan, ed., *The Theory of Corporate Finance.* Vol. 1 (Cheltenham, UK: Elgar, 1996), pp.35–90; previously published in 1976.
Jensen, M. C. and K. J. Murphy, "Performance Pay and Top-Management Incentives", *Journal of Political Economy* 98, April 1990: pp. 225–264.
Jensen, M. C. and R. S. Rubac, "The Market for Corporate Control: The Scientific Evidence", *Journal of Financial Economics* 11, 1983: pp. 5–55.
Kahn, J. A., "Inventories and the Volatility of Production", *American Economic Review* 77, September 1987: pp. 667–679.
Keeton, W., *Equilibrium Credit Rationing,* New York: Garland Press, 1979.
Keynes, J. M., *The general theory of employment, interest and money,* Harcourt Brace, New York, 1936.
Klein, B. and Leffler K. B., "The Role of Market Forces in Assuring Contractual Performance", *Journal of Political Economy* 89(4), August 1981: pp. 615–641.
Kuh, E. and J. Meyer, *The Investment Decision: An Empirical Study,* Cambridge: Harvard University Press, 1957.
Laffont, J. J. and J. Tirole, A *Theory of Incentives in Procurement and Regulation,* Cambridge, MA: The MIT Press, 1993.
Lamont, O., "Cash Flow and Investment: Evidence from Internal Capital Markets", *Journal of Finance,* LII (1997), pp. 83–109.
Leibenstein, H., "The Theory of Underemployment in Backward Economies," *Journal of Political Economy* 65, 1967: pp. 91–103.
Leitzinger, J. and J. E. Stiglitz, "Information Externalities in Oil and Gas Leasing," *Contemporary Policy Issues,* 5, March 1984, pp. 44–57.
Leland, H. and D. Pyle "Informational Asymmetries, Financial Structure, and Financial Intermediation", *Journal of Finance* 32(2), 1977: pp. 371–387.
Lucas, R. E., *Models of Business Cycles.* Basil Blackwell, New York, 1987.

Mailath, G., "Introduction: Symposium on Evolutionary Game Theory." *Journal of Economic Theory*, 57, 1992: pp. 259–277.
Mankiw, N.G., "Small Menu Costs and Large Business Cycles: A Macro-economic Model of Monopoly", *Quarterly Journal of Economics* 100, 1985: 529–537.
Manne, H., "Mergers and the Market for Corporate Control", *Journal of Political Economy* 73, 1965: 110–120.
March, J. G. and H. A. Simon, *Organizations*. John Wiley & Sons, 1958.
Marris R., *The Economic Theory of "Managerial" Capitalism* London: Macmillan, 1964.
Marschak, J., and Radner, R., *"Economic Theory of Teams"*, Yale University Press, New Haven, 1972.
Marshall, A., *Principles of economics*, London; New York: Macmillan and Co., 1890.
–, "The Old Generation of Economists and the New", *Quarterly Journal of Economics* 11(2), January 1897: pp. 115–135.
Mas-Colell, A., M. Whinston and J. Green, *Microeconomic Theory*, Oxford University Press, Oxford 1995.
Mayer, C., "Financial Systems, Corporate Finance, and Economic Development", in R. Glenn Hubbard (ed.), *Asymmetric Information, Corporate Finance and Investment*, Chicago, IL: The University of Chicago Press, 1990.
Meyer, J., and Kuh, E., *"The Investment Decision: An Empirical Study"* (Cambridge, MA: Harvard University Press, 1957).
Maynard Smith, J., and G. R. Price. "The Logic of Animal Conflict", *Nature* 246, 1973: pp. 15–18.
Mill, J. S., *Principles of Political Economy*, London: J. W. Parker, 1848.
Miller, M. and J. E. Stiglitz, "Bankruptcy protection against macro-economic shocks: the case for a 'super chapter 11'," World Bank Conference on Capital Flows, Financial Crises, and Policies, April 15, 1999.
Mincer, J., *Schooling, experience and earnings*, Columbia University Press, New York, 1974.
Mirrlees, J. A., "An Exploration in the Theory of Optimum Income Taxation", *The Review of Economic Studies* 38(2), April 1971: pp. 175–208.
–, "Optimal Taxation in a Two-Class Economy", *Journal of Public Economics* 4, February 1975a.
–, The Theory of Moral Hazard and Unobservable Behaviour I", mimeo., Nuffield College, 1975b.
–, "The Optimal Structure of Incentives and Authority within an Organization", *Bell Journal of Economics and Management Science*, Spring 1976.
Modigliani, F., and M. Miller, "The Cost of Capital, Corporation Finance, and the Theory of Investment", *American Economic Review*, June 1958: pp. 261–297.
Modigliani, F. and M. H. Miller, "Dividend Policy, Growth, And The Valuation Of Shares", *Journal of Business* 34(4), 1961: pp. 411–433.
Morck, R., A. Shleifer and R. W. Vishny, "Management Ownership and Market Valuation: An Empirical Analysis," *Journal of Financial Economics* 20, 1988: pp 293–315.
Moynihan, P. D., *Secrecy: The American Experience*, Yale University Press, 1998.
Murphy, K. J., "Corporate Performance and Managerial Remuneration: An Empirical Analysis," *Journal of Accounting and Economics* 7, 1985: pp. 11–42.
Myers, S. C. and N. S. Majluf, "Corporate Financing and Investment Decisions when Firms have Information that Investors do not have", *Journal of Financial Economics* 13 (2), June 1984: pp. 187–222.
Myerson, R., "Incentive Compatibility and the Bargaining Problem", Econometrica, 47, 1979, pp. 61–73.
Nalebuff, B. and J. E. Stiglitz, "Information, Competition and Markets," *American Economic Review*, 73(2), May 1983a: pp. 278–284.
–, "Prizes and Incentives: Toward a General Theory of Compensation and Competition," *Bell Journal*, 14(1), Spring 1983b: pp. 21–43.
Nalebuff, B., A. Rodriguez, and J. E. Stiglitz, "Equilibrium Unemployment as a Worker Screening Device," NBER Working Paper 4357, May 1993.

Nelson, R. and S. Winter, *An Evolutionary Theory of Economic Change.* Belknap Press of Harvard University Press: Cambridge, MA, 1982.

–, "Neoclassical vs. Evolutionary Theories of Economic Growth: Critique and Prospectus," in *The Economics of Innovation.* Christopher Freeman, ed. International Library of Critical Writings in Economics, no. 2. Elgar, Brookfield, VT, 1990: pp. 3–22.

Newbery, David, and J. E. Stiglitz, "Sharecropping: Risk Sharing and the Importance of Imperfect Information," in J.A. Roumasset, et al. (eds.), *Risk Uncertainty and Development,* SEARCA, A/D/C, 1976, pp. 311–341.

–, "The Choice of Techniques and the Optimality of Market Equilibrium with Rational Expectations," *Journal of Political Economy,* 90(2), April 1982, pp. 223–246.

–, "Pareto Inferior Trade", *Review of Economic Studies,* 51(1), January 1984, pp. 1–12.

Phelps, E. S. and Winter, S.G., "Optimal price policy under atomistic competition", in E.S. Phelps et al. *Microeconomic Foundations of Employment and Inflation Theory,* New York: Norton, 1970.

Phelps, E. S., "Money-wage dynamics and labor-market equilibrium", *Journal of Political Economy* 76(4), Part 2, August 1968: pp. 678–711.

Phelps, E. S., "The Statistical Theory of Racism and Sexism", *The American Economic Review* 62(4), September 1972: pp. 659–661.

Pigou, A. C., *The Economics of Welfare,* London: Macmillan & Co, 1920.

–, *Quarterly Journal of Economics,* Volume 98, Supplement, 1983.

Radner, R.,"Competitive Equilibrium under Uncertainty", *Econometrica,* 36, 1968, pp.31–58.

–, "Existence of Equilibrium of Plans, Prices, and Price Expectations in a sequence of markets", *Econometrica,* 40, 1972, pp. 289–303.

–, "A Note on Unanimity of Stockholders' Preferences Among Alternative Production Plans: A Reformulation of the Ekern-Wilson Model", *Bell Journal of Economics,* 5, 1974, pp. 181–184.

–, "Rational Expectations Equilibrium: Generic Existence and the Information Revealed by Prices", *Econometrica,* 47, 1979, pp. 655–678.

Radner, R. and J. E. Stiglitz, "A Nonconcavity in the Value of Information," in Marcel Boyer and Richard Khilstrom (eds.), *Bayesian Models in Economic Theory,* Elsevier Science Publications, 1984, pp. 33–52.

Ramsey, F. P., "A Contribution to the Theory of Taxation", *Economic Journal* 37, 1927: pp. 47–61.

Rey, P. and J. E. Stiglitz "Moral Hazard and Unemployment in Competitive Equilibrium", Unpublished Manuscript, University of Toulouse, July 1996.

Riley, J. G., "Informational Equilibrium", *Econometrica* 47, 1979: pp. 331–360.

–, "Silver signals: Twenty-five years of screening and signaling", *Journal of Economic Literature* 39(2), June 2001: pp. 432–478.

Robinson, J., "The Economics of Imperfect Competition", Macmillan, London, 1933.

Rodriguez, A. and J. E. Stiglitz, "Equilibrium Unemployment, Testing, and the Pure Theory of Selection," Paper presented at NBER/CEPR Conference on Unemployment and Wage Determination, Boston, October 1991a.

–, "Unemployment and Efficiency Wages: The Adverse Selection Model," Paper presented at NBER/CEPR Conference on Unemployment and Wage Determination, Boston, October 17–19, 1991b.

Rosen, S., "Implicit Contracts: A Survey", *Journal of Economic Literature* 23(3), September 1985: pp. 1144–1175.

Ross, S. A., "The Economic Theory of Agency: The Principals Problem," *American Economic Review* LXII, May 1973: pp. 134–139.

–, "The determination of financial structure: The incentive signalling approach", *Bell Journal of Economics* 8, 1977: pp. 23–40.

Rothschild, M. and J. E. Stiglitz, "Equilibrium in Competitive Insurance Markets: An Essay on the Economics of Imperfect Information," *Quarterly Journal of Economics,* 90(4), November 1976, pp. 629–649.

–, "A Model of Employment Outcomes Illustrating the Effect of the Structure of Information on the Level and Distribution of Income," *Economic Letters* 10, 1982: pp. 231–236.

–, "Competition and Insurance Twenty Years Later," *Geneva Papers on Risk and Insurance Theory;* 22(2), December 1997: pages 73–79.

Sah, R. K., "Fallibility in Human Organizations and Political Systems" (in Symposium: Organizations and Economics), *Journal of Economic Perspectives* 5(2), Spring 1991: pp. 67–88.

Sah, R., and J. E. Stiglitz, "Human Fallibility and Economic Organization,", *American Economic Review,* 75(2), May 1985, pp. 292–296.

–, "The Architecture of Economic Systems: Hierarchies and Polyarchies", *American Economic Review,* 76(4), September 1986, pp. 716–727.

–, "Committees, Hierarchies and Polyarchies", *The Economic Journal,* 98, June 1988a: pp. 451–470.

–, "Qualitative Properties of Profit-Maximizing K-out-of-N Systems Subject to Two Kinds of Failure," *IEEE Transactions on Reliability,* 37(5), December 1988b: pp. 515–520.

–, "Sources of Technological Divergence between Developed and Less Developed Countries," in G. Calvo, *et al.* (eds.), *Debt, Stabilizations and Development: Essays in Memory of Carlos Diaz-Alejandro,* Basil Blackwell, 1989a, pp. 423–46.

–, "Technological Learning, Social Learning and Technological Change," in S. Chakravarty (ed.), *The Balance between Industry and Agriculture in Economic Development,* MacMillan Press/International Economic Association, 1989b, pp. 285–298.

–, "The Quality of Managers in Centralized Versus Decentralized Organizations", *Quarterly Journal of Economics* 106(1), February 1991: pp.289–25.

–, *Peasants versus City-Dwellers: Taxation and the Burden of Economic Development,* Clarendon Press, Oxford, 1992.

Salop, S. and J. E. Stiglitz, "Bargains and Ripoffs: A Model of Monopolistically Competitive Price Dispersions," *Review of Economic Studies,* 44, October 1977, pp. 493–510. (Reprinted in S.A. Lippman and D.K. Levine (eds.), *The Economics of Information,* Edward Elgar, 1995, pp. 198–215.).

–, "The Theory of Sales: A Simple Model of Equilibrium Price Dispersion with Identical Agents", *American Economic Review,* 72(5), December 1982, pp. 1121–1130.

–, "Information, Welfare and Product Diversity," in G. Feiwel (ed.), *Arrow and the Foundations of the Theory of Economic Policy,* London: MacMillan, 1987, pp. 328–340.

Salop, S., "The Noisy Monopolist: Information, Price Dispersion and Price Discrimination", *Review of Economic Studies* 44(3), October 1977: pp 393–406.

Samuelson, P.A., *Foundations of Economic Analysis,* Cambridge MA: Harvard University Press, 1947.

Sappington, D. and J. E. Stiglitz, "Information and Regulation," in E. Bailey (ed.), *Public Regulation,* London: MIT Press, 1987a, pp. 3–43.

–, "Privatization, Information and Incentives," , *Journal of Policy Analysis and Management,* 6(4), 1987b, pp. 567–582.

Schultz, T. W., "Capital Formation by Education" *The Journal of Political Economy* 68 (6), December 1960: pp. 571–583.

Shakespeare, W., *As you like it,* (Act 2, Scene 7), New York: Cambridge University Press, [1599] 2000.

Shapiro, C. and J. E. Stiglitz, "Equilibrium Unemployment as a Worker Discipline Device," *American Economic Review,* 74(3), June 1984, pp. 433–444.

–, "Equilibrium Unemployment as a Worker Discipline Device: Reply", *American Economic Review,* 75(4), September 1985a, pp. 892–893.

–, "Can Unemployment be Involuntary? Reply", *American Economic Review,* 75(5), December 1985b, pp. 1215–1217.

Shapiro, C., "Premiums for High Quality Products as Returns to Reputations", *Quarterly Journal of Economics* 98(4), November 1983, pp. 659–680.

Shell, K., (ed.), *Essays on the Theory of Optimal Economic Growth,* Cambridge MA: MIT Press, 1967.

Shiller, R. J., *"Irrational Exuberance",* Princeton University Press, Princeton NJ, 2000.

Shleifer, A. and R. W. Vishny, "Management Entrenchment: The Case of Manager-Specific Assets", *Journal of Financial Economics* 25, 1989: 123–139.

–, "A Survey of Corporate Governance," *The Journal of Finance* 52(2), 1997: pp. 737–783.

–, *"The Grabbing Hand: Government Pathologies and Their Cures"*. Cambridge: Harvard University Press. 1998.

Simon H. A., "Organizations and Markets", *Journal of Economic Perspectives* 5(2), Spring 1991: pp. 25–44.

Singh, R., "Takeover bidding with toeholders: The case of the Owners Curse", *Review of Financial Studies* 11: pp. 679–704.

Simonde de Sismondi, J. C. L., *Political Economy,* NY: Kelley, [1814] 1966.

Smith, A. *An Inquiry into the Nature and Causes of The Wealth of Nations,* University of Chicago Press February 1977. (First published 1776).

Spence, M., *Market Signaling: Information Transfer in Hiring and Related Processes,* Cambridge MA: Harvard University Press, 1974.

–, "Job Market Signalling", *Quarterly Journal of Economics,* August 1973: pp. 355–379.

Stern, N. and J. E. Stiglitz, "A Framework for a Development Strategy in a Market Economy", in E. Malinvaud and A.K. Sen, eds. *Development Strategy and the Management of the Market Economy.* Oxford: Clarendon Press, 1997, pp. 253–295.

Stigler, G. J., "The economics of information", *The Journal of Political Economy* 69(3), 1961: pp. 213–225.

–, "Imperfections in the Capital Market," *Journal of Political Economy* 75(3), 1967: pp. 287–92.

Stiglitz, J. E., "A Re-Examination of the Modigliani-Miller Theorem," *American Economic Review,* 59(5), December 1969a: pp. 784–793.

–, "Rural-Urban Migration, Surplus Labor and the Relationship Between Urban and Rural Wages," *East African Economic Review,* 1–2, December 1969b: pp. 1–27.

–, "On the Optimality of the Stock Market Allocation of Investment", *Quarterly Journal of Economics,* 86(1), February 1972a: pp. 25–60.

–, "Some Aspects of the Pure Theory of Corporate Finance: Bankruptcies and Take-Overs," *Bell Journal of Economist,* 3(2), Autumn 1972b, pp. 458–482.

–, "Approaches to the Economics of Discrimination," *American Economic Review,* 62(2), May 1973a, pp. 287–295. (Reprinted in W. Darity and C. Boshamer (eds.), *Economics and Discrimination,* Edward Elgar Publishing, 1993.)

–, "Taxation, Corporate Financial Policy and the Cost of Capital", *Journal of Public Economics,* 2, February 1973b: pp. 1–34.

–, "Alternative Theories of Wage Determination and Unemployment in L.D.C.'s: The Labor Turnover Model," *Quarterly Journal of Economics,* 88(2), May 1974a, pp. 194–227.

–, "Incentives and Risk Sharing in Sharecropping", *Review of Economic Studies,* 41, April 1974b: pp. 219–255.

–, "On the Irrelevance of Corporate Financial Policy," *American Economic Review,* 64(6), December 1974c: pp. 851–866.

–, "Theories of Discrimination and Economic Policy," In *Patterns of Racial Discrimination,* G. von Furstenberg, *et al.* (eds.), D.C. Heath and Company (Lexington Books), 1974d, pp. 5–26.

–, "Incentives, Risk and Information: Notes Toward a Theory of Hierarchy," *Bell Journal of Economics,* 6(2), Autumn 1975a, pp. 552–579.

–, "Information and Economic Analysis," in J.M. Parkin and A.R. Nobay, eds. *Current Economic Problems* (Cambridge: Cambridge University Press), 1975b: pp. 27–52.

–, "The Theory of Screening, Education and the Distribution of Income," *American Economic Review,* 65(3), June 1975c: pp. 283–300.

–, "The Efficiency of Market Prices in Long Run Allocations in the Oil Industry," in *Studies in Energy Tax Policy,* G. Brannon (ed.), Cambridge: Ballinger Publishing, 1975d, pp. 55–99.

–, "The Efficiency Wage Hypothesis, Surplus Labor and the Distribution of Income in L.D.C.'s," *Oxford Economic Papers,* 28(2), July 1976: pp. 185–207.

–, "Monopoly, Non-Linear Pricing and Imperfect Information: The Insurance Market," *Review of Economic Studies,* 44, October 1977a, pp. 407–430.
–, "Symposium on the Economics of Information: Introduction," *Review of Economic Studies,* 44(138), October 1977b, pp. 389–391.
–, "Equilibrium in Product Markets with Imperfect Information," *American Economic Review,* 69(2), May 1979a: pp. 339–345.
–, "On Search and Equilibrium Price Distributions," In *Economics and Human Welfare: Essays in Honor of Tibor Scitovsky,* M. Boskin (ed.), York: Academic Press Inc., 1979b, pp. 203–236.
–, "Pareto Optimality and Competition," *Journal of Finance,* 36(2), May 1981, pp. 235–251.
–, "Alternative Theories of Wage Determination and Unemployment: The Efficiency Wage Model," in *The Theory and Experience of Economic Development: Essays in Honor of Sir Arthur W. Lewis,* M. Gersovitz, *et al.* (eds.), London: George Allen & Unwin, 1982a, pp. 78–106.
–, "The Inefficiency of the Stock Market Equilibrium," *Review of Economic Studies,* XLIX, April 1982b: pp. 241–261.
–, "Information and Capital Markets," in *Financial Economics: Essays in Honor of Paul Cootner,* William F. Sharpe and Cathryn Cootner (eds.), Prentice Hall, New Jersey, 1982c, pp. 118–158.
–, "Ownership, Control and Efficient Markets: Some Paradoxes in the Theory of Capital Markets," in *Economic Regulation: Essays in Honor of James R. Nelson,* Kenneth D. Boyer and William G. Shepherd (eds.), Michigan State University, 1982, pp. 311–341.
–, "Self-Selection and Pareto Efficient Taxation," *Journal of Public Economics,* 17, 1982e: pp. 213–240.
–, "The Structure of Labor Markets and Shadow Prices in L.D.C.'s," in *Migration and the Labor Market in Developing Countries,* R. Sabot (ed.), Boulder, Colo.: Westview, 1982f, pp. 13–64.
–, "Utilitarianism and Horizontal Equity: The Case for Random Taxation," *Journal of Public Economics,* 18, 1982g, pp. 1–33.
–, "Risk, Incentives and Insurance: The Pure Theory of Moral Hazard," *The Geneva Papers,* January 1983, 8(26), pp. 4–32.
–, "Information, Screening and Welfare," In *Bayesian Models in Economic Theory,* Marcel Boyer and Richard Khilstrom (eds.), Elsevier Science Publications, 1984a, pp. 209–239.
–, "Price Rigidities and Market Structure," *American Economic Review,* 74(2), May 1984b: pp. 350–356.
–, "Credit Markets and the Control of Capital," *Journal of Money, Banking, and Credit,* 17(2), May 1985a: pp. 133–152.
–, "Economics of Information and the Theory of Economic Development," *Revista De Econometria,* 5(1), April 1985b: pp. 5–32.
–, "Equilibrium Wage Distribution," *Economic Journal,* 95, September 1985c: pp. 595–618.
–, "Information and Economic Analysis: A Perspective," *Economic Journal,* 95(0), 1985d, pp. 21–41.
–, "The New Development Economics," *World Development,* 14(2), 1986a: pp. 257–265.
–, "Theories of Wage Rigidities," in *Keynes' Economic Legacy: Contemporary Economic Theories,* J.L. Butkiewicz, *et al.* (eds.), New York: Praeger Publishers, 1986b, pp.153–206.
–, "Theory of Competition, Incentives and Risk," in *New Developments in the Theory of Market Structure,* J.E. Stiglitz and F. Mathewson (eds.), MacMillan/MIT Press, 1986c, pp.399–449.
–, "The Causes and Consequences of the Dependence of Quality on Prices," *Journal of Economic Literature* 25(1) March 1987a: pp. 1–48.
–, "Competition and the Number of Firms in a Market: Are Duopolies More Competitive Than Atomistic Markets?" *Journal of Political Economy,* 95(5), 1987b, pp. 1041–1061.
–, "Design of Labor Contracts: Economics of Incentives and Risk-Sharing," in *Incentives, Cooperation and Risk Sharing,* H. Nalbantian (ed.), Totowa, NJ: Rowman & Allanheld, 1987c, pp.47–68.

–, "Learning to Learn, Localized Learning and Technological Progress," in *Economic Policy and Technological Performance,* P. Dasgupta and Stoneman (eds.), Cambridge University Press, 1987d, pp. 125–153.
–, "On the Microeconomics of Technical Progress," in *Technology Generation in Latin American Manufacturing Industries,* Jorge M. Katz (ed.), The Macmillan Press Ltd. 1987e, pp. 56–77.
–, "Efficient and Optimal Taxation and the New New Welfare Economics," in *Handbook on Public Economics,* A. Auerbach and M. Feldstein (eds.), North Holland: Elsevier Science Publishers, 1987f: pp. 991–1042.
–, "Sharecropping," in *The New Palgrave: A dictionary of Economics,* MacMillan Press, 1987g.
–, "Technological Change, Sunk Costs, and Competition," *Brookings Papers on Economic Activity* 3, 1987h.
–, "The Wage-Productivity Hypothesis: Its Economic Consequences and Policy Implications," In *Modern Developments in Public Finance,* M.J. Boskin (ed.), Basil Blackwell, 1987i, pp. 130–165.
–, "Human Nature and Economic Organization," Jacob Marashak Lecture, presented at Far Eastern Meetings of the Econometric Society, October 1987j.
–, "Economic Organization, Information, and Development," in *Handbook of Development Economics,* H. Chenery and T.N. Srinivasan (eds.), Elsevier Science Publishers, 1988a, pp. 185–201.
–, "Money, Credit, and Business Fluctuations," *Economic Record,* 64(187), December 1988b: pp. 62–72.
–, "On the Relevance or Irrelevance of Public Financial Policy," in *The Economics of Public Debt,* (Proceedings of the 1986 International Economics Association Meeting), Macmillan Press, 1988c: pp. 4–76.
–, "Why Financial Structure Matters," *Journal of Economic Perspectives,* 2(4), 1988d: pp. 121–126.
–, *The Economic Role of the State,* A. Heertje (ed.), Basil Blackwell and Bank Insinger de Beaufort NV, 1989a, pp. 9–85.
–, "Financial Markets and Development," *Oxford Review of Economic Policy,* 5(4), 1989b: pp. 55–68.
–, "Imperfect Information in the Product Market," in *Handbook of Industrial Organization,* 1, Elsevier Science Publishers, 1989c, pp. 769–847.
–, "Incentives, Information and Organizational Design," *Empirica,* 16(1), January 1989d: pp. 3–29.
–, "Markets, Market Failures and Development," *American Economic Review,* 79(2), May 1989e: pp. 197–203.
–, "Monopolistic Competition and the Capital Market," in *The Economics of Imperfect Competition and Employment – Joan Robinson and Beyond,* G. Feiwel (ed.), New York: New York University Press, 1989f, pp. 485–507.
–, "Mutual Funds, Capital Structure, and Economic Efficiency," in *Theory of Valuation – Frontiers of Modern Financial Theory, Vol. 1,* S. Bhattacharya and G. Constantinides (eds.), Totowa, NJ: Rowman and Littlefield, 1989g, pp. 342–356.
–, "Principal and Agent," in *The New Palgrave: Allocation, Information and Markets,* J. Eatwell, et al. (eds.), MacMillan Press, London, 1989h, pp. 241–253.
–, "Rational Peasants, Efficient Institutions and the Theory of Rural Organization," in *The Economic Theory of Agrarian Institutions,* P. Bardhan (ed.), Oxford: Clarendon Press, 1989i, pp. 18–29.
–, Reflections on the State of Economics: 1988," *Economic Record,* March 1989j, pp. 66–72.
–, "Using Tax Policy to Curb Speculative Short-Term Trading," *Journal of Financial Services Research,* 3(2/3), December 1989k, pp. 101–115.
–, "Some Retrospective Views on Growth Theory presented on the occasion of the Celebration of Robert Solow's 65th Birthday," in *Growth/Productivity/Unemployment,* P. Diamond (ed.), Cambridge, Mass.: MIT Press, 1990a, pp. 50–68.

–, "Peer Monitoring and Credit Markets," *World Bank Economic Review,* 4(3), September 1990b: pp. 351–366.

–, "Another Century of Economic Science," *Economic Journal* Anniversary Issue, 101(404), January 1991a, pp. 134–141; *The Future of Economics,* J.D. Hey (ed.), Blackwell Publishers, 1992, pp. 134–141.

–, "Development Strategies: The Roles of the State and the Private Sector," in *Proceedings of the World Bank's Annual Conference on Development Economics 1990,* 1991b, pp. 430–35.

–, "Introduction to Symposium on Organizations and Economics," *Journal of Economic Perspectives,* 5(2), Spring 1991c, pp. 15–24.

–, "The Invisible Hand and Modern Welfare Economics," in *Information Strategy and Public Policy,* D. Vines and A. Stevenson (eds.), Oxford: Basil Blackwell, 1991f pp. 12–50.

–, "Some Theoretical Aspects of the Privatization: Applications to Eastern Europe," *Revista di Politica Economica,* December 1991d, pp. 179–204.

–, "The Economic Role of the State: Efficiency and Effectiveness" *Efficiency and Effectiveness in the Public Domain. The Economic Role of the State,* T.P. Hardiman and M. Mulreany (eds.), Institute of Public Administration, 1991e: pp. 37–59.

–, "Banks versus Markets as Mechanisms for Allocating and Coordinating Investment," in *The Economics of Cooperation: East Asian Development and the Case for Pro-Market Intervention,* J.A. Roumasset and S. Barr (eds.), Westview Press, Boulder, 1992a, pp. 15–38.

–, "Capital Markets and Economic Fluctuations in Capitalist Economies," *European Economic Review,* 36, North-Holland, 1992b, pp. 269–306.

–, "Contract Theory and Macroeconomic Fluctuations," in *Contract Economics,* L. Werin and H. Wijkander (eds.), Basil Blackwell, 1992c: pp. 292–322.

–, "The Design of Financial Systems for the Newly Emerging Democracies of Eastern Europe," in *The Emergence of Market Economies in Eastern Europe,* C. Clague and G.C. Rausser (eds.), Cambridge: Basil Blackwell, 1992d pp. 161–184.

–, "Explaining Growth: Competition and Finance," *Rivista di Politica Economica (Italy),* 82(169), November 1992e, p. 225.

–, "Introduction: S&L Bailout," in *The Reform of Federal Deposit Insurance: Disciplining the Government and Protecting Taxpayers,* J. Barth and R. Brumbaugh, Jr. (eds.), Harper Collins Publishers, 1992f, pp. 1–12.

–, "Methodological Issues and the New Keynesian Economics," *Alternative Approaches to Macro-economics,* A. Vercelli and N. Dimitri (eds.), Oxford University Press, 1992g, pp. 38–86.

–, "Prices and Queues as Screening Devices in Competitive Markets," in *Economic Analysis of Markets and Games: Essays in Honor of Frank Hahn,* D. Gale and O. Hart (eds.), Cambridge: MIT Press, 1992h: pp. 128–166. (IMSSS Technical Report No. 212, Stanford University, August 1976.).

–, "Notes on Evolutionary Economics: Imperfect Capital Markets, Organizational Design, Long-run Efficiency." Paper presented at a conference at Osaka University, 1992i.

–, "The Role of the State in Financial Markets", *Proceeding of the World Bank Conference on Development Economics,* Washington, D.C., World Bank, 1993a: pp. 41–46.

–, "Consequences of Limited Risk Markets and Imperfect Information for the Design of Taxes and Transfers: An Overview," in K. Hoff, A. Braverman, and J. Stiglitz (eds.) *The Economics of Rural Organization: Theory, Practice, and Policy.* New York: Oxford University Press for the World Bank. 1993b.

–, "Perspectives on the Role of Government Risk-Bearing within the Financial Sector," in *Government Risk-bearing,* M. Sniderman (ed.), Norwell, Mass.: Kluwer Academic Publishers, 1993c: pp. 109–30.

–, "Some Theoretical Aspects of the Privatization: Applications to Eastern Europe," *Privatization Processes in Eastern Europe,* M. Baldassarri, L. Paganetto and E.S. Phelps (eds.), St. Martin's Press, Rome, 1993d, pp. 179–204.

–, "Economic Growth Revisited," *Industrial and Corporate Change,* 3(1), 1994a: pp. 65–110.

–, "Endogenous Growth and Cycles," *Innovation in Technology, Industries, and Institutions,* Y. Shionoya and M. Perlman (eds.), The University of Michigan Press, 1994b, pp. 121–56.

–, *Whither Socialism?* Cambridge, Mass.: MIT Press, 1994c.

–, "Interest Rate Puzzles, Competitive Theory and Capital Constraints," in *Economics in a Changing World,* Fitoussi, Jean-Paul ed., (Proceedings of the Tenth World Congress of the International Economic Association, Moscow, Volume 5. Economic Growth and Capital and Labour markets.) IEA Conference Volume 111, New York: St. Martin's Press, 1995a: pp. 145–75.

–, "Social Absorption Capability and Innovation," in *Social Capability and Long-Term Economic Growth,* Bon Ho Koo and D.H. Perkins (eds.), New York: St. Martin's Press, 1995b, pp. 48–81.

–, "Some Lessons from the East Asian Miracle," *World Bank Research Observer,* 11(2), August 1996, pp. 151–77.

–, "The Role of Government in Economic Development," in *Annual World Bank Conference on Development Economics 1996,* M. Bruno and B. Pleskovic (eds.), The World Bank, 1997a. pp. 11–23.

–, "The Role of Government in the Economies of Developing Countries," in E. Malinvaud and A.K. Sen, eds. *Development Strategy and the Management of the Market Economy. Oxford:* Clarendon Press, 1997b, pp. 61–109.

–, "More Instruments and Broader Goals: Moving Toward the Post-Washington Consensus, The 1998 Wider Annual Lecture, Helsinki, January, 1998a .

–, "Towards a New Paradigm for Development: Strategies, Policies and Processes." 9th Raul Prebisch Lecture delivered at the Palais des Nations, Geneva, UNCTAD, October 19, 1998b.

–, "Pareto Efficient Taxation and Expenditure Policies, With Applications to the Taxation of Capital, Public Investment, and Externalities," presented at conference in honor of Agnar Sandmo. January 1998c.

–, "Interest Rates, Risk, and Imperfect Markets: Puzzles and Policies", *Oxford Review of Economic Policy* 15(2), 1999a, pp 59–76.

–, "Knowledge for Development: Economic Science, Economic Policy, and Economic Advice", *Proceedings from the Annual Bank Conference on Development Economics 1998.* World Bank, Washington D.C. Keynote Address, 1999b: pp 9–58.

–, "On Liberty, the Right to Know and Public Discourse: The Role of Transparency in Public Life" (Paper presented at Oxford Amnesty Lecture), 1999c.

–, "Toward a General Theory of Wage and Price Rigidities and Economic Fluctuations", *American Economic Review* 89(2), May 1999d: pp. 75–80.

–, "Responding to Economic Crises: Policy Alternatives for Equitable Recovery and Development." *The Manchester School* 67(5) Special Issue 1999e, pp. 409–427.

–, "Whither Reform? Ten Years of the Transition", *Proceedings of the Annual Bank Conference on Development Economics* 1999, Washington, D.C.: World Bank, 2000a: pp. 27–56.

–, "Capital Market Liberalization, Economic Growth, and Instability" in *World Development,* Vol. 28, No. 6, pp. 1075–1086, 2000b.

–, "Formal and Informal Institutions" in *Social Capital: A Multifaceted Perspective.* P. Dasgupta and I. Serageldin (eds.), The World Bank: Washington, DC, 2000c: pp. 59–68.

–, "The Contributions of the Economics of Information to Twentieth Century Economics," *Quarterly Journal of Economics,* November, 2000d, pp. 1441–1477.

–, "Democratic Development as the Fruits of Labor," Working Paper, *Progressive Economics Papers,* January 2000e.

–, "Some Elementary Principles of Bankruptcy" in Governance, Equity and Global Markets (Proceedings of Annual Bank Conference for Development Economics in Europe June 21–23, 1999) La Documentation Francaise, 2000f.

–, "Challenges in the Analysis of the Role of Institutions in Economic Development," *Villa Borsig Workshop Series 2000: The Institutional Foundations of a Market Economy.* Gudrun Kochendorfer-Lucius and Boris Pleskovic (eds.), German Foundation for International Development (DSE), 2001a: pp 15–28.

–, "From Miracle to Recovery: Lessons from Four Decades of East Asian Experience," *Rethinking the East Asian Miracle.* Shahid Yusuf ed. World Bank, Washington, D.C., 2001b.

–, "Principles of Financial Regulation: A Dynamic Approach," *The World Bank Observer* 16(1), Spring 2001c: pp. 1–18.
–, "Crisis y Restructuración Financiera: el Papel de la Banca Central" Cuestiones Económicas 17(2), 2001d: pp. 3–24.
–, "Quis Custodiet Ipsos Custodes?" in *Governance, equity, and global markets: the Annual Bank Conference on Development Economics, Europe,* J. E. Stiglitz and Pierre-Alain Muet (eds.) World Bank, New York, Oxford University Press. 2001e: pp 22–54.
–, "New Perspectives on Public Finance: Recent Achieves and Future Challenges", *Journal of Public Economics* (84), forthcoming, 2002.
Stiglitz, J. E. and A. Weiss, "Credit Rationing in Markets with Imperfect Information," *American Economic Review,* 71(3), June 1981: pp. 393–410.
–, "Alternative Approaches to the Analysis of Markets with Asymmetric Information," *American Economic Review,* 73(1), March 1983a, pp. 246–249.
–, "Incentive Effects of Termination: Applications to the Credit and Labor Markets," *American Economic Review,* 73(5), December 1983b, pp. 912–927.
–, "Credit Rationing and Collateral," in *Recent Developments in Corporate Finance,* Jeremy Edwards, *et al.* (eds.), New York: Cambridge University Press, 1986, pp. 101–135.
–, "Credit Rationing: Reply" , *American Economic Review,* March 1987, pp. 228–231.
–, "Banks as Social Accountants and Screening Devices for the Allocation of Credit", *Greek Economic Review,* 12(0), Supplement, Autumn 1990, pp. 85–118.
–, "Asymmetric Information in Credit Markets and Its Implications for Macro-economics," *Oxford Economic Papers,* 44(4), October 1992, pp. 694–724.
–, "Sorting Out the Differences Between Screening and Signaling Models," in M.O.L. Bacharach, M.A.H. Dempster and J.L. Enos, eds., *Mathematical Models in Economics.* Oxford University Press, Oxford, 1994.
Stiglitz, J. E. and M. Wolfson, "Taxation, Information, and Economic Organization," *Journal of the American Taxation Association,* 9(2), Spring 1988, pp. 7–18. (Paper presented for delivery to the American Accounting Association, August 1987.).
Stiglitz, J. E. and S. Yusuf "Development Issues: Settled and Open" in *Frontiers of Development Economic: The Future in Perspective,* Gerald M. Meier and Joseph E. Stiglitz (Eds.), Oxford University Press, May 2000, pp 227–268.
Stulz, R., "Managerial Control of Voting Rights: Financing Policies and the Market for Corporate Control," *Journal of Financial Economics* 20, 1988: pp. 25–54.
Thaler, W. *et al.*, "Anomalies" *Journal of Economic Perspectives* 11 (1), 1997.
–, "Anomalies" *Journal of Economic Perspectives* 2(1–4), 1988.
–, "Anomalies" *Journal of Economic Perspectives* 3 (1–2, 4), 1989.
–, "Anomalies" *Journal of Economic Perspectives* 4(1–4), 1990.
–, "Anomalies" *Journal of Economic Perspectives* 5(1), 1991.
–, "Anomalies" *Journal of Economic Perspectives* 9(2, 4), 1995.
Thaler, W., "Anomalies" *Journal of Economic Perspectives* 1(2), 1987.
Todaro, M., "A Model of Labor Migration and Urban Unemployment in Less Developed Countries", *American Economic Review* (59), 1969: pp. 138–48.
Townsend, R., "Optimal contracts and competitive markets with costly state verifications", *Journal of Economic Theory* 21, October 1979: pp. 265–93.
Varian, H., "A Model of Sales", *American Economic Review, Papers and Proceedings,* 70(4), 1980, pp. 651–659.
Visser, B., "Binary Decision Structures and the Required Detail of Information", European University Institute, Economic Department, *Working Paper 89/1,* February 1998.
Waldman M., "Job Assignments, Signaling and Efficiency", *Rand Journal of Economics* 15, 1984: pp. 255–267.
Weiss, A., "Job Queues and Layoffs in Labor Markets with Flexible Wages", *The Journal of Political Economy* 88(3), June 1980: pp. 526–538.
–, "Human Capital vs. Signaling Explanation of Wages and Sorting Models of Education and Training", *Journal of Economic Perspectives* 9(4), Fall 1995: pp. 133–154.

Werin, L. and H. Wijkander (eds.), *Contract Economics,* Blackwell Publishers, Oxford, UK, 1992. (Proceedings of *Contract: Determinants, Properties and Implications,* 1990 Nobel Symposium 77, Saltsjöbaden, Sweden.)

Williamson, J., "What Washington Means by Policy Reform", in Williamson (ed.), *Latin American Adjustment: How Much Has Happened?* Institute of International Economics, Washington D.C. April 1990.

Wilson, R., "Competitive Bidding with Disparate Information", *Management Science* 15, 1969: pp. 446–448.

–, "A Bidding Model of Perfect Competition", *Review of Economic Studies* 44, 1977: pp. 511 – 518.

World Bank (ed.), *Knowledge for Development: 1998/99 World Development Report,* Washington D.C.: The World Bank, 1999.

Weibull, J. W., *Evolutionary Game Theory.* Cambridge, MA: MIT Press, 1996.

Yabushita, S., "Theory of Screening and the Behavior of the Firm." *American Economic Review,* March 1983, 73, pp. 242–245.

Economic Sciences 2002

DANIEL KAHNEMAN

"for having integrated insights from psychological research into economic science, especially concerning human judgement and decision-making under uncertainty"

and

VERNON L. SMITH

"for having established laboratory experiments as a tool in empirical economic analysis, especially in the study of alternative market mechanisms"

THE SVERIGES RIKSBANK (BANK OF SWEDEN) PRIZE IN ECONOMIC SCIENCES IN MEMORY OF ALFRED NOBEL

Speech by Professor Lars-Göran Nilsson of the Royal Swedish Academy of Sciences.
Translation of the Swedish text.

Your Majesties, Your Royal Highnesses, Ladies and Gentlemen,

Economic theory relies on the assumption that economic agents may be likened to a "homo oeconomicus". This fictitious individual is usually governed by self-interest and makes his economic decisions by rationally evaluating the consequences of different alternatives, even in complex situations where the outcome is difficult to predict. Despite such strong assumptions, this approach has proved to be highly rewarding and has enhanced our understanding of many economic phenomena.

Empirical testing of postulates in economic theory confronts theoretical predictions with findings from real-world markets and economies. In general, however, since "field data" are affected by factors which scarcely allow for control and measurement, the identification of causal relationships is problematic. Whereas economists have had to overcome such obstacles by using ingenious statistical methods, many natural scientists have been able to rely on controlled experiments to test their theories.

These common descriptions of theoretical and empirical economic science may well have historical validity. But nowadays, they both have to be modified. With increasing confidence, researchers in psychological economics have been able to demonstrate that in some situations, individuals do not behave like "homo oeconomicus". Researchers in experimental economics have developed methods for controlled laboratory experiments in economics. A number of scholars have contributed to this development, including previous Laureates: Maurice Allais and Herbert Simon thus brought psychological perspectives into decision theory while John Nash and Reinhard Selten conducted early experimental studies. But this year's Laureates are the key figures in these two fields.

Daniel Kahneman has enriched economic analysis with fundamental insights from cognitive psychology, in particular regarding behavior under uncertainty. In collaboration with the late Amos Tversky, he conducted a series of classical experiments to reveal how human *judgement* under uncertainty adheres to systematic rules of thumb or shortcuts. They showed, for example, that most experimental subjects attribute equal credence to the mean values in small and large samples. This "law of small numbers" is contrary to the law of large numbers in probability theory, that is, the certainty in estimates of the mean value of a population provided by the sample mean increases with sample size. Systematic errors in probability estimates may have important consequences, particularly in financial markets. A timely illustration is that most of us have to choose a pension fund. If we adhere to the law of small numbers, funds with short-term returns well above average will attract many investors, even if this favourable outcome is due entirely to chance.

Kahneman has also formulated a new theory for decision-making under uncertainty, known as *prospect theory*. This theory can capture behavioral patterns in human decision-making better than traditional economic theory. A key element in prospect theory is that individuals compare uncertain outcomes with a reference level which depends on the decision situation, instead of evaluating the outcome according to an absolute scale. A further element is that individuals' perception of probabilities is to some extent allowed to deviate from real predictions.

Whereas Kahneman studied human judgment and decisions on an individual basis, Vernon Smith has analyzed the interaction among individuals on markets. A reoccurring feature throughout his research is the development of feasible methods for carrying out economic experiments. The difficulties which arise in controlled experiments, where thinking people make economic decisions in the laboratory, are altogether different from those in experiments with elementary particles or cells. Smith has demonstrated ways of coping with these problems.

In one of his first experiments, Smith divided his subjects into buyers and sellers, after which he allowed them to bid for a good in accordance with given rules. Even though the subjects had not been informed about demand and supply conditions, Smith found that the prices in the laboratory converged towards a level close to the theoretical equilibrium price, where supply equals demand. Subsequent experiments verified that the general result was robust, but that price adjustment systematically depended on the precise rules governing the trade.

Auctions are used in many contexts, for example, in sales of government bonds and, in recent years, in privatization of former monopolies and distribution of transmission rights for mobile telephones. Economic theory makes clear predictions regarding the outcome of different auction methods, but they are difficult to test solely on the basis of observational data. Smith was able to conduct experiments that proved systematic relationships between the auction method and the average selling price, which in some cases coincide with – but in others deviate from – theoretical predictions.

In recent years, Smith has also demonstrated that experiments can be used in more complex situations, where economic theory does not provide precise results. In the same way that wind tunnel tests with prototypes can guide engineers before a real airplane is sent into the air, Smith has shown that laboratory experiments can guide economists before they launch new market methods, for instance in connection with deregulation or privatization.

Professor Kahneman,
Insights from cognitive psychology have been instrumental in establishing new theoretical and empirical results; in ongoing research, they guide thought-provoking attempts to reformulate many aspects of economic and financial theory. The new bridges across disciplines can largely be attributed to your innovative research on the boundary between economics and psychology.

Professor Smith,
Economics used to be regarded as a non-experimental science. This is no longer so; nowadays, economic experiments are routinely conducted in specialized labs all over the world. Scale or ethics may limit economic experimentation, but the methods you have developed continue to enrich our empirical toolbox.

Both of you have laid the foundations for an exciting renewal of economic research. It is a great honour for me to express, on behalf of the Royal Swedish Academy of Sciences, our warmest congratulations. I now ask you to step forward and receive your Prizes from His Majesty the King.

Daniel Kahneman

DANIEL KAHNEMAN

EARLY YEARS

I was born in Tel Aviv, in what is now Israel, in 1934, while my mother was visiting her extended family there; our regular domicile was in Paris. My parents were Lithuanian Jews, who had immigrated to France in the early 1920s and had done quite well. My father was the chief of research in a large chemical factory. But although my parents loved most things French and had some French friends, their roots in France were shallow, and they never felt completely secure. Of course, whatever vestiges of security they'd had were lost when the Germans swept into France in 1940. What was probably the first graph I ever drew, in 1941, showed my family's fortunes as a function of time – and around 1940 the curve crossed into the negative domain.

I will never know if my vocation as a psychologist was a result of my early exposure to interesting gossip, or whether my interest in gossip was an indication of a budding vocation. Like many other Jews, I suppose, I grew up in a world that consisted exclusively of people and words, and most of the words were about people. Nature barely existed, and I never learned to identify flowers or to appreciate animals. But the people my mother liked to talk about with her friends and with my father were fascinating in their complexity. Some people were better than others, but the best were far from perfect and no one was simply bad. Most of her stories were touched by irony, and they all had two sides or more.

In one experience I remember vividly, there was a rich range of shades. It must have been late 1941 or early 1942. Jews were required to wear the Star of David and to obey a 6 p.m. curfew. I had gone to play with a Christian friend and had stayed too late. I turned my brown sweater inside out to walk the few blocks home. As I was walking down an empty street, I saw a German soldier approaching. He was wearing the black uniform that I had been told to fear more than others – the one worn by specially recruited SS soldiers. As I came closer to him, trying to walk fast, I noticed that he was looking at me intently. Then he beckoned me over, picked me up, and hugged me. I was terrified that he would notice the star inside my sweater. He was speaking to me with great emotion, in German. When he put me down, he opened his wallet, showed me a picture of a boy, and gave me some money. I went home more certain than ever that my mother was right: people were endlessly complicated and interesting.

My father was picked up in the first large-scale sweep for Jews, and was interned for six weeks in Drancy, which had been set up as a way station to the extermination camps. He was released through the intervention of his firm, which was directed (a fact I learned only from an article I read a few years ago) by the financial mainstay of the Fascist anti-Semitic movement in France in the 1930s. The story of my father's release, which I never fully understood, also involved a beautiful woman and a German general who loved her. Soon afterward, we escaped to Vichy France, and stayed on the Riviera in relative safety, until the Germans arrived and we escaped again, to the center of France. My father died of inadequately treated diabetes, in 1944, just six weeks before the D-day he had been waiting for so desperately. Soon my mother, my sister, and I were free, and beginning to hope for the permits that would allow us to join the rest of our family in Palestine.

I had grown up intellectually precocious and physically inept. The ineptitude must have been quite remarkable, because during my last term in a French lycée, in 1946, my eighth-grade physical-education teacher blocked my inclusion in the Tableau d'Honneur–the Honor Roll–on the grounds that even his extreme tolerance had limits. I must also have been quite a pompous child. I had a notebook of essays, with a title that still makes me blush: "What I write of what I think." The first essay, written before I turned eleven, was a discussion of faith. It approvingly quoted Pascal's saying "Faith is God made perceptible to the heart" ("How right this is!"), then went on to point out that this genuine spiritual experience was probably rare and unreliable, and that cathedrals and organ music had been created to generate a more reliable, ersatz version of the thrills of faith. The child who wrote this had some aptitude for psychology, and a great need for a normal life.

ADOLESCENCE

The move to Palestine completely altered my experience of life, partly because I was held back a year and enrolled in the eighth grade for a second time–which meant that I was no longer the youngest or the weakest boy in the class. And I had friends. Within a few months of my arrival, I had found happier ways of passing time than by writing essays to myself. I had much intellectual excitement in high school, but it was induced by great teachers and shared with like-minded peers. It was good for me not to be exceptional anymore.

At age seventeen, I had some decisions to make about my military service. I applied to a unit that would allow me to defer my service until I had completed my first degree; this entailed spending the summers in officer-training school, and part of my military service using my professional skills. By that time I had decided, with some difficulty, that I would be a psychologist. The questions that interested me in my teens were philosophical–the meaning of life, the existence of God, and the reasons not to misbehave. But I was discovering that I was more interested in what made people believe in God than I was in whether God existed, and I was more curious about the origins of people's peculiar convictions about right and wrong than I was about ethics. When I went for vocational guidance, psychology emerged as the top recommendation, with economics not too far behind.

I got my first degree from the Hebrew University in Jerusalem, in two years, with a major in psychology and a minor in mathematics. I was mediocre in math, especially in comparison with some of the people I was studying with–several of whom went on to become world-class mathematicians. But psychology was wonderful. As a first-year student, I encountered the writings of the social psychologist Kurt Lewin and was deeply influenced by his maps of the life space, in which motivation was represented as a force field acting on the individual from the outside, pushing and pulling in various directions. Fifty years later, I still draw on Lewin's analysis of how to induce changes in behavior for my introductory lecture to graduate students at the Woodrow Wilson School of Public Affairs at Princeton. I was also fascinated by my early exposures to neuropsychology. There were the weekly lectures of our revered teacher Yeshayahu Leibowitz–I once went to one of his lectures with a fever of 41 degrees Celsius; they were simply not to be missed. And there was a visit by the German neurosurgeon Kurt Goldstein, who claimed that large wounds to the brain eliminated the capacity for abstraction and turned people into concrete thinkers. Furthermore, and most exciting, as Goldstein described them, the boundaries that separated abstract from concrete were not the ones that philosophers would have set. We now know that there was little substance to Goldstein's assertions, but at the time the idea of basing conceptual distinctions on neurological observations was so thrilling that I seriously considered switching to medicine in order to study neurology. The Chief of Neurosurgery at the Hadassah Hospital, who was a neighbor, wisely talked me out of that plan by pointing out that the study of medicine was too demanding to be undertaken as a means to any goal other than practice.

THE MILITARY EXPERIENCE

In 1954, I was drafted as a second lieutenant, and after an eventful year as a platoon leader I was transferred to the Psychology branch of the Israel Defense Forces. There, one of my occasional duties was to participate in the assessment of candidates for officer training. We used methods that had been developed by the British Army in the Second World War. One test involved a leaderless group challenge, in which eight candidates, with all insignia of rank removed and only numbers to identify them, were asked to lift a telephone pole from the ground and were then led to an obstacle, such as a 2.5-meter wall, where they were told to get to the other side of the wall without the pole touching either the ground or the wall, and without any of them touching the wall. If one of these things happened, they had to declare it and start again. Two of us would watch the exercise, which often took half an hour or more. We were looking for manifestations of the candidates' characters, and we saw plenty: true leaders, loyal followers, empty boasters, wimps–there were all kinds. Under the stress of the event, we felt, the soldiers' true nature would reveal itself, and we would be able to tell who would be a good leader and who would not. But the trouble was that, in fact, we could not tell. Every month or so we had a "statistics day," during which we would get feedback from the officer-training school, indicating the accuracy of our ratings of candidates' potential. The story was always the same: our ability to predict performance at the school was negligible. But the next day, there would be another batch of candidates to be taken to the obstacle field, where we would face them with the wall and see their true natures revealed. I was so impressed by the complete lack of connection between the statistical information and the compelling experience of insight that I coined a term for it: "the illusion of validity." Almost twenty years later, this term made it into the technical literature (Kahneman and Tversky, 1973). It was the first cognitive illusion I discovered.

Closely related to the illusion of validity was another feature of our discussions about the candidates we observed: our willingness to make extreme predictions about their future performance on the basis of a small sample of behavior. In fact, the issue of willingness did not arise, because we did not really distinguish predictions from observations. The soldier who took over when the group was in trouble and led the team over the wall was a leader at that moment, and if we asked ourselves how he would perform in officer-training, or on the battlefield, the best bet was simply that he would be as good a leader then as he was now. Any other prediction seemed inconsistent with the evidence. As I understood clearly only when I taught statistics some years later, the idea that predictions should be less extreme than the information on which they are based is deeply counterintuitive.

The theme of intuitive prediction came up again, when I was given the major assignment for my service in the Unit: to develop a method for interviewing all combat-unit recruits, in order to screen the unfit and help allocate soldiers to specific duties. An interviewing system was already in place, administered by a small cadre of interviewers, mostly young women, themselves recent graduates from good high schools, who had been selected for their outstanding performance in psychometric tests and for their interest in psychology. The interviewers were instructed to form a general impression of a recruit and then to provide some global ratings of how well the recruit was expected to perform in a combat unit. Here again, the statistics of validity were dismal. The interviewers' ratings did not predict with substantial accuracy any of the criteria in which we were interested.

My assignment involved two tasks: first, to figure out whether there were personality dimensions that mattered more in some combat jobs than in others, and then to develop interviewing guidelines that would identify those dimensions. To perform the first task, I visited units of infantry, artillery, armor, and others, and collected global evaluations of the performance of the soldiers in each unit, as well as ratings on several personality dimensions. It was a hopeless task, but I didn't realize that then. Instead, spending weeks and months on complex analyses using a manual Monroe calculator with a rather iffy handle, I invented a statistical technique for the analysis of multi-attribute heteroscedastic data, which I used to produce a complex description of the psychological requirements of the various units. I was capitalizing on chance, but the technique had enough charm for one of my graduate-school teachers, the eminent personnel psychologist Edwin Ghiselli, to write it up in what became my first published article. This was the beginning of a lifelong interest in the statistics of prediction and description.

I had devised personality profiles for a criterion measure, and now I needed to propose a predictive interview. The year was 1955, just after the publication of "Clinical versus statistical prediction" (Meehl, 1954), Paul Meehl's classic book in which he showed that clinical prediction was consistently inferior to actuarial prediction. Someone must have given me the book to read, and it certainly had a big effect on me. I developed a structured interview schedule with a set of questions about various aspects of civilian life, which the interviewers were to use to generate ratings about six different aspects of personality (including, I remember, such things as "masculine pride" and "sense of obligation"). Soon I had a near-mutiny on my hands. The cadre of interviewers, who had taken pride in the exercise of their clinical skills, felt that they were being reduced to unthinking robots, and my confident declarations–"Just make sure that you are reliable, and leave validity to me"–did not satisfy them. So I gave in. I told them that after completing "my" six ratings as instructed, they were free to exercise their clinical judgment by generating a global evaluation of the recruit's potential in any way they pleased. A few months later, we obtained our first validity data, using ratings of the recruits' performance as a criterion. Validity was much higher than it had been. My recollection is that we achieved correlations of close to .30, in contrast to about .10 with the previous methods. The most instructive finding was that the interviewers' global evaluation, produced at the end of a structured interview, was by far the most predictive of all the ratings they made. Trying to be reliable had made them valid. The puzzles with which I struggled at that time were the seed of the paper on the psychology of intuitive prediction that Amos Tversky and I published much later.

The interview system has remained in use, with little modification, for many decades. And if it appears odd that a twenty-one-year-old lieutenant would be asked to set up an interviewing system for an army, one should remember that the state of Israel and its institutions were only seven years old at the time, that improvisation was the norm, and that professionalism did not exist. My immediate supervisor was a man with brilliant analytical skills, who had trained in chemistry but was entirely self-taught in statistics and psychology. And with a B.A. in the appropriate field, I was the best-trained professional psychologist in the military.

GRADUATE SCHOOL YEARS

I came out of the Army in 1956. The academic planners at the Hebrew University had decided to grant me a fellowship to obtain a PhD abroad, so that I would be able to return and teach in the psychology department. But they wanted me to acquire some additional polish before facing the bigger world. Because the psychology department had temporarily closed, I took some courses in philosophy, did some research, and read psychology on my own for a year. In January of 1958, my wife, Irah, and I landed at the San Francisco airport, where the now famous sociologist Amitai Etzioni was waiting to take us to Berkeley, to the Flamingo Motel on University Avenue, and to the beginning of our graduate careers.

My experience of graduate school was quite different from that of students today. The main landmarks were examinations, including an enormous multiple-choice test that covered all of psychology. (A long list of classic studies preceded by the question "Which of the following is *not* a study of latent learning?" comes to mind.) There was less emphasis on formal apprenticeship, and virtually no pressure to publish while in school. We took quite a few courses and read broadly. I remember a comment of Professor Rosenweig's on the occasion of my oral exam. I should enjoy my current state, he advised, because I would never again know as much psychology. He was right.

I was an eclectic student. I took a course on subliminal perception from Richard Lazarus, and wrote with him a speculative article on the temporal development of percepts, which was soundly and correctly rejected. From that subject I came to an interest in the more technical aspects of vision and I spent some time learning about optical benches from Tom Cornsweet. I audited the clinical sequence, and learned about personality tests from Jack Block and from Harrison Gough. I took classes on Wittgenstein in the philosophy department. I dabbled in the philosophy of science. There was no particular rhyme or reason to what I was doing, but I was having fun.

My most significant intellectual experience during those years did not occur in graduate school. In the summer of 1958, my wife and I drove across the United States to spend a few months at the Austen Riggs Clinic in Stockbridge, Massachusetts, where I studied with the well-known psychoanalytic theorist David Rapaport, who had befriended me on a visit to Jerusalem a few years earlier. Rapaport believed that psychoanalysis contained the elements of a valid theory of memory and thought. The core ideas of that theory, he argued, were laid out in the seventh chapter of Freud's "Interpretation of Dreams," which sketches a model of mental energy (cathexis). With the other young people in Rapaport's circle, I studied that chapter like a Talmudic text, and tried to derive from it experimental predictions about short-term memory. This was a wonderful experience, and I would have gone back if Rapaport had not died suddenly later that year. I had enormous respect for his fierce mind. Fifteen years after that summer, I published a book entitled "Attention and Effort," which contained a theory of attention as a limited resource. I realized only while writing the acknowledgments for the book that I had revisited the terrain to which Rapaport had first led me.

Austen Riggs was a major intellectual center for psychoanalysis, dedicated primarily to the treatment of dysfunctional descendants of wealthy families. I was allowed into the case conferences, which were normally scheduled on Fridays, usually to evaluate a patient who had spent a month of live-in observation at the clinic. Those attending would have received and read, the night before, a folder with detailed notes from every department about the person in question. There would be a lively exchange of impressions among the staff, which included the fabled Erik Erikson. Then the patient would come in for a group interview, which was followed by a brilliant discussion. On one of those Fridays, the meeting took place and was conducted as usual, despite the fact that the patient had committed suicide during the night. It was a remarkably honest and open discussion, marked by the contradiction between the powerful retrospective sense of the inevitability of the event and the obvious fact that the event had not been foreseen. This was another cognitive illusion to be understood. Many years later, Baruch Fischhoff wrote, under my and Amos Tversky's supervision, a beautiful PhD thesis that illuminated the hindsight effect.

In the spring of 1961, I wrote my dissertation on a statistical and experimental analysis of the relations between adjectives in the semantic differential. This allowed me to engage in two of my favorite pursuits: the analysis of complex correlational structures and FORTRAN programming. One of the programs I wrote would take twenty minutes to run on the university mainframe, and I could tell whether it was working properly by the sequence of movement on the seven tape units that it used. I wrote the thesis in eight days, typing directly on the purple "ditto" sheets that we used for duplication at the time. That was probably the last time I wrote anything without pain. The paper itself, by sharp contrast, was so convoluted and dreary that my teacher, Susan Ervin, memorably described the experience of reading it as "wading through wet mush." I spent the summer of 1961 in the ophthalmology department, doing research on contour interference. And then it was time to go home to Jerusalem, and start teaching in the psychology department at the Hebrew University.

TRAINING TO BECOME A PROFESSIONAL

I loved teaching undergraduates and I was good at it. The experience was consistently gratifying because the students were so good: they were selected on the basis of a highly competitive entrance exam, and most were easily PhD material. I took charge of the basic first-year statistics class and, for some years, taught both that course and the second-year course in research methods, which also included a large dose of statistics. To teach effectively I did a lot of serious thinking about valid intuitions on which I could draw and erroneous intuitions that I should teach students to overcome. I had no idea, of course, but I was laying the foundation for a program of research on judgment under uncertainty. Another course I was teaching concerned the psychology of perception, which also contributed quite directly to the same program.

I had learned a lot in Berkeley, but I felt that I had not been adequately trained to do research. I therefore decided that in order to acquire the basic skills I would need to have a proper laboratory and do regular science–I needed to be a solid short-order cook before I could aspire to become a chef. So I set up a vision lab, and over the next few years I turned out competent work on energy integration in visual acuity. At the same time, I was trying to develop a research program to study affiliative motivation in children, using an approach that I called a "psychology of single questions." My model for this kind of psychology was research reported by Walter Mischel (1961a, 1961b) in which he devised two questions that he posed to samples of children in Caribbean islands: "You can have this (small) lollipop today, or this (large) lollipop tomorrow," and "Now let's pretend that there is a magic man ... who could change you into anything that you would want to be, what would you want to be?" The answer to the latter question was scored 1, if it referred to a profession or to an achievement-related trait, otherwise 0. The responses to these lovely questions turned out to be plausibly correlated with numerous characteristics of the child and the child's background. I found this inspiring: Mischel had succeeded in creating a link between an important psychological concept and a simple operation to measure it. There was (and still is) almost nothing like it in psychology, where concepts are commonly associated with procedures that can be described only by long lists or by convoluted paragraphs of prose.

I got quite nice results in my one-question studies, but never wrote up any of the work, because I had set myself impossible standards: in order not to pollute the literature, I wanted to report only findings that I had replicated in detail at least once, and the replications were never quite perfect. I realized only gradually that my aspirations demanded more statistical power and therefore much larger samples than I was intuitively inclined to run. This observation also came in handy some time later.

My achievements in research in these early years were quite humdrum, but I was excited by several opportunities to bring psychology to bear on the real world. For these tasks, I teamed up with a colleague and friend, Ozer Schild. Together, we designed a training program for functionaries who were to introduce new immigrants from underdeveloped countries, such as Yemen, to modern farming practices (Kahneman and Schild, 1966). We also developed a training course for instructors in the flight school of the Air Force. Our faith in the usefulness of psychology was great, but we were also well aware of the difficulties of changing behavior without changing institutions and incentives. We may have done some good, and we certainly learned a lot.

I had the most satisfying Eureka experience of my career while attempting to teach flight instructors that praise is more effective than punishment for promoting skill-learning. When I had finished my enthusiastic speech, one of the most seasoned instructors in the audience raised his hand and made his own short speech, which began by conceding that positive reinforcement might be good for the birds, but went on to deny that it was optimal for flight cadets. He said, "On many occasions I have praised flight cadets for clean execution of some aerobatic maneuver, and in general when they try it again, they do worse. On the other hand, I have often screamed at cadets for bad execution, and in general they do better the next time. So please don't tell us that reinforcement works and punishment does not, because the opposite is the case." This was a joyous moment, in which I understood an important truth about the world: because we tend to reward others when they do well and punish them when they do badly, and because there is regression to the mean, it is part of the human condition that we are statistically punished for rewarding others and rewarded for punishing them. I immediately arranged a demonstration in which each participant tossed two coins at a target behind his back, without any feedback. We measured the distances from the target and could see that those who had done best the first time had mostly deteriorated on their second try, and vice versa. But I knew that this demonstration would not undo the effects of lifelong exposure to a perverse contingency.

My first experience of truly successful research came in 1965, when I was on sabbatical leave at the University of Michigan, where I had been invited by Jerry Blum, who had a lab in which volunteer participants performed various cognitive tasks while in the grip of powerful emotional states induced by hypnosis. Dilation of the pupil is one of the manifestations of emotional arousal, and I therefore became interested in the causes and consequences of changes of pupil size. Blum had a graduate student called Jackson Beatty. Using primitive equipment, Beatty and I made a real discovery: when people were exposed to a series of digits they had to remember, their pupils dilated steadily as they listened to the digits, and contracted steadily when they recited the series. A more difficult transformation task (adding 1 to each of a series of four digits) caused a much larger dilation of the pupil. We quickly published these results, and within a year had completed four articles, two of which appeared in *Science*. Mental effort remained the focus of my research during the subsequent year, which I spent at Harvard. During that year, I also heard a brilliant talk on experimental studies of attention by a star English psychologist named Anne Treisman, who would become my wife twelve years later. I was so impressed that I committed myself to write a chapter on attention for a Handbook in Cognitive Psychology. The Handbook was never published, and my chapter eventually became a rather ambitious book. The work on vision that I did that year was also more interesting than the work I had been doing in Jerusalem. When I returned home in 1967, I was, finally, a well-trained research psychologist.

THE COLLABORATION WITH AMOS TVERSKY

From 1968 to 1969, I taught a graduate seminar on the applications of psychology to real-world problems. In what turned out to be a life-changing event, I asked my younger colleague Amos Tversky to tell the class about what was going on in his field of judgment and decision-making. Amos told us about the work of his former mentor, Ward Edwards, whose lab was using a research paradigm in which the subject is shown two bookbags filled with poker chips. The bags are said to differ in their composition (e.g., 70:30 or 30:70 white/red). One of them is randomly chosen, and the participant is given an opportunity to sample successively from it, and required to indicate after each trial the probability that it came from the predominantly red bag. Edwards had concluded from the results that people are "conservative Bayesians": they almost always adjust their confidence interval in the proper

Amos Tversky.

direction, but rarely far enough. A lively discussion developed around Amos's talk. The idea that people were conservative Bayesian did not seem to fit with the everyday observation of people commonly jumping to conclusions. It also appeared unlikely that the results obtained in the sequential sampling paradigm would extend to the situation, arguably more typical, in which sample evidence is delivered all at once. Finally, the label of 'conservative Bayesian' suggested the implausible image of a process that gets the correct answer, then adulterates it with a bias. I learned recently that one of Amos's friends met him that day and heard about our conversation, which Amos described as having severely shaken his faith in the neo-Bayesian idea. I do remember that Amos and I decided to meet for lunch to discuss our hunches about the manner in which probabilities are "really" judged. There we exchanged personal accounts of our own recurrent errors of judgment in this domain, and decided to study the statistical intuitions of experts.

I spent the summer of 1969 doing research at the Applied Psychological Research Unit in Cambridge, England. Amos stopped there for a few days on his way to the United States. I had drafted a questionnaire on intuitions about sampling variability and statistical power, which was based largely on my personal experiences of incorrect research planning and unsuccessful replications. The questionnaire consisted of a set of questions, each of which could stand on its own–this was to be another attempt to do psychology with single questions. Amos went off and administered the questionnaire to participants at a meeting of the Mathematical Psychology Association, and a few weeks later we met in Jerusalem to look at the results and write a paper.

The experience was magical. I had enjoyed collaborative work before, but this was something different. Amos was often described by people who knew him as the smartest person they knew. He was also very funny, with an endless supply of jokes appropriate to every nuance of a situation. In his presence, I became funny as well, and the result was that we could spend hours of solid work in continuous mirth. The paper we wrote was deliberately humorous–we described a prevalent belief in the "law of small numbers," according to which the law of large numbers extends to small numbers as well. Although we never wrote another humorous paper, we continued to find amusement in our work–I have probably shared more than half of the laughs of my life with Amos.

And we were not just having fun. I quickly discovered that Amos had a remedy for everything I found difficult about writing. No wet-mush problem for him: he had an uncanny sense of direction. With him, movement was always forward. Progress might be slow, but each of the myriad of successive drafts that we produced was an improvement–this was not something I could take for granted when working on my own. Amos's work was always characterized by confidence and by a crisp elegance, and it was a joy to find those characteristics now attached to my ideas as well. As we were writing our first paper, I was conscious of how much better it was than the more hesitant piece I would have written by myself. I don't know exactly what it was that Amos found to like in our collaboration–we were not in the habit of trading compliments–but clearly he was also having a good time. We were a team, and we remained in that mode for well over a decade. The Nobel Prize was awarded for work that we produced during that period of intense collaboration.

At the beginning of our collaboration, we quickly established a rhythm that we maintained during all our years together. Amos was a night person, and I was a morning person. This made it natural for us to meet for lunch and a long afternoon together, and still have time to do our separate things. We spent hours each day, just talking. When Amos's first son Oren, then fifteen months old, was told that his father was at work, he volunteered the comment "Aba talk Danny." We were not only working, of course–we talked of everything under the sun, and got to know each other's mind almost as well as our own. We could (and often did) finish each other's sentences and complete the joke that the other had wanted to tell, but somehow we also kept surprising each other.

We did almost all the work on our joint projects while physically together, including the drafting of questionnaires and papers. And we avoided any explicit division of labor. Our principle was to discuss every disagreement until it had been resolved to mutual satisfaction, and we had tie-breaking rules for only two topics: whether or not an item should be included in the list of references (Amos had the casting vote), and who should resolve any issue of English grammar (my dominion). We did not initially have a concept of a senior author. We tossed a coin to determine the order of authorship of our first paper, and alternated from then on until the pattern of our collaboration changed in the 1980s.

One consequence of this mode of work was that all our ideas were jointly owned. Our interactions were so frequent and so intense that there was never much point in distinguishing between the discussions that primed an idea, the act of uttering it, and the subsequent elaboration of it. I believe that many scholars have had the experience of discovering that they had expressed (sometimes even published) an idea long before they really understood its significance. It takes time to appreciate and develop a new thought. Some of the greatest joys of our collaboration–and probably much of its success–came from our ability to elaborate each other's nascent thoughts: if I expressed a half-formed idea, I knew that Amos would be there to understand it, probably more clearly than I did, and that if it had merit he would see it. Like most people, I am somewhat cautious about exposing tentative thoughts to others–I must first make sure that they are not idiotic. In the best years of the collaboration, this caution was completely absent. The mutual trust and the complete lack of defensiveness that we achieved were particularly remarkable because both of us–Amos even more than I–were known to be severe critics. Our magic worked only when we were by ourselves. We soon learned that joint collaboration with any third party should be avoided, because we became competitive in a threesome.

Amos and I shared the wonder of together owning a goose that could lay golden eggs – a joint mind that was better than our separate minds. The statistical record confirms that our joint work was superior, or at least more influential, than the work we did individually (Laibson and Zeckhauser, 1998). Amos and I published eight journal articles during our peak years (1971–1981), of which five had been cited more than a thousand times by the end of 2002. Of our separate works, which in total number about 200, only Amos' theory of similarity (Tversky, 1977) and my book on attention (Kahneman, 1973) exceeded that threshold. The special style of our collaborative work was recognized early by a referee of our first theoretical paper (on representativeness), who caused it to be rejected by *Psychological Review*. The eminent psychologist who wrote that review – his anonymity was betrayed years later – pointed out that he was familiar with the separate lines of work that Amos and I had been pursuing, and considered both quite respectable. However, he added the unusual remark that we seemed to bring out the worst in each other, and certainly should not collaborate. He found most objectionable our method of using multiple single questions as evidence – and he was quite wrong there as well.

THE SCIENCE '74 ARTICLE AND THE RATIONALITY DEBATE

From 1971 to 1972, Amos and I were at the Oregon Research Institute (ORI) in Eugene, a year that was by far the most productive of my life. We did a considerable amount of research and writing on the availability heuristic, on the psychology of prediction, and on the phenomena of anchoring and overconfidence–thereby fully earning the label "dynamic duo" that our colleagues attached to us. Working evenings and nights, I also completely rewrote my book on *Attention and Effort,* which went to the publisher that year, and remains my most significant independent contribution to psychology.

At ORI, I came into contact for the first time with an exciting community of researchers that Amos had known since his student days at Michigan: Paul Slovic, Sarah Lichtenstein, and Robyn Dawes. Lewis Goldberg was also there, and I learned much from his work on clinical and actuarial judgment, and from Paul Hoffman's ideas about paramorphic modeling. ORI was one of the major centers of judgment research, and I had the occasion to meet quite a few of the significant figures of the field when they came visiting, Ken Hammond among them.

Some time after our return from Eugene, Amos and I settled down to review what we had learned about three heuristics of judgment (representativeness, availability, and anchoring) and about a list of a dozen biases associated with these heuristics. We spent a delightful year in which we did little but work on a single article. On our usual schedule of spending afternoons together, a day in which we advanced by a sentence or two was considered quite productive. Our enjoyment of the process gave us unlimited patience, and we wrote as if the precise choice of every word were a matter of great moment.

We published the article in *Science* because we thought that the prevalence of systematic biases in intuitive assessments and predictions could possibly be of interest to scholars outside psychology. This interest, however, could not be taken for granted, as I learned in an encounter with a well-known American philosopher at a party in Jerusalem. Mutual friends had encouraged us to talk about the research that Amos and I were doing, but almost as soon as I began my story he turned away, saying, "I am not really interested in the psychology of stupidity."

The *Science* article turned out to be a rarity: an empirical psychological article that (some) philosophers and (a few) economists could and did take seriously. What was it that made readers of the article more willing to listen than the philosopher at the party? I attribute the unusual attention at least as much to the medium as to the message. Amos and I had continued to practice the psychology of single questions, and the *Science* article–like others we wrote–incorporated questions that were cited verbatim in the text. These questions, I believe, personally engaged the readers and convinced them that we were concerned not with the stupidity of Joe Public but with a much more interesting issue: the susceptibility to erroneous intuitions of intelligent, sophisticated, and perceptive individuals such as themselves. Whatever the reason, the article soon became a standard reference as an attack on the rational-agent model, and it spawned a large literature in cognitive science, philosophy, and psychology. We had not anticipated that outcome.

I realized only recently how fortunate we were not to have aimed deliberately at the large target we happened to hit. If we had intended the article as a challenge to the rational model, we would have written it differently, and the challenge would have been less effective. An essay on rationality would have required a definition of that concept, a treatment of boundary conditions for the occurrence of biases, and a discussion of many other topics about which we had nothing of interest to say. The result would have been less crisp, less provocative, and ultimately less defensible. As it was, we offered a progress report on our study of judgment under uncertainty, which included much solid evidence. All inferences about human rationality were drawn by the readers themselves.

The conclusions that readers drew were often too strong, mostly because existential quantifiers, as they are prone to do, disappeared in the transmission. Whereas we had shown that (some, not all) judgments about uncertain events are mediated by heuristics, which (sometimes, not always) produce predictable biases, we were often read as having claimed that people cannot think straight. The fact that men had walked on the moon was used more than once as an argument against our position. Because our treatment was mistakenly taken to be inclusive, our silences became significant. For example, the fact that we had written nothing about the role of social factors in judgment was taken as an indication that we thought these factors were unimportant. I suppose that we could have prevented at least some of these misunderstandings, but the cost of doing so would have been too high.

The interpretation of our work as a broad attack on human rationality – rather than as a critique of the rational-agent model – attracted much opposition, some quite harsh and dismissive. Some of the critiques were normative, arguing that we compared judgments to inappropriate normative standards (Cohen, 1981; Gigerenzer, 1991, 1996). We were also accused of spreading a tendentious and misleading message that exaggerated the flaws of human cognition (Lopes, 1991, and many others). The idea of systematic bias was rejected as unsound on evolutionary grounds (Cosmides & Tooby, 1996). Some authors dismissed the research as a collection of artificial puzzles designed to fool undergraduates. Numerous experiments were conducted over the years, to show that cognitive illusions could "be made to disappear" and that heuristics had been invented to explain "biases that do not exist" (Gigerenzer, 1991). After participating in a few published skirmishes in the early 80's, Amos and I adopted a policy of not criticizing the critiques of our work, although we eventually felt compelled to make an exception (Kahneman and Tversky, 1996).

A young colleague and I recently reviewed the experimental literature, and concluded that the empirical controversy about the reality of cognitive illusions dissolves when viewed in the perspective of a dual-process model (Kahneman and Frederick, 2002). The essence of such a model is that judgments can be produced in two ways (and in various mixtures of the two): a rapid, associative, automatic, and effortless intuitive process (sometimes called System 1), and a slower, rule-governed, deliberate and effortful process (System 2) (Sloman, 1996; Stanovich and West, 1999). System 2 'knows" some of the rules that intuitive reasoning is prone to violate, and sometimes intervenes to correct or replace erroneous intuitive judgments. Thus, errors of intuition occur when two conditions are satisfied: System 1 generates the error and System 2 fails to correct. In this view, the experiments in which cognitive illusions were "made to disappear" did so by facilitating the corrective operations of System 2. They tell us little about the intuitive judgments that are suppressed.

If the controversy is so simply resolved, why was it not resolved in 1971, or in 1974? The answer that Frederick and I proposed refers to the conversational context in which the early work was done:

> A comprehensive psychology of intuitive judgment cannot ignore such controlled thinking, because intuition can be overridden or corrected by self-critical operations, and because intuitive answers are not always available. But this sensible position seemed irrelevant in the early days of research on judgment heuristics. The authors of the "law of small numbers" saw no need to examine correct statistical reasoning. They believed that including easy questions in the design would insult the participants and bore the readers. More generally, the early studies of heuristics and biases displayed little interest in the conditions under which intuitive reasoning is preempted or overridden – controlled reasoning leading to correct answers was seen as a default case that needed no explaining. A lack of concern for boundary conditions is typical of "young" research programs, which naturally focus on demonstrating new and unexpected effects, not on making them disappear. (Kahneman and Frederick, 2002, p. 50).

What happened, I suppose, is that because the 1974 paper was influential it altered the context in which it was read in subsequent years. Its being misunderstood was a direct consequence of its being taken seriously. I wonder how often this occurs.

Amos and I always dismissed the criticism that our focus on biases reflected a generally pessimistic view of the human mind. We argued that this criticism confuses the medium of bias research with a message about rationality. This confusion was indeed common. In one of our demonstrations of the availability heuristic, for example, we asked respondents to compare the frequency with which some letters appeared in the first and in the third position in words. We selected letters that in fact appeared more frequently in the third position, and showed that even for these letters the first position was judged more frequent, as would be predicted on the idea that it is easier to search through a mental dictionary by the first letter. The experiment was used by some critics as an example of our own confirmation bias, because we had demonstrated availability only in cases in which this heuristic led to bias. But this criticism assumes that our aim was to demonstrate biases, and misses the point of what we were trying to do. Our aim was to show that the availability heuristic controls frequency estimates *even when that heuristic leads to error* – an argument that cannot be made when the heuristic leads to correct responses, as it often does.

There is no denying, however, that the name of our method and approach created a strong association between heuristics and biases, and thereby contributed to giving heuristics a bad name, which we did not intend. I recently came to realize that the association of heuristics and biases has affected me as well. In the course of an exchange of messages with Ralph Hertwig (no fan of heuristics and biases), I noticed that the phrase "judging by representativeness" was in my mind a label for a cluster of errors in intuitive statistical judgment. Judging probability by representativeness is indeed associated with systematic errors. But a large component of the process is the judgment *of* representativeness, and that judgment is often subtle and highly skilled. The feat of the master chess player who instantly recognizes a position as "white mates in three" is an instance of judgment of representativeness. The undergraduate who instantly recognizes that enjoyment of puns is more representative of a computer scientist than of an accountant is also exhibiting high skill in a social and cultural judgment. My long-standing failure to associate specific benefits to the concept of representativeness was a revealing mistake.

What did I learn from the controversy about heuristics and biases? Like most protagonists in debates, I have few memories of having changed my mind under adversarial pressure, but I have certainly learned more than I know. For example, I am now quick to reject any description of our work as demonstrating human irrationality. When the occasion arises, I carefully explain that research on heuristics and biases only refutes an unrealistic conception of rationality, which identifies it as comprehensive coherence. Was I always so careful? Probably not. In my current view, the study of judgment biases requires attention to the interplay between intuitive and reflective thinking, which sometimes allows biased judgments and sometimes overrides or corrects them. Was this always as clear to me as it is now? Probably not. Finally, I am now very impressed by the observation I mentioned earlier, that the most highly skilled cognitive performances are intuitive, and that many complex judgments share the speed, confidence and accuracy of routine perception. This observation is not new to me, but did it always loom as large in my views as it now does? Almost certainly not.

As my obvious struggle with this topic reveals, I thoroughly dislike controversies where it is clear that no minds will be changed. I feel diminished by losing my objectivity when in point-scoring mode, and downright humiliated when I get angry. Indeed, my phobia for professional anger is such that I have allowed myself for many years the luxury of refusing to referee papers that might arouse that emotion: If the tone is snide, or the review of the facts more tendentious than normal, I return the paper back to the editor without commenting on it. I consider myself fortunate not to have had too many of the nasty experiences of professional quarrels, and am grateful for the occasional encounters with open minds across lines of sharp debate (Ayton, 1998; Klein, 2000).

PROSPECT THEORY

After the publication of our paper on judgment in *Science* in 1974, Amos suggested that we study decision-making together. This was a field in which he was already an established star, and about which I knew very little. For an introduction, he suggested that I read the relevant chapters of the text "Mathematical Psychology," of which he was a co-author (Coombs, Dawes and

Tversky, 1970). Utility theory and the paradoxes of Allais and Ellsberg were discussed in the book, along with some of the classic experiments in which major figures in the field had joined in an effort to measure the utility function for money by eliciting choices between simple gambles.

I learned from the book that the name of the game was the construction of a theory that would explain Allais's paradox parsimoniously. As psychological questions go, this was not a difficult one, because Allais's famous problems are, in effect, an elegant way to demonstrate that the subjective response to probability is not linear. The subjective non-linearity is obvious: the difference between probabilities of .10 and .11 is clearly less impressive than the difference between 0 and .01, or between .99 and 1.00. The difficulty and the paradox exist only for decision theorists, because the non-linear response to probability produces preferences that violate compelling axioms of rational choice and are therefore incompatible with standard expected utility theory. The natural response of a decision theorist to the Allais paradox, certainly in 1975 and probably even today, would be to search for a new set of axioms that have normative appeal and yet permit the non-linearity. The natural response of psychologists was to set aside the issue of rationality and to develop a descriptive theory of the preferences that people actually have, regardless of whether or not these preferences can be justified.

The task we set for ourselves was to account for observed preferences in the quaintly restricted universe within which the debate about the theory of choice has traditionally been conducted: monetary gambles with few outcomes (all positive), and definite probabilities. This was an empirical question, and data were needed. Amos and I solved the data collection problem with a method that was both efficient and pleasant. We spent our hours together inventing interesting choices and examining our preferences. If we agreed on the same choice we provisionally assumed that other people would also accept it, and we went on to explore its theoretical implications. This unusual method enabled us to move quickly, and we constructed and discarded models at a dizzying rate. I have a distinct memory of a model that was numbered 37, but cannot vouch for the accuracy of our count.

As was the case in our work on judgment, our central insights were acquired early and, as was the case in our work on judgment, we spent a vast amount of time and effort before publishing a paper that summarized those insights (Kahneman and Tversky, 1979). The first insight came as a result of my naïveté. When reading the mathematical psychology textbook, I was puzzled by the fact that all the choice problems were described in terms of gains and losses (actually, almost always gains), whereas the utility functions that were supposed to explain the choices were drawn with wealth as the abscissa. This seemed unnatural, and psychologically unlikely. We immediately decided to adopt changes and/or differences as carriers of utility. We had no inkling that this obvious move was truly fundamental, or that it would open the path to behavioral economics. Harry Markowitz, who won the Nobel Prize in economics in 1990, had proposed changes of wealth as carriers of utility in 1952, but he did not take this idea very far.

The shifts from wealth to changes of wealth as carriers of utility is significant because of a property of preferences that we later labeled *loss-aversion:* the response to losses is consistently much more intense than the response to corresponding gains, with a sharp kink in the value function at the reference point. Loss aversion is manifest in the extraordinary reluctance to accept risk that is observed when people are offered a gamble on the toss of a coin: most will reject a gamble in which they might lose $20, unless they are offered more than $40 if they win. The concept of loss aversion was, I believe, our most useful contribution to the study of decision making. The asymmetry between gains and losses solves quite a few puzzles, including the widely noted and economically irrational distinction that people draw between opportunity costs and 'real' losses. Loss aversion also helps explain why real-estate markets dry up for long periods when prices are down, and it contributes to the explanation of a widespread bias favoring the status quo in decision making. Finally, the asymmetric consideration of gains and losses extends to the domain of moral intuitions, in which imposing losses and failing to share gains are evaluated quite differently. But of course, none of that was visible to Amos and me when we first decided to assume a kinked value function – we needed that kink to account for choices between gambles.

Another set of early insights came when Amos suggested that we flip the signs of outcomes in the problems we had been considering. The result was exciting. We immediately detected a remarkable pattern, which we called "reflection": changing the signs of all outcomes in a pair of gambles almost always caused the preference to change from risk averse to risk seeking, or vice-versa. For example, we both preferred a sure gain of $900 over a .9 probability of gaining $1,000 (or nothing), but we preferred a gamble with a .9 probability of losing $1,000 over a sure loss of $900. We were not the first to observe this pattern. Raiffa (1968) and Williams (1966) knew about the prevalence of risk-seeking in the negative domain. But ours was apparently the first serious attempt to make something of it.

We soon had a draft of a theory of risky choice, which we called "value theory" and presented at a conference in the spring of 1975. We then spent about three years polishing it, until we were ready to submit the article for publication. Our effort during those years was divided between the tasks of exploring interesting implications of our theoretical formulation and developing answers to all plausible objections. To amuse ourselves, we invented the specter of an ambitious graduate student looking for flaws, and we labored to make that student's task as thankless as possible. The most novel idea of prospect theory occurred to us in that defensive context. It came quite late, as we were preparing the final version of the paper. We were concerned with the fact that a straightforward application of our model implied that the value of the prospect ($100, .01; $100, .01) is larger than the value of ($100, .02). The prediction is wrong, of course, because most decision makers will spontaneously transform the former prospect into the latter and treat them as equivalent in subsequent operations of evaluation and choice. To eliminate the problem we proposed that decision-makers, prior to evaluating the prospects, perform an editing operation that collects similar outcomes and adds their probabilities. We went on to propose several other editing operations that provided an explicit and psychologically plausible defense against a variety of superficial counter-examples to the core of the theory. We had succeeded in making life quite difficult for that pedantic graduate student. But we had also made a truly significant advance, by making it explicit that the objects of choice are mental representations, not objective states of the world. This was a large step toward the development of a concept of framing, and eventually toward a new critique of the model of the rational agent.

When we were ready to submit the work for publication, we deliberately chose a meaningless name for our theory: "prospect theory." We reasoned that if the theory ever became well known, having a distinctive label would be an advantage. This was probably wise.

I looked at the 1975 draft recently, and was struck by how similar it is to the paper that was eventually published, and also by how different the two papers are. Most of the key ideas, most of the key examples, and much of the wording were there in the early draft. But that draft lacks the authority that was gained during the years that we spent anticipating objections. "Value theory" would not have survived the close scrutiny that a significant article ultimately gets from generations of scholars and students, who only are obnoxious if you give them a chance.

We published the paper in *Econometrica*. The choice of venue turned out to be important; the identical paper, published in *Psychological Review*, would likely have had little impact on economics. But our decision was not guided by a wish to influence economics. *Econometrica* just happened to be the journal where the best papers on decision-making to date had been published, and we were aspiring to be in that company.

And there was another way in which the impact of prospect theory depended crucially on the medium, as well as the message. Prospect theory was a formal theory, and its formal nature was the key to the impact it had in economics. Every discipline of social science, I believe, has some ritual tests of competence, which must be passed before a piece of work is considered worthy of attention. Such tests are necessary to prevent information overload, and they are also important aspects of the tribal life of the disciplines. In particular, they allow insiders to ignore just about anything that is done by members of other tribes, and to feel no scholarly guilt about doing so. To serve this screening function efficiently, the competence tests usually focus on some aspect of form or method, and have little or nothing to do with substance. Prospect theory passed such a test in economics, and its observations became a legitimate (though optional) part of the scholarly discourse in that discipline. It is a strange and rather arbitrary process that selects some pieces of scientific writing for relatively enduring fame while committing most of what is published to almost immediate oblivion.

FRAMING AND MENTAL ACCOUNTING

Amos and I completed prospect theory during the academic year of 1977 to 1978, which I spent at the Center for Advanced Studies at Stanford, while he was visiting the psychology department there. Around that time, we began work on our next project, which became the study of framing. This was also the year in which the second most important professional friendship in my life–with Richard Thaler–had its start.

A framing effect is demonstrated by constructing two transparently equivalent versions of a given problem, which nevertheless yield predictably different choices. The standard example of a framing problem, which was developed quite early, is the 'lives saved, lives lost' question, which offers a choice between two public-health programs proposed to deal with an epidemic that is threatening 600 lives: one program will save 200 lives, the other has a 1/3 chance of saving all 600 lives and a 2/3 chance of saving none. In this version, people prefer the program that will save 200 lives for sure. In the second version, one program will result in 400 deaths, the other has a 2/3 chance of 600 deaths and a 1/3 chance of no deaths. In this formulation most people prefer the gamble. If the same respondents are given the two problems on separate occasions, many give incompatible responses. When confronted with their inconsistency, people are quite embarrassed. They are also quite helpless to resolve the inconsistency, because there are no moral intuitions to guide a choice between different sizes of a surviving population.

Amos and I began creating pairs of problems that revealed framing effects while working on prospect theory. We used them to show sensitivity to gains and losses (as in the lives example), and to illustrate the inadequacy of a formulation in which the only relevant outcomes are final states. In that article, we also showed that a single-stage gamble could be rearranged as a two-stage gamble in a manner that left the bottom-line probabilities and outcomes unchanged but reversed preferences. Later, we developed examples in which respondents are asked to make simultaneous choices in two problems, A and B. One of the problems involves gains and elicits a risk-averse choice; the other problem involves losses and elicits risk-seeking. A majority of respondents made both these choices. However, the problems were constructed so that the combination of choices that people made was actually dominated by the combination of the options they had rejected.

These are not parlor-game demonstrations of human stupidity. The ease with which framing effects can be demonstrated reveals a fundamental limitation of the human mind. In a rational-agent model, the agent's mind functions just as she would like it to function. Framing effects violate that basic requirement: the respondents who exhibit susceptibility to framing effects wish their minds were able to avoid them. We were able to conceive of only two kinds of mind that would avoid framing effects: (1) If responses to all outcomes and probabilities were strictly linear, the procedures that we used to produce framing effects would fail. (2) If individuals maintained a single canonical and all-inclusive view of their outcomes, truly equivalent problems would be treated equivalently. Both conditions are obviously impossible. Framing effects violate a basic requirement of rationality which we called invariance (Kahneman and Tversky, 1984) and Arrow (1982) called extensionality. It took us a long time and several iterations to develop a forceful statement of this contribution to the rationality debate, which we presented several years after our framing paper (Tversky and Kahneman, 1986).

Another advance that we made in our first framing article was the inclusion of riskless choice problems among our demonstrations of framing. In making that move, we had help from a new friend. Richard Thaler was a young economist, blessed with a sharp and irreverent mind. While still in graduate school, he had trained his ironic eye on his own discipline and had collected a set of pithy anecdotes demonstrating obvious failures of basic tenets of economic theory in the behavior of people in general–and of his very conservative professors in Rochester in particular. One key observation was the endowment effect, which Dick illustrated with the example of the owner of a bottle of old wine, who would refuse to sell it for $200 but would not pay as much as $100 to replace it if it broke. Sometime in 1976, a copy of the 1975 draft of prospect theory got into Dick's hands, and that event made a significant difference to our lives. Dick realized that the endowment effect, which is a genuine puzzle in the context of standard economic theory, is readily explained by two assumptions derived from prospect theory. First, the carriers of utility are not states (owning or not owning the wine), but changes–getting the wine or giving it up. And giving up is weighted more than getting, by loss aversion. When Dick learned that Amos and I would be in Stanford in 1977/8, he secured a visiting appointment at the Stanford branch of the National Bureau of Economic Research, which is located on the same hill as the Center for Advanced Studies. We soon became friends, and have ever since had a considerable influence on each other's thinking.

The endowment effect was not the only thing we learned from Dick. He had also developed a list of phenomena of what we now call "mental accounting." Mental accounting describes how people violate rationality by failing to maintain a comprehensive view of outcomes, and by failing to treat money as fungible. Dick showed how people segregate their decisions into separate accounts, then struggle to keep each of these accounts in the black. One of his compelling examples was the couple who drove through a blizzard to a basketball game because they had already paid for the tickets, though they would have stayed at home if the tickets had been free. As this example illustrates, Dick had independently developed the skill of doing "one-question economics." He inspired me to invent another story, in which a person who comes to the theater realizes that he has lost his ticket (in one version), or an amount of cash equal to the ticket value (in another version). People report that they would be very likely still to buy a ticket if they had lost the cash, presumably because the loss has been charged to general revenue. On the other hand, they describe themselves as quite likely to go home if they have lost an already purchased ticket, presumably because they do not want to pay twice to see the same show.

BEHAVIORAL ECONOMICS

Our interaction with Thaler eventually proved to be more fruitful than we could have imagined at the time, and it was a major factor in my receiving the Nobel Prize. The committee cited me "for having integrated insights from psychological research into economic science ....". Although I do not wish to renounce any credit for my contribution, I should say that in my view the work of integration was actually done mostly by Thaler and the group of young economists that quickly began to form around him, starting with Colin Camerer and George Loewenstein, and followed by the likes of Matthew Rabin, David Laibson, Terry Odean, and Sendhil Mullainathan. Amos and I provided quite a few of the initial ideas that were eventually integrated into the thinking of some economists, and prospect theory undoubtedly afforded some legitimacy to the enterprise of drawing on psychology as a source of realistic assumptions about economic agents. But the founding text of behavioral economics was the first article in which Thaler (1980) presented a series of vignettes that challenged fundamental tenets of consumer theory. And the respectability that behavioral economics now enjoys within the discipline was secured, I believe, by some important discoveries Dick made in what is now called behavioral finance, and by the series of "Anomalies" columns that he published in every issue of the *Journal of Economic Perspectives* from 1987 to 1990, and has continued to write occasionally since that time.

In 1982, Amos and I attended a meeting of the Cognitive Science Society in Rochester, where we had a drink with Eric Wanner, a psychologist who was then vice-president of the Sloan Foundation. Eric told us that he was interested in promoting the integration of psychology and economics, and asked for our advice on ways to go about it. I have a clear memory of the answer we gave him. We thought that there was no way to "spend a lot of money honestly" on such a project, because interest in interdisciplinary work could not be coerced. We also thought that it was pointless to encourage psychologists to make themselves heard by economists, but that it could be useful to encourage and support the few economists who were interested in listening. Thaler's name surely came up. Soon after that conversation, Wanner became the president of the Russell Sage Foundation, and he brought the psychology/economics project with him. The first grant that he made in that program was for Dick Thaler to spend an academic year (1984–85) visiting me at the University of British Columbia, in Vancouver.

That year was one of the best in my career. We worked as a trio that also included the economist Jack Knetsch, with whom I had already started constructing surveys on a variety of issues, including valuation of the environment and public views about fairness in the marketplace. Jack had done experimental studies of the endowment effect and had seen the implications of that effect for the Coase theorem and for issues of environmental policy. We made a very good team: Jack's wisdom and imperturbable calm withstood the stress of Dick's boisterous temperament and of my perfectionist anxieties and intellectual restlessness.

We did a lot together that year. We conducted a series of market experiments involving real goods (the "mugs" studies), which eventually became a standard in that literature (Kahneman, Knetsch and Thaler, 1990). We also conducted multiple surveys in which we used experimentally varied vignettes to identify the rules of fairness that the public would apply to merchants, landlords, and employers(Kahneman, Knetsch and Thaler, 1986a). Our central observation was that in many contexts the existing situation (e.g., price, rent, or wage) defines a "reference transaction," to which the transactor (consumer, tenant, and employee) has an entitlement–the violation of such entitlements is considered unfair and may evoke retaliation. For example, cutting the wages of an employee merely because he could be replaced by someone who would accept a lower wage is unfair, although paying a lower wage to the replacement of an employee who quit is entirely acceptable. We submitted the paper to the *American Economic Review* and were utterly surprised by the outcome: the paper was accepted without revision. Luckily for us, the editor had asked two economists quite open to our approach to review the paper. We later learned that one of the referees was George Akerlof and the other was Alan Olmstead, who had studied the failures of markets to clear during an acute gas shortage.

One question that arose during this research was whether people would be wiling to pay something to punish another agent who treated them "unfairly", and in some circumstances would share a windfall with a stranger in an effort to be "fair". We decided to investigate these ideas using experiments for real stakes. The games that we invented for this purpose have become known as the ultimatum game and the dictator game. Alas, while writing up our second paper on fairness (Kahneman, Knetsch and Thaler, 1986b) we learned that we had been scooped on the ultimatum game by Werner Guth and his colleagues, who had published experiments using the same design a few years earlier. I remember being quite crestfallen when I learned this. I would have been even more depressed if I had known how important the ultimatum game would eventually become.

Most of the economics I know I learned that year, from Jack and Dick, my two willing teachers, and from what was in fact my first experience of communicating across tribal boundaries. I was also much impressed by an experimental game that Dick Thaler, James Brander, and I invented and called the N* game. The game is played by a group of, say, fifteen people. On each trial, a number $0 < N^* < 15$ is announced. The participants then make simultaneous choices of whether or not to "enter." Those who decide to enter announce their choice simultaneously. The payoff to the N entrants depends on their number, according to the following formula: $\$.25(N^* - N)$. We played the game a few times, once with the faculty of the psychology department at U.B.C. The results, although not surprising to an economist, struck me as magical. Within very few trials, a pattern emerged in which the number of entrants, N, was within 1 or 2 of N*, with no obvious systematic tendency to be higher or lower than N*. The group was doing the right thing collectively, although conversations with the participants and the obvious statistical analyses did not reveal any consistent strategies that made sense. It took me some time to realize that the magic we were observing was an equilibrium: the pattern we saw existed because no other pattern could be sustained. This idea had not been in my intellectual bag of tools. We never formally published the N* game–I described it informally in Kahneman (1987)–but it has been taken up by others (Erev & Rapoport, 1998).

That was the closest my research ever came to core economics, and since that time I have been mostly cheering Thaler and behavioral economics from the sidelines. There has been much to cheer about. As a mark of the progress that has been made, I recall a seminar in psychology and economics that I co-taught with George Akerlof, after Anne Treisman and I had moved from the University of British Columbia to Berkeley in 1986. I remember being struck by the reverence with which the rationality assumption was treated even by a free thinker such as George, and also by his frequent warnings to the students that they should not let themselves be seduced by the material we were presenting, lest their careers be permanently damaged. His advice to them was to stick to what he called "meat-and-potatoes economics," at least until their careers were secure. This opinion was quite common at the time. When Matthew Rabin joined the Berkeley economics department as a young assistant professor and chose to immerse himself in psychology, many considered the move professional suicide. Some fifteen years later, Rabin had earned the Clark medal, and George Akerlof had delivered a Nobel lecture entitled "Behavioral Macroeconomics."

Eric Wanner and the Russell Sage Foundation continued to support behavioral economics over the years. I was instrumental in the idea of using some of that support to set up a summer school for graduate students and young faculty in that field, and I helped Dick Thaler and Colin Camerer organize the first one, in 1994. When the fifth summer school convened in 2002, David Laibson, who had been a participant in 1994, was tenured at Harvard and was one of the three organizers. Terrance Odean and Sendhil Mullainathan, who had also participated as students, came back to lecture as successful researchers with positions in two of the best universities in the world. It was a remarkable experience to hear Matthew Rabin teach a set of guidelines for developing theories in behavioral economics – including the suggestion that the standard economic model should be a special case of the more complex and general models that were to be constructed. We had come a long way.

Although behavioral economics has enjoyed much more rapid progress and gained more respectability in economics than appeared possible fifteen years ago, it is still a minority approach and its influence on most fields of economics is negligible. Many economists believe that it is a passing fad, and some hope that it will be. The future may prove them right. But many bright young economists are now betting their careers on the expectation that the current trend will last. And such expectations have a way of being self-fulfilling.

LATER YEARS

Anne Treisman and I married and moved together to U.B.C. in 1978, and Amos and Barbara Tversky settled in Stanford that year. Amos and I were then at the peak of our joint game, and completely committed to our collaboration. For a few years, we managed to maintain it, by spending every second weekend together and by placing multiple phone calls each day, some lasting several hours. We completed the study of framing in that mode, as well as a study of the 'conjunction fallacy' in judgment (Tversky and Kahneman, 1983). But eventually the goose that had laid the golden eggs languished, and our collaboration tapered off. Although this outcome now appears inevitable, it came as a painful surprise to us. We had completely failed to appreciate how critically our successful interaction had depended on our being together at the birth of every significant idea, on our rejection of any formal division of labor, and on the infinite patience that became a luxury when we could meet only periodically. We struggled for years to revive the magic we had lost, but in vain.

We were again trying when Amos died. When he learned in the early months of 1996 that he had only a few months to live, we decided to edit a joint book on decision-making that would cover some of the progress that had been made since we had started working together on the topic more than twenty years before (Kahneman and Tversky, 2000). We planned an ambitious preface as a joint project, but I think we both knew from the beginning that we would not be granted enough time to complete it. The preface I wrote alone was probably my most painful writing experience.

During the intervening years, of course, we had continued to work, sometimes together sometimes with other collaborators. Amos took the lead in our most important joint piece, an extension of prospect theory to the multiple-outcome case in the spirit of rank-dependent models. He also carried out spectacular studies of the role of argument and conflict in decision-making, in collaborations with Eldar Shafir and with Itamar Simonson, as well as influential work on violations of procedural invariance in collaborations with Shmuel Sattath and with Paul Slovic. He engaged in a deep exploration of the mathematical structure of decision theories with Peter Wakker. And, in his last years, Amos was absorbed in the development of support theory, a general approach to thinking under uncertainty that his students have continued to explore. These are only his major programmatic research efforts in the field of decision-making–he did much more.

I, too, kept busy, and also kept moving. Anne Treisman and I moved to UC Berkeley in 1986, and from there to Princeton in 1993, where I happily took a split appointment that located me part-time in the Woodrow Wilson School of Public Affairs. Moving East also made it easier to maintain frequent contacts with friends, children and adored grandchildren in Israel.

Over the years I enjoyed productive collaborations with Dale Miller in the development of a theory of counterfactual thinking (Kahneman and Miller, 1986), and with Anne Treisman, in studies of visual attention and object perception. In addition to the work on fairness and on the endowment effect that we did with Dick Thaler, Jack Knetsch and I carried out studies of the valuation of public goods that became quite controversial and had a great influence on my own thinking. Further studies of that problem with Ilana Ritov eventually led to the idea that the translation of attitudes into dollars involves the almost arbitrary choice of a scale factor, leading some people who have quite similar values to state very different values of their willingness to pay, for no good reason (Kahneman, Ritov and Schkade, 1999). With David Schkade and the famous jurist Cass Sunstein I extended this idea into a program of research on arbitrariness in punitive damage decisions, which may yet have some influence on policy (Sunstein, Kahneman, Schkade and Ritov, 2002).

The focus of my research for the past fifteen years has been the study of various aspects of experienced utility – the measure of the utility of outcomes as people actually live them. The concept of utility in which I am interested was the one that Bentham and Edgeworth had in mind. However, experienced utility largely disappeared from economic discourse in the twentieth century, in favor of a notion that I call decision utility, which is inferred from choices and used to explain choices. The distinction could be of little relevance for fully rational agents, who presumably maximize experienced utility as well as decision utility. But if rationality cannot be assumed, the quality of consequences becomes worth measuring and the maximization of experienced utility becomes a testable proposition. Indeed, my colleagues and I have carried out experiments in which this proposition was falsified. These experiments exploit a simple rule that governs the assignment of remembered utility to past episodes in which an agent is passively exposed to a pleasant or unpleasant experience, such as watching a horrible film or an amusing one (Frederickson and Kahneman, 1993), or undergoing a colonoscopy (Redelmeier and Kahneman, 1993). Remembered utility turns out to be determined largely by the peak intensity of the pleasure or discomfort experienced during the episode, and by the intensity of pleasure or discomfort when the episode ended. The duration of the episode has almost no effect on its remembered utility. In accord with this rule, an episode of 60 seconds during which one hand is immersed in painfully cold water will leave a more aversive memory than a longer episode, in which the same 60 seconds are followed by another 30 seconds during which the temperature rises slightly. Although the extra 30 seconds are painful, they provide an improved end. When experimental participants are exposed to the two episodes, then given a choice of which to repeat, most choose the longer one (Kahneman, Fredrickson, Schreiber and Redelmeier, 1993). In these and in other experiments of the same kind (Schreiber and Kahneman, 2000), people make wrong choices between experiences to which they may be exposed, because they are systematically wrong about their affective memories Our evidence contradicts the standard rational model, which does not distinguish between experienced utility and decision utility. I have presented it as a new type of challenge to the assumption of rationality (Kahneman, 1994).

Most of my empirical work in recent years has been done in collaboration with my friend David Schkade. The current topic of our research is a study of well-being that builds on my previous research on experienced utility. We have assembled a multi-disciplinary team for an attempt to develop tools for measuring welfare, with the design specification that economists should be willing to take the measurements seriously.

Another major effort went into an essay that attempted to update the notion of judgment heuristics. That work was done in close collaboration with a young colleague, Shane Frederick. In the pains we took in the choice of every word it came close to matching my experiences with Amos (Kahneman and Frederick, 2002). My Nobel lecture is an extension of that essay.

One line of work that I hope may become influential is the development of a procedure of *adversarial collaboration,* which I have championed as a substitute for the format of critique-reply-rejoinder in which debates are currently conducted in the social sciences.[1] Both as a participant and as a reader I have been appalled by the absurdly adversarial nature of these exchanges, in which hardly anyone ever admits an error or acknowledges learning anything from the other. Adversarial collaboration involves a good-faith effort to conduct debates by carrying out joint research – in some cases there may be a need for an agreed arbiter to lead the project and collect the data. Because there is no expectation of the contestants reaching complete agreement at the end of the exercise, adversarial collaborations will usually lead to an unusual type of joint publication, in which disagreements are laid out as part of a jointly authored paper. I have had three adversarial collaborations, with Tom Gilovich and Victoria Medvec (Gilovich, Medvec and Kahneman, 1998), with Ralph Hertwig (where Barbara Mellers was the agreed arbiter, see Mellers, Hertwig and Kahneman, 2001), and with a group of experimental economists in the UK (Bateman et *al.*, 2003). An appendix in the Mellers *et al.* article proposes a detailed protocol for the conduct of adversarial collaboration. In another case I did not succeed in convincing two colleagues that we should engage in an adversarial collaboration, but we jointly developed another procedure that is also more constructive than the reply-rejoinder format. They wrote a critique of one of my lines of work, but instead of following up with the usual exchange of unpleasant comments we decided to write a joint piece, which started by a statement of what we did agree on, then went on to a series of short debates about issues on which we disagreed (Ariely, Kahneman, & Loewenstein, 2000). I hope that more efficient procedures for the conduct of controversies will be part of my legacy.

PART 2 – EULOGY FOR AMOS TVERSKY (JUNE 5, 1996)

People who make a difference do not die alone. Something dies in everyone who was affected by them. Amos made a great deal of difference, and when he died, life was dimmed and diminished for many of us.

[1] Although I did not know it, I was not the first to propose this procedure in psychology: an adversarial collaboration had been reported by Latham, Erez, & Locke (1988).

There is less intelligence in the world. There is less wit. There are many questions that will never be answered with the same inimitable combination of depth and clarity. There are standards that will not be defended with the same mix of principle and good sense. Life has become poorer.

There is a large Amos-shaped gap in the mosaic, and it will not be filled. It cannot be filled because Amos shaped his own place in the world, he shaped his life, and even his dying. And in shaping his life and his world, he changed the world and the life of many around him.

Amos was the freest person I have known, and he was able to be free because he was also one of the most disciplined.

Some of you may have tried to make Amos do something he did not want to do. I don't think that there are many with successes to recount. Unlike many of us, Amos could not be coerced or embarrassed into chores or empty rituals. In that sense he was free, and the object of envy for many of us. But the other side of freedom is the ability to find joy in what one does, and the ability to adapt creatively to the inevitable. I will say more about the joy later. The supreme test of Amos's ability to accept what cannot be changed came in the last few months. Amos loved living. Death, at a cruelly young age was imposed on him, before his children's lives had fully taken shape, before his work was done. But he managed to die as he had lived – free. He died as he intended. He wanted to work to the last, and he did. He wanted to keep his privacy, and he did. He wanted to help his family through their ordeal, and he did. He wanted to hear the voices of his friends one last time, and he found a way to do that through the letters that he read with pleasure, sadness and pride, to the end.

There are many forms of courage, and Amos had them all. The indomitable serenity of his last few months is one. The civic courage of adopting principled and unpopular positions is another, and he had that too. And then there is the heroic, almost reckless courage, and he had that too.

My first memory of Amos goes back to 1957, when someone pointed out to me a thin and handsome lieutenant, wearing the red beret of the paratroopers, who had just taken the competitive entrance exam to the undergraduate program in Psychology at Hebrew University. The handsome lieutenant looked very pale, I remember. He had been wounded.

The paratrooper unit to which he belonged had been performing an exercise with live fire in front of the general staff of the Israel Defense Forces and all the military attaches. Amos was a platoon commander. He sent one of his soldiers carrying a long metal tube loaded with an explosive charge, which was to be slid under the barbed wire of the position they were attacking, and was to be detonated to create an opening for the attacking troops. The soldier moved forward, placed the explosive charge, and lit the fuse. And then he froze, standing upright in the grip of some unaccountable attack of panic. The fuse was short and the soldier was certainly about to be killed. Amos leapt from behind the rock he was using for cover, ran to the soldier, and managed to jump at him and bring him down just before the charge exploded. This was how he was wounded. Those who have been soldiers will recognize this act as one of almost unbelievable presence of mind and bravery. It was awarded the highest citation available in the Israeli army.

Amos almost never mentioned this incident, but some years ago, in the context of one of our frequent conversations about the importance of memory in our lives, he mentioned it and said that it had greatly affected him. We can probably appreciate what it means for a 20-year old to have passed a supreme test, to have done the impossible. We can understand how one could draw strength from such an event, especially if – as was the case for Amos – achieving the almost impossible was not a once-off thing. Amos achieved the almost impossible many times, in different contexts.

Amos' almost impossible achievements, as you all know, extended to the academic life. Amos derived some quiet pleasure from one aspect of his record: by a large margin, he published more articles in *Psychological Review*, the prestigious theory journal of the discipline, than anyone else in the history of that journal, which goes back more than 100 years. He had two pieces in press in *Psychological Review* when he died.

But other aspects of the record are even more telling than this statistic. The number of gems and enduring classics sets Amos apart even more. His early work on transitivity violations, elimination by aspects, similarity, the work we did together on judgment, prospect theory and framing, the Hot Hand, the beautiful work on the disjunction effect and Argument-Based Choice, and most recently an achievement of which Amos was particularly proud: Support Theory.

How did he do it? There are many stories one could tell. Amos' lifelong habit of working alone at night while others slept surely helped, but that wouldn't quite do it. Then there was that mind – the bright beam of light that would clear out an idea from the fog of other people's words, the inventiveness that could come up with six different ways of doing anything that needed to be done. You might think that having the best mind in the field and the most efficient work style would suffice. But there was more.

Amos had simply perfect taste in choosing problems, and he never wasted much time on anything that was not destined to matter. He also had an unfailing compass that always kept him going forward. I can attest to that from long experience.

It is not uncommon for me to write dozens of drafts of a paper, but I am never quite sure that they are actually improving, and often I wander in circles. Almost everything I wrote with Amos also went through dozens of drafts, but when you worked with Amos you just knew. There would be many drafts, and they would get steadily better.

Amos and I wrote an article in *Science* in 1974. It took us a year. We would meet at the van Leer Institute in Jerusalem for 4–6 hours a day. On a good day we would mark a net advance of a sentence or two. It was worth every minute. And I have never had so much fun. When we started work on Prospect Theory it was 1974, and in about 6 months we had been through 30-odd versions of the theory and had a paper ready for a conference. The paper had about 90% of the ideas of Prospect Theory, and quite properly did not impress anyone. We spent the better part of the following four years debugging it, trying to anticipate every objection.

What kept us at it was a phrase that Amos often used: "Let's do it right". There was never any hurry, any thought of compromising quality for speed. We could do it because Amos said the work was important, and you could trust him when he said that. We could also do it because the process was so intensely enjoyable.

But even that is not all. To understand Amos' genius – not a word I use lightly – you have to consider a phrase that he was using increasingly often in the last few years: "Let us take what the terrain gives". In his growing wisdom Amos believed that Psychology is almost impossible, because there is just not all that much we can say that is both important and demonstrably true. "Let us take what the terrain gives" meant not over-reaching, not believing that setting a problem implies it can be solved.

The unique ability Amos had – no one else I know comes close – was to find the one place where the terrain will yield (for Amos, usually gold) – and then to take it *all*. This skill in taking it all is what made so many of Amos' papers not only classics, but definitive. What Amos had done did not need redoing.

Whether or not to over-reach was a source of frequent, and frequently productive tension between Amos and me over nearly 30 years. I have always wanted to do more than could be done without risk of error, and have always taken pride in preferring to be approximately right rather than precisely wrong. Amos thought that if you pick the terrain properly you won't have to choose, because you can be precisely right. And time and time again he managed to be precisely right on things that mattered. Wisdom was part of his genius.

Fun was also part of Amos' genius. Solving problems was a lifelong source of intense joy for him, and the fact that he was richly rewarded for his problem solving never undermined that joy.

Much of the joy was social. Almost all of Amos' work was collaborative. He enjoyed working with colleagues and students, and he was supremely good at it. And his joy was infectious. The 12 or 13 years in which most of our work was joint were years of interpersonal and intellectual bliss. Everything was interesting, almost everything was funny, and there was the recurrent joy of seeing an idea take shape. So many times in those years we shared the magical experience of one of us saying something which the other would understand more deeply than the speaker had done. Contrary to the old laws of information theory, it was common for us to find that more information was received than had been sent. I have almost never had that experience with anyone else. If you have not had it, you don't know how marvelous collaboration can be . . .

REFERENCES

Ariely, D., Kahneman, D. & Loewenstein, G. (2000). Joint comment on "When does duration matter in judgment and decision making". *Journal of Experimental Psychology:* General, 129, 524–529.

Arrow, K. J. (1982). Risk perception in psychology and economics. *Economic Inquiry, 20,* 1–9.

Ayton, P. (1998). How bad is human judgment? In Forecasting with judgment, G. Wright & P. Goodwin (Eds.). West Sussex, England: John Wiley & Sons.

Bateman, I., Kahneman, D., Munro, A., Starmer, C. & Sugden, R. (2003). Is there loss aversion in buying? An adversarial collaboration. (under review).

Cohen, L.J. (1981). Can human irrationality be experimentally demonstrated? *The Behavioral and Brain Sciences,* 4, 317–331.

Coombs, C.H., Dawes, R.M., Tversky, A. (1970). Mathematical Psychology: An elementary introduction. Oxford, England: Prentice-Hall.

Cosmides, L. & Tooby, J. (1996). Are humans good intuitive statisticians after all? Rethinking some conclusions from the literature on judgment under uncertainty. *Cognition,* 58, 1–73.

Erev, I. & Rapoport, A. (1998). Coordination, "magic", and reinforcement learning in a market entry game. *Games and Economic Behavior,* 23, 146–175.

Gigerenzer, G. (1991). How to make cognitive illusions disappear: Beyond 'heuristics and biases'. In W. Stroebe & M. Hewstone (Eds.), *European review of social psychology,* (Vol. 2, 83–115). Chichester, England: Wiley.

Gigerenzer, G. (1996). On narrow norms and vague heuristics: A rebuttal to Kahneman and Tversky (1996). *Psychological Review, 103,* 592–596.

Gilovich, T., Medvec, V.H., & Kahneman, D. (1998). Varieties of regret: A debate and partial resolution. *Psychological Review, 105,* 602–605.

Kahneman, D., & Schild, E.O. (1966). Training agents of social change in Israel: Definitions of objectives and a training approach. *Human Organization, 25,* 323–327.

Kahneman, D. (1973). *Attention and Effort.* Englewood Cliffs, NJ: Prentice-Hall.

Kahneman, D., & Tversky, A. (1973). On the psychology of prediction. *Psychological Review, 80,* 237–251.

Kahneman, D., & Tversky, A. (1979). Prospect theory: An analysis of decisions under risk. *Econometrica, 47,* 313–327.

Kahneman, D., & Tversky, A. (1984). Choices, values and frames. *American Psychologist, 39,* 341–350.

Kahneman, D., Knetsch, J., & Thaler, R. (1986a). Fairness as a constraint on profit seeking: Entitlements in the market. *The American Economic Review, 76,* 728–741.

Kahneman, D., Knetsch, J., & Thaler, R. (1986b). Fairness and the assumptions of economics. *Journal of Business, 59,* S285–S300.

Kahneman, D., Knetsch, J., & Thaler, R. Experimental tests of the endowment effect and the Coase theorem. *Journal of Political Economy,* 1990, *98(6),* 1325–1348.

Kahneman, D., & Miller, D.T. (1986). Norm theory: Comparing reality to its alternatives. *Psychological Review, 93,* 136–153.

Kahneman, D. (1987). Experimental economics: A psychological perspective. In R. Tietz, W. Albers and R. Selten (Eds.), *Modeling Bounded Rationality,* 11–20.

Kahneman, D., Fredrickson, D.L., Schreiber, C.A., & Redelmeier, D.A. (1993). When more pain is preferred to less: Adding a better end. *Psychological Science, 4,* 401–405.

Kahneman, D. (1994). New challenges to the rationality assumption. *Journal of Institutional and Theoretical Economics, 150,* 18–36. Reprinted as Kahneman, D. New challenges to the rationality assumption. *Legal Theory, 3,* 1997, 105–124.

Kahneman, D., & Tversky, A. (1996). On the reality of cognitive illusions: A reply to Gigerenzer's critique. *Psychological Review, 103,* 582–591.

Kahneman, D., Ritov, I., and Schkade, D. (1999). Economic preferences or attitude expressions? An analysis of dollar responses to public issues. *Journal of Risk and Uncertainty, 19,* 220–242. Reprinted as Ch. 36 in Kahneman, D, and Tversky, A. (Eds.), *Choices, Values and Frames.* New York: Cambridge University Press and the Russell Sage Foundation, 2000.

Kahneman, D, and Tversky, A. (Eds.), *Choices, Values and Frames.* New York: Cambridge University Press and the Russell Sage Foundation, 2000.

Kahneman, D., and Frederick, S. (2002). Representativeness revisited: Attribute substitution in intuitive judgment. In T. Gilovich, D. Griffin and D. Kahneman (Eds.) *Heuristics and Biases: The Psychology of Intuitive Judgment.* New York: Cambridge University Press, 2002.

Klein, G. (2000). The fiction of optimization. In *Bounded rationality: The adaptive toolbox,* G. Gigerenzer & R. Selton (Eds.). Cambridge, USA: The MIT Press. 103–121.

Latham, G., Erez, M. & Locke, E. (1988), Resolving Scientific Disputes by the Joint Design of Crucial Experiments by the Antagonists: Application to the Erez-Latham Dispute Regarding Participation in Goal-Setting. *J. of Applied Psychology, 73,* 753–772.

Laibson, D. & Zeckhauser, R. (1998). Amos Tversky and the ascent of behavioral economics. *Journal of Risk and Uncertainty, 16,* 7–47.

Lopes, (1991). The rhetoric of irrationality. *Theory and Psychology, 1,* 65–82.

Meehl, P.E. (1954). Clinical versus statistical prediction: A theoretical analysis and a review of the evidence. Minneapolis: University of Minnesota Press.

Mellers, A., Hertwig, R., and Kahneman, D. (2001). Do frequency representations eliminate conjunction effects? An exercise in adversarial collaboration. *Psychological Science, 12,* 269–275.

Mischel, W. (1961a). Preference for delayed reinforcement and social-responsibility. *Journal of Abnormal and Social Psychology, 62,* 1–15.

Mischel, W. (1961b). Delay of gratification, need for achievement, and acquiescence in another culture. *Journal of Abnormal and Social Psychology, 62,* 543–560.

Raiffa, H. (1968). Decision analysis: Introductory lectures on choices under uncertainty. Reading, MA: Addison-Wesley.

Schreiber, C.A., & Kahneman, D. (2000). Determinants of the remembered utility of aversive sounds, *Journal of Experimental Psychology:* General, *129,* 27–42.

Sloman, S.A. 1996. The empirical case for two systems of reasoning. *Psychological Bulletin, 119,* 3–22.

Stanovich, K. E. (1999). *Who is Rational?: Studies of Individual Differences in Reasoning.* Lawrence Erlbaum. Mahwah, New Jersey.

Sunstein, C., Kahneman, D., Schkade, D., & Ritov, I. (2002). Predictably incoherent judgments. *Standard Law Review.*

Thaler, R. (1980). Toward a positive theory of consumer choice. *Journal of Economic Behavior and Organization, 39,* 36–90.

Tversky, A., & Kahneman, D. (1974). Judgment under uncertainty: Heuristics and biases. *Science, 185,* 1124–1131.

Tversky, A. (1977). Features of similarity. *Psychological Review, 84,* 327–352.

Tversky, A., & Kahneman, D. (1983). Extensional vs. intuitive reasoning: The conjunction fallacy in probability judgment. *Psychological Review,* 293–315.

Tversky, A., & Kahneman, D. (1986). Rational choice and the framing of decisions. *Journal of Business, 59,* S251–0S278.

Williams, A.C. (1966). Attitudes toward speculative risks as an indicator of attitudes toward pure risks. *Journal of Risk and Insurance, 33,* 577–586.

MAPS OF BOUNDED RATIONALITY: A PERSPECTIVE ON INTUITIVE JUDGMENT AND CHOICE

Prize Lecture, December 8, 2002

by

DANIEL KAHNEMAN*

Princeton University, Department of Psychology, Princeton, NJ 08544, USA.

The work cited by the Nobel committee was done jointly with the late Amos Tversky (1937–1996) during a long and unusually close collaboration. Together, we explored the psychology of intuitive beliefs and choices and examined their bounded rationality. This essay presents a current perspective on the three major topics of our joint work: heuristics of judgment, risky choice, and framing effects. In all three domains we studied intuitions – thoughts and preferences that come to mind quickly and without much reflection. I review the older research and some recent developments in light of two ideas that have become central to social-cognitive psychology in the intervening decades: the notion that thoughts differ in a dimension of accessibility – some come to mind much more easily than others – and the distinction between intuitive and deliberate thought processes.

Section 1 distinguishes two generic modes of cognitive function: an intuitive mode in which judgments and decisions are made automatically and rapidly, and a controlled mode, which is deliberate and slower. Section 2 describes the factors that determine the relative accessibility of different judgments and responses. Section 3 explains framing effects in terms of differential salience and accessibility. Section 4 relates prospect theory to the general

* This essay revisits problems that Amos Tversky and I studied together many years ago, and continued to discuss in a conversation that spanned several decades. The article is based on the Nobel lecture, which my daughter Lenore Shoham helped put together. It builds on an analysis of judgment heuristics that was developed in collaboration with Shane Frederick (Kahneman and Frederick, 2002). Shane Frederick, David Krantz, and Daniel Reisberg went well beyond the call of friendly duty in helping with this effort. Craig Fox, Peter McGraw, Daniel Read, David Schkade and Richard Thaler offered many insightful comments and suggestions. Kurt Schoppe provided valuable assistance, and Geoffrey Goodwin and Amir Goren helped with scholarly fact-checking. My research is supported by NSF 285-6086 and by the Woodrow Wilson School for Public and International Affairs at Princeton University. A different version of this article is to appear in the American Economic Review (December 2003).

proposition that changes and differences are more accessible than absolute values. Section 5 reviews an attribute substitution model of heuristic judgment. Section 6 describes a particular family of heuristics, called prototype heuristics. Section 7 concludes with a review of the argument.

1. INTUITION AND ACCESSIBILITY

From its earliest days, the research that Tversky and I conducted was guided by the idea that intuitive judgments occupy a position – perhaps corresponding to evolutionary history – between the automatic operations of perception and the deliberate operations of reasoning. Our first joint article examined systematic errors in the casual statistical judgments of statistically sophisticated researchers (Tversky & Kahneman, 1971). Remarkably, the intuitive judgments of these experts did not conform to statistical principles with which they were thoroughly familiar. In particular, their intuitive statistical inferences and their estimates of statistical power showed a striking lack of sensitivity to the effects of sample size. We were impressed by the persistence of discrepancies between statistical intuition and statistical knowledge, which we observed both in ourselves and in our colleagues. We were also impressed by the fact that significant research decisions, such as the choice of sample size for an experiment, are routinely guided by the flawed intuitions of people who know better. In the terminology that became accepted much later, we held a two-system view, which distinguished intuition from reasoning. Our research focused on errors of intuition, which we studied both for their intrinsic interest and for their value as diagnostic indicators of cognitive mechanisms.

The two-system view

The distinction between intuition and reasoning has been a topic of considerable interest in the intervening decades (among many others, see Epstein, 1994; Hammond, 1996; Jacoby, 1981, 1996; and numerous models collected by Chaiken & Trope, 1999; for comprehensive reviews of intuition, see Hogarth, 2002; Myers, 2002). In particular, the differences between the two modes of thought have been invoked in attempts to organize seemingly contradictory results in studies of judgment under uncertainty (Kahneman & Frederick, 2002; Sloman, 1996, 2002; Stanovich, 1999; Stanovich & West, 2002). There is considerable agreement on the characteristics that distinguish the two types of cognitive processes, which Stanovich and West (2000) labeled System 1 and System 2. The scheme shown in Figure 1 summarizes these characteristics: The operations of System 1 are fast, automatic, effortless, associative, and difficult to control or modify. The operations of System 2 are slower, serial, effortful, and deliberately controlled; they are also relatively flexible and potentially rule-governed. As indicated in Figure 1, the operating characteristics of System 1 are similar to the features of perceptual processes. On the other hand, as Figure 1 also shows, the operations of System 1, like those of System 2, are not restricted to the processing of current stimulation. Intuitive judgments deal with concepts as well as with percepts, and can be evoked by language.

In the model that will be presented here, the perceptual system and the intuitive operations of System 1 generate *impressions* of the attributes of objects of perception and thought. These impressions are not voluntary and need not be verbally explicit. In contrast, *judgments* are always explicit and intentional, whether or not they are overtly expressed. Thus, System 2 is involved in all judgments, whether they originate in impressions or in deliberate reasoning. The label 'intuitive' is applied to judgments that directly reflect impressions. As in several other dual-process models, one of the functions of System 2 is to monitor the quality of both mental operations and overt behavior (Gilbert, 2002; Stanovich & West, 2002). In the anthropomorphic terms that will be used here, the explicit judgments that people make (whether overt or not) are endorsed, at least passively, by System 2. Kahneman and Frederick (2002) suggested that the monitoring is normally quite lax, and allows many intuitive judgments to be expressed, including some that are erroneous.

Shane Frederick (personal communication, April 2003) has used simple puzzles to study cognitive self-monitoring, as in the following example: "A bat and a ball cost $1.10 in total. The bat costs $1 more than the ball. How much does the ball cost?" Almost everyone reports an initial tendency to answer "10 cents" because the sum $1.10 separates naturally into $1 and 10 cents, and 10 cents is about the right magnitude. Frederick found that many intelligent people yield to this immediate impulse: 50% (47/93) of Princeton students, and 56% (164/293) of students at the University of Michigan gave the wrong answer. Clearly, these respondents offered a response without checking it. The surprisingly high rate of errors in this easy problem illustrates how lightly the output of System 1 is monitored by System 2: people are not accus-

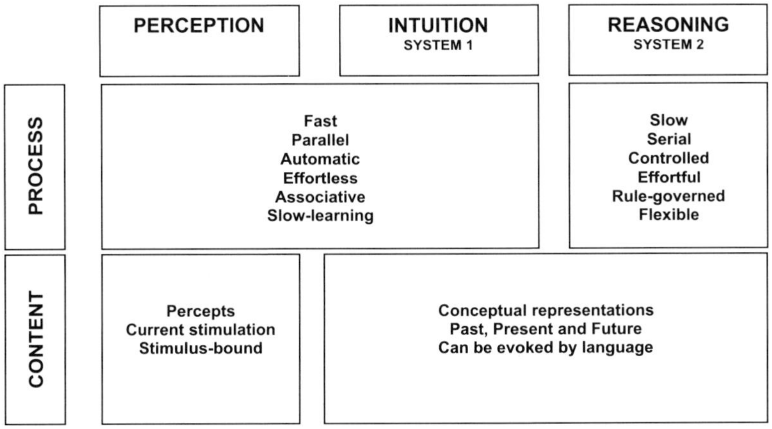

Figure 1.

tomed to thinking hard, and are often content to trust a plausible judgment that quickly comes to mind. Remarkably, errors in this puzzle and in others of the same type were significant predictors of relative indifference to delayed rewards (high discount rates), and of cheating.

The accessibility dimension

The core concept of the present analysis of intuitive judgments and preferences is *accessibility* – the ease with which particular mental contents come to mind (Higgins, 1996). A defining property of intuitive thoughts is that they come to mind spontaneously, like percepts. To understand intuition, then, we must understand why some thoughts are accessible and others are not. The concept of accessibility is applied more broadly in this treatment than in common usage. Category labels, descriptive dimensions (attributes, traits), values of dimensions, all can be described as more or less accessible, for a given individual exposed to a given situation at a particular moment.

For an illustration of differential accessibility, consider Figures 2a and 2b. As we look at the object in Figure 2a, we have immediate impressions of the height of the tower, the area of the top block, and perhaps the volume of the tower. Translating these impressions into units of height or volume requires a deliberate operation, but the impressions themselves are highly accessible. For other attributes, no perceptual impression exists. For example, the total area that the blocks would cover if the tower were dismantled is not perceptually accessible, though it can be estimated by a deliberate procedure, such as multiplying the area of a block by the number of blocks. Of course, the situation is reversed with Figure 2b. Now the blocks are laid out and an impression of total area is immediately accessible, but the height of the tower that could be constructed with these blocks is not.

Some relational properties are accessible. Thus, it is obvious at a glance

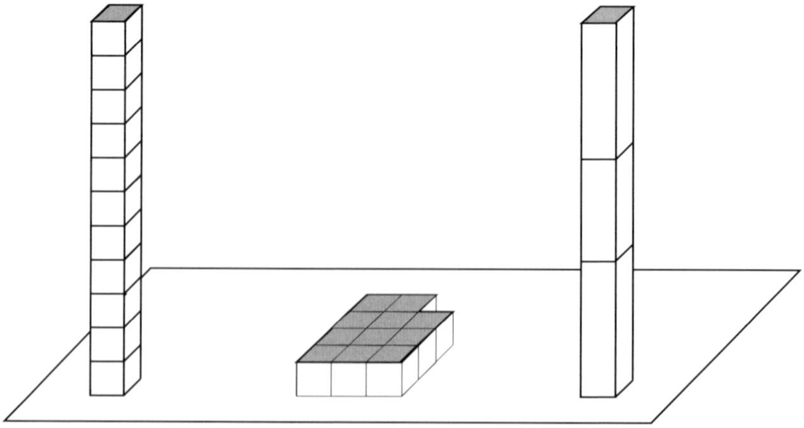

Figure 2a. *Figure 2b.* *Figure 2c.*

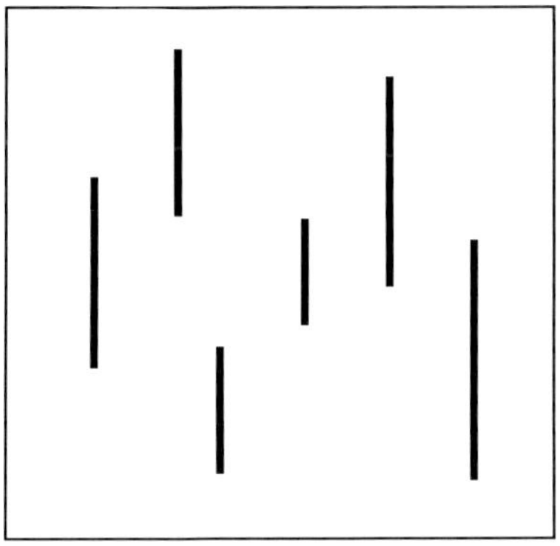

Figure 3.

that Figures 2a and 2c are different, but also that they are more similar to each other than either is to Figure 2b. And some statistical properties of ensembles are accessible, while others are not. For an example, consider the question "What is the average length of the lines in Figure 3?" This question is easy. When a set of objects of the same general kind is presented to an observer – whether simultaneously or successively – a representation of the set is computed automatically, which includes quite precise information about the average (Ariely, 2001; Chong & Treisman, in press). The representation of the prototype is highly accessible, and it has the character of a percept: we form an impression of the typical line without choosing to do so. The only role for System 2 in this task is to map this impression of typical length onto the appropriate scale. In contrast, the answer to the question "What is the total length of the lines in the display?" does not come to mind without considerable effort.

These perceptual examples serve to establish a dimension of accessibility. At one end of this dimension we find operations that have the characteristics of perception and of the intuitive System 1: they are rapid, automatic, and effortless. At the other end are slow, serial and effortful operations that people need a special reason to undertake. Accessibility is a continuum, not a dichotomy, and some effortful operations demand more effort than others. The acquisition of skill selectively increases the accessibility of useful responses and of productive ways to organize information. The master chess player does not see the same board as the novice, and the skill of visualizing the tower that could be built from an array of blocks could surely be improved by prolonged practice.

Determinants of accessibility

As it is used here, the concept of accessibility subsumes the notions of stimulus salience, selective attention, and response activation or priming. The different aspects and elements of a situation, the different objects in a scene, and the different attributes of an object – all can be more or less accessible. What becomes accessible in any particular situation is mainly determined, of course, by the actual properties of the object of judgment: it is easier to see a tower in Figure 2a than in Figure 2b, because the tower in the latter is only virtual. Physical salience also determines accessibility: if a large green letter and a small blue letter are shown at the same time, 'green' will come to mind first. However, salience can be overcome by deliberate attention: an instruction to look for the smaller letter will enhance the accessibility of all its features. Motivationally relevant and emotionally arousing stimuli spontaneously attract attention. All the features of an arousing stimulus become accessible, including those that are not linked to its motivational or emotional significance. This fact is known, of course, to the designers of billboards.

The perceptual effects of salience and of spontaneous and voluntary attention have counterparts in the processing of more abstract stimuli. For example, the statements 'Team A beat team B' and 'Team B lost to team A' convey the same information. Because each sentence draws attention to its subject, however, the two versions make different thoughts accessible. Accessibility also reflects temporary states of priming and associative activation, as well as enduring operating characteristics of the perceptual and cognitive systems. For example, the mention of a familiar social category temporarily increases the accessibility of the traits associated with the category stereotype, as indicated by a lowered threshold for recognizing manifestations of these traits (Higgins, 1996; for a review, see Fiske, 1998). And the "hot" states of high emotional and motivational arousal greatly increase the accessibility of thoughts that relate to the immediate emotion and current needs, and reduce the accessibility of other thoughts (George Loewenstein, 1996).

Some attributes, which Tversky and Kahneman (1983) called *natural assessments*, are routinely and automatically registered by the perceptual system or by System 1, without intention or effort. Kahneman and Frederick (2002) compiled a list of natural assessments, with no claim to completeness. In addition to physical properties such as size, distance and loudness, the list includes more abstract properties such as similarity (e.g., Tversky & Kahneman, 1983), causal propensity (Kahneman & Varey, 1990; Heider, 1944; Michotte, 1963), surprisingness (Kahneman & Miller, 1986), affective valence (e.g., Bargh, 1997; Cacioppo, Priester, & Berntson, 1993; Kahneman, Ritov, & Schkade, 1999; Slovic, Finucane, Peters, & MacGregor, 2002; Zajonc, 1980), and mood (Schwarz & Clore, 1983). Accessibility itself is a natural assessment – the routine evaluation of cognitive fluency in perception and memory (e.g., Jacoby & Dallas, 1981; Johnson, Dark, & Jacoby, 1985; Schwarz & Vaughn, 2002; Tversky & Kahneman, 1973).[1]

[1] The availability heuristic is based on an assessment of accessibility, in which frequencies or probabilities are judged by the ease with which instances come to mind. Tversky and I were responsible for this terminological confusion (Tversky and Kahneman, 1973).

Figure 4.

Figure 4 illustrates the effect of context on accessibility. An ambiguous stimulus that is perceived as a letter in a context of letters is seen as a number in a context of numbers. The figure also illustrates another point: the ambiguity is suppressed in perception. This aspect of the demonstration is spoiled for the reader who sees the two versions in close proximity, but when the two lines are shown separately, observers will not spontaneously become aware of the alternative interpretation. They 'see' the interpretation that is the most likely in its context, but have no subjective indication that it could be seen differently. Similarly, in bi-stable pictures such as the mother/daughter figure or the Necker cube, there is no perceptual representation of the instability. And almost no one (for a report of a tantalizing exception, see Wittreich, 1961) is able to see the Ames room as anything but rectangular, even when fully informed that the room is distorted, and that the photograph does not provide enough information to specify its true shape. As the transactionalists who built the Ames room emphasized, perception is a choice of which we are not aware, and we perceive what has been chosen.

The unpredictability that is perceived as inherent to some causal systems is psychologically distinct from epistemic uncertainty, which is attributed to one's own ignorance (Kahneman & Tversky, 1982b). Competing propensities are often perceived – as they are when we watch a close horse race. And counterfactual alternatives to what happened are also perceived – we can see a horse that was catching up at the finish as 'almost winning the race' (Kahneman & Varey, 1990). In contrast to competing propensities, however, competing interpretations of reality appear to suppress each other: we do not see each horse in a close finish as both winning and losing. Epistemic uncertainty and ambiguity are not natural assessments.

Uncertainty is poorly represented in intuition, as well as in perception. Indeed, the concept of judgment heuristics was invented to accommodate the observation that intuitive judgments of probability are mediated by attributes such as similarity and associative fluency, which are not intrinsically related to uncertainty. The central finding in studies of intuitive decisions, as described by Klein (1998), is that experienced decision makers working under pressure, such as captains of firefighting companies, rarely need to choose between options because in most cases only a single option comes to their mind. The options that were rejected are not represented. Doubt is a phenomenon of

System 2, a meta-cognitive appreciation of one's ability to think incompatible thoughts about the same thing.

As this discussion illustrates, much is known about the determinants of accessibility, but there is no general theoretical account of accessibility and no prospect of one emerging soon. In the context of research in judgment and decision making, however, the lack of a theory does little damage to the usefulness of the concept. For most purposes, what matters is that empirical generalizations about the determinants of accessibility are widely accepted – and, of course, that there are procedures for testing their validity. For example, the claims about differential accessibility of different attributes in Figures 2 and 3 appealed to the consensual judgments of perceivers, but claims about accessibility are also testable in other ways. In particular, judgments of relatively inaccessible properties are expected to be substantially slower and more susceptible to interference by concurrent mental activity. Some tasks can be performed even while retaining several digits in memory for subsequent recall, but the performance of more effortful tasks will collapse under cognitive load.

Considerations of accessibility and analogies between intuition and perception play a central role in the programs of research that I will briefly review in what follows. Framing effects in decision making (Section 3) arise when different descriptions of the same problem highlight different aspects of the outcomes. The core idea of prospect theory (Section 4) is that changes and differences are much more accessible than absolute levels of stimulation. Judgment heuristics, which explain many systematic errors in beliefs and preferences are explained in Section 5 by a process of attribute substitution: people sometimes evaluate a difficult attribute by substituting a more accessible one. Variations in the ability of System 2 to correct or override intuitive judgments are explained by variations in the accessibility of the relevant rules (Section 6). Diverse manifestations of the differential accessibility of averages and sums are discussed in Section 7.

2. FRAMING EFFECTS

In Figure 2, the same property (the total height of a set of blocks) is highly accessible in one display and not in another, although both displays contain the same information. This observation is entirely unremarkable – it does not seem shocking that some attributes of a stimulus are automatically perceived while others must be computed, or that the same attribute is perceived in one display of an object but must be computed in another. In the context of decision making, however, similar observations raise a significant challenge to the rational-agent model. The assumption that preferences are not affected by variations of irrelevant features of options or outcomes has been called extensionality (Arrow, 1982) and invariance (Tversky & Kahneman, 1986). Invariance is an essential aspect of rationality, which is violated in demonstrations of *framing effects* such as the Asian disease problem (Tversky & Kahneman, 1981):

> **Problem 1** – The Asian Disease
>
> Imagine that the United States is preparing for the outbreak of an unusual Asian disease, which is expected to kill 600 people. Two alternative programs to combat the disease have been proposed. Assume that the exact scientific estimates of the consequences of the programs are as follows:
>
> If Program A is adopted, 200 people will be saved
>
> If Program B is adopted, there is a one-third probability that 600 people will be saved and a two-thirds probability that no people will be saved
>
> Which of the two programs would you favor?

In this version of the problem, a substantial majority of respondents favor program A, indicating risk aversion. Other respondents, selected at random, receive a question in which the same cover story is followed by a different description of the options:

> If Program A' is adopted, 400 people will die
>
> If Program B' is adopted, there is a one-third probability that nobody will die and a two-thirds probability that 600 people will die

A clear majority of respondents now favor program B', the risk-seeking option. Although there is no substantive difference between the versions, they evidently evoke different associations and evaluations. This is easiest to see in the certain option, because outcomes that are certain are over-weighted relative to outcomes of high or intermediate probability (Kahneman & Tversky, 1979). Thus, the certainty of saving people is disproportionately attractive, and the certainty of deaths is disproportionately aversive. These immediate affective responses respectively favor A over B and B' over A'. As in Figures 2a and 2b, the different representations of the outcomes highlight some features of the situation and mask others.

The question of how to determine whether two decision problems are 'the same' or different does not have a general answer. To avoid this issue, Tversky and I restricted framing effects to discrepancies between choice problems that decision makers, upon reflection, consider effectively identical. The Asian disease problem passes this test: respondents who are asked to compare the two versions almost always conclude that the same action should be taken in both. Observers agree that it would be frivolous to let a superficial detail of formulation determine a choice that has life and death consequences.

In another famous demonstration of an embarrassing framing effect, McNeill, Pauker, Sox and Tversky (1982) induced different choices between surgery and radiation therapy, by describing outcome statistics in terms of survival rates or mortality rates. Because 90% short-term survival is less threatening than 10% immediate mortality, the survival frame yielded a substantially higher preference for surgery. The framing effect was no less pronounced among experienced physicians than it was among patients.

Shafir (1993) presented respondents with problems in which they played the role of a judge in adjudicating the custody of a child between divorcing parents. Each parent was described by a list of attributes. One of the descriptions was richer than the other: it contained more negative and more positive attributes. The framing of the instruction was varied. Some respondents were asked which custody request should be accepted, others decided which request should be rejected. The rich description was favored under both instructions, presumably because the respondents attended to its many advantages in deciding which custody request to accept, and to its many disadvantages in deciding about rejection.

A large-scale study by LeBoeuf and Shafir (in press) examined an earlier claim that framing effects are reduced, in a between-subjects design, for participants with high scores on 'need for cognition' (Smith & Levin, 1996). The original effect was not replicated in the more extensive study. However, LeBoeuf, and Shafir (2003) showed that more thoughtful individuals do show greater consistency in a within-subject design, where each respondent encounters both versions of each problem. This result is consistent with the present analysis. Respondents characterized by an active System 2 are more likely than others to notice the relationship between the two versions and to ensure the consistency of the responses to them. Thoughtfulness confers no advantage in the absence of a relevant cue, and is therefore irrelevant to performance in the between-subjects design.

Framing effects are not restricted to decision-making: Simon and Hayes (1976) documented an analogous observation in the domain of problem solving. They constructed a collection of transformation puzzles, all formally identical to the tower of Hanoi problem, and found that these 'problem isomorphs' varied greatly in difficulty. For example, the initial state and the target state were described in two of the versions as three monsters holding balls of different colors. The state transitions were described in one version as changes in the color of the balls, and in the other as balls being passed from one monster to another. The puzzle was solved much more easily when framed in terms of motion. The authors commented that "It would be possible for a subject to seek that representation which is simplest, according to some criterion, or to translate all such problems into the same, canonical, representation..." but "subjects will not employ such alternative strategies, even though they are available, but will adopt the representation that constitutes the most straightforward translation..." (Simon & Hayes, 1976, p 183).

Passive adoption of the formulation given appears to be a general principle, which applies as well to these puzzles, to the displays of Figure 2, and to the standard framing effects. People do not spontaneously compute the height of a tower that could be built from an array of blocks, and they do not spontaneously transform the representation of puzzles or decision problems. It is of interest, however, that some specialized perceptual and cognitive systems exhibit a limited ability to generate canonical representations for particular types of stimuli. Having seen a face once from a particular angle, for example, observers will recognize it from another angle, and they will also identify a black and white picture of it, or even a contour drawing. But even the versatile face-recognition module has its limitations: its performance is quite poor in recognizing familiar faces that are shown upside down. The brain mechanisms that support the comprehension of language also have a substantial ability to strip the surface details and get to the gist of meaning in an utterance, but this ability is limited as well. Few of us are able to recognize '137 x 24' and '3,288' as 'the same' number without going through some elaborate computations. Invariance cannot be achieved by a finite mind.

The impossibility of invariance raises significant doubts about the descriptive realism of rational-choice models (Tversky & Kahneman, 1986). Absent a system that reliably generates appropriate canonical representations, intuitive decisions will be shaped by the factors that determine the accessibility of different features of the situation. Highly accessible features will influence decisions, while features of low accessibility will be largely ignored. Unfortunately, there is no reason to believe that the most accessible features are also the most relevant to a good decision.

3. CHANGES OR STATES: PROSPECT THEORY

A general property of perceptual systems is that they are designed to enhance the accessibility of changes and differences (Palmer, 1999). Perception is *reference-dependent*: the perceived attributes of a focal stimulus reflect the contrast between that stimulus and a context of prior and concurrent stimuli. Figure 5 illustrates reference dependence in vision. The two enclosed squares have the same luminance, but they do not appear equally bright. The point of the demonstration is that the brightness of an area is not a single-parameter function of the light energy that reaches the eye from that area. An account of perceived brightness also requires a parameter for a reference value (often called adaptation level), which is influenced by the luminance of neighboring areas.

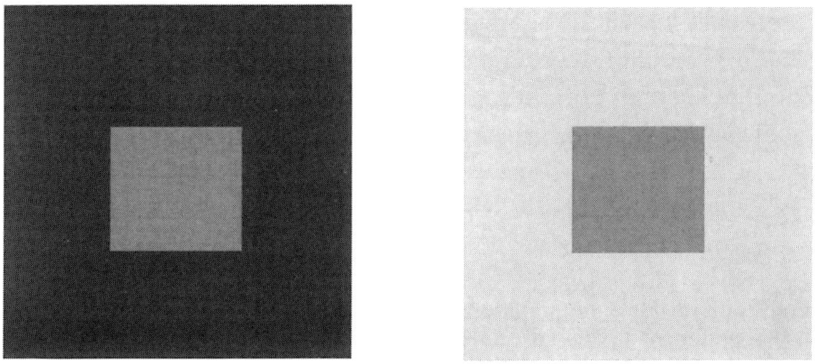

Figure 5.

The reference value to which current stimulation is compared also reflects the history of adaptation to prior stimulation. A familiar demonstration involves three buckets of water of different temperatures, arranged from cold on the left to hot on the right, with tepid in the middle. In the adapting phase, the left and right hands are immersed in cold and hot water, respectively. The initially intense sensations of cold and heat gradually wane. When both hands are then immersed in the middle bucket, the experience is heat in the left hand and cold in the right hand.

Reference-dependence in choice

The facts of perceptual adaptation were in our minds when Tversky and I began our joint research on decision making under risk. Guided by the analogy of perception, we expected the evaluation of decision outcomes to be reference-dependent. We noted, however, that reference-dependence is incompatible with the standard interpretation of Expected Utility Theory, the prevailing theoretical model in this area. This deficiency can be traced to the brilliant essay that introduced the first version of expected utility theory (Bernoulli, 1738).

One of Bernoulli's aims was to formalize the intuition that it makes sense for the poor to buy insurance and for the rich to sell it. He argued that the increment of *utility* associated with an increment of wealth is inversely proportional to initial wealth, and from this plausible psychological assumption he derived that the utility function for wealth is logarithmic. He then proposed that a sensible decision rule for choices that involve risk is to maximize the expected utility of wealth (the moral expectation). This proposition accomplished what Bernoulli had set out to do: it explained risk aversion, as well as the different risk attitudes of the rich and of the poor. The theory of expected utility that he introduced is still the dominant model of risky choice. The language of Bernoulli's essay is prescriptive – it speaks of what is sensible or reasonable to do – but the theory is also intended to describe the choices of reasonable men (Gigerenzer *et al.*, 1989). As in most modern treatments of decision making, there is no acknowledgment of any tension between prescription and description in Bernoulli's essay. The idea that decision makers evaluate outcomes by the utility of final asset positions has been retained in economic analyses for almost 300 years. This is rather remarkable, because the idea is easily shown to be wrong; I call it Bernoulli's error.

Bernoulli's model is flawed because it is *reference-independent*: it assumes that the value that is assigned to a given state of wealth does not vary with the decision maker's initial state of wealth.[2] This assumption flies against a basic principle of perception, where the effective stimulus is not the new level of

[2] What varies with wealth in Bernoulli's theory is the response to a given *change* of wealth. This variation is represented by the curvature of the utility function for wealth. Such a function cannot be drawn if the utility of wealth is reference-dependent, because utility then depends not only on current wealth but also on the reference level of wealth.

stimulation, but the difference between it and the existing adaptation level. The analogy to perception suggests that the carriers of utility are likely to be gains and losses rather than states of wealth, and this suggestion is amply supported by the evidence of both experimental and observational studies of choice (see Kahneman & Tversky, 2000). The present discussion will rely on two thought experiments, of the kind that Tversky and I devised when we developed the model of risky choice that we called Prospect Theory (Kahneman & Tversky, 1979).

Problem 2

Would you accept this gamble?

50% chance to win $150
50% chance to lose $100

Would your choice change if your overall wealth were lower by $100?

There will be few takers of the gamble in Problem 2. The experimental evidence shows that most people will reject a gamble with even chances to win and lose, unless the possible win is at least twice the size of the possible loss (e.g., Tversky & Kahneman, 1992). The answer to the second question is, of course, negative.

Next consider Problem 3:

Problem 3

Which would you choose?

lose $100 with certainty

or

50% chance to win $50
50% chance to lose $200

Would your choice change if your overall wealth were higher by $100?

In Problem 3, the gamble appears much more attractive than the sure loss. Experimental results indicate that risk seeking preferences are held by a large majority of respondents in choices of this kind (Kahneman & Tversky, 1979). Here again, the idea that a change of $100 in total wealth would affect preferences cannot be taken seriously.

Problems 2 and 3 evoke sharply different preferences, but from a Bernoullian perspective the difference is a framing effect: when stated in terms of final wealth, the problems only differ in that all values are lower by $100 in Problem 3 – surely an inconsequential variation. Tversky and I examined many choice pairs of this type early in our explorations of risky choice, and concluded that the abrupt transition from risk aversion to risk seeking could not plausibly be explained by a utility function for wealth. Preferences appeared to be determined by attitudes to gains and losses, defined relative to a reference point, but Bernoulli's theory and its successors did not incorporate a reference point. We therefore proposed an alternative theory of risk, in which the carriers of utility are gains and losses – changes of wealth rather than states of wealth. Prospect theory (Kahneman & Tversky, 1979) embraces the idea that preferences are reference-dependent, and includes the extra parameter that is required by this assumption.

The distinctive predictions of prospect theory follow from the shape of the value function, which is shown in Figure 6. The value function is defined on gains and losses and is characterized by four features: (1) it is concave in the domain of gains, favoring risk aversion; (2) it is convex in the domain of losses, favoring risk seeking; (3) Most important, the function is sharply kinked at the reference point, and *loss-averse* – steeper for losses than for gains by a factor of about 2–2.5 (Kahneman, Knetsch, & Thaler, 1991; Tversky & Kahneman, 1992). (4) Several studies suggest that the functions in the two domains are fairly well approximated by power functions with similar exponents, both less than unity (Swalm, 1966; Tversky & Kahneman, 1992). However, the value function is not expected to describe preferences for losses that are large relative to total assets, where ruin or near-ruin is a possible outcome.

Bernoulli's error – the assumption that the carriers of utility are final states – is not restricted to decision making under risk. Indeed, the error of reference-independence is built into the standard representation of indifference maps. It is puzzling to a psychologist that these maps do not include a representation of the decision maker's current holdings of various goods – the counterpart of the reference point in prospect theory. The parameter is not included, of course, because consumer theory assumes that it does not matter.

The wealth frame

The idea that the carriers of utility are changes of wealth rather than asset positions was described as the cornerstone of prospect theory (Kahneman & Tversky, 1979, p. 273). This statement implied that choices are always made by considering gains and losses rather than final states, but that proposition

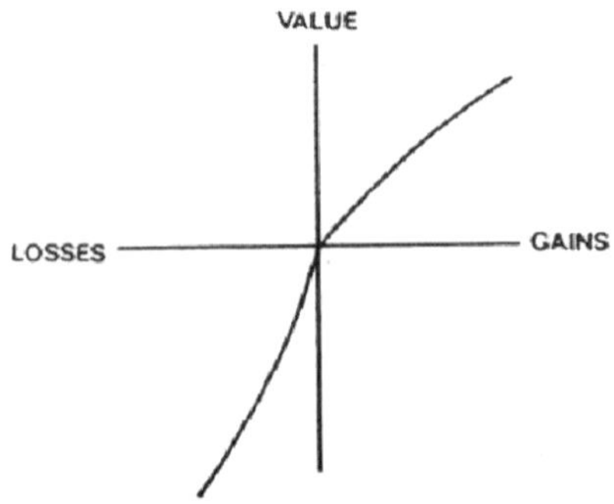

Figure 6.

must be qualified. The analysis of accessibility and framing that was presented earlier suggests a more moderate alternative, in which (1) decision problems can be formulated either in terms of wealth or in terms of changes; (2) the two formulations may lead to different preferences. For an example, consider Problem 4:

Problem 4

Please estimate your total wealth, call it W

Which of these situations is more attractive:

You own W

or

50% chance that you own W – $100
50% chance that you own W + $150

Informal experiments with problems of this type have consistently yielded a mild preference for the uncertain state of wealth, and a strong impression that the stakes mentioned in the question are entirely negligible.

In terms of final states of wealth, Problem 4 is identical to Problem 2. Furthermore, most respondents will agree, upon reflection, that the difference between the problems is inconsequential – too slight to justify different choices. Thus, the discrepant preferences observed in these two problems satisfy the definition of a framing effect.

The manipulation of accessibility that produces this framing effect is straightforward. The gamble of Problem 2 is likely to evoke an evaluation of the emotions associated with the immediate outcomes, and the formulation will not bring to mind thoughts of overall wealth. In contrast, the formulation of Problem 4 favors a view of the uncertainty as trivially small in relation to W, and includes no mention of gains or losses. In this perspective it is hardly surprising that the two problems elicit different representations, and therefore different preferences.

Over the centuries, Bernoulli's theory and its successors have been applied to decision problems in which outcomes are almost always formulated in terms of gains and losses, without any explicit mention of either current or final states of wealth. The assumption implicit in applications of expected utility theory is that outcomes described as gains or losses are first transformed into final asset states, then evaluated in that representation. In light of the preceding discussion of framing, the hypothesis of a transformation is highly implausible, and the different responses observed in Problems 2 and in Problem 4 provide direct evidence against it.

The same argument also applies in the other direction. Consider a decision maker who is only presented with Problem 4. Prospect theory assumed a preliminary operation of editing, in which prospects are reframed in simpler terms, prior to evaluation. But Problem 2 is not a simpler version of Problem 4; it includes gains and losses, which are not mentioned in Problem 4. The discussion of framing suggests that Problem 4 will be evaluated as it is stated – in terms of states of wealth. Indeed, some real-world choices are made in that frame. In particular, financial advisors and decision analysts often insist on formulating outcomes in terms of assets when they elicit their clients' preferences. Prospect theory is unlikely to provide an accurate description of decisions made in the wealth frame.

In experimental research as well as in the real world, the overwhelming majority of decisions are framed as gains and losses. There has been no systematic study of the choices that people make in the wealth frame, but one of the important properties of these choices is not in doubt: they will generally be closer to risk neutrality than when the equivalent outcomes are framed as gains and losses. The wealth frame favors risk neutrality in two ways. First, this frame eliminates any mention of losses, and therefore eliminates loss aversion. Second, in analogy with a familiar principle of perception, the outcomes of small bets will appear less significant when considered in the context of much larger amounts of wealth.

If Bernoulli's formulation is transparently incorrect as a descriptive model of risky choices, as has been argued here, why has this model been retained for so long? The answer may well be that the assignment of utility to wealth is an aspect of rationality, and therefore compatible with the general assumption of rationality in economic theorizing.

Consider Problem 5.

Problem 5

Two persons get their monthly report from a broker:

A is told that her wealth went from 4M to 3M
B is told that her wealth went from 1M to 1.1M

"Who of the two individuals has more reason to be satisfied with her financial situation?"

"Who is happier today?"

Problem 5 highlights the contrasting interpretations of utility in theories that define outcomes as states or as changes. In Bernoulli's analysis only the first of the two questions is relevant, and only long-term consequences matter. Prospect theory, in contrast, is concerned with short-term outcomes, and the value function presumably reflects an anticipation of the valence and intensity of the emotions that will be experienced at moments of transition from one state to another (Kahneman, 2000a, b; Mellers, 2000). Which of these concepts of utility is more useful? For descriptive purposes, the more myopic notion is superior, but the prescriptive norms of reasonable decision making favor the long-term view. The Bernoullian definition of relevant outcomes is a good fit in a rational-agent model.

It is worth noting that an exclusive concern with the long term may be prescriptively sterile, because the long term is not where life is lived. Utility cannot be divorced from emotion, and emotion is triggered by changes. A theory of choice that completely ignores feelings such as the pain of losses and the regret of mistakes is not only descriptively unrealistic. It also leads to prescriptions that do not maximize the utility of outcomes as they are actually experienced – that is, utility as Bentham conceived it (Kahneman, 1994, 2000c; Kahneman, Wakker, & Sarin, 1997).

4. ATTRIBUTE SUBSTITUTION: A MODEL OF JUDGMENT BY HEURISTIC

The first joint research program that Tversky and I undertook was a study of various types of judgment about uncertain events, including numerical predictions and assessments of the probabilities of hypotheses. We reviewed this work in an integrative article (Tversky & Kahneman, 1974), which aimed to show "that people rely on a limited number of heuristic principles which reduce the complex tasks of assessing probabilities and predicting values to simpler judgmental operations. In general, these heuristics are quite useful, but sometimes they lead to severe and systematic errors." (p. 1124). The second paragraph of that article introduced the idea that "the subjective assessment of probability resembles the subjective assessments of physical quantities such as distance or size. These judgments are all based on data of limited validity, which are processed according to heuristic rules." The concept of *heuristic* was illustrated by the role of the blur of contours as a potent determinant of the perceived distance of mountains. The observation that reliance on blur as a distance cue will cause distances to be overestimated on foggy days and underestimated on clear days was the example of a heuristic-induced *bias*. As this example illustrates, heuristics of judgment were to be identified by the characteristic errors that they inevitably cause.

Three heuristics of judgment, labeled representativeness, availability and anchoring, were described in the 1974 review, along with a dozen systematic biases, including non-regressive prediction, neglect of base-rate information, overconfidence and overestimates of the frequency of events that are easy to recall. Some of the biases were identified by systematic errors in estimates of known quantities and statistical facts. Other biases were identified by systematic discrepancies between the regularities of intuitive judgments and the principles of probability theory, Bayesian inference or regression analysis. The article defined the so-called "heuristics and biases approach" to the study of intuitive judgment, which has been the topic of a substantial research literature (Kahneman, Slovic, & Tversky, 1982; Gilovich, Griffin, & Kahneman, 2002) and has also been the focus of substantial controversy.

Shane Frederick and I recently revisited the conception of heuristics and biases, in the light of developments in the study of judgment and in the broader field of cognitive psychology in the intervening three decades (Kahneman & Frederick, 2002). The new model departs from the original formulation of heuristics in three significant ways: (i) it proposes a common process of attribute substitution to explain how judgment heuristics work; (ii) it extends the concept of heuristic beyond the domain of judgments about uncertain events; (iii) it includes an explicit treatment of the conditions under which intuitive judgments will be modified or overridden by the monitoring operations associated with System 2.

Attribute substitution

The 1974 article did not include a definition of judgmental heuristics. Heuristics were described at various times as principles, as processes, or as sources of cues for judgment. The vagueness did no damage, because the research program focused on a total of three heuristics of judgment under uncertainty, which were separately defined in adequate detail. In contrast, Kahneman and Frederick (2002) offered an explicit definition of a generic heuristic process of *attribute substitution*: A judgment is said to be mediated by a heuristic when the individual assesses a specified *target attribute* of a judgment object by substituting a related *heuristic attribute* that comes more readily to mind. This definition elaborates a theme of the early research, that people who are confronted with a difficult question sometimes answer an easier one instead. Thus, a person who is asked "What proportion of long-distance relationships break up within a year?" may answer as if she had been asked "Do instances of swift breakups of long-distance relationships come readily to mind?" This would be an application of the availability heuristic. A respondent asked to assess the probability that team A will beat team B in a basketball tournament may answer by mapping an impression of the relative strength of the two teams onto the probability scale (Tversky & Koehler, 1994). This could be called a "relative strength heuristic". In both cases, the target attribute is low in accessibility and another attribute, which is (i) related to the target, and (ii) highly accessible, is substituted in its place.

The word 'heuristic' is used in two senses in the new definition. The noun refers to the cognitive process, and the adjective in 'heuristic attribute' specifies the substitution that occurs in a particular judgment. For example, the representativeness heuristic is defined by the use of representativeness as a heuristic attribute to judge probability. The definition excludes anchoring effects, in which judgment is influenced by temporarily raising the accessibility

Figure 7.

of a particular *value* of the target attribute. On the other hand, the definition of the concept of heuristic by the process of attribute substitution greatly extends its range of application.

For a perceptual example of attribute substitution, consider the question: "What are the sizes of the two horses in Figure 7, as they are shown on the page?" The images are in fact identical in size, but the figure produces a compelling illusion. The target attribute that the observer is instructed to report is two-dimensional size, but the responses actually map an impression of three-dimensional size onto units of length that are appropriate to the required judgment. In the terms of the model, three-dimensional size is the heuristic attribute. As in other cases of attribute substitution, the illusion is caused by differential accessibility. An impression of three-dimensional size is the only impression of size that comes to mind for naïve observers – painters and experienced photographers are able to do better – and it produces a perceptual illusion in the judgment of picture size. The cognitive illusions that are produced by attribute substitution have the same character: an impression of one attribute is mapped onto the scale of another, and the judge is normally unaware of the substitution.

Direct tests of attribute substitution

An experiment described by Kahneman and Tversky (1973) illustrates a cognitive illusion that arises from attribute substitution. It also illustrates a particularly strict test of the hypothesis of substitution, in a research paradigm that Kahneman and Frederick (2002) labeled the *heuristic elicitation* design. Participants were given the following description of a fictitious graduate student, which was shown along with a list of nine fields of graduate specialization.

> Tom W. is of high intelligence, although lacking in true creativity. He has a need for order and clarity, and for neat and tidy systems in which every detail finds its appropriate place. His writing is rather dull and mechanical, occasionally enlivened by somewhat corny puns and by flashes of imagination of the sci-fi type. He has a strong drive for competence. He seems to have little feel and little sympathy for other people and does not enjoy interacting with others. Self-centered, he nonetheless has a deep moral sense. (p.127)

Participants in a ***representativeness*** group ranked the nine fields of specialization by the degree to which Tom W. "resembles a typical graduate student" (in that field). Participants in a ***base-rate*** group evaluated the relative frequencies of the nine fields of graduate specialization. The description of Tom W. was deliberately constructed to make him more representative of the less populated fields: the rank correlation between the averages of representativeness rankings and of estimated base rates was -.65. Finally, participants in the ***probability*** group ranked the nine fields according to the likelihood of Tom W.'s specializing in each. These respondents were graduate students in psychology at major universities. They were given information that was intended to discredit the evidence of the personality sketch, namely that it had been written by a psychologist when Tom W. was in high school, on the basis of personality tests of dubious validity.

A description based on unreliable information should be given little weight, and predictions made in the absence of valid evidence should revert to base rates. Statistical logic therefore dictates that the correlation between judgments of probability and of representativeness should be negative in this problem. In contrast, the hypothesis of attribute substitution implies that the ranking of fields by the two measures should coincide. The results are shown in Figure 7. The correlation between the mean judgments of representativeness and of probability is nearly perfect (.97), supporting attribute substitution.

Another study in the same design involved one of the best-known characters in the heuristics and biases literature.

> Linda is 31 years old, single, outspoken and very bright. She majored in philosophy. As a student she was deeply concerned with issues of discrimination and social justice and also participated in antinuclear demonstrations.

Respondents were shown the description of Linda and a list of eight possible outcomes describing her present employment and activities. The two critical items in the list were #6 ("Linda is a bank teller") and the conjunction item #8 ("Linda is a bank teller and active in the feminist movement"). The other six possibilities were unrelated and miscellaneous (e.g., elementary school teacher, psychiatric social worker). As in the Tom W. problem, some respondents ranked the eight outcomes by representativeness; others ranked the same outcomes by probability. The correlation between the mean rankings was .99. Furthermore, the proportion of respondents who ranked the conjunction (item #8) higher than its constituent (#6) was about the same for representativeness (85%) and for probability (89%). The ordering of the two items is quite reasonable for judgments of similarity: Linda does resemble the

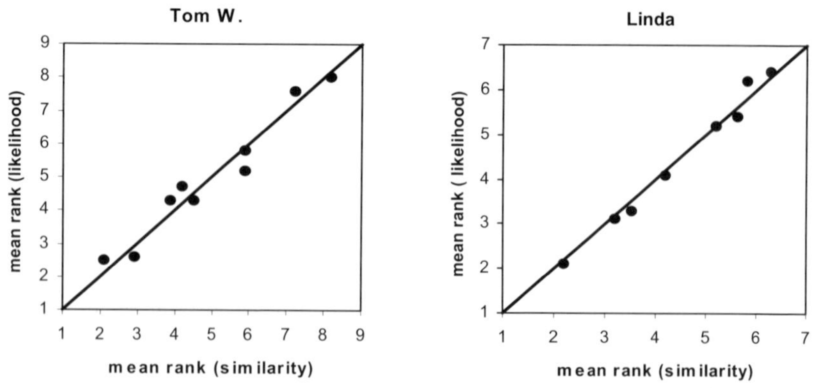

Figure 8.

image of a feminist bank teller more than she resembles a stereotypical bank teller. However, the reliance on representativeness as a heuristic attribute yields a pattern of probability judgments that violates monotonicity, and has been called the 'conjunction fallacy' (Tversky & Kahneman, 1983).

The results shown in Figure 8 are especially compelling because the responses were rankings. The large variability of the average rankings of both attributes indicates highly consensual responses, and nearly total overlap in the systematic variance. Stronger support for attribute-substitution could hardly be imagined, and it is surprising that this evidence was not acknowledged in subsequent debates about the validity of judgment heuristics. Other tests of representativeness in the heuristic elicitation design have been equally successful (Bar-Hillel & Neter, 2002; Tversky & Kahneman, 1982). The same design was also applied extensively in studies of support theory (Tversky & Koehler, 1994; for a review see Brenner, Koehler & Rottenstreich, 2002). In one of the studies reported by Tversky and Koehler (1994), participants rated the probability that the home team would win in each of 20 specified basketball games, and later provided ratings of the relative strength of the two teams, using a scale in which the strongest team in the tournament was assigned a score of 100. The correlation between normalized strength ratings and judged probabilities was .99.

The essence of attribute substitution is that respondents offer a reasonable answer to a question that they have not been asked. An alternative interpretation that must be considered is that the respondents' judgments reflect their understanding of the question they were asked. This may be true in some situations: it is not unreasonable to interpret a question about the probable outcome of a basketball game as referring to the relative strength of the competing teams. But the idea that judgments signify a commitment to the interpretation of the target attribute does not generally hold. For example, it is highly unlikely that educated respondents have a concept of probability that coincides precisely with similarity, or that they are unable to distinguish picture size from object size. A more plausible hypothesis is that an evaluation of the heuristic attribute comes immediately to mind, and that its associative relationship with the target attribute is sufficiently close to pass the monitoring of a permissive System 2. Respondents who substitute one attribute for another are not confused about the question that they are trying to answer – they simply fail to notice that they are answering a different one. And when they do notice the discrepancy, they either modify the intuitive judgment or abandon it altogether.

The new heuristics

As illustrated by its use in the interpretation of the visual illusion of Figure 7, the definition of judgment heuristics by the mechanism of attribute substitution applies to many situations in which people make a judgment that is not the one they intended to make. There is no finite list of heuristic attributes. Kahneman and Frederick (2002) illustrated this conception by a study by Strack, Martin, and Schwarz (1988), in which college students answered a survey that included these two questions: "How happy are you with your life in general?" and "How many dates did you have last month?". The correlation between the two questions was negligible when they occurred in the order shown, but it rose to 0.66 when the dating question was asked first. The model of attribute substitution suggests that the dating question automatically evokes an affectively charged evaluation of one's satisfaction in that domain of life, which lingers to become the heuristic attribute when the happiness question is subsequently encountered. The underlying correlation between the target and heuristic attributes is surely higher than the observed value of 0.66, which is attenuated by measurement error. The same experimental manipulation of question order was used in another study to induce the use of marital satisfaction as a heuristic attribute for well-being (Schwarz, Strack, & Mai, 1991). The success of these experiments suggests that *ad hoc* attribute substitution is a frequent occurrence.

The idea of an ***affect heuristic*** (Slovic *et al.*, 2002) is probably the most important development in the study of judgment heuristics in the last decades. There is compelling evidence for the proposition that every stimulus evokes an affective evaluation, which is not always conscious (see reviews by Zajonc, 1980, 1997; Bargh, 1997). Affective valence is a natural assessment, and therefore a candidate for substitution in the numerous responses that express attitudes. Slovic and his colleagues (Slovic *et al.*, 2002) discuss how a basic affective reaction can be used as the heuristic attribute for a wide variety of more complex evaluations, such as the cost/benefit ratio of technologies, the safe concentration of chemicals, and even the predicted economic performance of industries. Their treatment of the affect heuristic fits the present model of attribute substitution.

In the same vein, Kahneman and Ritov (1994) and Kahneman, Ritov, and Schkade (1999) proposed that an automatic affective valuation – the emotional core of an attitude – is the main determinant of many judgments and behaviors. In the study by Kahneman and Ritov (1994), 37 public causes were ranked by average responses to questions about (i) the importance of the issues, (ii) the size of the donation that respondents were willing to make, (iii) political support for interventions, and (iv) the moral satisfaction associated with a contribution. The rankings were all very similar. In the terms of the present analysis, the same heuristic attribute (affective valuation) was mapped onto the distinct scales of a wide range of target attributes. Similarly, Kahneman, Schkade, and Sunstein (1998) interpreted jurors' assessments of punitive awards as a mapping of outrage onto a dollar scale of punishments. In an article titled "Risk as Feelings", Loewenstein, Weber, Hsee, and Welch (2001), offered a closely related analysis in which emotional responses, such as the intensity of fear, govern diverse judgments (e.g., ratings of the probability of a disaster).

In terms of the scope of responses that it governs, the natural assessment of affect should join representativeness and availability in the list of general-purpose heuristic attributes. The failure to identify the affect heuristic much earlier, as well as its enthusiastic acceptance in recent years, reflect significant changes in the general climate of psychological opinion. It is worth noting that in the early 1970's the idea of purely cognitive biases appeared novel and distinctive, because the prevalence of motivated and emotional biases of judgment was taken for granted by the social psychologists of the time. There followed a period of intense emphasis on cognitive processes, in psychology generally and in the field of judgment in particular. It took another thirty years to achieve what now appears to be a more integrated view of the role of affect in intuitive judgment.

5. THE ACCESSIBILITY OF CORRECTIVE THOUGHTS

The present treatment assumes that System 2 is involved in all voluntary actions – including overt expressions of the intuitive judgments that originated in System 1. This assumption implies that errors of intuitive judgment involve failures of both systems: System 1, which generated the error, and System 2 which failed to detect and correct it (Kahneman & Tversky, 1982a). To illustrate this point, Kahneman and Frederick (2002) revisited the perceptual analogy that Tversky and Kahneman (1974) had used to explain how judgment heuristics generate biases: blur is a good cue to the distance of mountains, but reliance on this cue causes predictable errors of distance estimation on sunny or hazy days. The analogy was apt, but the analysis of the perceptual example neglected an important fact. Observers know, of course, whether the day is sunny or hazy, and they could use this knowledge to counteract the bias – but most often they do not. Contrary to what the early treatment implied, the use of blur as a cue does not inevitably lead to bias in the judgment of distance – the illusion could just as well be described as a failure to assign adequate negative weight to ambient haze. The effect of haziness on *impressions* of distance is a failing of System 1: the perceptual system is not designed to correct for this variable. The effect of haziness on *judgments* of distance is a separate failure of System 2. Analogous failures can be identified in other errors of intuitive judgment.

It is useful to consider how System 2 might have intervened in the problems of Tom W. and Linda that were described in an earlier section.

> "Tom W. does look like a library science person, but there are many more graduate students in Humanities and Social Sciences. I should adjust my rankings accordingly." "Linda cannot be more likely to be a feminist bank teller than to be a bank teller. I must rank these two outcomes accordingly"

These hypothetical samples of reasoning illustrate two ways in which intuitive judgments can be corrected. In the Tom W. example, the individual becomes aware of a factor that was not part of the intuitive judgment, and makes an effort to adjust accordingly. In the Linda example, the individual recognizes that the question can be answered by applying a decisive logical rule, which makes intuitions to the contrary irrelevant. Both would come under the rubric of "statistical heuristics", which people are sometimes capable of deploying in their reasoning about uncertain events (Nisbett, Krantz, Jepson, & Kunda, 1983/2002).

Neither of these examples of reasoning exceeds the intellectual reach of the graduate students at major universities whose rankings were shown in Figure 8. However, the data indicate that very few respondents actually came up with corrections. The puzzle is the same as in the blur illusion: why did these people not put their knowledge to good use? In the context of the present treatment, the question can be rephrased: Why did the statistical heuristics not become accessible when they were needed?

An important part of the answer is that attribute substitution is a silent process: the respondents who judge probability as if they had been asked to judge representativeness are not self-conscious about what they are doing. The substitute attribute is pertinent to the task, and its value comes to mind with little or no effort and with high confidence. There is therefore little reason for respondents to question their judgment, perhaps even less than in the bat-and-ball problem that was mentioned earlier. In contrast, the accessibility of statistical heuristics is often low, but it can be enhanced in at least two ways: by increasing the vigilance of the monitoring activities, or by providing stronger cues to the relevant rules.

A substantial research program was mounted by Nisbett, Krantz and their colleagues to investigate the factors that control the accessibility of statistical heuristics (Nisbett *et al.*, 1983/2002). For example, Nisbett *et al.* studied formally identical problems in several domains. They found that statistical reasoning was most likely to be evoked in the context of games of chance, occasionally evoked in situations involving sports, but relatively rare when the problems concerned the psychology of individuals. They also showed that the explicit mention of a sampling procedure facilitated statistical thinking (Nisbett *et al.*, 1983; see also Gigerenzer, Hell, & Blank, 1988). Zukier and Pepitone (1984) found that respondents were more likely to use base-rate information when instructed to think as statisticians than when instructed to emulate psychologists. Agnoli and Krantz (1989) found that brief training in the logic of sets improved performance in a simple version of the Linda problem. Considerations of accessibility are evidently relevant to the activation of statistical reasoning, not only to attribute substitution.

Nisbett, Krantz and their colleagues drew a sharp distinction between their statistical heuristics and the intuitive heuristics, which they described as "rapid and more or less automatic judgmental rules of thumb" (2002, p. 510). In the same vein, the present treatment assigns the competing heuristics to different cognitive systems. Attribute substitution has been described as an operation of System 1, which occurs automatically and effortlessly. In contrast, the statistical heuristics illustrate the rule-governed reasoning of System 2 (Sloman, 1996), which is deliberate and demands some effort. It is worth noting that the intervention of System 2 and the application of statistical heuristics and other rules do not guarantee a correct response. The rules that people apply in deliberate reasoning are sometimes false.

An implication of the view of intuition that has been proposed here is that statistical training does not eradicate intuitive heuristics such as representativeness, but only enables people to avoid some biases under favorable circumstances. The results shown in Figure 8, which were collected from statistically knowledgeable graduate students, support this prediction. In the absence of strong cues to remind them of their statistical knowledge, these respondents made categorical predictions like everybody else – by representativeness. However, statistical sophistication made a difference in a stripped-down version of the Linda problem, which required respondents to compare the probabilities of Linda being "a bank teller" or "a bank teller who is active in the feminist movement" (Tversky & Kahneman, 1983). The incidence of errors remained high for the statistically naïve even in that transparent version, but the error rate dropped dramatically among the sophisticated.

The efficacy of System 2 is impaired by time pressure (Finucane, Alhakami, Slovic, & Johnson, 2000) by concurrent involvement in a different cognitive task (Gilbert, 1989, 1991, 2002), by performing the task in the evening for 'morning people' and in the morning for 'evening people' (Bodenhausen, 1990), and, surprisingly, by being in a good mood (Isen, Nygren, & Ashby, 1988; Bless *et al.*, 1996). Conversely, the facility of System 2 is positively correlated with intelligence (Stanovich & West, 2002), with 'need for cognition' (Shafir & LeBoeuf, 2002), and with exposure to statistical thinking (Nisbett *et al.*, 1983; Agnoli & Krantz, 1989; Agnoli, 1991).

The observation that it is possible to design experiments in which 'cognitive illusions disappear' has sometimes been used as an argument against the usefulness of the notions of heuristics and biases (for example, Gigerenzer, 1991). In the present framework, however, there is no mystery about the conditions under which illusions appear or disappear. An intuitive judgment that violates a rule which the respondent accepts will be overridden, if the rule comes early enough to the respondent's mind. This argument is not circular, because we have adequate scientific knowledge (as well as widely shared folk knowledge) about the conditions that facilitate or impede the accessibility of logical or statistical rules.

The examples of possible corrections in the Tom W. and Linda problems illustrated two possible outcomes of the intervention of System 2: the intuitive judgment may be adjusted, or else rejected and replaced by another conclusion. A general prediction can be made about the former case, which is certainly the most frequent. Because the intuitive impression comes first, it is likely to serve as an anchor for subsequent adjustments, and corrective adjustments from anchors are normally insufficient. Variations on this theme are common in the literature (Epley & Gilovich, 2002; Epstein, 1994; Gilbert, 2002; Griffin & Tversky, 1992; Sloman, 2002; Wilson, Centerbar, & Brekke, 2002).

The methodological implication of this analysis is that intuitive judgments and preferences are best studied in between-subject designs. Within-subject designs with multiple trials encourage the adoption of simplifying strategies in which answers are computed mechanically, without delving into the specifics of each problem. Factorial designs are particularly undesirable, because they provide an unmistakable cue that every factor that is manipulated must be relevant to the judgment (Kahneman & Frederick, 2002). It is inappropriate to study intuitive judgments in conditions that are guaranteed to destroy their intuitive character. The difficulties of these experimental designs were noted long ago by Kahneman and Tversky (1982a), who pointed out that "Within-subject designs are associated with significant problems of interpretation in several areas of psychological research (Poulton, 1975). In studies of intuition, they are liable to induce the effect that they are intended to test" (p. 500). Unfortunately, this methodological caution has been widely ignored.

6. PROTOTYPE HEURISTICS

This section introduces a family of prototype heuristics, which share a common mechanism and a remarkably consistent pattern of cognitive illusions, analogous to the effects observed in the Tom W. and in the Linda problems (Kahneman & Frederick, 2002). Prototype heuristics can be roughly described as the substitution of an average for a sum – a process that has been extensively studied by Anderson in other contexts (e.g., Anderson, 1981, ch. pp. 58–70; 1991a,b). The section also discusses the conditions under which System 2 prevents or reduces the biases associated with these heuristics.

Extensional and prototype attributes

The target assessments in several significant tasks of judgment and decision making are *extensional attributes* of categories or sets. The value of an extensional attribute in a set is an aggregate (not necessarily additive) of the values over its extension. Each of the following tasks is illustrated by an example of an extensional attribute and by the relevant measure of extension. The argument of this section is that the extensional attributes in these tasks are low in accessibility, and are therefore candidates for heuristic substitution.

(i) category prediction (e.g., *the probability that the set of bank tellers contains Linda / the number of bank tellers*);
(ii) pricing a quantity of public or private goods (e.g., *the personal dollar value of saving a certain number of birds from drowning in oil ponds / the number of birds*);
(iii) global evaluation of a past experience that extended over time (e.g., *the overall aversiveness of a painful medical procedure / the duration of the procedure*);
(iv) assessment of the support that a sample of observations provides for a hypothesis (e.g., *the probability that a specified sample of colored balls has been drawn from one urn rather than another / the number of balls*).

Extensional attributes are governed by a general principle of conditional adding, which dictates that each element of the set adds to the overall value an amount that depends on the elements already included. In simple cases, the value is additive: the total length of the set of lines in Figure 3 is just the sum of their separate lengths. In other cases, each positive element of the set increases the aggregate value, but the combination rule is non-additive (typically sub-additive).[3]

A category or set which is sufficiently homogeneous to have a prototype can also be described by its *prototype attributes*. Where extensional attributes are akin to a sum, prototype attributes are averages. As the display of lines in Figure 3 illustrated, prototype attributes are often highly accessible. This observation is well-documented. Whenever we look at, or think about, an ensemble or category that has a prototype, information about the prototype becomes accessible. The classic discussion of basic-level categories included demonstrations of the ease with which features of the prototype come to mind (Rosch & Mervis, 1975). Even earlier, Posner and Keele (1968, 1970) had reported experiments in which observers were exposed on many trials to various distortions of a single shape. The prototype shape was never shown, but observers erroneously believed that it had been presented often. More recently, several studies in social psychology have shown that exposure to the name of a familiar social category increases the accessibility of the traits that are closely associated with its stereotype (see Fiske, 1998).

Because of their high accessibility, the prototype attributes are natural candidates for the role of heuristic attributes. A ***prototype heuristic*** is the label for the process of substituting an attribute of a prototype for an extensional attribute of its category (Kahneman & Frederick, 2002). The original instance of a prototype heuristic was the use of representativeness in category prediction. The probability of Linda being a bank teller is an extensional variable, but her resemblance to a typical bank teller is a prototype attribute.

Two tests of prototype heuristics

Because extensional and prototypical attributes are governed by characteristically different rules, the substitution of a prototype attribute for an extensional attribute entails two testable biases: extension neglect and violations of monotonicity. Tests of the two hypotheses are discussed in turn.

Tests of extension neglect

Doubling the frequencies of all values in a set will not affect prototype attributes, because measures of central tendency depend only on relative frequencies. In contrast, the value of an extensional attribute will increase monotonically with extension. The hypothesis that judgments of a target attribute are mediated by a prototype heuristic gains support if the judgments are insensitive to variations of extension.

The proposition that extension is neglected in a particular judgment has the character of a null hypothesis: it is strictly true only if all individuals in the

[3] If the judgment is monotonically related to an additive scale (such as the underlying count of the number of birds), the formal structure is known in the measurement literature as an "extensive structure" (Luce, Krantz, Suppes & Tversky, 1990, Chapter 3). There also may be attributes that lack any underlying additive scale, in which case the structure is known in the literature as a "positive concatenation structure" (Luce *et al.*, 1990, Chapter 19, vol. III, p. 38).

sample are completely insensitive to variations of extension. The hypothesis will be rejected, in a sufficiently large study, if even a small proportion of participants show some sensitivity to extension. The chances of some individuals responding to extension are high a priori, because educated respondents are generally aware of the relevance of this variable (Kahneman & Frederick, 2002). Everyone agrees that WTP for saving birds should increase with the number of birds saved, that extending a painful medical procedure by an extra period of pain makes it worse, and that evidence from larger samples is more reliable. Complete extension neglect is therefore an unreasonably strict test of prototype heuristics. Nevertheless, this extreme result can be obtained under favorable conditions, as the following examples show:

- The study of Tom W. (see Figure 8) illustrated a pattern of *base-rate neglect* in categorical prediction. This finding is robust when the task requires a ranking of multiple outcomes (Kahneman & Tversky, 1973). As noted in the preceding section, the sophisticated participants in this experiment were aware of the base-rates and were capable of using this knowledge in their predictions – but the thought of doing so apparently occurred to almost none of them. Kahneman and Tversky also documented almost complete neglect of base-rates in an experiment (the engineer/lawyer study) in which base-rates were explicitly stated. However, the neglect of explicit base-rate information in this design is a fragile finding (see Kahneman & Frederick, 2002; Koehler, 1996, Evans, Handley, Over, & Perham, 2002).
- Participants in a study by Desvousges *et al.*, (1993) indicated their willingness to contribute money to prevent the drowning of migratory birds. The number of birds that would be saved was varied for different sub-samples. The estimated amounts that households were willing to pay were $80, $78 and $88, to save 2,000, 20,000, or 200,000 birds, respectively. Frederick and Fischhoff (1998) reviewed numerous other demonstrations of *scope neglect* in studies of willingness to pay (WTP) for public goods. For example, Kahneman and Knetsch found that survey respondents in Toronto were willing to pay almost as much to clean up the lakes in a small region of Ontario or to clean up all the lakes in that province (reported by Kahneman, 1986).
- In a study described by Redelmeier and Kahneman (1996), patients undergoing colonoscopy reported the intensity of pain every 60 seconds during the procedure (see Figure 9), and subsequently provided a global evaluation of the pain they had suffered. The correlation of global evaluations with the duration of the procedure (which ranged from 4 to 66 minutes in that study) was .03. On the other hand global evaluations were correlated ($r = .67$) with an average of the pain reported on two occasions: when pain was at its peak, and just before the procedure ended. For example, patient A in Figure 9 reported a more negative evaluation of the procedure than patient B. The same pattern of *duration neglect* and Peak/End evaluations has been observed in other studies (Fredrickson & Kahneman, 1993; see Kahneman, 2000b, 2000c for a discussion).

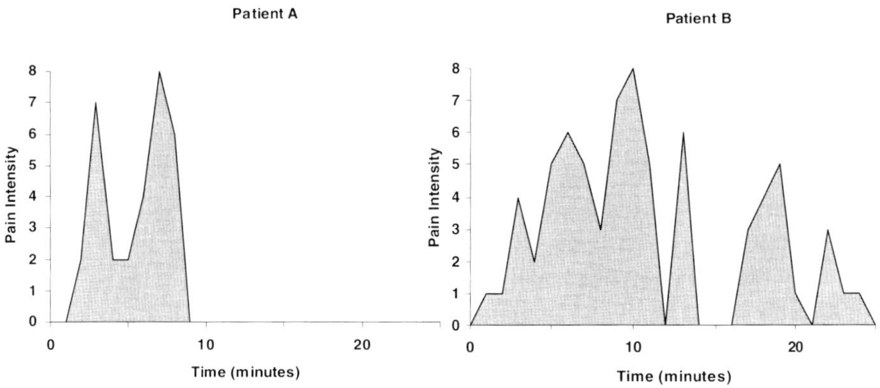

Figure 9. Pain intensity reported by two colonoscopy patients.

In light of the findings discussed in the preceding section, it is useful to consider situations in which people will *not* neglect extension completely. Extension effects are expected, in the present model, if the individual (i) has information about the extension of the relevant set; (ii) is reminded of the relevance of extension; and (iii) is able to detect that her intuitive judgments neglect extension. These conditions are least likely to hold – and complete neglect most likely to be observed – when the judge evaluates a single object and when the extension of the set is not explicitly mentioned. At the other extreme, the conditions for a positive effect of extension are all satisfied in psychologists' favorite research design: the within-subject factorial experiment, in which values of extension are crossed with the values of other variables in the design. As noted earlier, this design provides an obvious cue that the experimenter considers every manipulated variable relevant, and it enables participants to ensure that their judgments exhibit sensitivity to all these variables. The factorial design is therefore especially inappropriate for testing hypotheses about biases of neglect (Kahneman & Frederick, 2002).

In spite of these objections, within-subject factorial designs have been used in several experimental studies of extension neglect. Figure 10 illustrates the remarkably consistent *additive extension effect* that has emerged in these experiments (Schreiber & Kahneman, 2000). In each of the experiments, the extension variable has a slight but significant effect, and combines additively with other information. The additivity is noteworthy, because it is normatively inappropriate. For each panel of Figure 10, a compelling normative argument can be made for a quasi-multiplicative rule in which the lines should fan out.[4] The observed pattern is compatible with a process of anchoring and adjustment: the intuitive judgment provides an anchor, and small adjustments from that anchor are made to accommodate the role of extension.

[4] Anderson (1996, p. 253) has described several other situations in which variables that should be combined multiplicatively are combined additively.

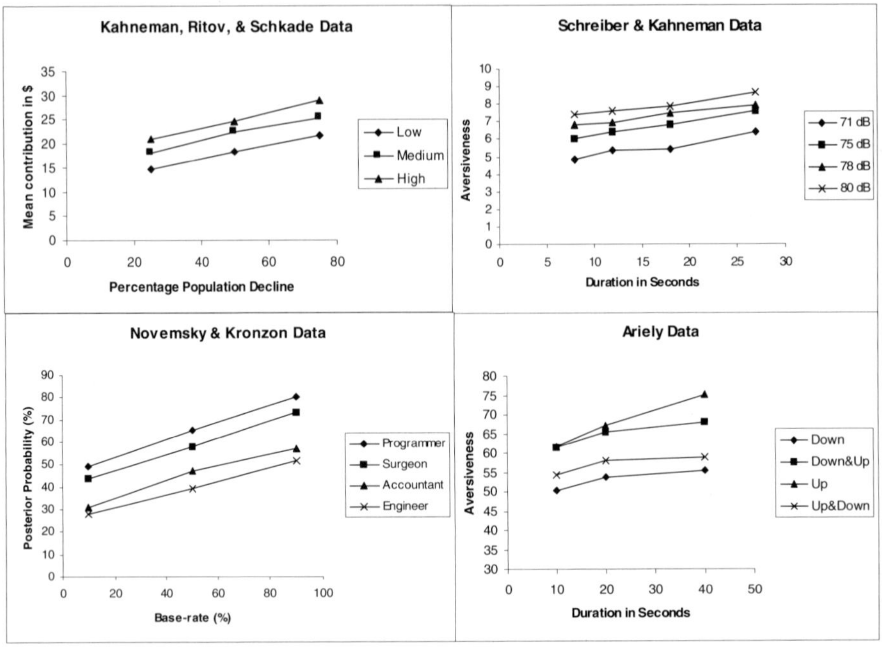

Figure 10. (a) Willingness to pay to restore damage to species that differ in popularity as a function of the damage they have suffered (from Kahneman, Ritov, & Schkade, 1999); (b) Global evaluations of aversive sounds of different loudness as a function of duration for subjects selected for their high sensitivity to duration (from Schreiber & Kahneman, 2000); (c) Ratings of probability for predictions that differ in representativeness as a function of base-rate frequency (from Novemsky & Kronzon, 1999); (d) Global evaluations of episodes of painful pressure that differ in temporal profile as a function of duration (Ariely, 1998).

Tests of monotonicity

Extensional variables, like sums, obey monotonicity. The sum of a set of positive values is at least as high as the maximum of its subsets. In contrast, the average of a subset can be higher than the average of a set that includes it. Violations of monotonicity are therefore bound to occur when an extensional attribute is judged by a prototype attribute: it must be possible to find cases in which adding elements to a set causes the judgment of the target variable to decrease. This test of prototype heuristics is less demanding than the hypothesis of extension neglect, and violations of monotonicity are compatible with some degree of sensitivity to extension (Ariely & Loewenstein, 2000). Nevertheless, violations of monotonicity in important tasks of judgment and choice are the strongest source of support for the hypothesis that prototype attributes are substituted for extensional attributes in these tasks.

- Conjunction errors, which violate monotonicity, have been demonstrated in the Linda problem and in other problems of the same type. There are no documented exceptions to the predicted pattern when the judgments are obtained in a between-subjects design, or when the two critical outcomes are embedded in a longer list (Tversky & Kahneman, 1982, 1983; Mellers, Hertwig, & Kahneman, 2001). Tversky and Kahneman (1983) also found that statistically naïve respondents made conjunction errors even in a direct comparison of the critical outcomes. As in the case of extension neglect, however, conjunction errors are less robust in within-subject conditions, especially when the task involves a direct comparison (see Kahneman & Frederick, 2002 for a discussion).

- Hsee (1999) asked participants to price sets of dinnerware offered in a clearance sale. One of the sets (A) consisted of 24 pieces, all in good condition. The other set included the same 24 pieces, plus 16 additional pieces, of which 7 were in a good condition and 9 were broken. When each respondent evaluated only one set, mean willingness to pay (WTP) was $33 for the smaller set and $23 for the larger set ($p < .01$). In contrast, participants who evaluated both sets were consistently willing to pay more for the larger set. List (2002) observed similar violations of dominance with a different good (sets of baseball cards), in a real market situation.
- Problems of the following kind have been used in several experiments (Kahneman & Tversky, 1972; Griffin & Tversky, 1992).

  A sample has been drawn from one of two urns. One urn contains 70% red balls and 30% white balls. The proportions are reversed in the other urn. What is the probability that each of these samples was drawn from the predominantly red urn?

  A sample of three red balls and zero white balls (3R, 0W)
  A sample of four red balls and three white balls (4R, 3W)
  A sample of seven red balls and three white balls (7R, 3W)

  The extensional target variable here is the degree of support for the 'red' hypothesis relative to the 'white' hypothesis. The normative solution is straightforward: posterior probability (the target attribute) is determined by an additive combination over sample elements – the difference between the number of red and white balls in the sample. The psychological solution is equally straightforward: the prototype attribute (the heuristic) is an average of support, which corresponds to the proportion of red balls in the sample. Thus, the addition of (4R, 3W) to (3R, 0W) raises the value of the target attribute but reduces the value of the heuristic attribute. This particular example is fictitious, but the pattern of findings indicates that respondents would derive much more confidence from (3R, 0W) than from (7R, 3W) (Kahneman & Tversky, 1972; Griffin & Tversky, 1992).
- A randomized clinical experiment was conducted as a follow-up to the colonoscopy study described earlier. For half the patients, the instrument was not immediately removed when the clinical examination ended. Instead, the physician waited for about a minute, leaving the instrument stationary. The experience during the extra period was uncomfortable, but the procedure guaranteed that the colonoscopy never ended in severe pain. Patients reported significantly more favorable global evaluations in this experimental condition than in the control condition (Redelmeier,

Katz, & Kahneman, in press). Violations of dominance have also been confirmed in choices. Kahneman, Fredrickson, Schreiber, and Redelmeier (1993) exposed participants to two cold-pressor experiences, one with each hand: a "short" episode (immersion of one hand in 14°C water for 60 seconds), and a "long" episode (the short episode, plus an additional 30 seconds during which the water was gradually warmed to 15°C). When they were later asked which of the two experiences they preferred to repeat, a substantial majority chose the long trial. This pattern of choices is predicted from the Peak/End rule of evaluation, which was described earlier. The same pattern of results was found with unpleasant sounds of variable loudness and duration (Schreiber & Kahneman, 2000).

The consistency of the results observed in diverse studies of prototype heuristics suggests the need for a unified interpretation, and challenges interpretations that only apply to a single domain. A number of authors have offered competing interpretations of base-rate neglect (Cosmides & Tooby, 1996; Koehler, 1996), insensitivity to scope in WTP (Kopp, 1992), and duration neglect (Ariely & Loewenstein, 2000). In general however, these interpretations are specific to a particular task, and would not carry over to demonstrations of extension neglect in the other tasks that have been discussed here. Similarly, the attempts to describe the conjunction fallacy as a miscommunication between experimenter and respondent (Dulany & Hilton, 1991; Hilton & Slugoski, 2001) do not explain analogous violations of monotonicity in the cold-pressor experiment and in the pricing of private goods. In contrast, the account offered here (and developed in greater detail by Kahneman & Frederick, 2002) is equally applicable to diverse tasks that require an assessment of an extensional target attribute.

The findings obtained in choices and joint evaluations confirm the existence of two distinct ways of choosing, which were already identified in prospect theory (Kahneman & Tversky, 1979). In the non-analytic procedure that I have called "choosing by liking" (Kahneman, 1994), the individual considers the global evaluation of the two options separately, and selects the one that has the higher global value, without detailed comparison of the options. Choice by global value was the basic mechanism assumed in prospect theory. However, prospect theory also introduced the idea that if the individual detects that one option dominates the other, the dominant option will be chosen without consulting their separate valuations. The same mechanisms apply to problems of judgment, such as the case of Linda, where some statistically sophisticated individuals detect that one of the sets includes the other and respond accordingly, ignoring representativeness. In Hsee's dinnerware study (1998), respondents chose by liking in separate evaluation, and chose by dominance in joint evaluation.

Joint evaluation is not sufficient to guarantee choice by dominance; it is also necessary for the decision makers to realize explicitly that one of the options is strictly better than the other. This requirement was not satisfied in the cold-pressor experiment. Although the participants were exposed to both experiences (joint evaluation), they did not notice that the long episode contained all the pain of the short one, and then some extra pain. Most respondents would have made a different choice if they had understood the structure of the options.

The normative logic of belief and choice is extensional, and it requires appropriate valuation of extensional attributes, which include both probability and utility. The examples that were discussed in this section demonstrate a pervasive departure from extensional logic, in the intuitive evaluation of both evidence and outcomes. The substitution of prototype attributes for extensional attributes appears to be a general characteristic of System 1, which is incompatible with both Bayesian beliefs and utility maximization.

CONCLUSIONS

The starting point of the present analysis was the observation that complex judgments and preferences are called 'intuitive' in everyday language if they come to mind quickly and effortlessly, like percepts. Another basic observation was that judgments and intentions are normally intuitive in this sense, but can be modified or overridden in a more deliberate mode of operation. The labels 'System 1' and 'System 2' were associated with these two modes of cognitive functioning.

The preceding sections elaborated a single generic proposition: "Highly accessible impressions produced by System 1 control judgments and preferences, unless modified or overridden by the deliberate operations of System 2." This template sets an agenda for research: to understand judgment and choice we must study the determinants of high accessibility, the conditions under which System 2 will override or correct System 1, and the rules of these corrective operations. Much is known about each of the three questions.

First, consider the ways in which the concept of accessibility was used here. Framing effects were attributed to the fact that alternative formulations of the same situation make different aspects of it accessible. The core idea of prospect theory, that the normal carriers of utility are gains and losses, invoked a general principle that changes are relatively more accessible than absolute values. Judgment heuristics were explained as the substitution of a highly accessible heuristic attribute for a less accessible target attribute. Finally, the proposition that averages are more accessible than sums unified the analysis of prototype heuristics. A recurrent theme was that different aspects of problems are made accessible in between-subjects and in within-subject experiments, and more specifically in separate and joint evaluations of stimuli. In all these cases, the discussion appealed to rules of accessibility that are independently plausible and sometimes quite obvious.

The status of accessibility factors in psychological theorizing is, in principle, similar to the status of perceptual grouping factors. In both cases there is no general theory, only a list of powerful empirical generalizations that provide a sound basis for experimental predictions and for models of higher-level phenomena. Unlike Gestalt principles, which were catalogued a long time ago, a comprehensive list of the factors that influence accessibility is yet to be drawn. The list will be long, but many of its elements are already known. For example, it is safe to assume that similarity is more accessible than probability, that changes are more accessible than absolute values, and that averages are more accessible than sums. Furthermore, each of these assumptions can be verified independently by multiple operations, including measurements of reaction time, susceptibility to interference by secondary tasks, and asymmetric priming. Assumptions about accessibility are incompletely theorized, but they need not be vague and they can do genuine explanatory work.

The present discussion of accessibility effects has been restricted to the differential accessibility of attributes (dimensions) on which judgment objects vary, such as length or price, similarity and probability, (Kahneman & Frederick, 2002). A similar analysis could be applied to the accessibility of particular values of attributes, such as 'six feet' or 'two dollars'. Highly accessible values are generally overweighted, and when considered as possible answers to a question they become potent anchors (Epley & Gilovich, 2002; Strack & Mussweiler, 1997; Chapman & Johnson, 2002). The effects of salience and anchoring play a central role in treatments of judgment and choice. Indeed, anchoring effects are among the most robust phenomena of judgment, and overweighting of salient values is likely to be the mechanism that explains why low-probability events sometimes loom large in decision making. The analysis of accessibility could readily be extended to deal with these observations.

The claim that cognitive illusions will occur unless they are prevented by System 2 sounds circular, but it is not. Circular inferences are avoidable because the role of System 2 can be independently verified in several ways. For example, the assumption that System 2 is vulnerable to interference by competing activities suggests that manifestations of intuitive thought that are normally inhibited may be expressed when people are placed under cognitive load. Another testable hypothesis is that intuitive judgments that are suppressed by System 2 still have detectable effects, e.g., in priming subsequent responses.

Principles of accessibility determine the relative power of the cues to which the monitoring functions of System 2 respond. For example, we know that differences between options are more salient in joint than in separate evaluation, and that any variable which is manipulated in a factorial design will attract some attention. Other cues can be found in the wording of problems and in the context of previous tasks. Many apparent inconsistencies in the literature on judgment heuristics are easily resolved within this framework (Kahneman & Frederick, 2002). A judgment bias that appears in some situations but not in others usually provides information about the factors that control corrective operations. As already noted, the attribution of the variability of intuitive judgments to System 2 is a source of readily testable hypotheses. It suggests, for example, that intelligence will be correlated with susceptibility to biases only in problems that provide relatively weak cues to the correct solution. In the absence of cues, there is no opportunity for intelligence or sophistication to manifest itself. When cues are abundant, at the other extreme, even the moderately intelligent will find them (Kahneman, 2000a; Stanovich & West, 1999, 2002).

The model suggests four ways in which a judgment or choice may be made:

(i) no intuitive response comes to mind, and the judgment is produced by System 2.

(ii) an intuitive judgment or intention is evoked, and
   a. is endorsed by System 2;
   b. serves as an anchor for adjustments that respond to other features of the situation;
   c. is identified as incompatible with a subjectively valid rule, and blocked from overt expression.

There is of course no way to ascertain precisely the relative frequencies of these outcomes, but casual observation suggests the following ordering, from most to least frequent:

(iia) – (iib) – (i) – (iic)

Most behavior is intuitive, skilled, unproblematic and successful (Klein, 1998). In some fraction of cases, a need to correct the intuitive judgments and preferences will be acknowledged, but the intuitive impression will be the anchor for the judgment. Under-correction is more likely than over-correction in such cases. A conservative general prediction is that variables that are neglected in intuition will remain underweighted in considered judgments.

The analysis of intuitive thinking and choice that has been presented here provides a framework which highlights commonalities between lines of research that are usually studied separately. In particular, the psychology of judgment and the psychology of choice share their basic principles, and differ mainly in content. At a more specific level, prototype heuristics solve structurally similar problems in diverse domains, where they yield closely similar patterns of results. Furthermore, the principles are not specific to the domain of judgment / decision making. The analogy between intuition and perception has been especially fruitful in identifying the ways in which intuitive thought differs from deliberate reasoning, and the notions of accessibility and dual-process analyses play a fundamental role in several domains of social and cognitive psychology.

A general framework such as the one offered here is not a substitute for domain-specific concepts and theories. For one thing, general frameworks and specific models make different ideas accessible. Novel ideas and compelling examples are perhaps more likely to arise from thinking about problems at a lower level of abstraction and generality. However, a broad framework can be useful if it guides a principled search for analogies across domains, to identify common processes and to prevent overly narrow interpretations of findings.

REFERENCES

Agnoli, F. (1991). Development of judgmental heuristics and logical reasoning: Training counteracts the representativeness heuristic. *Cognitive Development, 6,* 195–217.

Agnoli, F., & Krantz, D. H. (1989). Suppressing natural heuristics by formal instruction: The case of the conjunction fallacy. *Cognitive Psychology, 21,* 515–550.

Anderson, N. H. (1981). *Foundations of information integration theory.* New York: Academic Press.

Anderson, N. H. (1991a). *Contributions to information integration theory* (Vol. I: Cognition). Hillsdale, NJ: Erlbaum.

Anderson, N. H. (1991b). *Contributions to information integration theory* (Vol. II: Social). Hillsdale, NJ: Erlbaum.

Anderson, N. H. (1996). *A functional theory of cognition.* Hillsdale, NJ: Erlbaum.

Ariely, D. (1998). Combining experiences over time: The effects of duration, intensity changes, and on-line measurements on retrospective pain evaluations. *Journal of Behavioral Decision Making, 11,* 19–45.

Ariely, D. (2001). Seeing sets: Representation by statistical properties. *Psychological Science, 12,* 157–162.

Ariely, D., & Loewenstein, G. (2000). When does duration matter in judgment and decision making? *Journal of Experimental Psychology: General, 129,* 524–529.

Arrow, K. J. (1982). Risk perception in psychology and economics. *Economic Inquiry, 20,* 1–9.

Bar-Hillel, M., & Neter, E. (2002). How alike is it versus how likely is it: A disjunction fallacy in probability judgments. In T. Gilovich, D. Griffin & D. Kahneman (Eds.), *Heuristics and Biases* (pp.82–97). New York: Cambridge University Press, 2002, 82–97.

Bargh, J. A. (1997). The automaticity of everyday life. In R. S. Wyer, Jr. (Ed.), *The automaticity of everyday life: Advances in social cognition* (Vol. 10, pp.1–61). Mahwah, NJ: Erlbaum.

Bernoulli, D. (1954). Exposition of a new theory on the measurement of risk, *Econometrica, 22,* 23–36. (Original work published 1738).

Bless, H., Clore, G. L., Schwarz, N., Golisano, V., Rabe, C., & Wolk, M. (1996). Mood and the use of scripts: Does a happy mood really lead to mindlessness? *Journal of Personality and Social Psychology, 71,* 665–679.

Bodenhausen, G. V. (1990). Stereotypes as judgmental heuristics: Evidence of circadian variations in discrimination. *Psychological Science, 1,* 319–322.

Brenner, L. A., Koehler, D. J., & Rottenstreich, Y. (2002). Remarks on support theory: Recent advances and future directions. In T. Gilovich, D. Griffin & D. Kahneman (Eds.), *Heuristics and Biases* (pp. 489–509). New York: Cambridge University Press.

Cacioppo, J. T., Priester, J. R., & Berntson, G. G. (1993). Rudimentary determinants of attitudes. II: Arm flexion and extension have differential effects on attitudes. *Journal of Personality and Social Psychology, 65,* 5–17.

Chaiken, S., & Trope, Y. (Eds.). (1999). *Dual-process theories in social psychology.* New York: Guilford Press.

Chapman, G. B., & Johnson, E. J. (2002). Incorporating the irrelevant: Anchors in judgments of belief and value. In T. Gilovich, D. Griffin & D. Kahneman (Eds.), *Heuristics and biases* (pp.120–138). New York: Cambridge University Press.

Chong, S. C., & Treisman, A. (2003). Representation of statistical properties. *Vision Research,* in press.

Cosmides, L., & Tooby, J. (1996). Are humans good intuitive statisticians after all? Rethinking some conclusions from the literature on judgment and uncertainty. *Cognition, 58,* 1–73.

Desvousges, W. H., Johnson, F., Dunford, R., Hudson, S., Wilson, K., & Boyle, K. (1993). Measuring natural resource damages with contingent valuation: Tests of validity and reliability. In J. A. Hausman (Ed.), *Contingent valuation: A critical assessment* (pp. 91–159). Amsterdam: North Holland.

Dulany, D. E., & Hilton, D. J. (1991). Conversational implicature, conscious representation, and the conjunction fallacy. *Social Cognition, 9*, 85–110.

Epley, N., & Gilovich, T. (2002). Putting adjustment back in the anchoring and adjustment heuristic. In T. Gilovich, D. Griffin & D. Kahneman (Eds.), *Heuristics and Biases* (pp. 139–149). New York: Cambridge University Press.

Epstein, S. (1994). Integration of the cognitive and psychodynamic unconscious. *American Psychologist, 49*, 709–724.

Evans, J. St. B. T., Handley, S. J., Over, D. E., & Perham, N. (2002). Background beliefs in Bayesian inference. *Memory and Cognition, 30*, 179–190.

Finucane, M. L., Alhakami, A., Slovic, P., & Johnson, S. M. (2000). The affect heuristic in judgments of risks and benefits. *Journal of Behavioral Decision Making, 13*, 1–17.

Fiske, S. (1998). Stereotyping, prejudice, and discrimination. In D. T. Gilbert & S. T. Fiske (Eds.), *The handbook of social psychology* (4th ed., Vol. 1, pp. 357–441). New York: McGraw-Hill.

Frederick, S. W., & Fischhoff, B. (1998). Scope (in)sensitivity in elicited valuations. *Risk, Decision, and Policy, 3*, 109–123.

Fredrickson, B. L., & Kahneman, D. (1993). Duration neglect in retrospective evaluations of affective episodes. *Journal of Personality and Social Psychology, 65*, 45–55.

Gigerenzer, G. (1991). How to make cognitive illusions disappear: Beyond "heuristics and biases." In W. Stroebe & M. Hawthorne (Eds.), *European Review of Social Psychology* (Vol. 2, pp. 83–115). Chichester, UK: Wiley.

Gigerenzer, G., Hell, W. & Blank, H. (1988). Presentation and content – the use of base rates as a continuous variable. *Journal of Experimental Psychology: Human Perception and Performance, 14*, 513–525.

Gigerenzer, G., Swijtink, Z., Porter, T., Daston, L., Beatty, J., & Krueger, L. (1989). *The empire of chance: How probability changed science and everyday life.* Cambridge, UK: Cambridge University Press.

Gilbert, D. T. (1989). Thinking lightly about others: Automatic components of the social inference process. In J. Uleman & J. A. Bargh (Eds.), *Unintended thought* (pp. 189–211). Englewood Cliffs, NJ: Prentice-Hall.

Gilbert, D. T. (1991). How mental systems believe. *American Psychologist, 46*, 107–119.

Gilbert, D. T. (2002). Inferential correction. In T. Gilovich, D. Griffin & D. Kahneman (Eds.), *Heuristics and biases* (pp.167–184). New York: Cambridge University Press.

Gilovich, T., Griffin, D., & Kahneman, D. (Eds.). (2002). *Heuristics and Biases.* New York: Cambridge University Press.

Griffin, D. W., & Tversky, A. (1992). The weighing of evidence and the determinants of confidence. *Cognitive Psychology, 24*, 411–435.

Hammond, K. R. (1996). *Human judgment and social policy: Irreducible uncertainty, inevitable error, unavoidable injustice.* New York: Oxford University Press.

Heider, F. (1944). Social perception and phenomenal casuality. *Psychological Review, 51*, 358–374.

Higgins, E. T. (1996). Knowledge activation: Accessibility, applicability, and salience. In E. T. Higgins & A. Kruglanski (Eds.), *Social psychology: Handbook of basic principles* (pp.133–168). New York: Guilford Press.

Hilton, D. J., & Slugoski, B. R. (2001). Conversational processes in reasoning and explanation. In A. Tesser & N. Schwartz (Eds.), *Blackwell handbook of social psychology.* (Vol. 1: Intraindividual processes, pp.181–206). Oxford, UK: Blackwell.

Hogarth, R. M. (2001). *Educating intuition.* Chicago: University of Chicago Press.

Hsee, C. K. (1998). Less is better: When low-value options are valued more highly than high-value options. *Journal of Behavioral Decision Making, 11*, 107–121.

Hsee, C. K. (1999). Value seeking and prediction decision inconsistency: Why don't people take what they predict they'll like the most? *Psychonomic Bulletin and Review, 6*, 555–561.

Isen, A. M., Nygren, T. E., & Ashby, F. G. (1988). Influence of positive affect on the subjective utility of gains and losses: It is just not worth the risk. *Journal of Personality and Social Psychology, 55*, 710–717.

Jacoby, L. L. (1991). A process dissociation framework: Separating automatic from intentional uses of memory. *Journal of Memory and Language, 30*, 513–541.

Jacoby, L. L. (1996). Dissociating automatic and consciously controlled effects of study/test compatibility. *Journal of Memory and Language, 35*, 32–52.

Jacoby, L. L., & Dallas, M. (1981). On the relationship between autobiographical memory and perceptual learning. *Journal of Experimental Psychology: General, 110*, 306–340.

Johnston, W. A., Dark, V. J., & Jacoby, L. L. (1985). Perceptual fluency and recognition judgments. *Journal of Experimental Psychology: Learning, Memory, and Cognition, 11*, 3–11.

Kahneman, D. (1986). Comment. In, R. G. Cummings, D. S. Brookshire & W. D. Schultze (Eds.), *Valuing Environmental Goods* (pp.185–193). Totowa, NJ: Rowman & Allenheld.

Kahneman, D. (1994). New challenges to the rationality assumption. *Journal of Institutional and Theoretical Economics, 150*, 18–36.

Kahneman, D. (2000a). A psychological point of view: Violations of rational rules as a diagnostic of mental processes (Commentary on Stanovich and West). *Behavioral and Brain Sciences, 23*, 681–683.

Kahneman, D. (2000b). Experienced utility and objective happiness: A moment-based approach. In D. Kahneman & A. Tversky (Eds.), *Choices, values, and frames* (pp.673–692). New York: Cambridge University Press.

Kahneman, D. (2000c). Evaluation by moments: Past and future. In D. Kahneman and A. Tversky (Eds.), *Choices, values, and frames* (pp.693–708). New York: Cambridge University Press.

Kahneman, D., & Frederick, S. (2002). Representativeness revisited: Attribute substitution in intuitive judgment. In T. Gilovich, D. Griffin & D. Kahneman (Eds.), *Heuristics and Biases* (pp. 49–81). New York: Cambridge University Press.

Kahneman, D., Fredrickson, D. L., Schreiber, C. A., & Redelmeier, D. A. (1993). When more pain is preferred to less: Adding a better end. *Psychological Science, 4*, 401–405.

Kahneman, D., Knetsch, J., & Thaler, R. (1991). The endowment effect, loss aversion, and status quo bias, *Journal of Economic Perspectives, 5*, 193–206.

Kahneman, D., & Miller, D. T. (1986). Norm theory: Comparing reality to its alternatives. *Psychological Review, 93*, 136–153.

Kahneman, D., & Ritov, I. (1994). Determinants of stated willingness to pay for public goods: A study in the headline method. *Journal of Risk and Uncertainty, 9*, 5–38.

Kahneman, D., Ritov, I., & Schkade, D. (1999). Economic preferences or attitude expressions? An analysis of dollar responses to public issues. *Journal of Risk and Uncertainty, 19*, 220–242.

Kahneman, D., Schkade, D. A., & Sunstein, C. R. (1998). Shared outrage and erratic awards: The psychology of punitive damages. *Journal of Risk and Uncertainty, 16*, 49–86.

Kahneman, D., Slovic, P. & Tversky, A. (Eds.). (1982). *Judgment under uncertainty: Heuristics and biases.* New York: Cambridge University Press.

Kahneman, D., & Tversky, A. (1972). Subjective probability: A judgment of representativeness. *Cognitive Psychology, 3*, 430–454.

Kahneman, D., & Tversky, A. (1973). On the psychology of prediction. *Psychological Review, 80*, 237–251.

Kahneman, D., & Tversky, A. (1979). Prospect theory: An analysis of decisions under risk. *Econometrica, 47*, 313–327.

Kahneman, D., & Tversky, A. (1982a). On the study of statistical intuitions. In D. Kahneman, P. Slovic & A. Tversky (Eds.). *Judgment under uncertainty: Heuristics and biases* (pp.493–508). New York: Cambridge University Press.

Kahneman, D., & Tversky, A. (1982b). Variants of uncertainty. *Cognition, 11*, 143–157.

Kahneman, D., & Tversky, A. (Eds.). (2000). *Choices, values, and frames.* New York: Cambridge University Press.

Kahneman, D., & Varey, C. A. (1990). Propensities and counterfactuals: The loser that almost won, *Journal of Personality and Social Psychology, 59*, 1101–1110.

Kahneman, D., Wakker, P. P., & Sarin, R. (1997). Back to Bentham? Explorations of experienced utility. *Quarterly Journal of Economics, 112*, 375–405.

Klein, G. (1998). *Sources of power: How people make decisions.* Cambridge: MIT Press.
Koehler, D. J. (1996). A strength model of probability judgments for tournaments. *Organizational Behavior and Human Decision Making Processes, 66,* 16–21.
Kopp, R. (1992). Why existence value should be used in cost-benefit analysis. *Journal of Policy Analysis and Management, 11,* 123–130.
LeBoeuf, R. A., & Shafir, E. (2003). Deep thoughts and shallow frames: On the susceptibility to framing effects. *Journal of Behavioral Decision Making,* in press.
List, J. (2002). Preference reversals of a different kind: The more is less phenomenon. *American Economic Review, 92,* 1636–1643.
Loewenstein, G. (1996). Out of control: Visceral influences on behavior. *Organizational Behavior and Human Decision Processes, 65,* 272–292.
Loewenstein, G., Weber, E. U., Hsee, C. K., & Welch, N. (2001). Risk as feelings. *Psychological Bulletin, 127,* 267–286.
Luce, R. D., Krantz, D. H., Suppes, P., & Tversky A. (1990). *Foundations of measurement* (Vol. 3: Representation, axiomatization, and invariance). San Diego, CA: Academic Press.
McNeil, B. J., Pauker. S. G., Sox, H. C., & Tversky, A. (1982). On the elicitation of preferences for alternative therapies. *New England Journal of Medicine, 306,* 1259–1262.
Mellers, B. (2000). Choice and the relative pleasure of consequences. *Psychological Bulletin, 126,* 910–924.
Mellers, B., Hertwig, R., & Kahneman, D. (2001). Do frequency representations eliminate conjunction effects? An exercise in adversarial collaboration. *Psychological Science, 12,* 269–275.
Michotte, A. (1963). *The perception of causality* (T. R. Miles & E. Miles, Trans.). New York: Basic Books.
Myers, D. G. (2002). *Intuition: Its powers and perils.* New Haven, CT: Yale University Press.
Nisbett, R. E., Krantz, D. H., Jepson, C., & Kunda, Z. (1983). The use of statistical heuristics in everyday inductive reasoning. *Psychological Review, 90,* 339–363.
Nisbett, R. E., Krantz, D. H., Jepson, C., & Kunda, Z. (2002). The use of statistical heuristics in everyday inductive reasoning. In T. Gilovich, D. Griffin & D. Kahneman (Eds.), *Heuristics and Biases* (pp.510–533). New York: Cambridge University Press.
Novemsky, N., & Kronzon, S. (1999). How are base-rates used, when they are used: A comparison of Bayesian and additive models of base-rate use. *Journal of Behavioral Decision Making, 12,* 55–69.
Palmer, S. E. (1999). *Vision science: Photons to phenomenology.* Cambridge, MA: The MIT Press.
Posner, M. I., & Keele, S. W. (1968). On the genesis of abstract ideas. *Journal of Experimental Psychology, 77,* 353–363.
Posner, M. I., & Keele, S. W. (1970). Retention of abstract ideas. *Journal of Experimental Psychology, 83,* 304–308.
Poulton, E. C. (1975). Range effects in experiments with people. *American Journal of Psychology, 77,* 353–363.
Redelmeier, D., & Kahneman, D. (1996). Patients' memories of painful medical treatments: Real-time and retrospective evaluations of two minimally invasive procedures. *Pain, 66,* 3–8.
Redelmeier, D. A., Katz, J., & Kahneman, D. (in press). Memories of colonoscopy: A randomized trial. *Pain.*
Rosch, E., & Mervis, C. B. (1975). Family resemblances: Studies in the internal structure of categories. *Cognitive Psychology, 7,* 573–605.
Rottenstreich, Y., & Tversky, A. (1997). Unpacking, repacking, and anchoring: Advances in support theory. *Psychological Review, 104,* 406–415.
Schreiber, C. A., & Kahneman, D. (2000). Determinants of the remembered utility of aversive sounds. *Journal of Experimental Psychology: General, 129,* 27–42.
Schwarz, N., & Clore, G. L. (1983). Mood, misattribution, and judgments of well-being: Informative and directive functions of affective states. *Journal of Personality and Social Psychology, 45,* 513–523.

Schwarz, N., Strack, F., & Mai, H. P. (1991). Assimilation and contrast effects in part-whole question sequences: A conversational logic analysis. *Public Opinion Quarterly, 55*, 3–23.

Schwarz, N., & Vaughn, L. A. (2002). The availability heuristic revisited: Ease of recall and content of recall as distinct sources of information. In T. Gilovich, D. Griffin & D. Kahneman (Eds.), *Heuristics and biases* (pp. 103–119). Cambridge: Cambridge University Press.

Shafir, E. (1993). Choosing versus rejecting: Why some options are both better and worse than others. *Memory & Cognition, 21*, 546–556.

Shafir, E., & LeBoeuf, R. A. (2002). Rationality. *Annual Review of Psychology, 53*, 419–517.

Simon, H. A., & Hayes, J. R. (1976). Understanding process: Problem isomorphs. *Cognitive Psychology, 8*, 165–190.

Sloman, S. A. (1996). The empirical case for two systems of reasoning. *Psychological Bulletin, 119*, 3–22.

Sloman, S. A. (2002). Two systems of reasoning. In T. Gilovich, D. Griffin & D. Kahneman (Eds.), *Heuristics and biases* (pp.379–396). Cambridge: Cambridge University Press.

Slovic, P., Finucane, M., Peters, E., & MacGregor, D. G. (2002). The affect heuristic. In T. Gilovich, D. Griffin & D. Kahneman (Eds.), *Heuristics and biases* (pp.397–420). Cambridge: Cambridge University Press.

Smith, S. M., & Levin, I. P. (1996). Need for cognition and choice framing effects. *Journal of Behavioral Decision Making, 9*, 283–290.

Stanovich, K. E. (1999). *Who is rational? Studies of individual differences in reasoning.* Mahwah, NJ: Erlbaum.

Stanovich, K. E., & West, R. F. (1999). Discrepancies between normative and descriptive models of decision making and the understanding / acceptance principle. *Cognitive Psychology, 38*, 349–385.

Stanovich, K. E., & West, R. F. (2000). Individual differences in reasoning: Implications for the rationality debate. *Behavioral and Brain Sciences, 23*, 645–665.

Stanovich, K. E., & West, R. F. (2002). Individual differences in reasoning: Implications for the rationality debate. In T. Gilovich, D. Griffin & D. Kahneman (Eds.), *Heuristics and biases* (pp.421–440). Cambridge: Cambridge University Press.

Strack, F., Martin, L. L., & Schwarz, N. (1988). Priming and communication: The social determinants of information use in judgments of life-satisfaction. *European Journal of Social Psychology, 18*, 429–442.

Strack, F., & Mussweiler, T. (1997). Explaining the enigmatic anchoring effect: Mechanisms of selective accessibility. *Journal of Personality and Social Psychology, 73*, 437–446.

Swalm, R. O. (1966). Utility theory: Insights into risk taking. *Harvard Business Review, 44*, 123–136.

Tversky, A., & Kahneman, D. (1971). Belief in the law of small numbers. *Psychological Bulletin, 76*, 105–110.

Tversky, A., & Kahneman, D. (1973). Availability: A heuristic for judging frequency and probability, *Cognitive Psychology, 5*, 207–232.

Tversky, A., & Kahneman, D. (1974). Judgment under uncertainty: Heuristics and biases. *Science, 185*, 1124–1131.

Tversky, A., & Kahneman, D. (1981). The framing of decisions and the psychology of choice. *Science, 211*, 453–458.

Tversky, A., & Kahneman, D. (1982). Evidential impact of base rates. In D. Kahneman, P. Slovic & A. Tversky (Eds.), *Judgment under Uncertainty: Heuristics and Biases* (pp.153–160). New York: Cambridge University Press.

Tversky, A., & Kahneman, D. (1983). Extensional vs. intuitive reasoning: The conjunction fallacy in probability judgment. *Psychological Review, 90*, 293–315.

Tversky, A., & Kahneman, D. (1986). Rational choice and the framing of decisions. *Journal of Business, 59*, S251–0S278.

Tversky, A., & Kahneman, D. (1991). Loss aversion in riskless choice: A reference-dependent model. *Quarterly Journal of Economics, 106*, 1039–1061.

Tversky, A., & Kahneman, D. (1992). Advances in prospect theory: Cumulative representation of uncertainty, *Journal of Risk and Uncertainty, 5*, 297–323.

Tversky, A., & Koehler, D. J. (1994). Support theory: A nonextensional representation of subjective probability. *Psychological Review, 101*, 547–567.

Wilson, T. D., Centerbar, D. B., & Brekke, N. (2002). Mental contamination and the debiasing problem. In T. Gilovich, D. Griffin & D. Kahneman (Eds.), *Heuristics and biases* (pp.185–200). Cambridge: Cambridge University Press.

Wittreich, W. J. (1961). The Honi phenomenon: A case of selective perceptual distortion. In F. P. Kilpatrick (Ed.), *Explorations in transactional psychology* (pp. 188–202). New York: New York University Press.

Zajonc, R. B. (1980). Feeling and thinking: Preferences need no inferences. *American Psychologist, 35*, 151–175.

Zajonc, R. B. (1997). Emotions. In D.T. Gilbert, S.T. Fiske, & G. Lindzey (Eds.), *Handbook of social psychology* (4th Ed., Vol. 1, pp. 591–632). New York: Oxford University Press.

Zukier, H., & Pepitone, A. (1984). Social roles and strategies in prediction: Some determinants in the use of base-rate information. *Journal of Personality and Social Psychology, 47*, 349–360.

Vernon L. Smith

VERNON L. SMITH

THE EARLY YEARS TO 1975

I was born Vernon Lomax Smith in Wichita, on the flat plains of Kansas, January 1, 1927 in the years leading to the Great Depression. Like many of my generation I am a product of the strange circumstances of survival, and of successes built on tragedy. This narrative is written from memory and impressions, which are notoriously subject to error. Therefore I have carefully verified certain dates and events from family records, newspaper clippings and published Wichita history that provide some mileposts for accuracy checks.

Grover Bougher, my mother's first husband and father of her two oldest children, was a fireman–they shoveled coal and maintained their locomotive's steam pressure–on the Santa Fe railroad. I have a letter Grover wrote to his brother, George, a Private in the American Expeditionary Force, dated October 3, 1918, postmarked in Newton, Kansas on the 4th. On October 5, Grover was killed instantly in a train wreck – not uncommon at the time – when his passenger train engine and its cars were diverted, by a manual cut-over switch left open, onto the sidetrack, colliding with a waiting freight engine. The letter was returned to Newton, postmarked the following April with a notation by the Command P.O. that George had been killed on September 17, 1918 fighting the war in France. Neither brother knew of the other's death. When Grover was killed, my grandfather to be had been laid up for some weeks with a badly injured leg caused by another railroad accident. He was an engineer on the Missouri Pacific Railroad, and was injured as he and his fireman leaped from the engine cab when one of the drive shafts bolted loose from the drive wheel and flailed up through the cab's wood flooring.

Grover's tragedy proved pivotal. The life insurance money provided to my mother by the Santa Fe Railroad, and augmented by a retail job selling shoes, guaranteed a less arduous survival to a twenty-two year old widow with two girls, age 3 and 4.5. In those days aid to dependent children came from family and friends, in this case her parents, whose home she moved into. My maternal grandfather and his twin brother had been orphaned at age 3–4, and were sent to a relative's nearby farm, boys being in demand for farm labor.

Fortune smiled for us all when my father Vernon Chessman Smith (1890–1954), a machinist who had apprenticed in Cleveland Ohio, met my mother, Lulu Belle Lomax (Bougher) (1896–1957) in Wichita, and was delighted to find a warm and caring woman already with a family. My mother often mentioned that she had not intended to have any more children, but my father so loved children, particularly her daughters, that it was unthinkable for her not to have one child by him. If I had been a girl, my name would have been Verna. My father had a brother, Norman (1888–1946), a wildcat driller who had followed his father, a tool dresser, into the oil fields, and a sister, Izella (1892–1918), who died in the great flu epidemic, two months after Grover Bougher had widowed my mother.

The life insurance money was invested in a farm located about 45 miles from Wichita, which was to become our sole means of survival during the difficult years, 1932–1934. A machinist with the Bridgeport Machine Co., maker of oil field equipment, my father was laid off in 1932 for lack of enough work, and the three of us moved to the farm located near Milan, Kansas. My older sisters remained in Wichita, one finishing High School, the other having left high school, and married in 1931.

The farm brought hard work and hard times for my parents–our house had no indoor water, electricity or toilet facilities–but for me it yielded memories of adventure, and learning about chickens (one of which I befriended as a pet until its penchant for following us into the house resulted in a broken neck as the screen door slammed shut behind my mother), milk cows, hogs, gardens, grain crops, priming well pumps, Coleman Lanterns and Kansas windstorms. The farm proved an invigorating childhood with ample opportunity for daily, fatherly lessons in 'how things work' – an interest I have carried the breadth of my life. I learned when and how to milk cows and put them to pasture, feed the hogs, chickens and horse (we could afford only one horse, and perforce had to borrow another for plowing), and to tag along and watch my father repair fences, gates, hog sheds, and barn doors, store hay in the barn loft and shoot rabbits for the table with his father's 1890 vintage lever action Winchester 12 Gauge shotgun.

From my mother I learned about cooking on a wood stove in the Kansas prairie where there is precious little wood, so we supplemented by burning dried corncobs, and–euphemistically–dried sun-baked 'cow chips.' The early settlers had burned Buffalo (sic, Bison) chips, as had the Indians before them. Decades latter I learned that the first Americans who crossed to Alaska on the land bridge from Siberia burned Mammoth chips, and I felt connected to those ancient peoples of 14,000 years ago. I can still memory-taste the fresh buttermilk pancakes and hot buttermilk biscuits–both made with lard!–that were cooked on the top, or in the oven, of that ancient iron stove. If the egg basket was empty, I can remember being sent to the chicken coop to gather fresh warm eggs, occasionally containing two yolks, for the pancakes. I also remember my mother axing the head of a chicken for the table, noting that she did not relish that necessity. Yes, long hours and a hard life for my parents, but for a six to seven year old every new day dawned with fresh excitement when you have not a care in the world, and so much to learn and witness.

At age six I took my place alongside more seasoned farm children for primary education in the classic rural one-room schoolhouse. A neighbor, Mr. Hemburger, had the distinction of being able to read and write, and therefore was deemed fully equipped to be our grade school teacher. A wise decision, I think, although my mother was always a bit irritated when he used the word "ain't," a completely grammatical contraction of which English has many; Mom was something of a language maven. Each morning my teacher/neighbor faced six rows of desks. The first row on his right, where I sat, was grade 1, the second row to his left, grade 2 and so on for all six grades. After some first row recitation, and left with an assignment, I had the opportunity to listen in on the second and third grade recitation lessons – the grades seated closest to me. As I later became aware, this classroom implemented the original progressive system, in which you were part of a single seamless community consisting of six grades. At the end of grade 1, Mr. Hemburger gave me a note to take home to my mother, stating unceremoniously, that 'Vernon can read the second grade reader and therefore next year he will be in the third grade.' There were of course only three subjects–reading, writing and arithmetic. Reading was the litmus test; if you were less strong in arithmetic, or writing, the next year you could participate along with those in the row on your left, before Mr. Hemberger got to your row. The whole purpose of this management style was to move each person along at her own pace of accomplishment, get her through school and into farm work where she could be useful. I understand that the earliest achievement tests showed high performance in Kansas and Nebraska because of these rural schools.

In 1934 my father returned to Bridgeport Machine for part time work, and subsequently full time work. This was fortuitous, as we lost ownership of the farm to the mortgage bank, unable to meet payments on the loan, and we had to move back to Wichita. This confirmed my mother's political commitment to socialism, but my father seemed to take it in stride. At some point in the 1930's this man refused to apply for help from WPA (the Works Project Administration–my grandfather always said that WPA meant 'we piddle around') because he considered it demeaning, a point of contention with my mother who thought he was being completely unreasonable. In 1940 he lost his job permanently when the independent entrepreneur owner of Bridgeport, A. A. Bushaw, closed his factory rather than cede control of his oil field equipment factory to President Franklin Roosevelt's defense industry production. (Of course, the plant was taken over–by Culiver Aircraft–and used for defense, then war production). My father changed employment to the Coleman Lantern Company for about a year, and then he went to work for Stearman Aircraft, which had been purchased by Boeing in 1938. Lloyd Stearman manufactured the famous PT-13 and PT-17 Kaydet biplane that was a U.S. Primary Trainer then and through much of World War II. In 1941 Boeing started construction of Plant II, where the B-29 was to be built, and the Stearman plant was renamed the Boeing-Wichita Plant I. By 1945, 1000 B-29s and over 10,000 Kaydets had been manufactured by Boeing-Wichita.

Wichita and farm life were separated by location, intellectual and economic activity. The city had homegrown a surprising breadth of business life. Beech, Stearman and Cessna Aircraft, Coleman Lantern Company, Fred Dold meatpacking, and the Fred Koch, Jack Vickers and other petroleum companies provided tangible initial evidence of the machinery of markets, specialization and globalization. Bold independent actions by Coleman, Cessna, Beech, Koch, and many others, instilled a mid-western sense of freedom and entrepreneurship (if not always unqualified patriotism, as with Bushaw). When Walter Beech died, his wife, Olive Ann Beech, cofounder of their company, took over the management of Beech Aircraft to become one of the great early women executives. She built it into an internationally successful manufacturer of light planes, and continued to be active on the Board well into her eighties.

After my stellar first grade academic achievements, I continued to perform well in the city primary schools–except for penmanship, which was not my forte. My school performance, however, deteriorated beginning in the eighth grade and all through high school. I found High school very uninspiring–young coeds were far and away more interesting–but I always expected to go to college. I vividly recall that my mother helped me with my English homework when we were learning to diagram sentences in the 9–10th grades, and complaining about the deterioration in the quality of the public schools, circa 1941–2. She had learned to diagram sentences in the 7–8th grades. It was not evident to me why one should learn it in any grade, but what did I know? I have often wondered whether my mother's socialist constructions would have survived her pragmatism, and the reality of poor performance in socialist controlled production as well as education.

In the 9th grade I began my first wage work for the West Side Drug store delivering prescriptions and sundries on my bicycle to customers who called in orders. I still have my original social security card signed when I was 13. (To my mother, social security was a great invention. Not realizing that it was just a tax, she wanted me to enroll early. Here I sit 63 years later receiving SS payments of $1900 per month. I wonder what the payments would be if SS had been vested). Between deliveries I waited on customers, learned to 'soda jerk' on an old fashion drug store fountain (cokes, milk and malt shakes, ice cream Sundays and sodas, etc.). I was paid fifty cents for a six-hour shift plus occasional tips. In 1941 I finished at Allison Intermediate School (grades 7–9), and started at North High School, commuting by bicycle about 5 miles from home to school. On the way was a restaurant and fountain called the OK Drive Inn, owned and operated by Don Eaton, who was a restaurateur known to my family for years. Throughout the 1930's my mother home-baked desserts that Don bought for his restaurant–angel food cake, chocolate devil food cake and Boston cream pie were most common–for 25 cents each. At age 14, with my soda fountain experience, Don offered me a job at $1 per day, summers and weekends. That seemed like good wages to me. I remembered in the early 1930s my father made $1 a day working as a temporary construction carpenter making and installing windows. I operated the fountain, learned to cook and Don later gave me a raise to $8 per six-day week.

In the summer of 1943, at age 16, I applied for an entry level job at Boeing Aircraft, and went to work at an incredible–to me–starting wage of 60 cents per hour, with a 10 cent premium for working the grave yard shift from midnight to 8 am. I was earning $5.60 per day. I also attended summer school at

North High so that when the fall term started I could graduate in January 1944 by taking only two courses. In that way I could finish High School and continue at Boeing. It was very demanding, but did not become burdensome until the following December when Boeing converted from three 8-hour shifts to two 10 hour shifts per day. I made it through, and two months later, on January 20, I graduated.

At Boeing, because of my high school training in electricity principles and practice, I was in the Functional Testing Department where I studied the training manuals for the Central Fire Control (gun operation) System on the B-29. It was the first high altitude bomber with pressurized cabin for the crew–pilot, co-pilot, engineer, bombardier, nose gunner, two side gunners, an upper gunner and a tail gunner. The gun turrets were each remotely controlled by gun sights with electro mechanical selsyn (self synchronous) motors located in the heated and pressurized cabin areas. My division had responsibility for trouble shooting the system and aligning the gun sights with the firing trajectories. We learned about compensating for windage jump as the spinning bullets emerged from the barrels into the high velocity air, and 'leading the target' to account for differential air speed between source and target. This was the first Buck Rogers armament system, and it was fascinating. Some time after I got up to speed I requested and was granted transfer to the second shift flight crew. On this assignment, I would be part of the crew that did the final alignment checks on the system, and fire tested all the guns on the ground. There was a large abutment of stacked wood beams backed by an earth fill into which all the guns were fired. Each plane was set parallel to the firing range. The lower aft, lower forward and upper aft turrets (two fifty caliber machine guns in each) and the upper forward (four fifties) were aligned on the target range, and we fired 25 rounds through each gun. The plane was then turned 90 degrees and the tail turret, consisting of two fifties and a 20 mm cannon, were also fire tested, except that the air force required 50 rounds to be fired through the cannon; I never quite understood why it was called a cannon, as it spit out rounds like a machine gun. We pulled all the barrels and loading bolts, cleaned and reinstalled them in the guns, the air force bought the plane, and it was flown to its base. I was turning 17 years old and Boeing was actually paying me to do this thing called 'work!' It ended in August 1944, after 15 months, when I resigned to begin college.

Our sole family 'intellectual' was my mother's uncle, Sullivan Lomax, who injured his leg as a child in a farm accident. It was not set properly, and left him handicapped. Being ill suited for arduous farm work, he studied law at the University of Kansas, passed the Kansas Bar exam, and practiced law in Cherryvale, Kansas his entire life. My mother and indeed all of us were proud of him! Consequently, neither I, nor my parents, or anyone in my family, or any neighbor or friend, had any idea how to go about choosing a college. So, I went to the city library, found a book on choosing a college, and learned among other things that the 'best' college in the United States was Caltech. Being naïve and impetuous I decided that I should prepare myself to enter Caltech, as, without preparation, my 'C' average in High School would not even qualify me to take the entrance exam. A serious Quaker College, Friend's University, was located near my home in West Wichita. I enrolled in physics, chemistry, calculus, astronomy and literature courses for one year, earned top grades, and sat for the entrance exams for Caltech.

The exam consisted of problems: how fast must a snowball be thrown against a wall to melt on impact? Lets see now, if the mass of the snowball is 'm,' and its velocity, 'v,' then its kinetic energy is $(1/2)\ mv^2$. Since it takes C (was it 528?) calories of heat energy to convert each gram of snowball (ice) into water, you had only to equate Cm with the kinetic energy, and solve for 'v' with suitable account taken of units.

I passed, took the Santa Fe's California Limited passenger train west out of Newton through La Junta, Colorado, Tucumcari, Clovis, Gallop and Albuquerque, New Mexico; Winslow, Flagstaff and Kingman, Arizona; and Barstow, California, arriving in Los Angeles in September, 1945. It was 'all the way on the Santa Fe,' as the concessionaire would announce in each car as he went through with peanuts, gum, candy, pop and cigarettes. This route would become familiar in the next four years, whether I was traveling by train or driving the parallel Route 66.

Caltech was a meat grinder like I could never have imagined. I studied night, day, weekends and survived hundreds of problems, but what a joy to take freshman chemistry from Linus Pauling, hear physics lectures by J. Robert Oppenheimer on his frequent visits to Caltech, attend a visiting lecture by Bertrand Russell, and regularly see von Karman, Anderson, Zwicky, Tolman, Millikan and other legendary figures of that time, on campus.

I was majoring in physics, but switched to electrical engineering, which was in the same division (Mathematics, Physics and EE) as a senior. In this way I did not have to take the dreaded "Smyth's course," required for physics majors, but not EE, and received my BS on schedule in 1949. At the time I relished the unbending facts and mathematics of physics/engineering. Then, as a senior, I took an economics course and found it very intriguing–you could actually learn something about the economic principles underlying the claims of socialism, capitalism and other such 'isms.' Curious about advanced economics, I went to the Caltech library, stumbled upon two books, Samuelson's *Foundations*, and von Mises' *Human Action.* From the former, it was clear that economics could be done like physics, but from the latter there seemed to be much in the way of reasoning that was not like physics. I also subscribed to the *Quarterly Journal of Economics*, and one of the first issues had a paper by Hollis Chenery on Engineering Production Functions. So, economics was also like engineering! I had not a hint then as to how much those first impressions would be changed in my thinking over the decades to follow. But in 1962, my book, *Investment and Production,* would have a chapter on engineering production functions.

After graduating in engineering I went to the University of Kansas to get an MA in economics as a vehicle for allowing me to decide if I wanted to continue in economics. At KU I took classes from Dick Howey: price theory, math economics, imperfect competition, but significantly, a full year course in the

Development of Economic Thought. Howey was a surviving member of an endangered species, a History of Economic Thought scholar, but it was from him that I learned what scholarship really meant. To be good at whatever you did, you needed to acquire knowledge of all the supporting structure, tools and primary sources of inspiration. If you were Howey, that meant knowing mathematics and being fluent in French, German and Italian. As one who just barely knew English, he much impressed me. His model seemed just right and it generalized to whatever might interest you. With Dick as a mentor, I decided economics was for me, and I continued by pursuing an economics Ph.D. at Harvard beginning in 1952. I met Joyce Harkleroad at KU. We were married in 1950. A year later she gave birth to twins, Deborah and Eric in that order, and I was part of a rapidly growing family.

At Harvard, I had macroeconomics from Alvin Hansen–the foremost American Keynesian, but he was also very eclectic. You read everything from Foster and Catchings to Hayek, and not only Keynes, his interpreters and critics–Hicks, Samuelson, Metzler, Friedman, etc. The Keynesian economics was tempered by the dry wit of Gottfried Haberler, the sarcasm of Wassily Leontief, Guy Orcutt's deeply serious search for the messages hidden in all data, Alexander Gershenkron who lectured on 'ven Breetan vas ze voikshop of ze woild,' and a coterie of graduate students trying to make sense of it all for their own careers. When Fritz Machlup visited, I wondered how the two polite Austrians–he and Haberler–would determine which one would get through a door first. Schumpeter was no longer alive, but his ghost was lurking in the halls with Haberler countering any claims that inflation ('ze monster' to Schumpeter), if not too large, was good for the soul and spirit of the economy.

For micro I supplemented with courses Samuelson taught down the Charles River at MIT. After Caltech, Harvard seemed easy, and I got virtually straight A's. I remember that my classmate Dick Quant and I always scored high, and close together, on exams. But at best we were vying for second–the top score always went to Barbara Jay, who married an artist and dropped out before dissertation time. Graduate school is an endurance test, but was not that demanding for me after having survived the undergraduate meat grinder.

In the Spring of 1955, as I was finishing my PhD dissertation, and Joyce was typing it, my second daughter, Torrie, was born, and in August we moved to my first teaching post, at Purdue University, nestled in comfortably familiar Midwestern plains. In the Autumn semester, 1955, I taught Principles of Economics, and found it a challenge to convey basic microeconomic theory to students. Why/how could any market approximate a competitive equilibrium? I resolved that on the first day of class the following semester, I would try running a market experiment that would give the students an opportunity to experience an actual market, and me the opportunity to observe one in which I knew, but they did not know what were the alleged driving conditions of supply and demand in that market.

But let me backtrack to 1952. Many generations of Harvard graduate students had been exposed to E. H. Chamberlin's beginning graduate course in Monopolistic Competition. On the first day he would set the stage for the semester using a classroom demonstration experiment showing that competitive price theory was an unrealistic idealization of the real world. He gave half the class buyer reservation values, and the other half seller reservation costs. The value/cost environment was like Böhm-Bawerk's (1884/1959, book III, pp 207– 235; 432–436) representation of supply and demand in a horse market with multiple buyers and sellers in two-sided competition – perhaps Chamberlin's source of inspiration. I knew Böhm-Bawerk because of Dick Howey's course, but I did not pick up on this similarity until much later. Chamberlin, unlike Böhm-Bawerk's description, had the buyers and sellers circulate, form pairs, and bargain over a bilateral trade; if successful the price was posted on the blackboard; if not successful, each would seek a new trading partner. This continued until the market was closed. The prices in sequence were volatile and failed to support the equilibrium prediction. Chamberlin used this first-day exercise to set the stage for his theory of monopolistic competition. I decided to use the same value/cost setup but changed the institution. Secondly, I decided to repeat the experiment for several trading periods to allow the traders to obtain experience and to adapt over time, as in Marshall's conception of the dynamics of competition. For the institution, I reasoned that if you were going to show that the competitive model did not work, then you should choose a more competitive trading procedure, so that when the competitive model failed to predict the outcomes, you would have a stronger case than had been made by Chamberlin. I went to the Purdue Library and found a book by Lefler, *The Stock Market* (1951), giving details on the bid/ask double auction used in the stock and commodity Exchanges. In January 1956 I carried out my plan. To my amazement the experimental market converged 'quickly' to near the predicted equilibrium price and exchange volume, although there were 'only' 22 buyers and sellers, none of whom had any information on supply and demand except their own private cost or value. I thought perhaps that it was an accident of symmetry in the buyer and seller surpluses. I shot that idea down with an experiment later using a design in which the seller surplus was much greater than that of the buyers. Thus did I seem to have stumbled upon an engine for testing ideas inside and outside traditional economic theory.

Over the years 1956–1960 I continued to do many variations on this original experiment, altering the supply and demand environment, examining shifts in the demand or supply, varying the trading rules and introducing cash rewards showing that they made a difference. I gradually became persuaded that the subjects, without intending to, had revealed to me a basic truth about markets that was foreign to the literature of economics. I reported my early experiments–crude as they were compared with what I would later learn to do–in a paper, accepted for publication in *The Journal of Political Economy*, 1962, after two revisions, four negative referee reports and an initial rejection. (See, Smith, *Papers in Experimental Economics, Cambridge University Press,* 1991, pp 157–158).

During these years most of my research and teaching dealt with capital and investment theory, and corresponding pricing problems (Smith, 1961, *Investment and Production*, Harvard University Press). In 1961–1962 I was a visiting associate professor at Stanford, and at the beginning of the Autumn quarter had the significant experience of meeting Sydney Siegel and discovering that we had both been doing experimental economics. Unknown to both of us at the time, Reinhard Selten had also been pioneering economics experiments in Germany. Syd–a truly powerful experimental intellect–strongly influenced me in becoming committed to experimental economics, but he died unexpectedly at age 45 within a few weeks of our meeting. Eventually, I read all of his publications, including his classic, *Nonparametric Statistics*, and his two books coauthored with L. Fouraker (1960, 1963). Syd was not only a master experimentalist; he also used theory and statistics with skill in the design and analysis of experiments.

The growth of my research interests in experiment, together with a modest literature by myself, Siegel, Fouraker and Siegel, Edwards in choice under uncertainty, Anatol Rapoport in Prisoners Dilemma, and others in experimental matrix games, led me to initiate a graduate seminar in experimental economics at Purdue in 1963, which continued until my departure in 1967. In that first seminar I had thirteen students, including Don Rice, Hugo Sonnenschein, Norm Weldon, and Tom Muench, whose careers I have followed. I published new papers in experimental economics in 1964 (with Don Rice), another in 1964, then in 1965 and 1967. Several working papers by students and faculty were also spawned by this effort. In 1963 and again in 1964, under the enabling and supporting influence of Dick Cyert, Jim March (and probably Herb Simon in the background), Lester Lave and I conducted Ford Foundation faculty summer research workshops at Carnegie Mellon. With several experimental papers in the pipeline, and a seminar going, experimental economics was becoming much more than a hobby for me.

In 1967 Joyce, Eric, Deborah, Torrie and I moved to Sherborn, Massachusetts, where we would live until 1972, with Joyce serving in her first position as a Unitarian minister. I was able to get a tenured professorship, first at Brown University, then in 1968 at the University of Massachusetts. Our children had finished high school by 1972, and I accepted a fellowship at the Center for Advanced Study in the Behavioral Sciences, 1972–1973. During all of this period my research turned to the economics of uncertainty, financial theory of the firm, and natural resource economics, but I continued to think about experimental economics and to use it in teaching. This was good in that my brain was continuing to work on experiments, and I was developing a fresh perspective. Also, Charles Plott and I talked experiments (for example the idea of induced valuation) on many bass fishing trips to Lake Powell. At the Center, thanks to the encouragement of the anthropologist, Bob Heiser, I wrote my 'Pleistocene Extinctions' paper, and submitted it to the AER. After a year's delay I received a letter of rejection along with three favorable referee reports. The editor explained that he had been unconvinced by the first two, sought a third report, and was still not convinced. So I sent it to the

Journal of Political Economy (1975) along with the letter and the three reports; the editor sent it to one referee, it was accepted and published in about six weeks.

While at the Center I continued to be in touch with Charles Plott, who wanted to join me in 'getting into experimental economics.' Caltech offered me a Sherman Fairchild Distinguished Scholar position for one year, and this provided the vehicle for us to offer a seminar for student credit in the Spring quarter of 1974. Charlie and I updated my old outline and notes from Purdue, and we had regular meetings attended by three paying customers (including an undergraduate, Ross Miller), and several faculty, including Mo Fiorina, John Ferjohn, Roger Noll, Jim Quirk, Lance Davis and Bill Riker, also a visiting Fairchild scholar that academic year from Rochester. Bill had done some political science game theory experiments and we were off and running. Afterwards at Caltech, experiments, including political economy, would be central to their teaching and research program. Later Bill reported that he had agreed to write a paper for an editor on experimental methods in political science, but after the course reversed his decision, because the seminar had changed his thinking about experiments, and he wanted to reflect more on the experience. I think that story summarizes well the intellectual ferment produced that semester.

As an interesting side-note, I had developed what I called the "Theory of Induced Valuation," in lecture notes in my Purdue Seminar sometime in the period 1963–65. I talked from those notes in our Caltech seminar in 1974. Charlie pointed out to me that these ideas were catching hold and he and others needed something to cite so at some point I included them in a methods write-up in the Caltech working paper series. Later, I did a write-up of induced valuation for the American Economic Review (1976) and it was finally published long after its original genesis. The Nobel citation included that paper.

Except for some loose publication ends for me to complete in resource economics, I was firmly back into experiments, and Charlie, Mo, John and others were creating experimental public choice. I stayed on in 1974–75 with a joint appointment at Caltech and USC, we wrote up our experiments for Miller, Plott and Smith (Quarterly Journal of Economics, 1977) (this must have been the first scientific paper in economics with an undergraduate coauthor), Charlie and I wrote our paper on comparing institutions for the Review of Economic Studies (1978), and I started the experiments that would lead to a series of papers testing the incentive properties of various public good mechanisms (1977–1984).

I considered staying on at Caltech; also, going to Northwestern, where I had close friends like John Hughes and Stan Reiter, but I feared the tug of a silver cord, and that 'you can't go home again.' I was looking for new opportunity; I could not describe it, but I thought I would know it when I saw it. In 1974 I gave a seminar at the University of Arizona. Rene Manes, a student from Purdue days, was Dean of the College of Business, and they were interested in bringing me to Arizona. I returned in 1975 to give another seminar, visited with their administration, and sensed that this was what I was looking for. They had some recruiting successes in the College, but had much work ahead in building the faculty. Most impressive, however, was a committed top administration: John Schafer, President; Gary Munsinger as Vice President, and Al Weaver, a tough minded Provost. I decided to move to Tucson. Carol Breckner moved with me. Subsequently we married and our son, Joshua, was born in 1981.

In retrospect that was a good decision. I was there for 26 years, before leaving for George Mason University. That is a long and exciting story that continued the basic work begun at Purdue, which formed the primary citation by the Nobel Foundation. That story begs to be told, but I cannot possibly do it justice in the limited time and space I have for this narrative.

Stay tuned.

CONSTRUCTIVIST AND ECOLOGICAL RATIONALITY IN ECONOMICS[1]

Prize Lecture, December 8, 2002

by

VERNON L. SMITH,[2]

Interdisciplinary Center for Economic Science, George Mason University, Fairfax, VA 22030-4444, USA.

When we leave our closet, and engage in the common affairs of life, (reason's) conclusions seem to vanish, like the phantoms of the night on the appearance of the morning; and 'tis difficult for us to retain even that conviction, which we had attained with difficulty… (Hume, 1739/, p 507).

…we must constantly adjust our lives, our thoughts and our emotions, in order to live simultaneously within different kinds of orders according to different rules. If we were to apply the unmodified, uncurbed rules (of caring intervention to do visible 'good') of the…small band or troop, or…our families…to the (extended order of cooperation through markets), as our instincts and sentimental yearnings often make us wish to do, we would *destroy* it. Yet if we were to always apply the (noncooperative) rules of the extended order to our more intimate groupings, we would *crush* them. (Hayek, 1988, p 18). (Italics are his, parenthetical reductions are mine).

We have become accustomed to the idea that a natural system like the human body or an ecosystem regulates itself. To explain the regulation, we look for feedback loops rather than a central planning and directing body. But somehow our intuitions about self-regulation do not carry over `to the artifi-

[1] The title was suggested to me in the paper by Joel Norman, "Two Visual Systems and Two Theories of Perception: An Attempt to Reconcile the Constructivist and Ecological Approaches, "Behavioral and Brain Sciences, 2002. After finishing this paper I found that my use of the term below had been used by Gigerenzer, *et al.* (1999), for application to "fast and frugal decision making," by individuals: "A heuristic is ecologically rational to the degree that it is adapted to the structure of an environment." (p. 13). Hayek, in the citations below identifies both kinds of rationality.

[2] Doing experimental economics has changed the way I think about economics. There are many reasons for this, but one of the most prominent is that designing and conducting experiments forces you to think through the process rules and procedures of an institution. Few, like Einstein, can perform detailed and imaginative mental experiments. Most of us need the challenge of real experiments to discipline our thinking. In this paper I hope to indicate how my thinking has been changed in some detail. I am indebted to Syd Siegel for technical and conceptual inspiration; to John Hughes, Stan Reiter, and the Purdue faculty from 1955 to 1967 for warm tolerant support beginning with my first experiment; to Charles Plott, Charles Holt and Martin Shubik for many valuable encounters over the years on institutional and experimental issues; to students, visitors, the current ICES team, and especially to my growing but tolerating family who have made all these years the best years of my life.

cial systems of human society. (Thus)...the...disbelief always expressed by (my) architecture students (about)...medieval cities as marvelously patterned systems that had mostly just "grown" in response to myriads of individual decisions. To my students a pattern implied a planner... The idea that a city could acquire its pattern as "naturally" as a snowflake was foreign to them. (H. Simon, 1981/1996, p 33).

Historically, a recurrent theme in economics is that the values to which people respond are not confined to those one would expect based on the narrowly defined canons of rationality. These roots go back to Adam Smith (1759, 1776) who examined the moral sympathies that characterize natural human sociality.[3] Contrary to vulgar impressions, in Smith's view, each individual defined and pursued his own interest in his own way, and individuals were mischaracterized by the metaphor, 'economic man.' (Cf Hayek, 1991, p 120). This careless scholarship fails to recognize the key proposition articulated by the Scottish philosophers: to do good for others, does **not** require deliberate action to further the perceived interest of others. As Mandeville so succinctly put it, "The worst of all the multitude did something for the common good." (See Mandeville's poem, 'The Grumbling Hive' or 'Knaves Turned Honest,' 1705; quoted in Hayek, 1991, p 82). Many contemporary scholars, and not only popular writers, have reversed Mandeville's proposition, and argued that the standard socio-economic science model (SSSM) requires, justifies and promotes selfish behavior.[4] On the contrary, because enforceable rights can never cover every margin of decision, opportunism in all relational contracting and exchange across time are costs, not benefits, in achieving long-term value from trade; an ideology of honesty[5] means that people play the game of 'trade,' rather than 'steal,' although crime may often pay the rational lawbreaker who always chooses dominant strategies. Nor does non-selfish behavior in ordinary market transactions prevent those transactions from promoting specialization and creating wealth.

Cultures that have evolved markets have enormously expanded resource specialization, created commensurate gains from exchange, and are wealthier than those that have not. This proposition says nothing about the necessity of human selfishness–the increased wealth of particular individuals can be used for consumption, investment, to pay taxes, for Macarthur Fellows, gifted

[3] Economists are largely untouched by Smith's first great work, which was eclipsed by the Wealth of Nations. Thus, one of the profession's best known historian of economic thought, "found these two works in some measure basically inconsistent," Viner (1991). For a contrary interpretation see Smith (1998). Many of the references herein to my own and co-authored work have been reprinted in Smith (1991, 2000).

[4] That A implies B in no sense allows the reverse statement. But why would we economists confuse necessary with sufficient conditions? The text from Hume provides the answer. No one can consistently apply rational logical principles to everything he or she does; if there are cognitive costs in every application then the effort cost will often exceed the benefits. (Smith and Szidarovszky (2002). Theorists live by proving theorems, and when in this mode we rarely make such errors. A missing chapter in the study of bounded rationality is its application to understanding, and accepting with a little humility, the severe limitations it imposes on our development of economic theory.

[5] North (1981) has emphasized the importance of ideology in promoting economic growth.

to the symphony, the Smithsonian, or the poor.[6] Markets economize on the need for virtue, but do not eliminate it.

Research in economic psychology[7] has prominently reported examples where 'fairness' considerations are said to contradict the rationality assumptions of the standard socio-economic science model, or SSSM. But experimental economists have reported mixed results on rationality: people are often better (e.g. in two-person anonymous interactions), in agreement with (e.g. in flow supply and demand markets), or worse (e.g. in asset trading), in achieving gains for themselves and others than is predicted by rational analysis. Patterns in these contradictions and confirmations provide important clues to the implicit rules or norms that people may follow, and can motivate new theoretical hypotheses for examination in both the field and the laboratory. The pattern of results greatly modifies the prevailing, and I believe misguided, rational SSSM, and richly modernizes the unadulterated message of the Scottish philosophers.

I. ON TWO FORMS OF RATIONALITY

The organizing principle throughout this paper is the simultaneous existence of two rational orders. I shall try to make the case that both orders are distinguishing characteristics of what we are as social creatures; that both are essential to understanding and unifying a large body of experience from socio-economic life and the experimental laboratory, and in charting relevant new directions for economic theory as well as experimental-empirical programs.

Constructivist rationality

The first concept of a rational order derives from the SSSM going back to the seventeenth century. The SSSM is an example of what Hayek has called constructivist rationality (or 'constructivism'), which stems particularly from Descartes (also Bacon and Hobbes),[8] who believed and argued that all worth-

[6] In the Potlatch, some wealth–created in part by private property rights in fishing grounds–was publicly destroyed.

[7] I will use the term 'economic psychology' generally to refer to cognitive psychology as it has been applied to economic questions, and to a third sub-field of experimental methods in economics recently product-differentiated as 'behavioral economics,' (Mullainathan and Thaler, 2001), and further differentiated into 'behavioral game theory.' (Camerer, 2002, in press); the original foundations were laid by W. Edwards, D. Kahneman, A. Rappoport, P. Slovic and A. Tversky to name some of the most prominent.

[8] In the 19th century Bentham and John Stuart Mill were among the leading constructivists. Bentham (and the utilitarians) sought to "...remake the whole of...(British)...law and institutions on rational principles." (Hayek, 1960, p 174). Mill introduced the much-abused constructivist concept of (but not the name) 'natural monopoly'. To Mill it was transparently wasteful and duplicative to have two or more mail carriers operating on the same route. He is the intellectual father of the U.S. and other postal monopolies around the world, their resistance to innovation, and their demise in the face of the privatization movement in some countries and the growth of superior substitutes in others. Mill could not imagine that it would be efficient for two cities to be connected by two parallel railroad tracks. (Mill, 1848/1900, Vol 1, p 131, p 141–2, Vol 2, p 463). Mill died in 1873. I would conjecture that by that date, or soon thereafter, men with grade school educations had become rich constructing the first parallel route railroads. These emergent contradictions to constructivist natural monopoly are examples of what we shall call ecological rationality, as detailed below.

while social institutions were and should be created by conscious deductive processes of human reason.[9] In economics the SSSM leads to rational predictive models of decision that motivate research hypotheses that experimentalists have been testing in the laboratory since mid twentieth century. Although the test results tend to be confirming in impersonal market exchange, the results are famously and recalcitrantly mixed in 'personal exchange,' notably in a great variety of two person extensive form games where some half of the people attempt and frequently succeed when risking cooperation, even when anonymously paired.[10] These results have motivated constructivist extensions of game theory based on other-regarding, in addition to own-regarding, preferences (e.g. Bolton, 1991; Rabin, 1993), and on 'learning'–the idea that the predictions of the SSSM might be approached over time by trial-and-error adaptation processes (Erev and Roth, 1998; Camerer and Ho, 1999).

An alternative and perhaps complimentary explanation of some of these contradictions to theory is that people may use social-grown norms of trust and reciprocity[11] (including equity, meaning to each according to his justly earned desert; i.e., equality of opportunity, not outcome) to achieve cooperative states superior to individually rational defection outcomes. We will report some experimental tests designed to separate competing preference and reciprocity theories of behavior in personal exchange. Although reciprocity seems to be a leader in the comparisons we summarize, its strength is not uniform across all tests, and much remains to be learned about the hidden recesses of meaning in human behavior and the circumstances in which cooperative or non-cooperative behavior is manifest.[12] Technically, the issue is how most productively to model agent 'types' by extending game theory so that types are an integral part of its **predictive** content, rather than merely imported as an ex post technical explanation of experimental results. For example, moves can signal types, and effect decision, which explains why game

[9] "...Descartes contended that all the useful human institutions were and ought to be deliberate creation(s) of conscious reason...a capacity of the mind to arrive at the truth by a deductive process from a few obvious and undoubtable premises." (Hayek, 1967, p 85).

[10] Behavioral economists have made a cottage industry of showing that the SSSM assumptions seem to apply almost nowhere to real decisions. This is because their research program has been a deliberate search in the tails of distributions for "Identifying the ways in which behavior differs from the standard model..." (Mullainathan and Thaler 2001), a search that can only succeed.

[11] Dissatisfied with the utilitarian approach because its predictions fail to account for the observed importance of instructions/procedures, we began investigating the reciprocity hypothesis in Hoffman, *et al.* (1994). Mechanically, utilities can serve as intermediate placeholders for reciprocal trust, but, as surface indicators, serve poorly to generate new hypotheses designed to understand interactive processes. Good theory must be an engine for generating testable hypotheses, and utility theory runs out of fuel quickly. Utility values are seen as providing the ultimate 'given' data, and the conversation stops.

[12] I am reminded of a department head from Hewlett-Packard visiting our lab. I naively assumed that he would be most interested in demonstrations of some of our market experiments. Not so. He was more interested in the 'trust' experiments. Why? He saw the HP management problem as one of getting teams to cooperate internally by building trust and trustworthiness, while being vigorous competitors externally. Could the trust games serve as a measurement and teaching tool for helping to solve this problem? This nicely illustrates the tension in Hayek's two-worlds quote in the text.

form matters, and why payoffs available, but foregone, can effect outcomes. These elements must be part of the internal structure of the theory such that outcomes become predictions conditional on the elementary characteristics of players who read each other's intentions. If successful, many of the basic results in game theory would become special cases of the extended theory.

In market experiments–where cooperation can occur through the coordination function of prices produced by, but simultaneously resulting from, interaction with individual choice behavior–the results are more commonly in accord with standard competitive models that maximize group welfare. This professional victory is hollowed by the failure of standard theory to predict the 'surprisingly'[13] weak conditions under which the results obtain.[14]

Thus, for tractability, Cartesian rationalism provisionally assumes or 'requires' agents to possess complete payoff and other information – far more than could ever be given to one mind. In economics the resulting exercises are believed to sharpen economic thinking, as if-then parables. Yet, these assumptions are unlikely to approximate the level of ignorance that has conditioned either individual behavior, or our evolved institutions, as abstract norms or rules independent of particular parameters, which have survived as part of the world of experience.[15] The temptation is to ignore this reality because it is poorly understood, and does not yield to our familiar but inadequate modeling tools, and to proceed in the implicit belief that our parables capture what is most essential about what we observe. Having sharpened our understanding on Cartesian complete information parables we carry these tools into the world for application without all the necessary caveats that reflect the tractability constraints imposed by our bounded professional cognitive capacities as theorists.

In summary, constructivism uses reason to deliberately create rules of action, and create human socioeconomic institutions that yield outcomes deemed preferable, given particular circumstances, to those produced by alternative arrangements. Although constructivism is one of the crowning

[13] Wilson, (1992, p 256) discusses an efficiency theorem, and suggests that the phenomenon is 'perhaps unsurprising.' It is, nowadays, but few believe it; also, theory has lagged well behind the evidence, and yields inadequate testable insight into the process dynamics operating in different institutions.

[14] I want to acknowledge correspondence with Charles Plott and add the following: Although this is a giant victory for the economic theory of markets it simultaneously demonstrates that the theory is incomplete. The unexpectedly weak conditions under which the results obtain are good news for market performance, but not such good news for the scientific community because it demonstrates that we do not understand why markets work as they do. You do not have to have large numbers of agents, each an insignificant part of the whole–3 or 4 buyers and as many sellers is entirely adequate in a wide range of economic environments; they do not have to have complete or perfect or common information–each can have only private information; nor is it required that individuals make decisions systematically, or be economically sophisticated.

[15] Throughout the paper I will use 'environment' to mean the collection of agent values (preferences) that define the gains from trade; 'institution' to refer to the language (messages), rules of message exchange and contract in a market; and 'behavior' for agent message choices conditional on the environment and institution. (Smith, 1982).

achievements of the human intellect, it is important to remain sensitive to the fact that human institutions and most decision making is not guided primarily, if at all, by constructivism. Emergent arrangements, even if initially constructivist in form, must have survival properties that take account of opportunity costs and environmental challenges invisible to our modeling efforts.

Limitations and distractions of constructivist rationality

Since our theories and thought processes about social systems involve the conscious and deliberate use of reason, it is necessary to constantly remind ourselves that human activity is diffused and dominated by unconscious, autonomic, neuropsychological systems that enable people to function effectively without always calling upon the brain's scarcest resource– attentional and reasoning circuitry. This is an important economizing property of how the brain works. If it were otherwise, no one could get through the day under the burden of the selfconscious monitoring and planning of every trivial action in detail.[16] Also, no one can express in thoughts, let alone words, all that he or she knows, and does not know but might call upon, or need to discover, for some purposive action. Imagine the strain on the brain's resources if at the supermarket a shopper were required to explicitly evaluate his preferences for every combination of the tens of thousands of grocery items that are feasible for a given budget. Such mental processes are enormously opportunity-costly and implicitly our brain knows, if our conscious mind does not know, that we must avoid incurring opportunity costs that are not worth the benefit.[17] The challenge of any unfamiliar action or problem appears first to trigger a search by the brain to bring to the conscious mind what one knows that is related to the decision context. Context triggers autobiographic experiential memory, which explains why context surfaces as a nontrivial treatment, particularly in small group experiments. The brain (including the entire neurophysiological system) takes over directly in the case of familiar, mastered tasks, and plays the equivalent of lightening chess when the 'expert'

[16] "If we stopped doing everything for which we do not know the reason, or for which we cannot provide a justification...we would probably soon be dead." Hayek (1988, p 68).

[17] Expected utility theory is for teaching (as Wassily Leontief once suggested), but also for the constructivist modeling of consistent choice. It seems inadequate for the prediction, or the ecological understanding, of behavior. Its inadequacy for prediction has been plainly emphasized in the many contributions of Tversky and Kahneman (see their 1986 paper for an excellent summary statement), some of which have been qualified and reinterpreted in the work of Gigerenzer, *et al.* (1999). The results are far more encouraging in the context of markets, where subjects are not consciously maximizing. See, e.g. Smith (1991, 2000) and Plott (2001). Berg, Dickhaut and McCabe (1994), in a significant paper, find that the measurement of risk aversion varies with the type of market institution or procedure used in extracting risk measures from decisions. See Smith and Szidarovszky (2002) for a constructivist utilitarian treatment of decision whose reward outcome requires cognitive costs to be incurred: objective rationality is not subjectively rational, and therefore it is not optimal for the individual to apply the objectively 'optimal' prescriptions.

trades, plays Beethoven's Fifth piano concerto, or connects with a 95 mile/hour fast ball–all without self aware 'thinking' by the mind.

We fail utterly to possess natural mechanisms for reminding ourselves of the brain's offline activities and accomplishments. This important proposition has led Gazzaniga (1998) to ask why the brain fools the mind into believing it is in control.[18] And to Hayek, who thoroughly understood this proposition, what was the 'fatal conceit'? "The idea that the ability to acquire skills stems from reason." The constructivist mind makes a fatal 'error,' blinding itself to understanding, as we are warned, "one should never suppose that our reason is in the higher critical position and that only those moral rules are valid that reason endorses." (Hayek, 1988, p 21). But the anthropocentric (- morphic) mind routinely makes this significant error.

Most of our operating knowledge[19] we do not remember learning. Natural language is the most prominent example, but also music and virtually everything that constitutes our developmental socialization. We learn the rules of a language and of efficient social intercourse, without explicit instruction, simply by exposure to family and extended family social networks. (Pinker, 1994; Kagan and Lamb, 1987; Kagan, 1994; Fiske, 1991).

That the brain is capable of off-line subconscious learning is shown by experiments with amnesiacs who are taught a new task. They learn to perform well, but memory of having learned the task escapes them. (Knowlton, Mangels, and Squire, 1996).

Ecological rationality

These considerations lead to the second concept of a rational order, as an undesigned ecological system that emerges out of cultural and biological evolutionary[20] processes: home grown principles of action, norms, traditions, and

[18] "By the time we think we know something – it is part of our conscious experience – the brain has already done its work. It is old news to the brain, but fresh to 'us.' Systems built into the brain do their work automatically and largely outside of our conscious awareness. The brain finishes the work half a second before the information it processes reaches our consciousness . . . We are clueless about how all this works and gets effected. We don't plan or articulate these actions. We simply observe the output . . . The brain begins to cover for this 'done deal' aspect of its functioning by creating in us the illusion that the events we are experiencing are happening in real time – not before our conscious experience of deciding to do something." (Gazzaniga, 1998, pp. 63–64).

[19] Hayek (1967, p 44) notes that "...modern English usage does not permit generally to employ the verb 'can' (in the sense of the German können) to describe all those instances in which an individual merely 'knows how' to do a thing...(including)... the capacity to act according to rules which we may be able to discover but which we need not be able to state in order to obey them."

[20] Many recognize that evolutionary processes are necessarily co-evolutionary, but there is also deep denial of this, and bias, that all is due to 'culture' (which is even more poorly understood than biology), leading Pinker (2002) to investigate why. Heritable abstract function can become dormant, atrophied or mal-functional in the absence of initializing input on a developmental time schedule for the brain's vision, language and socialization circuitry. That these processes are co-evolutionary is evident in the study of twins (Segal, 1999). Deconstructivist reports argue that these studies exhibit many of the usual data and statistical identification problems (Goldberger, 1979), but the need is for positive revisionist analysis.

'morality'.[21] Ecological rationality uses reason– rational reconstruction–to examine the behavior of individuals based on their experience and folk knowledge, who are 'naïve' in their ability to apply constructivist tools to the decisions they make; to understand the emergent order in human cultures; to discover the possible intelligence embodied in the rules, norms and institutions of our cultural and biological heritage that are created from human interactions but not by deliberate human design. People follow rules without being able to articulate them, but they can be discovered. This is the intellectual heritage of the Scottish philosophers, who described and interpreted the social and economic order they observed.

An eighteenth century precursor of Herbert Simon, David Hume was concerned with the limits of reason, the bounds on human understanding, and with scaling back the exaggerated claims of Cartesian constructivism. To Hume, rationality was phenomena that reason discovers in emergent institutions. Thus, "the rules of morality...are not conclusions of (our) reason." (Hume, 1739/1985, II, 235). Adam Smith developed the idea of emergent order for economics. Truth is discovered in the form of the intelligence embodied in rules and traditions that have formed, inscrutably, out of the ancient history of human social interactions. This is the antithesis of the anthropocentric belief that if an observed social mechanism is functional, somebody in the unrecorded past must have used reason consciously to create it to serve its perceived intended purposes.[22]

In experimental economics the eighteenth century Scottish tradition is revealed in the observation of emergent order in numerous studies of existing market institutions such as the continuous double auction (CDA).[23] To para-

[21] 'Morality' refers to any maxim of cohesive social behavior that survives the test of time, and is prominently represented by the great 'shalt not' prohibitions of the leading world religions: thou shalt not: (1) steal, (2) covet the possessions of others, commit (3) murder, (4) adultery or (5) bear false witness. The first two define and defend property rights in the product of one's labor, and all resources accumulated by such labor, enabling the emergence of the extended order of mind through markets. The last three commandments protect the sanctity of social exchange–the external order of the mind. These modest exclusionary constraints leave an immense scope for freedom within their bounds. Corollaries, like the Buddhist live-and-let-live version of the golden rule, are explicit in this respect: "do not unto others as you would have them not do unto you."

[22] In cultural and biological evolution, order arises from mechanisms for generating variation to which is applied mechanisms for selection. I am indebted to Todd Zywicki, who, at a recent Liberty Fund conference on 'Hayek, Experiment and Freedom,' observed that reason is good at providing variation, but not selection. Constructivism is indeed an engine for generating variation, but is far too limited in its ability to comprehend and apply all the relevant facts to serve the process of selection, which is better left to ecological processes.

[23] What experimentalists have unintentionally brought to the table is a methodology for objectively testing the Scottish-Hayekian hypotheses under scientific controls. This answers the question Milton Friedman is said to have raised concerning the validity of Hayek's theory/reasoning: "how would you know?" (I am unable to provide a reference). Economic historians e.g. North (1981), and political economists, e.g. Elinor Ostrom (1982), have long explored the intelligence and efficacy embodied in emergent socioeconomic institutions that solve, or fail to solve, problems of growth and resource management. They study 'natural' ecological experiments from which we have learned immeasurably.

phrase Adam Smith, people in these experiments are led to promote group welfare enhancing social ends that are not part of their intention. This principle is supported by hundreds of experiments whose environments and institutions (sealed bid, posted offer and others besides CDA) may exceed the capacity of formal game theoretic analysis to articulate predictive models. But they do not exceed the functional capacity of collectives of incompletely informed human decision makers, whose autonomic mental algorithms coordinate behavior through the rules of the institution–social algorithms–to generate high levels of measured performance.

Acknowledging and investigating the workings of unseen processes are essential to the growth of our understanding of social phenomena, and enable us to probe beyond the anthropocentric limitations of constructivism.

Both kinds of rationality have influenced the design and interpretation of experiments in economics. Thus, if people in certain contexts make choices that contradict our formal theory of rationality, rather than conclude that they are irrational, some ask why, reexamine maintained hypotheses including all aspects of the experiments–procedures, payoffs, context, instructions, etc.–and inquire as to what new concepts and experimental designs can help us to better understand the behavior. What is the subjects' perception of the problem that they are trying to solve?

Finally, understanding decision requires knowledge beyond the traditional bounds of economics,[24] a challenge to which Hume and Smith were not strangers.[25] This is manifest in the recent studies of the neural correlates of strategic interaction (Kevin McCabe calls it neuroeconomics) using fMRI and other brain imaging technologies. That research explores the neurocorreleates of intentions or "mind reading," and other hypotheses about information, choice, and own versus other payoffs in determining interactive behavior.

The above themes will be illustrated and discussed in a wide variety of examples drawn from economics, law, experimental economics and psychology. I will begin with impersonal exchange through markets, drawing on the learning from experiments and field observations to illustrate how the contrast between constructive and ecological rationality informs learning from observation. Then I will examine personal exchange, particularly in the context of two person extensive form games, asking why constructivist models are of limited success in predicting behavior in single play games, even when subjects are anonymously matched.

[24] I importune students to read narrowly within economics, but widely in science. Within economics there is essentially only one model to be adapted to every application: optimization subject to constraints due to resource limitations, institutional rules and /or the behavior of others, as in Cournot-Nash equilibria. The economic literature is not the best place to find new inspiration beyond these traditional technical methods of modeling.

[25] Thus, for Hayek, "an economist who is only an economist cannot be a good economist."

II. IMPERSONAL EXCHANGE: THE EXTENDED ORDER OF THE MARKET

How are the two concepts of a rational order related?

Constructivism takes as given the social structures generated by emergent institutions that we observe in the world, and proceeds to model it formally. An example would be the Dutch auction or its alleged isomorphic equivalent, the sealed bid auction. (Vickery, 1961; Milgrom and Weber, 1982). Constructivist models need not ask why or how an auction institution arose or what were the ecological conditions that created it; or why there are so many distinct auction institutions. In some cases it is the other way around. Thus, revenue equivalence theorems show that the standard auctions generate identical expected outcomes, which, if taken literally, leave no modeled economic reason for choosing between them.

More generally, using rational theory, one represents an observed socio-economic situation with an abstract interactive game tree. Contrarily, the ecological concept of rationality asks from whence came the structure captured by the tree? Why this social practice, from which we can abstract a particular game, and not another? Were there other practices and associated game trees that lacked survival properties and were successfully invaded by what we observe? There is a sense in which ecological systems, whether cultural or biological, must necessarily be, or are in the process of becoming, rational: they serve the fitness needs of those who unintentionally created them through their interactions. Constructivist mental models are based on assumptions about behavior, structure and the value-knowledge environment. These assumptions might be correct, incorrect or irrelevant, and the models may or may not lead to rational action in the sense of serving well the needs of those to whom the models apply. As theorists the professional charge for which we are paid is to formulate and prove theorems. A theorem is a mapping from assumptions into testable or observable implications. The demands of tractability loom large in this exercise, and to get anything much in the way of results it is necessary to consider both the assumptions and their implications as variables. Few game theorists, building on the assumption that agents always choose dominant strategies, believed this to characterize the behavior of all agents in all situations. Hence, the near universal justification of theory as an exercise in 'understanding.' But the temptation is to believe that our 'castles in the sky' (as W. Brock would say) have direct meaning in our worlds of experience and proceed to impose them where it may not be ecologically rational to do so.

To understand what is–the tip of the knowledge iceberg–requires understanding of a great deal that is not. In the laboratory we can not only rationally reconstruct counterfactuals, as in economic history, but also use experiments to test and examine their properties. Let us look at two contemporary examples.

Deregulating Airline Routes

Airline route deregulation brought an unanticipated reorganization of the network, called the hub-and-spoke system. (See e.g., Donahue, 2002). This is an ecologically rational response, apparently anticipated by none of the constructivist arguments for deregulation, and predicted by no one. Nor could it have been uncovered, I submit, in 1978 by surveys of airline managers, or by marketing surveys of airline customers. Unknown to both managers and customers was the subsequently revealed decision preferences of customers who unknowingly favored frequency of daily departure and arrival times–a preference that had to be discovered through market experimentation. Nonstop service between secondary cities was simply not sustainable in a deregulated world of free choice. The only way to achieve efficiency, both the demand for frequency of service and profitable load factors, among secondary cities was for the flights to connect through hubs. Hence, the hypothesis that a rational ecological equilibrium emerged to dominate repeated constructivist attempts, by business entrants and start-ups, to satisfy an incompatible set of constraints provided by the microstructure of demand, profitability and technology.

Might it have been otherwise if airport runway rights, or 'slots', had been an integral part of the deregulation of airline routes, and the time-of-day spot pricing of slots had emerged to reflect hub congestion costs? (Rassenti, Smith and Bulfin, 1982). We do not know, but the effect of this hypothetical counterfactual on the viability of hub bypass could be assessed in laboratory experiments. As in all studies of what is not, the challenge is to estimate the parameters that would implement the appropriate economic environment.

The California Energy Crisis

A second, and very troubling, example is the circumstances leading to the California energy crisis. As in other regions of the country and the world, deregulation was effected as a planned transition with numerous political compromises. In California it took the form of deregulating wholesale markets and prices while continuing to regulate retail prices at fixed hourly rates over the daily and seasonal cycles in consumption. The utilities negotiated an increase in these average retail rates to meet the revenue requirements of capital investments that were 'stranded' (i.e., were believed to be unable to recover their costs under competition). This preoccupation with the past, and with average revenue/cost thinking by regulators and regulated alike, ill prepared the state for the consequences of having no dynamic mechanisms for prioritizing the end use consumption of power.

As expected, traditional volatility in the marginal cost of generated electricity was immediately translated into volatile intra-day wholesale prices. What was not expected was that a combination of low rainfall (reducing Pacific Northwest hydroelectric output), growth in demand, unseasonably hot weather, generators down on normal maintenance schedules, etc., caused the temporary normal daily peaking of prices to be greatly accentuated, and to be much more lasting than had occurred earlier in the Midwest and South.

Events of small probability happen at about the expected frequency, and since there are many such events the unexpected is not that unlikely. Constructivist planning failed to provide for retail competition to experiment with programs allowing consumers to save money by enabling their lower priority uses of power to be interrupted in times of supply stress. Interruptible deliveries are a direct substitute for both energy supply and energy reserves, and are an essential means of assuring adequate capacity and reserves that cover all the various supply contingencies faced by the industry.

Because of the regulatory mandate that all demand must be served at a fixed price, the planning did not allow for the early introduction of demand responsive retail prices and technologies to enable peak consumption to be reduced. Instead of mechanism design we had fixed retail price 'design' to generate average revenue that was supposed to cover average cost, and it failed. The regulatory thought process is as follows: the function of price is to provide revenue, and the function of revenue is to cover cost. But this is the antithesis of the market function of price. For neither management nor the regulators was it natural to think in terms of profiting from selling less power. Yet that was precisely the route by which the California distributors could have avoided the loss of an estimated $15 billion: every peak kilowatt-hour not sold at the average retail rate would have saved up to ten times that amount of energy cost. Static technology, and the utter fantasy that all load can always be served, were protected from innovation by the legally franchised local wires monopoly. An entrant could not seek to win customers by offering discounts for switching from peak to off peak consumption, and, at the entrant's investment risk, installing the required control devices on end-use appliances. This legacy–long entrenched, and jealously sheltered by local franchised monopolies after deregulation–gave California dispatchers no alternative but to trap people in elevators and shut down high-end computer programming facilities at critical times of peak power shortage.

All power delivery systems are vulnerable to a combination of unfavorable events that will produce short supplies at peak demand. Constructivism alone, without competitive trial-and-error ecological experimentation with retail delivery technologies and consumer preferences, cannot design mechanisms that process all the distributed knowledge that individuals either possess or will discover, and that is relevant to finding an efficient mix of both demand and supply responsiveness.[26]

[26] This is illustrated by a November 6, 2002 press release by Puget Sound Energy. "PSE Proposes to End Pilot Time-of-Use Program Ahead of Schedule: PSE's time-of-use (TOU) program was created in 2000 during the energy crisis and was intended to provide financial incentives for customers to shift some of their electricity consumption to less expensive, off-peak times of the day. The program was restructured in July 2002 to reflect a calmer energy market. Since that time it has resulted in most participants' bills being slightly higher than on flat rates...Reynolds (a PSE spokesman) said, 'However, when exploring new territory, you need to be able to recognize when the program is not working as you had hoped...and begin a rigorous analysis of the program and how it could be successfully restructured for the future energy marketplace.'" It is because no one knows what will work best that you have to open retailing up to the field experi-

Economic Systems Design

What can we learn from experiments about how demand responsiveness could impact energy shortages as in the California crisis? Rassenti, Smith and Wilson (2002a) measure this impact by creating a market in which a modest and achievable 16% of peak retail demand can be interrupted voluntarily at discount prices by wholesale energy providers. In the experiments, demand cycles through four levels each 'day' and is expressed in the wholesale market with two contrasting experimental treatments: (1) robot buyers who reveal all demand at the spot market clearing price; (2) four profit motivated human buyers who are free to bid strategically in the market to obtain the lowest available prices. In each case bids to supply power are entered by five profit motivated human suppliers. In the passive demand treatment prices average much above the benchmark competitive equilibrium, and are very volatile. In the treatment with human buyers, prices approach the competitive equilibrium, and price volatility becomes minuscule. By empowering wholesale buyers, in addition to sellers, to bid strategically in their own interest, even though 84% of peak demand is 'must serve,' buyers are able to effectively discipline sellers and hold prices at competitive levels.[27]

This example illustrates the use of the laboratory in economic systems design. In these exercises we can test-bed alternative market auction rules and

ment called "free entry and exit." One experimental possibility is a contract that would share the inheritently unknown and unpredictable savings with the customer. When a total cannot be known in advance, use a proportionality rule. New Zealand's tradable fish catch quotas were originally specified in quantities, and were redesigned as proportions of the changing quantity available. (Oral communication with Maurice McTigue, 2002). An advantage of laboratory experiments is that these kinds of errors are exposed, and corrective alternatives tested, at very low cost.

[27] The most widely agreed upon design failure in the California crisis was the rule preventing the distribution utilities from engaging in long term contracts to supply power. (Wilson, 2002, p. 1332). Beware this simplistic popular explanation: it is a two-wrongs-make-a-right argument: yes, of course, given that you were going to protect the monopoly power of the distribution utilities to tie the rental of the wires to the metering and sale of energy at a fixed regulated price, then one way to protect them temporarily from the consequent wholesale price volatility might be to encourage long term contracts at a fixed average delivery cost. But suppliers will want higher prices and/or short-term contracts if they anticipate shortages–you cannot get blood out of a turnip; long contracts work to lower cost only to the extent that suppliers are surprised by high spot prices, but when it comes time to renegotiate expiring contracts they will not replicate the error. California discovered this when they intervened to sign long-term contracts, and encountered high prices. This whole argument turns the design problem on its head. You must (1) remove the legal power of the local wires monopoly to prevent competing energy suppliers from contracting with customers to discount off-peak energy, charge premiums for peak energy, and install the supporting control devices; (2) let this competition determine the dynamic price structure, and investment required to implement it; (3) simultaneously, let financial instruments evolve to hedge whatever risk is left over as prices become less volatile. Financial instruments can hedge price volatility, not load volatility. Only demand responsive interruptible loads can relieve supply stress and provide the demand side reserves that reduce the risk of lost load. No one mind or collective can anticipate and plan the needed mix of technologies to enable the market to manage demand. Therefore it is essential to remove all entry barriers, and allow firms to experiment through competition to discover and innovate efficient ways of organizing retail delivery systems. Claims that short run retail demand is 'notoriously' inelastic miss the point: how would you know if loan-shedding technology is inflexible? Competition and incentives to innovate have never been part of the structure.

the effect of transmission constraints on generator supply behavior (Backerman*et al.*, 2001), vary the degree of market concentration, or 'power' in a non-convex environment (Dentin*et al.*, 2001), compare the effect of more or less strategic demand responsiveness (Rassenti, Smith and Wilson, 2002a), study network and multiple market effects also in a non-convex environment (Olson *et al.*, 2003), and test bed markets to inform, but not finalize, market liberalization policy (Rassenti, Smith and Wilson, 2002b). For a survey of many examples, see McCabe, Rassenti, and Smith (1991).

The two types of rational order are both expressed in the experimental methodology developed for economic systems design. This branch of experimental economics uses the lab as a test bed to examine the performance of proposed new institutions, and modifies their rules and implementation features in the light of the test results. The proposed designs are initially constructivist, although most applications, such as the design of electricity markets or auctions for spectrum licenses, are far too complicated for formal analysis. (Rassenti, Smith and Wilson, 2002a; Banks, *et al.*, 2003).

But when a design is modified in the light of test results, the modifications tested, modified again, retested, and so on, one is using the laboratory to effect an evolutionary adaptation as in the ecological concept of a rational order. If the final result is implemented in the field, it certainly undergoes further evolutionary change in the light of practice, and of operational forces not tested in the experiments because they were unknown, or beyond current laboratory technology.[28] In fact this evolutionary process is essential if institutions, as dynamic social tools, are to be adaptive and responsive to changing conditions. How can such flexibility be made part of their design? We do not know because no one can foresee what changes will be needed.

Market Institutions and Performance

Non-cooperative or Cournot-Nash competitive equilibrium (CE) theory has conventionally offered two specifications concerning the preconditions for achieving a CE: (1) agents require complete, or 'perfect', information on the equations defining the CE; also common knowledge–all must know that all know that all know that they have this information. In this way all agents have common expectations of a CE and their behavior must necessarily produce it; (2) another tradition, popularly articulated in textbooks, and showing, perhaps, more sensitivity for plausibility, has argued for a weaker requirement that agents need only be price takers in the market.

The alleged 'requirement' of complete, common or perfect information is vacuous: I know of no predictive theorem stating that when agents have such information their behavior produces a CE, and in its absence their behavior

[28] People often ask, What are the limits of laboratory investigation? I think any attempt to define such limits is very likely to be bridged by the subsequent ingenuity and creativity (the primary barriers at any one time) of some experimentalist. Twenty-five years ago I could not have imagined being able to do the kinds of experiments that today have become routine in our laboratories. Experimentalists also include many of us who see no clear border separating the lab and the field.

fails to produce a CE. If such a theorem existed, it could help us to design the experiments that could test these dichotomous predictions. I suggest that the idea that agents need complete information is derived from introspective error: as theorists **we** need complete information to calculate the CE. But this is not a theory of how information or its absence causes agent behavior to yield or not a CE. It is simply an unmotivated statement declaring, without evidence, that every agent is a constructivist in exactly the same sense as are we as theorists. And the claim that it is 'as if' agents had complete information, helps not a wit to understand the wellsprings of behavior. What is missing are models of the process whereby agents go from their initial circumstances, and dispersed information, using the algorithms of the institution to update their status, and converge (or not) to the predicted equilibrium.[29]

As a theory the price-taking parable is also a non-starter: who makes price if all agents take price as given? If it is the Walrasian auctioneer, why have such processes been found to be so inefficient? (Bronfman, *et al.*, 1996).

Hundreds of experiments in the past 40 years (Smith, 1962, 1982; Davis and Holt, 1993; Kagel and Roth, 1995; Plott, 2001) demonstrate that complete information is not necessary for a CE to form out of a self-ordering interaction between agent behavior and the rules of information exchange and contract in a variety of different institutions, but most prominently in the continuous bid/ask double auction (CDA).[30] That complete information also

[29] The inherent difficulty in equilibrium modeling of the CDA is shown by the fact that so few have even attempted. Wilson (1985, 1987), characteristically, has had the courage and competence to log progress. Friedman (1984) uses an unconventional no-congestion assumption to finesse Nash-Cournot analysis, concluding efficiency and a final competitive clearing price. Wilson (1987) uses standard assumptions of what is common knowledge– number of buyers (sellers), each with inelastic demand (supply) for one unit, preferences linear in payoffs, no risk aversion or wealth effects, valuations jointly distributed, and agent capacity to "compute equilibrium strategies and select one equilibrium in a way that is common knowledge." (p 411). This is an abstract as-if-all-agents-were-game-theorists constructivist model of a thought process that no game theorist would or does use when participating in a CDA. The model itself generates its own problems, such as degeneracy in the endgame when there is only one buyer and seller left who can feasibly trade– a problem that is not a problem for the subjects, who do not know this, and see imperfectly informed buyers and sellers still attempting to trade and thereby disciplining price. Extra marginal traders provide opportunity cost endgame constraints on price. Agents need have no understanding of opportunity cost in order for their behavior to be shaped by it. Wilson recognizes these considerations: "The crucial deficiencies, however, are inescapable consequences of the game-theoretic formulation." (1987, p 411) We are squarely up against the limitations–perhaps the dead end ultimate consequences–of Cartesian constructivism. We have not a clue, any more than the so-called 'naïve' subjects in experiments, how it is that our brains so effortlessly solve the equilibration problem in interacting with other brains though the CDA (and other) institutions. We model not the right world to capture this important experimental finding.

[30] See Ketcham, *et al.*, (1984) for a comparison of CDA with the posted offer (PO) retail pricing mechanism. CDA converges more rapidly and is more efficient than PO. So why does not CDA invade and displace PO? It is the high cost of training every retail clerk to be an effective negotiator for the firm. Institutions reflect the fine structure of opportunity cost, and the loss of exchange efficiency in PO is more than offset by the distributional productive efficiency of the mass retailing innovation of the 1880s that led price policy to be centralized. As I write, those policies are being modified on the internet where prices can be adjusted to the opportunity cost characteristics of buyers, such as how many other internet sites they have visited. (Deck and Wilson 2002). Institutional changes in response to innovations like mass retailing are part of the emergence of an ecologically rational equilibrium.

may not be sufficient for a CE is suggested (the samples are small) by comparisons showing that convergence is slowed or fails under complete information in certain environments. (Smith, 1976, 1980).

An interesting contribution by Gode and Sunder (Hereafter GS; see Sunder 2002, and the references it contains) is to demonstrate that an important component of the emergent order observed in these market experiments derives from the institution, not merely the presumed rationality of the individuals. Efficiency is necessarily a joint product of the rules of the institution and the behavior of agents. What Sunder and his coauthors have shown is that in the double auction market for a single commodity (we know not yet how far it can be generalized), efficiency is high even with 'zero' intelligence robot agents, each of whom chooses bids (asks) completely at random from all those that will not impose a loss on the agent. Thus, agents who are not rational constructivist profit maximizers, and use no learning or updating algorithms, achieve most of the possible social gains from trade using this institution. Does this example illustrate in a small way those "super-individual structures within which individuals found great opportunities...(and that)...could take account of more factual circumstances than individuals could perceive, and in consequence...is in some respects superior to, or 'wiser' than, human reason..."? (Hayek, 1988, p 77, 75).

We do not know if the GS results generalize to multiple market settings as discussed in the next paragraph. Miller (2002), however, has shown that in a very elementary two-market environment–inter-temporally separated markets for the same commodity–the GS results are qualified. Complex price dynamics, including 'bubbles,' appear, and there is loss of efficiency, although the loss is not substantial. On average the decline is apparently from around 94% to 88%.

In multiple market trading in nonlinear interdependent demand environments, each individual's maximum willingness-to-pay for a unit of commodity A depends on the price of B, and vice versa, and in this more complex economy double auction markets also converge to the vector of CE prices and trading volumes. A two-commodity example is reported in Smith (1986), based on nonlinear demand (CES payoff function) and linear supply functions found in Williams and Smith (1986); also see Williams, *et al.*, (2000). In these experiments, numerical tables based on the preference and cost information defining the general equilibrium solution of four nonlinear equations in two prices and two quantities are dispersed among the undergraduate subjects. They buy and sell units of each of the two commodities in a series of trading periods. Prices and trading volume converge, after several trading periods, to the CE defined by the nonlinear equations. The subjects would not have a clue as to how to solve the equations mathematically. The experimenter applies the tools of constructivist reason to solve for the benchmark CE, but in repeat play this 'solution' emerges from the spontaneous order created by the subjects trading under the rules of the double auction market institution. Numerous other experiments with many simultaneous interdependent markets show similar patterns of convergence (Plott, 1988, 2001).

The Iowa Electronic Market

What evidence do we have that the laboratory efficiency properties of continuous double auction trading apply also in the field? One of the best sources of evidence, I believe, is found in the Iowa Electronic Market (IEM) used widely around the world. (Forsythe, *et al.*, 1992, 1999) These markets are used to study the efficacy of futures markets in aggregating widely dispersed information on the outcomes of political elections, or any well defined extra-laboratory event, such as a change in the discount rate by the FED. The 'laboratory' is the internet. The 'subjects' are all who log on and buy an initial portfolio of claims on the final event outcomes; they consist of whom ever logs in, and are not any kind of representative or 'scientific' sample as in the polls with which they are paired. The institution is the open book double auction.

In the IEM, traders make a market in shares representing pari-mutuel claims on the popular vote (or winner-take-all) outcome of an election, referendum, etc. For example the first IEM was on the 1988 Presidential Election. Each person wanting to trade shares deposits a minimum sum, $35, with the IEM and receives a trading account containing $10 cash for buying additional shares, and ten elemental portfolios at $2.50 each, consisting of one share of each of the candidates–Bush, Dukakis, Jackson, and 'rest-of-field.' Trading occurs continuously in an open-book bid-ask market for several months, and everyone knows that the market will be called (trading suspended) in November on election day, when the dividend paid on each share is equal to the candidate's fraction of the popular vote times $2.50. Hence if the final two candidates and all others receive popular vote shares (53.2%, 45.4%, 1.4%), these proportions (times $2.50) represent the payoff to a trader for each share held. Consequently, at any time t, normalizing on $1, the price of a share (÷$2.50), reflects the market expectation of that candidate's share of the total vote. A price, $0.43 means the market predicts that the candidate will poll 43% of the vote. Other forms of contract that can be traded in some IEMs include winner-take-all, or number of seats in the House, and so on.

The IEM data set includes 49 markets, 41 worldwide elections and 13 countries. Several results stand out: the closing market prices, produced by a non-representative sample of traders, show lower average absolute forecasting error (1.5%) than the representative exit poll samples (1.9%); in the subset of 16 national elections, the market outperforms the polls in 9 of 15 cases; in the course of several months preceding the election outcome, the market predictions are consistently much less volatile than the polls; generally, larger and more active markets predict better than smaller, thinner markets; surveys of the market traders show that their share holdings are biased in favor of the candidates they themselves prefer.

In view of this last result why do markets outperform the polls? Forsythe, *et al.*, (1992) argue that it's their marginal trader hypothesis. Those who are active in price 'setting,' that is, in entering limit bids or asks, are found to be less subject to this bias, than those traders accepting (selling and buying 'at market') the limit bids and asks. Polls record unmotivated, representative, average opinion. Markets record motivated marginal opinion that cannot be described as 'representative.' This analysis helps to provide a good mechanical, if not ultimate, understanding of how human interaction with the rules of a bid/ask CDA yield efficient predictions.[31]

We have seen that markets economize on information, understanding, the number of agents, and individual rationality. Can they also economize on the need for external intervention to protect particular interests, if all are empowered by the trading institution to act in their individual interests?

Strategy Proof-ness: theory and behavior

Preferences are private and unobservable, and institutions have to rely on the messages reported by agents, not their true preferences. This follows from the fact that no one mind has all the information known together by all those in the market. It is therefore possible for an agent to affect prices and outcomes in a market by strategically misreporting preferences. This prospect has motivated the literature seeking strategy-proof mechanisms: "an allocation mechanism is strategy-proof if every agent's utility-maximizing choice of what preferences to report depends only on his own preferences and not on his expectations concerning the preferences that other agents will report." (Satterthwaite, 1987, p. 519). This requires each agent to have a dominant strategy to report true preferences, and has led to impossibility theorems establishing the nonexistence of such a mechanism under certain conditions.

In view of such negative theoretical results and the narrow conditions under which solutions have been investigated, it is important to ask what people actually do in experimental environments in which the experimenter induces preferences privately on individual subjects. We know what is impossible, but what is possible in more open-ended systems than are modeled by theory? Is it possible that when all are free to choose from a large space of strategies,

[31] Other markets besides the IEM are known to have efficient information aggregating properties. Pari-mutuel racetrack markets are an example where, interestingly, the environment is much like the IEM: the settlements occur at a well defined end-state known to all agents, unlike stock market trading where expectations float continuously with no clear value revelation endpoint. "The racetrack betting market is surprisingly efficient. Market odds are remarkably good estimates of winning probabilities. This implies (sic) that race track bettors have considerable expertise, and that the markets should be taken seriously." (Thaler and Ziemba 1988, p 169). It is surprising to behavioral economists because their methodology is restricted to looking for deviations from the standard model. What is unusual here is that in racetracks they have found reportable evidence for efficient outcomes. For those who follow experimental economics, IEM and similar controlled-environment market studies, efficiency is not only commonplace (if not universal), it cannot be attributed to agents with "considerable expertise." The agents are mostly naïve, although they get repeat interaction experience, which, from the evidence, clearly gives them expertise enough. But, as in the IEM and experimental markets, race track markets are not perfect: there are inefficiencies in the 'place' and 'show' options and the favorite-long-shot bias, with the latter more pronounced in the last two races of the day. Various hypotheses have been offered to explain these inefficiencies, but more significant is that computer programs have been written to arbitrage (yielding returns of some 11% per bet), the place, show and long-shot inefficiencies. (It is my understanding that good profits have been accumulated on these programs, so far without neutralizing the arbitrage opportunities–let the good times roll!)

ecologically rational strategies will emerge that immunize against strategic manipulation? Given that information is inherently dispersed, has society evolved institutions in which forms of behavior arise that result in practical if not universal solutions to the problem of strategy proof-ness?

The double auction is a well-known example yielding CE in a wide range of economic environments including small numbers. Are there other examples, and if there are, what are the strategic behavioral mechanisms that people adopt to achieve strategy proof-ness?

One example is the sealed bid-offer auction: in each contract period the submitted bids are ordered from highest to lowest, the offers (asks) from lowest to highest, with the intersection (cross) determining the uniform clearing price and volume exchanged. (See Cason and Friedman, Friedman, and Wilson in Friedman and Rust (1991). Also see Smith, Williams, Bratton and Vannoni (1982) for comparative studies of different versions of the sealed bid-offer mechanism and the continuous double auction.

In experiments with stationary supply and demand, initially both buyers and sellers greatly under-reveal their true individual willingness to buy or sell. Volume is very low (10–15% of optimal), the market is inefficient and each agent can see that at the initial clearing price they are leaving money on the table. In repeat play they increase revelation, but mostly of units near the last period's clearing price. As volume increases and the clearing price closes in on the CE, the realized inverse demand and supply become very flat near the true clearing price with many tied or nearly tied bids and asks that exceed the capacity of any single buyer or seller. At this steady state, and given this behavior, if anyone withholds purchases or sales she is denied an allocation as other more competitively traded units substitute for hers. This results in a 'behavioral strategy proof equilibrium.' Such is the power of motivated, privately informed agents in trial-and-error repeat interaction.

These experimental results make it plain that the theoretical condition for a strategy-proof equilibrium–that each agent have a dominate strategy to reveal true willingness-to-pay or willingness-to-accept for all units, and not just units near the margin–is much too strong. The above description from blind two-sided auctions, however, also shows that there is a social cost to the achievement of a strategy-proof equilibrium: blind two-sided auctions converge more slowly to the competitive equilibrium than continuous double auctions, and upon converging, may not be quite as efficient if agents occasionally attempt manipulation, are disciplined, and return to the full exchange volume.

A second example is the uniform price double auction (UPDA), a real-time continuous feedback mechanism clearing all trades at a single price in each trading period. This is a 'designer market' invented by experimentalists who asked, 'Can we combine the continuous information feedback advantages of the double auction with the uniform price (zero within-period volatility) advantages of the sealed bid-offer auction?' As we have seen above, with blind bidding several repeat interactions are required to reach optimality, with many lost trades in the process. Can we accelerate the price discovery process by continuously feeding back information on the tentative state of the market, and allowing bids (asks) to be adjusted within each period?

This institution is made possible by high-speed computer and communication technology. It comes in several flavors, or variations on the rules. In all versions at each time, $t \leq T$ = time market is 'called' (closed), the tentative clearing price, p_t, is displayed and each agent knows the acceptance state of all her bids (asks). This allows bids and asks to be adjusted in real time. See the chapter by McCabe, Rassenti and Smith in Friedman and Rust (1991, pp. 311–316) for a report of 49 UPDA experiments comparing these different versions with the continuous double auction. UPDA exhibits even more under-revelation of demand and supply than the blind twosided auction discussed above, but efficiency tends to be much higher, especially in the first periods, and, in one form, (endogenous close, open book, the 'other side' rule with conditional time priority) exceeds that of the continuous double auction.

Experiments using UPDA in a randomly fluctuating supply and demand environment routinely exhibit efficiencies of 95–100%, sometimes with as little as 5–10% of the available surplus revealed. This is shown in Table 1 for summary data from UPDA experiment up 43. Most agents enter bids (asks) equal to or near the clearing price as it is continuously displayed in real time. It is of course true, hypothetically, that if all agents reveal their true demand or supply with the exception of one intra-marginal buyer or seller, then that agent can manipulate the price to his or her advantage. But this parable is irrelevant. The relevant question is what behavior is manifest when every agent has the potential for manipulating the price. Without knowledge or understanding of the whole, and without design or intention, the participants use the rules at their disposal to achieve three properties observed by the experimenter: (1) high efficiency, (2) maximum individual profit given the behavior of all other agents, and (3) protection from manipulation by their protagonists.[32] This ecological result illustrates the perceptive insight of Hayek (1988, p. 19–20). "Rules alone can unite an extended order . . . Neither all ends pursued, nor all means used, are known or need be known to anybody, in order for them to be taken account of within a spontaneous order. Such an order forms of itself . . . "

[32] Space prevents me from dealing fully with the many important issues raised when a subset of agents have asymmetric advance information on product quality or value characteristics. The analysis shows that such conditions generate market failure or inefficiency. Some of these problems, however, arise because the analysis is inadequate in examining both sides of the market, and the implications of the information content of prices. Experiments have established that constructivist inefficiency is often alleviated by one of several ecologically rational response mechanisms: competition among sellers for reputations, quality (brand) signaling, product warranties, and the aggregation of private asymmetric information into public price patterns that self correct the alleged problems. See e.g. Miller and Plott (1985); Plott and Wilde (1982); Plott and Sunder (1982, 1988); Camerer and Weigelt (1988).

Table 1.

(Pe, Qe) = equilibium price and quantity.

(Pr, Qr) = realized price and quantity

Eff% = efficiency, % max surplus

Rev% = % of surplus revealed

Summary of Results; up 43;5,5

	P_e	Q_e	P_r	Q_r	Eff%	Rev%
1	295	18	300	16	91%	22%
2	405	18	400	18	100%	7%
3	545	18	540	18	100%	14%
4	460	18	448	18	92%	14%
5	360	18	350	18	100%	9%
6	500	18	500	18	98%	12%
7	260	18	250	17	96%	26%
8	565	18	553	15	92%	28%
9	300	18	300	18	100%	28%
10	610	18	610	18	100%	33%
11	365	18	350	15	85%	88%
12	550	18	558	15	88%	55%
13	450	18	450	18	100%	31%
14	410	18	410	18	100%	5%
15	485	18	484	19	89%	39%
			μ = 17.3		95%	27%
			σ = 1.3		5	21

Gresham's Law: if it isn't Cournot-Nash, why is it a law?

In this section I have given many examples of institutions in which the CE theory of markets predicts their observed behavior. Do we have contrary examples? Yes. Gresham's Law: bad money drives out good. This 'law', while sometimes claimed to be an observed phenomena in countries all over the world, is not a Cournot-Nash equilibrium.[33] If currencies A and B are both available, A having an intrinsic worth while B is worthless fiat money, then the theory predicts that A will drive out B. This is because each agent believes other agents are rational, and will accept only A in exchange. Each agent will therefore avoid getting stuck with the inferior B by accepting only A, which becomes the dominant circulating medium of exchange, while B is 'horded.' Experiments have confirmed that if both types of money are initially available, subjects use only the superior currency (an interest bearing consol) as a medium of exchange. But in treatments in which subjects first experience a history of using fiat money, it being the only medium of exchange available, and then the consol is introduced, subjects continue trading with the fiat money, hording the interest bearing consol. (Camera, Noussair and Tucker, 2001). This is entirely rational if each agent believes others will accept the fiat money in exchange and this belief is supported by experience. Think of Gresham's Law as a belief equilibrium in which theory alone is unable to predict when it might occur. (Ledyard, 1986).

Complementing these results, another experimental study shows that when fiat money is the only currency. It will be used even under the condition that it is abandoned and replaced with a new fiat money issue at the end of a finite horizon. In this study the real economy is found to suffer some loss in efficiency relative to the use of 'backed' (commodity) money, but the economy does not collapse even in short horizon treatments. Collapse in real sector efficiency is observed only when a 'government' sector prints fiat money to purchase real goods from the private sector. Moreover, additional experimental tests show that the collapse cannot be due to the resulting inflation, but to interference with the real price discovery of markets when some agents are able to crowd out private real purchases with printing press money.[34] (Deck, McCabe and Porter, 2001).

Psychology and Markets

Psychologists and 'behavioral economists' who study decision behavior almost uniformly report results contrary to rational theory. (Hogarth and Reder,

[33] Hayek (1967, p 318) notes that Gresham's Law is not due to Gresham nor is it a 'law' in the theoretical sense, and "...as a mere empirical rule is practically worthless." In the 1920s when people started using dollars and other hard currencies in substitution for the depreciating mark, the claim emerged that Gresham's Law was wrong–that it was the other way around.

[34] This is demonstrated by comparison experiments in which there are no government agents, but fiat money is inflated each period by the average rate that is observed in those experiments with government agents present.

1987). It was not always so,[35] but the focus on 'anomalies', beginning in the 1970s converted the emerging discovery enterprise into a search for contradictions between reports of behavior and the caricatures[36] of mainstream theory that constitute much of its core. Psychologists, to their credit, have maintained an intensive program examining the behavioral nature of these contradictions to the classical model. For example Siegel (1959) and Fouraker and Siegel (1963) reported both confirmations and contradictions, and used the pattern to propose improved models. Similarly, in prospect theory Kahneman and Tversky (1979) have proposed modifications in both the utility and probability weighting functions of standard expected utility theory.[37] Research strategies that focus on the study of errors, however, can distort professional beliefs, to say nothing of popular representations, if the primary emphasis is on the failures, to the exclusion of the predictive successes, of the theory. [38]

Psychology, Economics and the Two Kinds of Rationality

Curiously, the image of economists and psychologists as protagonists obscures their underlying agreement on foundations. Both rely upon constructivism:

[35] "Prior to 1970 or so, most researchers in judgement and decision-making believed that people are pretty good decision–makers... Since then, however, opinion has taken a decided turn for the worse, though the decline was not in any sense demanded by experimental results. Subjects did not suddenly become any less adept at experimental tasks nor did experimentalists begin to grade their performance against a tougher standard. Instead, researchers began selectively to emphasize some results at the expense of others." "The view that people are irrational is real in the sense that people hold it to be true. But the reality is mostly in the rhetoric." (Lopes, 1991, p 66, 80).

[36] I say 'caricatures' because economics has long offered much in the way of theoretical exceptions to the core neoclassical model of self-interested market competition: externalities in choice, public good effects, and 'anomalies' in choice under uncertainty requiring explanation. (Markowitz, 1952; Friedman and Savage, 1948). But it is the neoclassical assumption of self-interested agents that has been the most productive of theoretical results and therefore is a prominent and easy target of criticism.

[37] Their most important contributions in prospect theory were in empirical tests demonstrating the relevance of two ideas suggested originally by Markowitz (1952): the idea that the theory applies to changes in wealth (income) relative to the individual's current asset state, and that people are risk preferring in losses and risk averse in gains. This much is consistent with standard expected utility theory, which requires only that the prizes of choice can be ordered, and therefore applies either to wealth or income. Which prizes the theory is best applied to, has always seemed to me to be inherently a subject for empirical determination. If applied to wealth, the theory starts to infringe on preference theory over time, long recognized as especially difficult modeling terrain.

[38] As I see it experimental market economics and behavioral economics are in principle complementary. Experimental economists study market performance (rationality) given individual valuations, while cognitive psychologists study the valuations (rationality) of individuals. If the objects traded are prospects the appropriate valuations are their "cash values," whether based on expected utility, prospect theory (Kahneman and Tversky, 1979), or some other representation. Thus Plott and Uhl (1981) study experimental markets in which the items traded are gambles, and report convergence to a CE defined by demand and supply based on the expected values of the gambles. But the connective interface between rationality at the individual and at the market level and how institutions modulate the interface has not been well explored. Markets do their thing with whatever are the values–rational, irrational, or nonrational–that are provided by individuals.

(1) to the extent that markets are rational[39] or irrational,[40] this derives directly and only from the rationality or irrationality of agents[41]; (2) individual rationality is a self-aware, calculating process of maximization[42]; (3) predominantly both are reluctant to allow that naïve, unsophisticated agents can achieve socially optimal ends without comprehension of the whole, as well as their individual parts, implemented by deliberate action (there is no 'magic,' and no room for the GS zero intelligence traders); (4) consequently, psychologists test the rationality of individual decisions largely by asking for subject responses to choice problems to discover how they 'reason.' Rather than challenge this constructivist view, economists, subject to the identical vision (how do agents consciously think?), are critical of the question-response survey methods used in cognitive psychology: the stakes are zero or too low,[43] and the subjects are too unsophisticated, inexperienced or untrained to allow a serious researcher to find out how 'real agents, really think.' Many psychologists appear to find irrationality everywhere, and many economists appear to see the findings as everywhere irrelevant. To these economists, how agents think indeed exhausts the core of empirical economics; psychologists merely 'fail' to properly implement their investigation of this core.[44]

In point of fact opinion surveys can provide important insights: sometimes survey findings can be tested more rigorously with reward motivated choices in the laboratory or the field and are found to have predictive content (e.g., the asymmetry between losses and gains in wealth). Sometimes what people actually do completely contradicts what they say, and sometimes you cannot find out by asking because the agents themselves do not know what they will do or are doing. For example:

- Comparisons of risk preferences under low and high monetary stakes have shown that actual reward levels have a statistically significant effect on decision, but that the qualitative conclusions from hypothetical choice response surveys

[39] For example the double auction markets discussed above.
[40] Experimental asset markets bubble and crash on the long path of experience to equilibrium. (Smith, *et al.*, 1988; Porter and Smith, 1994). For a new study of subject experience and asset bubbles see Dufwenberg, *et al.* (2002).
[41] Thus, even a "...monopolist...has to have a full general equilibrium model of the economy." (Arrow, 1987, p 207). Also see note 30 above on racetrack market efficiency, and the inference that the bettors must therefore have considerable expertise. Thus, market rationality is automatically assumed to derive entirely from individual rationality.
[42] Here is a particularly clear statement of decision as rational constructivist action: "Incentives do not operate by magic: they work by focusing attention and by prolonged deliberation." (Tversky and Kahneman, 1987, p 90).
[43] The use of cash or other reward medium in decision behavior experiments is listed by Hertwig and Ortmann, (2001) as one of the key differences between psychology and economics experiments. The controversy over paying subjects, however, is rapidly being eroded as cognitive psychologists and experimental economists join with neurobiologists–including those who are informed on animal behavior models – and subjects are paid salient rewards.
(Breiter *et al.*, 2001; McCabe, *et al.*, 2001; Thut *et al.*, 1997).
[44] Kahneman clearly does not see people as irrational except in the narrow context used in economic modeling based on dominant choice. In fact he describes his empirical findings contradicting the SSSM as having been easy, thanks to the implausibility to any psychologist of the SSSM. See the Nobel Foundation interview of the 2002 Nobel Laureates in economics at http://www.nobel.se/economics/laureates/2002/kahneman-interview.html.

are not refuted by studies using very high stakes–the accumulated payoffs average three times subjects' normal monthly living expenses. (Kachelmeier and Shehata, 1992; also see Binswanger, 1980 for similar findings).

- Consider the double auction in classroom demonstration experiments: in debriefings afterwards students deny that there is any kind of quantitative model that could predict their market price and exchange volume, or that they were able to maximize their profits; but a participant with an envelope containing the predictions provided in advance, opens it showing that this consensus is false. The dispersed private value/cost information is aggregated into prices that are at the equilibrium and each agent is maximizing his or her profit given the behavior of all others. Here there is indeed a kind of 'magic', but only, I think, in not being well understood or modeled at the game theoretic level of individual choice.[45] Our bounded rationality as economic theorists is far more constraining on economic science, than the bounded rationality of privately informed agents is constraining on their ability to maximize the gains from exchange.
- In asset trading, participant survey responses reflect the disconnect between their information on fundamental value and their puzzling experience of a price bubble and crash generated on the long path to the rational expectations equilibrium. (Schwartz and Ang, 1989)
- Opinion polls administered to the IEM traders show the same judgment biases that psychologists and political scientists find in public opinion polls, but these biases did not interfere with the market's ability to predict the popular vote outcomes. (Forsythe *et al.*, 1992).
- In preference reversal survey experiments subjects report many inconsistent choices: gamble A is preferred to B but a subject will sell A for less than B. Arbitraging the subjects' cash motivated choices quickly reduces these inconsistencies (Chu and Chu, 1990, p 906), and it has been shown that the inconsistencies are unbiased random errors under some, but not all, conditions (Cox and Grether, 1996; also see Soper and Gigliotti, 1993, where choice intransitivity is studied directly and the errors are found to be random).
- Kahneman, Knetsch and Thaler (1986; hereafter KKT) provide many examples in which respondents are asked to rate the fairness,[46] on a four-point scale, of elementary business actions in competitive environments. In one

[45] At the macro-market level, convergence, and cases of stable and unstable equilibrium, are well predicted by the classical Walrasian adjustment model, but the paths taken, including jumps across alternative unstable equilibria, are not well predicted by the model. See the outstanding summary by Plott (2001). The disconnect with choice behavior is evident in the following: Walrasian dynamics makes ad hoc assumptions about price adjustments in response to excess demand saying nothing about the corresponding payoff motivation of the agents who drive the price changes. Walrasian dynamics is a story about the tatonnement mechanism in which there are no disequilibrium trades, whereas Plott's (2001) summary is about continuous double auction trading with a great many disequilibrium trades.

[46] The descriptor 'fairness' has so many meanings in different contexts that I believe it is best to avoid the term entirely in experimental science except where it is explicitly modeled and the model tested in environments where subjects make decisions on the basis of the defining parameters of the model; then the descriptor 'fair' and its ambiguity can be avoided altogether. This is the way it is used in the utilitarian definitions by Franciosi, *et al.* (1994), in Fehr and Schmidt (1999), and

case a hardware store raises the price of snow shovels from $15 to $20 after a snowstorm. 82% of the respondents consider this action either unfair or very unfair. Franciosi, *et al.* (1995) substitute the words 'acceptable' for 'fair' and 'unacceptable' for 'unfair'[47] and add one additional sentence to this KKT example: "The store does this to prevent a stock out for its regular customers since another store has raised its price to $20." Now only 32% rate the action unfavorably. This exercise suggests the possible sensitivity of survey results to emotive words and/or perceived 'justification' in terms of impersonal market forces.

Note that it is in private information environments, where the market is aggregating information far beyond the reach of what each individual knows, and is able to comprehend, that the solicited opinions are so far off the mark. The surveys yield no useful understanding because the subjects have none to relate. In the complete information asset market, subjects are aware of its fundamental value structure, and come to have common expectations through an experiential process of repetition; i.e. initial common information is not sufficient to induce common expectations.[48] They play myopically and their expressed bafflement ('prices rise without cause') reflects this myopia. These comments suggest that much insight might be obtained from the systematic study of the conditions under which survey results are robustly informative and the conditions where they are not.

Fairness: an Experimental Market Test

In developing a descriptive theory[49] of the 'reference transaction', KKT state that what is considered 'fair' may change: "Terms of exchange that are ini-

Bolton and Ockenfels (2000). Of course it is appropriate to use the descriptor if the purpose is to see how its instructional use might have an emotive affect on behavior. The emotive content of 'fairness' is clear in the important work of Zajac (1995), who has also examined the rhetoric of fairness arguments as self-interest serving in the Florida, 2000, election controversy. (Zajac, 2002).

[47] KKT state that "...the phrase 'it is fair,' is simply an abbreviation for a substantial majority of the population studied thinks it is fair." (KKT, 1986, p 201). But their main interest is in whether firm behavior is affected by community norms. Whether or not an action is 'acceptable' would seem to be just as important in determining firm behavior as whether or not it is 'fair.' If the two terms map into different attitudes, then there is inherent ambiguity in specifying the effect on firm behavior.

[48] This interpretation is consistent with asset trading experiments using undergraduates, small businesspersons, corporation managers and over-the-counter traders. (Suchanek *et al.*, 1988, Porter and Smith....). Exceptions using inexperienced subjects, to my knowledge, have only been observed with advanced graduate students. (McCabe and Smith, 2000–PNAS).

[49] This methodology is driven by the untenable belief that general theories can be derived directly from observations if you just have enough data (see Smith, 2002, and the references therein). "Perhaps the most important lesson learned from these studies is that the rules of fairness cannot be inferred either from conventional economic principles or from intuition and introspection. In the words of Sherlock Holmes in ' The Adventure of the Copper Beaches': 'Data! Data! Data! I cannot make bricks without clay.' " KKT (1986, p115–116). Neither can a predictive theory of 'fairness' be inferred from any amount of the KKT data. If N 'fairness' rules are discovered by trial and error modifications in the survey questionnaires, you cannot reject the hypothesis that there is an N + 1st variation that will identify a new one. More data will not help, as the fairness concept is used here as a word that provides no effective means of modifying standard theory to correct for its predictive flaws.

tially seen as unfair may in time acquire the status of a reference transaction." (KKT, 1991, p 203). This paves the way for the adaptation of 'fairness beliefs' to changes in the competitive equilibrium. Although the competitive model is the one that has static predictive content, its prediction is silent as to how long it will take to respond to a change in parameters. KKTs arguments are not predictive, but they tell a story about why markets might be sluggish in responding to change. How good is their story?

Franciosi, *et al.* (1995), state a preference model of optimal choice that allows for a utilitarian trade-off between own-consumption and 'fairness'. For example, the utility of two commodities (x,z) is given by: $u(x, z) = z + ax - (b/2)\, x^2 - \alpha x[(\pi/\pi_0) - 1]$, in which the seller's profit, π, relative to a reference profit, π_0, appears as an 'externality' in the buyer's utility function. The usual maximization subject to an income constraint yields the inverse demand equation: $p = a - bx - \alpha[(\pi/\pi_0) - 1]$. Thus, for $\alpha > 0$ any change in the environment that increases a firm's profit relative to the reference profit has an external effect that lowers the buyer's inverse demand for units x. If $\alpha = 0$, then we have the standard own-maximizing theory. Consequently, Franciosi, *et al.* (1995) can test the hypothesis, never using the word 'fairness,' that if subject buyers have a utilitarian concern for profits not being increased relative to a baseline then after a change from the baseline this should alter the observed equilibrium relative to the standard predicted equilibrium with no external effect, $\alpha = 0$. In a posted offer market giving KKT their best shot (sellers cannot see each other's posted prices, and therefore cannot knowingly emulate or undercut each other's prices). Franciosi, *et al.* (1995) find that when $\alpha = 0$ (implemented by either no disclosure, or by marginal cost justifying disclosure) the market converges quickly to the new competitive equilibrium. When $\alpha > 0$ (implemented by profit π and π_0 disclosure) prices converge more slowly, but precisely, to the new equilibrium. Hence, under conditions most favorable to a 'fairness' effect, the response dynamics is changed, but not the equilibrium as predicted by the standard competitive model. The discipline of the market swamps all but a transient 'fairness' effect. If sellers can see each others prices, I would predict a much smaller 'fairness' effect, if any.

III. PERSONAL SOCIAL EXCHANGE

One of the most intriguing discoveries of experimental economics is that (1) as we have seen, people invariably behave non-cooperatively in small and large group 'impersonal' market exchange institutions; (2) many (up to half in single play; over 90% in repeat play) cooperate in 'personal' exchange (two-person extensive form games); (3) yet in both economic environments all interactions are between anonymous players. In this section I shall attempt to summarize some of the most compelling evidence of cooperation in personal exchange–in the field as well as the laboratory–and review some of the test results designed to discriminate among the more prominent predictive hypotheses for modeling cooperative behavior. Whatever might be the most useful way to model and explain cooperation, unaided by market incentives, my working hypothesis throughout is that it is a product of an unknown mix of cultural and biological evolution, with the biology providing abstract function defining potential, and culture shaping the emergent forms that we observe. But to motivate the whole exercise in thought, I will begin with a discussion of some persistent cross-cultural social practices from business, law, anthropology and American economic history.

How might a social rule (practice, norm) emerge, become a cultural fixture, and be widely emulated? I will use a parable to illustrate how a rule for 'bargaining in good faith' might become established.

In bargaining over the exchange price between a buyer and seller, suppose the seller begins by announcing a selling price, the buyer responds with a lower buying price, the seller reduces his asking price, and so on. In this concessionary process it is considered bad form for the buyer (or seller), once having made a concession, to return to a lower (or higher) price. This violates a principle of 'bargain in good faith.' (See Siegel and Fouraker, 1960). How might this come about? One can suppose that those who fail to bargain in good faith would be less likely to be sought out by others for repeat transactions. Such behavior raises transactions cost by increasing the time it takes to complete a sale. Trading pairs would be expected to self-select, tending to isolate the more time consuming bargainers, and it would take them longer to find those willing to tolerate the time cost of bargaining. Such practices–inherently economizing in this parable–might then become part of a cultural norm, powerful enough to be codified ultimately in contract law and in stock exchange rules. Proposition: in this manner collectives discover law in those rules that persist long enough to become entrenched practices. In this example the emergent rule reduces transaction cost, leaving open the classical question of how equilibrium can be characterized in bilateral bargaining.

Spontaneous Order without the Law[50]

The early 'law-givers' did not make the law they 'gave'; they studied social traditions and informal rules and gave voice to them, as God's, or natural, law.[51]

[50] Experimental studies have inquired as to whether emergent norms of cooperation and constructivist incentive schemes are substitutes, the latter crowding out the former. See Bohnet, *et al.* (2001) and Fehr and Gachter (2000) for studies suggesting that they are substitutes (formal rules undermine informal cooperative norms), and Lazzarini, *et al.* (2002) for new results suggesting that they are complements–contracts facilitate the self-enforcement of relational elements beyond contractibility. I would hypothesize that both must be true: constructivist rules ultimately must pass fitness tests of ecological rationality. Formal rules that are incompatible with informal rules will be modified or eliminated; those that are compatible will persist. Hence, at any time-slice in history, both must necessarily be observed across all socioeconomic experiments.

[51] "...all early (my insertion: as in Sumar with the beginning of writing) 'law-giving' consisted in efforts to record and make known a law that was conceived as unalterably given. A 'legislator' might endeavor to purge the law of supposed corruptions, or to restore it to its pristine purity, but it was not thought that he could make new law... But if nobody had the power or intention to change the law...this does not mean that law did not continue to develop." (Hayek, 1973, p 81).

The common lawyer, Sir Edward Coke, championed 17th century social norms as law commanding higher authority than the king. Remarkably, these forces prevailed, paving the way for the rule of law in England.[52] Similarly, the cattlemen's associations, land clubs, and mining districts in the American West all fashioned their own rules for establishing property rights and enforcing them: the brand on the hindquarters of his calf was the cattlemen's indelible ownership signature on his property, enforced by gunmen hired through his cattle club;[53] squatter's rights were defended ably (possession is nine points of the law?) by the land clubs composed of those brave enough to settle wilderness lands in advance of veterans exercising their land script claims, and of settlers under the Homestead Act; mining claims were defined, established and defended by the guns of the mining clubbers, whose rules were later to become part of public mining law. (Anderson and Hill, 1975; Umbeck, 1977). For over a century, the Maine lobstermen have established rights, used threats, then force, to defend exclusive individual lobster fishing territories in the ocean. (Acheson, 1975). Eskimo polar bear hunting teams awarded the upper half of the bear's skin (prized for its long mane hairs used to line women's boots) to that person who first fixed his spear in the prey. (Freuchen, 1961). Extant hunter-gatherers have evolved sharing customs for the products of communal hunting and gathering. For example the Ache of Eastern Paraguay share the volatile products of the hunt widely within the tribe, while the low variance products of gathering are shared only within the nuclear family. (Hawkes, 1990; Kaplan and Hill, 1985).

Ellickson Out-Coases Coase

Using the rancher/farmer parable, Coase (1960) argued that if there were no costs of transacting, then theoretically efficiency could not depend on who was liable for damages to crops caused by stray animals. Legal liability gives the rancher an incentive to employ cost-efficient measures to control straying cattle. But if she were not liable, then in a world of zero transactions cost, victims would be led in their own interest to negotiate a settlement paying the rancher to undertake the same efficient control measures induced by legal liability. In so doing, trespass victims save the cost of crop damage, assumed to

[52] What allowed the rule of 'natural' or found law to prevail in England "...was the deeply entrenched tradition of a common law that was not conceived as the product of anyone's will but rather as a barrier to all power, including that of the king–a tradition which Edward Coke was to defend against King James I and Francis Bacon, and which Matthew Hale at the end of the seventeenth century masterly restated in opposition to Thomas Hobbes." (Hayek, 1973, p 85; also see pp 167, 173–4).

[53] These voluntary private associations for sharing the cost of a common good–policing–were subsequently undermined by statehood, and the publicly financed local sheriff as the recognized monopoly law enforcement officer. This observation contradicts the myth that a central function of government is to 'solve' the free rider problem in the private provision of public goods. Here we have the reverse: the incentive of the cattlemen's clubs was to free ride on the general taxpayer, assigning the sheriff the task of enforcing property rights in cattle. The same free riding occurs with school busing programs, and in publicly provided education itself in which government financing need not require government provision.

be more than the cost of cattle control–otherwise it is inefficient to control them. The externality is internalized by market negotiation incentives. Curiously, the Coase Theorem–that in the absence of transactions cost efficiency does not depend upon the locus of liability–was controversial. It was clearly intended as a kindly spoof of oversimplified theories that, in particular, ignored transactions cost.[54] The real problem, addressed brilliantly by Coase, was to deal with the question of efficient liability rules in a world of significant transactions cost. He then proceeded to use the transactions cost framework to examine the problem of social cost in a variety of legal precedents and cases.[55]

In the beginning Shasta County California was governed by 'open range' law, meaning that in principle ranchers are not legally liable for damages resulting from their cattle accidentally trespassing on unfenced land. Then, in 1945 a California law authorized the Shasta County Board of Supervisors to substitute a 'closed range' ordinance in sub regions of the County. Dozens of conversions have occurred since this enabling law. Under a closed range law the rancher is strictly liable–even if not negligent–for damage caused by his livestock. Elickson (1991), out- Coased Coase by, in effect, asking, 'given that this county applies the polar legal rules used in Coase's illustration, how do neighbors in Shasta County actually handle the problem of stray cattle?' The answer: "Neighbors in fact are strongly inclined to cooperate, but they achieve cooperative outcomes not by bargaining from legally established entitlements,[56] as the parable supposes, but rather developing and enforcing adaptive norms of neighborliness that trump formal legal arrangements. Although the route chosen is not the one that the parable anticipates, the end reached is exactly the one that Coase predicted: coordination to mutual advantage without supervision by the state."[57] (Ellikson, 1991. p 4). Thus, Shasta County citizens, including judges, attorneys and insurance adjustors, do not have full working knowledge of formal local trespass law.[58] Citizens notify owners and help catch the trespassing animal; use mental accounting (reciprocity) to settle debts, e.g. a rancher, whose cattle have strayed may tell the victim to come down and take some hay, or if your goat eats my tomato

[54] Later game theoretic formulations have allowed that with two or more alternatives there may exist 'standoff equilibria' that stall agreement in Coase bargaining. (See Myerson, 1991, p 506). These cases may limit extensions of the Coase Theorem, but do not I think detract from its essential message that the locus of liability was irrelevant.

[55] Coase (1974) also noticed that the light house was frequently cited by theorists as an example of a 'pure' public good. As was his style (to confront the casual parables of theory that finessed certain costs by fiat), his response in effect was, 'well, lets see what people have done who actually operate lighthouses, or who use the services of lighthouses.' It turned out that early lighthouses were private enterprise, not government, solutions to a public good problem, and the alleged inevitability of free riding was solved by the owner who contracted with port authorities to collect lighthouse fees when ships arrived portside to load or unload cargo.

[56] These are the outside options or threat points in game theory.

[57] The same results emerge in laboratory experiments reported by Hoffman and Spitzer (1985)

[58] Under open range the animal owner is liable for intentional trespass, trespass of a lawful fence, and trespass by goats, whatever the circumstances, suggesting the hypothesis that goat behavior had long been recognized in pastoral norms and now captured in codified law.

plants, you offer to help me replant them; use negative gossip, complain to officials, submit informal claims for money (but not though a lawyer) to punish deviant neighbors; rarely use lawyers to seek monetary compensation; share the building of fences, most often by a rule of proportionality–you pay more if you have more animals than your neighbor; ignore fence law as irrelevant; and do not change fence obligations with the planting of crops. Finally, contrary to the Coasian parable the main cost of trespass is not from crop damage, but from highway collisions that kill animals and damage property.

Extensive Form Interactions between Anonymously Paired Individuals

Cooperation has also emerged in anonymous two person extensive form games in laboratory experiments. Although such behavior is contrary to rational prescriptions, it is not inconsistent with our examples of spontaneous order without externally imposed law.

Why do we study anonymous interactions in the laboratory? The model of non-repeated game theory is about strangers without a history or a future (Rosenthal, 1982), but anonymity has long been used in small group experiments to control for the unknown complexities of natural social intercourse. (Siegel and Fouraker, 1960). It is well documented that face-to-face interaction swamps subtler procedural effects in yielding cooperative outcomes. (Hoffman and Spitzer, 1985; Roth, in Kagel and Roth, 1995). But more important, I believe it is this condition that provides the greatest scope for exploring the human instinct for social exchange, and how it is affected by context, reward and procedural conditions that vary elements of social distance. Again, studying what is not helps us to understand what is.

Perception and the Internal Order of the Mind: why context matters

Two decision tasks, represented by the same abstract game tree may lead to different responses because they occur in different contexts. Why? The answer may be found in the process by which we perceive the external world. Hayek (1952)[59] was a pioneer in developing a theory of perception, which anticipated recent contributions to the neuroscience of perception. It is natural for our minds to suppose that experience is formed from the receipt of sensory impulses that reflect unchanging attributes of external objects in the environment. Instead, Hayek proposed that our current perception results from a relationship between external impulses and our past experience of similar conditions. Categories formed in the mind are based on the relative frequency with which current and past perceptions coincide. Memory consists of external stimuli that have been modified by processing systems whose

[59] The Sensory Order was not published until 1952 when Hayek revised a manuscript, originally written in the 1920's, entitled "What is Mind?"

[60] The interdependence between perception and memory is revealed by the different descriptions of the same event by two eyewitnesses. (Gazzaniga, Ivry and Mangun, 1998, pp 484–6).

organization is conditioned by past experience.[60] (Hayek, 1952 p. 64, 165). There is a "constant dynamic interaction between perception and memory, which explains the . . . identity of processing and representational networks of the cortex that modern evidence indicates." "Although devoid of mathematical elaboration, Hayek's model clearly contains most of the elements of those later network models of associative memory..." (Fuster, 1999, p. 88–9).

Hayek's model captures the idea that, in the internal order of the mind, perception is selforganized: abstract function combines with experience to determine network connectivity and expansion.[61] Loss can occur either from lack of function or the stimulus of developmental experience. Block or distort sensory input, and function is impaired; impair function by brain lesions or inherited deficiency, and development is compromised.

This model is consistent with the hypothesis that the mind is organized by interactive modules (circuits) that are specialized for vision, for language learning, for socialization and a host of other functions. (See Cosmides and Tooby, 1992; Pinker, 1995). In this view, mind is the unconscious product of co-evolution between the biological and cultural development of our brains that distinguished us from other primates. It was what made reason possible. Our folk predilection for believing in the 'blank slate' concept of mind (Pinker, 2002) makes plain that this interpretation of mind is just as consonant with our direct experience as was once the idea that the earth is flat, or that witches had to be destroyed. In each case to escape from the folk perception requires the falsifying indirect evidence, based on reason, to become part of our 'felt' experience. Constructivist rationality then becomes ecologically rational.

Experimental procedures

The experiments I will report will show how social context can be important in the interactive decision behaviour we observe. This possibility follows from the autobiographical character of memory and the manner in which past encoded experience interacts with current sensory input in creating memory. I will be reporting the results of decision-making in single play, two-person, sequential-move game trees. Subject instructions do not use technical and role-suggestive words like 'game,' 'play,' 'players, 'opponent,' and 'partner' (except where variations on the instructions are used as systematic treatments to

[61] Built into your brain is the maintained hypothesis that the world around you is stationary. Look at the wall and move your eyes back and forth with head still. The wall does not move. Now press your eyeball with your finger through the eyelid from the side. The wall moves as you jiggle your eyeball. Why the difference? When you flex the eye muscles and move your eyes back and forth, a copy of the signal goes to the occipital cortex to offset apparent movement of the wall so that the net perception is that of a stationary wall. This stabilizing self ordered system for seeing also makes you vulnerable to optical illusions of motion. Moving your eyes back and forth between the tunnel gate and your airplane as it docks, you ambiguously 'sense' that either the gate or the plane, or both, is in motion. The ambiguity is resolved only when the gate, or plane, stops.

[62] See Burnham, McCabe and Smith (2000), discussed below, for a study comparing the effect of using 'partner' and 'opponent' in a trust game.

identify their effect)[62]; rather reference is made to the 'decision tree,' 'decision maker 1' (DM1) or 2 (DM2), and 'your counterpart,' etc. The purpose is to provide a baseline context, which avoids emotive words that might trigger unintended meanings by the experimenter.[63] I do not mean that the baseline is "neutral," a concept that is not clearly definable, given that context effects can depend on autobiographical experience. The effect of instructional variation on decision is an empirical matter and any particular set of instructions must always be considered a treatment unless the observations are shown to be robust to changes in the instructions. All observations must be seen as a joint product of experimental procedures and the theoretical hypotheses, implemented by particular parameters that it is our intention to test. This is not unique to laboratory observations, but a characteristic also of field observations, and the whole of science. (See Smith, 2002 for examples from physics, astronomy and experimental economics). It is therefore important to understand how procedures as well as different parameterizations (games, payoffs) affect behaviour.

Subjects are recruited in advance for an economics experiment. Upon arrival at the appointed time they register, receive a show-up fee, and are assigned to a private computer terminal in a large room with 40 stations. Commonly there are 11 other people, well spaced throughout the room, in the experiments reported below. After everyone has arrived each person logs into the experiment reads through the instructions for the experiment, responds to instructional questions, and learns that he or she is matched anonymously with another person in the room, whose identity will never be known, and vice versa. This does not mean that a subject knows nothing about their matched counterpart. For example, it may appear evident that he or she is another 'like' person, such as an undergraduate, or an industry executive with whom one may feel more-or-less an in-group identity. Obviously, each person imports into the experiment a host of different past experiences and impressions that are likely to be associated with the current experiment.

The Context of Decision: The Ultimatum Game Example

Consider the ultimatum game, a two-stage two-person game with the following abstract form: for each pair the experimenter makes a fixed sum of money, m, available (e.g. m will be 10 one-dollar bills, or 10 ten-dollar bills); player 1 moves first offering $0 \leq x \leq m$ units of the money to player 2, player 1 retaining $m - x$; player 2 then responds by either accepting the offer, in which case player 1 is paid $m - x$, and player 2 is paid x, or rejecting the offer, in which case each player receives nothing.

Below I report ultimatum results from four different instructional/proce-

[63] It is not meaningful or helpful to talk about 'experimenter effects.' There are instructional and procedural effects, including the presence or absence of an experimenter, what he/she knows or does not know (as in double blind behavioral experiments), and what he/she does or does not do. All of the elementary operations used to implement an experiment are treatments that may or may not have a significant effect on observed outcomes.

dural treatments (contexts) that have the same underlying abstract game structure. In each case imagine that you are player 1. See Hoffman *et al.*, (1994; hereafter HMSS) for instructional details, and for references to the literature and the origins of the ultimatum game.

'Divide $10.' You and your counterpart have been 'provisionally allocated $10,' and randomly assigned to positions. Your task as player 1 is to 'divide' the $10 by filling out a form that will then go to your counterpart who will accept or reject it.

'Contest entitlement.' The 12 people in the room each answer the same 10 questions on a general knowledge quiz. Your score is the number of questions answered correctly; ties are broken in favor of the person who first finished the quiz. The scores are ranked from 1 (highest) through 12 (lowest). Those ranked 1–6 are informed that they have earned the right to be person player 1, the other six will be players 2.

'Exchange.' Player 1 is a seller, and 2 is a buyer. A table lists the buyer and seller profit for each price $0, $1, $2, . . . , $10 charged by the seller, and the buyer chooses to buy or not buy. The profit of the seller is the price chosen; the profit of the buyer is ($10 – price). Each receives nothing if the buyer refuses to buy.

'Contest/Exchange.' This treatment combines Contest with Exchange; i.e. the sellers and buyers in Exchange are selected by the contest scoring procedure. In one version the total amount is 10 one-dollar bills, and in the second it is 10 ten-dollar bills.

Whatever the context there is a game theoretic concept of equilibrium (sub-game perfect) that yields the same prediction in all four treatments (Selten, 1975): player 1 offers the minimum unit of account, $1 ($10) if m = $10 ($100), and player 2 accepts the offer. This follows from the assumption that each player is self interested in the narrow sense of always choosing the largest of two immediate payoffs for herself; that this condition is common knowledge for the two players; and that player 1 applies backward induction to the decision problem faced by player 2, conditional on player 1's offer. Thus player 1 reasons that any positive payoff is better than zero for player 2 and therefore, player 1 need only offer x = $1 ($10).

One difficulty with this analysis is that, depending on context, the interaction may be interpreted as a social exchange between the two anonymously matched players who in day-today experience read intentions into the actions of others. (Baron-Cohen, 1995). Suppose the situation is perceived as a social contract as follows: if player 2 has an entitlement to more than the minimum unit of account, then an offer of less than the perceived entitlement (say, only $1, or even $2–$3) may be rejected by some players 2. Player 1, introspectively anticipating this possible mental state of player 2, might then offer $4 or $5 to insure acceptance of his offer. Alternatively, player 1 might enjoy (get utility from) giving money to his counterpart. The point is simply that there are alternative models to that of sub-game perfection that predict choices in the ultimatum game, and these alternatives leave wide latitude for the possibility of context affecting the behaviour of both players. Abstract game theory can embrace these alternatives through the artifice of 'types'–utilities, or beliefs states such as trust, trustworthy, reciprocation, etc. Ultimately the predictive success of such models depends on relating task descriptions defining context to autobiographical characteristics of individuals that are then identified by types that in turn determine behaviour. The point that needs emphasis is that it is easy to go from 'types' (traditionally utility or beliefs about states) to game theoretic choice; the hard part is to relate 'types' to characteristics of the individual's memory-sensory system. Given the directions of neuroscience and the learning from brain imaging, I do not think this is an impossible order.

Observe that in 'Divide $10' the original $10 is allocated imprecisely to both players. Moreover, a common definition of the word 'divide' (Webster) includes the separation of some divisible quantity into equal parts. Finally, random devices are recognized as a standard mechanism for 'fair' (equal) treatment. Consequently, the instructions might be interpreted as suggesting that the experimenter is engaged in the 'fair' treatment of the subjects cueing them to be 'fair' to each other.

As an alternative, Contest deliberately introduces a pre-game procedure that requires player 1 to 'earn' the right to be the first mover. This may cue some insipient norm of just desert based on the pre-game quiz.

In Exchange the ultimatum game is imbedded in the gains from exchange from a transaction between a buyer and a seller. In an exchange, both the buyer and the seller are made better off, and buyers in our culture may accept the right of a seller to move first by quoting a price.

Contest/Exchange combines the implicit property right norm of a seller with a mechanism for earning the property right.

Table 2 summarizes the results from two different studies of ultimatum game bargaining with stakes of either 10 one-dollar or 10 ten-dollar bills for each of N pairs of players, where N varies from 23 to 33 subject pairs.

1. Comparing Divide $10 with Divide $100 under the random entitlement we observe a trivial difference in the amount offered between the low stakes (43.7%) and the 10-fold increase in the stakes (44.4%). Also, there is no significant difference in the percentage rate at which offers are rejected, 8.3% and 3.7% respectively.

2. When Exchange is combined with an earned entitlement the increase in stakes lowers the offer percentage from 30.8% for $10 stakes to 27.8% for $100 stakes, but this difference is within the normal range of sampling error using different groups of subjects and is not significant. Surprisingly, however, this minuscule decline in the mean offer causes the rejection rate to go up from 12.5% to 21.7%. Three of four subject players 1 offering $10 are rejected, and one offer of $30 is rejected in the game with $100 stakes. As has been shown in trust/punishment games, this behavior is associated with a strong human propensity to incur personal cost to punish those who are perceived as cheaters, even under strict anonymity.

3. We note that comparing the Divide $10/Random entitlement condition with the Exchange entitlement, the offer percentage declines from 43.7% to

Table 2. Mean Percentage Offered by Treatment in Ultimatum Games[1]

Context	Measure	$10 Stakes			$100 Stakes		
Random Entitlement		Divide $10	Exchange	Exchange, Strategic Prompt	Divide $100	Exchange	Exchange (grad students)[3]
	Mean	43.7 %	37.1 %	41.7 %	44.1 %	NA	NA
	N	24	24	24	27	NA	NA
	(% Rejected)[2]	(8.3%)	(8.3%)	(12.5%)	(3.7 %)	NA	NA
Earned Entitlement	Mean	36.2 %	30.8 %	39.6 %	NA	27.8 %	28.8 %
	N	24	24	24	NA	23	33
	(% Rejected)[2]	(0)	(12.5 %)	(2.9 %)	NA	(21.7 %)	(21.2 %)

[1] Source: Data from Hoffman, *et al.* (1994) and Hoffman, McCabe, and Smith (1996a). See the references for the statistical significance of pair wise comparisons as discussed in the text.
[2] Refers to percentage of the N pairs in which the second player rejects the offer of the first.
[3] The graduate students were visiting participants in an introductory workshop in experimental economics. These are new data not previously reported.

37.1%, and comparing the former to the Earned entitlement the decline is from 43.7% to 36.2%, both reductions being statistically significant. Even more significant is the reduction form 43.7% to 30.8% when the Earned and Exchange Entitlements are combined. Moreover, in all four of these comparisons the rejection rate is null or modest (0 to 12.5%).

4. The small proportion of the offers that were rejected, except when the stakes were $100 in the Earned/Exchange context and the mean offers declined to a low of 27.8%, indicates that players 1 read their counterparts well, and as the context is altered, normally offer a sufficient amount to avoid being rejected. The one exception shows clearly that pushing the edge, even if it seems justified by the higher stakes, may invite an escalation of rejections.

These data indicate that context is important in the ultimatum game: the percentage offered varies by over a third as we move from the highest (44%) to the lowest (28%) measured effect. Like variation is reported in cross-cultural experiments: a comparison of two hunter-gather and five modern cultures reveals variation from a high of 48% (Los Angeles subjects) to a low of 26% (Machiguenga subjects from Peru). (Heinrich, 2000). These comparisons used care in attempted to control for instructional differences across different languages, but this is inherently problematic, given the nature of perception, in that one cannot be sure that the instructions, translations, payoffs, or the procedures for handling the subjects, control adequately for con-

Table 3. Dictator Giving: With and Without Gains from Exchange and Social History

Treatments	Standard Dictator Game Giving		Double Blind[2] Dictator Giving Under Gains from Exchange[3]			
	Single Blind	Double Blind 2	Baseline		Social History	
Player Role	FHSS[1]	HMSS[2]	Sent (Player 1)	Returned (Player 2)	Sent (Player 1)	Returned (Player 2)
Mean Percent Given Of Total Available	23.3	10.5	51.6	27.2[4]	53.6	35.5[4]
Mean Percent Given By Top 50% Givers	38.3	21.0	74.4	49.4	82.7	55.8

[1] Data from Forsythe, *et al.* (1994), replicated by Hoffman, McCabe, and Smith (1996b).
[2] Data from Hoffman, *et al.* (1994), Double Blind 2.
[3] Data from Berg, Dickhaut and McCabe (1995). Their procedures are different, but are nearest to those of Double Blind 2 in HMSS.
[4] Since the sender amount is tripled, if the receivers return an average of 33.3 percent, then the average amount returned will equal (pay back) the amount sent.

text across cultures. In each culture one needs to vary the instructions/procedures and observe the sampling distribution of outcomes, then compare the sample distributions across cultures.

These instructional treatment effects call into question the extent to which one can define what is meant by "unbiased" instructions. If results are robust with respect to instructional changes, this can only be established empirically. Without such studies no claims can be made concerning the relative 'neutrality' of instructions. The main lesson is that, because of the nature of perception and memory, context should matter, and in the ultimatum game the variation of observed results with systematic instructional changes designed to alter context shows clearly that context can and does matter. Experimenters, subject to the same perception/memory variations, are likely to disagree as to what is 'neutral.'

Dictator Games with and without Gains from Exchange

The ultimatum game is converted into a dictator game by removing the right of the second mover to veto the offer of the first. Forsythe, *et al.* (1994; hereafter FHSS) note that if the observed tendency toward equal split of the prize is due primarily to 'fairness'–a social norm of just division–then it should be of little consequence if this right is eliminated. But if it is the prospect of rejection–however irrational–that tempers the amount offered by Player 1, then the outcomes should be materially affected by removing the right of rejection, which converts the ultimatum game into what is called the dictator game. Thus a significant reduction in the mean percent offered in the dictator game would be consistent with the second hypothesis, while no significant reduction would be consistent with the first. Comparing the results in Table 3, column 1 with those for Divide $10, Random Entitlement in Table 2, we see that the mean dictator offer is only 23.3% compared with the mean ultimatum offer of 43.7%. FHSS conclude that fairness alone cannot account for behavior in the ultimatum game. This is correct, but, equally of interest, why are dictators giving away nearly a quarter of their endowment? This research puzzle was picked up by HMSS who conjectured that such generosity might be, at least in part, a consequence of the incompleteness of anonymity. In all the games prior to the HMSS study the members of each player pair were anonymous with respect to each other but not with respect to the experimenter who knew every person's decision. Hence, they introduced a "double blind" treatment category (two versions) in which the protocol made it transparent that no one, including the experimenter, could learn the decisions of any player. Data from the second version, Double Blind 2, are reported in Table 3. In this treatment mean dictator offers decline to only 10.5%. Consequently, context–in this case social connectedness or distance–has an important affect on dictator transfers.[64] These issues are explored more fully in Hoffman, McCabe and Smith (1996b) who vary social distance by varying the instructional and protocol parameters that define various versions of single and double blind dictator games. Also reported in Table 3 is the percent given by the top 50% of the most generous dictators: 38.3% for Single Blind and 21% for Double Blind.

Berg, Dickhaut and McCabe (1995, hereafter BDM) modify the dictator game to introduce gains from 'exchange.'[65] Their investment trust two-stage dictator game also uses the Double Blind 2 protocol: dictators in room A send any portion of their $10 (0 to $10) to their random counterpart in room B. People in both rooms know that if $x is sent by anyone, it is tripled, so that the counterpart receives $3x. Thus, the most generous offer, $10, yields a gain to $30. The counterpart can then respond by sending any part (0 to $3x) of the amount received back to his or her matched sender. Now an exchange with gains to both parties is possible, and BDM ask if this context is a significant treatment. Note that the analysis of the game is no different than the onestage dictator game: by the principle of backward induction Player 1 can see that Player 2's interest is to keep all the money received, and therefore nothing should be sent. The fact that the sender's transfer will be tripled is irrelevant. But it is not irrelevant if both players see the interaction as an exchange based on trust by Player 1 and trustworthiness by Player 2.

[64] These double blind procedures and treatment effects have been replicated by two other investigations (Eckel and Grossman (1996) and Burnham (1998)).
Bolton, Katok, and Zwick (1998), using a different double blind procedure failed to replicate the results, suggesting that procedures matter and interact with the double blind condition.

[65] For a recent extension and replication of the BDM findings see Pillutla, *et al.* (2002). Also see Ortmann, *et al.* (2002).

In Table 3 sender Players 1 now give 51.6%, when the transfer is tripled, compared with 23.3%, when it is not. Furthermore, the top 50% of the givers send 74.4% of the money, up from 38.3%. This shows how the tripled pie shifts the distribution toward larger transfers by Players 1. But on average the senders do not quite break even: an average of 27.2% of the amount received by Players 2 is returned to Players 1 (break even would be 33.3% since x is tripled). In the social history treatment the instructions and protocol are the same as described above except that the second treatment group is shown the distribution of amounts transferred and returned for the first group. Comparing the social history with the baseline mean percent given and returned reveals the effect of being exposed to the decision data of the first group. Social history does not cause a reduction in transfers, which actually increases marginally from 51.6% to 53.6%. The average percent returned increases from 27.2% to 35.5%, just above the breakeven level.

These results are not explicable by the canons of traditional game theory that assumes self-interested (in the sense of always choosing larger payoffs) types. By introducing gains from the investment by Player 1, who can only benefit if Player 2 perceives the process as an exchange calling for payment for services rendered, dictator giving more than doubles. And the effect of social history does not precipitate a decline in investment nor in the return to Players 2– in fact both increase slightly. The same behaviors have been observed in chimpanzee and capuchin monkey communities. (deWaal, 1989 and 1997). Should such trusting and trustworthy behaviors be diminished in human communities characterized by the maxim that "the rules of morality are not...conclusions of (our) reason?"

Trust Games

Ultimatum and dictator games have been studied extensively, but are much too simple to allow an adequate understanding of some of the underlying behavior manifest in them. It is tempting to over interpret them in terms of a mixed utility for own and other reward. The potential for greatly expanding what can be learned is illustrated in Table 3 where BDM extended the dictator game to a two-stage game with gains from voluntary exchange. We turn therefore to a somewhat richer class of two-person extensive form trust games in which equilibrium play, cooperation, and the prospect of defection can be studied in a richer parameter space than the ultimatum game.[66]

Figure 1 is a typical "trust" game tree.[67] Play starts at the top of the tree, node x1, with Player 1 who can move right, which stops the game yielding the

[66] Space does not permit examining also the effect of being able to punish defection. See McCabe, Rassenti and Smith (1996) for a more complete report of trust games with and without punishment of defection and with a wide variety of matching protocols.

[67] As indicated above, the word "trust" never appears in the instructions. Of interest, however, is that the subjects use this word when you ask them openended questions about their analysis and perceptions of the game. "Its all a question of whether you can trust your partner." Neither do we use the word "partner."

upper payoff to player 1, $10, and the lower payoff to player 2, $10, or move down in which case Player 2 chooses a move at node x2. If Player 2's move is right, Player 1 receives $15, and Player 2, $25. This is the cooperative (C) outcome. If, however, player 2 moves down the payoffs to 1 and 2 are respectively $0 and $40. This is the defection (D) outcome, in which Player 2 defects on Player 1's offer to cooperate. The sub-game perfect equilibrium (SPE) is $10 for each player. This follows because at node 1 Player 1 can apply backward induction by observing that if play reaches node x2, Player 2's dominant choice is to defect. Seeing that this is the case, Player 1's dominant choice is to move right at the top of the tree, yielding the SPE outcome.

These game theoretic assumptions are very strong. As we see from the above discussion, however, they have the dubious merit of allowing 'unambiguous' predictions to be made about behavior.[68] We particularly want to note that if every player is exactly like every other player, and is strictly self-interested, there is no room for "mind reading," or inferring intentions from actions, and no room for more sophisticated and subtle action in the self-interest.

To illustrate, suppose that you have been through the standard economics course in game theory and that you are in the position of Player 2 in Figure 1. Consequently, you expect Player 1 to move right at the top of the tree. He doesn't. He moves down, and it is your turn. Surely he did not move down because he prefers $0 to $10, or expects you to defect. He must think that you think that he wants you to choose C. Whatever else can he have in mind? Maybe he cannot do backward induction, or thinks you are not self-interested. So how are you going to respond? He is making it possible for you to increase your payoff by 150%, and his by 50%, compared with the SPE. He is not even asking for the larger share of the pie that his action has created! According to reciprocity theory, if you choose C, you will reciprocate his inferred intentions, and complete an exchange–exactly in the same way that you trade favors, services and goods across time with your closer friends and associates in life (except for those who are victims of antisocial personality disorder, or sociopaths, and are unable to maintain social relations based on reciprocity)[69]; also in the same way that you do not hesitate to leave a 'tip' ("to

[68] Except see Smith, 2002, wherein it is shown that if, in addition to the research hypothesis derived from game theory (e.g., Cournot-Nash or SPE), there is one auxiliary hypothesis (e.g., payoffs are adequate, types have been accurately defined, or subjects are sophisticated), then either the theoretical hypothesis is not falsifiable, or it has no predictive content. The belief, however, persists that the predictions of game theory are sharp and unambiguous. (See, e.g. Camerer, *et al.*, 2001).

[69] "Sociopaths, who comprise only 3–4% of the male population and less than 1% of the female population, are thought to account for 20% of the United States prison population and between 33% and 80% of the population of chronic criminal offenders. Furthermore, whereas the 'typical' U.S. burglar is estimated to have committed a median five crimes per year before being apprehended, chronic offenders–those most likely to be sociopaths–report committing upwards of 50 crimes per year and sometimes as many as two or three hundred. Collectively, these individuals are thought to account for over 50% of all crimes in the U.S." (See Mealy, 1995, p523, and pp 587– 599 for references and caveats; also Lyyken, 1995).

insure promptness?") for good service at a restaurant even in a foreign city. Without a conscious thought you often say, "I owe you one," in response to an acquaintance's favor. So you might choose C with hardly a thought, or, since he will never know your identity, upon closer reflection, you may think that it just makes no sense not to take the $40. Although you are not a clinical sociopath, here is an opportunity to cut a corner and no one can know. As Player 1 in Figure 1 are you certain that you would want to play SPE?[70]

In regard to this reciprocity analysis of the game, we should note that the game in Figure 1 is a much reduced-form version of the BDM game: think of Player 1 as sending $10, which becomes $30; Player 2 can either split the $30 equally with Player 1, giving the imputation C, or Player 2 can keep it all, yielding the D outcome. But there is another difference, one of context. In the experiment using Figure 1 the subjects play an abstract game, one that is not embedded in a BDM-type story about sending $10 upstairs, which becomes $30, and the receiver can either keep it all or split the gain made possible by the sender. But given the BDM outcomes reported above we should not be too surprised that some subject pairs might end at C.

The outcomes are shown in Figure 1 for 24 undergraduate subjects: 50% move down, and of these 75% "reciprocate."

Why So Much Cooperation?

My co-authors and I have interpreted the outcome C as due to reciprocity. But there are other interpretations; e.g., that the subjects are game theoretically unsophisticated or have nonselfish preferences. The effect of subjects on outcomes is an empirical matter, and is most important, but cannot be pursued here in depth. It is essential to programs concerned with extending game theory to 'player types.' Subject background diversity and resulting choice behavior can help inform the identification and classification of 'types,' whether reciprocators, sophisticates or utilitarian. (See McCabe and Smith, 2001; McCabe, *et al.*, 2001).

Is It The Subjects? Undergraduate's vs Graduates

In the above trust game nearly half the Players 1 forego the sure thing, SP, and threequarters of the responses are cooperative. We have often heard such results dismissed as a consequence of using naïve subjects. (This dismissal has the logical implication that the original theoretical hypothesis is either not falsifiable or has no predictive content. See footnote 68). McCabe and Smith (2000) examined this explanation using advanced graduate students from the population a sample of whom participated in the $100

[70] This thought process may explain why, in data reported by Corelli, McCabe and Smith (2000) comparing faculty with undergraduate subjects, the faculty take much longer (and earn less money) than the undergraduates to decide whether to offer cooperation, and whether to defect. Yet given knowledge of game theory, and knowing that one's counterpart has the equivalent knowledge, what is there to think about?

Figure 1. Invest $10 Trust Game: Frequency of Play

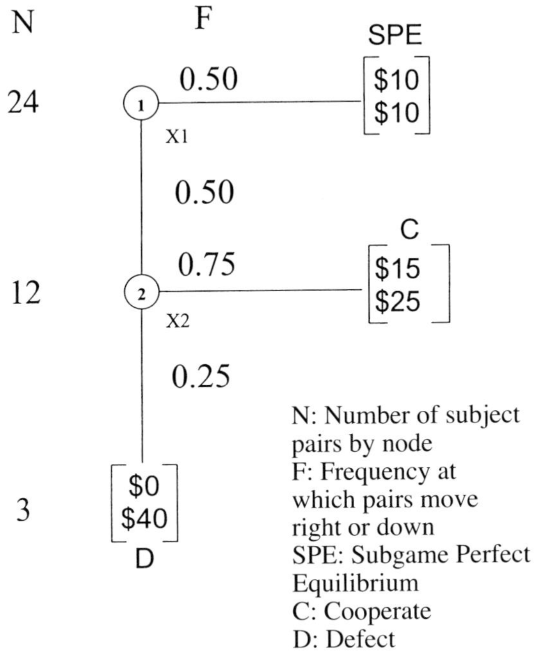

Exchange/Entitlement version of the ultimatum game reported in Table 2 showing almost identical results for graduate and undergraduate students. They used the trust game shown in Figure 1. For comparison, McCabe and Smith (2000) used the undergraduate data shown in Figure 1. In both groups 50% of Players 1 offer cooperation, while 75% of the undergraduate and 64% of the graduate student Players 2 reciprocate. See Figure 2. However naïve undergraduates are alleged to be, these tests suggest that graduate students with training in economic theory are capable of showing very similar behavior in this extensive form game, and in the ultimatum game reported in Table 2.

Is it Utility for Other?

Bolton (1991), Rabin (1993), Fehr and Schmidt (1999), Bolton and Ockenfels (2000) have proposed useful preference models of decision that aim at accounting for behavior in a variety of experiments, most particularly ultimatum and dictator games. The idea behind these models is that we can explain cooperation in bargaining games by saying that people have a taste for altruism or for 'fair' outcomes (or a distaste for 'unfair' outcomes), where fairness is understood as payoff equity, as in Franciosi, *et al.* (1995). The hypothesis is that subjects seek to maximize these adjusted utilities. It is only the intrinsic properties of outcomes that are assumed to drive behavior; what alternatives the players faced at a previous decision node are irrelevant. This means that intentions, as reflected in the move choices, are assumed to be su-

Figure 2. Invest $10 Trust Game Comparing Undergraduates (U) and Graduates (G)

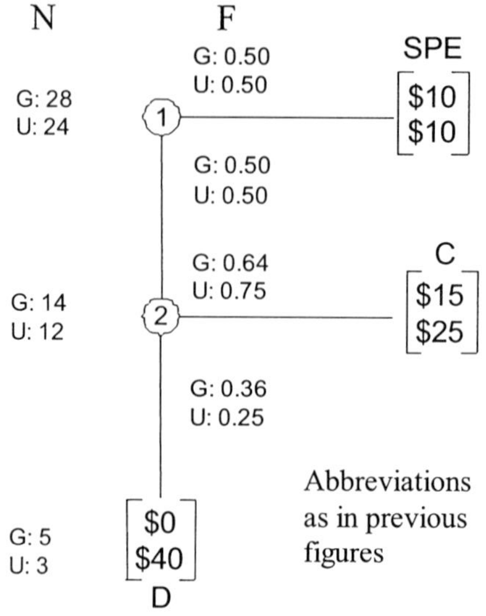

perfluous in the interactions between the parties. The former approach identifies utility types. The latter identifies types who signal intentions, who are into reading move signals, and risk misidentifying reciprocity vs defection types. The important testable distinctions are that the former are immune to instructional procedures and to path dependency–the opportunity costs of foregone options; this constitutes the core of the research program of my coauthors and me. This program leads naturally to an understanding of its own limitations as well as that of the utilitarian program, i.e., both types may be needed.

Other-regarding preference models are unable to account for our previous data demonstrating that procedures and context variables matter. In the ultimatum game data reported above where the context is varied from "Divide $10" to "Context/Exchange", ostensibly the utilities to the participants are the same under each ultimatum condition. However, behavior varies dramatically. These models also cannot explain the results reported above in the single versus double-blind protocol in dictator games, and the dramatic change in dictator behavior in the BDM investment trust game. Clearly, the behavior is much more variable than is expected from outcome-based utility models.

An altruistic utility interpretation of cooperation can be invoked in trust games like that in Figure 1: Player 2 may move down because her utility for reward is increasing in both own and other payoff. In Figure 3 is a trust game that enables us to distinguish subjects who cooperate from motivations of altruism, and those whose cooperation derives from reciprocity in an exchange. The game starts at the top, node x1, with Player 1 who can move right, which stops the game yielding the upper payoff to player 1, $7, and the lower payoff to player 2, $14, or move down in which case Player 2 chooses a move at node x2 If the move is right, each player gets $8. If player 2 moves down, player 1 can then move right at node x3 yielding $10 for each, or down, yielding $12 for player 1 and $6 for player 2. The sub-game perfect equilibrium (SPE) is $8 for each player. This follows because at node x1, player 1 can apply backward induction by observing that if play reaches node x3, Player 1 will want to move down. But Player 2, also using backward induction will see that at node x2 he should move right. Since right at node x2 yields a higher payoff to Player 1, at node x1 player 1 will conclude that he should move down. Hence, the SPE outcome would prevail by the logic of self-interested players who always choose dominant strategies, and apply the principle of backward induction.

If Player 1 has other regarding preferences (altruism) and is willing to incur some cost to greatly increase the Payoff to player 2, Player 1 may move right at x1. His payoff of $7 is only one-eighth smaller than his payoff at the SPE, and yields $14 for player 2. Hence, at a cost of $1 to himself, player 1 can increase his counterpart Player 2's payoff by $6. Player 1 need have only a modest preference for an increase in Player 2's welfare to induce him to move right because of the 6 to 1 return for the other player over the cost to Player 1.

At x2, Player 2 may move down signaling to Player 1 that such a move enables both to profit (gains from exchange), provided that at x3 Player 1 cooperates by reciprocating Player 2's favor. Alternatively at x3 Player 1 can defect (D) on the offer to cooperate by choosing his dominate strategy, and move down.

The outcome frequencies for the trust game (N = 26 pairs) are entered directly on the tree in Figure 3. The first result – overwhelmingly decisively – is that no Player 1 chooses the A (altruistic) outcome; all choose to pass to Player 2 seeking a higher payoff for themselves, and being content to give Player 2 a smaller payoff than is achieved at A, depending upon the final outcome of the move sequence. Secondly, 46% offer to cooperate (down), and 50% reciprocate.

Utility vs Exchange. Does Opportunity Cost Matter?

If reciprocity is perceived as an exchange in which each player gains relative to the default outcome (SPE), then the cooperative outcome must yield an increase in the size of the prize to be split between the two players. (See McCabe, Rigdon, and Smith, 2002). Also, Player 2 must believe that (i) Player 1 made a deliberate choice to make this outcome possible, and (ii) incurred an opportunity cost in doing so, i.e., gave up a smaller certain payoff risking a still smaller payoff if C is not attained. It then becomes credible to Player 2 that Player 1 did a favor for Player 2, and reasonably can expect reciprocal action in return. Notice that our argument is in the form of a constructivist theory that need not characterize the subjects' reasoning, even if it has predictive accuracy; i.e., constructive rationality may predict emergent ecologically rational outcomes, just as CE theory predicts market outcomes not part of the conscious intentions of the agents. McCabe, *et al.* (2001), however, report fMRI brain imaging data supporting the hypothesis that subjects who cooperate use the 'mind reading' circuit modules in their brains (See Baron-Cohen, 1995). This circuitry is not activated in subjects who choose not to co-operate (SPE). In responding to post experiment questions asking them to write their impressions of their decisions, subjects frequently report that the experiment is all about whether you can trust your counterpart. They do not refer to returning a favor, to reciprocity, an exchange, fairness, etc., suggesting that if their actions are driven by reciprocity motives, such are not part of a self-aware reasoning process.

Reciprocity reasoning motivated the alternative game trees shown in Figure 4 designed to test reciprocity against utility interpretations of choice. In Figure 4(a) if Player 1 moves down at the top the potential prize increases from $40 to $50. Player 2 can defect at a cost to Player 1, and can clearly infer that Player 1 deliberately enabled the outcome to increase from ($20, $20) to ($25, $25). But in Figure 4(b) Player 2 can see that Player 1 was presented with no voluntary choice to move down. Consequently, Player 1 incurred no opportunity cost to enable Player 2 to achieve C. Player 1 did nothing intentionally for Player 2, and according to reciprocity reasoning, Player 2 incurred no implied debt that needed to be repaid. Player 2 can thus move down with impunity. Consequently, reciprocity theory predicts a greater frequency of right moves by Players 2 in Figure 4(a) than in Figure 4(b). Since only outcomes matter, both own and other-regarding utility theories predict no difference in Player 2's choices between Figures 4 (a) and 4 (b). In fact, as shown by the frequency data on the trees, a third of the Players 2 on the right play C, whereas nearly twice that many choose C in the left game.

Intentions have also been found to matter in a study of ultimatum bargaining: "...we show that identical offers in an ultimatum game trigger vastly different rejection rates depending on the other offers available to the proposer." (Falk, Fehr and Fischbacher, 1999, p 2).

Extensive Versus Normal Form Games

A fundamental principle of game theory is that rational behavior is invariant to the form– extensive or normal–of the game. Behavior in the extensive and normal forms has been compared by Schotter, Wiegelt and Wilson (1994), Rapoport (1997), and McCabe, Smith and LePore (1998). All three reject the invariance principle, but in the first study the rationality principles they proposed to explain the invariance either failed to predict the differences, "or they were not what we expected." (Schotter, Wiegelt and Wilson, 1994, pp. 446–447). Rapoport provides two versions of the "Battle-of-the-Sexes" game to show how order-of-play information in the extensive form allows players to better coordinate their actions. McCabe, Smith and LePore (1998) argue that the important principle that allows better coordination "derives from the human capacity to read another person's thoughts or intentions by placing themselves in the position and information state of the other person." (p.

Figure 3. Trust Game with Altruism: Frequency of Play

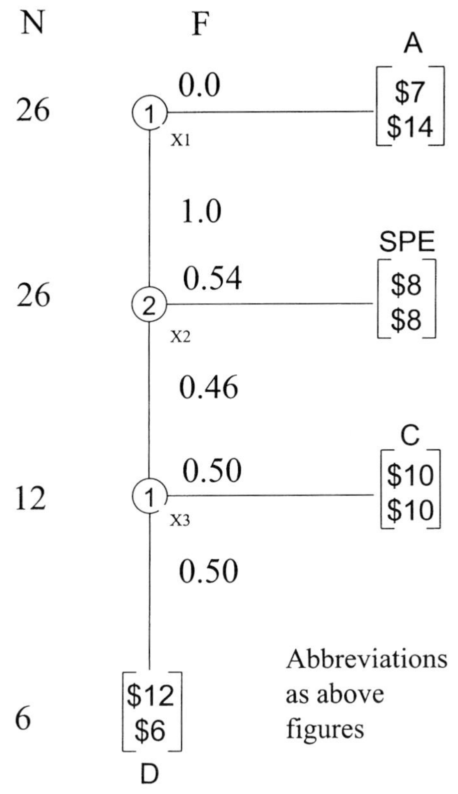

4404). This "mind reading" to detect intentions underlies reciprocity. We summarize here the findings of McCabe, Smith and LePore (1998) for the trimmed version of the game they study, which is the game we have depicted in Figure 3.

In the extensive form of the game in Figure 3, Player 2 sees the move of Player 1 before Player 2 chooses to move. In this form of the game intentions can be clearly communicated along the lines storied above. In the normal (or strategic) form of the same game each player chooses a move at each node without knowing whether that node will actually be reached in the move sequence. Decisions are thus contingent on the node being reached and may be irrelevant in determining the payoffs. In the normal form, therefore we can present the game as an n x m matrix of the n = 3 strategies of Player 1–right at node x1, right or down at node x3, and the m = 2 strategies of Player 2, right or down at node x2. Players 1 and 2 each simultaneously choose among these alternatives not knowing the choice of the other.

McCabe, Smith and LePore (1998) predict that Players 2 will move down at x2, with higher frequency in the extensive than the normal from. They also predict higher rates of cooperation by Players 1 (and lower defection rates) in

Table 4. Branch Conditional Outcomes for One-shot Game: Extensive Versus Normal Form Outcome Extensive Form Frequency Normal Form

Outcome	Extensive Form Frequency	Normal Form Frequency
($7, $14)	$\frac{0}{26} = 0.0$	$\frac{0}{24} = 0.0$
Left Branch Play	$\frac{12}{26} = 0.46$	$\frac{7}{24} = 0.29$
($8, $8)	$\frac{6}{12} = 0.50$	$\frac{1}{7} = 0.14$
($12, $6)	$\frac{6}{12} = 0.50$	$\frac{6}{7} = 0.86$

the extensive than normal forms. Neither own- or otherregarding utility theory can support these predictions. The data are shown in Table 4: 46% of the Players 1 offer to cooperate in the extensive form, only 29% in the normal form. Similarly, they observe a 50% cooperative rate by Players 2 in the extensive form, but only 14% in the normal form.

These results and that of others cited above imply that the extensive and normal forms are not played as if they were the same games. Players' moves signal intentions that are not the same when actually experienced in extensive form as when imagined in a mental experiment corresponding to the normal form. I would argue that experience and its memory in life is an extensive process that encodes context along with outcome. The brain is not naturally adapted to solve all sequential move problems by reducing them to a single strategy vector as in a highly structured game. Apparently, we have a built-in tendency to wait, observe, then decide–a process that conserves cognitive resources by applying them only to contingencies that are realized, and avoids the need for revision, given the inevitable surprises in the less structured games of life.[71] Constructivist modeling glosses over distinctions of which we are unaware that govern the ecology of choice. Experimental designs conditioned only by constructivist thinking, ill prepare us to collect the data that can inform needed revisions in our thinking. It is both cost effective

[71] Any such natural process must be deliberately overcome, constructively, in situations where nature serves us poorly.

Figure 4a. Voluntary Trust Game

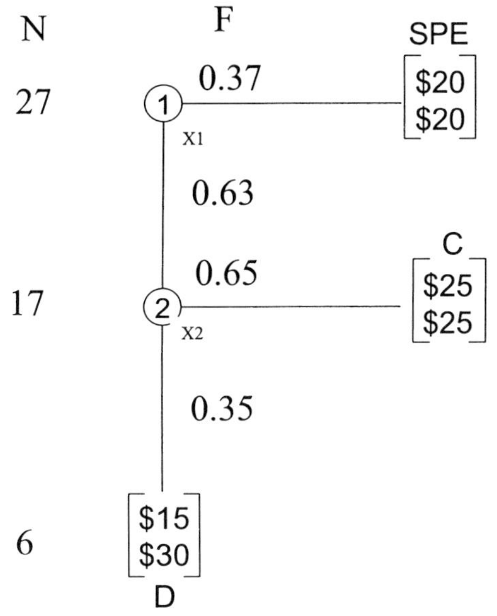

Figure 4b. Involuntary Trust Game

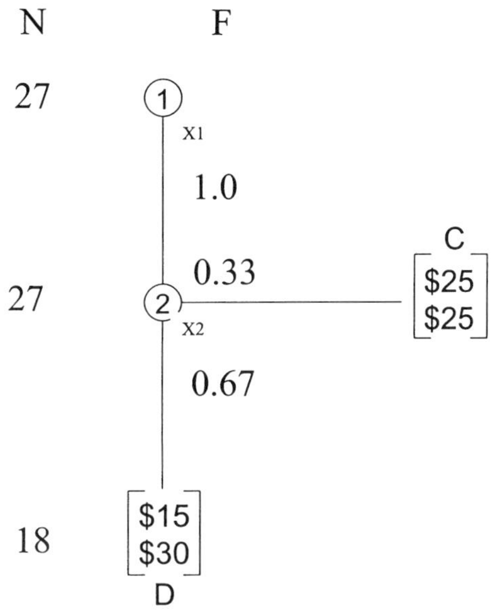

and faithful to game theoretic assumptions in experiments to collect move data from each subject under all contingencies, but it distorts interpretability if game forms are not equivalent. The assumptions of game theory, such as those leading to the logical equivalence of the two game forms, should not be imposed on experimental designs, thereby constraining our understanding of behavior beyond those assumptions.

Neuroeconomics

Neuroeconomics is concerned with studying the connections between how the mind/brain works–the internal order of the mind–and behavior in (1) individual decision making, (2) social exchange and (3) institutions such as markets. The working hypothesis is that the brain has evolved different, but interdependent, adaptive mechanisms for each of these tasks involving experience, memory and perception. The tools include brain imaging technology and the existence of patients with localized brain lesions associated with specific loss of certain mental functions.

Decision making has drawn the attention of neuroscientists who study the deviant behavior of neurological patients with specific brain lesions, such as front lobe (ventromedial prefrontal) damage. Such patients have long been known to be challenged by tasks involving planning and coordination over time, although they score normally on batteries of psychological tests. (Damasio, 1994). A landmark experimental study of such patients (compared with controls) in individual decision making under uncertainty is that of Bechara *et al.* (1997). Starting with (fictional) endowments of $2000, each subject on each trial, draws a card from one of four freely chosen decks, (A, B, C, D). In decks (A, B) each card has a payoff value of $50, whereas in decks (C, D), each is worth $100. Also, the $100 decks contain occasional large negative payoff cards, while the $50 decks have much smaller negative payoff cards. All this must be learned from single card draws in a sequence of trials, with a running tally of cumulative payoff value. A subject performs much better by learning to avoid the $100 decks in favor of the $50 decks. By period 60, normal control subjects have learned to draw only from the $50, (C, D) decks, while the brain damaged subjects continue to sample disadvantageously the $100, (A, B) decks. Furthermore, the control subjects shift to the (C, D) decks before they are able to articulate why, in periodic questioning. Also, they pre-register emotional reactions to the (A, B) decks as measured by real time skin conductivity test (SCT) readings. But the brain damaged patients tend to verbally rationalize continued sampling of the (A, B) decks, and some types (with damaged amygdala) register no SCT response. Results consistent with those of Bechara *et al.* (1997) have been reported by Goel *et al.* (1997) who study patient performance in a complex financial planning task.

Over 50 years ago experiments with animal behavior demonstrated that motivation was based on relative or foregone reward – opportunity cost – and not on an absolute scale of values generated by the brain. Thus Zeaman (1949) reported experiments in which rats were trained to run for a large reward motivated goal. When shifted to a small reward, the rats responded by running more slowly than they would to the small reward only. A control group began with a small reward and shifted to a large one, and these rats immediately ran faster than if the large reward alone was applied. Monkeys similarly respond to comparisons of differential rewards. It is now established that orbitofrontal cortex (just above the eyes) neuron activity in monkeys enable them to discriminate between rewards that are directly related to the animals' relative, as distinct from absolute, preference among rewards such as cereal, apple and raisins (in order of increasing preference in monkeys). (Tremblay and Schultz, 1999).

Thus suppose A is preferred to B is preferred to C based on choice response. Then neuronal activity is greater for A than for B when the subject is viewing A and B, and similarly for B and C when comparing B and C. But the activity associated with B is much greater when compared with C than when it is compared with A. This is contrary to what one would expect to observe if A, B and C are coded on a fixed properties scale rather than a relative scale (Tremblay and Schultz, 1999, p. 706).

These studies have a parallel significance for humans. Prospect theory proposes that the evaluation of a gamble depends not on the total asset position but focuses myopically on the opportunity cost, gain or loss, relative to one's current asset position. There is also asymmetry – the effect of a loss looms larger than the effect of gain of the same magnitude. (Kahneman and Tversky, 1979). Mellers *et al.* (1997) have shown that the emotional response to the outcome of a gamble depends on the perceived value and likelihood of the outcome and on the foregone outcome. It feels better (less bad) to receive $0 from a gamble when you forgo +$10 than when you forgo +$90. (They use the term "counterfactual" rather than "opportunity cost" to refer to the alternative that might have prevailed). Thus, our ability to form opportunity cost comparisons receive important neurophysiological support from our emotional circuitry. Breiter *et al.* (2001) use these same principles in the design of a functional magnetic imaging (fMRI) study of human hemodynamic responses to both the expectation and experience of monetary gains and losses under uncertainty. They observed significant activation responses in the amygdala and orbital gyrus, with both activations increasing with the expected value of the gamble. There was also some evidence that the right hemisphere is predominantly active for gains, and the left for losses–a particularly interesting possibility inviting deeper examination, perhaps by imaging splitbrain subjects in the same task.

The effect of paying subjects is informed by Thut *et al.* (1997) who compare brain activation under monetary rewards with the feedback of an 'OK' reinforcement in a dichotomous choice task. The monetary rewards yielded a significantly higher activation of the orbitofrontal cortex and other related brain areas. (Also see Schultz, 2000, 2002).

The neural correlates of individual decision-making were extended, by McCabe *et al.* (2001), to an fMRI study of behavior in two person strategic interactions in extensive form trust games like those in Figures 1 to 4. The prior hypothesis, derived from reciprocity theory, the theory-of-mind literature, and supported by imaging results from individual studies of cued thought processes (Fletcher *et al.* 1995), was that cooperators would show greater activation in the prefrontal cortex (specifically BA-8) and supporting circuitry, than non cooperators. The control, for comparison with the mental processes used when a subject is playing a human, is for the subject to play a computer knowing the programmed response probabilities and therefore having no need to interpret moves as intentions. The predicted activations were significantly greater, relative to controls, for cooperators than non cooperators, and are consistent with the reciprocity interpretation of behavior discussed above.

IV. CONCLUSIONS

Cartesian constructivism applies reason to the design of rules for individual action, to the design of institutions that yield socially optimal outcomes, and constitutes the standard socioeconomic science model. But most of our operating knowledge, and ability to decide and perform is non-deliberative. Our brains conserve attentional, conceptual and symbolic thought resources because they are scarce, and proceeds to delegate most decision-making to autonomic processes (including the emotions) that do not require conscious attention. Emergent arrangements, even if initially constructivist, must have survival properties that incorporate opportunity costs and environmental challenges invisible to constructivist modeling. This leads to an alternative, ecological concept, of rationality: an emergent order based on trial-and-error cultural and biological evolutionary processes. It yields home- and socially-grown rules of action, traditions and moral principles that underlie property rights in impersonal exchange, and social cohesion in personal exchange. To study ecological rationality we use rational reconstruction–for example, reciprocity or other regarding preferences–to examine individual behavior, emergent order in human culture and institutions, and their persistence, diversity and development over time. Experiments enable us to test propositions derived from these rational reconstructions.

The study of both kinds of rationality has been prominent in the work of experimental economists. This is made plain in the many direct tests of the observable implications of propositions derived from economic and game theory. It is also evident in the great variety of experiments that have reached far beyond the theory to ask why the tests have succeeded, failed, or performed better (under weaker conditions) than was expected. What have we learned, not as final truth, but as compelling working hypotheses for continuing examination?

1. Markets constitute an engine of productivity by supporting resource specialization through trade and creating a diverse wealth of goods and services.

2. Markets are rule-governed institutions providing algorithms that select, process and order the exploratory messages of agents who are better informed as to their personal circumstances than that of others. As precautionary probes by agents yield to contracts, each becomes more certain of what must be given in order to receive. Out of this interaction between minds through the intermediary of rules the process aggregates the dispersed asymmetric information, converging more-or-less rapidly to competitive equilibria if they exist. Each experimental market carries its own unique mark with a different dynamic path.

3. All this information is captured in the static or time variable supply and demand environment and must be aggregated to yield efficient clearing

prices. We can never fully understand how this process works in the world because the required information is not given, or available, to any one mind. Thus, for many the arguments of the Scottish philosophers and of Hayek are obscure and mystical. But we can design experiments in which the information is not given to any participant, then compare market outcomes with efficient competitive outcomes and gauge a market institution's performance.

4. The resulting order is invisible to the participants, unlike the visible gains they reap. Agents discover what they need to know to achieve outcomes optimal against the constraining limits imposed by others.

5. Rules emerge as a spontaneous order–they are found–not deliberately designed by one calculating mind. Initially constructivist institutions undergo evolutionary change adapting beyond the circumstances that gave them birth. What emerges is a form of "social mind" that solves complex organization problems without conscious cognition. This "social mind" is born of the interaction among all individuals through the rules of institutions that have to date survived cultural selection processes.

6. This process accommodates trade offs between the cost of transacting, attending and monitoring, and the efficiency of the allocations so that the institution itself generates an order of economy that fits the problem it evolved to solve. Hence, the hundreds of variations on the fine structure of institutions, each designed without a designer to accommodate disparate conditions, but all of them subservient to the reality of dispersed agent information.

7. We understand little about how rule systems for social interaction and markets emerge, but it is possible in the laboratory to do variations on the rules, and thus to study that which is not.

8. Markets require enforcement–voluntary or involuntary–of the rules of exchange. These are: the right possession, it's transference by consent, and the performance of promises (Hume). Voluntary enforcement occurs when people in the market reward good services with gratuities or 'tips,' an example, perhaps, of an emergent cultural norm in which people recognize that tips are part of an informal exchange. If self or community enforcement conditions are not present, the result is unintended consequences for the bad, as markets are compromised or may fail. The game of 'trade' must not yield to the game of 'steal.'

9. Reciprocity, trust and trustworthiness are important in personal exchange where formal markets are not worth their cost, yet there are gains from exchange to be captured. They are also important in contracting as not every margin of gain at the expense of other can be anticipated and formalized in written contracts.

10. People are not required to be selfish; rather the point of the Scottish philosophers was that people did not have to be good to produce good. Markets economize on information, understanding, rationality, numbers of agents, and virtue.

11. Markets in no way need destroy the foundation upon which they probably emerged–social exchange between family, friends and associates. This is supported in the studies reported by Heinrich (2000). Thus, individuals can

be habitual social exchangers and vigorous traders as well, but as in Hayek's 'two worlds' text, the ecologically rational co-existence of personal and impersonal exchange is not a self-aware Cartesian construct. Consequently, there is the ever-present danger that the rules of 'personal exchange' will be applied inappropriately to govern or modify the extended order of markets. Equally dangerous, the rules of impersonal market exchange may be applied inappropriately to our cohesive social networks.

12. New brain imaging technologies have motivated neuroeconomic studies of the internal order of the mind and its links with the spectrum of human decision from choice among fixed gambles to choice mediated by market and other institutional rules. We are only at the beginning of this enterprise, but its promise suggests a fundamental change in how we think, observe and model decision in all its contexts.

REFERENCES

Acheson, James (1975), The Lobster Fiefs: Economic and Ecological Effects of Territoriality in the Maine Lobster Industry." *Human Ecology,* 3, pp. 183–207.

Anderson, T., and P. J. Hill (1975), "The Evolution of Property Rights: A Study of the American West," *Journal of Law and Economics,* 18, pp. 163–179.

Arrow, Kenneth (1987), "," in *Rational Choice,* edited by R. Hogarth and M. Reder. Chicago: University of Chicago Press.

Backerman, S., S. Rassenti, and V. L. Smith (2000), Efficiency and Income Shares in High Demand Energy Network: "Who Receives the Congestion Rents When a Line is Constrained?" *Pacific Economic Review,* 5, pp. 331–347.

Banks, J., M. Olson, S. Rassenti and V. Smith (2003),"Theory, Experiment and the Federal Communications Commission Spectrum Auctions," *Journal of Economic Behavior and Organization,* in press.

Backerman, S., M. Denton, S., Rassenti, and V. L. Smith (2001), "Market Power in a Deregulated Electrical Industry," *Journal of Decision Support Systems,* 30, pp. 357–381.

Baron-Cohen, S. (1995), Mindblindness: An Essay on Autism and Theory of Mind. Cambridge, MA: MIT Press.

Bechara, A., H. Damasio, D. Tranel and AR. Damascio (1997), "Deciding advantageously before knowing the advantageous Strategy," *Science* 275, pp. 1293–1295.

Berg, J., J. Dickhaut, and K. McCabe (1994), "Risk Preference Instability Across Institutions: A Dilemma," Working paper, Carlson School of Management, University of Minnesota.

Berg, J., J. Dickhaut, and K. McCabe (1995), "Trust, Reciprocity, and Social History," *Games and Economic Behavior,* 1995, 10, pp. 122–142.

Binswanger, H. P. (1980), "Attitudes Toward Risk: Experimental Measurement in Rural India." *American Journal of Agricultural Economics,* 63, 395–407.

Bohnet, I., B. Frey, and S. Huck (2001), "More Order with Less Law: on Contract Enforcement, Trust, and Crowding." *American Political Science Review,* 95, pp 131–51.

Bolton, G., A. Ockenfels. (2000), "ERC: A Theory of Equity, Reciprocity, and Competition" *American Economic Review,* 90, pp. 166–193.

Bolton, G., E. Katok, and R. Zwick (1998), "Dictator Game Giving: Rules of Fairness Versus Acts of Kindness," *International Journal of Game Theory,* 27, pp. 269–299.

Bolton, Gary E. (1991), "A Comparative Model of Bargaining: Theory and Evidence." *American Economic Review,* 81, pp. 1096–136.

Brandts, Jordi, and C. A. Holt (1991), "An Experimental Test of Equilibrium Dominance in Signaling Games," *American Economic Review.*

Breiter, HC., I. Aharon, D. Kahneman, A. Dale and P. Shizgal (2001), "Functional imaging of neural responses to expectancy and experience of monetary gains and losses," *Neuron* 30, pp. 619–639.

Bronfman, Corrine, Kevin McCabe, Dave Porter, Stephen Rassenti, and Vernon L. Smith (1996), "An Experimental Examination of the Walrasian Tatonnement Mechanism," *Rand Journal,* 27, pp. 681–699.

Burnham, T. (1998), "Engineering Altruism: An Experimental Investigation of Anonymity and Gift Giving." Manuscript. Kennedy School of Government, Harvard University.

Burnham, T., K. McCabe and V. Smith (2000), "Friend-or-foe Intentionality Priming in an Extensive Form Game," *Journal of Economic Behavior and Organization,* 44, pp. 1–17.

Camera, G. C. Noussair and S. Tucker (2001), "Rate-of-Return Dominance and Efficiency in an Experimental Economy." Department of Economics, Krannert School of Management, Purdue University.

Camerer, C. F. and T-H Ho (1999), "Experience-weighted Attraction Learning in Normal Form Games, " *Econometrica,* 67, pp. 827–874.

Camerer, C., T. Ho, and J. Chong (2001), "Behavioral Game Theory: Thinking, Learning, and Teaching." Nobel Symposium on Behavioral and Experimental Economics, Stockholm, December.

Camerer, Colin (2002), Behavioral Game Theory: Experiments on Strategic Interaction. Princeton: Princeton University Press.

Cason, Timothy and Daniel Friedman (1993), "An Empirical Analysis of Price Formation in Double Auction Markets," in *The Double Auction,* edited by J. Friedman and J. Rust. Redwood City, CA.: Addison-Wesley.

Coase, R. (1960), "The problem of Social Cost." *Journal of Law and Economics,* 3, pp. 1–44.

Coase, R. (1974), "The Lighthouse in Economics." *Journal of Law and Economics,* 17, pp. 357–76.

Copeland, T. E. and Daniel Friedman (1987), "The Effect of Sequential Information Arrival on Asset Markets: An Experimental Study," *Journal of Finance,* 42, 763–797.

Corelli, K. McCabe and V. L. Smith (2000), "Theory-of-Mind Mechanism in Personal Exchange." Proceedings 13th Annual Toyota Conference on Affective Minds, Chapter 26 in *Affective Minds,* edited by G. Hatano, N. Okada and H. Tanabe. Amsterdam: Elsevier.

Cosmides, L. and J. Tooby (1992), "Cognitive Adaptations for Social Exchange," in J. Barkow, L. Cosmides, and J. Tooby (eds.), *The Adapted Mind.* New York: Oxford University Press, pp. 163–228.

Cox, J., and D. Grether (1996), "The Preference Reversal Phenomenon: Response Mode, Markets and Incentives." *Economic Theory,* 7, pp. 381–405.

Damasio, A. R. (1994), Descartes Error: Emotion, Reason, and the Human Brain. New York: Putnam.

Davis, Douglas and Charles Holt (1993), *Experimental Economics.* Princeton: Princeton University Press.

Deck, C. and B. Wilson (2002), "Tracking Customer Search to Price Discriminate," Working Paper, Interdisciplinary Center for Economic Science, George Mason University.

Deck, Cary, K. McCabe and D. Porter (2001), "Why Stable Fiat Money Hyperinflates: Results from an Experimental Economy." Department of Economics, University of Arkansas.

Dentin, M., S. Rassenti, and V. L. Smith (2001), "Spot Market Mechanism Design and Competitivity Issues in Electric Power," *Journal of Economic Behavior and Organization,* 44, 435–453.

de Waal, F. B. M. (1997), "Food-transfers Through Mesh in Brown Capuchins," *Journal of Comparative Psychology,* 111, pp. 370–378.

de Waal, F. B. M. (1989), "Food Sharing and Reciprocal Obligations Among Chimpanzees," *Journal of Human Evolution,* pp.433–459.

Donahue, George (2002), "The US Air Transportation System: A Bold Vision for Change," paper prepared for the Commission on the Future of the US Airspace Industry, September 19.

Dufwenberg, M., T. Lindqvist and E. Moore (2002), "Bubbles and experience: An experiment on speculation." Working Paper, Department of Economics, Stockholm University.

Eckel, C. and P. Grossman (1996), "Altruism in Anonymous Dictator Games," *Games and Economic Behavior*, 16, pp. 181–191.

Elikson, Robert C. (1991), Order Without Law: How Neighbors Settle Disputes. Cambridge: Harvard University Press.

Erev, I., and A. Roth (1998), "Predicting How People Play Games: Reinforcement Learning in Experimental Games with Unique, Mixed-Strategy Equilibria," *American Economic Review*, 88, pp. 848–881.

Falk, A., E. Fehr and U. Fischbacher (1999), "On the Nature of Fair Behavior," Working Paper No 17, ISSN 1424-0459, University of Zurich, August.

Fehr, E. and K. M. Schmidt (1999), "A Theory of Fairness, Competition, and Cooperation," *Quarterly Journal of Economics*, 114, pp. 817–868.

Fehr, E., and S. Gachter (2000), "Do Incentive Contracts Crowd Out Voluntary Cooperation?" Working Paper, Institute for Empirical Research in Economics, University of Zurich.

Fiske, A. P. (1991), The Structures of Social Life: The Four Elementary Forms of Human Relations. New York: Free Press.

Forsythe, R., F. Nelson, G. R. Neumann and J. Wright (1992), "Anatomy of an experimental political stock market," *American Economic Review*, 82:1142–1161.

Forsythe, R., T. A. Rietz and T.W. Ross (1999), Wishes, expectations and actions: Price formation in Election Stock Markets. *Journal of Economic Behavior and Organization*, 39: 83–110.

Forsythe, R., J. L. Horowitz, N. E. Savin, and M. Sefton (1994), "Fairness in Simple Bargaining Experiments," *Games and Economic Behavior*, 6, pp. 347–369.

Fouraker, Lawrence, and Sidney Siegel (1963), Bargaining Behavior. New York: McGraw Hill.

Franciosi, R., P. Kujal, R. Michelitsch, V. L. Smith, and G. Deng (1995), "Fairness: Effect on Temporary and Equilibrium Prices in Posted Offer Markets," *Economic Journal*, 105, pp. 938–950.

Freuchen, P. (1961), Book of the Eskimos. Clevland: World Publishing.

Friedman, Daniel (1984), "On the Efficiency of Double Auction markets," *American Economic Review*, 74, pp. 60–72.

Friedman, Daniel (1991), "," in The Double Auction, edited by J. Friedman and J. Rust.

Friedman, Milton and L. J. Savage (1948), "The Utility Analysis of Choices Involving Risk," *Journal of Political Economy*, 56, pp. 279–304.

Fletcher, P., Happe, F., Frith, U., Baker, S., Dolan, R., Frakowiak, R., and Frith, C. (1995), Other Minds in the Brain: A Functional Imaging Study of 'Theory of Mind' in Story Comprehension Cognition 57: 109–128.

Fuster, J. (1999), *Memory in the Cerebral Cortex*. Cambridge, MA: MIT Press.

Gazzaniga, M., R. Ivry and G. Mangun, (1998), *Cognitive Neuroscience*. New York: Norton.

Gazzaniga, Michael S. (1998), *The Mind's Past*. Berkeley: University of California Press.

Gigerenzer, Gerd, Peter M. Todd, and the ABC Research Group (1999), Simple Heuristics That Make Us Smart. New York: Oxford.

Goel, V., J. Grafman, J. Tajik, S. Gana and D. Danto (1997), "A study of the performance of patients with frontal lobe lesions in a financial planning task," *Brain* 120, pp. 1805–1822.

Goldberger, A. (1979), Heritability, *Economica*, 46, pp. 327–47.

Hawkes, K. (1990), "Showing Off: Tests of an Hypothesis about Men's Foraging Goals. *Ethnology and Evolutionary Biology*, 12, pp. 29–54.

Hayek, F.,(1952), *The Sensory Order*. Chicago: University of Chicago Press.

Hayek, F. A. (1960), *The Constitution of Liberty*. Chicago: Chicago University Press.

Hayek, F. A. (1967), *Studies in Philosophy Politics and Economics*. Chicago: Chicago University Press.

Hayek, F. A. (1991), *The Trend of Economic Thinking*. Chicago: University of Chicago Press.

Hayek, F. (1988), *The Fatal Conceit*. Chicago: University of Chicago Press.

Hayek, F.A. (1973), *Law, Legislation, and Liberty*, vol I, Rules and Order. Chicago: University of Chicago.

Heinrich, J. (2002), "Does Culture Matter in Economic Behavior?," *American Economic Review*, September 2000, pp. 973–979.

Hertwig, R. and A. Ortmann (2001), "Experimental Practices in Economics: A Methodological Challenge for Psychologists?" *Behavioral and Brain Sciences*, 24, pp. 383–451.

Hoffman, E., K. McCabe, K. Shachat, and V. Smith. (1994), "Preferences, Property Rights, and Anonymity in Bargaining Games," *Games and Economic Behavior*, 7, pp. 346–380.

Hoffman, E., K. McCabe and V. L. Smith (1996a), "On Expectations and the Monetary Stakes in Ultimatum Games," *International Journal of Game Theory*, pp. 289–301.

Hoffman, E., and M. Spitzer (1985), "Entitlements, Right and Fairness: An Experimental Examination of Subject's Concepts of Distributive Justice." *Journal of Legal Studies*, 14, pp. 259–97.

Hoffman, E., K. McCabe, and V. L. Smith (1996b), "Social Distance and Other-Regarding Behavior in Dictator Games," *American Economic Review*, 86, pp. 653–660.

Hoffman, E., K. McCabe, and V. L. Smith (2000), "The Impact of Exchange Context on the Activation of Equity in Ultimatum Games," *Experimental Economics*, 3, pp. 5–9.

Hogarth, Robin and Melvin Reder (1987), *Rational Choice*. Chicago: University of Chicago.

Holt, Charles (1995), "Industrial Organization,' Chapter 5 in *The Handbook of Experimental Economics*, edited by J. Kagel and A. Roth. Princeton: Princeton University press.

Hume, David (1739/1985), *A Treatise of Human Nature*. London: Penguin Books.

Kachelmeier, S. J. and M. Shehata (1992), "Examining Risk Preferences Under High Monetary Incentives: Evidence from the People's republic of China." *American Economic Review*, December, 82, pp. 1120–1141.

Kagan, J. (1994), *Galen's Prophecy*. New York: Basic Books.

Kagan, J. and S. Lamb (1987), *The Emergence of Morality in Young Children*. Chicago: University of Chicago press.

Kagel, John and Alvin Roth (1995), *Handbook of Experimental Economics*. Princeton: Princeton University Press.

Kahneman, D., and A. Tversky (1979), "Prospect Theory: An Analysis of Decision Under Risk," *Econometrica*, 47, pp. 263–91.

Kahneman, Daniel, J. Knetsch, and R. Thaler (1986), "Fairness as a Constraint on Profit Seeking: Entitlements in the Market." *American Economic Review*, 76, pp. 728–741.

Kahneman, Daniel, J. Knetsch and R, Thaler (1991), "Fairness and the Assumptions of Economics," in *Quasi Rational Economics*, edited by R. Thaler. New York: Russell Sage Foundation.

Kaplan, H. and K. Hill. (1985), "Food Sharing among Ache Foragers: Tests of Explanatory Hypotheses," *Current Anthropology*, 26, pp. 223–246.

Ketcham, J., V. L. Smith, and A. Williams (1984), "A Comparison of Posted-Offer and Double-Auction Pricing Institutions," *Review of Economic Studies*, 51, 595–614.

Knowlton, B., J. Mangels, and L. Squire (1996), "A Neostriatal Habit Learning System in Humans. *Science* 273, pp. 1399–402.

Lazzarini, S., G. Miller, and T. Zenger (2002), "Order with Some Law: Complementarity vs Substitution of Formal and Informal Arrangements." Interdisciplinary Conference on trust and Reciprocity in Experimental Economics, October 11–12, 2002, Washington University, St. Louis.

Ledyard, J. (1986), "The Scope of the Hypothesis of Bayesian Equilibrium," *Journal of Economic Theory*, 39, pp. 59–82.

Lopes, Lola (1991), "The Rhetoric of Irrationality," *Psychology and Theory*, 1, 65–82.

Lyyken, D. T. (1995), The Antisocial Personalities. Earlbaum.

Markowitz, H. (1952), "The Utility of Wealth," *Journal of Political Economy*, 60, pp. 151–8.

McCabe, K., D. Houser, L. Ryan, V. L. Smith, and T. Trouard (2001), "A functional imaging study of cooperation in two-person reciprocal exchange," Proceedings of the National Academy of Sciences, 98, pp. 11832–11835.

McCabe, K. and V. L. Smith (2000), "A Comparison of Naïve and Sophisticated Subject Behavior with Game Theoretic Predictions," Proceedings of the National Academy of Sciences, 97, pp. 3777–3781.

McCabe, K. and V. L. Smith (2001), "Goodwill Accounting and the Process of Exchange," in G. Gigerenzer and R. Selten (eds.), *Bounded Rationality the Adaptive Toolbox.* Cambridge, MA: MIT Press, pp. 319–340.

McCabe, K., M. Rigdon, and V. L. Smith (2002), "Positive Reciprocity and Intentions in Trust Games," to appear, *Journal of Economic Behavior and Organization.*

McCabe, K., S. Rassenti and V. L. Smith (1996), "Game Theory and Reciprocity in Some Extensive Form Experimental Games." Proceedings National Academy of Sciences, 93, pp. 13421–8.

McCabe, K., S. Rassenti, and V. L. Smith (1991), "Smart Computer-Assisted Markets," *Science,* 254, pp. 534–538.

McCabe, K., D. Houser, L. Ryan, V. Smith, and T. Trouard (2001), "A Functional Imaging Study of Cooperation in Two-Person Reciprocal Exchange," Proceedings of the National Academy of the Sciences, 98, pp. 11832–11835.

McCabe, K., V. Smith, and M. LePore (2000), "Intentionality Detection and `Mindreading': Why Does Game Form Matter?" Proceedings of the National Academy of the Sciences, 97, pp. 4404–4409.

McCabe, Kevin, Stephen Rassenti, and Vernon L. Smith (1991), "," in The Double Auction, edited by J. Friedman and J. Rust.

Mealy, Linda (1995), "The Sociobiology of Sociopathy." *Behavioral and Brain Sciences,* 18, September, pp. 523–599.

Mellers, B. A., A. Schwartz, K. Ho and J. Ritov) (1997), Decision Affect Theory: How we feel about risky options. *Phychological Science,* 8, p. 423–429.

Milgrom, Paul on subject sophistication, stakes Milgrom, Paul R. and Robert J. Weber (1982), "A Theory of Auctions and Competitive Bidding." *Econometrica,* 50, pp. 1089–1122.

Mill, John Stuart (1848/1900), *Principles of Political Economy,* Vol. 1 and 2. London: The Colonial Press.

Miller, Ross (2002), "Don't Let Your Robots Grow Up to Be Traders," Working Paper, Miller Risk Advisors.

Miller, Ross and C. Plott (1985), "Product Quality Signalling in Experimental Markets," *Econometrica,* 53, pp. 837–872.

Mullainathan, Sendhil, and Richard Thaler (2001), "Behavioral Economics," in *International Encyclopedia of the Social and Behavioral Sciences.* Pergamon, Oxford.

North, Douglass C. (1981), *Structure and Change in Economic History.* New York: Norton.

Olson, M., S. Rassenti, V. Smith, and M. Rigdon, (2003), "Market Design and Motivated Human Trading Behavior in Electricity Markets," to appear *Institute of Industrial Engineering Transactions.*

Ortmann, A., J. Fitzgerald, and C. Boening (2000). "Trust, Reciprocity, and Social History," *Experimental Economics,* 3(1), pp.81–100.

Ostrom, Eleanor (1990), *Governing the Commons.* Cambridge: Cambridge University Press.

Pillutla, M., D. Malhotra, and J.K. Murnighan (2002), "Attributions of Trust and the Calculus of Reciprocity," (in press) *Journal of Experimental Social Psychology.*

Pinker, Steven (1994), *The Language Instinct.* New York: William Morrow.

Pinker, Steven (2002), *The Blank Slate.* New York: Viking.

Plott, C. and S. Sunder (1982), "Efficiency of Experimental Security Markets with Insider Information: An Application of Rational-Expectations Models," *Journal of Political Economy,* 90, pp. 663–698.

Plott, C., and L. Wilde (1982), "Professional Diagnosis vs. Self-Diagnosis: An Experimental Examination of Some Special features of markets with Uncertainty," in *Research in Experimental Economics,* vol 2, edited by V. L. Smith. Greenwich Conn.: JAI Press, pp. 63–112.

Plott, C., and S. Sunder (1988), "Rational Expectations and the Aggregation of Diverse Information in Laboratory Securities Markets," *Econometrica,* 56, pp. 1085–1118.

Plott, Charles (1988), "Research on Pricing in a Gas Transportation Network." Office of Economic policy Technical Report no. 88-2. Federal Energy Regulatory Commission, Washington, D.C., July 1988.

Plott, Charles (2001), "Equilibrium, Equilibration, Information and Multiple Markets: From Basic Science to Institutional Design," Nobel Symposium, Behavioral and Experimental Economics. Grand Hotel Saltsjöbaden, December 4–6.

Plott, Charles and J. T. Uhl (1981), "Competitive Equilibrium with Middlemen." *Southern Economic Journal,* 47, pp. 1063–71.

Porter, D. and V. L. Smith (1994), "Stock Market Bubbles in the Laboratory," *Applied Mathematical Finance,* 1, pp. 111–127.

Rabin, Mathew, (1993), "Incorporating Fairness into Game Theory and Economics." *American Economics Review* 83(5): 1281–302.

Rapoport, A. (1997), "Order of Play in Strategically Equivalent Games in Extensive Form," *International Journal of Game Theory,* 26, pp. 113–136.

Rassenti, S., V. L. Smith and B. Wilson (2002a), "Controlling Market Power and Price Spikes in Electricity Networks: Demand side Bidding," Working Paper, Interdisciplinary Center for Economic Science, George Mason University, Arlington. VA.

Rassenti, S., V. L. Smith, and B. Wilson (2002b), "Using Experiments to Inform the Privatization/Deregulation Movement in Electricity," *The Cato Journal,* 21, pp. 515–544.

Rassenti, S., V. L. Smith, and R. Bulfin (1982), "A Combinatorial Auction Mechanism for Airport Time Slot Allocation," *Bell Journal of Economics* 13, pp. 402–417.

Rosenthal, R. (1982), "Games of Perfect Information, Predatory Pricing, and the Chain Store Paradox," *Journal of Economic Theory,* 25, pp. 92–100.

Satterthwaite, Mark (1987), "Strategy–Proof Allocation mechanisms," in *The New Palgrave,* Vol 4, edited by J. Eatwell, M. Milgate, and P. Newman. London: Macmillan, pp. 518–20.

Schotter, A., K. Wiegelt, and C. Wilson (1994), "A Laboratory Investigation of Multiperson Rationality and Presentation Effects," *Games and Economic Behavior,"* 6, pp. 445–68.

Schultz, W. (2000), "Multiple reward signals in the brain." *Nature Reviews: Neuroscience,* 1, pp. 199–207.

Schultz, W. (2002), "Getting Formal with Dopamine and Reward," *Neuron,* 36, pp. 241–263.

Schwartz, T. and J. S. Ang (1989), "Speculative Bubbles in the Asset Market: An Experimental Study." Paper presented at the American Finance Association meeting. Atlanta, December.

Segal, Nancy (1999), *Entwined Lives.* New York: Plume.

Selten, R. "Re-examination of the Perfectness Concept for Equilibrium Points in Extensive Games," *International Journal of Game Theory,* 1975, pp. 25–55.

Siegel, Sidney (1959), "Theoretical Models of Choice and Srategy behavior," *Psychometrik* 24, pp. 303–316.

Siegel, Sidney, and L. Fouraker (1960), *Bargaining and Group Decision Making.* New York: McGraw-Hill.

Simon, Herbert (1981/1996), *The Sciences of the Artificial.* 3rd edition. Cambridge, MA: The MIT Press.

Smith, Adam (1759/1982), *The Theory of Moral Sentiments.* Indianapolis: Liberty Classics.

Smith, Adam (1776/1981), *An Enquiry into the Nature and Causes of the Wealth of Nations.* Indianapolis: Liberty Fund.

Smith, K., J. Dickhaut, K. McCabe, and J. Pardo (2002), "Neuronal substrates for choice under ambiguity, risk, gains, and losses," *Management Science.*

Smith, V. L. (1998), "The Two Faces of Adam Smith," Distinguished Guest Lecture, *Southern Economic Journal,* 65, pp. 1–19.

Smith, V. L. and F. Szidarovszky (2002), "Monetary Rewards and Decision Cost in Strategic Interactions", edited by M. Augier, and J. March, *Models of a Man: Essays in Memory of Herbert A. Simon.* Cambridge Mass.: MIT Press.

Smith, Vernon L. (1962), "An Experimental Study of Competitive Market Behavior," *Journal of Political Economy*, 70, pp.111–37.

Smith, Vernon L. (1976), Experimental Economics: Induced Value Theory, *American Economic Review Proceedings*, 66, pp. 274–79.

Smith, Vernon L. (1980), "Relevance of Laboratory Experiments to Testing resource Allocation Theory," in *Evaluation of Econometric Models*, edited by J. Kmenta, and J. B. Ramsey. New York: Academic Press.

Smith, Vernon L. (1982), "Microeconomic Systems as an Experimental Science, *American Economic Review.*

Smith, Vernon L. (1991), Papers in *Experimental Economics.* Cambridge: Cambridge University Press.

Smith, Vernon L. (2000), *Bargaining and Market Behavior.* Cambridge: Cambridge University Press.

Smith, Vernon L. (2002), "Method in Experiment: Rhetoric and Reality," *Journal of Experimental Economics.*

Smith, Vernon L. (1986), "Experimental Methods in the Political Economy of Exchange," *Science*, 234, pp. 167–73.

Smith, Vernon L., Arlington Williams, Kenneth Bratton and Michael Vannoni (1982), "Competitive market Institutions: Double Auctions vs Sealed Bid-Offer Auctions," *American Economic Review*, 72, pp. 58–77.

Smith, Vernon L., Gerry Suchanek and Arlington Williams (1988), "Bubbles, Crashes and Endogenous Expectations in Experimental Spot Asset Markets," *Econometrica*, 56, pp. 49–51.

Soper, Barry, and G. Gigiolotti (1993), "Intransitive Cycles: Rational Choice or random Error," *Theory and decision*, 35, pp. 311–336.

Sunder, Shyam (2002), "Market as Artifact: Aggregate Efficiency from Zero Intelligence Traders," in *Models of a Man: Essays in Memory of Herbert A. Simon.* Cambridge Mass.: MIT Press.

Thaler, Richard, and W. T. Ziemba (1988), "Parimutuel Betting Markets: Racetracks and Lotteries," *Journal of Economics perspectives*, 2, pp. 161–174.

Thut, G., W. Schultz, U. Roelcke *et al.* (1997), "Activation of the human brain by monetary reward," *NeuroReport*, 8, pp. 1225–1228.

Tversky, Amos and Daniel Kahneman (1987), "," in *Rational Choice*, edited by R. Hogarth and M. Reder. Chicago: University of Chicago Press.

Tversky, Amos and Daniel Kahneman (1987), "Rational Choice and The Framing of Decisions," *Rational Choice* edited by R.M. Hogarth and M. W. Reder. Chicago: University of Chicago Press.

Umbeck, John (1977), "The California Gold Rush: A Study of Emerging Property Rights," *Explorations in Economic History*, 14, pp. 197–226.

Vickery, William (1961), "Counterspeculation, Auctions, and Competitive Sealed Tenders." *Journal of Finance*, 16, pp. 8–37.

Viner, Jacob (1991), "Adam Smith", in *Essays on the Intellectual History of Economics*, edited by D. Irvin. Princton: Princton University Press, pp. 248–61.

Williams, Arlington and Vernon L. Smith (1986), "Simultaneous Trading in Two Competitive Markets" manuscript, Indiana University Department of Economics, Bloomington, Indiana.

Williams, Arlington, Vernon L. Smith, John O. Ledyard and Steven Gjerstad (2000), Concurrent Trading in Two Experimental Markets with Demand Interdependence." *Journal of Economic Theory*, 16, pp. 511–528.

Wilson, R. B. (1987), "On Equilibria of Bid-Ask Markets," in *Arrow and the Ascent of Modern Economic Theory*, edited by G. Feiwel. New York: NYU Press, pp. 375–414.

Wilson, R. (2002), "Architecture of Power Markets," *Econometrica*, 70, pp. 1299–1340.

Wilson, R. B. (1992), '"Strategic Analysis of Auctions," in *Handbook of Game Theory*, edited by R. Aumann and S. Hart. Amsterdam: North-Holland, pp. 227–279.

Wilson, R. B (1991), "Design of Efficient Trading Procedure" in *The Double Auction,* edited by J. Friedman and J. Rust.
Zajac, E. E. (1995), *Political Economy of Fairness.* Cambridge, Mass.: MIT Press.
Zajac, E.E. (2002), "What Fairness-and-Denial Research Could Have Told the Florida Supreme Court (and Rest of Us)," *The Independent Review,* VI, pp. 377–97.

Economic Sciences 2003

ROBERT F. ENGLE III

"for methods of analyzing economic time series with time-varying volatility (ARCH)"

and

CLIVE W. J. GRANGER

"for methods of analyzing economic time series with common trends (cointegration)"

THE SVERIGES RIKSBANK (BANK OF SWEDEN) PRIZE IN ECONOMIC SCIENCES IN MEMORY OF ALFRED NOBEL

Speech by Professor Torsten Persson of the Royal Swedish Academy of Sciences.
Translation of the Swedish text.

Your Majesties, Your Royal Highnesses, Ladies and Gentlemen,

In modern society, every day of our lives the media deluge us with numbers on key economic variables: inflation, unemployment, interest rates, stock prices and much more. For most readers or viewers these are observations more or less similar to weather reports. But for us as researchers they are integral parts of a massive flow of data which, over time, gives rise to economic time series. Such time series are vital, not only for basic researchers who develop and test economic theory, but also for practitioners who require clear understanding and reliable forecasts as a basis for public policy or private decisions.

A prerequisite for the work of both researchers and practitioners is statistical methods well adopted to economic theory and economic data. Observations of business cycles and the weather are both cyclical, but economic time series have other specific features that distinguish them from meteorological ones. Scientific breakthroughs in the borderland between economics and statistics have therefore prevented statistical pitfalls, paved the way for new research, and opened the door for entirely new applications.

Clive Granger solved a particularly difficult problem concerning the complex interplay among macroeconomic variables over time. For example, when analyzing the effects of households' income and wealth on their consumption in the long run, it is difficult to distinguish adjustment towards a long-run relationship from short-run fluctuations in data. As we know, the value of wealth is highly affected by fluctuating share prices and property values. Moreover, like most macroeconomic variables, consumption, income and wealth do not fluctuate around given values over time, but around stochastic trends. When traditional statistical methods are applied to such nonstationary time series, the resulting relationships are often misleading, sometimes even nonsensical.

During the 1980s Granger succeeded in showing that systems of nonstationary variables are often driven by a single underlying common trend. He minted the term cointegration to describe such systems and demonstrated that cointegration provides a key to reliable statistical inference. Granger's methods are powerful tools that have wholly transformed work with time series, among both researchers and forecasters. Put simply, the methods naturally separate the dynamics in an economic system into forces that generate adjustment to long-run equilibrium and forces that only lead to short-run fluctuations.

During the same period, Robert Engle worked on another aspect of time series, to some extent inspired by two earlier Laureates. Theoretical work by Friedman and Lucas had shown that uncertainty, volatility, in macroeconomic variables could shape economic relationships, such as the sensitivity of unemployment to inflation: the slope of the well-known Phillips curve. Natural questions were then if, and how, volatility was changing over time; Engle devised the so-called ARCH method precisely to identify and analyze such patterns in the data.

It soon became clear, however, that the principal applications of the method would be in financial economics rather than macroeconomics. Investors who choose between stocks and bonds, firms which try to determine the value of derivatives, banks which want to limit the risk of large capital losses, all require forecasts on the riskiness of returns, that is, their volatility. Time series for returns on stocks, bonds and currencies also exhibit distinct patterns. Turbulent periods with high volatility on markets are followed by calmer periods. ARCH methods allows the forecaster to take account of these patterns which had not been possible before. The methods are now indispensable tools for risk evaluation throughout the world. They also became the starting point for a new field of research. Engle's breakthrough is a striking example of basic research, stirred by curiosity, which engendered unexpected applications in wholly new areas.

Dear Professor Engle,

Your contribution to economic sciences paved the way for the new field of financial econometrics. Your ARCH methods have unleashed a flood of applications, which help investors in financial markets to forecast volatility and manage their risks.

Dear Professor Granger,

Your contribution to economic sciences has transformed research and forecasting with macroeconomic time series. Your cointegration methods have given researchers and practitioners a statistical tool-kit to model and estimate economic dynamics.

It is a great honor and a privilege for me to convey to you, on behalf of the Royal Swedish Academy of Sciences, our warmest congratulations. I now ask you to receive the Prize from the hands of His Majesty the King.

ROBERT F. ENGLE III

"Wake up, Robin", a gentle hand shook my shoulder. "Let's go." It was so very early but I loved those mornings when my father would wake me and take me on an adventure. When I was a boy and we were camping, we would leave in the quiet morning hours to enjoy the lake together, and attempt to catch some fish. He was an experienced fisherman and a kindly teacher. While he was in graduate school at Cornell and the nation was still in the aftermath of the Great Depression, he traded fish and hunted meat for room and board. I did love those mornings and their crisp dawns.

My mother says that my father truly enjoyed having a son. My two years younger twin sisters felt that he didn't quite know how to enjoy them. But, I wasn't aware of those things then. So many of my childhood memories involve him. All the excursions into science were shaped by his knowledge and enthusiasm. As a Ph.D. chemist at Dupont, he also had access to many materials. So when my friend, Peter Hotz, and I decided to build and shoot off rockets, my Dad supplied different chemicals and a notebook. With each rocket we built, he would help us construct an explosive recipe. We had to write down the ingredients measuring carefully. He taught us to vary one ingredient at a time and then measure the effects. We recorded everything neatly. By the time he was finished, we had learned the scientific method and we had learned the math of measuring the distance that each rocket traveled. Of course, we also varied the rocket design. It was the way science should be done, passionately and carefully.

There were some experiments that Peter and I didn't tell him about. Like the time that we built mazes and caught flies to go through them. We found it difficult to measure their progress while they were flying, so we varied the experiment by removing their wings. It's a little painful to think about those boyish decisions now.

He also had a wonderfully equipped workshop where he built furniture and fixed all manner of things. One of my favorite tools was the lathe. My mother said that she always appreciated my constructions! As time progressed, the combination of the science explorations and the workshop led to many science fair entries culminating in the project that won the Philadelphia Science Fair in my Senior year of high school. For that experiment, I built a Van de Graff generator and ran experiments with it on X-ray transmission rates for thin metal sheets. The generator had a big copper toilet float to collect the static electricity and the X-ray tube was an old medical discard. A Geiger counter with homemade electronics recorded each X-ray photon as it passed through the test sample. It was pretty exciting stuff.

My mother was the unsung hero. She loved parenting the three of us and was always thinking up creative projects. We still watch the home slide shows she made of us and the neighborhood kids acting out fairy tales. She made the costumes, wrote the plays, and drove us to scenic locations around Philadelphia (the haunted house, the secret garden, etc). We all loved them. Except when I was supposed to kiss my sister, Sleeping Beauty, to awake her from the long sleep. I faked that part.

She also supervised our homework and made us feel that doing well in school was a wonderful thing. When I was in junior high school, she arranged for me to go to the Science Library at her alma mater, Swarthmore College. It was a small, beautiful place with wood shelves and books to the ceiling. I relished the time there looking through many books dreaming of when I would be able to really master science and be in the "big time".

Both of my parents nurtured my dreams and me. It was an idyllic childhood in many ways. We lived in a large somewhat ancient three-story house on 15 acres in Media, Pennsylvania just outside of Philadelphia. Both of my parents grew up in Philadelphia. My father, Robert Fry Engle, Jr., was named after his father who owned a lovely large hotel on the Jersey shore called the Engleside. Summers were spent in Beach Haven and school years in Philadelphia. My Dad didn't really like the hotel business and told stories about eating in the kitchen with the staff so that he didn't have to fuss every night with fancy clothes and fancy food. He loved to sail and won many races. We still have silver bowls and dishes from these events. Instead of the hotel business he headed off to Cornell where he earned a Ph.D. in chemistry.

The Engles were a Quaker (Society of Friends) family who emigrated from Cambridge, England in the 1600's. We assume that they came to escape religious persecution and set up their lives in Pennsylvania with the other Quakers. My great-grandfather, Robert Barkley Engle built the Engleside in 1876. A wonderful history of this has been recounted by John Bailey Lloyd in his book *Eighteen Miles of History* on Long Beach Island. The hotel was very successful for a time but two things eventually led to its demise. One was the spread of the use of the automobile. Families use to pack up and go to the beach for a month at a time bringing their servants with them. Once the bridges were built and cars became more common (and servants less common), families took shorter vacations bringing fewer people along. The second factor had to do with my grandmother, Sarah Atkinson. As a strict Quaker, she didn't believe in drinking and insisted that the hotel be dry. This opened up an opportunity for nearby hotels who then benefited from the additional revenue.

My father proposed to my mother on one of the round towers of the hotel. My mother said that she thought she was marrying into a rich family with a wonderful hotel. The hotel went bankrupt and was torn down a mere 4 years later. My father never seemed to regret the demise of the hotel. Probably he was relieved to know that he could proceed with his science and not be called in to take over a business that did not interest him.

Recently, my wife, Marianne and I went to find the location of the

Engleside. There is a park and another small hotel (also called the Engleside) on the land. Many of the old-timers recounted stories of the wonderful days of the Engleside. It gave us great pleasure. My mother also told me that she and my father took me to the Engleside when I was a baby just before it closed.

My mother's family had American, French, and Welsh origins. Her father, William Vernon Phillips, immigrated to Philadelphia as a young man with his three brothers and two sisters. They came from Cardiff and worked in the scrap metal business. Vernon had great success. His import and export iron and steel business, F.R. Phillips and Sons was based in Philadelphia and Milan, Italy. He was also President of the Phillips-Laffitte Company and Chairman of the Board of the Perry Buston Doane Company. He served as mayor of his town, president of his country club, and deacon in his church. During World War I he was Chief of the War Industry Board in Washington, D.C. and on the Council of National Defense. After the Great War, he received the Knight of the Crown of Italy from the King. His obituary called him "an eminent statesman and capitalist." He was clearly a busy man!

He married Florence Starr, a native of Philadelphia in 1912. They had three children, Billy, Isabel, and Mary whom they nicknamed Murry. In tragic succession, Isabel died of then unknown childhood ailments when she was 7, Billy was killed in an automobile accident when he was 16, and Vernon died of a heart attack in 1931 after the Crash of 1929. Murry and Florence were left on their own. They had to move from their beautiful home to smaller quarters. Murry remembers the sadness and loneliness of this time. One of her favorite memories is of the European tour that she took with her mother when she was 18. The pictures of that trip show a tall, slim beautifully dressed young woman full of charm and grace. She attended Swarthmore College majoring in French and then took numerous postgraduate courses in education at the University of Pennsylvania. Although an Episcopalian, she attended Friends schools throughout her life. When she married Bob Engle, she decided to join him in the Society of Friends and has been active her whole life in the Quaker community.

Once her children were older, she started to teach French at Media Friends School and eventually became its head. She sheparded the school through the addition of a junior and senior high school and a building campaign. She remained on its board for many years contributing both expertise and funds for new buildings and programs.

After she and my father married in 1939, they moved to Syracuse. I was born there on November 10, 1942 and soon after we moved back to the Philadelphia area in Swarthmore. These were happy times. I was named Robert Fry Engle III after my father and grandfather. Small Fry for short! They also had a favorite Springer spaniel named Dukie. My father had taken up ice dancing and there are pictures of my parents skating on ponds and at the Philadelphia Skating Club and Humane Society. They would hook up a record player to a car battery and play music while they skated outdoors.

Two years later, in December 1944, my twin sisters, Patricia Lee (Patty) and

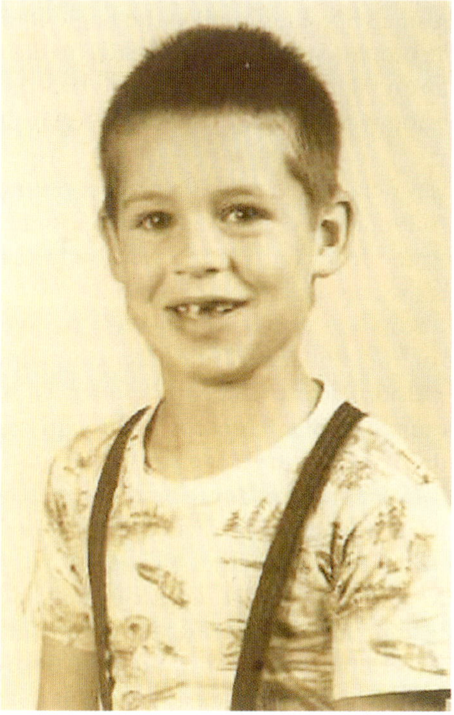

Rob with no teeth.

Sally Starr were born. It was a shock to have three children. Grandmother Florence Starr (nicknamed Twinkle) helped by taking me over to her apartment where I had a wonderful time visiting the giant steam engine trains and learning card games. In 1947, our family moved a few miles away to a big, old house in Media that the Engles called home until my mother sold the house following my father's death in 1983.

I was a very active child and adolescent. I loved science, sports, music, and friends. Our yard was so big that we crafted a sloping baseball diamond. After school, my friends would bicycle over and we would play until it got dark or our mothers' called. Eventually in high school I learned to play lacrosse and played goalie on the high school team. I began to play the tuba in junior high school. My teacher said that any tuba player should also know the string bass! I loved the instrument, took private lessons from Fred Maresch, a bass player of the Philadelphia Orchestra and was named to the All State Orchestra. Later, I played in the symphonies at Williams College, Cornell University, and MIT. Eventually my bass was stolen and I took up the cello. I still have my cello but it doesn't get much exercise.

I graduated as Valedictorian of Penncrest High School in 1960. Ours was the second graduating class of the newly built school. There are some things that I said in my valedictory address that I still believe. I talked about the need for science to be both relevant and sensitive to the needs of humanity and I emphasized the importance of a balanced life. I am still happiest when I can do research that others can apply widely and when my days have some time for ice dancing or skiing, cultural activities, traveling, and being with my wife and children.

My four years at Williams College were filled with fun, growing up, and more science. I decided to call myself "Rob" as it was more masculine and mature. I still use this today. I majored in Physics, joined the Beta Theta Pi fraternity, and played more lacrosse. In my sophomore year, I was named to the All American Team as a lacrosse goalie, which was quite a thrill. By senior year I was nominated to Phi Beta Kappa. Another delight was roaming all over the countryside going to the women's colleges looking for dates and parties on the weekends! I seemed to have one close girlfriend each year. Some of my best friends were made in the fraternity house although tragically, two of them, Stan Allen and Dave Kershaw, died young. They would have hooted with pleasure over the Nobel honor.

Academically, I started Physics and Math at the sophomore level since I had done advanced work and lots of outside reading in high school. A small event happened in my senior year that would have great consequences. I could take one more elective to finish out my courses. I almost took the religion course that everyone said was great, but I decided instead to try Introductory Economics. My roommate, Walt Nicholson, and many of my fraternity brothers were economics majors and spent hours discussing economic issues. I loved the course. It was interesting and came easily to me. Who could have predicted that this one elective would later serve as the catalyst that changed the course of my life?

During my senior year, my advisors in Physics encouraged me to apply to graduate school. It seemed natural since I had always dreamed of being a scientist. But something was lacking. I was losing my passion for physics. I did finally apply at the last minute and was accepted at Cornell and UC Berkeley. I called to accept Berkeley, but it was lunchtime. By the time they called back, my advisors had suggested I go to the famous labs at Cornell and so I did, following in my father's footsteps. I graduated from Williams Cum Laude with Highest Honors in Physics and went off to Ithaca, New York.

Graduate school had its own pleasures. I lived initially in Sage Hall, which was the graduate student dorm. It was wonderful to be on campus with both men and women. I began to date a girl who was an ice skater who took me to the Cornell Figure Skating Club to learn ice dancing. I was very pleased to be in an environment with families and skaters of all ages. As a child my father tried to get me to skate with him, but I had no interest. Now, I needed a new sport since my lacrosse days were over. Ice-skating began to look like a lot of fun. Men are always in short supply in ice dancing so there were plenty of talented pretty girls to help teach me. There was also Eddie Collins, a former Canadian competitor, who took me on as student. The girl friend quit the club and me, but I have enjoyed ice dancing since then.

I worked in Professor Watt Webb's lab doing low temperature physics and studied quantum mechanics from Nobel Laureate Hans Bethe. Watt Webb was a great advisor with lots of insight and creativity and the study of superconductivity was certainly exciting. However by mid-year, I realized that I did not want to spend the rest of my life as a physicist. Physics wasn't what I expected, or maybe, what I expected was what I realized I did not want anymore. Working in the bowels of a building on projects that interested very few people in the world held less interest for me. After agonizing over these feelings and talking to my friends, I approached Alfred Kahn, chairman of the Economics department at Cornell. I asked if his department would be interested in considering me for their Ph.D. program. Serendipitously, he said that an NDEA fellowship had just become available because the intended recipient had turned it down. He offered it to me but said that I needed to make an immediate decision or they would offer it to someone else. My head spinning, I accepted the offer. Now, I had to tell my father and Professor Webb. Both were supportive but with heavy hearts. My father had trained me to be a scientist and now I was leaving for one of those "soft" science fields. At that point, neither he nor I realized how important all that scientific training would be in my contributions to economics.

I loved economics. I attacked it with an energy that I had lost. I took undergraduate classes to make up my deficits in knowledge while I finished my Masters in Physics on using nuclear magnetic resonance to study the performance of a high temperature-superconducting magnet. Intriguingly, both superconductivity and NMR, now named MRI, were awarded Nobel prizes this year! In fact the superconductivity lab next to Webb's had been honored by the prize in 1996 and they were in the audience this year.

As I began the graduate program, my new advisor, Ta Chung Liu, was in Taiwan working with Chiang Kai Shek on their economic development plan. I took courses in Econometrics from Berndt Stigum where we read Malinvaud in its new English edition, and with John Fei who introduced me to modern microeconomics. My knowledge of math and statistics was put to use instantly. I took Kiefer's probability and Wolfowitz's statistics. I was extremely happy.

The next year, Ta Chung was back and I took his Econometrics class which gave me a solid basis for understanding the field. He was working on his third model of the U.S. economy. He had built an annual model and a quarterly model, having beaten the enormous Brookings Project to this goal. Now he was building a monthly model with all the new data and econometric problems that engendered. I learned trade from Ron Jones and Jaroslav Vanek, growth and development from John Fei and economic history from Woody Fleisig. It was so much fun. I found that I could solve the problems easily but quickly got stuck if I needed to formulate a problem. The casual discussions of short run and long run elasticities always required tremendous thought. It was probably ten years before I really absorbed the economic way of thinking.

The years spent in graduate school passed quickly. A few summers were spent in Washington, D.C. at the Bureau of the Budget doing program budgeting. I worked for John Deutsch who later became CIA director. It was there that I first tried to solve a cost benefit problem for public transportation. I recognized that land use was endogenous in the long run and this was critical for the analysis. This was my introduction to urban economics. I met John Kain and Charles Schultz.

As the years passed, my work became more focused on time series econometrics. Ta Chung suggested that I try to theoretically analyze the relationship between the different time scales for economic modeling. I was able to use some of my physics skills by formulating the problem in the frequency domain and applying Clive Granger's "typical spectral shape" for an economic time series. This was my first introduction to his work.

In January of 1968 another important event occurred. After a ski trip to Aspen, Colorado with friends, I returned to start the second semester. There was a party down the street and a beautiful new young woman caught my eye. She had graduated early from a California college and was just beginning graduate study in Child Development at Cornell. Her name was Marianne Eger and she became my wife in August 1969.

We were first good friends and then I asked her to come with me and my friend Linus Schrage on a week-long canoe trip to the Algonquin Wilderness in Canada. She had never slept in a tent or been in a canoe but she thought it might be fun. Her sense of adventure has been a hallmark of our married life. We love traveling the world, hiking, skiing, and snorkeling while meeting new people and appreciating natural environments. We have come to understand many of the world views that exist on this planet. Our children have embraced the sense of adventure and we continue to have great fun together.

She is also a wonderful intellectual companion and mother. Although I do not understand the intricacies of psychological theory and she, likewise, is not a trained economist, we discuss our ideas and careers with each other at length. And our children, Lindsey and Jordan, are the joys of our lives. I consider myself a very fortunate man.

Marianne was born in Presov, Slovakia and immigrated to the USA in 1949 when she was 2. Her mother, Edith Elefant, grew up in Kosice and was a teenage survivor of Auschwitz. Her parents perished there. She met her husband, Albert Bela Eger, at a recuperation spa after the war. He was a resistance fighter from Presov. After WW II, the Communists made life uncomfortable and they left after an assassination attempt. They were fortunate to receive a visa and joined his brother and her sister in Baltimore, Maryland. They had to leave the Eger fortune behind and like many immigrants, found a way to reinvent their lives. Bela became an accountant, Edith, a bookkeeper. Marianne, meanwhile, went to nursery school. The family moved to El Paso, Texas to pursue more lucrative opportunities. El Paso was good to the family but Marianne was ready to leave. She went to Whittier College on scholarship, graduated early and then went on to a Cornell.

Although our marriage made finishing her Ph.D. more difficult, Marianne did receive it 1978, two years after our daughter Lindsey, was born. She has gone on to have a very successful career as a clinical child psychologist and as a sports psychologist. She has an active speaking career. She even wrote a weekly food column for a number of years.

But I've gotten ahead of my story. We married on August 10, 1969. On that

Rob, Marianne, Jordan and Lindsey in Williamstown 2002.

day, I turned in my dissertation, received my Ph.D. and we left Cornell for good to take my first academic job at MIT. It was strange to arrive at a place with so many famous economists, none of whom were particularly interested in time series. For one overlapping year, Christopher Sims was at Harvard and a few years later, Jerry Hausman came to MIT. They were both helpful and enjoyable to talk with.

The first summer, 1970, I developed the theory for Band Spectrum Regression and attended the World Congress of the Econometric Society in Cambridge, England. I met economists there who have become lifelong friends and collaborators – Clive Granger, Ken Wallis, David Hendry. I began to go to London and the LSE every chance I could to pursue my fascination with time series. But finding my place was still complicated at MIT.

I enjoyed the teaching and the students there. Many of my students from that time have gone on to do quite well themselves: Larry Summers, Larry Backow, Ric Mishkin, Hal White, and many others. I even received an Outstanding Teacher of the Year Award from the graduate students. But I thought that my research needed a new focus.

Frank Fisher, Bob Solow, and Jerry Rothenberg encouraged me to join them on a new project to build a model of the city of Boston. A fellow economist and friend from Cornell, Tom O'Brien, was research head of the Boston Redevelopment Authority. Over the next 5 years and with many graduate students, the model took shape. I became an urban economist publishing very elaborate statistical models in a field not known for its mathematical sophistication.

Although MIT promoted me to Associate Professor, it was clear that I would not get tenure there. I wanted to work more in time series and I was attracted to Clive Granger's interest in spectral analysis. At a meeting in Washington, D.C., I asked him if his new university, UCSD, had any openings.

He said he'd check and I was invited to La Jolla, California to give a talk there. It was mid-winter, they housed me in a lovely hotel on the beach, a Williams Beta, Dick Attiyeh, was Economics Department Chair, Clive Granger had recently arrived – it was irresistible. I was hired as an Urban Economist and for years I did teach their urban economics course.

It was the beginning of a golden time for time series econometrics. Clive and I began an econometric seminar series, hired Hal White and later Jim Hamilton. We had funding for visitors and the best and brightest came from all over the world. We had numerous visits from David Hendry, Svend Hylleberg, Søren Johannson, Katerina Juselius, Timo Teräsvirta, Ken Wallis, Grayham Mizon, Tony Hall, Adrian Pagan, Max King, Giampierro Gallo, Tony Espasa, Keith MacLaren, Bernt Stigum, Eilev Jansen, Øivind Eitrheim, Helmut Lütkepohl, Hermann van Dijk and many others.

I took a sabbatical at LSE in 1979. Lindsey was then 2 and we rented a lovely row house in Hampstead with a back garden and a study in the back of the first floor. It was there that a new idea came.

I was interested in Milton Friedman's conjecture that inflation uncertainty was a central cause of business cycles. Investors who did not know what prices and wages would be in the future might invest less. To test this, a time series model was needed with variances that could change over time. There were two tools that came together to solve this problem. I had done a lot of work with the Kalman Filter and recognized that a one step predictive density would be sufficient to define a likelihood function. The second tool was a test. Clive had recently proposed a test for bilinear time series models. He came by my computer one day before I left and suggested I square the residuals and then fit an autoregression. To my amazement, it was quite significant. I suspected that this test was the optimal Lagrange Multiplier test for some new type of model, but not the bilinear model. I was later to discover that it is indeed the optimal test for ARCH and it is so called today.

Lunch and tea at the LSE were very stimulating times for me. Each day I would get a little further on this new model and would talk with Sargan or Durbin or Hendry or Harvey about its properties and my proofs. David Hendry eventually named it AutoRegressive Conditional Heteroskedasticity and offered to have Frank Srba program it. We applied it to UK inflation data and the ARCH model was launched.

Looking back now, one might think that new ideas are easy to publish. At least for me, they are not. It took quite a bit of rewriting and persuading to finally get it accepted in *Econometrica*. In fact, I don't think that any of my papers have had an easy time of it!

Coming back to La Jolla, I was pleased that two events had occurred. The ARCH model was on its way and so was our son, Jordan, who was born in May 1980. I became very interested in Clive's new concept of low frequency correlation that he called cointegration. It seemed to me that the new tests for unit roots of Dickey and Fuller, which had been so successfully applied by Nelson and Plosser, could be extended to this case. So I constructed an econometric approach to estimation and testing of cointegrated systems.

The ARCH Cafe in Sydney. My favorite!

Initially we wrote two joint papers and presented these at a time series meeting at UC Davis. There was a lot of discussion with many opinions as to whether this was a big or a small innovation. We decided to put these together but again, it took rewriting and persuasion, before *Econometrica* accepted this one too. Clive lost patience and published another version of the paper in the Oxford Bulletin.

Also, my excellent students, Mark Watson and Tim Bollerslev were busy. Mark had carried the Kalman Filter and state space models to a wide range of problems in macroeconometrics. We wrote a paper combining factor analysis and time series modeling and called it DYMIMIC. His first job was at Harvard where he worked with Jim Stock on models of leading indicators. This eventually became an official NBER business cycle forecasting model. Tim took the ARCH model, added a moving average and created GARCH. The GARCH model is an infinite order ARCH model with a geometrically declining set of weights. This extension made the model even more useful. The simplest GARCH model often performs successfully in a wide range of data.

Although these lines of research are now the most visible, there were a lot of other interesting things going on. I had visited LSE in 1975 on a Ken Wallis grant. There I learned about Lagrange Multiplier Tests and wrote a series of papers of which the Handbook of Econometrics survey is the one that gets the most attention. I gave a talk at C.O.R.E. and got into a big argument with Jean Francois Richard on the meaning of exogeneity. Afterward we looked up Koopmans' definition and realized there were two different notions which we dubbed weak and strong exogeneity. The difference between these two was Clive's concept of "Granger Causality" which was being used as a test for exogeneity by many authors. We invited David Hendry to join us, added a characterization of "super exogeneity" to deal with the "Lucas Critique" and wrote a quite controversial paper. After the dust settled, the paper was published by *Econometrica* and the profession has more or less accepted these exogeneity concepts.

Ramu Ramanathan, Clive and I founded a small consulting company, QUERI, that was dedicated to doing econometric research. We spent many happy hours on EPRI (Electric Power Research, Inc.) and other projects working with excellent graduate students to estimate better electricity demand systems, or load factor systems, or weather sensitivity models. These models have found an important place in electric utilities and in EPRI research, but only the spline model done with John Rice has received much academic attention. I wonder whether we would have been involved in the California energy crisis if QUERI had still be in existence?

I loved going to the European meetings of the Econometric Society. Time series was a big part of the program each summer. The meetings were invariably in nice places and we developed long term friendships that were renewed annually. By the mid 80's these meetings featured multiple sessions on cointegration and ARCH. It was so exciting to see the new directions people were taking this research. We kept working to keep up with these fast flowing fields of research. Each year we would have several students working on these topics. Many of these students have had highly successful careers in and out of universities.

The profession rapidly developed a wide range of extensions of ARCH and GARCH models. Dan Nelson who sadly passed away at a very early age, introduced the Exponential GARCH model called the EGARCH. This model allowed an asymmetric response to returns. This was followed by many versions with names – TARCH, GJR-GARCH, NARCH, VGARCH, APARCH, FIGARCH, FIE-GARCH, STARCH, SWARCH, CES-GARCH, SQGARCH, component GARCH and many more. It was an exciting time. Students such as Gary Lee, Ding, Raul Susmel, Victor Ng, Ted Hong, and Ray Chou contributed to this growing literature.

As my research career developed, so did my ice skating hobby. I began skating with Brigit Luciani and we competed in many adult competitions. We often were successful in regional competitions. I passed my gold dance test around 1990 and shortly after that we did a week long workshop with Jane Torvill and Christopher Dean, legendary innovative ice dance champions. Finally, the United States Figure Skating Association agreed to have a national adult skating competition. The first year was 1995 in Wilmington Delaware. There were 21 teams and we eventually ended up 4th. We were very pleased. In 1996 we managed to move up to second place. Later I began skating with Dr. Wendy Buchi and we were again quite successful, placing second in 1999. I've had lots of incredible coaches over the years including Barret Brown, Michelle Ford, Jeannie Miley, Kent Weigle, Tatiana Navka, Judy Blumberg, and now Natalia Dubova and Eve Chalom. When I am skating, economics is far away. I always return refreshed and ready to carry on.

Ultimately, my interests gravitated more and more to finance. My colleagues David Lilien and Mike Rothschild and wonderful graduate students, Russ Robins, Victor Ng, Ken Kroner, Mustafa Choudhury and Aaron Smith helped me see this new way of thinking. The trade-off between risk and return was a central feature of financial analysis and the ARCH model had a mechanism for measuring this. We called it the ARCH-M model. A multivariate version with Tim Bollerslev and Jeff Wooldridge generalized the Capital

David Hendry and Rob after a great meal at the Waterside Inn outside London.

Asset Pricing Model, CAPM. Options markets traded volatility and gave a quantitative validation of the ARCH models. Alex Kane, Jaesun Noh and I explored the possibility of using GARCH to trade options; it was temporarily successful. We flirted with the idea of managing money or investing our own but ultimately didn't take that route. I ran several conferences in San Diego on the ARCH model designed for both academics and practitioners. I remember being so delighted that finance faculty such as Michael Brennan, Eduardo Schwartz and Bill Schwert came. It was a peek into a new profession. I knew Michael from MIT where I had stepped in to be part of his thesis committee when I first arrived. He was about my age and we still joke about how he is my first student. The rest of the committee was Franco Modigliani and Myron Scholes – a hat trick!

Gradually this new area of research became known as financial econometrics. It is the development of statistical tools specifically designed for financial applications. At conferences and meetings there were now quite a few sessions on financial econometrics. At UCSD we developed a specialization in financial econometrics. The arrival of Bruce Lehman and Allan Timmerman were very important in buttressing the finance side of this research area.

As these ideas spread around the globe, I was increasingly asked to give long workshops or mini-courses. This was fun as a travel experience and introduced me to students I still meet. The first was in Nairobi where Marianne and I were able to spend time with Jim Tobin and his wife. We did a short course at Peoples University in Beijing in 1995 flanked by Gregory Chow and Angus Deaton. Mini-courses in Maastrict, Bagni di Lucca, Helsinki, Uppsala, Madrid, London, Sydney, Stockholm, Vienna, Vaasa, and Rotterdam followed and gave opportunities for me to survey research in particular areas.

Joint work with Sharon Kozicki, Farshid Vahid, Joao Issler and Raul Susmel introduced another idea into econometrics - common features. This is a generalization of factor analysis that has applications to cointegrated systems, multivariate ARCH models and many areas of economics. The goal is to simplify multivariate systems into a small number of variables that endow the system with its typical features. In this case the features are common. This simplifies analysis in a way that is widely used in financial research. I will be surprised if there aren't important research developments using common features in the next few years.

Somewhat later Simone Manganelli and I developed a new approach to measuring the extremes of a distribution. This method quantifies the probability of large losses on a portfolio by predicting the future quantiles. It has the tastiest name of any of my models, the CAViaR model. It stands for conditional autoregressive value at risk. Peter Hansen came up with this clever mnemonic. The CAViaR model uses the theory of regression quantiles in a time series context to give an updating formula for the Value at Risk (extreme quantile) of a portfolio.

In the early 1990's I gave my first talks to financial practitioners. In a series of RISK meetings and Q-Group meetings, I introduced the audience to ARCH models and learned about the fascinating questions facing practitioners doing risk management and derivatives trading. I began a consulting project at Salomon Brothers in building seven of the World Trade Center. This project with Joe Mezrich and Eric Sorensen was to incorporate the GARCH model into a series of client oriented trading systems. Volatility forecasts and trading strategies were proposed based on innovative models. Advanced software developed by Pat Burns and Aslihan Salih, was used to structure client and proprietary portfolio strategies. I learned a great deal from this experience and made many contacts throughout the financial world.

I was asked to serve on the steering committee of a Zurich Financial Services company, Olsen and Associates, who were doing path breaking work on the analysis of very high frequency financial data. They were partly data vendors who delivered tick by tick currency and other data to a collection of European clients, and partly model builders. Richard Olsen and Michel Dacarogna proposed joint academic/practitioner conferences on the use of these data. In the first high frequency data conference, the same data set was analyzed by statisticians, economists, physicists, financial practitioners, and traders. The comparison was fascinating and highly informative.

Jeff Russell and I wrestled with the question of what we could learn from such high frequency data. Every way of handling the data in calendar time involved a loss of information. One day we realized that we could treat the time between trades as a random variable itself and model the speed of trading. We developed the Autoregressive Conditional Duration or ACD model for this purpose. It is a Poisson process with an intensity that is conditional on the past information. Financial data show variations in trading rates that can be called duration clustering. The model we proposed had the same structure as the GARCH model and recognizes the close relation between trading inten-

Rob and Wendy Buchi in National Adult Ice Dance competion in Lake Placid 1997.

sity and volatility. The simple ACD(1,1) very rapidly led to generalizations with different functional forms, error densities and types of data. Initially we only observed quotes so we built a model for the time it took for prices to move a fixed amount. The ACD model of such price durations is really an alternative volatility model. Then we obtained transactions data and modeled the time between trades. In the Fisher Schultz Lecture that I gave in Istanbul, I combined the time between trades and the prices at which trades occurred into an "ultra high frequency" or tick by tick GARCH model.

Although there was a lot of interest in the statistical model of trade arrivals, some economists at the time thought this was a model of the least interesting variable in finance. I was convinced that the trading frequency measured a fundamental heartbeat of financial markets. Clearly it reflected the flow of information. It turns out also to be closely related to measures of liquidity. I began reading the literature on market microstructure and soon came to Maureen O'Hara and David Easley(1992). Maureen was also on the Olsen steering committee and I recognized that the speed of trading was related to information flow in their model and had a direct link with measures of liquidity such as bid-ask spread and price impact. In papers with Alfonso

Dufour, Joe Lange and Andrew Patton, we showed that when markets are more active, in the sense that the time between trades is short, they are less liquid. Information flows correspond to illiquid markets over time.

This research leads naturally to an interest in timing of trades to achieve good execution. Several years later, a group at Morgan Stanley headed by Robert Ferstenberg and Rohit d'Soza approached me and I have spent many interesting days with them developing a microstructure approach to optimizing and evaluating trades. We have become good friends as we push this frontier between theory and practice.

New York was a very exciting place to visit when I was consulting for Salomon. Now that Lindsey and Jordan were both on their own, I convinced Marianne to spend the fall semester of 1999 visiting NYU in the finance department. I knew many people there. My sister, Patty, had also moved there to work as the child development officer for UNICEF. Joel Hasbrouck was the leading microstructure econometrician; Steve Figlewski, who was a student of mine many years ago at MIT, was a leading empirical options researcher, and my recent student Josh Rosenberg was there. The semester was too short. I saw the financial markets at work and got to know more finance faculty. We ate well and played hard. When NYU offered me a permanent position, I took it and we moved in September 2000. I thought we would stay for only a year, but even that was not enough. Eventually I retired from UCSD, becoming an emeritus professor. We maintain close ties with San Diego as we have a house there where we spend summers and have lots of friends. UCSD has kept my office and I still see a few students.

Since I have been in New York, my work has actually moved back to volatility models, but in large multivariate systems. The extension of ARCH models from univariate processes to multivariate processes began in the early 1980's. Ken Kroner and I introduced one new family, he and Victor Ng introduced another and Tim Bollerslev introduced a third. However, there have not yet been many empirical applications of these models. This is because they are difficult to specify, estimate and interpret. In a new general class of models called Dynamic Conditional Correlation or DCC models, I have developed a potential solution. This class is parsimonious and appears to give satisfactory performance for both small and large systems. In a series of lectures at Erasmus University in May 2003, this model was fully described and these lectures will soon appear as a Princeton University Press monograph.

To evaluate alternative covariance matrices, I have developed a loss function with Riccardo Colacito, based on the effectiveness for asset allocation. The same model can be applied to Credit Risk as the correlation between defaults is determined by the dynamic structure of the covariance matrix and the tail properties of the model. New high frequency volatility models have come out of research with Giampiero Gallo and models for the volatility of volatility have been developed with Isao Ishida. The new and interesting research topics that have opened up since I have been in New York are a constant source of stimulation.

While professional interests have always been important in my life, so have my family and my hobbies. Marianne and I have had a wonderful busy time raising Lindsey and Jordan. We stay as close as we can to them and over the years they have traveled with us all over the world. Lindsey was always a fine student and devoted ballerina. Her warm, friendly personality and her strong determination have led to much success for her and a good time for us. She has been a wonderful sister to her younger brother. When she was a baby, she would come to my office one day a week and sleep on a mat behind a chair to take her nap. She would come to lunch with Clive and the other economists. Unfortunately, all that good input didn't lead to a career in economics! She graduated from Princeton Cum Laude in anthropology and has now finished a Ph.D. in developmental psychology at UCLA. In May, 2003, she married Justin Richland, JD, a legal anthropologist from Los Angeles, also finishing his Ph.D. They both hope to have careers in academia.

Jordan is the outgoing charmer. He is a wonderful athlete, excellent soccer player, and has a probing mind. He graduated from Williams College in English literature with a certificate in theater and is now in Los Angeles working as an actor and cinematographer. During his college years, he spent 2 semesters at the University of Cape Town, South Africa. He was very affected by the country and its people. Our trip with him to Botswana was a highlight for us. Jordan can talk to anyone comfortably and learn about them. He is also an excellent writer. His career path will be an interesting one. As a brother and a son, he is a pleasure for all of us. He has had lots of girlfriends and was especially sorry that the Swedish princesses did not seem interested in him!!

My sisters Sally and Patty have also had very successful careers and I am so proud of them. It is remarkable how many parallels there are among us. I guess it must be something about either genetics or our upbringing. Sally received her Ph.D. in Anthropology and has been teaching at Wellesley for 30 years. She developed an interest in the relation between legal systems and cultural systems. This lead to books on Urban Danger in Boston, the ways of Getting Justice and Getting Even in and outside the Massachusetts court system, law, culture and the U.S. colonization in Hawaii, human rights and the U.N. and lots of papers with sharp insights into modern society. She was president of the Law and Society Association and a regular visitor at the American Bar Foundation. She is now being courted by NYU and the University of Pennsylvania. Maybe there will be another Engle in New York.

Patty received her Ph.D. in psychology at Stanford and has spent a career studying cross cultural child development focusing often on the role of nutrition. She has been involved in projects in Guatemala, Nicaragua, Peru, Uganda, India, and many other places. Her academic publications describe many of these research settings; her students and colleagues at her long time university, California State University at San Louis Obisbo, were able to hear about these first hand. Her current position as Senior Advisor for Child Development at UNICEF in New York gives her scope to pursue the goal of child health from a broad perspective. She has become a vocal advocate for global children as she works to improve the quality of life in so many different cultures.

A stable, happy home life is good for all of us and allows us each to focus on our careers knowing that when we are back together, there is more to share. As a family we love food, wine, music, opera, art, theater, traveling, hiking, fishing, and watching sports. Separately we have our individual career paths and our hobbies. It makes for a rich interaction. I still ice skate 2-3 times a week. I enjoy skating with Wendy Buchi when I am in La Jolla. Marianne is learning to play golf. Lindsey runs with her dogs, Jordan finds soccer games and surfs when he can.

The Nobel Prize in Economics is an incredible recognition for the work that my students, colleagues and I have done over the years. We all worked hard but we were also lucky that the financial applications were so important. It continues to amaze me how far this simple idea has traveled. I am starting a Financial Econometrics Research Center at NYU to foster the continuing development of this field.

As I look back over my career, this Prize is the high point. I find myself reflecting with great affection on smaller, perhaps less dramatic, moments. These are moments of insight; moments that started a new research topic or recognized a connection between things previously thought to be distinct. These are also moments of family time – wonderful moments with Lindsey and Jordan, sharing ideas, eating, hiking, skiing and yes, even fishing - and moments with my lifelong companion and soul-mate, Marianne. It has been already a lengthy and varied career but I think I am only part way through it. There are many exciting adventures in our future and I am looking forward to ever so many special moments more.

RISK AND VOLATILITY: ECONOMETRIC MODELS AND FINANCIAL PRACTICE

Nobel Lecture, December 8, 2003[1]

by

ROBERT F. ENGLE III

New York University, Department of Finance (Salomon Centre), 44 West Fourth Street, New York, NY 10012-1126, USA.

INTRODUCTION

The advantage of knowing about risks is that we can change our behavior to avoid them. Of course, it is easily observed that to avoid all risks would be impossible; it might entail no flying, no driving, no walking, eating and drinking only healthy foods and never being touched by sunshine. Even a bath could be dangerous. I could not receive this prize if I sought to avoid all risks. There are some risks we choose to take because the benefits from taking them exceed the possible costs. Optimal behavior takes risks that are worthwhile. This is the central paradigm of finance; we must take risks to achieve rewards but not all risks are equally rewarded. Both the risks and the rewards are in the future, so it is the expectation of loss that is balanced against the expectation of reward. Thus we optimize our behavior, and in particular our portfolio, to maximize rewards and minimize risks.

This simple concept has a long history in economics and in Nobel citations. Markowitz (1952) and Tobin (1958) associated risk with the variance in the value of a portfolio. From the avoidance of risk they derived optimizing portfolio and banking behavior. Sharpe (1964) developed the implications when all investors follow the same objectives with the same information. This theory is called the Capital Asset Pricing Model or CAPM, and shows that there is a natural relation between expected returns and variance. These contributions were recognized by Nobel prizes in 1981 and 1990.

Black and Scholes (1972) and Merton (1973) developed a model to evaluate the pricing of options. While the theory is based on option replication arguments through dynamic trading strategies, it is also consistent with the CAPM. Put options give the owner the right to sell an asset at a particular

[1] This paper is the result of more than two decades of research and collaboration with many many people. I would particularly like to thank the audiences in B.I.S., Stockholm, Uppsala, Cornell and the University de Savoie for listening as this talk developed. David Hendry, Tim Bollerslev, Andrew Patton and Robert Ferstenberg provided detailed suggestions. Nevertheless, all lacunas remain my responsibility.

price at a time in the future. Thus these options can be thought of as insurance. By purchasing such put options, the risk of the portfolio can be completely eliminated. But what does this insurance cost? The price of protection depends upon the risks and these risks are measured by the variance of the asset returns. This contribution was recognized by a 1997 Nobel prize.

When practitioners implemented these financial strategies, they required estimates of the variances. Typically the square root of the variance, called the volatility, was reported. They immediately recognized that the volatilities were changing over time. They found different answers for different time periods. A simple approach, sometimes called *historical volatility*, was and remains widely used. In this method, the volatility is estimated by the sample standard deviation of returns over a short period. But, what is the right period to use? If it is too long, then it will not be so relevant for today and if it is too short, it will be very noisy. Furthermore, it is really the volatility over a future period that should be considered the risk, hence a forecast of volatility is needed as well as a measure for today. This raises the possibility that the forecast of the average volatility over the next week might be different from the forecast over a year or a decade. Historical volatility had no solution for these problems.

On a more fundamental level, it is logically inconsistent to assume, for example, that the variance is constant for a period such as one year ending today and also that it is constant for the year ending on the previous day but with a different value. A theory of dynamic volatilities is needed; this is the role that is filled by the ARCH models and their many extensions that we discuss today.

In the next section, I will describe the genesis of the ARCH model, and then discuss some of its many generalizations and widespread empirical support. In subsequent sections, I will show how this dynamic model can be used to forecast volatility and risk over a long horizon and how it can be used to value options.

THE BIRTH OF THE ARCH MODEL

The ARCH model was invented while I was on sabbatical at the London School of Economics in 1979. Lunch in the Senior Common Room with David Hendry, Dennis Sargan, Jim Durbin and many leading econometricians provided a stimulating environment. I was looking for a model that could assess the validity of a conjecture of Milton Friedman (1977) that the unpredictability of inflation was a primary cause of business cycles. He hypothesized that the level of inflation was not a problem; it was the uncertainty about future costs and prices that would prevent entrepreneurs from investing and lead to a recession. This could only be plausible if the uncertainty were changing over time so this was my goal. Econometricians call this heteroskedasticity. I had recently worked extensively with the Kalman Filter and knew that a likelihood function could be decomposed into the sum of its predictive or conditional densities. Finally, my colleague Clive Granger with whom I share this prize, had recently developed a test for bilinear time series models based on the dependence over time of squared residuals. That is, squared residuals often were autocorrelated even though the residuals themselves were not. This test was frequently significant in economic data; I suspected that it was detecting something besides bilinearity but I didn't know what.

The solution was *autoregressive conditional heteroskedasticity* or ARCH, a name invented by David Hendry. The ARCH model described the forecast variance in terms of current observables. Instead of using short or long sample standard deviations, the ARCH model proposed taking weighted averages of past squared forecast errors, a type of weighted variance. These weights could give more influence to recent information and less to the distant past. Clearly the ARCH model was a simple generalization of the sample variance.

The big advance was that the weights could be estimated from historical data even though the true volatility was never observed. Here is how this works. Forecasts can be calculated every day or every period. By examining these forecasts for different weights, the set of weights can be found that make the forecasts closest to the variance of the next return. This procedure, based on Maximum Likelihood, gives a systematic approach to the estimation of the optimal weights. Once the weights are determined, this dynamic model of time varying volatility can be used to measure the volatility at any time and to forecast it into the near and distant future. Granger's test for bilinearity turned out to be the optimal or Lagrange Multiplier test for ARCH and is widely used today.

There are many benefits to formulating an explicit dynamic model of volatility. As mentioned above, the optimal parameters can be estimated by Maximum Likelihood. Tests of the adequacy and accuracy of a volatility model can be used to verify the procedure. One-step and multi-step forecasts can be constructed using these parameters. The unconditional distributions can be established mathematically and are generally realistic. Inserting the relevant variables into the model can test economic models that seek to determine the causes of volatility. Incorporating additional endogenous variables and equations can similarly test economic models about the consequences of volatility. Several applications will be mentioned below.

David Hendry's associate, Frank Srba wrote the first ARCH program. The application that appeared in Engle (1982) was to inflation in the U.K. since this was Friedman's conjecture. While there was plenty of evidence that the uncertainty in inflation forecasts was time varying, it did not correspond to the U.K. business cycle. Similar tests for U.S. inflation data, reported in Engle (1983), confirmed the finding of ARCH but found no business cycle effect. While the trade-off between risk and return is an important part of macroeconomic theory, the empirical implications are often difficult to detect as they are disguised by other dominating effects, and obscured by the reliance on relatively low frequency data. In finance, the risk/return effects are of primary importance and data on daily or even intra-daily frequencies are readily available to form accurate volatility forecasts. Thus finance is the field in which the great richness and variety of ARCH models developed.

GENERALIZING THE ARCH MODEL

Generalizations to different weighting schemes can be estimated and tested. The very important development by my outstanding student Tim Bollerslev (1986), called Generalized Autoregressive Conditional Heteroskedasticity or GARCH, is today the most widely used model. This essentially generalizes the purely autoregressive ARCH model to an autoregressive moving average model. The weights on past squared residuals are assumed to decline geometrically at a rate to be estimated from the data. An intuitively appealing interpretation of the GARCH (1,1) model is easy to understand. The GARCH forecast variance is a weighted average of three different variance forecasts. One is a constant variance that corresponds to the long run average. The second is the forecast that was made in previous period. The third is the new information that was not available when the previous forecast was made. This could be viewed as a variance forecast based on one period of information. The weights on these three forecasts determine how fast the variance changes with new information and how fast it reverts to its long run mean.

A second enormously important generalization was the Exponential GARCH or EGARCH model of Dan Nelson (1992) who prematurely passed away in 1995 to the great loss of our profession as eulogized by Bollerslev and Rossi (1995). In his short academic career, his contributions were extremely influential. He recognized that volatility could respond asymmetrically to past forecast errors. In a financial context, negative returns seemed to be more important predictors of volatility than positive returns. Large price declines forecast greater volatility than similarly large price increases. This is an economically interesting effect that has wide ranging implications to be discussed below.

Further generalizations have been proposed by many researchers. There is now an alphabet soup of ARCH models that include: AARCH, APARCH, FIGARCH, FIEGARCH, STARCH, SWARCH, GJR-GARCH, TARCH, MARCH, NARCH, SNPARCH, SPARCH, SQGARCH, CESGARCH, Component ARCH, Asymmetric Component ARCH, Taylor-Schwert, Student-t-ARCH, GED-ARCH, and many others that I have regrettably overlooked. Many of these models were surveyed in Bollerslev, Chou and Kroner (1992), Bollerslev (1994), Engle (2002b), and Engle and Ishida (2002). These models recognize that there may be important non-linearity, asymmetry and long memory properties of volatility and that returns can be non-normal with a variety of parametric and non-parametric distributions.

A closely related but econometrically distinct class of volatility models called Stochastic Volatility or SV models have also seen dramatic development. See for example, Clark (1973), Taylor (1986), Harvey, Ruiz and Shephard (1994), Taylor (1994). These models have a different data generating process which makes them more convenient for some purposes but more difficult to estimate. In a linear framework, these models would simply be different representations of the same process; but in this non-linear setting, the alternative specifications are not equivalent, although they are close approximations.

MODELING FINANCIAL RETURNS

The success of the ARCH family of models is attributable in large measure to the applications in finance. While the models have applicability for many statistical problems with time series data, they find particular value for financial time series. This is partly because of the importance of the previously discussed trade-off between risk and return for financial markets, and partly because of three ubiquitous characteristics of financial returns from holding a risky asset. Returns are almost unpredictable, they have surprisingly large numbers of extreme values and both the extremes and quiet periods are clustered in time. These features are often described as *unpredictability, fat tails* and *volatility clustering.* These are precisely the characteristics for which an ARCH model is designed. When volatility is high, it is likely to remain high, and when it is low it is likely to remain low. However, these periods are time limited so that the forecast is sure to eventually revert to less extreme volatilities. An ARCH process produces dynamic, mean reverting patterns in volatility that can be forecast. It also produces a greater number of extremes than would be expected from a standard normal distribution, since the extreme values during the high volatility period are greater than could be anticipated from a constant volatility process.

The GARCH (1,1) specification is the workhorse of financial applications. It is remarkable that one model can be used to describe the volatility dynamics of almost any financial return series. This applies not only to US stocks but also to stocks traded in most developed markets, to most stocks traded in emerging markets, and to most indices of equity returns. It applies to exchange rates, bond returns and commodity returns. In many cases, a slightly better model can be found in the list of models above, but GARCH is generally a very good starting point.

The widespread success of GARCH (1,1) begs to be understood. What theory can explain why volatility dynamics are similar in so many different financial markets? In developing such a theory, we must first understand why asset prices change. Financial assets are purchased and owned because of the future payments that can be expected. Because these payments are uncertain and depend upon unknowable future developments, the fair price of the asset will require forecasts of the distribution of these payments based on our best information today. As time goes by, we get more information on these future events and re-value the asset. So at a basic level, financial price volatility is due to the arrival of new information. Volatility clustering is simply clustering of information arrivals. The fact that this is common to so many assets is simply a statement that news is typically clustered in time.

To see why it is natural for news to be clustered in time, we must be more specific about the information flow. Consider an event such as an invention that will increase the value of a firm because it will improve future earnings and dividends. The effect on stock prices of this event will depend on economic conditions in the economy and in the firm. If the firm is near bankruptcy, the effect can be very large and if it is already operating at full capacity, it may be small. If the economy has low interest rates and surplus labor, it may be easy to develop this new product. With everything else equal, the response will be greater in a recession than in a boom period. Hence we are not surprised to find higher volatility in economic downturns even if the arrival rate of new inventions is constant. This is a slow moving type of volatility clustering that can give cycles of several years or longer.

The same invention will also give rise to a high frequency volatility clustering. When the invention is announced, the market will not immediately be able to estimate its value on the stock price. Agents may disagree but be sufficiently unsure of their valuations that they pay attention to how others value the firm. If an investor buys until the price reaches his estimate of the new value, he may revise his estimate after he sees others continue to buy at successively higher prices. He may suspect they have better information or models and consequently raise his valuation. Of course, if the others are selling, then he may revise his price downward. This process is generally called *price discovery* and has been modeled theoretically and empirically in market microstructure. It leads to volatility clustering at a much higher frequency than we have seen before. This process could last a few days or a few minutes.

But to understand volatility we must think of more than one invention. While the arrival rate of inventions may not have clear patterns, other types of news surely do. The news intensity is generally high during wars and economic distress. During important global summits, congressional or regulatory hearings, elections or central bank board meetings, there are likely to be many news events. These episodes are likely to be of medium duration, lasting weeks or months.

The empirical volatility patterns we observe are composed of all three of these types of events. Thus we expect to see rather elaborate volatility dynamics and often rely on long time series to give accurate models of the different time constants.

MODELING THE CAUSES AND CONSEQUENCES OF FINANCIAL VOLATILITY

Once a model has been developed to measure volatility, it is natural to attempt to explain the causes of volatility and the effects of volatility on the economy. There is now a large literature examining aspects of these questions. I will only give a discussion of some of the more limited findings for financial markets.

In financial markets, the consequences of volatility are easy to describe although perhaps difficult to measure. In an economy with one risky asset, a rise in volatility should lead investors to sell some of the asset. If there is a fixed supply, the price must fall sufficiently so that buyers take the other side. At this new lower price, the expected return is higher by just enough to compensate investors for the increased risk. In equilibrium, high volatility should correspond to high expected returns. Merton (1980) formulated this theoretical model in continuous time, and Engle, Lilien and Robins (1987) pro-

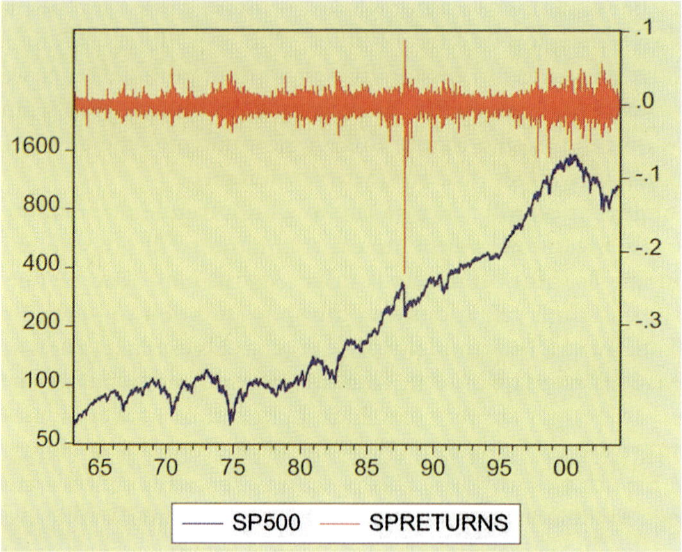

Figure 1. S&P 500 Daily Prices and Returns from January 1963 to November 2003.

posed a discrete time model. If the price of risk were constant over time, then rising conditional variances would translate linearly into rising expected returns. Thus the mean of the return equation would no longer be estimated as zero, it would depend upon the past squared returns exactly in the same way that the conditional variance depends on past squared returns. This very strong coefficient restriction can be tested and used to estimate the price of risk. It can also be used to measure the coefficient of relative risk aversion of the representative agent under the same assumptions.

Empirical evidence on this measurement has been mixed. While Engle *et al.* (1987) find a positive and significant effect, Chou, Engle and Kane (1992), and Glosten, Jagannathan and Runkle (1993), find a relationship that varies over time and may be negative because of omitted variables. French, Schwert and Stambaugh (1987) showed that a positive volatility surprise should and does have a negative effect on asset prices. There is not simply one risky asset in the economy and the price of risk is not likely to be constant, hence the instability is not surprising and does not disprove the existence of the risk return trade-off, but it is a challenge to better modeling of this trade-off.

The causes of volatility are more directly modeled. Since the basic ARCH model and its many variants describe the conditional variance as a function of lagged squared returns, these are perhaps the proximate causes of volatility. It is best to interpret these as observables that help in forecasting volatility rather than as causes. If the true causes were included in the specification, then the lags would not be needed.

A small collection of papers has followed this route. Andersen and Bollerslev (1998b) examined the effects of announcements on exchange rate

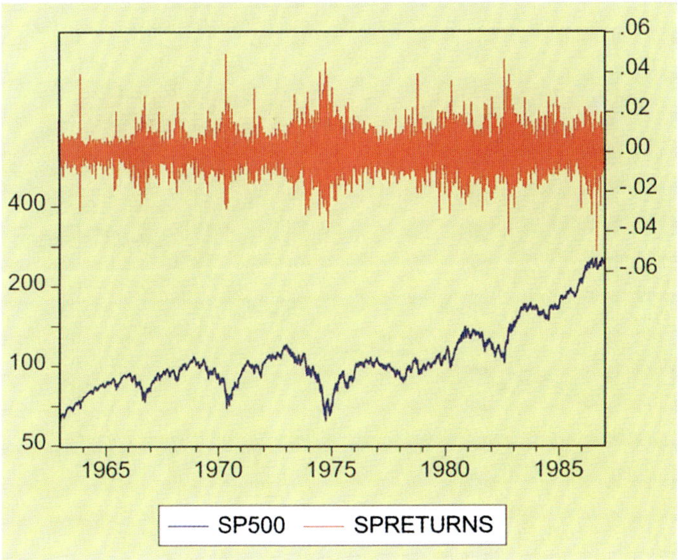

Figure 2. S&P 500 Daily Before 1987.

volatility. The difficulty in finding important explanatory power is clear even if these announcements are responsible in important ways. Another approach is to use the volatility measured in other markets. Engle, Ng and Rothschild (1990) find evidence that stock volatility causes bond volatility in the future. Engle, Ito and Lin (1990) model the influence of volatility in markets with earlier closing on markets with later closing. For example, they examine the influence of currency volatilities in European, Asian markets and the prior day US market on today's US currency volatility. Hamao, Masulis and Ng (1990), Burns, Engle and Mezrich (1998), and others have applied similar techniques to global equity markets.

AN EXAMPLE

To illustrate the use of ARCH models for financial applications, I will give a rather extended analysis of the Standard and Poors 500 Composite index. This index represents the bulk of the value in the US equity market. I will look at daily levels of this index from 1963 through late November 2003. This gives a sweep of US financial history that provides an ideal setting to discuss how ARCH models are used for risk management and option pricing. All the statistics and graphs are computed in EViews™ 4.1.

The raw data are presented in (Figure 1) where prices are shown on the left axis. The rather smooth lower curve shows what has happened to this index over the last 40 years. It is easy to see the great growth of equity prices over the period and the subsequent decline after the new millennium. At the

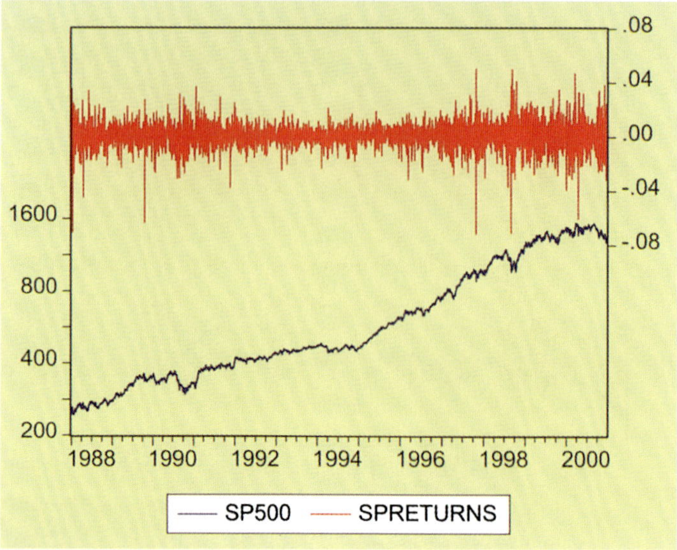

Figure 3. S&P 500 1988 to 2000.

beginning of 1963 the index was priced at $63 and at the end it was $1035. That means that one dollar invested in 1963 would have become $16 by November 21, 2003 (plus the stream of dividends that would have been received as this index does not take account of dividends on a daily basis). If this investor were clever enough to sell his position on March 24, 2000, it would have been worth $24. Hopefully he was not so unlucky as to have purchased on that day. Although we often see pictures of the level of these indices, it is obviously the relative price from the purchase point to the sale point that matters. Thus economists focus attention on returns as shown at the top of the figure. This shows the daily price change on the right axis (computed as the logarithm of the price today divided by the price yesterday). This return series is centered around zero throughout the sample period even though prices are sometimes increasing and sometimes decreasing. Now the most dramatic event is the crash of October 1987 which dwarfs all other returns in the size of the decline and subsequent partial recovery.

Other important features of this data series can be seen best by looking at portions of the whole history. For example, (Figure 2) shows the same graph before 1987. It is very apparent that the amplitude of the returns is changing. The magnitude of the changes is sometimes large and sometimes small. This is the effect that ARCH is designed to measure and that we have called volatility clustering. There is however another interesting feature in this graph. It is clear that the volatility is higher when prices are falling. Volatility tends to be higher in bear markets. This is the asymmetric volatility effect that Nelson described with his EGARCH model.

Looking at the next sub-period after the 87 crash in (Figure 3), we see the

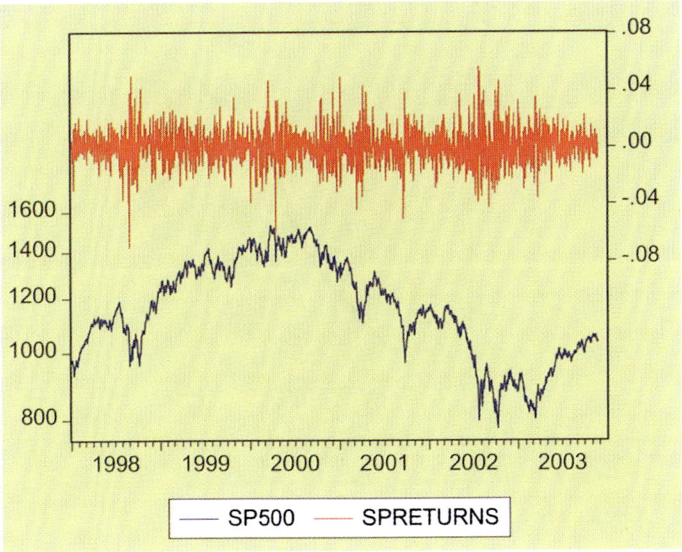

Figure 4. S&P 500 1998 to 2003.

record low volatility period of the middle '90's. This was accompanied by a slow and steady growth of equity prices. It was frequently discussed whether we had moved permanently to a new era of low volatility. History shows that we didn't. The volatility began to rise as stock prices got higher and higher reaching very high levels from 1998 on. Clearly, the stock market was risky from this perspective but investors were willing to take this risk because the returns were so good. Looking at the last period since 1998 in (Figure 4), we see the high volatility continue as the market turned down. Only at the end of the sample, since the official conclusion of the Iraq war, do we see substantial declines in volatility. This has apparently encouraged investors to come back into the market which has experienced substantial price increases.

We now show some statistics that illustrate the three stylized facts mentioned above: almost unpredictable returns, fat tails and volatility clustering. Some features of returns are shown in Table I. The mean is close to zero relative to the standard deviation for both periods. It is .03% per trading day or about 7.8% per year. The standard deviation is slightly higher in the 90's.

Table I. S&P 500 Returns.

SAMPLE	FULL	SINCE 1990
Mean	.0003	.0003
Standard Deviation	.0094	.0104
Skewness	-1.44	-.10
Kurtosis	41.45	6.78

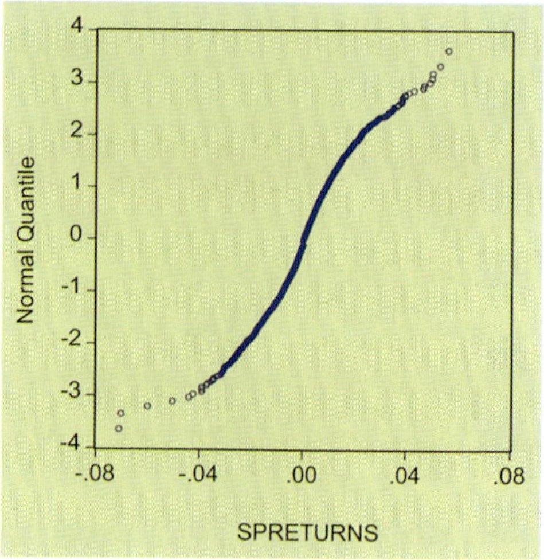

Figure 5. Quantile Plot of S&P500 Returns Post 1990.

These standard deviations correspond to annualized volatilities of 15% and 17%. The skewness is small throughout.

The most interesting feature is the kurtosis which measures the magnitude of the extremes. If returns are normally distributed, then the kurtosis should be three. The kurtosis of the nineties is substantial at 6.8, while for the full sample it is a dramatic 41. This is strong evidence that extremes are more substantial than would be expected from a normal random variable. Similar evidence is seen graphically in (Figure 5), which is a quantile plot for the post 1990 data. This is designed to be a straight line if returns are normally distributed and will have an s-shape if there are more extremes.

The unpredictability of returns and the clustering of volatility can be concisely shown by looking at autocorrelations. Autocorrelations are correlations calculated between the value of a random variable today and its value some days in the past. Predictability may show up as significant autocorrelations in returns, and volatility clustering will show up as significant autocorrelations in squared or absolute returns. (Figure 6) shows both of these plots for the post 1990 data. Under conventional criteria[2], autocorrelations bigger than .033 in absolute value would be significant at a 5% level. Clearly, the return autocorrelations are almost all insignificant while the square returns have all autocorrelations significant. Furthermore, the squared return autocorrelations are all positive which is highly unlikely to occur by chance. This figure gives powerful evidence for both the unpredictability of returns and the clustering of volatility.

Now we turn to the problem of estimating volatility. The estimates called

[2] The actual critical values will be somewhat greater as the series clearly are heteroskedastic. This makes the case for unpredictability in returns even stronger.

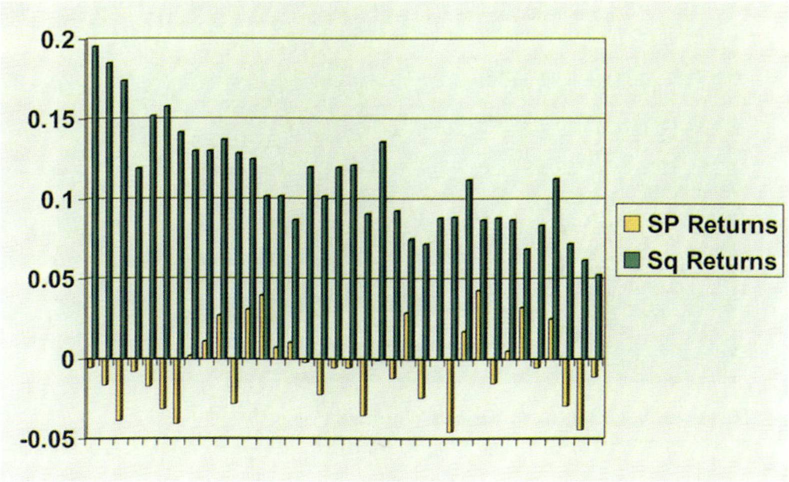

Figure 6. Return and Squared Return Autocorrelations

historical volatility are based on rolling standard deviations of returns. In (Figure 7) these are constructed for 5 day, one year, and five year windows. While each of these approaches may seem reasonable, the answers are clearly very different. The 5 day estimate is extremely variable while the other two are much smoother. The 5 year estimate smoothes over peaks and troughs that the other two see. It is particularly slow to recover after the 87 crash and particularly slow to reveal the rise in volatility in 1998–2000. In just the same way, the annual estimate fails to show all the details revealed by the 5 day volatility. However, some of these details may be just noise. Without any true measure of volatility, it is difficult to pick from these candidates.

The ARCH model provides a solution to this dilemma. From estimating the unknown parameters based on the historical data, we have forecasts for each day in the sample period and for any period after the sample. The natural first model to estimate is the GARCH (1,1). This model gives weights to the unconditional variance, the previous forecast, and the news measured as the square of yesterday's return. The weights are estimated to be (.004, .941, .055) respectively[3]. Clearly the bulk of the information comes from the previous day forecast. The new information changes this a little and the long run average variance has a very small effect. It appears that the long run variance effect is so tiny that it might not be important. This is incorrect. When forecasting many steps ahead, the long run variance eventually dominates as the importance of news and other recent information fades away. It is naturally small because of the use of daily data.

In this example, we will use an asymmetric volatility model that is some-

[3] For a conventional GARCH model defined as $h_{t+1} = \omega + \alpha r_t^2 + \beta h_{t+1}$, the weights are $(1-\alpha-\beta, \beta, \alpha)$.

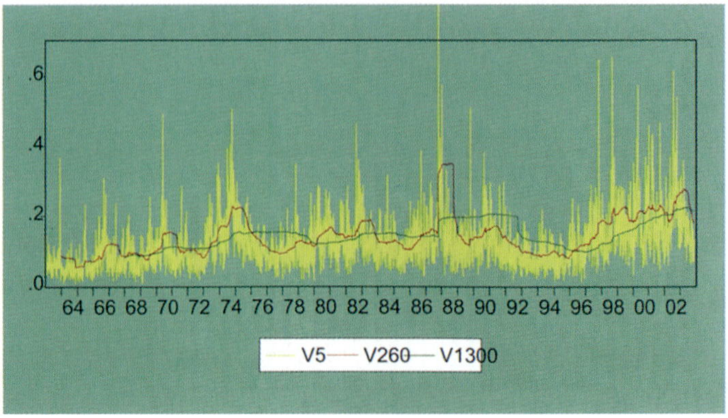

Figure 7. Historical Volatilties with Various Windows.

times called GJR-GARCH for Glosten, *et al.* (1993) or TARCH for Threshold ARCH, Zakoian (1994). The statistical results are given in Table II. In this case there are two types of news. There is a squared return and there is a variable that is the squared return when returns are negative, and zero otherwise. On average, this is half as big as the variance, so it must be doubled implying that the weights are half as big. The weights are now computed on the long run average, the previous forecast, the symmetric news and the negative news. These weights are estimated to be (.002, .931, .029, .038) respectively[4]. Clearly the asymmetry is important since the last term would be zero otherwise. In fact negative returns in this model have more than 3 times the effect of positive returns on future variances. From a statistical point of view, the asymmetry term has a t-statistic of almost 20 and is very significant.

The volatility series generated by this model is given in (Figure 8). The series is more jagged than the annual or 5 year historical volatilities, but is less

Table II. TARCH estimates of SP500 Return Data.

Dependent Variable: SP
Method: ML - ARCH (Marquardt)
Date: 11/24/03 Time: 09:27
Sample(adjusted): 1/03/1963 11/21/2003
Included observations: 10667 after adjusting endpoints
Convergence achieved after 22 iterations
Variance backcast: ON

	Coefficient	Std. Error	z-Statistic	Prob.
C	0.000301	6.67E-05	4.512504	0.0000
	Variance Equation			
C	4.55E-07	5.06E-08	8.980473	0.0000
ARCH(1)	0.028575	0.003322	8.602582	0.0000
(RESID<0)*ARCH(1)	0.076169	0.003821	19.93374	0.0000
GARCH(1)	0.930752	0.002246	414.4693	0.0000

[4] If the model is defined as $h_t = \omega + \beta h_{t-1} + \alpha r_{t-1}^2 + \gamma r_{t-1}^2 I_{r_{t-1}<0}$, then the weights are $(1-\alpha-\beta-\frac{\gamma}{2}, \beta, \alpha, \frac{\gamma}{2})$.

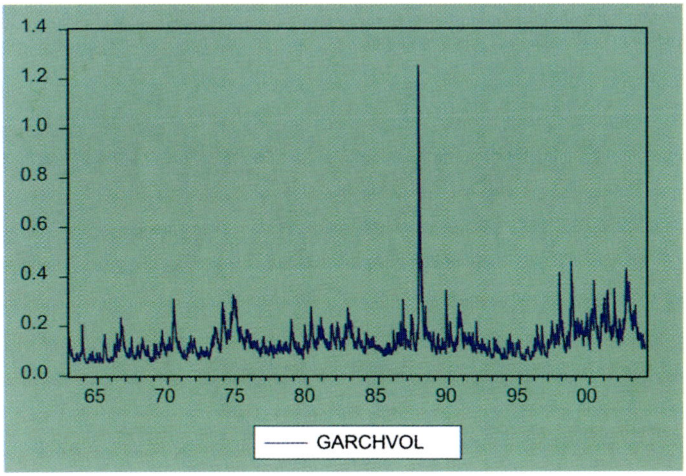

Figure 8. GARCH Volatilties.

variable than the 5 day volatilities. Since it is designed to measure the volatility of returns on the next day, it is natural to form confidence intervals for returns. In (Figure 9) returns are plotted against plus and minus three TARCH standard deviations. Clearly the confidence intervals are changing in a very believable fashion. A constant band would be too wide in some periods and too narrow in others. The TARCH intervals should have 99.7% probability of including the next observation if the data are really normally distributed. The expected number of times that the next return is outside the interval should then be only 29 out of the more than 10,000 days. In fact, there are 75 indicating that there are more outliers than would be expected from normality.

Additional information about volatility is available from the options market. The value of traded options depends directly on the volatility of the underlying asset. A carefully constructed portfolio of options with different strikes will have a value that measures the option market estimate of future volatility under rather weak assumptions. This calculation is now performed by the CBOE for S&P500 options and is reported as the VIX. Two assumptions that underly this index are worth mentioning. The price process should be continuous and there should be no risk premia on volatility shocks. If these assumptions are good approximations, then implied volatilities can be compared with ARCH volatilities. Because the VIX represents the volatility of one-month options, the TARCH volatilities must be forecast out to one month.

The results are plotted in (Figure 10)[5]. The general pattern is quite similar, although the TARCH is a little lower than the VIX. These differences can be

[5] The VIX is adjusted to a 252 trading day year.

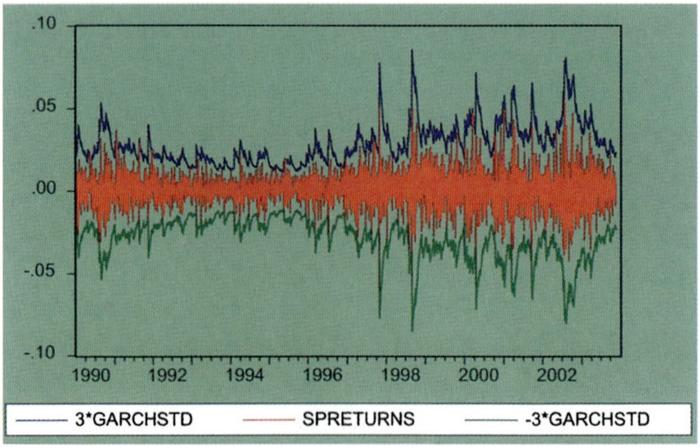

Figure 9. GARCH Confidence Intervals: 3 standard deviations.

attributed to two sources. First the option pricing relation is not quite correct for this situation and does not allow for volatility risk premia or non-normal returns. These adjustments would lead to higher options prices and consequently implied volatilities that were too high. Secondly, the basic ARCH models have very limited information sets. They do not use information on earnings, wars, elections, etc. Hence the volatility forecasts by traders should be generally superior; differences could be due to long lasting information events.

This extended example illustrates many of the features of ARCH/GARCH models and how they can be used to study volatility processes. We turn now to financial practice and describe two widely used applications. In the presentation, some novel implications of asymmetric volatility will be illustrated.

FINANCIAL PRACTICE – VALUE AT RISK

Every morning in thousands of banks and financial services institutions around the world, the Chief Executive Officer is presented with a risk profile by his Risk Management Officer. He is given an estimate of the risk of the entire portfolio and the risk of many of its components. He would typically learn the risk faced by the firm's European Equity Division, its US Treasury Bond Division, its Currency Trading Unit, its Equity Derivative Unit, and so forth. These risks may even be detailed for particular trading desks or traders. An overall figure is then reported to a regulatory body although it may not be the same number used for internal purposes. The risk of the company as a whole is less than the sum of its parts since different portions of the risk will not be perfectly correlated.

The typical measure of each of these risks is Value at Risk, often abbreviated as VaR. The VaR is a way of measuring the probability of losses that could occur to the portfolio. The 99% one day VaR is a number of dollars that the

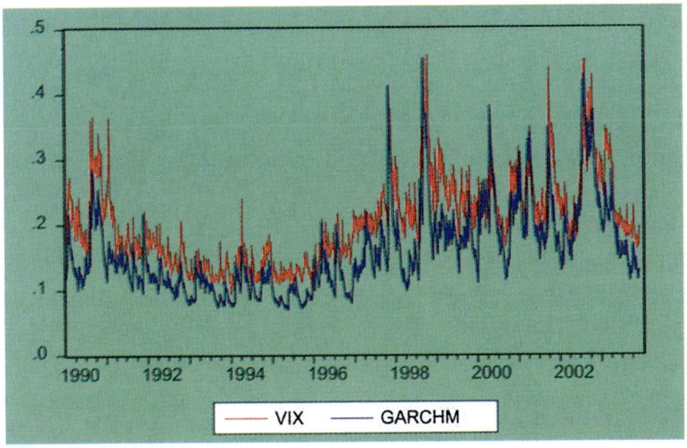

Figure 10. Implied Volatilities and GARCH Volatilities.

manager is 99% certain will be worse than whatever loss occurs on the next day. If the one-day VaR for the currency desk is $50,000, then the risk officer asserts that only on 1 day out of 100 will losses on this portfolio be greater than $50,000. Of course this means that on about 2.5 days a year, the losses will exceed the VaR. The VaR is a measure of risk that is easy to understand without knowing any statistics. It is however, just one quantile of the predictive distribution and therefore it has limited information on the probabilities of loss.

Sometimes the VaR is defined on a multi-day basis. A 99% 10 day VaR is a number of dollars that is greater than the realized loss over 10 days on the portfolio with probability .99. This is a more common regulatory standard but is typically computed by simply adjusting the one-day VaR as will be discussed below. The loss figures assume that the portfolio is unchanged over the 10 day period which may be counterfactual.

To calculate the VaR of a trading unit or a firm as a whole, it is necessary to have variances and covariances, or equivalently volatilities and correlations, among all assets held in the portfolio. Typically, the assets are viewed as responding primarily to one or more risk factors that are modeled directly. Riskmetrics™ for example, uses about 400 global risk factors. BARRA uses industry risk factors as well as risk factors based on firm characteristics and other factors. A diversified U.S. equity portfolio would have risks determined primarily by the aggregate market index such as the S&P 500. We will carry forward the example of the previous section to calculate the VaR of a portfolio that mimics the S&P.

The one day 99% VaR of the S&P can be estimated using ARCH. From historical data, the best model is estimated, and then the standard deviation is calculated for the following day. In the case of S&P on November 24, this forecast standard deviation is .0076. To convert this into VaR we must make an assumption about the distribution of returns. If normality is assumed, the

1% point is –2.33 standard deviations from zero. Thus the value at risk is 2.33 times the standard deviation or in the case of Nov 24, it is 1.77%. We can be 99% sure that we will not lose more than 1.77% of portfolio value on Nov 24. In fact the market went up on 24th so there were no losses.

The assumption of normality is highly questionable. We observed that financial returns have a surprising number of large returns. If we divide the returns by the TARCH standard deviations, the result will have a constant volatility of one but will have a non-normal distribution. The kurtosis of these "de-volatized returns" or "standardized residuals" is 6.5, which is much less than the unconditional kurtosis, but is still well above normal. From these de-volatized returns, we can find the 1% quantile and use this to give a better idea of the VaR. It turns out to be 2.65 standard deviations below the mean. Thus our portfolio is riskier than we thought using the normal approximation. The one day 99% VaR is now estimated to be 2%.

A 10 day value at risk is often required by regulatory agencies and is frequently used internally as well. Of course, the amount a portfolio can lose in 10 days is a lot greater than it can lose in one day. But how much greater is it? If volatilities were constant, then the answer would be simple; it would be the square root of 10 times as great. Since the 10-day variance is 10 times the one day variance, the 10-day volatility multiplier would be the square root of 10. We would take the one day standard deviation and multiply it by 3.16 and then with normality we would multiply this by 2.33 giving 7.36 times the standard deviation. This is the conventional solution in industry practice. For November 24, the 10-day 99% VaR is 5.6% of portfolio value.

However, this result misses two important features of dynamic volatility models. First, it makes a difference whether the current volatilities are low or high relative to the long run average, so that they are forecast to increase or decrease over the next 10 days. Since the volatility is relatively low in November, the TARCH model will forecast an increase over the next 10 days. In this case, this effect is not very big as the standard deviation is forecast to increase to .0077 from .0076 over the 10-day period.

More interesting is the effect of asymmetry in variance for multi-period returns. Even though each period has a symmetric distribution, the multi-period return distribution will be asymmetric. This effect is simple to understand but has not been widely recognized. It is easily illustrated with a two-step binomial tree, (Figure 11), as used in elementary option pricing models. In the first period, the asset price can either increase or decrease and each outcome is equally likely. In the second period, the variance will depend upon whether the price went up or down. If it went up, then the variance will be lower so that the binomial branches will be relatively close together. If the price went down, the variance will be higher so that the outcomes will be further apart. After two periods, there are four outcomes that are equally likely. The distribution is quite skewed, since the bad outcome is far worse than if the variance had been constant.

To calculate the VaR in this setting, a simulation is needed. The TARCH model is simulated for 10 days using normal random variables and starting

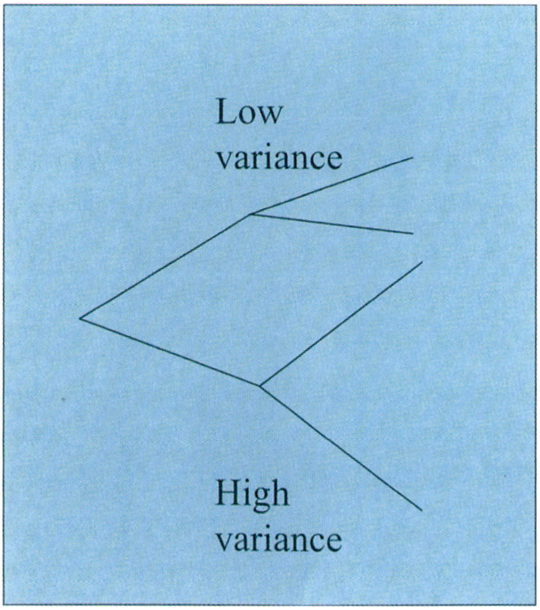

Figure 11. Two Period Binomial Tree with Asymmetric Volatility.

from the values of November 21.[6] This was done 10,000 times and then the worst outcomes were sorted to find the Value at Risk corresponding to the 1% quantile. The answer was 7.89 times the standard deviation. This VaR is substantially larger than the value assuming constant volatility.

To avoid the normality assumption, the simulation can also be done using the empirical distribution of the standardized residuals. This simulation is often called a bootstrap; each draw of the random variables is equally likely to be any observation of the standardized residuals. Thus the October '87 crash observation could be drawn once or even twice in some simulations but not in others. The result is a standard deviation multiplier of 8.52 that should be used to calculate VaR. For our case the November 24, 10 day, 99% VaR is 6.5% of portfolio value.

FINANCIAL PRACTICE – VALUING OPTIONS

Another important area of financial practice is valuation and management of derivatives such as options. These are typically valued theoretically assuming some particular process for the underlying asset and then market prices of the derivatives are implied by the parameters of the underlying process. This

[6] In the example here, the simulation was started at the unconditional variance so that the time aggregation effect could be examined alone. In addition, the mean was taken to be zero but this makes little difference over such short horizons.

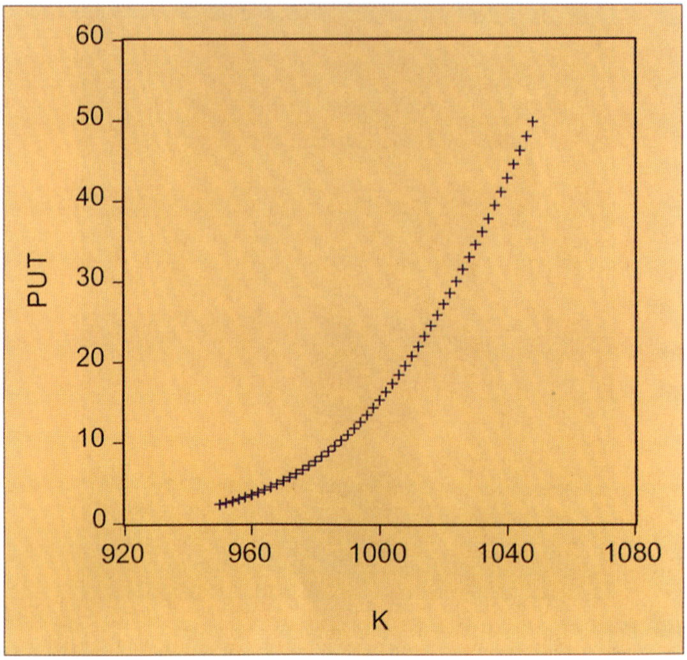

Figure 12. Put Prices from GARCH Simulation.

strategy is often called "arbitrage free pricing." It is inadequate for some of the tasks of financial analysis. It cannot determine the risk of a derivative position since each new market price may correspond to a different set of parameters and it is the size and frequency of these parameter changes that signify risk. For the same reason, it is difficult to find optimal hedging strategies. Finally, there is no way to determine the price of a new issue or to determine whether some derivatives are trading at discounts or premiums.

A companion analysis that is frequently carried out by derivatives traders is to develop fundamental pricing models that determine the appropriate price for a derivative based on the observed characteristics of the underlying asset. These models could include measures of trading cost, hedging cost and risk in managing the options portfolio.

In this section, a simple simulation based option pricing model will be employed to illustrate the use of ARCH models in this type of fundamental analysis. The example will be the pricing of put options on the S&P 500 that have 10 trading days left to maturity.

A put option gives the owner the right to sell an asset at a particular price, called the strike price, at maturity. Thus if the asset price is below the strike, he can make money by selling at the strike and buying at the market price. The profit is the difference between these prices. If however, the market price is above the strike, then there is no value in the option. If the investor holds the underlying asset in a portfolio and buys a put option, he is guaranteed to

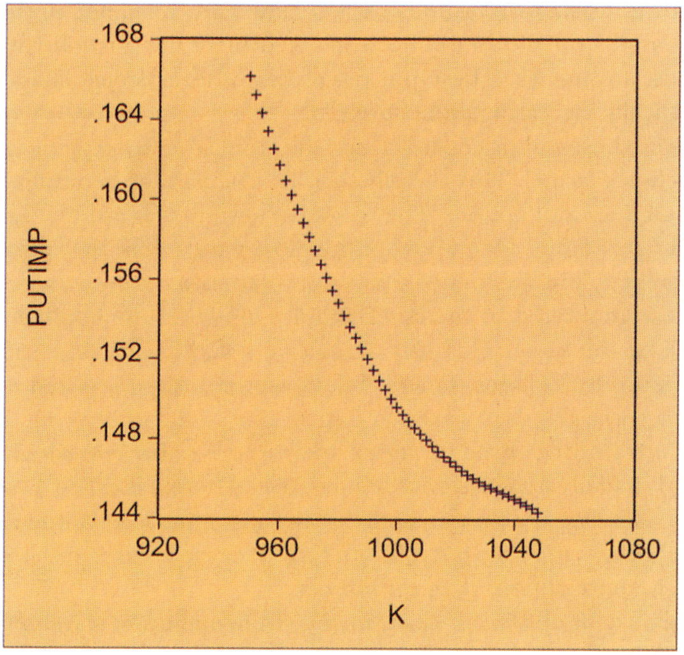

Figure 13. Implied Volatilties from GARCH Simulation.

have at least the strike price at the maturity date. This is why these options can be thought of as insurance contracts.

The simulation works just as in the previous section. The TARCH model is simulated from the end of the sample period, 10,000 times. The bootstrap approach is taken so that non-normality is already incorporated in the simulation. This simulation should be of the "risk neutral" distribution, i.e. the distribution in which assets are priced at their discounted expected values. The risk neutral distribution differs from the empirical distribution in subtle ways so that there is an explicit risk premium in the empirical distribution which is not needed in the risk neutral. In some models such as the Black-Scholes, it is sufficient to adjust the mean to be the risk free rate. In the example, we take this route. The distribution is simulated with a mean of zero, which is taken to be the risk free rate. As will be discussed below, this may not be a sufficient adjustment to risk neutralize the distribution.

From the simulation, we have 10,000 equally likely outcomes for 10 days in the future. For each of these outcomes we can compute the value of a particular put option. Since these are equally likely and since the riskless rate is taken to be zero, the fair value of the put option is the average of these values. This can be done for put options with different strikes. The result is plotted in (Figure 12). The S&P is assumed to begin at 1000 so a put option with a strike of 990 protects this value for 10 days. This put option should sell for $11. To protect the portfolio at its current value would cost $15 and to be certain that it was at least worth 1010 would cost \$21. The VaR calculated in the previous section was \$65 for the 10 day horizon. To protect the portfolio at this point would cost around \$2. These put prices have the expected shape; they are monotonically increasing and convex.

However, these put prices are clearly different from those generated by the Black- Scholes model. This is easily seen by calculating the implied volatility for each of these put options. The result is shown in (Figure 13). The implied volatilities are higher for the out-of-the-money puts than they are for the at-the-money puts and the in-the-money put volatilities are even lower. If the put prices were generated by the Black-Scholes model, these implied volatilities would all be the same. This plot of implied volatilities against strike is a familiar feature for options traders. The downward slope is called a "volatility skew" and corresponds to a skewed distribution of the underlying assets. This feature is very pronounced for index options, less so for individual equity options, and virtually non-existent for currencies where it is called a "smile". It is apparent that this is a consequence of the asymmetric volatility model and correspondingly, the asymmetry is not found for currencies and is weaker for individual equity options than for indices.

This feature of options prices is strong confirmation of asymmetric volatility models. Unfortunately, the story is more complicated than this. The actual options skew is generally somewhat steeper than that generated by asymmetric ARCH models. This calls into question the risk neutralization adopted in the simulation. There is now increasing evidence that investors are particularly worried about big losses and are willing to pay extra premiums to avoid them. This makes the skew even steeper. The required risk neutralization has been studied by several authors such as Rosenberg and Engle (2002), Bates (2003) and Jackwerth (2000).

NEW FRONTIERS

It has now been more than 20 years since the ARCH paper appeared. The developments and applications have been fantastic and well beyond anyone's most optimistic forecasts. But what can we expect in the future? What are the next frontiers?

There appear to be two important frontiers of research that are receiving a great deal of attention and have important promise for applications. These are high frequency volatility models and high dimension multivariate models. I will give a short description of some of the promising developments in these areas.

Merton was perhaps the first to point out the benefits of high frequency data for volatility measurement. By examining the behavior of stock prices on a finer and finer time scale, better and better measures of volatility can be achieved. This is particularly convenient if volatility is only slowly changing so that dynamic considerations can be ignored. Andersen and Bollerslev (1998a) pointed out that intra-daily data could be used to measure the performance of daily volatility models. Andersen, Bollerslev, Diebold and Labys

(2003) and Engle (2002b) suggest how intra-daily data can be used to form better daily volatility forecasts.

However the most interesting question is how to use high frequency data to form high frequency volatility forecasts. As higher and higher frequency observations are used, there is apparently a limit where every transaction is observed and used. Engle (2000) calls such data *ultra high frequency* data. These transactions occur at irregular intervals rather than equally spaced times. In principle, one can design a volatility estimator that would update the volatility every time a trade was recorded. However, even the absence of a trade could be information useful for updating the volatility so even more frequent updating could be done. Since the time at which trades arrive is random, the formulation of ultra high frequency volatility models requires a model of the arrival process of trades. Engle and Russell (1998) propose the Autoregressive Conditional Duration or ACD model for this task. It is a close relative of ARCH models designed to detect clustering of trades or other economic events; it uses this information to forecast the arrival probability of the next event.

Many investigators in empirical market microstructure are now studying aspects of financial markets that are relevant to this problem. It turns out that when trades are clustered, the volatility is higher. Trades themselves carry information that will move prices. A large or medium size buyer will raise prices, at least partly because market participants believe he could have important information that the stock is undervalued. This effect is called price impact and is a central component of *liquidity risk,* and a key feature of volatility for ultra high frequency data. It is also a central concern for traders who do not want to trade when they will have a big impact on prices, particularly if this is just a temporary impact. As financial markets become ever more computer driven, the speed and frequency of trading will increase. Methods to use this information to better understand the volatility and stability of these markets will be ever more important.

The other frontier that I believe will see substantial development and application is *high dimension* systems. In this presentation, I have focused on the volatility of a single asset. For most financial applications, there are thousands of assets. Not only do we need models of their volatilities but also of their correlations. Ever since the original ARCH model was published there have been many approaches proposed for multivariate systems. However, the best method to do this has not yet been discovered. As the number of assets increase, the models become extremely difficult to accurately specify and estimate. Essentially there are too many possibilities. There are few published examples of models with more than 5 assets. The most successful model for these cases is the constant conditional correlation model, CCC, of Bollerslev (1990). This estimator achieves its performance by assuming that the conditional correlations are constant. This allows the variances and covariances to change but not the correlations.

A generalization of this approach is the Dynamic Conditional Correlation, DCC, model of Engle (2002a). This model introduces a small number of parameters to model the correlations, regardless of the number of assets. The volatilities are modeled with univariate specifications. In this way, large covariance matrices can be forecast. The investigator first estimates the volatilities one at a time, and then estimates the correlations jointly with a small number of additional parameters. Preliminary research on this class of models is promising. Systems of up to 100 assets have been modeled with good results. Applications to risk management and asset allocation follow immediately. Many researchers are already developing related models that could have even better performance. It is safe to predict that in the next several years, we will have a set of useful methods for modeling the volatilities and correlations of large systems of assets.

REFERENCES

Andersen, T. G., and Bollerslev, T. (1998a), "Answering the Skeptics: Yes, Standard Volatility Models Do Provide Accurate Forecasts," *International Economic Review*, 39, 885–905.

Andersen, T. G., and Bollerslev, T. (1998b), "Deutsche Mark-Dollar Volatility: Intraday Activity Patterns, Macroeconomic Announcements, and Longer Run Dependencies," *Journal of Finance. February*, 53, 219–265.

Andersen, T. G., Bollerslev, T., Diebold, F. X., and Labys, P. (2003), "Modeling and Forecasting Realized Volatility," *Econometrica*, 71, 579–625.

Bates, D. S. (2003), "Empirical Option Pricing: A Retrospection," *Journal of Econometrics*, 116, 387–404.

Black, F., and Scholes, M. (1972), "The Valuation of Option Contracts and a Test of Market Efficiency," *Journal of Finance*, 27, 399–417.

Bollerslev, T. (1986), "Generalized Autoregressive Conditional Heteroskedasticity," *Journal of Econometrics*, 31, 307–327.

Bollerslev, T. (1990), "Modelling the Coherence in Short-Run Nominal Exchange Rates: A Multivariate Generalized ARCH Model," *Review of Economics and Statistics. August*, 72, 498–505.

Bollerslev, T., Chou, R. Y., and Kroner, K. F. (1992), "ARCH Modeling in Finance: A Review of the Theory and Empirical Evidence," *Journal of Econometrics. April May*, 52, 5–59.

Bollerslev, T., Engle R., Nelson D. (1994), "ARCH Models," in *Handbook of Econometrics* (Vol. Volume IV), ed. R. Engle and D. McFadden, Amsterdam: North Holland, pp. 2959–3038.

Bollerslev, T., and Rossi, P. E. (1995), "Dan Nelson Remembered," *Journal of Business and Economic Statistics. October*, 13, 361–364.

Burns, P., Engle, R. F., and Mezrich, J. (1998), "Correlations and Volatilities of Asynchronous Data," *Journal of Derivatives*, 1–12.

Chou, R., Engle, R. F., and Kane, A. (1992), "Measuring Risk-Aversion from Excess Returns on a Stock Index," *Journal of Econometrics*, 52, 201–224.

Clark, P. K. (1973), "A Subordinated Stochastic Process Model with Finite Variance for Speculative Price," *Econometrica*, 41, 135–156.

Engle, R. (1982), "Autoregressive Conditional Heteroskedasticity with Estimates of the Variance of U.K. Inflation," *Econometrica*, 50, 987–1008.

Engle, R. (2002a), "Dynamic Conditional Correlation: A Simple Class of Multivariate Generalized Autoregressive Conditional Heteroskedasticity Models," *Journal of Business & Economic Statistics*, 20, 339–350.

Engle, R. (2002b), "New Frontiers for ARCH," *Journal of Applied Econometrics*, 17, 425–446.

Engle, R., and Ishida, I. (2002), "Forecasting Variance of Variance: The Square-Root, the Affine, and the CEV Garch Models," *Department of Finance Working Papers, New York University*.

Engle, R. F. (1983), "Estimates of the Variance of U.S. Inflation Based Upon the ARCH Model," *Journal of Money, Credit, and Banking*, 15, 286–301.

Engle, R. F. (2000), "The Econometrics of Ultra-High-Frequency Data," *Econometrica. January*, 68, 1–22.

Engle, R. F., Ito, T., and Lin, W. L. (1990), "Meteor-Showers or Heat Waves – Heteroskedastic Intradaily Volatility in the Foreign-Exchange Market," *Econometrica*, 58, 525–542.

Engle, R. F., Lilien, D. M., and Robins, R. P. (1987), "Estimating Time Varying Risk Premia in the Term Structure: The ARCH -M Model," *Econometrica. March*, 55, 391–407.

Engle, R. F., Ng, V. K., and Rothschild, M. (1990), "Asset Pricing with a Factor-ARCH Covariance Structure: Empirical Estimates for Treasury Bills," *Journal of Econometrics. July Aug*, 45, 213–237.

Engle, R. F., and Russell, J. R. (1998), "Autoregressive Conditional Duration: A New Model for Irregularly Spaced Transaction Data," *Econometrica. September*, 66, 1127–1162.

French, K. R., Schwert, G. W., and Stambaugh, R. F. (1987), "Expected Stock Returns and Volatility," *Journal of Financial Economics*, 19, 3–29.

Friedman, M. (1977), "Nobel Lecture: Inflation and Unemployment," *Journal of Political Economy*, 85, 451–472.

Glosten, L. R., Jagannathan, R., and Runkle, D. E. (1993), "On the Relation between the Expected Value and the Volatility of the Nominal Excess Return on Stocks," *Journal of Finance*, 48, 1779–1801.

Hamao, Y., Masulis, R. W., and Ng, V. (1990), "Correlations in Price Changes and Volatility across International Stock Markets," *Review of Financial Studies*, 3, 281–307.

Harvey, A. C., Ruiz, E., and Shephard, N. (1994), "Multivariate Stochastic Variance Models," *Review of Economic Studies*, 61, 247–264.

Jackwerth, J. C. (2000), "Recovering Risk Aversion from Option Prices and Realized Returns," *Review of Financial Studies*, 13, 433–451.

Markowitz, H. M. (1952), "Portfolio Selection," *Journal of Finance*.

Merton, R. C. (1973), "Theory of Rational Options Pricing," *Bell Journal of Economics and Management Science*, 4, 141–183.

Merton, R. C. (1980), "On Estimating the Expected Return on the Market: An Exploratory Investigation," *Journal of Financial Economics*, 8, 323–361.

Rosenberg, J. V., and Engle, R. F. (2002), "Empirical Pricing Kernels," *Journal of Financial Economics*, 64, 341–372.

Sharpe, W. (1964), "Capital Asset Prices: A Theory of Market Equilibrium under Conditions of Risk," *Journal of Finance*, 19, 425–442.

Taylor, S. J. (1986), *Modeling Financial Time Series*, John Wiley.

Taylor, S. J. (1994), "Modeling Stochastic Volatility : A Review and Comparative Study," *Mathematical Finance*, 4, 183–204.

Tobin, J. (1958), "Liquidity Preference as Behavior Towards Risk," *Review of Economic Studies*, 25, 65–86.

Zakoian, J. M. (1994), "Threshold Heteroskedastic Models," *Journal of Economic Dynamics & Control*, 18, 931–955.

Clive W. J. Granger

CLIVE W.J. GRANGER

I was born in Swansea in the Principality of Wales in September 1934 and named Clive William John Granger. The "William John" names were traditional Granger boy's names and my mother liked the name Clive because some popular musician at the time had it. My father, Edward John Granger, and his wife Evelyn (both English) left Wales with me when I was about one year old to go to Lincoln in Eastern England. He was a commercial traveler for a well respected firm called Chivers that made jams, marmalades, jellies, and so forth. He traveled around whatever area he was directed to by the company and took orders for the products from wholesalers and individual grocers. My memory of Wales in this early period is non-existent but it did qualify me to play rugby for Wales, if I had been good enough. I did not get the Welsh ability to sing, unfortunately.

I can remember little about Lincoln except for the night of September 3, 1939, when war was declared and everyone cried. At about ten pm the air raid warning sirens went off and we all huddled nervously under the kitchen table. Of course, I now realize that the probability of a Nazi bomber flying over Lincoln on the first day of the war was extremely slight; it was just a wake-up call for the English people that a real war was upon them.

A year or so later my father went off to war to serve as a driver of large support vehicles for the Royal Air Force, first in the south of England and later in North Africa. My mother had three brothers serving in the forces, but we were a fortunate family as they and my father all returned unhurt. Whilst my father was away my mother and I moved to Cambridge to stay with her mother, who was a very short, fierce woman who had brought up many children and had a very strong personality. She was a professional cook and could make a great meal out of almost nothing, a worthwhile ability during the shortages of the war. Earlier in her career she had cooked for gentry and it was said that she once cooked for Queen Victoria. When she was just starting out she had worked as a very junior cook at Windsor Castle and her two sons had played with the princes Edward and George, both later Kings of England.

Later we moved across Cambridge to stay with my father's parents. My grandfather repaired shoes in his own shop and sold shoes in a successful small business. I went to a local primary school, did well in mathematics but not much else. A teacher told my mother that "I would never become successful," which illustrates the difficulties of long-run forecasting on inadequate data.

At the age of 11 I passed the necessary exams and was accepted by the

Cambridgeshire High School for Boys, where I performed fairly well but showed no particular ability. The headmaster was Mr. Newton-John, who later moved to Australia and had a famous daughter, Olivia.

At this stage of my life I had largely drifted through, just taking things as they came. I had no clear-cut ambition or long-term plan, and that policy has generally continued. My career has largely been determined by a sequence of "luck breaks," which will be discussed below.

LUCKY BREAK #1

My first lucky break was in 1946 when my father returned from the war and his job took him to Nottingham. He bought a nice house in a middle-class suburb called West Bridgeford and I would cycle many miles each day to and from the Grammar School, which was middle sized. At the end of the fifth form, the year when most of the students left and entered the job market, I asked my friends what they planned to do, and they all decided to stay on into the sixth-form, which prepares you for the A-level exams and possible entry to college. Until that time I had never considered going to university, I had expected to leave school at sixteen and work in a bank or an insurance company. My father was very supportive, even though my staying at school would be a drain on his finances. Sixth-form takes two years and I concentrated on Pure Mathematics, Applied Mathematics, and Physics. A decisive event took place, I believe, towards the end of the first year. In one of the classes we all had to stand up and state our planned career. By then I realized that I was quite good at mathematics, but I did not want a career in it, which I thought of as being a school teacher. I preferred to use mathematics in some practical fashion and thought that meteorology sounded promising. In those days I stuttered somewhat and when my turn came to stand up, I tried to say "meteorology" but found I could not get the word out, so I just said "statistics," thereby determining my future path.

It so happened that a particular strength at the West Bridgeford Grammar School was the quality of the mathematics teachers. Mr. Bradshaw and Mr. Midgley were both very well trained and I was told they had firsts at Oxford and/or Cambridge. They were still very enthusiastic about the subject and were very able to pass on this enthusiasm and their knowledge to the students. The fact that our sixth-form produce several First Class Degrees, several Ph.D's, and at least four Professors is largely due to this strong background in mathematics.

LUCKY BREAK #2

Applying to universities was a difficult process in those days as quite a small percentage of British youth went to university. Finding suitable courses that also had available places was not easy. However, I was told that the University of Nottingham was just starting the first joint degree in Mathematics and Economics which sounded ideal for my interests, so I applied and was quickly accepted. As far as I could tell, I was the first person anywhere in my family tree to go to university.

My courses in the first year at Nottingham were one third economics consisting of micro and national accounts taught by André Gabor and Brian Tew, with a lot of ability and enthusiasm. I also took large doses of pure and applied mathematics. To my delight I found pure mathematics not so difficult because of my training at Grammar School. At the end of the first year I switched to a Mathematics Degree and I eventually obtained my First. My only formal training in economics was in the first year where I attempted to reformulate what I was being taught in pure mathematical terms, but was usually unsuccessful.

LUCKY BREAK #3

On completing my degree I started a Ph.D. in statistics, although I knew very little about the topic. My supervisor was Professor Harry Pitt, who was an excellent pure mathematician and probabilist. He taught me by going through Harold Cramer's book on Mathematical Statistics which is very good text but makes no mention of data. I needed to find a thesis topic and I wanted something of relevance to economics. I went to our university library and found that they had only one book on Economic Time Series by H. T. Davis. I thought that this was both an appropriate topic and also that there must be plenty of opportunities, as there were so few books in the area. I still think that my judgement, made at the age of 22, was correct.

LUCKY BREAK #4

The next structural break in my life occurred after I had been doing research for just six months. As background, it is important to know that this was a time when British universities were expanding rapidly, particularly in certain fields which included statistics. Nottingham had received funding for a junior lecturer in statistics and advertised the position, but were embarrassed by having only a single applicant, even though he was from Cambridge and was very well qualified. The professors of the Mathematics Department asked me to apply and my initial reaction was to say no to the idea as I was not qualified and knew that I had little understanding of the area. They responded that I would not get the position anyway but it would be good experience for me to go through with the interview and be helpful to them, so how could I refuse? The selection committee was chaired by the Vice-Chancellor along with about fifteen full professors. The Vice-Chancellor and I had fought over certain undergraduate topics the previous year and my position had prevailed, so I knew for certain that did not help my chances of getting the job. As I knew that I would not get the position I was not at all nervous, and the Vice-Chancellor started the proceedings by making a kind remark about our previous battles and I actually enjoyed the interview. The other candidate came before the committee, got into a strong fight with the Vice-Chancellor, and did not make a good impression. The result was that I got the job. I was just 23 when I started the position in 1956 with what had to be a record low knowledge of statistics and no established teaching ability. What made it more difficult was that some of the students, returning from Army service (sometimes with battle experience) were older than me and had strong ambitions to learn and to get on with their life. I always found it difficult to accept that they should call me "sir."

One advantage was that I was the only person in the university calling himself a "statistician," so that I was visited by workers from many fields (geography, history, psychology, chemistry, and economic history) asking me questions. Each data set presented unique problems and being confronted with them provided excellent training for a young statistician that many beginners would not get these days with such emphasis on specialization. I even got a few publications from these studies. An even better outcome came from my work with Professor David Chambers, a good economic historian who would often send his research assistant, Patricia, over to ask me questions. She said "yes" to the right one from me and we were married in 1960, which is a significant part of "Lucky Break #4."

In 1959 I obtained a Ph.D. on "Testing for Non-stationariy" and applied for a Harkness Fellowship of the Commonwealth Fund. Apparently the Harkness family made a fortune selling saddles and leather wear for horses at the turn of the twentieth century but realizing that that industry may have a limited future, they lent a large sum of money to a friend called Rockefeller, who was having a problem with his oil company. From that investment the family became extremely wealthy, but died out in the mid-century, leaving large funds to various good projects, mostly medical research. Part of the funds went to the Harkness Fellowships, which were for about twenty young people from the United Kingdom, Australia, and New Zealand, mostly from academic subjects but also included artists, writers, and film makers. Each could spend either one or two years in the United States at any location they chose, being given sufficient funds to support themselves. In addition they had to agree to spend one month traveling around the country in December and three further months in the summer, again with all expenses paid.

LUCKY BREAK #5

I wrote to many major universities and had two positive responses, one from the Cowles' Commision at Yale, and the other from Morgenstern's Econometric Research Project at Princeton. As Oscar Morgenstern asked me to join his new "Time Series Project" I accepted with enthusiasm for a one year period. Getting the Harkness was certainly a lucky break as the fellowships were highly competitive and rarely went to candidates outside Oxford or Cambridge, and I was especially fortunate to go to Princeton.

When I arrived I found that the "Time Series Project" consisted of myself and Michio Hatanaka, an excellent econometrician who had recently finished a book on "Input-Output Analysis." He had done the calculations on the original Von Neumann computer at the Institute for Advanced Studies, which is a story in itself. However, Morgenstern had a specific project for us. His close friend, J. Von Neumann, a truly great mathematician, had told him that economists should be using the Fourier methods with their data, so Morgenstern had organized with John Tukey, a very famous Princeton statistician, to teach us how to do that. Tukey has a distinctly original way of teaching. We provided the data, he would describe what calculations he wanted us to do on the computer, Michio would do the programming and produce the results, and I would write mathematically what we were doing. John Tukey would then interpret the results and suggest a new set of calculations. This continued weekly for most of the academic year, by which time we had learnt a lot about filtering, the spectrum for a single series, and the cross-spectrum for a pair of series. This last topic was one that Tukey has been working on and was totally new. Michio and I realized that we had enough material for a book but we told John Tukey that we could not try to publish until he published his results. He said he was far too busy doing new research to publish, and that we should just go ahead, which we did. The book "Spectral Analysis in Economic Time Series" by Michio and myself appeared from Princeton University Press in 1969 and sold over three thousand copies, much to everyone's surprise. We tried to dedicate the book to Morgenstern and Tukey, but they would not allow it.

At the end of my academic year at Princeton, Pat and I were married in the Princeton University Chapel and we used the Harkness funds to finance a trip around the United States as an extended camping trip and honeymoon. After twelve thousand spectacular miles we still liked each other and I had acquired a beard.

I returned to Princeton the next two summers to work on stock market data. Two papers appeared in the journal *Kyklos*, on testing the random walk theory using spectral methods. In one of these, with Mike Godfrey and Oscar Morgenstern, we claimed the first published diagram in economics that was generated by a computer. It appeared in a cathode ray tube and was then photographed. During this period, in 1963, I wrote a very short paper on "The Typical Spectral Shape of An Economic Model." It was quickly submitted to *Econometrica* where it was accepted two years later with no referee reports, and essentially published three and a half years after submission. It has been cited often and I learned that a simple observation is enough to produce a successful paper, but you need patience with its appearance. I also published my second book, on commodity markets, written with Walt Labys, who left Harvard to study with me in Nottingham. A book with Morgenstern on the stock market and the one with Labys both appeared in 1970.

During this period I was also involved with André Gabor on some practical price research. To get data to test our theories and estimate models, we arranged with local supermarkets to conduct experiments in which we altered prices of popular products and recorded the change in sales. I believe that more economic micro-theory could be better tested by doing real world experiments rather than believing such an approach is impossible.

LUCKY BREAK #6

Around this time I thought that I should try to find a new line of research. In 1968 George Box and Gwilym Jenkins sent an advanced copy of their book "Time Series Analysis, Forecasting and Control" (published in 1970) and asked me for comments. I realized that I knew very little about forecasting and nothing about control. I decided that forecasting had great potential and applied for a grant to get a post-doctoral student to join me. The application was successful and I advertised around the world. I was rather surprised to get only one application, from Paul Newbold – a student of George Box, but one is all you need if the applicant is ideal. We were compatible, with a lot of common knowledge, but we had each been trained quite differently. He also proved to be a good writer, having received a good British education. Together we started a five year period of intense research, mostly on forecasting, leading to the publication of our book "Forecasting Economic Time Series" (Academic Press, 1976, second edition, 1986) which was widely used internationally in graduate courses.

During this period Paul and I conducted a small simulation study showing that if you take a pair of smooth, "highly autocorrelated" time series that are independent and put them into an ordinary least squares (OLS) regression, a surprisingly large number of times an incorrect, spurious, relationship is suggested by the standard statistical procedure. As many major economic publications used this type of analysis a lot of reconsideration of previous results had to be reconsidered. The size of the simulation was quite substantial at the time (1974) but would now be laughable. It shows that the usefulness of the result of a computer exercise depends on the quality of the question asked rather than the amount of computing undertaken.

LUCKY BREAK #7

In 1973 I was offered a professorship at the University of California, San Diego. Although I was certainly not unhappy at Nottingham, I had been there over twenty years from starting undergraduate studies to Professor of Applied Statistics and Econometrics and I thought that a change of scene was worth considering. We first decided to go for five years to see if we enjoyed California. We arrived in San Diego in August 1974 and several friends wrote advising me "not to retire," meaning do not spend all my time enjoying the sun and sand. By now the family consisted of Pat and myself, plus our children Mark William John, then aged ten and our daughter Claire Amanda Jane, aged six. The both eventually got their undergraduate degrees from California universities. Mark became a computer software developer and some of his earlier work was included in a movie that starred a future governor of California. Claire obtained her MA from Stanford in Molecular Biology and is now a science writer.

When I joined the Department of Economics at UCSD the theory group was already very strong but I was the only active research econometrician, although Paul Newbold came for the first year as a visitor to finish our book. That was soon to change.

LUCKY BREAK #8

In 1975 I was on a committee in Washington, DC chaired by Arnold Zellner. It discussed the organization of a conference on seasonal adjustment. Robert Engle, then at MIT, was on the same committee and during a break asked if I knew anywhere looking for a time series econometrician. I said that we were, so he visited, liked what he saw, and joined us. A year or so later Hal White came for a six month visit from Rochester, decided that we had the better climate, and accepted an offer. That is how a world ranked (top three) econometric group is formed. Take three active workers who interact, mix in a group of good students, and later add Jim Hamilton, Graham Elliott, and Allan Timmermann, and in under thirty years you produce a couple of Nobel Prizes, at least.

The students come from all over the world, and some started getting positions at good universities, which attracted further excellent students to us. If I start naming the better students I will only disappoint those that I leave out as there are so many that deserve mention. We claim to not only get good students, but also to have a particularly high value added.

Over the years we worked on a variety of questions including seasonal adjustment, aggregation, and several new types of time series models. These included the fractionally integrated model, done with Roselyn Joyeux, which has a so-called "long-memory property" and provided a discrete-time form of a continuous time model discussed by Benoit Mandelbroit. This whole area has resulted in a lot of interest by statisticians. Also considered was a variety of nonlinear models, including the bilinear model which produced a small book with an Australian visitor, Allan Anderson. Here the mathematics proved of interest but the models do not seem to be of great practical importance in economics. I also observed that a series could be serially uncorrelated but could still be forecast, nonlinearly, from its past. This produced a paper on "forecasting white noise" which produce reactions of surprise from those who thought the economic series were necessarily multivariate Gaussian processes. One observation that comes from this work was that squares of white noise series were not always white noise. I discussed this with Rob Engle and it might just have been the rolling pebble that much later produced the avalanche know as ARCH. Rob returned from a year at LSE with the ARCH model which we discussed frequently. As I was on the committees of his many students in the area so I learnt a lot about its development.

One of the benefits of joining an American university was the availability of sabbatical leaves plus long summer breaks when one could travel. The family made good use of these opportunities, plus some nice requests, and we spent lengthy periods at Oxford (Nuffield and All Souls), Cambridge (Trinity), Australian National University (Canberra), Aarhus (Denmark), and Victoria University (Wellington, New Zealand). At the last of these we had a splendid view of Haley's Comet, especially as the city shut off all the street lights for a couple of hours each night.

I find that traveling is usually enjoyable and certainly broadening both in general knowledge and also through cross-fertilization of ideas. Over my career I have visited over thirty countries.

LUCKY BREAK #9

The discovery, or invention, of cointegration was discussed in my Nobel Lecture and was a direct result of talking with a scholar from another university. It has an even bigger impact that causality, but cointegration was much less controversial and had more important applications.

The original theory of cointegration was from linear processes whereas causality theory had no such constraints. In 1993 Timo Teräsvirta and I wrote an overview of the field of nonlinear time series in economics which appears to have been helpful to people entering the field. This book appeared in the "Advanced Texts in Econometrics" series published by Oxford University Press. This series was edited by Grayham Mizon and myself, and was suggested by Andrew Schuler. Grayham and I agreed to edit the series provided that the books would be issued in both hard cover and paperback versions, and this seems to have been a successful strategy.

One of my latest projects involved analysis of a panel of data on the economy of regions in the Brazilian Amazon based on data collected every five years. The project was concerned with the dynamics and economics of the deforestation process going on in the Amazon forest which covers a huge area. With the help of a one year NSF grant a group was assembled which included Diana Weinhold (a former student) and Lykke Andersen visiting from the University of Aarhus in Denmark. We had available a very useful data set organized by Eustaquio Reis from Rio de Janeiro and built what seemed to be a useful model. The results were published in the book "The Dynamics of Deforestation and Economics Growth in the Brazilian Amazon," by L. Anderson, *et al.*, Cambridge University Press, 2003. This was an enjoyable and potentially important project from which I learnt a great deal.

As a schoolboy, aged around ten and living in Cambridge, England, I decided I did have a mild ambition, to see the year 2000. To achieve that I had to live to the age of sixty-six. In 1944, when I thought about this, such an age was by no means assured, many people did not make their mid-sixties. In 2000 Pat and I were living in La Jolla, next to the UCSD campus and quite near the ocean, Mark and his wife Kate were living in Sacramento in central California, and Claiare was about to move back to England.

In 2003 I decided to retire at the age of almost 69 after about 48 years of teaching. I was willing to give up my teaching and administrative duties in exchange for a reduced income and greater freedom of movement. My retirement date was July 31, 2003 and my long-term colleague, Rob Engle, retired from the department on the same day and moved permanently to New York. Pat and I started a visit to Christchurch on the South Island of New Zealand in that October. We greatly enjoy spending time in the Department of Economics at the University of Canterbury where we receive a warm welcome. We particularly like the spectacular Spring in the area.

LUCKY BREAK #10

At 3:00 am on October 8, 2003 a telephone call from Sweden turned our world upside down, and it will never return to normality. My colleagues at Nottingham, San Diego, and Canterbury were greatly excited, as were we. It seems all my lifetime friends, students, and acquaintances enjoyed the Prize as much as I did, which was terrific.

My story ends with a recipe for success. Do not start too high on the ladder, move to a good but not top university, work hard, have a few good ideas, chose good collaborators (I had over eighty in my career), attract some excellent students, wait twenty years or so, and then retire. It worked for Rob and I.

ADDENDUM

I have been asked if I consider myself to be naturally lucky. Certainly in my career the breaks have fallen my way. Sometimes I got a scholarship or an appointment at the right time, or I fell into good situations and others, particularly Rob, Hal, and Paul, accepted offers to join me. Even in general life I feel that I am often fortunate, coming across useful information or scarce parking spaces. I have never tried to use the ability by gambling but I do have friends who call on my name when trying to find somewhere to park their car, and they say that it works, even in Florence! I would like to thank my assistant, Mike Bacci, for handling all of the work involved with the Nobel presentations and essays, and much else.

TIME SERIES ANALYSIS, COINTEGRATION, AND APPLICATIONS

Nobel Lecture, December 8, 2003

by

CLIVE W.J. GRANGER

Department of Economics, University of California, San Diego, La Jolla, CA 92093-0508, USA.

The two prize winners in Economics this year would describe themselves as "Econometricians," so I thought that I should start by explaining that term.

One can begin with the ancient subject of Mathematics which is largely concerned with the discovery of relationships between deterministic variables using a rigorous argument. (A deterministic variable is one whose value is known with certainty.) However, by the middle of the last millennium it became clear that some objects were not deterministic, they had to be described with the use of probabilities, so that Mathematics grew a substantial sub-field known as "Statistics." This later became involved with the analysis of data and a number of methods have been developed for data having what may be called "standard properties."

However, in some areas of application, the data that they generated were found to be not standard, and so special sub-sub-fields needed to be developed. For example, Biology produced Biometrics, Psychology gave us Psychometrics, and Economics produced Econometrics.

There are many types of economic data, but the type considered by Rob Engle and myself is know as time series. Consider the measurement of unemployment rates which is an important measure of the health of the economy. Figures are gathered by a government agency and each month a new number is announced. Next month there will be another value, and so forth. String these value together in a simple graph and you get a "time series."

Rather than show a diagram, I would rather you use internal visualization (I think that you learn more that way). Suppose that you have a loosely strung string of pearls which you throw down, gently, onto a hard table top with the string of pearls roughly stretched out. You will have created a time series with time represented by the distance down the table, the size of the variable as the distance from the bottom edge of the table to a point, and the set of pearls giving the points in the series. As the placement of one pearl will impact where the next one lies, because they are linked together, this series will appear to be rather smooth, and will not have big fluctuations in value for one term to the next.

Time series can vary in many ways, some are gathered very often, others less frequently. Values for many important financial variables are known not merely daily, but can be found within seconds, if they change, such as highly traded stock prices or exchange rates. These are called "high frequency data" and are the input for Rob Engle's studies.

At the other extreme, some aspects of the overall, or "macro," economy, such as national income, consumption, and investment, may be available only quarterly for many countries, and only annually for others. Population data is also available only annually or less frequently. Many of these series are rather smooth, moving with local trends or with long swings, but the swings are not regular. It is this relative smoothness that makes them unsuitable for analysis with standard statistical procedures, which assumes data to have a property know as "stationarity." Many series in economics, particularly in finance and macroeconomics, do not have this property and can be called "integrated" or, sometimes incorrectly, "non-stationary." However, when expressed in terms of changes or rates of returns, these derived series appear closer to being stationary. The string of pearls would be "integrated" as it is a smooth series.

Methods to analyze a single integrated series had been proposed previously by Box and Jenkins (1970) and others, but the joint analysis of pairs, or more, of such series was missing an important feature. It turns out that the difference between a pair of integrated series can be stationary, and this property is known as "cointegration." More formally, two smooth series, properly scaled, can move and turn, but slowly, in similar but not identical fashions, but the distance between them can be stationary.

Suppose that we had two similar chains of pearls and we threw each on the table separately, but for ease of visualization, they do not cross one another. Each would represent smooth series but would follow different shapes and have no relationship. The distances between the two sets of pearls would also give a smooth series if you plotted it.

However, if the pearls were set in small but strong magnets, it is possible that there would be an attraction between the two chains, and that they would have similar, but not identical, smooth shapes. In that case, the distance between the two sets of pearls would give a stationary series and this would give an example of cointegration.

For cointegration, a pair of integrated, or smooth series, must have the property that a linear combination of them is stationary. Most pairs of integrated series will not have the property, so that cointegration should be considered as a surprise when it occurs. In practice, many pairs of macroeconomic series seem to have the property, as is suggested by economic theory.

Once we know that a pair of variables has the cointegration property it follows that they have a number of other interesting and useful properties. For example, they must both be cointegrated with the same hidden common factor. Further, they can be considered to be generated by what is know as the "error-correction model," in which the change of one of the series is explained in terms of the lag of the difference between the series, possibly after scaling, and lags of the differences of each series. The other series will be represented by a similar dynamic equation. Data generated by such a model is sure to be cointegrated. The error-correction model has been particularly important in making the idea of cointegration practically useful. It was invented by the well-known econometrician Dennis Sargan, who took some famous equations from the theory of economic growth and made them stochastic.

The early development of the cointegration idea was helped greatly by colleagues and friends in the Scandinavian countries, including Søren Johansen and Katarina Juselius in Copenhagen who developed and applied sophisticated testing procedures, Svend Hylleberg in Århus who extended the theory to seasonal data, and Eilev Jansen and his colleagues at the Bank of Norway, who successfully applied it to a large econometric model of Norway. To complete the set, Timo Teräsvirta, who is from Finland but now lives in Stockholm, helped develop models that were useful in nonlinear formulations of cointegration. I am delighted that they are all here as my guests.

The modern macro economy is large, diffuse, and difficult to define, measure, and control. Economists attempt to build models that will approximate it, that will have similar major properties so that one can conduct simple experiments on them, such as determining the impacts of alternative policies or the long-run implications of some new institution. Economic theorists do this using constraints suggested by the theory, whereas the econometrician builds empirical models using what is hopefully relevant data and which captures the main properties of the economy in the past. All models simply assume that the model is correct and extrapolate from there, but hopefully with an indication of uncertainty around future values.

Error-correction models have been a popular form of macro model in recent years, and cointegration is a common element. Applications have been considered using almost all major variables including investment, taxes, consumption, employment, interest rates, government expenditure, and so forth.

It is these types of equations that central banks, the Federal Reserve Bank, and various model builders have found useful for policy simulations and other considerations.

A potentially useful property of forecasts based on cointegration is that when extended some way ahead, the forecasts of the two series will form a constant ratio, as is expected by some asymptotic economic theory. It is this asymptotic result that makes this class of models of some interest to economic theorists who are concerned with "equilibrium." Whether the form of equilibria suggested by the models is related to that discussed by the theorists is unclear.

These ideas and models are fairly easily extended to many variables. Once the idea of cointegration (a name that was my own invention, incidentally) became public it was quickly picked up and used by many other econometricians and applied economists. There are now numerous citations and applications based on it. Rob Engle and I quickly realized that the concept of cointegration and its extensions could be used to explain and remove a variety of difficulties that we had observed in our own research and that of others. It seemed to be the missing piece in our approach to modeling groups of series.

An example is a problem known as "spurious regressions." It had been observed, by Paul Newbold and myself in a small simulation published in 1974, that if two independent integrated series were used in a regression, one chosen as the "dependent variable" and the other the "explanatory variable," the standard regression computer package would very often appear to "find" a relationship whereas in fact there was none. That is, standard statistical methods would find a "spurious regression." This observation lead to a great deal of reevaluation of empirical work, particularly in macroeconomics, to see if apparent relationships were correct or not. Many editors had to look again at their list of accepted papers. Putting the analysis in the form of an error-correction model resolves many of the difficulties found with spurious regression.

I am often asked how the idea of cointegration came about; was it the result of logical deduction or a flash of inspiration? In fact, it was rather more prosaic. A colleague, David Hendry, stated that the difference between a pair of integrated series could be stationary. My response was that it could be proved that he was wrong, but in attempting to do so, I showed that he was correct, and generalized it to cointegration, and proved the consequences such as the error-correction representation. I do not always agree with the philosopher Karl Popper, but in his book "The Logic of Scientific Discovery," according to Hacohen (2000), page 244, Popper believed the "discovery was not a matter of logic" but rather the application of methodology, which fits the discovery of cointegration. This insight intrigues me partly because Popper's book appeared almost exactly at the time of my birth, in September 1934. At this same time Popper was debating Heisenberg on the relevance of probability theory in physics. It happens to be the case that echoes of that debate still persists, but relating to economics. My position is that it is clear that we can best describe many of the movements of economic variables, and the resulting data, using probabilistic concepts. I should also point out that 1934 was also the year the J.M. Keynes finished the first draft of "The General Theory of Employment, Interest, and Money" although it was very many years before I became aware of this book.

As an aside, I wrote this lecture whilst visiting the Department of Economics of the University of Canterbury in New Zealand, where Karl Popper also spent some years after World War II.

Before considering the usefulness of the new methods of analysis, I would like to take a personal detour. This Prize has climaxed a year which started with me being named a Distinguished Fellow of the American Economic Association. Previously in my career, I have been Chair of two economics departments, yet I have received very little formal training in economics. One third of my first year as an undergraduate at the University of Nottingham was in economics, with introductions to micro and in national accounts, and that was it. Whatever other knowledge I have, it has come from living amongst economists for about forty years, by osmosis, attending seminars, having discussions with them, and general reading. My question is: does this say something about me, or something about the field of economics? I think it is true to say that I am not the first Nobel Prize winner in economics to have little formal training in economics. I wonder if economics has less basic core material than is necessary for fields such as mathematics, physics, or chemistry, say. Economics does have a multitude of different aspects, applications, and viewpoints which has to each form their own basis, at least in practice. Economic theory does seem to maintain common concepts and features but these may be quite simplistic and are not necessarily realistic.

Possibly because it is not tied down by too many central concepts but certainly because economics involves a myriad of topics, both theoretical and applied, it is a hot-bed of new ideas, concepts, approaches, and models. The availability of more powerful computing at low cost has just increased this activity even more.

In my reading I came across a statement (unfortunately I have forgotten who the author was) noting that "economics is a decision science, concerned with decision makers, such as consumers, employers, investors, and policy makers, in various forms of government, institutions, and corporations." I fully accept this viewpoint as it follows that the "purpose of economics is to help decision makers make better decisions." That statement is useful because it gives us a foundation with which we can compare and evaluate specific pieces of economic analysis. We can ask "how will a decision maker find this result useful?"

As I stated before, the main uses for the economic techniques that I helped develop, such as cointegration, was to build statistical models linking major economic variables that both fit the available data better and agree with the preconceptions of the model constructors about what the construction should look like. A major use of these models has been to provide short and medium term forecasts for important macro variables, such as consumption, income, investment, and unemployment, all of which are integrated series. The derived growth rates are found to be somewhat forecastable. Much less forecastable are inflation rates and returns from speculative markets, such as stocks, bonds, and exchange rates.

There are a number of stages to the forecasting process; getting the central forecast and then uncertainty bounds around it to give some idea of the risks involved in using this forecast. Finally, previous forecasts have to be gathered and evaluated. Hopefully any tendencies, trends, or swings in the errors can be detected so that one can learn and produce better forecasts in the future. The process of forecast evaluation, plus the use of combinations of forecasts from different series, is an on-going research project at the University of California, San Diego.

Forecasts do not just come from time series, but also from panels of data, which can be thought of as a group of series of a similar nature measured from different sources. An example would be monthly inflation rates from each of the Scandinavian countries. Once one is clear what is the purpose of the analysis, suitable techniques can be formulated.

I have recently been involved in such a project where the purpose is to study the future of the Amazon rainforest in Brazil. This forest covers an area larger than all the countries in the European Union put together, but it is being cut down quite rapidly. I was one of five authors who produce a report

(Anderson, *et al.,* Cambridge University Press (2003)) which includes a model that could forecast the decline of the forest under various policy scenarios. The forest is not being cut down for its timber, but to get at the land that the timber stands upon to produce food. Unfortunately, unlike European ex-forest land, its useful life span is often rather short, often becoming "fallow" within five years of being forested.

The advantage of being an academic econometrician is the possibility of working on data from many areas. I have run pricing experiments in real super markets, I have analyzed data from stock markets, commodity prices – particularly gold and silver prices, interest rates, considered electricity demand in small regions, the female labor force participation, river flooding, and even sun spots. All data present their own unique problems and I continue to find data analysis fascinating, particularly in economics.

There are plenty of disadvantages being a statistician working with economic data without very much training in the area, but occasionally it allows one to approach a problem from a different direction than that considered by most economists. As a statistician I am intrigued by the pure magnitude of some of the major economies, although economists pay little attention to this aspect of the real world. For example, in the United States there are about one hundred million households, so total consumption is the sum of all these household's consumptions. The sum over such a large number of families should have very special statistical properties, given various well-known limit theorems. If these properties are not observed this also has important implications. I think that these, and many other topics concerning aggregation, are worth further study.

An earlier concept that I was concerned with was that of causality. As a post-doctoral student in Princeton in 1959–1960, working with Professors John Tukey and Oskar Morgenstern, I was involved with studying something called the "cross-spectrum," which I will not attempt to explain. Essentially one has a pair of inter-related time series and one would like to know if there are a pair of simple relations, first from the variable X explaining Y and then from the variable Y explaining X. I was having difficulty seeing how to approach this question when I met Dennis Gabor who later won the Nobel Prize in Physics in 1971. He told me to read a paper by the eminent mathematician Norbert Wiener which contained a definition that I might want to consider. It was essentially this definition, somewhat refined and rounded out, that I discussed, together with proposed tests in the mid 1960's. The statement about causality has just two components:

1. The cause occurs before the effect; and
2. The cause contains information about the effect that that is unique, and is in no other variable.

A *consequence* of these statements is that the causal variable can help forecast the effect variable after other data has first been used. Unfortunately, many users concentrated on this forecasting implication rather than on the original definition.

At that time, I had little idea that so many people had very fixed ideas about causation, but they did agree that my definition was not "true causation" in their eyes, it was only "Granger causation." I would ask for a definition of true causation, but no one would reply. However, my definition was pragmatic and any applied researcher with two or more time series could apply it, so I got plenty of citations. Of course, many ridiculous papers appeared.

When the idea of cointegration was developed, over a decade later, it became clear immediately that if a pair of series was cointegrated then at least one of them must cause the other. There seems to be no special reason why there two quite different concepts should be related; it is just the way that the mathematics turned out.

As a brief aside for those of you with more technical training, what I have been telling you about so far has mostly been for concepts using linear models. Everything can be generalized to the nonlinear situation and recently efforts have been pushing into using similar concepts in conditional distributions, which is a very general form. It appears that causality will play a basic role in the generalization of the error-correction model, but that is still a work-in-progress.

I am not sure if the empirical studies on causation have proved to be so useful, although the debate relating to money supply and prices was interesting. The concept does help with the formulation of dynamic models in more useful ways.

I started this lecture talking about econometrics. We econometricians love numbers, so let me end with a few. The first two Nobel Prizes in Economics were to econometricians, Ragnar Frisch and Jan Tinbergen, for which we are very proud. In all there are now eight of us with the Prize, representing 15% of the Economics winners. However, in the current millennium, we represent about 44% of the winners, which I view as a healthy local trend.

Over my career and before today, I have met twenty-one Nobel Laureates: one in Physics (Dennis Gabor, 1970), one in Peace (Phillip Noel Baker, 1959), one in Chemistry (Harold Urey, 1934), plus 18 Prize winners in Economics. Without exception I have found them to be both very fine scholars and also having excellent personalities, willing to help a younger, inexperienced worker when seeking their advice or meeting them socially. I hope that I am able to live up to their very high standard.

REFERENCES

Lykke Andersen, C.W.J. Granger, Eustaquio Reis, Diana Weinhold, and Sven Wunder: "The Dynamics of Deforestation and Economic Growth in the Brazilian Amazon." Cambridge University Press, 2003.

M.H. Hacohen: "Karl Popper: The Formative Years, 1902–1945." Cambridge University Press, 2000.

K. Popper: "The Logic of Scientific Discovery." Hutchinson: London, 1959.

G. Box and G. Jenkins: "Time Series Analysis, Forecasting, and Control." Holden Day: San Francisco, 1970.

Economic Sciences 2004

FINN E. KYDLAND and EDWARD C. PRESCOTT

"for their contributions to dynamic macroeconomics: the time consistency of economic policy and the driving forces behind business cycles"

THE SVERIGES RIKSBANK (BANK OF SWEDEN) PRIZE IN ECONOMIC SCIENCES IN MEMORY OF ALFRED NOBEL

Speech written by Professor Torsten Persson, and presented by Professor Jörgen Weibull of the Royal Swedish Academy of Sciences.
Translation of the Swedish text.

Your Majesties, Your Royal Highnesses, Ladies and Gentlemen,

Brilliant scientific insights change our outlook on the world so that, as time goes by, we come to regard them as obvious. At first, however, the new ideas may appear foolish, particularly when they contradict the predominant view. This year's Laureates in Economic Sciences have seen their ideas make the journey from the foolish to the obvious – not only once, but twice.

The predominant view of business cycles and economic policy during the first half of the 1970s relied on Keynes's ideas and experience from the severe crises in the 1930s. In this view, business cycles could always be stabilized by government authorities. They should have full discretion, for instance to choose lower unemployment at the expense of higher inflation. Researchers could use so-called business-cycle models to provide underpinnings for such decisions by showing how inflation and unemployment were affected by lower interest rates or higher public expenditure.

The stable economic growth in the Western world during the 1950s and 1960s appeared to confirm this set of ideas. But the turbulent economic environment of the 1970s was an unwelcome wake-up call. Previously robust relationships in business-cycle models broke down. Economic policy failed and resulted in stagflation – concurrent inflation and unemployment. Researchers had indeed identified the shortcomings of their approaches, but there did not seem to be any feasible alternatives.

Among these frustrated researchers was Finn Kydland, who had recently received a U. S. Ph.D. and taken a job at the Norwegian School of Economics in Bergen. When advisor from Carnegie Mellon, Edward Prescott, was in Bergen as a visiting professor, the two entered into a rewarding collaboration. In 1977, the duo demonstrated – contrary to prevailing theory – that society could gain from prior commitment to economic policy. The origins of this startling conclusion lie in households' and firms' expectations. The article showed why decision-makers with complete short-run discretion to vary interest rates and expenditures are often unable to credibly announce, and adhere to, a desirable long-run policy. This time consistency problem provided a common explanation for phenomena which had hitherto been interpreted as disparate policy failures, for example the inflationary spirals in Western economies as of the mid–1970s.

The Laureates' work has stimulated new and extensive research on what types of policies are credible and politically feasible, questions which earlier analyses had never even posed. As a result, the entire discussion of economic policy has shifted from isolated measures to policymaking institutions. Practical examples include reforms of central banks and budget processes in many countries, including Sweden, over the last 10–15 years.

One summer, a few years later, Kydland and Prescott returned to Bergen, where they initiated a new project on business cycles. In 1982, they once again published results which reverberated throughout the academic community. According to established theory, variations in demand drove business cycles, but the Laureates pointed to driving forces on the supply side of the economy. They had in mind not only the oil-price shocks and productivity slowdown of the 1970s. Their new results revealed that fluctuations in the growth rate of technology could explain most of the postwar pattern in U.S. business cycles. Later on, the IT boom of the 1990s turned out to be an explicit example.

This analysis was unique also in other ways. Business cycles were the cumulative result of innumerable forward-looking decisions in households and firms, coordinated by wages, prices and interest rates. Such microeconomic foundations provide more robust results than earlier models, where the relationships were formulated at the macro level. Another novel feature was the method to calibrate a model with information from micro studies and generate synthetic time series for important macro variables by simulation. The model became a laboratory for large-scale economic experiments.

Dear Professor Kydland, Dear Professor Prescott,

At first, many economists found your ideas about economic policy design and the driving forces behind business cycles quite foolish. After passing this first test of a brilliant insight, most of your ideas have also passed the second test. Commitment vs. discretion in economic policy and cycles driven by supply as well as demand shocks are obvious to economists of today, as is the value of microeconomic underpinnings for quantitative macroeconomic modeling. Your work opened up far-reaching fields of research. It also changed our outlook on economic policy and the practice of institution design, especially in central banking.

It is a great honor and a privilege for me to convey to you, on behalf of the Royal Swedish Academy of Sciences, our warmest congratulations. I now ask you to receive your Prizes from His Majesty the King.

FINN E. KYDLAND

THE CRUCIAL DECISION

In the winter of 1968, Sten Thore, who was then a professor of economics at the Norwegian School of Economics and Business Administration (abbreviated *NHH* in Norwegian), where I was finishing up my three undergraduate years, made me an offer that would change dramatically the path I was to take for the rest of my life. I had gone to the business school in the expectation that I would eventually become a business manager. But when Sten asked if I would like to be his research assistant (vitenskapelig assistent), I agreed without thinking about what would turn out to be one of the most crucial decisions of my life.

It is interesting that I would be employed by the Department of Economics (to which Sten belonged as a faculty member), as I had not shown any more interest in the economics classes than in business. Admittedly, as business schools go, the curriculum at NHH included a substantial focus on economics. The department housed several economists who were highly visible internationally.

During my studies, I had made a couple of wise (or perhaps just lucky!) decisions. The curriculum did not permit any flexibility, except in two ways. One was to choose two elective areas of concentration, which students were to pursue by taking one course for each area per semester during the first two years. These elective tracks could be selected among four foreign languages, economic geography, economic history, law, and mathematics. I chose mathematics as one of the two (German being the other). I even took two math courses beyond the four-course sequence required for the elective.

Another source of flexibility was that the curriculum called for three relatively advanced courses, to be selected from an extensive list. My second wise decision was to take, as one of the three, the one offered by Sten Thore. In this course, we read from Howard's book on *Dynamic Programming and Markov Processes* and several rather mathematical articles from journals such as *Operations Research* and *Management Science.* I wrote my first computer program (in FORTRAN) doing dynamic programming, a tool I've used repeatedly ever since. After I had finished the course, Sten recommended to me a summer job at the local shipbuilding company to work on a computer program designed to determine a reasonable ship size for any particular route, given the available data on tonnage to be shipped and the per-unit time it took to load and unload it. Mathematically, it was an application of fractional programming – linear constraints and an objective function consisting of the ratio of two linear expressions.

As I said, Sten encouraged me to become a research assistant as I was approaching the end of my studies rather than take a job in industry. (He saved me from a boring life!) But then, after I had worked a few months as his research assistant, Sten informed me that he would be going on leave for a year to Carnegie-Mellon University, starting in January, and would I like to do my research-assistant duties there, and I agreed again. I postponed that move, however, until the summer, as Liv Kjellevold and I had married in August 1968, and Liv was finishing her last year as a nursing student. The second half of 1969 was when my fate was sealed – I would be an academic, and economics would be my field.

THE EARLY YEARS

There had been virtually no indication earlier in my life that such an outcome might even be a possibility. I grew up in Søyland (although born on the farm of my mother's parents in the neighboring township of Bjerkreim), a small area of the township Gjesdal, about 40 km south of Stavanger. There were seven farms and us. One of the neighboring farms was my grandfather's. My father, Martin, was the eldest son and therefore in line to take it over. He decided, however, to buy a truck – the first in the area to do so. He would base his living largely on a milk route between Søyland and the nearest diary, in Ålgård, 15 km away, and also on hauling other goods (and, in the spring, sheep to better pastures, returning them in the autumn) for the farmers. Eventually, he expanded to two trucks. My mother, Johanna, worked at home until all the kids (six of us, of whom I'm the eldest) were grown. I've been told that my father did well in school, although neither of my parents tried to influence their children in terms of career paths. In fact, it came as a surprise to both when I ended up as an academic.

The elementary school, in which all the pupils, except for my siblings and me, were farmers' kids, did seven years divided in three classes. We met twice a week in the first three years and three times a week during the remaining ones. The education wasn't especially "active." I was the only one in my class to go beyond elementary school. As a 15-year old, I went off to Bryne to attend Rogaland offentlege landsgymnas, the nearest high school. The need to rent a room was obvious, and probably half the pupils did so, as the distance to home made it infeasible for any of us otherwise to get to school in the morning in time for classes. Most pupils came from rural areas, as the cities typically had at least one high school.

This particular high school required an entrance exam, which I passed easily. As with all high schools in those days, one had to choose a concentration. This high school offered two, one emphasizing math and physics, and one placing a greater weight on foreign languages (although we all had English, French, and German for at least three years). Some high schools (but not this one) also had a concentration in topics oriented towards business and economics.

The education was exceptional. I've sometimes claimed that I knew more math at the end of high school than a typical American business or economics major, even at a university as highly ranked as Carnegie Mellon, know at the end of college. (As a consequence of my personal experience through my first 12 years of schooling, my bias has been to pooh-pooh the need for intensive education in elementary school, believing it is better to allow the pupils more time for play while they're kids, and instead to emphasize the importance of great high-school education.) Whether because the student body was more select than at most other high schools or because the teaching was first rate (or both), this high school always ranked highly in terms of number of *preseterister* – those students who had the grade of *very good* or *excellent* (the latter almost impossible to achieve) in absolutely all subjects. Indeed, to achieve the status of preseterist was regarded as important enough all over Norway to be worthy of photos in the local newspaper. In my case, I missed that distinction because of my grade in one subject: Norwegian composition. But my point score was still high enough to offer me the choice of just about all the university majors (the only exception being, I thought at the time, theoretical physics).

My initial inclination was to apply to the university for engineering studies, not out of a deep interest in engineering, but more for the simple reason that I had had an easy time with math and thought that's where that skill would be rewarded handily. Still, I had a nagging doubt about that decision. So to give me extra time to think about it, I applied for a one-year teaching position at the elementary school in Oltedal, the second-largest town in Gjesdal, and got it. In those days, the shortage of elementary-school teachers meant that such temporary hires straight out of high school were not uncommon. Thus, I spent a year teaching fifth and sixth graders in all subjects on Mondays through Fridays and second and third graders in Norwegian on Saturdays.

The year at Oltedal elementary school turned out to be important for my future. One of the other three teachers I'd see during lunch and other breaks was Harald Aarrestad who taught a junior-high-school class in the same school building. This program was nonaccredited, meaning that the students, at the end of the two years, would have to take their final exams in all fields at an accredited junior high school in a different town or city, but while they were in school, they could live at home. Aarrestad had taken the initiative to start this program and taught all the subjects. Further evidence of his energy and imagination was that he had started and was running two small businesses. I found him to be an extremely interesting person. Because his accountant was making lots of mistakes, he encouraged me to take a correspondence course in accounting and then promptly hired me as his accountant, a job I could easily do in my spare time. This experience gave me insight also in what it meant to run a business, a subject about which I had hitherto known nothing. Business hadn't been among the fields I had even considered for study. But by the end of the year, I decided to apply to NHH.

I had thought that, with my high-school grades, theoretical physics was the only field unavailable to me. I was wrong – NHH rejected me! Business education in Norway was a relatively young field – NHH had been started in 1936. The class size was only 60 students, and these students came from all over Norway. I learnt later that NHH gave preference to students graduating from the business concentration (which wasn't even offered at my high school). With that concentration, one could be admitted with a considerably lower high-school GPA than mine. Evidently, in those days, there was no appreciation for the notion that, in business and economics, mathematical ability could more than make up for lack of background in business subjects!

An option open to me was to study for a supplementary exam (in economics, law, business correspondence in English, German, and French, even in typewriting, which has served me well ever since!) to make my high-school education equivalent to that in the business orientation. This could be done through correspondence courses, which is what I decided to do. In the meantime, Aarrestad encouraged me to stay for another year in Oltedal, teach two subjects in his junior-high program, continue to do the accounting for him, and be fully in charge of running one of his two businesses (which imported tropical fish from Holland and distributed them to retail stores all over Norway) on a profit-sharing basis. As a result of being busier than expected, I was far from being finished with my correspondence courses at the end of the year, so I decided I might as well get my one-year mandatory military service out of the way and continue my correspondence courses while in the army. The following May, in 1965, I took the exams in Sortland, the location of the nearest high school with business concentration, during a two-week leave from the army and did well enough to be admitted to NHH starting that August. Four years later, I was off to the United States.

DOCTORAL STUDENT

Liv and I arrived in the United States in July 1969, and I still remember vividly when Sten Thore first took me to the Graduate School of Industrial Administration (GSIA) at Carnegie-Mellon University. We entered the building through the back entrance and immediately, on the back steps, met two professors to whom Sten introduced me. One was Herb Simon.

My formal status at GSIA was visiting student. Although I was there to work half time for Sten, I still signed up for three core economics courses: macroeconomics by Martin Bronfenbrenner, econometrics by Marty Geisel, and general equilibrium theory by John Ledyard (intended for second-year students, but my mathematics elective at NHH, along with subsequent math courses there, made it eminently manageable for me). Moreover, I decided, probably with the encouragement of Sten, to take linear programming from Egon Balas. About a month into the semester (while still doing a moderate amount of work for Sten), I came to the realization that to make it in research I needed a doctoral degree. I applied, and was promptly accepted in the doctoral program.

In December, Sten and his family returned to Norway and we were on our own, although I was still supported financially by NHH. Nonlinear programming by Egon Balas was a useful course for me. So were statistical decision theory taught by Morris DeGroot and microeconomics by Mort Kamien. But the most unusual course that first spring was economic fluctuations by Bob Lucas. He started out with basic mathematics, such as Kuhn-Tucker theory and functional equations, interspersed with economic applications. One day, sometime after the midpoint, Bob started setting up a model. In the following class he told us to scrap everything he had said the last time. He started over again, making a simplifying assumption or two, and then, over the course of the next couple of lectures, took the analysis to its conclusion. Later, we realized we had seen his paper "Expectations and the Neutrality of Money," for which he was later to get the Nobel Prize, being developed right there in front of our eyes.

GSIA was (and is) unusual in at least two ways. One was the small class size, which promoted a co-operative environment among the students. Also, there was relatively little course work. Most of the material taught was foundational, with emphasis on tools to put the student right on the research frontier. Important requirements were the first- and second-year summer research papers. My first-year paper was entitled "Duality in Fractional Programming," a topic that came to me partly because of the project for the shipbuilder in Bergen, partly because of all the mathematical programming I was taking. The paper ended up being my first serious publication, in *Naval Research Logistics Quarterly*, which my professors told me was ranked third in the operations research field. My main advisor was Bob Kaplan, later to become the dean of GSIA, whose specialty was dynamic programming (but who years later moved into accounting).

My second-year summer paper also involved dual prices, this time in hierarchical linear programs, and it was published in *Management Science*. By that time, I had become interested in an economic topic that went under the name of "the assignment problem." It had generated a substantial literature. The idea was, within the system-of-equations framework dominating macroeconomics at the time, that fiscal policy was more effective at achieving certain goals and monetary policy was effective at others. If the right instruments were assigned to the right targets, the economy would function quite well, while if the wrong assignment was chosen, the economy would function poorly and could, in the worst case, even be unstable. My idea was to think of the monetary and fiscal policymakers as separate decision makers with different goals, such that all the target variables would enter each objective function, but with different relative weights. Thus, a dynamic game resulted. Moreover, because of the differences in policymaking process for the alternative instruments, it made sense to me to think of the fiscal policy maker as dominant in the sense that he went first in every period, with the monetary policy maker a follower. This set-up represented an alternative to the symmetric noncooperative (Nash) solution.

In August 1971, I happened to run into a new professor who temporarily had been placed in a windowless office (presumably due to his arrival well before the start of classes), which later served for years as the mail room. He introduced himself to me as Ed Prescott and asked what I was working on. Evidently, he liked what I told him, and showed me some game-theoretic research he had done in an oligopoly context.

By the following spring, I had taken a course from Dave Cass who, like Ed Prescott, had arrived in GSIA in time for the 1971–72 academic year. I had had some conversations with him, and among other things told him about one of my findings, that even in the symmetric noncooperative case, the outcome was different when the solution was regarded as a policy rule in a recursive way as opposed to a *sequence* of decisions for the entire future. Dave asked me to prove it, as this finding went counter to the well-known property in single-player control theory that the solutions in what can be called policy space, on the one hand, and sequence space, on the other, give identical outcomes. Of course, once Dave saw the proof, he bought it right away. Moreover, I argued that the solution in policy space represented a more reasonable equilibrium from an economic standpoint.

That spring, I presented my thesis proposal to the faculty. The main element, motivated primarily by my version of the assignment problem, represented an application of dynamic game theory. Immediately after the faculty's deliberations, Bob Kaplan, who had been my main advisor up to that point, came to my PhD carrel with the outcome. In addition to informing me that I had passed, he told me that Ed Prescott had insisted on becoming the chairman of my committee. All along I had thought it would be Dave Cass (who still was to be a member of the committee, as was Kaplan). Thus started in earnest years of productive and much-appreciated interaction with Prescott.

THE 1977 PAPER…

After four years of PhD work, I defended my dissertation in time to graduate in May 1973. It was time to return to Bergen. While Cass and Prescott had both suggested I would do well on the U.S. job market, I felt obliged to take a position offered me by NHH. They had provided full financial aid for my studies. But one thing remained to be done. In April, around the time the final draft of my thesis was turned in, Ed had shown me a new paper by Bob Lucas. Its title (at least in its final draft) was "Econometric Policy Evaluation: A Critique." Ed had given it to me to consider whether one of the models Bob had used as examples of his critique could be banged into my dominant-player framework, with a government objective added to Bob's general set-up. In their *Econometrica* article on "Investment under Uncertainty" two years earlier, Bob and Ed had shown, using a dynamic industry model with capital accumulation, that the competitive equilibrium could be obtained quite simply by solving a particular stand-in consumer-surplus problem. So we thought why not do something similar, but then add that the industry was affected by cyclical investment-tax-credit policy? We submitted an abstract to the June Stochastic Economics and Control Conference, an annual conference that had recently started up at the initiative, I believe, of David Kendrick and Gregory Chow, and then we worked like crazy to get it in shape.

So while Liv and our one-year-old son Martin left for Norway at the end of May as planned, I stayed behind for an extra month to work on the paper and to attend the conference. I was pleased (as was Ed, I'm sure) with the attention the paper got.

The first year at NHH was frustrating as it was clear that modern macroeconomics was not the school's strength. Soon I came up with the idea of inviting Ed to spend a year at NHH. He seemed interested, and I set the wheels in motion to drum up financial support for his stay. I succeeded, and Ed and his family showed up in time for the 1974–75 academic year. By that time, two significant things had happened. In my thesis, although describing three different solutions to the dominant-player game – the recursive without commitment, the commitment solution in policy space, and the commitment solution in sequence space – I had calculated examples of only the first, in part because that's the one I argued was *the* candidate for an equilibrium. Also, the other two were much harder to calculate. During my first semester of teaching, I had identified an exceptional undergraduate, Nina Bjerkedal, whom I encouraged to become my research assistant. I gave her the task of writing a FORTRAN program to calculate the profits of a dominant firm on the assumption that it could commit to its optimal policy. It turned out these profits beat those of the otherwise time-consistent outcome by an astounding margin. Moreover, when Ed arrived, he had clearly warmed to the idea that the focus of our paper had to be a comparison with and without commitment. We expected the result that the time-consistent solution could represent quite an undesirable outcome.

Our progress initially was slow because Ed was busy with other matters and I was in the middle of getting out three papers based on my dissertation. One contained a description of the solutions that I argued, from an economic standpoint, represented dynamic equilibrium outcomes in symmetric noncooperative games and in dominant-player games (*International Economic Review* 1975), one was on the assignment problem (*Annals of Economic and Social Measurement* 1976), and one focused on dynamic dominant-player games (*Journal of Economic Theory* 1977).

When Ed and I finally got going on our paper in the spring, we first worried about two key issues. Our intuition was that the difference between the two solutions was greater when a lot of inherent dynamics was present in the model. Sticking to our stochastic model of capital accumulation in the face of government stabilization policy using the investment tax credit, we introduced "time-to-build" into the model *in combination with* the standard cost of adjustment. Secondly, we had realized, after we wrote our 1973 paper, that we needed to make sure the rest of the economy was treated explicitly as being inhabited by atomistic agents (not treated as one player). Ultimately, the appendix dealt with how to solve that issue (the "big K–little k" problem).

I had submitted my assignment-problem paper to a stochastic control conference to take place in Boston in May. At some point early in the conference, Gregory Chow announced a session for work in progress. I signed up to talk about Ed's and my paper, and was told I could go first. All hell broke loose. Everyone was trying to locate the error. Admittedly, we had chosen a rather provocative title for our first draft: "On The Inapplicability of Optimal Control for Policy Making." I was certain nothing was wrong. With all my experience in dynamic dominant-player games, I knew time inconsistency had to be an issue. I suppose at that point, after what happened at that presentation, I realized our findings could generate considerable attention. Moreover, as a consequence of the difficulty people had in understanding the time inconsistency, we decided to add, for expository reasons, a Phillips-curve example to our investment-tax-credit example before we resubmitted our revised version of the paper to the *Journal of Political Economy*. As I recall, it was motivated by a model in a recent paper by Phelps and Taylor. Of course, that example has turned out to be used a lot by subsequent writers.

With the rules-vs-discretion paper pretty much done, I dabbled in industrial organization for a while, especially pushing further the dominant-firm model from my dissertation. I had gone on leave for the academic year 1976–77 to the University of Minnesota (never to return, as it turned out, to Norway for any permanent position). While in Minneapolis, I was invited to visit Carnegie-Mellon University the following year. During that year, I was offered an associate-professor position, which I accepted.

...AND THE 1982 PAPER

By that time, Prescott and I had started to work on business cycles. Some of the computer programs used in our 1977 article could be adapted quite easily to calculating dynamic equilibriums of business-cycle models. In the beginning, we considered models in which we made the technology linear and the representative household's utility function quadratic. We included technology shocks, but at first, in large part because of Lucas's 1972 article, we didn't think we could do without monetary shocks. For an NBER conference in 1978, we wrote a paper that was somewhat schizophrenic. It contained a business cycle model, but also evaluated stabilization policy. The main idea behind the latter was that changes in taxes were costly as a way to balance the government budget over the cycle. Instead the "slack" should be picked up by fluctuations in government debt. In the end, we were asked to reduce the length of the paper for the resulting conference volume published by the NBER in 1980, and we had to leave out much of that material.

Instead, we wrote another paper on policy – a standard growth model with labor and capital taxes financing government purchases – and made the point that capital taxes should be low to maximize the representative consumer's welfare. At the same time, lack of commitment was likely to lead to capital taxes that were much higher than optimal. That paper, published in the 1980 *Journal of Economic Dynamics and Control*, also dispelled a common misunderstanding at the time, namely that time inconsistency originates from the policy maker's objective being different from those of the people. Our model economy is inhabited by millions of people who are all alike, and the government is assumed to have preferences that coincide with those of the representative household. Finally, the paper presents a way of determining the optimal policy (with commitment) through the use of a particular shadow price as a state variable. Variants of this basic method are still being used in many contexts.

A key breakthrough in Ed's and my continuing business cycle research was the realization that we could start with the basic growth model, with both production and utility functions in exponential forms and, to the extent necessary, approximate in order to make the computations tractable. Suddenly, the number of parameters was much smaller and their calibration transparent. For example, first-order conditions for the steady state implied relations between the parameters and steady-state values of the model aggregates, the latter with counterparts in corresponding average values in the data. With those averages quantified from the data, one could then map, through those first-order conditions, to the parameter values that would reproduce the steady-state values corresponding to the data. This procedure is called calibration.

The paper published in the 1980 NBER conference volume (titled *Rational Expectations and Economic Policy* and edited by Stanley Fischer) was our first real-business-cycle paper. That summer, we wrote the first draft of another paper, later to be published by *Econometrica* in 1982, in which we put our vastly improved calibration procedure to use. My first presentation of it took place at Cornell University in the early autumn of 1980 (in a job talk; evidently, the paper did not impress them, as I was told later that no offer would be forthcoming).

LOOSE ENDS

In our first two business-cycle papers Ed and I were surprised to find that including a role for money made very little difference to the model outcomes. Virtually all the "action" came from technology shocks and, moreover, they accounted surprisingly well for the data. In 1980, I wrote a first draft of a paper in which I focused on the role of money for the business cycle. I used two separate propagation mechanisms, one based on imperfect information in the spirit of Lucas's paper on "Expectations and the Neutrality of Money," and one in which there was a household trade-off between time and holdings of money. In the latter, the cyclical movement of the price level was in the right direction and of considerable magnitude, even when the central bank let the money stock grow steadily without fluctuations. The most interesting finding of the first part of the paper was that, while price shocks had the effect, as in Lucas 1972, of making people act in part as if these nominal shocks represented changes in real prices (because of the imperfect information), they also led people to react less to everything, including the real shocks, and the latter effect turned out to dominate, so that, for the calibrated economy, the larger is the variance of the price shocks resulting from central-bank behavior, the lower the business-cycle volatility. (Of course, this reduction in volatility is by no means welfare improving!)

While I gave this paper several times, and it was once on the program of the winter meetings of the Econometric Society, it continued to remain on the back burner in the sense that there always seemed to be projects with higher priority. In the end, I got the paper in shape to submit it to the *Journal of Monetary Economics* and got a favorable revise and resubmit. But then, in response to an invitation to a conference on the 100th anniversary of Ragnar Frisch's birth (whom I admire greatly and regard as having been well ahead of his time in the 1930s), I decided the paper fit well for that purpose and elected to use it there. The proceedings were to be published in a special volume of the *Econometric Society*. Unfortunately, the referee criticized the paper on issues related to the by then standard approximations (in my opinion a completely peripheral and inconsequential issue relative to the question addressed), and the editor, along with the conference organizer at the University of Oslo went along with the referee. At that point, three or four years after the *JME* referee report, I figured it was too late to resubmit it to them, so the paper remains unpublished (but often cited).

Much of my research immediately following upon the 1982 *Econometrica* article revolved around the labor market. The main anomaly relative to Ed's and my business-cycle model was the high cyclical hours-of-work volatility in U.S. data. We were convinced that a large part of the discrepancy was attributable to the simplicity of the abstraction. All model people were assumed to be alike. Literally speaking, all of the model's labor-input variation is in hours per worker, while, empirically, much more of it is in the form of changes in the number of workers (employment). This issue was dealt with beautifully by Gary Hansen in his 1985 *JPE* paper.

Another aspect of reality, not shared by our model, is the workforce's great variety of skills for market production. When Allan Meltzer called me sometime in the autumn of 1982 (while I was visiting the Hoover Institution for a year as a National Fellow) and asked me to write a paper for the 10th anniversary Carnegie-Rochester Conference to be held a year later, suggesting that the organizers would like a paper on the importance of contract theory for the business cycle, I was so convinced of the much greater importance of heterogeneity of workers' skills that I decided, without consulting Allan, that that was the labor-market topic I wanted to write about. So in the paper, entitled "Labor-Force Heterogeneity and the Business Cycle," I document with the help of data from the Panel Study of Income Dynamics (PSID) the vast differences in cyclical hours behavior depending on skills, and then construct a model with two skills categories, calibrated to what was known about the workforce if it is divided in two, according to skills. One implication of the model indeed turns out to be substantially greater work-hour variability than in the basic equal-skills model.

Part of the problem was that, given the form of the 1982 model, comparing its labor-input implications with aggregate hours of work could be quite misleading. A better measure would quality-adjust the hours of each worker before adding them up. That's what Ed Prescott and I did in a study a few years later. Based on data from the PSID, we found, for that sample, that the volatility of unweighted total hours was 40 percent greater than that of a weighted measure. This paper was published in 1993 in the Federal Reserve Bank of Cleveland's *Economic Review*.

Finally, as it was clear while working on our 1982 paper that greater intertemporal substitution of labor was a way to produce more labor-input volatility in the model, as an alternative to our standard utility function we had also introduced one that was nonseparable over time in leisure. As later shown in my above-mentioned labor-force heterogeneity paper, this utility function can be regarded as a stand-in for a particular household-production formulation. Still, we were somewhat in the dark as to what were reasonable values of the two additional parameters characterizing the nonseparability. In a subsequent study with Joe Hotz and Guilherme Sedlacek, published in *Econometrica* 1988, those parameters were estimated based on data from the PSID.

A prevalent misunderstanding in the early 1980s was that Ed and I had put forward our 1982 model as a way to "fit" the data. As this misunderstanding was still evident from the general discussion following the presentation of my 1984 paper at the Carnegie-Rochester Conference session, I took the opportunity, in a rejoinder to the discussant's comments, to state as precisely as I could what the question had been: If technology shocks were the only source of impulse to post-war U.S. business cycles, what portion of the cycle would remain? Our answer, based on that model, was over 50 percent. Importantly, this measurement was based on a calibrated model that was explicit about the dynamic decision problems faced by the model's people and businesses.

MY CO-AUTHORS

Throughout my academic careeer, I've had the great fortune to work with so many eminent researchers. I've already mentioned Hotz and Sedlacek. Prescott and I continued to do joint work off and on over the next decade. One focus was on variable capital utilization in the form of variation in the hours the capital is used. This general theme is reflected in our 1988 *Journal of Monetary Economics* paper and in our 1991 *Economic Theory* paper. As our business-cycle methodology received greater acceptance in the profession, we were also asked for methodological or expository contributions, which resulted, in particular, in our papers in the *Scandinavian Journal of Economics* 1991 and *Journal of Economic Literature* 1996.

The area of international macroeconomics has been ripe with puzzles and anomalies. An example is the fact that, between pairs of major countries, the cyclical consumption correlations are about the same as the corresponding output correlations. Another seeming anomaly is that, cyclically, the trade balance is the worst (that is, more negative) when one's goods are the cheapest. Beginning with a one-year stay at the Federal Reserve Bank of Minneapolis in 1989, David Backus, Patrick Kehoe, and I wrote several papers on the general subject of international real business cycles. Indeed, our first paper, in the *Journal of Political Economy* 1992, is entitled exactly that. We find, among other things, that the "consumption anomaly" mentioned above is quite robust, even under serious impediments to trade. Another paper was published in the *American Economic Review* 1994. In this paper, we find that the seeming anomaly involving the trade balance and the terms of trade is precisely what a calibrated model says should happen.

In the early 1990s, Bill Gavin encouraged me to become a research associate at the Federal Reserve Bank of Cleveland, which entailed occasional visits there. Slowly but surely we started to work on questions having to do with the role of money for the business cycle. When, after some time, Bill moved to the Federal Reserve Bank of St. Louis, he talked me into continuing to visit him there. This working relationship has resulted in several papers. One in the *Review of Economic Dynamics* 1999, for example, documents differences in postwar comovements of monetary aggregates with real GDP before and after 1980. The price level is still countercyclical in both subperiods, and the comovements of various real aggregates with real GDP are very similar. Then we go on to show that a monetary model with fully flexible prices, but with differences in policy regimes, can account for the different episodes. It is well known in policy circles that an important change in monetary policy did indeed take place during and after the Volcker era at the central bank. The subsequent work with Bill has, to some extent, been joint with others at the St. Louis Fed, in particular Rob Dittmar and Mike Pakko.

After Gavin had left the Cleveland Fed, I was still encouraged to continue visiting there for a couple of weeks a year. Over time, I started to work with Peter Rupert, first on measuring quality-weighted labor input based on Current Population Survey data, which are monthly, more up-to-date, and cover many more workers than does the PSID. After a while, we, along with Paul Gomme, also became interested in a major anomaly in the literature on the interaction of household and business activity, a literature that had sprung up in the early 1990s. The anomaly had to do with the degree of contemporaneousness of cyclical movements in household and business investment, with the former leading the latter. Our most significant paper so far made headway on that anomaly and was published in the *Journal of Political Economy* 2001.

In the mid 1990s, I was hired by the University of Texas, supposedly to help them build up the macro group. Unfortunately, while everyone in my family enjoyed Austin very much, in the end the administration's concept of keeping a promise was quite disappointing, and we unhappily left. But that stay had two longer-run consequences. Scott Freeman and I had talked about writing a paper about the interaction of money and output over the business cycle, using a novel model with both inside and outside money, and we finally completed it after I had left Texas. The paper ended up in the *American Economic Review* 2000. Subsequently, Scott and I wrote a follow-up paper for a conference at the Federal Reserve Bank of Cleveland, this time jointly also with Espen Henriksen, then a GSIA PhD student.

While in Austin, I was signed on as a research associate at the Federal

Reserve Bank of Dallas, a relationship that has continued to this day. While there, I have done research with D'Ann Petersen, Mark Wynne, and Carlos Zarazaga. The work with D'Ann represented the beginnings of a labor-input measurement project. Mark and I (along with Alan Ahearne, a former student of mine at Carnegie Mellon, now at the Federal Reserve Board) decided to investigate the reasons for Ireland's spectacular growth after 1990. Carlos and I embarked on a study of a much less successful nation – Argentina – and wrote a paper on its great depression in the 1980s, published in the *Review of Economic Dynamics* 2002.

Subsequently, Carlos and I decided to plug into our model – a standard version of the neoclassical growth model – the numbers for the period after 1990. To our great surprise, the model predicted that, while output from 1990 to 1998 had grown at a rapid pace by most standards, GDP and especially the capital stock should have grown much faster in light of the productivity growth that had taken place. This is a curious finding. Why should it be so? Did Argentina suffer from the "time-inconsistency disease" to such an extent that, even with the currency board instituted by former President Menem in 1990, the nation's credibility among investors still was much too low? This research highlights the dire situation in which Argentina found itself after it experienced a second and much faster-progressing great depression after 1998. By 2003, measured capital per working-age person had fallen an astounding 20 percent relative to 1982, with pessimistic implications for the average real wage as well as for the income distribution.

In the early 1990s, Michael Bordo came to visit Carnegie Mellon for an extended period. Our interaction during his stay resulted in two papers in which we interpret the history of the gold standard in light of the time-inconsistency of government policy and the need for a commitment mechanism to maintain credibility.

Dynamic macroeconomics, with the explicit analysis it entails of the decision problems of households and businesses, is not easy to teach and learn at the basic level. My impression over the past couple of decades is that the gulf between the research frontier and what's in undergraduate textbooks has grown wider and wider. So ten years ago, I started to use the computational experiment as a teaching tool in part of my semester-long course in intermediate macroeconomics. At first, the students would simply use the executable version of a FORTRAN program, with its rather crude input and output formats. A few years ago, during my annual summer visit to Bergen and NHH as part of my adjunct professor position, I was able to interest Solveig Bjørnestad of the Institute for Information Science at the University of Bergen in the idea that she and her students, in co-operation with me, could design and develop a learning environment that would be user friendly, perhaps even fun, for the students, with the goal that it would enhance dramatically their understanding of dynamic macro. This co-operative effort still continues. A detailed description of the approach and of the contents so far is written up in our joint 2004 paper.

During all of this, I have helped to raise four children: Marty, Eirik,

Camilla, and Kari. At times I've wondered if academic life took away too much time, which I otherwise could have spent with them. Some years ago, Liv and I parted ways. Liv claims that the extent of my travels took its toll. She has since remarried.

Almost two years ago, I had the incredible luck to stumble upon Tonya Schooler (now Kydland), a wonderful person, and we have been inseparable ever since. The complications of three academic careers (including her ex-husband's) combined with co-raising her school-age children, Joel and Rachel, took us, in August 2004, to the beautiful city of Vancouver. I accepted the Jeffrey Henley Chair in Economics at the University of California at Santa Barbara. Admittedly, Santa Barbara is still a long commute from Vancouver, but one in which Tonya has been happy to share. In the spring of 2004, the University of British Columbia had made me a nice offer, but their rule of mandatory retirement at 65, from which their provost refused to make an exception for me, was inconsistent with my desire to remain an academic and continue my research until I drop. I believe my co-researchers are happy I'm slowly but surely finding more time to get back into what I love to do. In my case, one of the benefits resulting from the Prize is the availability of funding to set up a major research institute at UCSB. Among other things, it will bring researchers from all over the world together for periods of time to brainstorm on important outstanding questions and anomalies in macroeconomics and finance.

QUANTITATIVE AGGREGATE THEORY

Prize Lecture, December 8, 2004

by

FINN E. KYDLAND

University of California, Santa Barbara and Carnegie Mellon University, Pittsburgh, USA.

I'm delighted to stand before so many people. I'm also very happy when I get to work with *models* with many people. That is the key to the framework for which Ed Prescott and I were cited by the Nobel committee: The people are introduced explicitly in the models. Their decision problems are fully dynamic – people are forward-looking. That is one of the prerequisites for what we ultimately seek, a framework in which we can evaluate economic policy.

The eminent researcher and 1995 Nobel laureate in economics, Bob Lucas, from whom I've learned a lot, wrote (Lucas, 1980): "One of the functions of theoretical economics is to provide fully articulated, artificial economic systems that can serve as laboratories in which policies that would be prohibitively expensive to experiment with in actual economies can be tested out at much lower cost... (696). Our task, as I see it...is to write a FORTRAN program that will accept specific economic policy rules as 'input' and will generate as 'output' statistics describing the operating characteristics of time series we care about, which are predicted to result from these policies" (709–10). The desired environments to which Lucas refers would make use of information on "*individual* responses [that] can be documented relatively cheaply...by means of...censuses, panels [and] other surveys..." (710). Lucas seems to suggest that economic researchers place people in desired model environments and record how they behave under alternative policy rules.

In practice, that is easier said than done. The key tool macroeconomists use is the *computational experiment.* Using it, the researcher performs precisely what I just described – places the model's people in the desired environment and records their behavior. But the purpose of the computational experiment is broader than simply to evaluate policy rules. The computational experiment is useful for answering a host of questions, in particular quantitative ones, that is, those for which we seek numerical answers. When evaluating government policy, the policy is stated in the form of a rule that specifies how the government will behave – what action to take under various contingencies – today and in the indefinite future. That's one reason it would be so difficult and prohibitively expensive to perform the alternative Lucas mentions, namely, to test the policies in actual economies.

THE COMPUTATIONAL EXPERIMENT

These models contain millions of people. My tiny laptop contains several such models. People are characterized by their preferences over goods and leisure into the indefinite future. Their budget constraints are explicit. They receive income from working and from owning capital, and their choices must remain within their budget constraints, given the prices they face – wage rates and interest rates, for example. In other words, these models are explicit about people's dynamic decision problems.

The models also contain thousands of businesses. Implied is a description of aggregate production possibilities – say, in the form of an aggregate production function. It describes the technology for converting inputs of capital and labor into output of goods, which can be used for consumption or to add to future productive capital – investment.

A key aspect of the production function is its description of the technology level and its change over time. It's a broad concept at this level of abstraction. Technological change encompasses anything that affects the transformation, given by the aggregate production function, of aggregate inputs of capital and labor into goods and services. It includes, of course, the usual outcomes of innovative activity, but also could include, again at this level of abstraction, factors such as oil shocks, new environmental regulations, changes in the legal constraints affecting the nature of contracting between workers and firms, government provision of infrastructure, and the loss in financial intermediation associated with banking panics – all elements one might want to study in more detail, depending on the question. But, for many questions, it makes perfect sense to include them implicitly as part of the technology level.

I've described two elements of typical models used for computational experiments: the millions of model inhabitants and the thousands of businesses. An essential aspect, however, is the calibration of the model environment. In a sense, models are measuring devices: they need to be calibrated, or otherwise we would have little faith in the answers they provide. In this sense, they are like thermometers. We know what a thermometer is supposed to register if we dip it into water with chunks of ice, or into a pot of boiling water. In the same sense, the model should give approximately correct answers to questions whose answers we already know. Usually, there are many such questions. In the context of business-cycle analysis, we know a lot about the long run of the economy, or we may use the Panel Study of Income Dynamics, say, for the United States or similar panel studies from other nations to collect the data to calibrate the model. Thus, the calibration is part of the action of making the quantitative answer as reliable as possible.

A computational experiment yields time series of the aggregate decisions of the model economy's people. Through the model formulation and its calibration, we have determined what the economic environment should look like. Then, the millions of people and the thousands of businesses in the economy make their decisions over time, and the computer records their decisions. We obtain time series as if we were confronted with an actual economy. These time series may be described statistically and compared with analogous statistics from the data for the nation under study. In a business-cycle study, these statistics may include standard deviations of detrended aggregates describing the amplitudes of their business-cycle movements, as well as correlation coefficients as measures of their comovements.

A SIMPLE EXAMPLE

Now I should like to walk you through a simple model – substantially simpler than that in Kydland and Prescott (1982), for example. It contains household and business sectors. To make it as straightforward as possible, I'll abstract from the government. For the same reason, there will be no foreign sector in this model. Moreover, for simplicity steady-state growth is zero. I have two main goals: to discuss the sense in which the model contains household and business sectors, and to give examples of what's involved in calibrating the parameters (see Cooley and Prescott 1995 for a detailed description of the practice of calibration, and Kydland 1995 for an elaborate example in which all the details have been worked out).

First, we have a description of the typical household's preferences in the form of a utility function to be maximized:

$$E\sum_{t=0}^{\infty}\beta^{t}\,\frac{(C_t^{\alpha}L_t^{1-\alpha})^{1-\sigma}-1}{1-\sigma}$$

Business cycles involve uncertainty about the future, so what one aims to maximize is *expected* (denoted by E) utility as a function of consumption, C, and leisure, L, over the indefinite future. It may seem a little far-fetched to be summing the utility from today (period zero, let's say) to infinity. I'll return to that assumption. The parameter β is a number slightly less than 1 and can be calibrated from knowledge of the long-run real interest. It simply describes the degree of people's impatience. Additional parameters are α and σ, also to be calibrated. I'll return to α in a minute. The parameter σ is what we may call a risk-aversion parameter, about which finance people know a lot. I could have picked a more general functional form in the class of so-called constant-elasticity-of-substitution functions. This particular one is consistent with the empirical observation that, as the U.S. real wage has doubled over the past decades, long-run hours worked per household have changed little.

The model formulation being presented is the statement of a planner's problem whose solution can be shown to be the equilibrium of an economy inhabited by millions of people with preferences such as this utility function. It contains a resource constraint,

$$C_t + I_t = z_t K_t^{\theta} N_t^{1-\theta} = r_t K_t + w_t N_t$$

which says that the sum of consumption and investment cannot exceed what the economy produces. The right-hand side of the first equality states that the economy produces output using capital – factories, machines, office buildings – along with the labor input of workers, and the technology level is denoted by z. In other words, this is total output – gross domestic product – as given by the production function, the specification of which is essential to all of macroeconomics. Moreover, GDP has to equal gross domestic income, the sum of capital and labor income, which appears on the right-hand side of the second equality.

In addition to this resource constraint, we have a constraint on time, which here can be devoted either to leisure or to labor input:

$$L_t + N_t = 1$$

The right-hand side equals 1; that is, without loss of generality I've chosen units so that if we add all the discretionary time – total time net of sleep and personal care – across people, it equals 1.

Then we have two relations representing key aspects of what makes an economy dynamic:

$$K_{t+1} = (1 - \delta) K_t + I_t$$

and

$$z_{t+1} = \rho z_t + \varepsilon_{t+1}$$

The first, where K_t denotes the capital stock at the beginning of period t, describes how the capital stock at any time depends on past investment decisions, where δ is the depreciation rate. Finally, the technology level is all-important because it's what, in this simple model, gives rise to uncertainty. If, as is borne out by the data, the parameter ρ is close to 1, the relation says that new technological innovations, given by ε, are long-lasting. One usually imagines that this random variable ε is drawn from a normal probability distribution, whose variance can be estimated from the data.

As we have seen, this simple economy already has a number of parameters we need to calibrate. One reason for presenting this model is so I can discuss two typical examples of calibration, namely of the parameters α in the utility functions and θ in the production function. Suppose we went to a panel of thousands of people and calculated the average of how much time they devote to market activity. That figure pins down, via a steady-state first-order condition, the value of α that makes this average identical in the model economy to that in the data. Similarly, with regard to the parameter θ, a property of the model is that if we look up National Income and Product Accounts data and find, say, that out of total gross domestic income, on the average 36 percent is compensation for capital input and 64 percent represents labor income, then that calibrates the parameter θ to 0.36.

I've used this model as a vehicle for talking about the two key sectors of the economy. The household sector contains lots of people characterized by the utility function – a description of the preferences over consumption and leisure into the indefinite future. The business sector is described by the technology for producing goods and services from capital and labor inputs. I have talked about the features that make this model dynamic, and about a key source of uncertainty. One could include many other such features. Ed Prescott mentioned in his lecture the so-called time-to-build assumption, which would make the model more detailed, as in the 1982 paper to which the Nobel committee refers. That model also contains inventories, as well as both permanent and temporary shocks. What to include depends on the question the model is designed to address. The question for which this framework was first put to use by Ed Prescott and me can be stated as follows: If technology shocks were the only source of impulse, what portion of business-cycle fluctuations would still have remained? The model produced a preliminary answer to that question: well over one-half, and that answer has pretty much been confirmed to be somewhere around 70 percent. The model provided measurement.

DOES BEING DIFFERENT MATTER?

Returning to the utility function, I assume in my prototype model above that preferences are given by some function that covers the entire future – goes to infinity. In other words, we have great power in setting up this economy: we can decide that people are immortal! That assumption turns out to be surprisingly innocuous for many questions. Of course it makes sense to check if it makes a difference and, as economists often conclude in many contexts, it depends. For many business-cycle questions, the answer is no. That's rather surprising. If you think about mortal people and their life-cycle behavior, typically they earn relatively little labor income early in their lives, then experience a substantial increase in income when they enter the middle stage, and finally, for those who live long enough, enter a period in which they will have retired from market work. In other words, the labor-earnings profile is decidedly hump-shaped. But we also know that people prefer a consumption stream that's much more even over time. So there will be a period in which they spend more than their income, then spend less for two or three decades, and finally revert to spending more than their labor income toward the end of their lives. Moreover, the behavior in various other ways typically is quite interesting at the beginning and end of one's working life.

Thus, it would seem that life-cycle behavior could matter substantially. Víctor Ríos-Rull (1996), however, finds for a typical business-cycle question such as the one I mentioned above that if we employ an economy with mortal consumers in which realistic life-cycle behavior is included, then as we aggregate across all of these people the time series in the computational experiments, we get approximately the same answer as in the immortal-consumer economy. Of course, there are a lot of questions for which life-cycle behavior does make a big difference. Among those are the economic impact on savings, interest rates, and tax rates of immigration, Social Security reform, and baby boomers' retirement, to mention a few.

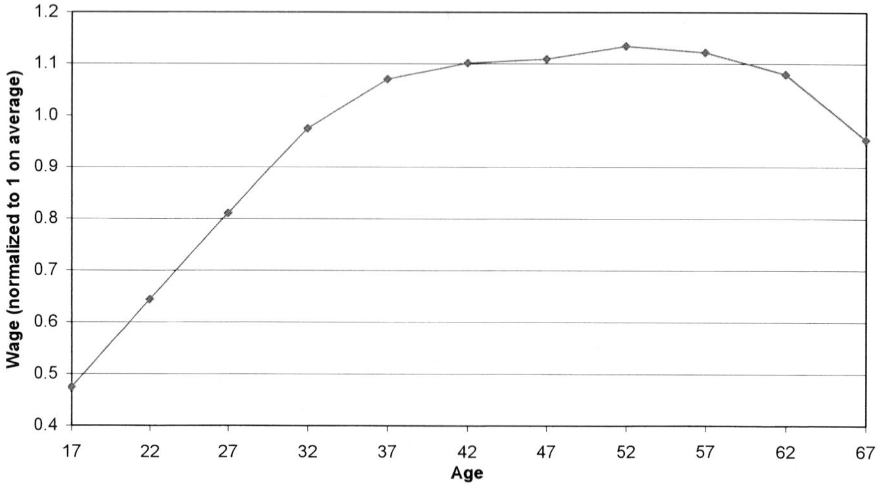

Figure 1. United States, Life-Cycle Wage Profiles. Source: Cross-sectional data based on 1990 US Census, as reported in Kjetil Storesletten (1995).

To give you a sense of how different people are and emphasize the need for including them when addressing *some* questions, I'll show you some numbers. Figure 1 displays the average life-cycle profile of people's efficiency of working in the market sector, as indicated by their real wage rates.

The graph shows a major reason for the hump-shaped profile of people's labor earnings depending on age. The curve is normalized so that it averages 1. It starts at around 0.5 and rises rapidly so that for a long time span later in people's working lives their efficiency is more than twice what it is when they enter the workforce. In addition to these life-cycle differences in workers' skills comes the fact that workers are quite different in their abilities as they enter the work force, depending on education and other factors. An interesting study of the aggregate implications of the interaction between, on the one hand, the labor input divided into low- and high-skilled workers and, on the other hand, the capital input divided into structures and equipment is in Krusell, Ohanian, Ríos-Rull, and Violante (2000). Their focus is on real-wage movements in particular. For a more elaborate discussion of cyclical implications, especially as they pertain to measured labor-input fluctuations, see Kydland and Petersen (1997), on which some parts of this lecture are based.

Figure 2 displays the age distribution of the U.S. population in 1994 and that projected to 2020. The vertical axis shows the percentage of people of different ages. You see the noticeable hump in 1994 roughly in the 30-to-40 age range. Predictably, there will be a corresponding hump in 2020. Of course, a reason to worry about this empirical pattern is that by 2020 many, if not most, of these baby boomers will have retired, putting a major strain on the

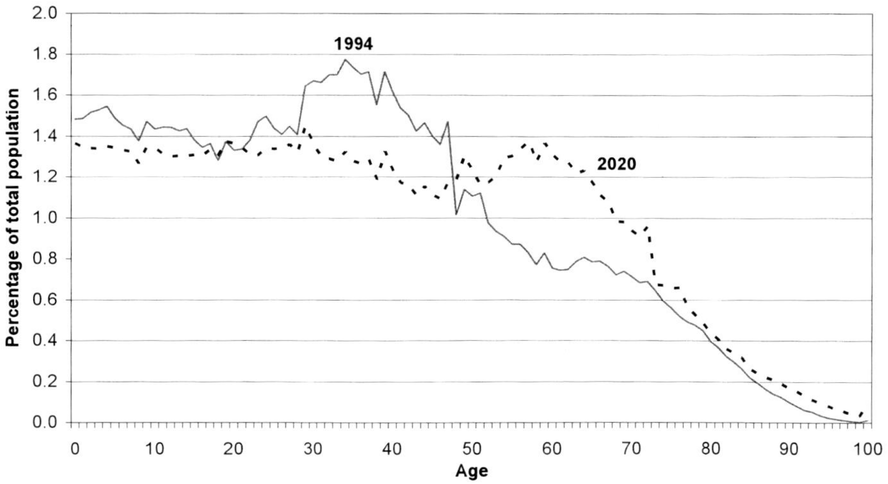

Figure 2. United States, Age Distribution of Population, 1994 and 2020. Source: US Census Bureau.

government budget constraint in general and the Social Security system in particular. A beautiful study of the effects the baby boomers in Spain (where immigration represents much less of a complication for the population dynamics than for the United States) may have on savings and real interest rates is in Ríos-Rull (2001).

Finally, Figure 3 tells us about the age distribution of immigrants to the United States. The curve for U.S. natives is the same as that for 1994 in Figure 2, except now each age group is five years wide and so the curve is smoother. The key message of the figure is that immigrants to the United States are relatively quite young.

These features of the data all correspond to elements that one may wish to add to a model of heterogeneous individuals – something we as economists have become adept at doing. When Víctor Ríos was my colleague at Carnegie Mellon University in the early 1990s, computers were not nearly as powerful as they are today. Víctor did early pioneering research with such models. Back then, some could take a long time – maybe a day or two – for the computer to calculate the model time series to analyze.

All of these features to which I've alluded – the age-dependent work efficiency, population dynamics, and so on – can and have been added to models such as those used by Víctor Ríos and others in the past decade. A student of Víctor's and mine at Carnegie Mellon, Kjetil Storesletten, now at the University of Oslo, made an interesting study of the interaction of immigration with government fiscal policy. Stark predictions have been made by people who do intergenerational accounting, suggesting that tax rates will have to rise

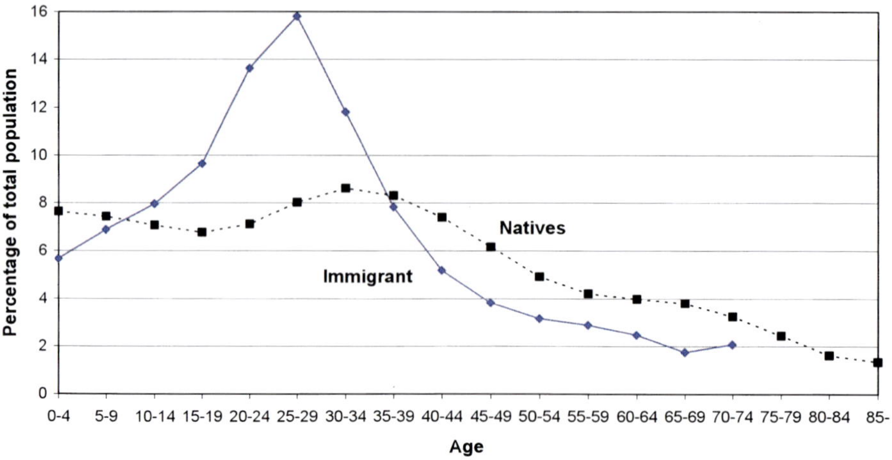

Figure 3. United States, Age Distribution of Natives and New Immigrants. Source: Immigration and Naturalization Services Yearbook (Years 1983-89), as reported in Kjetil Storesletten (1995).

substantially in the not-so-distant future in order for the government budget constraint to be satisfied. The interesting question Storesletten (2000) asks is, To what extent can one avoid that tax increase by raising the rate of immigration, especially if one could be selective in the immigrants to admit?

Our ability to compute equilibriums for economies with very different people has expanded dramatically in recent years, with many studies heavily influenced by the pioneering paper by Per Krusell and Tony Smith (1998). Today, we see interesting research with the implication, for example, that income and wealth distributions vary and evolve over time, for example Storesletten, Telmer and Yaron (2004). This exciting work is made possible through advances in our understanding of dynamic methodology, but also because of the power of today's computers.

NO MONEY?

A belief sometimes expressed is that this framework is used for analyzing real phenomena only. That's a huge misunderstanding. The same framework is used also to study monetary phenomena. For example, one could use it to ask the perennial question, Do monetary shocks cause business cycles?

[Before going on, I would like to say that there are two people whom I would have loved to see in Stockholm this week, but who will not be here because they have passed away. One is my father, Martin; the other Scott Freeman, who died some months ago. I've had the fortune to work with the greatest economist in the world, Ed Prescott. But Scott Freeman was not far behind. He was a tremendous economist, with great insight and innovative

Scott Freeman, The Thinker

ability. He and I did work on the interaction of monetary phenomena and real factors. In his memory, I've included two pictures. In the first, you see Scott in a pensive mood. In the second, he's enjoying himself at a party a few years ago.]

Here's a way to introduce money into a framework such as the one I've described to you. Suppose people purchase a whole variety of sizes of goods. We might as well say there's a continuum, from tiny to large. People make small purchases and large. Because of the cost of carrying out transactions using means of exchange (checks, for example) backed by interest-earning assets, it has to be optimal to make the small purchases using currency and the large purchases using these other means of exchange. The extent to which you want to use either becomes an economic decision whose incentives change over the cycle. They change for the choice of the proportion of the two means of exchange one wishes to hold, as well as for the frequency with which one replenishes one's liquid balances. The finding from this study with Scott Freeman (2000) is that money fluctuates procyclically even when the central bank does nothing. In other words, if one finds, as was the case over extended periods of U.S. history, that money moves up and down with output, that fact by itself says nothing about money causing output.

Because these models are inhabited by people, we can evaluate the welfare cost of inflation. In a project with Scott Freeman and Espen Henriksen (forthcoming), a Carnegie Mellon Ph.D. student, we did exactly that. We are now pushing that project further, asking, for example, what will happen if transaction costs drop over time, which already has happened and likely will continue to do so.

Scott in the quest for inspiration with co-author.

INTERNATIONAL BUSINESS CYCLES

I presented to you a closed-economy model. In the past 10 or 15 years, however, economists have put this framework to use to study the interaction of many nations. This is a particularly interesting field because anomalies abound for bright young (and even old) researchers to try to account for. Here's an example which, on the face of it, may seem like an anomaly: For many nations, cyclically the trade balance is the worst when one's goods are the cheapest. It turns out that once you write down a model in which nations trade, as for example Backus, Kehoe, and I did (1994), capital accumulation is important for the answer. Another factor is that there's "nonsynchronized" technological change in the different nations, which over time spills over from one nation to the next. The conclusion is that the empirical regularity to which I just referred is not an anomaly at all. It's what the model suggests would happen.

Here's a cute application. I loved to use it in my undergraduate course. I came across an article in the *Wall Street Journal* in April 1998 reporting that the International Monetary Fund dispatched representatives to Argentina, supposedly to convince the Argentine government to cool the economy. The reasons stated were threefold: (i) high growth rates, 6.5 to 7 percent annually, coming on top of strong growth that started in 1990, interrupted only by the Tequila crisis around 1995; (ii) export prices falling dramatically; and (iii) the trade deficit returning. Sound bad? As it turns out, these comovements are what a standard model would tell us to expect in an economy that's doing well. Our framework dictates that these three features, in combination, ought to be favorable. I should say that I have no way of knowing if the *Wall Street Journal* to some extent misstated the IMF's basis for going to Argentina. For example, the IMF may have been worried also about fiscal "overstimulation," as one might call it.

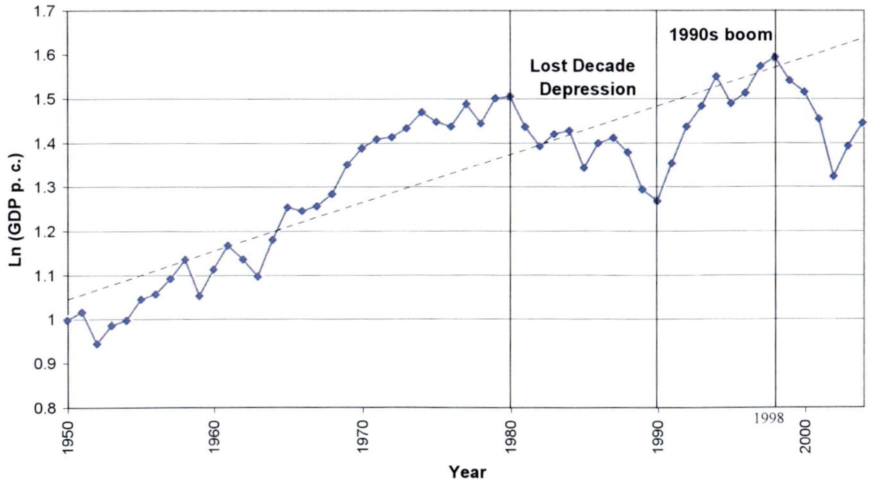

Figure 4. Argentina, GDP per working age person (Index).

THE CASE OF ARGENTINA

Recently, a number of studies of great depressions have been carried out. Many were put together for a conference at the Federal Reserve Bank of Minneapolis and will be collected in a volume edited by Tim Kehoe and Ed Prescott. The reasons I mention the great depression studies are twofold. First, people used to think great depressions are events of such magnitude that we need a separate framework to study them. I think this conference showed that any such suggestion is nonsense. The second reason is that this conference gave Carlos Zarazaga and me (2002) the impetus to study the case of Argentina, which had a great depression in the 1980s.

To give you a sense of what has happened in Argentina in the last 50 years, Figure 4 displays the log of its real GDP per person of working age. Logs are useful because constant growth rate translates into a straight line, and whether Argentina's GDP is as small as it was in the 1950s, or much larger in 1998, a one-cm deviation from trend, say, represents the same *percent* deviation. So that's how to read this picture. You see the dramatic decline in the 1980s – over 20 percent – during Argentina's "Lost Decade," qualifying it as a great depression. An even larger and much faster decline took place after 1998.

As already mentioned, Argentina's economy experienced an upturn in the 1990s. That episode, to Carlos and me (forthcoming), was even more interesting than the depression. Clearly, Argentina grew fast by most standards. The surprising thing was – and only the model could tell us this – when you put the numbers for total factor productivity growth into a standard model and calibrate it, the model says that investment should have been much greater in the 1990s. Of course, for that very reason, the capital stock should have been much larger by the end of the decade.

Figure 5 contains a picture of real GDP for Argentina, again in log scale.

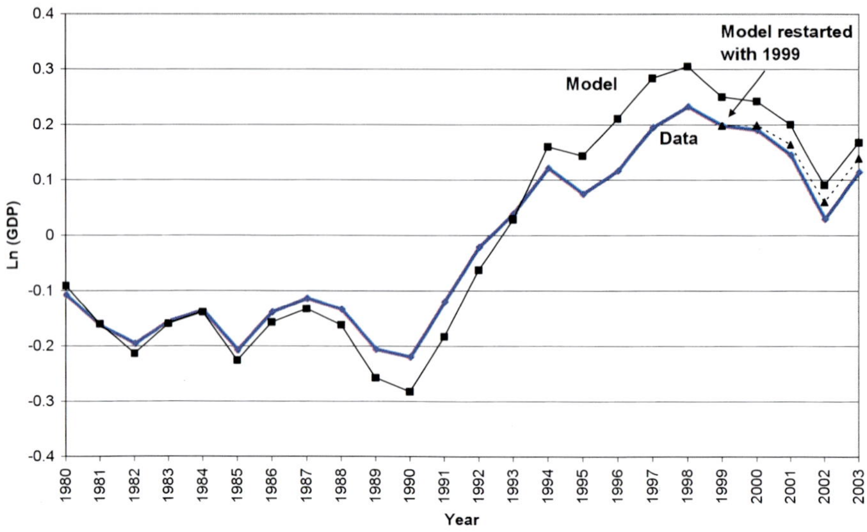

Figure 5. Argentina, GDP.

You can see the growth in the 1990s. Suppose we put into the model the actual numbers for total factor productivity measured by the method Robert Solow (1957) proposed for measuring them in a growth context. We use the period up to 1980 to estimate statistically the process for the technology level. The model accounts well for the great depression of the 1980s, and also for the downturn after 1999. The large discrepancy is for the 1990s where the model says that growth in the 1990s should have been much higher. The third curve is included to indicate what happens if we assume that the capital stock in 1999 is taken from the actual data for that year and then we start the model up again in 1999. The model accounts well for the remaining years.

What if we look more closely at the capital input? I mentioned it as representing the key anomaly. That is borne out in Figure 6, which displays an even greater discrepancy between model prediction and data for the 1990s than in the case of GDP. The difference in 1999 is almost 20 percent. As in Figure 5, the third curve displays the model prediction if we start with the 1999 capital stock so as to account for the remaining five years.

For Argentina, the data in Figure 7 must be extremely depressing because they show the fall in capital stock per working-age person (which would look more or less the same in per-capita terms). This represents the quantity of productive capacity in Argentina, given by the best measurements available. The capital stock in 2003, per person, was much lower than in 1982. The neoclassical growth model then would imply, as the data show, much lower wage rates, wage rates that were much, much lower than those that would have prevailed in Argentina if the economy had grown the way other nations' economies did. This is bad news for the future of Argentina's poor (and it

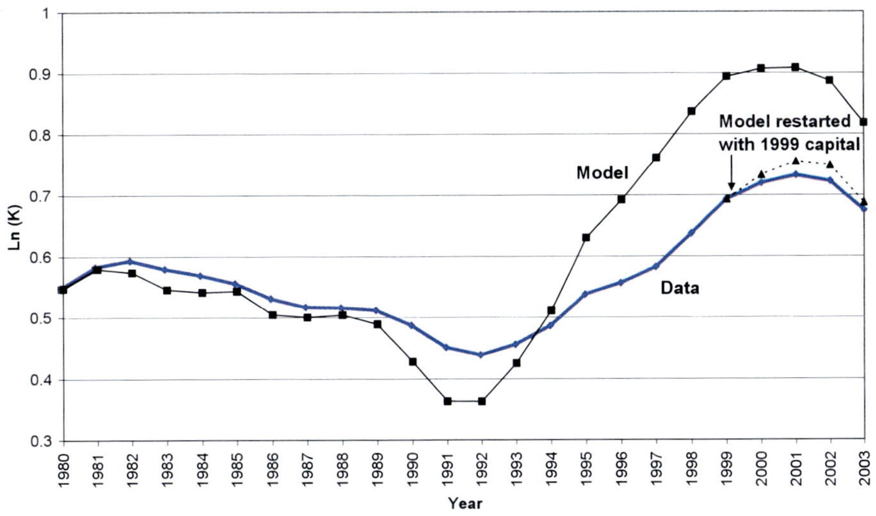

Figure 6. Argentina, Capital Input.

certainly has been so far). Clearly Argentina needs to grow at a rapid rate – not just 3 or 4 percent a year – to catch up. If it doesn't, then the poor will stay poor for a long time. People with relatively high human capital are likely to do reasonably well, but the wealth and income disparities will keep getting wider.

What are possible explanations for the 1990s? Measurement problem? In many nations like Argentina, the data are sometimes of poor quality. Moreover, aggregate series can be constructed from available data in different ways. A Ph.D. student at Carnegie Mellon, José de Anchorena (2004), tried an alternative way of constructing the capital series but reached the same conclusion.

Another possibility, and I'd like to return to it because it relates to our 1977 paper about which Ed Prescott talked in his lecture, is that the outcome for the 1990s in part is the result of what we may call the "time-inconsistency disease" due to bad policies in Argentina before 1990. People had fresh in their minds memories from the past, even if former President Carlos Menem and other politicians did their best to make Argentina a credible country in which to invest for the long run. Chances are, then, that Argentina still lacked the necessary credibility. There was considerable growth during the 1990s, but not nearly as much as Argentina should have experienced according to the neoclassical growth model. This conjecture needs to be investigated more rigorously, but is at least consistent with a growing body of literature (see, for example, Alvarez and Jermann 2000, Kehoe and Levine 2001, and Kehoe and Perri 2002) that predicts that fears of defaults and confiscations will have a "headwinds effect" on investment precisely when the economy is in the upswing.

Argentina has recovered in the past couple of years. I already mentioned

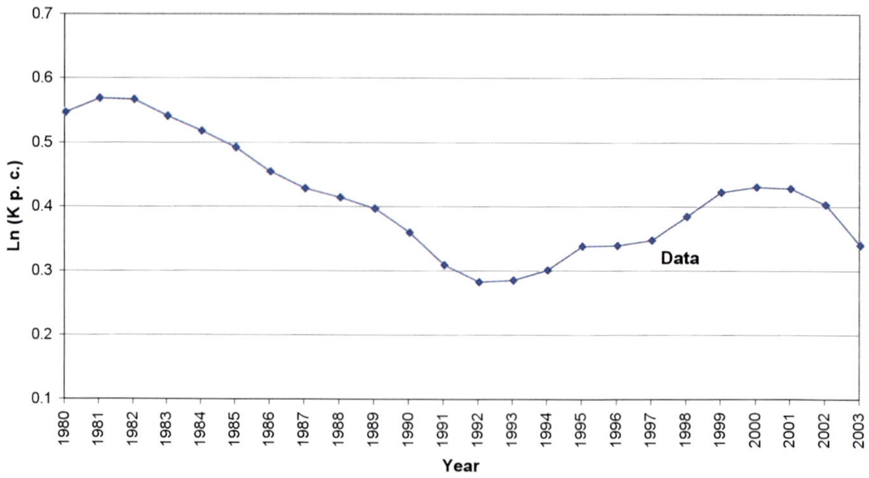

Figure 7. Argentina, Capital Input per working age person. Lower Capital: Lower Real Wages, Worse Distribution Of Income.

that if it doesn't happen at a rapid speed, if the gap is not closed, then the poor will stay poor for a long time. How will Argentina restore confidence? There's no easy answer. Once credibility has been lost, economists don't know much about how to restore it. What is needed is not a policy of patchwork for a year or two; Argentina needs a policy geared for the long run, with credible incentives for innovative activity and human and physical capital accumulation yielding returns far into the future.

CONCLUDING REMARKS

In this brief lecture, I've tried to give you a taste of the vast variety of questions, with the model details dictated accordingly, that have been addressed in macroeconomics in the past two decades, all within the framework that serves as the overall theme for this lecture: the decision problems of the models' people and businesses are explicit, and they are dynamic. I could have provided hundreds of references. Some of the ones I chose to include are authored or co-authored by researchers with whom I've enjoyed tremendously to interact. I'm delighted to have them here in Stockholm as my guests.

As there are many students in the audience, I'd like to conclude with some remarks about learning macroeconomics. Almost all interesting macroeconomic phenomena are dynamic; they are intertemporal. We need to consider forward-looking people. Unfortunately, dynamic macro is difficult for beginners to learn; it's not easy to do dynamics on paper. Perhaps mainly for that reason, in the past 20 years the gap between research and textbooks has grown wider and wider. What to do?

There are some recent attempts to bridge the gap. I like many aspects of Steve Williamson's (2005) recent textbook, for example. It may be amazing to you, however, that I've continued to use for so long (supplemented by my own notes) a textbook first published in 1974 by Merton Miller and Charles Upton (1986). It presents a dynamic framework with many of the features I have talked about, even life-cycle behavior. These two authors were simply great economists, and they included in their text the key elements they thought ought to be present in basic dynamic models of macroeconomics.

One possible remedy for teaching macroeconomics is to use the computer for computational experiments (see Bjørnestad and Kydland 2004). This tool, which has been so influential in modern research, can also help beginning and intermediate students to master dynamic macroeconomics. The students can compare model and real-economy cyclical statistics. The computer can generate plots of impulse responses. Shocks occur in every time period. It's hard in practice to disentangle the effects of each particular shock. As at least one occurs in every period, the shocks are not easy to observe and measure at the time they occur, and the effects of each are long-lasting. But model economies let us strengthen our intuition. For example, with an impulse response, one pretends that there hasn't been a shock for a long time – that the economy is in its steady state. Then we hit the model economy with a single shock or impulse and record what happens over a number time periods – a great aid to students' intuition.

I would like to stop there and just say: Takk for at dere alle kom for å høre på meg.

REFERENCES

Alvarez, Fernando and Urban J. Jermann, (2000): "Efficiency, Equilibrium, and Asset Pricing with Risk of Default," *Econometrica,* 68(4): 775–797.

Anchorena, José (2004): "Capital Accumulation, Sectoral Productivity and Real Exchange Rate." Carnegie Mellon University Working Paper.

Backus, David K., Patrick J. Kehoe and Finn E. Kydland (1994): "Dynamics of the Trade Balance and the Terms of Trade: The J-Curve?" *American Economic Review,* 84(1): 84–103.

Bjørnestad, Solveig and Finn E. Kydland (2004): "The Computational Experiment as an Educational Tool in Basic Macroeconomics." University of Bergen Working paper.

Cooley, Thomas F. and Edward C. Prescott (1995): "Economic Growth and Business Cycles." Frontiers of Business Cycle Research, T.F. Cooley (ed.), Princeton: Princeton University Press, 1–38.

Freeman, Scott and Finn E. Kydland (2000): "Monetary Aggregates and Output." *American Economics Review,* 90(5): 1125–1135.

Freeman, Scott, Espen Henriksen, and Finn E. Kydland (forthcoming): "The Welfare Cost of Inflation in the Presence of Inside Money." *Monetary Policy in Low-Inflation Economies,* D.E. Altig and E. Nosal (ed.), Cambridge University Press.

Kehoe, Patrick J. and Fabrizio Perri (2002): "International Business Cycles With Endogenous Incomplete Markets." *Econometrica,* 70(3): 907–928.

Kehoe, Timothy J. and David K. Levine (2001): "Liquidity Constrained Markets versus Debt Constrained Markets." *Econometrica,* 69(3): 575–598.

Krusell, Per and Anthony A. Smith, Jr. (1998): "Income and Wealth Heterogeneity in the Macroeconomy." *Journal of Political Economy,* 106(5): 867–896.

Krusell, Per, Lee E. Ohanian, José-Víctor Ríos-Rull, and Giovanni L. Violante (2000):

"Capital-Skill Complementarity and Inequality." *Econometrica,* 68(5): 1029–1053.
Kydland, Finn E. (1995): "Business Cycles and Aggregate Labor Market Fluctuations." Frontiers of Business Cycle Research, T.F. Cooley (ed.), Princeton: Princeton University Press, 126–156.
Kydland, Finn E. and D'Ann M. Petersen (1997): "Does Being Different Matter?" *Economic Review,* (Third Quarter), Federal Reserve Bank of Dallas.
Kydland, Finn E. and Edward C. Prescott (1977): "Rules Rather than Discretion: The Time Inconsistency of Optimal Plans." *Journal of Political Economy,* 85 (2) (June): 473–491.
Kydland, Finn E. and Edward. C. Prescott (1982): "Time to Build and Aggregate Fluctuations." *Econometrica,* 50(6): 1345–1370.
Kydland, Finn E. and Carlos E. J. M. Zarazaga (2002): "Argentina's Lost Decade." *Review of Economic Dynamics,* 5(1): 152–165.
Kydland, Finn E. and Carlos E. J. M. Zarazaga (forthcoming): "Argentina's Lost Decade and the Subsequent Recovery Capital Gap Puzzle," in *Great Depressions of the Twentieth Century,* Federal Reserve Bank of Minneapolis, Timothy J. Kehoe and Edward C. Prescott, editors.
Lucas, Robert E., Jr. (1980): "Methods and Problems in Business Cycle Theory." *Journal of Money, Credit and Banking,* 12(4): 696–715.
Miller, Merton H. and Charles W. Upton (1986): Macroeconomics, A Neoclassical Introduction. Chicago: The University of Chicago Press.
Ríos-Rull, José-Víctor (1996): "Life-Cycle Economies and Aggregate Fluctuations." *Review of Economic Studies,* 63: 465–90.
Ríos-Rull, José-Víctor (2001): "Population Changes and Capital Accumulation: The Aging of the Baby Boom." *The B.E. Journals in Macroeconomics: Advances in Macroeconomics,* 1(1), Article 7: 1–46.
Solow, Robert M. (1957): "Technical Change and the Aggregate Production Function." *Review of Economics and Statistics,* 39(3): 312–320.
Storesletten, Kjetil (1995): "On the Economics of Immigration," Ph D dissertation. Carnegie-Mellon University.
Storesletten, Kjetil (2000): "Sustaining Fiscal Policy Through Immigration." *Journal of Political Economy,* 108(2): 300–323.
Storesletten, Kjetil, Christopher I. Telmer and Amir Yaron (2004): "Consumption and Risk Sharing Over the Life Cycle." *Journal of Monetary Economics,* 51(3): 609–633.
Williamson, Stephen D. (2005): Macroeconomics. 2nd Ed., Boston: Pearson Addison Wesley.

Edward C Prescott

EDWARD C. PRESCOTT

I was born on December 26, 1940, in Glens Falls, New York, to Mathilde Helwig Prescott and William Clyde Prescott. My mother's parents were German immigrants. My mother was forced to drop out of high school at age 16 to care for her younger brother and sister after the death of their mother. Later, she managed to complete high school, and with the help of a family friend (whose name I wish I could remember) she continued with school and became a librarian. My mother's ambition and fortitude, even in hard times, were exceeded only by her generosity and kindness. My father told me it was she who insisted that he return to Penn State University to complete his education. He had dropped out of college in 1932 when his father lost his job in the Great Depression.

My father had dreams of being a writer, but ended up becoming an industrial engineer. Upon graduation from Penn State in 1935, he found a good job at the Imperial Wallpaper and Pigment Company in Glens Falls, New York. In 1935 he and my mother were married; a year later, my brother William III was born. My sister Prudence came next, in 1939. I was the third and last child. I was a shy and not very social child. I had dreams of doing something special. When a challenging problem came up, I attacked this problem with intensity until I solved it. We lived in Glens Falls throughout my childhood, except for two and a half years during World War II when my father worked for a defense firm in Bristol, Pennsylvania.

My father taught me how to play chess and we played until I gained the upper hand. History has a way of repeating itself. I taught my oldest son how to play chess when he was young and we played often until he became a much better chess player than I. My father and I also played golf. We had similar temperaments and this temperament was not that of a good golfer. We each got upset when we made a bad shot and you cannot play golf well when you are upset. I must admit that I derived great pleasure from the rare occasion when I beat him.

My father's company was acquired by Hercules Chemical, a multinational corporation, in the early 1960s. At the end of that decade my parents moved to Wilmington, Delaware, where my father became the comptroller of its international division. He retired and moved back to Glens Falls in 1974. Through discussion with him, I learned a lot about the way businesses operated. This was one reason why I liked my microeconomics course so much in my first year at Swarthmore College. The price theory that I learned in that course rationalized what I had learned from him about the way businesses operate. The other reason was the textbook used in that course, Paul A. Samuelson's *Principles of Economics*. I loved the way Samuelson laid out the theory in his textbook, so simply and clearly.

One thing that I remember from discussions with my father was the importance one person can have for the success of an organization. There was one such person, George Mellon, at my father's company. Mellon built Imperial into the dominant pigment producer in the world. George Mellon was just one of those special people that could make good things happen.

Glens Falls is an interesting small town located in the foothills of the Adirondack Mountains on the Hudson River. The town was once wealthy with lumber money. Residents chose not to let the railroad connecting Montreal and New York pass through the town, as that would detract from the community. Glens Falls had a number of high-tech businesses, including Imperial, which through research and development became the leading pigment producer in the world. There were also a number of small electronic and medical equipment firms, as well as an insurance company, a paper mill, and the capacitor division of General Electric Co.

In high school I spent a lot of time playing bridge at the home of a friend. I remember two large sculptures by David Smith that decorated the living room. I know these artworks were special because a dozen years later I saw them at a special exhibition of Smith's work in Washington, D.C. Douglas Crockwell, the father of this friend, was a famous illustrator who was a distant second to Norman Rockwell in number of covers done for the *Saturday Evening Post*. He showed me drawings that he prepared for the famous physicist Edward Teller. Not being an atomic physicist, they didn't mean much to me.

Another friend's father was a leading orthopedic surgeon who worked out of New York City, although he also had a local practice. He experimented with hypnosis in his local practice, and he let us watch when he hypnotized a patient. I tried to hypnotize someone once and was successful, but one time was enough. With its high-tech industries and interesting set of talented residents, Glens Falls in many ways was not a typical American small town.

But in many other ways, it was. We all played Little League baseball, played pickup basketball after school, and went skiing. There were Friday and Saturday community activities in town for the young people. The high school had an exceptional science program headed by Mr. Bosworth. A math course I vividly recall as special was Miss Mabel's plane geometry course. There I discovered a new "language" and learned the concept of a proof. The other math courses were good, but they were not the same. When I received a 99 on one of the New York State Regent Exams in mathematics (not plane geometry), Miss Mabel had tears in her eyes. She so much wanted me to have perfect scores in all the math exams! I felt bad about letting her down.

My goal was to make the high school basketball team, but being the second smallest and second youngest in my class of 160 put me at a disadvantage. I have always loved a challenge, so this didn't discourage me from sports. By the time I reached my senior year I had grown some (weight: 133 pounds) and made the varsity football team. I was a pretty good defensive back and the second-string quarterback. Our team was loaded with talent and easily won all our games. This experience was not exciting. There was no challenge. I also was a good pole vaulter, setting the school record in my senior year. This was a challenge and even though no one was concerned with pole vaulting except me and my coach, I was happy with myself that I met this challenge. I had other interests as well: I was an avid reader of science fiction and was enamored with the writings of the Fabian Socialists. I also played tournament bridge.

During the summers my friends and I all held jobs. I became a golf caddy when I was 12 and a camp counselor for troubled kids when I was 17. When I returned from college in the summers I worked in the paper mills, which paid well. This helped pay for college, but more importantly, I got to know, like, and respect my fellow workers who didn't have the opportunities I had.

Back in 1958, it was not hard to get into even the most prestigious universities. But I decided to go to Swarthmore College because it was less intimidating and somewhat less expensive than the Ivy League universities. Many years later my father told me that my mother had been disappointed in my decision. She had hoped that I would choose a more prestigious institution, but I have never been concerned with social status and prestige.

In high school I dreamed of being a rocket scientist, and therefore I majored in physics in college – probably the most demanding major at that time, given this was the *Sputnik* era. What disappointed me about Swarthmore was the dearth of intellectual discourse. Fellow students spent much of their time memorizing, rather than thinking and figuring things out. Nearly all were too idealogical to carry on an intellectual discussion. I could always predict what they would say. How anyone could defend the killing of tens of millions by Stalin and Mao was (and is) beyond me. This experience cured me of my socialistic leanings.

I have always had a need for physical activities and challenges. In college I played football for four years, and was the captain in my senior year. I enjoyed this diversion. Most of my teammates were the "non-intellects" – the engineers and premeds at Swarthmore. They had positive, cooperative attitudes and we worked well as a team. Winning or losing did not matter as much as playing as well as we could.

I dropped out of the physics honors program after my third year because I did not like the day-long laboratories. I liked to create things, and I found it difficult if not impossible to be careful and meticulous. Perhaps if the physics program had been more theoretical, I would have ended up a physicist rather than an economist. In my junior year I had taken an advanced seminar with the math honors students and liked it, so I switched to a math major in my senior year. That year I took a fascinating course in engineering economics taught by the charismatic professor Sam Carpenter. This led me to enroll in graduate school in operations research at Case Tech, which subsequently merged with Western University to become Case Western. I had no financial aid except for free room and board provided by a benefactor of Case. Given my financial situation, I worked intensely and completed the two-year master's degree program in 15 months. It was all work and no play, but what I learned in the operations research program at Case proved to be of great value in subsequent years. In particular, I learned some recursive methods in the queuing theory course and thoroughly enjoyed learning some probability theory in a course that used the Feller's classic text.

After earning my master's degree, I had to decide what to do next. If MIT had offered aid, I would have gone there. But they didn't, and the choice was between staying at Case or going to the Graduate School of Industrial Administration (GSIA) at Carnegie Tech (now Carnegie Mellon University) in Pittsburgh, Pennsylvania. I am not sure what led me to the decision that I made, but I chose GSIA with its multi-disciplinary program. In hindsight it was the right decision.

I truly enjoyed my graduate school days at GSIA. I arrived there as a student the same year Robert E. Lucas, Jr. (the 1995 Nobel Laureate in Economics) arrived as a freshly minted assistant professor. Under GSIA's system, there was an informal assignment of students to faculty. I was assigned to Michael C. Lovell, who became my dissertation advisor – although Morris M. DeGroot, a great statistician, played an important role in supervising my research. Mike and I wrote two joint papers, one on an interesting mathematic statistics problem and the other developing a business cycle model.

I learned something else from Mike that turned out to be important for the success of my career. I learned from him how to help students in that very difficult transition from student to researcher. What is key in this transition is that students gain confidence in their own judgment and that they learn to listen to, and even seek, criticism of their research papers. I think a number of my students have benefited from interacting with me. I know I have benefited greatly from interacting with them. When my former students contribute to the advancement of economics, I take great pleasure in their success.

I did not take many economics courses at GSIA, but the capital theory of Bob Lucas was important, as was the growth theory course that Mike Lovell and Mort Kamien taught. I took a number of courses outside of GSIA, and the one taught by Allen Newell, one of the fathers of artificial intelligence, was exciting. The reason I took Newell's course was that I found what Herbert A. Simon (1978 Nobel Laureate in Economics) said about artificial intelligence fascinating. Herb was a person who forced you to think and to take clean positions. With exceptional minds like these around, GSIA was an intellectually exciting place to be.

There was considerable interaction between the younger faculty and the graduate students. Bob Lucas, a junior faculty member, and I became lifelong friends. Much of the interaction occurred during the coffee times at 10:30 and 3:30. You could be certain Bob would be there, and the discussion would concern economics, broadly defined.

While at GSIA I received a generous fellowship and I worked hard. Having found a good group of friends, I partied hard as well. In September of 1964 I met Janet Dale Simpson. We were married June 5, 1965, the day before she graduated from Chatham College. Meeting Jan alone made my decision to go to GSIA the right one. There also were sporting activities, which I love. Carnegie

Tech had an exceptional intramural program, and we doctoral students along with some master's students had highly competitive teams in most sports. I even realized my high school dream of playing on a good basketball team! One year we were the intramural champions; another year we lost in the finals by two points.

After three years at GSIA, I left to join the faculty at the University of Pennsylvania in Philadelphia. There, my oldest son, Edward Simpson Prescott, and my daughter, Wynne Fraser Prescott, were born. The Penn years were good ones, though I must admit to a fear that I would not make it as a professor. The junior faculty members were bright and talented; I learned a lot from them. I have a great debt to Lawrence R. Klein (1980 Nobel Laureate in Economics), who provided summer support. I like models of the macroeconomy, and Larry Klein more than anyone is responsible for the development of this interest.

I benefited greatly from interaction with Larry Klein, and even more from Ned Phelps. He had the vision of the neoclassical synthesis; namely, providing the economic foundations for macroeconometric models. Ned posed the questions that had to be answered to unify macroeconometric models with the rest of economics. He ran the famous Conference on the Micro Foundations of Wage and Price Determination at Penn in 1969. Bob Lucas and a number of other people whose research was germane to this topic were there.

At the conference, Bob and I talked about the dominant firm problem in industrial organization and thought we had it solved. We ran into problems, however, and given that we were committed to presenting a paper at the summer Econometric Society meetings, we had to write something else. The paper we wrote in 1969 was "Investment under Uncertainty." To deal with this partial equilibrium problem, we embedded it in a general equilibrium framework.

In this framework the number of commodities was large, too many to even be counted. This is when I was introduced to Gerard Debreu's classic paper[1] on valuation equilibrium and Pareto optimum. Debreu's paper is less than five pages. The mathematics is beautiful. Each of the minimal number of assumptions is clearly specified and the welfare theorems established. I realized an economy that did not have the required mathematical structure with a given set of traded commodities often has the required structure with a richer set of traded commodities. This theory makes transparent Arrow-Debreu general equilibrium theory with event-contingent commodities. I learned that apparent market failures often disappear when mutually beneficial trades are not prohibited. This simple insight has been crucial in some of my most important papers. The Debreu paper makes clear the importance and power of good language.

[1] "Valuation Equilibrium and Pareto Optimum," *Proceedings of the National Academy of Sciences of the U.S.A.*, 40, 588-92, 1954.

Writing the "Investment under Uncertainty" paper transformed me into an economist. Before that I was more a statistician than an economist. I am an econometrician in Ragnar Frisch's original sense of the word; namely, someone dedicated to making neoclassical economics quantitative.

Among the highlights of my Penn experience was my interaction with one of the students there – Tom Cooley, who was (and remains) a family friend, and who subsequently became a valued collaborator. His dissertation supervisor was Larry Klein, but I also played a role in the supervision, and I like to take some of the credit for Tom developing into an exceptional economist.

In 1970 I was on leave as a Brookings Economic Policy Fellow assigned to the U.S. Department of Labor. When I returned, Penn had two new young faculty members that I came to admire greatly. They were Steve Ross and Tom Sargent. With colleagues like this, Penn was a very good place for me to be, but I was worried that I might not be granted tenure. When Richard Cyert, Dean of GSIA at Carnegie Mellon, called and made an attractive offer, I accepted.

Upon arriving at GSIA I met two advanced graduate students, Costas Azariadis and Finn Kydland. Even though they were more my colleagues than my students, I became their dissertation advisor and, like Tom Cooley, they became lifelong friends. The Ph.D. program became an exciting one. Credit for this goes to a number of people. David Cass and Bob Lucas played crucial roles and I think I did too.

After only one year, Dick Cyert moved to the presidency of Carnegie Mellon University, where he was critical in transforming it into a major research university. He is another example of one person being responsible for something happening. But even though this move was clearly good for the university, it was not good for GSIA. A dean who did not appreciate what he had (and did not understand the great tradition of the school) took actions that resulted in the departure of Dave Cass and Bob Lucas. I was saddened to see something good destroyed.

In 1973 our youngest son, Andy, was born. We joined the Chapel Gate Swimming and Tennis Club. I played tennis frequently. During this time tennis was how I got my exercise.

Jan, having an adventuresome soul, decided we would spend 1974–75 in Bergen, Norway, at the Norwegian School of Business and Economics, where Finn Kydland had become a faculty member. One thing that made it an adventure was that none of us spoke Norwegian and there were no English-speaking schools in Bergen. The visit turned out to be both personally and professionally rewarding. In the spring of 1975, Finn and I returned to the problem of policy selection in dynamic, uncertain environments. This time we got it right and found that the principle of optimality fails. Macro policy is a game, not a control problem as we had thought.

After returning from Norway, I decided to leave Carnegie Mellon as soon as a good opportunity arose. Finding a good match was not so easy, though. I was then established as an econometrician and was informally offered a good position in that area. But, I was no longer an econometrician. I found economics much more exciting, and upon my return to GSIA I chose not to teach the graduate econometrics course and instead taught an industrial organization course. A number of my students wrote innovative dissertations in this area. This was the rebirth of the field of industrial organization. The dissertations of Therese Flaherty, Chandra Kanodia, Charles Holt, Jean-Pierre Danthine, Edward Green, Barbara Spencer, Thore Johnsen, Léon Courville, and of course Finn Kydland, were all in this area. I wrote a couple of industrial organization papers with Michael Visscher, an assistant professor at Carnegie Mellon.

During this time I collaborated with Rajnish Mehra, the only Carnegie student other than Finn with whom I collaborated. In late 1979 we wrote "Equity Premium Puzzle" (which appeared in 1985) and "Recursive Competitive Equilibrium." The shift from trying to come up with models that fit the data to using theory and measurement to provide quantitative answers to questions was difficult for me, given the way I was programmed to think.

A bumper crop of exceptional economists came on the market in the mid-1970s, and Carnegie Mellon was fortunate to hire some of them. Upon my return I introduced a regular faculty seminar for these young faculty members. One of them, Rob Townsend, significantly altered my thinking about economics. He was a Neil Wallace student, and therefore one who uses the general equilibrium paradigm (as I do). But, he had been influenced by Leo Hurwicz's mechanism design thinking. Subsequently, in the late 1970s Rob and I introduced private information into classical valuation equilibrium theory in the sense of the Debreu paper I mentioned above. The commodity point we introduced turned out to be key to endogenizing the length of the workweek, which in turn is key in business cycle theory.

In 1978–79 I visited the University of Chicago as its Ford Foundation Research Professor. The following year I visited the Northwestern University economic department, where I took up running. This became my form of exercise for seven years until my knee gave way. That year at Northwestern I received an offer from the University of Minnesota. I accepted it, given that Minnesota had the best graduate program and was the leading producer of new assistant professors, with Thomas Sargent and Neil Wallace in macro. I think the success of the Minnesota program was due to its tradition of insisting that students first define terms, state their proposition, and then rigorously establish their proposition. With this approach, if you disagree with a conclusion, you have to disagree with one of the assumptions. The ample supply of ambitious, imaginative students was also crucial to the success of the program.

I began my association with the Federal Reserve Bank of Minneapolis in the fall of 1981, following in the footsteps of Tom Sargent and Neil Wallace. I had joined the Minnesota faculty in the fall of 1980, but was on leave at Northwestern's finance department most of that year so that my wife could complete the core part of her doctoral program in industrial psychology at Illinois Institute of Technology. A few years after beginning my association with the Federal Reserve Bank of Minneapolis, Gary Stern became president of the Bank, and Art Rolnick, director of research. Gary, a good economist, wanted a small set of top economists around him with whom to consult on a variety of economic matters. Under Art's leadership, this objective was achieved and the bank's research department became and still is a major center in macroeconomics research.

Minnesota did not hire me in macroeconomics, but rather in the field of industrial organization. I think the industrial organization group was excellent, with Herb Mohring, Rob Porter, and me. Rob's leaving was a great loss. Our efforts at replacing him were unsuccessful, but in going after Boyan Jovanovic and Ariel Pakes, we did go after the right people.

In Minnesota I became an applied game theorist – heavily involved in youth soccer. Here is how it happened. When I took my son Andy, then 8 years old, to the neighborhood park for the fall park board soccer program, I learned that Jan had signed me up as a coach. That evening I began my coaching career in a sport that I had never played. This was a challenge. Players from the local park board teams formed a traveling team that played in the late spring and summer. William A. George and I helped coach this team, and after a few years I took over the coaching. Bill was an exceptional manager, and I was not surprised when he later made Medtronic the leading medical equipment firm in the world. Here is another individual that made good things happen. I have limited coaching skills, but with the strong support of the parents over the years, the team attracted a talented set of players and we moved to the highest level of competition.

Soon these players became too good for me to coach, so I became the manager and hired a skilled coach to work with that team during the season. Given there was no one else available, I ran the entire Westside Football Club. While I was happy when a new generation came along to run the club, I was proud of the fact that the program did well under my stewardship. This was a challenge that I met.

The Minnesota economics department did as well in the 1980s as it had in the 1970s – in part due to the skills of the chair, Jim Simler. Here is another person that created an environment in which good things happened: consensus was reached quickly and there was hardly any politicking. This made the Minnesota department unique. The department had no required courses, a principle that served it well since its founding. The students who were betting their career made the decisions. If no one signed up for your graduate course, the course was dropped. Having this rule mitigates a time consistency problem.

I was fortunate to have worked with a large number of outstanding students at Minnesota. Minnesota grads have done more than any group to advance macroeconomics. They are special. I will mention Stephen Parente, who helped me coach soccer, because subsequently we had a long and fruitful collaboration culminating in our book *Barriers to Riches* (2000). The collaboration was inspired by Stephen's highly imaginative and original dissertation on growth. At the time everyone in the profession was concerned with what a country should do to foster growth. We took the opposite tack. Our position was that all market economies would be rich absent barriers to efficient production. To put it another way, to go fast, ease up on the brakes. In our studies we adopted the methodology that Finn and I developed for addressing business cycle questions.

Stephen is not only a great economist, but also a great cook. For a number of years Stephen's famous clam bakes were held at our house. He would have the lobsters flown in from Boston, where his family was still in the seafood business.

In the midst of these good times, an ominous development loomed in the department. One group could not attract students and insisted on the imposition of a required course sequence. At that point, I considered leaving and was thinking about Chicago. The commute would have been only a total of five hours per week. It is a great department and in many ways I was more a Chicagoan than a Minnesotan, as I had more interaction with the Chicago faculty than I did with the Minnesota faculty. Bob Lucas, Nancy Stokey, and Rob Townsend – all on the faculty at Chicago – had been collaborators in the past. In addition, I valued the interaction with Gary Becker, Lars Hansen, Jim Heckman, and Sherwin Rosen. Chicago had a large and respected graduate program, and I thought I could help make it better. But, there was a problem: One of the students in the program was Edward Simpson Prescott, my oldest son. It would have been unfair to him if I were to join the Chicago faculty while he was there.

In the mid-1990s, a new dean of Minnesota's College of Liberal Arts dramatically cut the size of the Minnesota economics department. The problems can be traced back to the politicization of the selection of the regents of the university. The regents had become representatives of special-interest groups instead of supporters of the mission of the university. In 1995 their plan to re-engineer the university included a proposal to eliminate tenure.

In 1998 I received offers from a number of departments, including Chicago, and the University of Minnesota chose not to match them. My oldest son was no longer a student at Chicago, and I accepted their offer. Except for the commute, I loved Chicago, which is in a class by itself when it comes to economics. I was depressed when I had to leave because of a family health problem. What particularly attracted me to Chicago was that it presented a challenge, and to repeat, I love challenges. In the single year I was there as a member of its economics faculty, I detected a rise in student morale. The students had gained a little confidence and become less intimidated by the profession. (Chicago can be an intimidating place, with all those gargoyles staring down at you.) After one year as a faculty member at Chicago, I was rehired and returned to troubled Minnesota.

Three good things happened after my return. At the Bank, I began a fruitful collaboration with Ellen McGrattan, in which we derived the implications of the neoclassical growth model that Finn and I used in the study of business cycles for the value of the stock market. The theory worked for predicting the value of the stock market as it had worked for predicting the magnitude and nature of business cycle fluctuations. When Ellen's (senior author) and my paper was accepted by the *Review of Economic Studies* in late November of 2004, I was a happy man. Needless to say, I was not the only happy person. Now, theory can be used to say whether the market is over- or under-valued, and by how much. The integration of the stock market into macro models has important ramifications for understanding the boom in employment and output in the United States during the late 1990s. These certainly are exciting times in macroeconomics, with so much progress being made using the methodology that Finn and I developed.

The second good thing was the teaching of an undergraduate macro course in modern macro. It turned out to influence my subsequent research. In that course I used the neoclassical growth model, which Finn and I used to study business cycles. I also used the same model, but with land a crucial input to production, to account for the 5,000 years prior to 1800 when there was little or no growth in living standards. One of the students in the class repeatedly asked the question, why use one production function for one period and another one for the other? He was a wise guy, but I liked him. His question was a good one, and was one that the profession should have been asking itself. Gary Hansen and I came up with the answer in our "Malthus to Solow" paper. We permitted both production functions to be used at all times. This unified the models of the two periods and accounted for the long transition commonly referred to as the Industrial Revolution. Economics owes a debt to that student.

The primary reason I taught this course was that I saw the need to develop material that could be used to teach modern macro. Typically, the material taught in undergraduate macro courses teaches the Keynesian macroeconomics models, which failed, and failed spectacularly, in the 1970s. I wish that I had just a little of the Samuelson genius and could write a great textbook for the teaching of modern macroeconomics. It is needed.

In that course, I wanted the students to use the theory to evaluate policy. Therefore, I made up an exercise in which they had to evaluate whether a consumption tax or an income tax is a better way to finance a transfer payment. The model economy that they used is basically the one that Finn and I use in our study of business cycles, but without technology shocks. The students came to me and said there had to be something wrong – they could not find any income tax rate that finances the transfer. I was sure they were wrong and did the exercise myself. They were right, there was none. This is when I realized the quantitative importance of the tax system for output and employment. This was the topic of my American Economic Association's 2002 Richard Ely Lecture and subsequent work establishing that tax rates account for most of the huge differences in labor supply across the major advanced industrial countries and for the large change in European labor supply over time.

The third good thing that happened upon my return was that my Bank colleagues Hal Cole and Lee Ohanian broke a taboo and used the neoclassical growth model to examine the Great Depression. What they found was eye-opening. This motivated Tim Kehoe and me to organize a conference where a number of scholars used the neoclassical growth model to analyze a number of depressions. In this project, I was fortunate to make a match with Fumio Hayashi. We studied the lost decade of Japanese growth that began in 1992. Treating total factor productivity (TFP) as exogenous, the theory accounts well for this episode. This TFP factor, which is so important in accounting for business cycle fluctuations, is also important for understanding periods of depression and prosperity. This is further support for Parente's and my position that the central issue in macroeconomics is to understand the mapping from policy arrangements to TFP levels.

In early 2003, my wife notified her company that she was retiring in January 2004. This made it possible for me to resign from Minnesota when the Minnesota administration refused to honor a written provision in my rehire agreement. This provision promised much-needed graduate student financial aid.

Once I was committed to leaving the University of Minnesota, the only question was where to go. We considered three places. My wife picked Arizona State University in Tempe, Arizona. One thing I particularly like about ASU is that its economics department is on track to become a great one. The people have good judgment. The department enjoys the strong support of administration, which is getting the needed resources. I welcome the challenge of helping to make the ASU economics department a great one.

THE TRANSFORMATION OF MACROECONOMIC POLICY AND RESEARCH

Prize Lecture, December 8, 2004

by

Edward C. Prescott*

Arizona State University, Tempe, and Federal Reserve Bank of Minneapolis, Minnesota, USA.

1. INTRODUCTION

What I am going to describe for you is a revolution in macroeconomics, a transformation in methodology that has reshaped how we conduct our science. Prior to the transformation, macroeconomics was largely separate from the rest of economics. Indeed, some considered the study of macroeconomics fundamentally different and thought there was no hope of integrating macroeconomics with the rest of economics, that is, with neoclassical economics. Others held the view that neoclassical foundations for the empirically determined macro relations would in time be developed. Neither view proved correct.

Finn Kydland and I have been lucky to be a part of this revolution, and my address will focus heavily on our role in advancing this transformation. Now, all stories about transformation have three essential parts: the time prior to the key change, the transformative era, and the new period that has been impacted by the change. And that is the story I am going to tell: how macroeconomic policy and research changed as the result of the transformation of macroeconomics from constructing a system of equations of the national accounts to an investigation of dynamic stochastic economies.

Macroeconomics has progressed beyond the stage of searching for a theory to the stage of deriving the implications of theory. In this way, macroeconomics has become like the natural sciences. Unlike the natural sciences, though, macroeconomics involves people making decisions based upon what they think will happen, and what will happen depends upon what decisions they make. This means that the concept of equilibrium must be dynamic, and – as we shall see – this dynamism is at the core of modern macroeconomics.

*Thanks to Dave Fettig, Tim Kehoe, Robert Lucas, Ellen McGrattan, Lee Ohanian, Richard Rogerson, and Art Rolnick for their helpful comments and the National Science Foundation for financial support (grant #0422539).

Before proceeding, I want to emphasize that the methodology that transformed macroeconomics is applicable to the study of virtually all fields of economics. In fact, the meaning of the word *macroeconomics* has changed to refer to the tools being used rather than just to the study of business cycle fluctuations.

As a result of the transformation, these are exciting times in macroeconomics. The methodology that Finn and I developed for the study of business cycle fluctuations is being used to advance learning not only in the area of business cycles but also in virtually all areas of economics. By using this methodology, researchers are able to apply theory and measurement to answer questions, define puzzles, and determine where better measurement is needed before specific questions can be answered.

Over the last five years, I have addressed the following questions using this methodology: What is the fundamental value of the stock market, and do fundamentals account for the large movements in the value of the stock market relative to gross domestic product that have occurred over time? Why did hours worked per adult fall by one-third in Western Europe, and not in Canada and the United States, in the 1970–1995 period? Why were market hours in the United States at the end of the 1990s 5 percent above what theory predicts? Why did Japan lose a decade of growth beginning in 1992, a decade when growth was at trend in the other advanced industrial countries?

Much of this recent research originates from my undergraduate teaching that began in the late 1990s. Until then, I had never taught a course in which macroeconomic questions were addressed using this methodology. The undergraduate course I taught was Quantitative Analysis of the Macroeconomy. I chose to teach this course because I felt there was a need to develop material that could be used in teaching what macroeconomics has become at the undergraduate level. I felt there was this need because Finn's and my work on the time consistency problem and developments in agency theory led me to the conclusion that having good macroeconomic policy requires having an educated citizenry that can evaluate macroeconomic policy. A second reason why I thought there was this need is that by introducing talented undergraduates to the excitement of modern macroeconomics, some would be influenced to pursue careers in economic research and would make important advances to economic science.

In the course I introduced the real business cycle model economy, which is the single sector growth model in which people decide how much of their income to consume and save and how much of their time endowment to allocate to the market. Motivated by Ragnar Frisch's Nobel address (1970), I call this model the neoclassical growth model because it incorporates the willingness of people to substitute as well as their ability to substitute.

One decision that people must make is how to allocate their time endowment, which is the most precious resource an individual has. Indeed, as my undergraduates figure out, the present value of their time endowment is approximately 5 million current U.S. dollars, which makes them all multimillionaires. Another crucial feature of any real business cycle model is that the model people decide how much to consume and how much to invest or equivalently save.

The course requires students to carry out quantitative analyses to address specific questions. They use the methodology that Finn and I developed for the study of business cycles to address policy issues. A typical exercise is to determine whether a proposal made by a public opinion leader or government official will have the intended consequence. One question they were assigned concerns financing of transfer payments. Their finding was totally counter to then-conventional wisdom. I will return to this finding later because it is an implication of Finn Kydland's and my business cycle theory.

2. THE TRANSFORMATION OF MACROECONOMIC POLICY

In this section I first describe what macroeconomic models were before the transformation and what they are after the transformation. Then I describe policy selection before and after the transformation. Before the transformation, what is evaluated is a policy *action given the current situation.* Policy discussions were in terms of questions such as whether the money supply should be increased or reduced. In his critique (1976), Robert Lucas established that questions such as these are not well posed in the language of dynamic economic theory.

After the transformation, what is evaluated is a policy *rule.* A policy rule specifies the current policy action as a function of the current economic situation. As Finn and I found, no best policy rule exists. Typically, the policy rule is best given that it will be followed in the future. Any such rule is by definition time-consistent, but except in empirically uninteresting cases, Finn and I show that time-consistent rules are not optimal; indeed, they lead to bad outcomes. All that can be hoped for is to follow a good rule, and this requires economic and political institutions that sustain this rule.

Macroeconomic Models before the Transformation

Macroeconomic models were systems of equations that determined current outcomes given the values of the current policy *actions,* values of predetermined variables, and values of any stochastic shocks. Thus, physical models and pre-transformation macro models have the same mathematical structure. The basic mathematical structure of both is

$$x_{t+1}=f(x_t,u_t,\varepsilon_t).$$

The state or position of the dynamic system at the beginning of period t is x_t, the control or policy variables are u_t, and the stochastic shocks are ε_t.

With the system-of-equations approach, each equation in the system is determined up to a set of parameters. The simple prototype system-of-equations macro model has a consumption function, an investment equation, a money demand function, and a Phillips curve. Behind all these equations were a rich empirical literature and, in the case of the consumption function, money demand function, and investment equation, some serious theoretical work. The final step was to use the tools of statistical estimation theory to select the parameters that define the function f.

I worked in this tradition. In my dissertation, I formulated the optimal policy selection problem as a Bayesian sequential decision problem. The problem is a difficult one because the policy actions taken today affect the distribution of the posterior distribution of the values of the coefficients of the equations.

The macroeconometric models organized the field. Success in macroeconomics was to have your equation incorporated into the macroeconometric models. Indeed, Lucas and I were searching for a better investment equation when in 1969 we wrote our paper "Investment under Uncertainty," a paper that was published two years later in 1971.

A key assumption in the system-of-equations approach is that the equations are *policy invariant*. As Lucas points out in his critique, which I delivered in 1973, this assumption is inconsistent with dynamic economic theory. His insight made it clear that there was no hope for the neoclassical synthesis – that is, the development of neoclassical underpinnings of the system-of-equations macro models.

Fortunately, with advances in dynamic economic theory an alternative set of tractable macro models was developed for drawing scientific inference. The key development was recursive competitive equilibrium theory in Lucas and Prescott (1971) and Lucas (1972). Equilibrium being represented as a set of stochastic processes with stationary transition probabilities was crucial to the revolution in macroeconomics.

Macroeconomic Models after the Transformation

Models after the transformation are dynamic, fully articulated model economies in the general equilibrium sense of the word *economy*. Model people maximize utility given the price system, policy, and their consumption possibility set; firms maximize profits given their technology set, the price system, and policy; and markets clear. Preferences, on the one hand, describe what people choose from a given choice set. Technology, on the other hand, specifies what outputs can be produced given the inputs. *Preferences and technology are policy invariant.* They are the data of the theory and not the equations as in the system-of-equations approach. With the general equilibrium approach, empirical knowledge is organized around preferences and technology, in sharp contrast to the system-of-equations approach, which organizes knowledge about equations that specify the behavior of aggregations of households and firms.

The Time Inconsistency of Optimal Policy

Before the transformation, optimal policy selection was a matter of solving what the physical scientists called a control problem. This is not surprising, given that the system-of-equations approach was borrowed from the physical sciences. With such systems, the principle of optimality holds – that is, it is best to choose at each point in time policy action that is best given the current situation and the rules by which policy will be selected in the future. The optimal policy is time-consistent, and dynamic programming techniques can be used to find the optimal policy as in the physical sciences. This is true even if there is uncertainty in the model economy.

Finn and I had read the Lucas critique and knew that for dynamic equilibrium models, only policy rules could be evaluated. This led us to search for a best rule to follow, where a rule specifies policy actions as a function of the state or position of the economy. We had worked on this problem before Finn left Carnegie Mellon to join the faculty of the Norwegian School of Business and Economics in 1973. In academic year 1974–1975 I visited the Norwegian School of Business and Economics, and in the spring of 1975 Finn and I returned to this problem. This is when we wrote our paper "Rules Rather than Discretion: The Inconsistency of Optimal Plans," one of the two papers for which Finn and I were awarded the Nobel Prize.

In previous research we had considered time-consistent stationary policy rules. These rules have the property that they are a fixed point of the mapping that specifies the best rule today as a function of the rule that will be used in the future. The fact that these rules were not optimal led us to our key insight: the best event-contingent policy plan is not time-consistent. By this I mean the continuation of a plan is not optimal at some future point in the event-time tree. For example, it is always best to tax the returns on existing capital but not tax the returns on new investments. The reason is that a tax on existing capital is a lump-sum tax and there is no associated distortion, whereas any taxes on future returns of current investments are distortionary. But capital investments today become existing capital tomorrow, and tomorrow the best policy action is to tax their returns.

This leads to the conclusion that being able to commit has value and that having discretion has costs. The only method of commitment is to follow rules. That is why we concluded that the time inconsistency of optimal plans necessitates following rules. Some societies have had considerable success in following good, but time-inconsistent, policy rules, and as a result their citizens enjoy a higher standard of living. Other societies have limited success in this regard, and as a result their citizens suffer economic hardships.

This need for rules in organizational settings has long been recognized. That is why all agree that rule by a good set of laws is desirable. Rule by law is a political institution to get around the time consistency problem. What was new in our research was that this principle holds for macroeconomic policy counter to what everyone thought at the time.

A Success in Following a Good Monetary Policy Rule

A notable example of a success in following a good, but time-inconsistent, rule is the one maintaining a low and stable inflation rate. Before describing an institution that is proving effective in getting commitment to this good rule in many countries, I will first describe one reason why the price stability policy rule is time-inconsistent.

Consider an economy in which the nominal wage rate is set above the market clearing level in some sectors, given the inflation rate specified by the rule. This outcome could be the result of industry insiders in each of a number of industries finding this action in their best interest, given the wages chosen by the insiders in other industries and the expected inflation rate. If the price stability policy rule is followed, ex post a distortion occurs that results in low employment. This distortion can be reduced by having inflation in excess of the amount specified by the rule. With the time-consistent monetary policy rule, inflation will be at that level where the marginal value of higher inflation in reducing the distortion will just equal the marginal cost of the higher inflation. The equilibrium outcome is high inflation and no reduction in the distortion. Commitment to the best rule will not result in high inflation, just the labor market distortion.

I turn now to an institution that is proving successful in sustaining this rule: an independent central bank. Members of this organization have a vested interest in following this rule, for if it is not followed, they would incur the risk that they would suffer in the future. If inflation has been excessive and a new administration is elected, people in the organization will be replaced and the size of the central bank cut. Thus, members of this organization have a vested interest in the rule being followed.

The increased stability of the economy and the improved performance of the payment and credit system may be due in part to the diffusion of findings of Finn's and my "Rules Rather than Discretion" paper. People now recognize much better the importance of having good macroeconomic institutions such as an independent central bank.

To find the time-consistent policy we *de facto* considered a game. In the simplest case, the value function of an individual is $v(k,K)$ and that of the policy maker $v(K,K)$, where k is a given individual's capital stock and K is the capital stock of all others. Note that within the class of policies that treat individuals anonymously, all individuals order policies in the same way as does the policy maker. At the first stage of each period, the policy maker selects the policy that is best for the representative individual and the rule by which policy will be selected in the future.

3. THE TRANSFORMATION OF MACROECONOMIC RESEARCH

The title of this address is "The Transformation of Macroeconomic Policy and Research." I turn now to the research part of the title. The methods used in macroeconomic research were different prior to Finn's and my paper, "Time to Build and Aggregate Fluctuations" (1982). The new methodology was developed in the summer of 1980 when Finn and I did the research and wrote the first draft of our "Time to Build" paper. We also wrote the first draft of this paper that summer.

Before specifying the new research methodology, I have to discuss what the key business cycle facts are and why they led economists to falsely conclude that business cycle fluctuations were not in large part equilibrium responses to real shocks. Then I will specify the methodology that Finn and I developed and used to quantitatively determine the consequences of these shocks for business cycle fluctuations.

I emphasize that what is important is the methodology and that this methodology can be and has been used to quantitatively determine the consequences of both nominal and real shocks. By using these methods, the

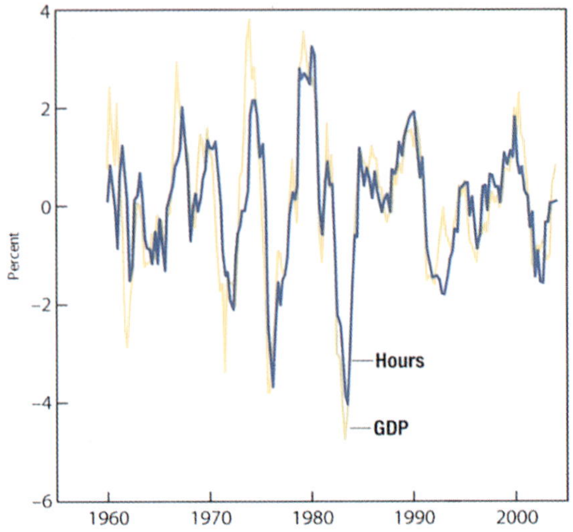

Figure 1. Deviations from Trend of U.S. GDP and Hours.

profession has learned so much. No longer do economists conjecture and speculate. Instead they make quantitative statements as to the consequences of various shocks and features of reality for business cycle fluctuations. This paper began a constructive and fruitful research program.

3.1 Business cycle facts

In the 1970s after the development of dynamic economic theory, it was clear that something other than the system-of-equations approach was needed if macroeconomics was to be integrated with the rest of economics. I want to emphasize that macroeconomics then meant business cycle fluctuations. Growth theory, even though it dealt with the same set of aggregate economic variables, was part of what was then called microeconomics, as was the study of tax policies in public finance.

Business cycles are fluctuations in output and employment about *trend.* But what is trend? Having been trained as a statistician, I naturally looked to theory to provide the definition of trend, with the plan to then use the tools of statistics to estimate or measure it. But theory provided no definition of trend, so in 1978 Bob Hodrick and I took the then-radical step of using an operational definition of trend.[1] With an operational definition, the concept is defined by the procedure used to determine the value of the concept.

[1] A shortened version of this 1978 Carnegie Mellon working paper, a copy of which I do not have, is a 1980 Northwestern University working paper. At the time, this paper was largely ignored because the profession was not using the neoclassical growth model to think about business cycle fluctuations. But once the then-young people in the profession started using the neoclassical growth model to think about business cycles, the profession found the statistics reported in this paper of interest.

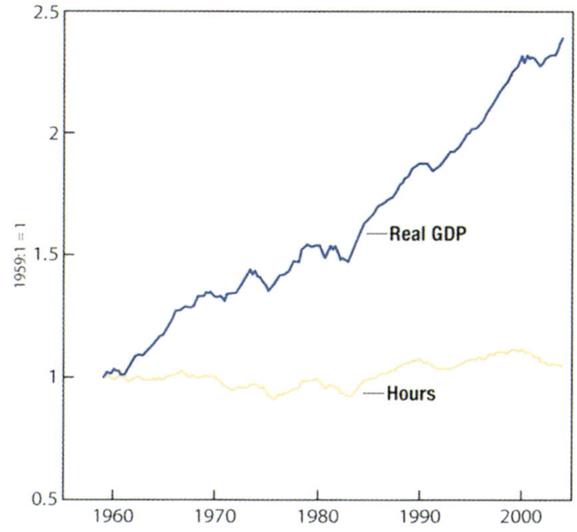

Figure 2. Indices of Per Capita Real GDP and Hours.

Our trend is just a well-defined statistic, where a statistic is a real valued function. Hodrick and Prescott's (1980) trend statistic mimics well the smooth curve that economists fit through the data. The family of trends we considered is one-dimensional. The one in the family that we used is the first one we considered. Later we learned that the actuaries use this family of smoothers, as did John von Neumann when he worked on ballistic problems for the U.S. government during World War II.[2] A desirable feature of this definition is that with the selection of smoothing parameters for quarterly time series, there are no degrees of freedom and the business cycle statistics are not a matter of judgment. Having everyone looking at the same set of statistics facilitated the development of business cycle theory by making studies comparable.

One set of key business cycle facts are that two-thirds of business cycle fluctuations are accounted for by variations in the labor input, one-third by variations in total factor productivity, and virtually zero by variations in the capital service input. The importance of variation in the labor input can be seen in Figure 1.

This is in sharp contrast to the secular behavior of the labor input and output, which is shown in Figure 2. Secularly, per capita output has a strong upward trend, while the per capita labor input shows no trend.

A second business cycle fact is that consumption moves procyclically; that is, the cyclical component of consumption moves up and down with the cyclical component of output. A third fact is that in percentage terms, invest-

[2] See Stigler's (1978) history of statistics.

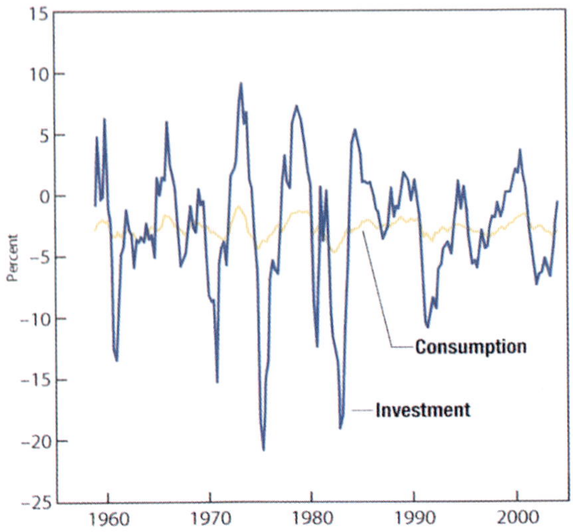

Figure 3. Deviations from Trend of U.S. Consumption and Investment.

ment varies 10 times as much as does consumption. Consequently, investment variation is a disproportionate part of cyclical output variation. This is shown in Figure 3.

3.2 Inference drawn from these facts

Now why did economists looking at these facts conclude that they ruled out total factor productivity and other real shocks as being a significant contributor to business cycle fluctuations? Their reasoning is as follows. Leisure and consumption are normal goods. The evidence at that time was that the real wage was acyclical, which implies no cyclical substitution effects and leaves only the wealth effect. Therefore, in the boom when income is high, the quantity of leisure should be high, when in fact it is low. This logic is based on partial equilibrium reasoning, and the conclusion turned out to be wrong.

In the 1970s a number of interesting conjectures arose as to why the economy fluctuated as it does. Most were related to finding a propagation mechanism that resulted in Lucas's monetary surprise shocks having persistent real effects. With this theory, leisure moves countercyclically in conformity with observations. The deviations of output and employment from trend are not persistent with this theory, but in fact they are persistent. This initiated a search for some feature of reality that when introduced gives rise to persistent real effects. To put it another way, economists searched for what Frisch called a propagation mechanism for the effects of monetary surprises.

Taylor (1980) and Fischer (1977) provided empirical and theoretical evidence in support of their conjecture that staggered nominal wage contracting might be the mechanism by which monetary shocks gave rise to persistent real effects on output and employment. Another conjectured mechanism of that era is the cost of changing nominal prices. In that era about the only people who argued that real shocks were the factor were Long and Plosser (1983). I say "in that era" because earlier, Wicksell (1907), Pigou (1927), and others held the view that real shocks were an important contribution to business cycles. My prior at the time we did the research for our "Time to Build" paper, and I think Finn's prior as well, was that business cycle fluctuations were induced by nominal and not real shocks.

3.3 Macroeconomics and growth theory before the "Time to Build" paper

Macroeconomics of the 1970s largely ignored capital accumulation. Growth theory was concerned with the long-term movements in the economic aggregates, whereas macroeconomics was concerned with the short-term movements. Virtually no connection was made between the then-dormant growth theory and the dynamic equilibrium theories of business cycles. Probably the reason was that short-term movements in output are accounted for in large part by movements in the labor input, whereas long-term growth in living standards is accounted for by increases in the capital service input and in total factor productivity. All these variables are per working-age person.

Kydland and I decided to use the neoclassical growth model to study business cycle fluctuations in the summer of 1980. The basic theoretical framework we developed came to be called the real business cycle model. The term *real* does not mean that the framework can be used only to answer questions concerning the consequences of real shocks. The real business cycle model is equally applicable to addressing the consequences of monetary shocks. I will not be discussing these monetary applications in this address because Kydland will in his address. This is appropriate given that he and his collaborators, and not I, are leaders in the study of the consequences of monetary policy for business cycles.

3.4 The methodology

This model builds on the contributions of many economists, many of whom have been awarded the Nobel Prize. The importance of the contributions of Simon Kuznets and Richard Stone in developing the national income and product accounts cannot be overstated. These accounts reveal a set of growth facts, which led to Solow's (1956) classical growth model, which Solow (1970) calibrated to the growth facts. This simple but elegant model accounts well for the secular behavior of the principal economic aggregates. With this model, however, labor supply is supplied inelastically and savings is behaviorally determined. There are people in the classical growth model economy, but they make no decisions. This is why I, motivated by Frisch's Nobel address delivered here in 1969, refer to this model as the classical growth model.

The steps in Finn's and my methodology are as follows.

Step 1: Start with the Neoclassical Growth Model

Central to the neoclassical growth model is the Solow–Swan aggregate production function. As explained in Solow (1956, n. 7), the theory underlying the aggregate production function is a theory of the income side of the national accounts.[3] With competitive factor and product markets and entry and exit of production units, factor claims against product exhaust product. In addition, output is maximized given the quantities of the factor inputs supplied.

The function F_t is the period t aggregate production function that specifies the output that is produced as a function of the inputs

$$c_t + x_t = y_t = F_t(k_t, l_t), \tag{1}$$

where c is consumption, x is investment, y is output, k is the capital service input, and l is the labor service input. One unit of capital provides one unit of capital services, and capital depreciates geometrically at rate δ. Thus,

$$k_{t+1} = (1-\delta)k_t + x_t. \tag{2}$$

We also introduced a multi-period requirement for building new capacity because we thought it might be an important shock propagation mechanism.[4]

For the growth model to be neoclassical, the savings-investment and labor-leisure decisions must be decisions of the households. Finn and I introduced an *aggregate* or stand-in household with preferences ordered by the expected discounted value of utility flows from consumption and leisure; that is, the household maximizes the expected value of

$$\sum_{t=0}^{\infty} \beta^t u(c_t, 1-h_t), \tag{3}$$

where c is consumption and $1-h$ is leisure. The aggregation theory underlying this aggregate household is based in part on the first welfare theory, namely, that a competitive equilibrium maximized some weighted average of individual utilities.

[3] For partial equilibrium models, this was recognized by Marshall and Wicksell at the end of the 19th century, but Solow saw it in the general equilibrium context.

[4] Hansen (1985) shows that this feature of reality is not central to understanding business cycle fluctuations and is best abstracted from.

Previously, others had effectively endogenized the savings decision by analyzing the optimal growth path because, by the second welfare theorem, the optimal path is the competitive equilibrium path for this model.[5] But in order for the model to be used to study business cycle fluctuations, the labor supply decision must be endogenized as well.[6]

Step 2: Modify the National Accounts to Be Consistent with the Theory

Prior to our work, macroeconomics was concerned with developing a theory of the national accounts statistics. Preferences and technology are the given, not the national accounts statistics. This means that we had to modify the national accounts to be consistent with the theoretical abstraction or model we used. The most important modification when studying business cycles is to treat consumer durable expenditures as an investment in the same way that expenditures on new housing and home improvement are treated as investments in the national accounts. Once this is done, services of consumer durables and consumer durable rental income must be imputed, in much the same way as is currently done for owner-occupied housing. This increases investment share of output and has consequences for the cyclical behavior of the economy. What led us to think about this issue is that consumer durable expenditures are highly variable, behaving very similarly to producer durable investments and not like consumer expenditures on nondurable goods and services.

Step 3: Restrict the Model to Be Consistent with the Growth Facts

The growth facts are that consumption and investment shares of output are roughly constant, as are labor and capital cost shares. All the variables and the real wage grow over time except for labor supply and the return on capital, which are roughly constant. This leads to a Cobb–Douglas production function. These facts also imply the constancy of the capital-output ratio and of the rental price of capital.

Two key growth facts are that the real wage and consumption grow at the same secular rate as does real output per capita, while labor supply displays no secular trend. This restricts the period utility function to be of the form

$$u(c,1-h) = \frac{(c\,g(1-l))^{1-\sigma}-1}{1-\sigma} \quad . \tag{4}$$

[5] Cass (1965) and Koopmans (1965) in deterministic situations establish the existence of an optimal path and characterize properties of this optimal path. Diamond (1965) studies the competitive equilibrium path in an economy with capital accumulation. In his economy, people live two periods. Brock and Mirman (1972) deal with the problem of optimal growth when there are stochastic shocks to the technology. These studies are in the nonquantitative theory tradition. Danthine and Donaldson (1981) compute the equilibrium process for the Brock and Mirman (1972) stochastic growth model.

[6] Auerbach, Kotlikoff, and Skinner (1983) carry out a deterministic dynamic applied general equilibrium analysis with endogenous labor supply in which they evaluate tax policies.

We set $\sigma = 1$. This parameter was not calibrated to growth observations. We made this choice based on a variety of evidence. The principal evidence used is comparisons of the return on capital for fast- and slow-growing economies. Fortunately, it turned out that our findings are not sensitive to this parameter, because at the time of our work, this key economic parameter had not been tightly tied down.

With $\sigma = 1$, the above utility function is

$$\log c + g(1-l). \tag{5}$$

The nature of the g function matters. The growth facts do not tie down the elasticity of substitution between consumption and leisure, and this parameter turned out to be key for deriving the predictions of the growth model for business cycle fluctuations. Subsequently, this key parameter has been tied down.

Step 4: Introduce a Markovian Shock Process

We wanted something in our model economy that led to labor supply errors and something to propagate these errors. Here, by "labor supply errors" I mean the difference between the optimal labor supply decision given individuals' information set and the decision that they would make if they observed the state of the economy without observation error. We introduced a total factor productivity shock that is independent over time and assumes that agents see the value of total factor productivity (TFP) with noise prior to making their labor supply decisions. We also introduced a second highly persistent autoregressive TFP shock. We introduced this shock because it is simple to do and we were curious to see what its consequences are. In order to use the Kalman filter, the two shocks and measurement errors are all normally distributed.

Step 5: Make a Linear Quadratic Approximation

The next step is to determine the steady state of the economy when the variances of the TFP shocks are zero. Then a linear quadratic economy is constructed, which has the same first two derivatives at the steady state. This linear quadratic economy displays the growth facts, and its equilibrium is easily computed. The behavior of this economy will be arbitrarily close to the economy we began with for sufficiently small variances of the two TFP shocks and the measurement errors. It turned out that it was extremely close even for variances far bigger than the ones we introduced.[7]

Step 6: Compute the Competitive Equilibrium Process

The next step is to compute the recursive competitive equilibrium stochastic process.

[7] Danthine and Donaldson (1981), who computed the exact equilibrium for the stochastic model using computationally intensive techniques, found this to be the case.

Step 7: Simulate the Model Economy

The equilibrium stochastic process is used to generate a time series realization of the model economy. If the number of observations in the period being considered is *N*, a time series of length significantly greater than *N* is generated and the last *N* observations considered. A longer time series is generated because we wanted a draw from the invariant distribution for the state of the economy as a starting point of the model's sample path.

Step 8: Examine the Key Business Cycle Statistics and Draw Scientific Inference

The last step is to compare the key business cycle statistics for the model and the actual economy. I emphasize that the identical statistics for the model and the actual economy are compared.

One important statistic is the standard deviation of the cyclical component of output. What we defined to be the cyclical component of output is first computed for the actual economy and the standard deviation determined. The identical procedure is followed for realizations of the equilibrium process of the model economy. This means the model is simulated to generate the time series of output and other series. Next the cyclical component of output is computed and its standard deviation determined. This is done many times so that the first two moments of the sampling distribution of the standard deviation of the model's cyclical output statistic can be determined.

If the sampling distribution of this statistic in question is concentrated about some number, this number relative to the statistic specifies how variable the economy would have been if TFP shocks were the only shocks. If the sampling distribution of this statistic is not concentrated, theory does not provide a precise accounting. But the sampling distribution is highly concentrated provided the number of quarterly observations is at least 100.

I emphasize that this is not a test in the sense of Neyman–Pearson statistical hypothesis tests, which are useful in the search for a model or law through induction. The way theory is tested is through successful use. The neoclassical growth model is tested theory.

4. USING THE METHODOLOGY IN BUSINESS CYCLE RESEARCH

Kydland and Prescott (1982) found, as reported in our paper "Time to Build and Aggregate Fluctuations," that if elasticity of substitution of labor supply is 3 and TFP shocks are highly persistent and of the right magnitude, then business cycles are what the neoclassical growth model predicts. This includes the amplitude of fluctuation of output, the serial correlation properties of cyclical output, the relative variability of consumption and investment, the fact that capital stock peaks and bottoms out later than does output, the cyclical behavior of leisure, and the cyclical output accounting facts.

Subsequently, Prescott (1986) found that the shocks were highly persistent and the TFP shocks of the right magnitude. Conditional on a labor supply elasticity close to 3, TFP shocks are *the* major contributor to fluctuations in the period 1954–1981 in the United States.

This finding turned out to be highly robust. Greenwood, Hercowitz, and Huffman (1988) find that if, on average, TFP shocks are non-neutral with regard to consumption and investment, the conclusions hold. Rotemberg and Woodford (1995) introduce imperfect competition and show that the finding is overthrown only if monopoly rents are far in excess of what they could be. With imperfect competition restricted to be consistent with labor cost share, Hornstein (1993) and Devereux, Head, and Lapham (1996) show that the importance of TFP shocks for business cycle fluctuations hardly changes. With the introduction of monopolistic competition, model-TFP shock variance is picked so that the model Solow-TFP variance matches the actual economy's Solow-TFP variance. In these monopolistic competitive worlds, Solow-TFP is a complex statistic and is not total factor productivity.

Investment in the model economy varies smoothly, as does aggregate investment in the actual economy. Investment at the plant level, however, is not smooth, and a natural question is whether this has consequences for modeling business cycles. Fisher and Hornstein (2000) find that having plants that make lumpy inventory investment in equilibrium does not change the estimates of the contribution of TFP shocks to fluctuations. For investment in plant and equipment, Thomas (2002) develops an economy that displays lumpy investment at the plant level. When calibrated to the growth facts and establishment investment statistics, the findings for business cycles using her abstraction are virtually the same as those using the neoclassical growth model.

Ríos-Rull (1995) uses a carefully calibrated overlapping generations model and finds that the estimated importance of TFP shocks for business cycle fluctuations does not change. Within this framework, Ríos-Rull (1994) then shuts down financial markets, so physical capital holdings is the only way to save. This extreme version of market incompleteness does not affect the estimate of the importance of TFP shocks. Introducing uninsurable idiosyncratic risk (see Krusell and Smith, 1998) does not affect the estimate either. Hansen and Prescott (2005) deal with capacity utilization constraints that are occasionally binding. With their introduction, the nature of the predictions for business cycles changes a little, but in a way that results in observations being in even closer conformity with theory.

Using this methodology, Danthine and Donaldson (1981) and Gomme and Greenwood (1995) investigate the consequences of various non-Walrasian features for business cycle fluctuations. There are interesting implications for relative variability of consumption for those with large capital ownership and those with no capital ownership.

Freeman and Kydland (2000) and Cooley and Hansen (1995) find that introducing money and a transaction technology does not alter the conclusion as to the importance of TFP shocks. Chari, Kehoe, and McGrattan (2000) find that nominal contracting does not either. They introduce staggered nominal contracting into the basic business cycle model and find that in such worlds, monetary shocks have effects that are persistent but too small to be an important contributor to business cycle fluctuations. In summary, introducing monetary factors did not alter Finn's and my finding that TFP shocks are the major contributor to business cycle fluctuations in the United States in the 1954–1980 period we consider in our "Time to Build" paper.

But in all cases, to generate business cycles of the magnitude and nature observed, the aggregate labor supply elasticity must be 3.[8] This attests to the robustness of the finding and focuses attention on this elasticity parameter. A variety of evidence that supports the number 3 had to be found before it was safe to conclude that the neoclassical growth model predicts business cycle fluctuations of the quantitative nature observed.

5. EVIDENCE THAT THE AGGREGATE ELASTICITY OF LABOR SUPPLY IS 3

A problem with the abstraction that many economists used to incorrectly conclude that labor supply is inelastic is that it has the prediction that everyone should make essentially the same percentage adjustment in hours worked. This is not the case. Over the business cycle, most of the variation in the aggregate number of hours worked is in the fraction of people working and not in the hours worked per worker. Looking at this observation, Rogerson (1984, 1988) studies a static world in which people either work a standard workweek or do not work. He shows that in this world, the aggregate elasticity of labor supply is infinite up to the point that the fraction employed is one.

Rogerson's aggregation result is every bit as important as the one giving rise to the aggregate production function.[9] In the case of production technology, the nature of the aggregate production function in the empirically interesting cases is very different from that of the individual production units being aggregated. The same is true for the aggregate or a stand-in household's utility function in the empirically interesting case.

Aggregate hours of labor supplied to the market per working-age person, l, equals the product of the fraction employed, e, and hours per employee, h; that is

$$l = eh. \tag{6}$$

If the principal margin of adjustment in l is the employment rate and not hours per employee, then aggregate labor supply elasticity will be much bigger than the elasticity of labor supply of the individuals being aggregated. Given that the principal margin of adjustment is e and not h, *the aggregate labor supply elasticity is much greater than the individual labor supply elasticity.*

[8] For reviews of many more business cycles studies, see *Frontiers of Business Cycle Research* (Cooley 1995).

[9] Rogerson uses the Prescott and Townsend (1984a, 1984b) lottery commodity point. This simplifies the analysis, but does not change the results because lottery equilibria are equivalent to Arrow–Debreu equilibria; see Kehoe, Levine, and Prescott (2002) and Prescott and Shell (2002).

Multiple margins determine e. Particularly important for males and single females is the fraction of potential working life that he or she works. This fraction is smaller if an individual retires earlier. For married females, Heckman and MaCurdy (1980) find that as the Rogerson theory predicts, their labor supply is highly elastic, with some estimates being as high as *10*. For all, weeks of vacation and the number of holidays is another important margin of adjustment in labor supply.

Hansen (1985) derives the consequence of the Rogerson (1988) assumption for business cycle fluctuations and develops a stand-in household for a type. He finds that in worlds with labor indivisibility, fluctuations induced by TFP shocks alone give rise to fluctuations *10* percent greater than those observed. This indicates that aggregate labor supply elasticity is not infinite as in his model world.

Hansen's findings led Finn and me to introduce both margins of labor supply adjustment. We numerically found the only margin used is e with the standard production function. The natural question is why? Hornstein and Prescott (1993) answer this question.[10] We permitted both margins to be adjusted. The key modification is that a worker's output y is

$$y = Ah\, k^{\theta}, \tag{7}$$

where h is the workweek length of this individual and k is the capital stock that this individual uses. A consequence is that payment per hour is an increasing function of h.

A key result is that all the growth facts hold for this modification of the neoclassical growth model. The important feature of this model is that capital used by one individual is not used by another in the period.

For the calibrated economy, the finding is that only the e margin is used except in extreme cases when all are employed. Only with $e = 1$ is $h > \bar{h}$, where $\bar{h}$ is the endogenously determined "standard" week length. A question, then, is why do we see any variation in h? My answer is that in worlds with "islands," some islands have $e = 1$ and $h > \bar{h}$ at a point in time. Here island i indicates occupation as well as location of work activity.

A question is: What is the real wage? The price of each workweek length is $w_{it}(h)$, where i denotes the island. If one naively assumes that an individual on island i is being paid real wage $w_{it}(h_{it})/h_{it}$ and regresses the logarithm of h_{it} on the log of this assumed wage, a small regression coefficient would be

[10] Many years prior, Sherwin Rosen (1978) had pointed out that workweeks of different lengths are different commodities and their price is not, in general, proportional to the length of the workweek. Introducing this feature of reality into an applied dynamic general equilibrium model of business cycles did not occur until Kydland and Prescott (1991). Earlier, Hansen and Sargent (1988) had two workweek lengths, straight time and overtime.

obtained in this island version of the Hornstein–Prescott world. Many ran this regression for full-time male workers and obtained a small coefficient as predicted by theory, independent of whether the micro or Frischian labor supply elasticity is big or small.

Thus, a low value of this regression coefficient does not imply low elasticity of aggregate labor supply elasticity, which is what matters for the study of business cycles and the evaluation of tax policies. A low value does not even indicate a low micro labor supply elasticity, which is a statement about preferences only. I emphasize that *aggregate labor supply elasticity is a statement about both preferences and technology*. Only for empirically uninteresting cases are the micro and macro elasticities equal.

Evidence from Consequence of Tax Rates across Countries and across Time

Good statistics are available on labor supply and tax rates across the major advanced industrial countries. My measure of aggregate labor supply is aggregate hours worked in the market sector divided by the number of working-age people.

Given that the effect of the marginal effective tax rate on labor supply depends on this elasticity, and given that tax rates vary considerably, these observations provide an almost ideal test of whether the aggregate labor supply elasticity is 3. The set of countries that Prescott (2004) studied are the G-7 countries, which are the large advanced industrial countries. The differences in marginal tax rates and labor supply are large; Canada, Japan, and the United States have rates near 0.40, and France, Germany, and Italy near 0.60.[11] The prediction, based on an aggregate labor supply elasticity of 3, that Western Europeans will work one-third less than North Americans and Japanese is confirmed.[12] Added evidence for an aggregate elasticity of 3 is that it explains why labor supply in France and Germany was nearly 50 percent greater during the 1970–1974 period than it is today.

Observations on aggregate labor supply across countries and across time imply a labor supply elasticity near 3.

Recent Evidence from Major Contractions and Expansions

Additional evidence is provided by the study of recent major contractions. The finding is that the elasticity of labor supply must be near 3 to account for the behavior of the labor supply in each case. Three advanced industrial countries with good economic statistics suffered a 20 percent or more loss in

[11] See Prescott (2004).

[12] The preference ordering used has a constant elasticity of substitution between consumption and leisure, not between consumption and labor supplied to the market. The elasticity of labor supply for our stand-in household is $(1 - h)/h$, where h is the fraction of productive time allocated to the market. Given that h in Europe is smaller than one-fourth of the U.S. number, the elasticity of labor supply there is even greater than 3 in Europe.

output per capita relative to a 2 percent trend in the last quarter to the 20th century. The countries are Japan in the 1990s and New Zealand and Switzerland in the 1970s and 1980s. The behavior of labor supply during these extended periods of nonbalanced growth implies the same labor supply elasticity as do business cycle fluctuations.[13]

Life Cycle Labor Supply Evidence

Recently, Imai and Keene (2004) examined the life cycle pattern of male labor supply. Real payments per hour are hump-shaped, as are hours worked over the working lifetime. The percentage size of the hump is greater for real payment per hour than for hours worked. This led some to conclude that male labor supply is inelastic; that is, the elasticity is less than 1. Imai and Keene take into consideration the value of the skills that younger workers acquire on the job – that is, the human capital they receive. This is part of total compensation and should be included in the wage. When it is, the lifetime wage schedule is much flatter than life cycle labor supply. Imai and Keene's estimate is 3.7. If this estimate rather than 3 is used, it would not change business cycle findings significantly. Further, the real interest rate implied by their analysis is close to the average real return on capital obtained using the neoclassical growth model and the national accounts.

An important difference between what labor economists estimate and what macroeconomists estimate is that labor economists use a constant elasticity of substitution utility function on consumption and labor supply, whereas macroeconomists use a constant elasticity of substitution on consumption and leisure.

A problem with many labor economists' estimates is that they maintain the hypothesis that people are not in organizational settings that have a fixed workweek length. Fitzgerald (1998) introduces team production with both supervisors and workers. Equilibrium is characterized by a fixed workweek length. The hours worked is not a choice variable of individuals. The individual choice variable is whether or not to work for this organization or for some other organization. In this world when people are promoted from worker to supervisor, their wages increase, but no change in hours worked occurs. Under the incorrect maintained hypothesis, these observations would lead to the conclusion that labor supply is perfectly inelastic, even if it is in fact large.

To summarize, aggregate observations imply that the aggregate labor supply elasticity is large. Aggregation theory implies that whenever the principal margin of adjustment is the fraction employed and not hours per person employed, the aggregate labor supply elasticity is large. This finding is consistent with all the micro observations, so no conflict arises between micro and macro observations.

[13] See the Kehoe and Prescott (2002) volume for a number of economic depression studies.

6. SIGNIFICANCE OF BUSINESS CYCLE RESEARCH

We learned that business cycle fluctuations are the optimal response to real shocks. The cost of a bad shock cannot be avoided, and policies that attempt to do so will be counterproductive, particularly if they reduce production efficiency. During the 1981 and current oil crises, I was pleased that policies were not instituted that adversely affected the economy by reducing production efficiency. This is in sharp contrast to the oil crisis in 1974 when, rather than letting the economy respond optimally to a bad shock so as to minimize its cost, policies were instituted that adversely affected production efficiency and depressed the economy much more than it would otherwise have been.

To summarize, concern has shifted away from business cycle fluctuations toward more important things. One important thing is setting up a good tax system. Finn's and my work sheds light on the most important economic parameter in the design of a tax system, the aggregate labor supply elasticity. In finding that technology shocks are important for fluctuations, our research program has been important in shifting the profession's attention to how economic institutions affect total factor productivity.

7. BEYOND BUSINESS CYCLE RESEARCH

The methodology that Finn and I developed and used to study business cycles is equally applicable to studying other phenomena. In this section I will briefly review three successful applications of this methodology and one very interesting open puzzle. While presenting evidence that the labor supply elasticity is 3, I already effectively reviewed one highly successful application – namely, my study assessing the role of taxes in accounting for the huge differences in labor supply across the advanced industrial countries and the huge fall in labor supply in Europe between the early 1970s and the mid-1990s.

Using the Methodology in the Stock Market Valuation Research

An interesting question is, why did the value of the stock market relative to GDP vary by a factor of 2.5 in the United States and 3 in the United Kingdom in the last half of the 20th century? Other variables display little secular variation relative to GDP, whether they are corporate after-tax profits or corporate physical capital relative to GDP.

Clearly the single sector neoclassical growth model does not suffice for studying the market value of corporate equity. The model must have both a corporate and noncorporate sector. Fortunately, the national accounts report the components of value added for the corporate sector as well as for government business, household business, and unincorporated business sectors. Various adjustments must be made to the accounts to bring them into conformity with the model, such as using producer prices for both inputs and outputs to the business sector.

An equilibrium relation develops when the market value of corporations is equal to the value of their productive assets. The capital accounts of the national accounts provide measures of the cost of replacing tangible capital.

But corporations also own large amounts of intangible capital, including organization capital, brand names, and patents, which also affect the market value of corporations. These assets cannot be ignored when determining what theory says the value of the stock market should be. This presents a problem for determining the fundamental value of the stock market – a problem that McGrattan and I solve (see McGrattan and Prescott, 2005a).

We find that the secular behavior of the value of the U.S. stock market is as theory predicts. What turns out to be important for the movement in the value of corporations relative to GDP are changes in tax and regulatory policies. If the tax rate on distributions by corporations is 50 percent rather than 0 percent, the value of corporations will be only half as large given the resource cost of their productive assets.

Our study uses a neoclassical growth model and connects the model to national income and product data, tax data, and sector balance sheet data. We submitted the paper to the *Review of Economic Studies,* a British journal. The editor rightfully insisted that we do the analysis for the U.K. stock market as well as for the U.S. stock market. We were nervous as to what theory and measurement would say and were happy when we found that the behavior of the value of the U.K. stock market was also in conformity to theory. Here is an example of the power of the macroeconomic methodology that Finn and I developed.

The excessive volatility of stock prices remains. Indeed, our study strengthens this puzzle. Stocks of productive capital vary little from year to year, whereas stock prices sometimes vary a lot. I am sure this volatility puzzle will, in the not too distant future, be resolved by some imaginative neoclassical economist. However, resolving the secular movement puzzle is progress.

This example illustrates how macroeconomics has changed as a result of the methodology that Finn and I pioneered. It is now that branch of economics in which applied dynamic equilibrium tools are used to study aggregate phenomena. The study of each of these aggregate phenomena is unified under one theory. This unification attests to the maturity of economic science when it comes to studying dynamic aggregate phenomena.

Using the Methodology to Study the Great U.S. Depression

The welfare gains from eliminating business cycles are small or negative. The welfare gains from eliminating depression and creating growth miracles are large. Cole and Ohanian (1999) broke a taboo and used the neoclassical growth model to study the Great U.S. Depression. One of their particularly interesting findings is that labor supply on a per adult basis in the 1935–1939 period was 25 percent below what it was before the Depression. Recently, Cole and Ohanian (2004) showed how New Deal cartelization could very well have been the reason for the low labor supply using neoclassical economics. The rapid recovery of the U.S. economy subsequent to the abandonment of these cartelization policies supports their theory.

Japan's Lost Decade of Growth

A more recent example is Japan's lost decade of growth, which was the 1992–2001 decade. Hayashi and Prescott (2002), treating TFP as exogenous, find that the neoclassical growth model predicts well the path of the principal aggregates. In particular it quantitatively predicts the large capital deepening and the associated fall in the return on capital. It quantitatively predicts the behavior of labor supply as well, which is further evidence for the high labor elasticity of labor supply.

A Business Cycle Puzzle

An economic boom in the United States began with an expansion relative to trend in early 1996 and continued to the fourth quarter of 1999. Then, a contraction set in and continued until the third quarter to 2001. At the peak, detrended GDP per working-age person was 4 percent above trend and labor supply 5 percent above average. None of the obvious candidates for the high labor supply were operating. There was no war with temporarily high public consumption that was debt financed; tax rates were not low; TFP measured in the standard way was not high; and there was no monetary surprise that would give rise to high labor supply. This is why I say this boom is a puzzle for the neoclassical growth model.

Why did people supply so much labor in this boom period? The work of McGrattan and Prescott (2005a), which determines the quantitative predictions of theory for the value of the stock markets, suggests an answer. The problem is one of *measurement*. During this period (see McGrattan and Prescott, 2005b), there is evidence that unmeasured investment was high, as was unmeasured compensation. Therefore, output and productivity were higher than the standard statistics indicate. The measurement problem is to come up with estimates of this expensed investment. With these improved measurements of economic activity, theory can be used to determine whether or not the puzzle has been solved.

This example illustrates the unified nature of aggregate economics today. The real business cycle model was extended and used to understand the behavior of the stock market, and that extended model in turn is now being used to resolve a business cycle puzzle.

8. RAGNAR FRISCH'S VISION REALIZED

I conclude this address with an ode to Frisch, who was awarded the first Nobel Prize in Economics in 1969. Frisch's Nobel address is entitled "From Utopian Theory to Practical Applications: The Case of Econometrics" (1970). He is the father of quantitative neoclassical economics, which is what he is referring to by the word *econometrics* in the title.[14]

[14] Frisch (1970, p. 12) reports that the English mathematician and economist Jevons (1835–1882) dreamed that we would be able to quantify neoclassical economics.

Prior to Frisch's creating the Econometric Society in 1930 and launching *Econometrica* in 1933, neoclassical economists did little to verify their theoretical results by statistical observations. Frisch writes in his Nobel address that the reason was in part the poor quality of statistics then available and in part that neoclassical theory was not developed with systematic verification in view. The American Institutionalists and German Historical schools pointed this out and advocated letting the facts speak for themselves. The impact of these schools on economic thought was minimal. To quote Frisch, "Facts that speak for themselves, talk in a very naive language" (1970, p. 16). Now theory derives its concepts from measurement, and in turn theory dictates new measurement. The latter is what McGrattan and I are currently doing to resolve the puzzle of why U.S. employment was so high at the end of the 1990s.

In the 1960s Frisch was frustrated by the lack of progress in his quest to making neoclassical economics quantitative and referred to much of what was being done then as "playometrics." It is a little unfair to criticize those studying business cycles at that time for not using the full discipline of neoclassical economics. All the needed tools were not yet part of the economist's tool kit. Some of these tools that are crucial to the study of business cycles are Lindal's extension of general equilibrium theory to dynamic environments; Savage's statistical decision theory as uncertainty is central to business cycles; Arrow and Debreu's extension of general equilibrium theory to environments with uncertainty; Blackwell's development of recursive methods which are needed in computation and in representation of a dynamic stochastic equilibrium; Lucas and Prescott's development of recursive competitive equilibrium theory;[15] and, of course, the computer.

Particularly noteworthy is Lucas's role in the macroeconomic revolution. In the very late 1960s and early 1970s he revolutionized macroeconomics by taking the position that neoclassical economics should be used to study business cycles. Others had dreamed of doing it, but Lucas actually figured out ways to do it. In his 1972 paper "Expectations and the Neutrality of Money," he creates and analyzes a dynamic stochastic neoclassical model that displays the Phillips curve, which is a key equation in the system-of-equations macro models. I can think of no paper in economics as important as this one. The key prediction based upon this theoretical analysis – namely, that there is no exploitable trade-off between inflation and employment – was confirmed in the 1970s when attempts were made to exploit the then perceived trade-off.

But Lucas's work is not *quantitative* dynamic general equilibrium, and only 10 years later did Finn and I figure out how to quantitatively derive the implications of theory and measurement for business cycle fluctuations using the full discipline of dynamic stochastic general equilibrium theory and

[15] This was further developed in Prescott and Mehra (1980). The published version of "Investment under Uncertainty" did not include the section formally defining the recursive equilibrium with policy and value functions depending on both an individual firm's capacity and the industry capacity and was an industry equilibrium analysis.

national accounts statistics. That we have learned that business cycles of the quantitative nature observed are what theory predicts is testimony to the grand research program of Ragnar Frisch and to the vision and creative genius of Robert Lucas.

On nearly every dimension I am in agreement with what Frisch advocated in his Nobel Prize address, but on one dimension I am not. Like Frisch, I am a fervent believer in the democratic process. The dimension on which I disagree is how economists and policy makers should interact. His view is that the democratic political process should determine the objective, and economists should then determine the best policy given this objective. My view is that economists should educate the people so that they can evaluate macroeconomic policy rules and that the people, through their elective representatives, should pick the policy rule. I emphasize that Finn and my "Rules Rather than Discretion" paper finds that public debate should be over rules and that rules should be changed only infrequently, with a lag to mitigate the time consistency problem.

REFERENCES

Auerbach, Alan J., Laurence J. Kotlikoff, and Jonathan Skinner. 1983. "The Efficiency Gains from Dynamic Tax Reform." *Int. Econ. Rev.* 24 (February): 81–100.

Brock, William A., and Leonard J. Mirman. 1972. "Optimal Economic Growth and Uncertainty: The Discounted Case." *J. Econ. Theory* 4 (June): 479–513.

Cass, David. 1965. "Optimal Growth in an Aggregate Model of Capital Accumulation." *Rev. Econ. Studies* 32 (April): 233–240.

Chari, V. V., Patrick J. Kehoe, and Ellen R. McGrattan. 2000. "Sticky Price Models of the Business Cycle: Can the Contract Multiplier Solve the Persistence Problem?" *Econometrica* 68 (September): 1151–1179.

Cole, Harold L., and Lee E. Ohanian. 1999. "The Great Depression in the United States from a Neoclassical Perspective." *Fed. Reserve Bank Minneapolis Q. Rev.* 23 (Winter): 2–24.

Cole, Harold L., and Lee E. Ohanian. 2004. "New Deal Policies and the Persistence of the Great Depression: A General Equilibrium Analysis." *J. Polit. Economy* 112 (August): 779–816.

Cooley, Thomas F., ed. 1995. *Frontiers of Business Cycle Research.* Princeton, N.J.: Princeton Univ. Press.

Cooley, Thomas F., and Gary D. Hansen. 1995. "Money and the Business Cycle." In *Frontiers of Business Cycle Research,* edited by Thomas F. Cooley. Princeton, N.J.: Princeton Univ. Press.

Danthine, Jean-Pierre, and John B. Donaldson. 1981. "Stochastic Properties of Fast vs. Slow Growing Economies." *Econometrica* 49 (July): 1007–1033.

Devereux, Michael B., Allen C. Head, and Beverly J. Lapham. 1996. "Monopolistic Competition, Increasing Returns, and the Effects of Government Spending." *J. Money, Credit, Banking* 28 (May): 233–254.

Diamond, Peter A. 1965. "National Debt in a Neoclassical Growth Model." *Amer. Econ. Rev.* 55 (December): 1126–1150.

Fischer, Stanley. 1977. "Long-Term Contracts, Rational Expectations, and the Optimal Money Supply Rule." *J. Polit. Economy* 85 (February): 191–205.

Fisher, Jonas D. M., and Andreas Hornstein. 2000. "(S, s) Inventory Policies in General Equilibrium." *Rev. Econ. Studies* 67 (January): 117–145.

Fitzgerald, Terry J. 1998. "Work Schedules, Wages, and Employment in a General Equilibrium Model with Team Production." *Rev. Econ. Dynam.* 1 (October): 809–834.

Freeman, Scott, and Finn E. Kydland. 2000. "Monetary Aggregates and Output." *Amer. Econ. Rev.* 90 (December): 1125–1135.

Frisch, Ragnar. 1970. "From Utopian Theory to Practical Applications: The Case of Econometrics." Lecture to the Memory of Alfred Nobel, June 17, 1970. www.nobelprize.org.
Gomme, Paul, and Jeremy Greenwood. 1995. "On the Cyclical Allocation of Risk." *J. Econ. Dynam. Control* 19 (January–February): 92–124.
Greenwood, Jeremy, Zvi Hercowitz, and Gregory W. Huffman. 1988. "Investment, Capacity Utilization, and the Real Business Cycle." *Amer. Econ. Rev.* 78 (June): 402–417.
Hansen, Gary D. 1985. "Indivisible Labor and the Business Cycle." *J. Monetary Econ.* 16 (November): 309–327.
Hansen, Gary D., and Edward C. Prescott. 2005. "Capacity Constraints, Asymmetries, and the Business Cycle." *Rev. Econ. Dynam.*, forthcoming.
Hansen, Gary D., and Thomas J. Sargent. 1988. "Straight Time and Overtime in Equilibrium." *J. Monetary Econ.* 21 (March–May): 281–308.
Hayashi, Fumio, and Edward C. Prescott. 2002. "The 1990s in Japan: A Lost Decade." *Rev. Econ. Dynam.* 5 (January): 206–235.
Heckman, James J., and Thomas E. MaCurdy. 1980. "A Life Cycle Model of Female Labour Supply." *Rev. Econ. Studies* 47 (Econometrics Issue, January): 47–74.
Hodrick, Robert J., and Edward C. Prescott. 1980. "Post-War U.S. Business Cycles: An Empirical Investigation." Discussion Paper 451, Northwestern University, Center for Mathematical Studies in Economics and Management Science. Published as Hodrick Robert J., and Edward C. Prescott. 1997. "Postwar U.S. Business Cycles: An Empirical Investigation." *J. Money, Credit, Banking* 29 (February): 1–16.
Hornstein, Andreas. 1993. "Monopolistic Competition, Increasing Returns to Scale, and the Importance of Productivity Shocks." *J. Monetary Econ.* 31 (June): 299–316.
Hornstein, Andreas, and Edward C. Prescott. 1993. "The Firm and the Plant in General Equilibrium Theory." In *General Equilibrium, Growth, and Trade II: The Legacy of Lionel McKenzie*, edited by Robert Becker, Michele Boldrin, Ronald Jones, and William Thomson. San Diego: Academic Press.
Imai, Susumu, and Michael P. Keene. 2004. "Intertemporal Labor Supply and Human Capital Accumulation." *Int. Econ. Rev.* 45 (May): 601–641.
Kehoe, Timothy J., David K. Levine, and Edward C. Prescott. 2002. "Lotteries, Sunspots, and Incentive Constraints." *J. Econ. Theory* 107 (November): 39–69.
Kehoe, Timothy J., and Edward C. Prescott. 2002. Introduction to "Great Depressions of the 20th Century." *Rev. Econ. Dynam.* 5 (January): 1–18.
Koopmans, Tjalling C. 1965. "On the Concept of Optimal Economic Growth." In Semaine d'étude sur le role de l'analyse économétrique dans la formulation de plans de développement. *Pontificiae Academiae Scientiarum Scripta Varia* 28, 1.
Krusell, Per, and Anthony A. Smith Jr. 1998. "Income and Wealth Heterogeneity in the Macroeconomy." *J. Polit. Economy* 106 (October): 867–896.
Kydland, Finn E., and Edward C. Prescott. 1977. "Rules Rather than Discretion: The Inconsistency of Optimal Plans." *J. Polit. Economy* 85 (June): 473–492.
Kydland, Finn E., and Edward C. Prescott. 1982. "Time to Build and Aggregate Fluctuations." *Econometrica* 50 (November): 1345–1370.
Kydland, Finn E., and Edward C. Prescott. 1991. "Hours and Employment Variation in Business Cycle Theory." *Econ. Theory* 1 (January): 63–82.
Long, John B., Jr., and Charles I. Plosser. 1983. "Real Business Cycles." *J. Polit. Economy* 91 (February): 39–69.
Lucas, Robert E., Jr. 1972. "Expectations and the Neutrality of Money." *J. Econ. Theory* 4 (April): 103–124.
Lucas, Robert E., Jr. 1976. "Econometric Policy Evaluation: A Critique." *Carnegie-Rochester Conf. Ser. Public Policy* 1: 19–46.
Lucas, Robert E., Jr. 1995. "Monetary Neutrality." Nobel Prize Lecture, December 7, 1995. www.nobelprize.org.
Lucas, Robert E., Jr., and Edward C. Prescott. 1971. "Investment under Uncertainty."

Econometrica 39 (September): 659–681.
McGrattan, Ellen R., and Edward C. Prescott. 2005a. "Taxes, Regulations, and the Value of U.S. and U.K. Corporations." *Rev. Econ. Studies* 72 (July), forthcoming.
McGrattan, Ellen R., and Edward C. Prescott. 2005b. "Productivity and the Post-1990 U.S. Economy." *Fed. Reserve Bank St. Louis Review* 87 (July/August), forthcoming.
Pigou, Arthur C. 1927. *Industrial Fluctuations.* London: Macmillan.
Prescott, Edward C. 1986. "Theory Ahead of Business Cycle Measurement." *Carnegie-Rochester Conf. Ser. Public Policy* 25 (Autumn): 11–44. Reprint, 1986, *Fed. Reserve Bank Minneapolis Q. Rev.* 10 (Fall): 9–22.
Prescott, Edward C. 2004. "Why Do Americans Work So Much More than Europeans?" *Fed. Reserve Bank Minneapolis Q. Rev.* 28 (July): 2–13.
Prescott, Edward C., and Rajnish Mehra. 1980. "Recursive Competitive Equilibrium: The Case of Homogeneous Households." *Econometrica* 48 (September): 1365–1379.
Prescott, Edward C., and Karl Shell. 2002. "Introduction to Sunspots and Lotteries." *J. Econ. Theory* 107 (November): 1–10.
Prescott, Edward C., and Robert M. Townsend. 1984a. "General Competitive Analysis in an Economy with Private Information." *Int. Econ. Rev.* 25 (February): 1–20.
Prescott, Edward C., and Robert M. Townsend. 1984b. "Pareto Optima and Competitive Equilibria with Adverse Selection and Moral Hazard." *Econometrica* 52 (January): 21–45.
Ríos-Rull, José-Víctor. 1994. "On the Quantitative Importance of Market Completeness." *J. Monetary Econ.* 34 (December): 463–496.
Ríos-Rull, José-Víctor. 1995. "Models with Heterogeneous Agents." In *Frontiers of Business Cycle Research,* edited by Thomas F. Cooley. Princeton, N.J.: Princeton Univ. Press.
Rogerson, Richard. 1984. *Topics in the Theory of Labor Markets.* Ph.D. thesis, University of Minnesota, September.
Rogerson, Richard. 1988. "Indivisible Labor, Lotteries and Equilibrium." *J. Monetary Econ.* 21 (January): 3–16.
Rosen, Sherwin. 1978. "The Supply of Work Schedules and Employment." In *Work Time and Employment.* Washington, D.C.: National Commission for Manpower Policy.
Rotemberg, Julio J., and Michael Woodford. 1995. "Oligopolistic Pricing and the Effects on Aggregate Demand on Economic Activity." *J. Polit. Economy* 100: 1153–1207.
Solow, Robert M. 1956. "A Contribution to the Theory of Economic Growth." *Q. J. Econ.* 70 (February): 65–94.
Solow, Robert M. 1970. *Growth Theory: An Exposition.* The Radcliffe Lectures, delivered at the University of Warwick, 1969. Oxford: Oxford Univ. Press.
Stigler, Stephen M. 1978. "Mathematical Statistics in the Early States." *Ann. Statistics* 6 (March): 239–265.
Taylor, John B. 1980. "Aggregate Dynamics and Staggered Contracts." *J. Polit. Economy* 88 (February): 1–23.
Thomas, Julia K. 2002. "Is Lumpy Investment Relevant for the Business Cycle?" *J. Polit. Economy* 110 (June): 508–534.
Wicksell, Knut. 1907. "The Enigma of Business Cycles." 1953 translation in *Int. Econ. Papers* 3: 58–74.

Economic Sciences 2005

ROBERT J. AUMANN and THOMAS C. SCHELLING

"for having enhanced our undestanding of conflcit and cooperation through game-theory analysis"

THE SVERIGES RIKSBANK (BANK OF SWEDEN) PRIZE IN ECONOMIC SCIENCES IN MEMORY OF ALFRED NOBEL

Speech by Professor Jörgen Weibull of the Royal Swedish Academy of Sciences. Translation of the Swedish text.

Your Majesties, Your Royal Highnesses, Honoured Laureates, Ladies and Gentlemen,

War and other conflicts have tormented mankind since time immemorial, more often than not with great suffering and extensive material losses. Yet many societies live in prosperity founded on cooperation and peaceful competition. Why do some groups, organizations and countries succeed in promoting cooperation while others suffer from conflict? Robert Aumann and Thomas Schelling approached this age-old question against the backdrop of the cold war, when an understanding of cooperation and conflict was imperative under the threat of nuclear war. Although they approached the topic from different angles – Aumann from mathematics and Schelling from economics – they shared a vision: that game theory had the potential to reshape the analysis of human interaction.

What, then, is game theory? It is all about strategic interaction. Such interaction may occur within or between families, local communities, firms, organizations or whole countries. In most instances, no single party, or "player", can determine the outcome single-handedly; the result of interaction depends on everyone's behavior. Just as in chess or bridge, a player's best move thus depends on the moves that have been and will be made by other players. Consequently, in strategic interactions each player acts on the information at his or her disposal, as well as on expectations of others' future actions. However, others' actions depend, in turn, on their information and expectations about your actions, so all players' actions, information and expectations are intertwined in a complex and fascinating pattern. The analysis of strategic interaction, with due regard to these complexities, is precisely what game theory is all about.

This year's Laureates have offered us new insights into the dynamic aspects of conflict and cooperation. Thomas Schelling showed how one party in a conflict can often strengthen its position by overtly worsening or limiting its own options – by "burning its ships". He also demonstrated that the capability to retaliate can be more useful than the capability to resist an attack, and that uncertain and gradual retaliation can be more credible and less costly than immediate and certain retaliation. These insights have proven to be of great relevance for conflict resolution and the avoidance of war. They have also prompted new developments in economics, in particular concerning our understanding of market competition. For example, a firm can sometimes increase its profit through strategic investment in a large and expensive plant. Even if its average production costs would rise, losses due to inefficient production may be outweighed by the gains generated by competitors' less aggressive behavior.

Robert Aumann laid the foundation for game-theory analysis of long-run relationships. In many real-world situations, interaction takes place not only once, but repeatedly, over an indefinite time horizon. An example is when competing firms make production decisions or set prices on a daily or monthly basis. Aumann's analysis of repeated games showed how repetition can enable cooperation, even among parties with strong conflicts of interest. The theory of repeated games – which continues to grow and flourish – has given us a more precise understanding of the conditions that facilitate cooperation and prevent conflict. For example, how does the level of cooperation in maintaining common-pool resources in local communities depend on their size and the frequency of interaction? Here, cooperation has positive effects. But this is not always the case. Firms in a market can more easily sustain a high collusive price level if they are few, interact frequently and are not short-sighted regarding their profit maximization. Although such cooperation may be advantageous for the firms in question, it usually harms a third party, the consumers, for whom conflict – in the form of price competition – is more favorable.

Robert Aumann and Thomas Schelling have been instrumental in the development of game theory and in its application to the social sciences. When today's economists, political scientists and sociologists analyze issues concerning conflict and cooperation, they almost without exception rely on their contributions.

Dear Dr. Aumann, Dear Dr. Schelling,

Thanks to your work, game theory has become the dominant tool for analyzing the age-old question of why some groups, organizations and countries succeed in fostering cooperation while others suffer from conflict.

Dr Aumann, you were the first to conduct a full-fledged and formal analysis of long-run relationships, so-called repeated games. The theory of repeated games has enhanced our understanding of cooperation among parties with conflicting interests. It has helped explain economic conflicts such as price wars and trade wars – as well as why some communities are more successful than others in managing common-pool resources, such as grasslands or irrigation systems.

Dr Schelling, you were the first to demonstrate the strategic importance of commitment and the difficulties associated with strategic coordination. These insights have proven to be of great relevance for conflict resolution and the avoidance of war. Your work has also prompted new developments in formal game theory and accelerated the use of game theory throughout the social sciences.

It is an honor and a privilege to convey to you, on behalf of the Royal Swedish Academy of Sciences, our warmest congratulations. I now ask you to receive your Prize from the hands of His Majesty the King.

Robert J. Aumann

ROBERT J. AUMANN

Being awarded the Prize in Economic Sciences in Memory of Alfred Nobel is a beautiful, fairy-tale experience, from beginning to end. It is not, however, conducive to research, writing, teaching, or indeed to any ordinary academic work. Instead, one is besieged by hundreds – indeed thousands – of demands to appear and speak at events and congresses, many of which have nothing at all to do with science, to underwrite good (and less good) causes, to sign and send autographs, to be photographed, to be interviewed, etc., etc., etc.

The reader should not misunderstand. This is not a complaint; a Nobelist is glad to do these things, it's worth it. Rather, it's an apology for the biography that follows. This biography was due on February 1, 2006, but I simply did not get to it. After many futile attempts on the part of the Nobel Foundation to wrest the biography from me, I was told that if it were not in by May 15, it would simply not be included. This alarmed me, so finally I started seriously working on it. But being serious did not help me; the requests for interviews, appearances, speeches, photographs, etc., etc., kept pouring in. Somehow, though, I did manage to devote a few minutes a day to the biography. Unfortunately (or perhaps fortunately) the result is rather haphazard and disorganized, jumping from topic to topic; but perhaps it is better – more interesting – that way than a more straight-laced essay would be.

I was born in June of 1930 in Frankfurt-am-Main, Germany, to an orthodox Jewish family. My father was a wholesale textile merchant, financially comfortable, whose family had lived in Germany for centuries; he had fought in World War I for the Germans, and been decorated. My mother grew up in London, and obtained a B.A. at University College, London – a somewhat unusual feat for women in the early 20th century. The Nazi regime in the thirties made life very difficult for Jews in Germany, and my parents saw the handwriting on the wall – realized that far worse was in the offing. In 1938 we obtained American visas with some difficulty, and emigrated from Frankfurt to New York. In that passage my parents lost all their assets, and had to work very hard to make a living; nevertheless, they gave their two children – my brother and me – excellent educations, and we had wonderful childhoods. We attended Jewish parochial schools, and obtained bachelor's degrees at the City College of New York.

In high school I had an extraordinary teacher of mathematics, Abraham Gansler, who taught me to love the subject. What attracted me most were the axioms, theorems, proofs, and constructions of Euclid's geometry. So in City

College, I decided to "major" in (emphasize) mathematics. I was mainly interested in classical mathematics: complex and real functions, Fourier series, differential geometry, and so on. Most of all, analytic and algebraic number theory, which I read voraciously, largely from the books of Edmund Landau. Number theory fascinated me because (i) the problems are very natural; (ii) they are simple to formulate, a schoolchild can understand them; (iii) the solutions are very difficult and deep, they require years of university study even to begin to fathom; and (iv) the whole subject was absolutely useless, had no practical applications, was a purely intellectual endeavor. The vogue of pure mathematics – the "purer," the better – was at its height in the mid-twentieth century, and, young and impressionable, I was drawn into it.

As is customary in American higher education, in addition to mathematics, I studied many other subjects: physics, chemistry, biology, bacteriology, geology, philosophy, English and German literature, history, writing, art, music, public speaking, film, … . There was even a course in economics, which baffled and bored me, and which I "dropped" after a few weeks. But many of the other courses left a deep impression. The best were those with a "hands-on" approach: the art course consisted almost exclusively of showing and analyzing (reproductions of) specific paintings and sculptures; the music course consisted almost exclusively of playing and analyzing specific musical compositions; the literature courses consisted almost exclusively of reading and analyzing specific literary works, mostly English poetry and German drama (an entire semester was devoted to Goethe's *Faust*). An extreme example was the course in geology. For three weeks we did nothing but learn the names of various kinds of rock, pieces of which were provided in the classroom. At the end of that period there was an examination: we were provided with twenty-five or thirty pieces of rock – not pictures, but the rocks themselves – which we had to identify. After that, we never saw the inside of the classroom again; the course consisted *exclusively* of field trips, all inside New York City and its immediate surroundings, all accessible by public transportation. I will never forget what I learned there – why rivers meander, what makes rocks different, dikes, glaciation, U- and V-shaped valleys, etc., etc.; when hiking in Israel and all over the world, I teach these things to my children and grandchildren, who do not have the benefit of such a marvellously broad education.

After completing a B.S. at "City," I entered the Massachusetts Institute of Technology (MIT) for graduate studies. At MIT I became interested in the more modern branches of mathematics, like algebraic topology, to which I was attracted by the excellent lectures of George W. Whitehead. I decided to do a Ph.D. with Whitehead in knot theory, a branch of algebraic topology that deals with the properties of knots (those tied in ropes). Like analytic number theory, knot theory deals with problems that (i) are very natural, have an immediacy that is even greater than that of the distribution of prime numbers or Fermat's last theorem; (ii) are simple to formulate, a schoolchild can understand them; (iii) have solutions that are very difficult and deep; and (iv) the whole subject was absolutely useless.

Whitehead gave me a very difficult problem – one that had been attacked unsuccessfully for a quarter of a century – namely, to show that knots are "aspheric" (we won't explain here what this means). I didn't solve this problem, but did establish asphericity for knots of a special kind: those that are "alternating." That means that when you draw the knot on a piece of paper, and follow along any component of the knot, then the undercrossings alternate with the overcrossings – as, for example, in the famous "Borromean Rings." My thesis was published in the *Annals of Mathematics* in 1956.

After completing the Ph.D., I went to work for an Operations Research consulting outfit – the "Analytical Research Group" (ARG) – affiliated with Princeton University's mathematics department, and located at the University's Forrestal Center for Applied Research. ARG did highly practical consulting. One of the problems that I was assigned had to do with defending a city from attack by a squadron of aircraft, a few of which are carrying nuclear weapons, but most of which are decoys. At MIT I had met John Nash – who in 1994 shared the Prize in Economic Sciences in Memory of Alfred Nobel with John Harsanyi and Reinhard Selten, and who came to MIT as a young instructor in the early fifties – and had heard a little about game theory from him. At the time it didn't interest me very much, but when I was assigned the problem about the decoys, I remembered the conversations with Nash, and figured that game theory had to be the right tool to attack this problem. So I studied some game theory – just enough for this problem – and then the subject started attracting me in its own right. The rest is history, as the saying goes.

Jews have been yearning for the land of Israel, and for Jerusalem, for close to 2000 years – ever since the destruction of the Temple by the Romans in the year 70, and the ensuing exile of the Jewish people. In our central prayer, which we recite three times a day, we ask the Lord to "return to Jerusalem Your city in mercy, and rebuild it and dwell therein." Jerusalem is mentioned many thousands of times in the scriptures, in our other prayers, in the Talmud, and indeed in all our sources. So when the state of Israel was established in 1948, my brother and I made a determination eventually to make our lives there. My brother fulfilled this ambition shortly thereafter, in 1950, but I decided first to complete my education. In 1953 I met an Israeli girl, Esther Schlesinger, who was visiting the United States; we were married in Brooklyn in April of 1955. In the fall of 1956 I took up a position as instructor of mathematics at the Hebrew University of Jerusalem, and have been there ever since. Esther and I had five beautiful children; the oldest, Shlomo, was killed in action in 1982, while serving in the Israeli Army in "Operation Peace for Galilee." At this writing, I have nineteen grandchildren and two great-grandchildren. Esther died of ovarian cancer in October of 1998, after we had enjoyed forty-four truly magnificent years together. In late November of 2005, about a week before being awarded the Prize in Economic Sciences in Memory of Alfred Nobel, I married Esther's widowed sister, Batya Cohn.

When the Prize was announced, the work of mine most prominently mentioned by the Committee was my 1959 paper "Acceptable Points in General Cooperative *n*-Person Games," which is perhaps the first rigorous treatment of repeated games that has some generality. Briefly put, the finding of that paper is that the strong equilibrium payoffs of a repeated game coincide with the core (more precisely, β-core) payoffs in the one-shot game. Frankly, I don't recall well the genesis of that paper. As mentioned above, I became interested in game theory while at Princeton in the years 1954–56. The 1957 Luce–Raiffa book *Games and Decisions,* which made a big impression on me, has an interesting – though inconclusive – discussion of repeated games, and this may have piqued my interest. I vividly recall working on "Acceptable Points" while at the Bureau of Standards in Washington in the summers of 1957 and 58; the yellow pads are still before my eyes. In the course of that work I became aware of what later became known as the "Folk Theorem" (see my 1981 "Survey of Repeated Games"), but it seemed to me at the time that it did not have sufficient mathematical depth to merit publication. That was a big mistake. Both "Acceptable Points" and the Folk Theorem are expressions of the relation between equilibrium behavior in the repeated game and cooperative behavior in the one-shot game; but while "Acceptable Points" is undoubtedly interesting, and much the deeper and more subtle, the Folk Theorem is by far the more fundamental and important.

At some point during the academic year 1959–60 I gave a colloquium lecture at the mathematics department of the Hebrew University; the colloquium is a weekly gathering of the entire department, at which a faculty member or guest talks about his own research or a related topic. I chose to discuss the von Neumann–Morgenstern "solutions" of cooperative *n*-person games, sometimes called *stable sets.* Historically, this is the first "solution concept" for cooperative games, and to this day it remains one of the most subtle and beautiful. Michael Maschler, an expert in the theory of functions of a complex variable, was in the audience; after the talk he asked a question. This question led to a lifelong scientific partnership with Maschler.

The specific question that Maschler asked led eventually to our 1964 joint paper on the *bargaining set* for coalitional (a.k.a. cooperative) games. In turn, this led to a very considerable literature, encompassing related concepts such as the *kernel* (Davis and Maschler 1965) and *nucleolus* (Schmeidler 1969). But I myself made only two additional contributions to this subject after 1964. One was a computation and tabulation of the kernels of several classes of games with up to five players, done jointly with Bezalel Peleg from the Hebrew University and Pinny Rabinowitz from the Weizmann Institute of Science; this work led to several conjectures on the structure of the kernel, which turned out to be very fruitful and led to important theoretical advances and a much better understanding of this structure. The other is the 1985 paper "Game-Theoretic Analysis of a Bankruptcy Problem from the Talmud," also joint with Maschler; it is an explanation of a difficult passage in the Babylonian Talmud (Ketubot 93a), the key to which was Schmeidler's nucleolus. This is undoubtedly the work of mine that is best known; not so much to the scientific public – though there, too, it is widely cited – but to the general public. I have lectured on it dozens – perhaps hundreds – of times, to scientific audiences as well as to high school students and teachers, synagogue groups, Talmudic academies, and so on. It has been quoted and explained and reworked by many different people, innumerable times; I cannot possibly keep track of it.

Another important joint work with Maschler is that on repeated games of incomplete information. This began as part of a project initiated by the United States Arms Control and Disarmament Agency (ACDA) in the mid-1960s, to help shape United States policy in the arms control negotiations that were taking place with the Soviet Union at that time. Involved in this project, in addition to Maschler and me, were John Harsanyi, Reinhard Selten, and Gerard Debreu – all three of whom eventually became Nobelists; Dick Stearns – eventually awarded the Turing prize in theoretical computer science; Herb Scarf and Harold Kuhn – eventually awarded the John von Neumann Prize in operations research theory; Jim Mayberry, whom I had gotten to know at ARG; and others. Several times a year the members of this stellar group would converge on Washington to discuss arms control and disarmament with each other and with the personnel of the agency; between meetings, we would work alone or in small groups in our home environments. I doubt that this work did indeed have much practical influence on policy, though one can never know; a side discussion with an agency staff member at lunch or during a coffee break can sometimes leave a deep impression – conscious or subconscious – that may eventually profoundly affect policy.

Be that as it may, the work of Maschler and me on repeated games of incomplete information, in which Dick Stearns also played an important role, spawned a large scientific literature. For many years the original work was difficult to obtain; it was available only in the form of the original ACDA reports, and one had to scrounge around for it. Eventually, in 1995, the original reports were published in book form by the MIT Press, together with extensive notes describing much of the subsequent work (up to 1995, of course). This book was awarded the Lanchester Prize of the Operations Research (OR) Society of America for the best OR book in 1995.

Maschler is by no means my only collaborator. I have collaborated – and am collaborating – with more than thirty scientists; a good part of my prize is attributable to them. Prominent among them is Lloyd Shapley, with whom I coauthored the 1974 book *Values of Non-Atomic Games;* it concerns games with many players, who impinge significantly on the outcome only when they form large coalitions, but not as individuals. Examples are national elections or large economies or markets. Another collaboration with Shapley concerns perfect equilibria in repeated games; it is a sharpening of the Folk Theorem, and it, too, was cited by the Nobel Committee. At around the same time that Lloyd and I were looking into this at the Rand Corporation in Santa Monica, California, in 1976, Ariel Rubinstein was doing a master's thesis – with Bezalel Peleg in Jerusalem – on precisely the same question, and he reached essentially the same conclusions that we did. Although it became widely known soon thereafter, this work was not published until 1994 – most appropriately, in a festschrift honoring Maschler.

Others with whom I've collaborated extensively – and intensively – throughout the years include Jacques Drèze, Mordecai Kurz, Sergiu Hart, Bezalel Peleg, Adam Brandenburger, Frank Anscombe, Abraham Neyman, Benjy Weiss, Micha Perles, Joe Kruskal, Roger Myerson, and others. At this writing I'm collaborating with Roberto Serrano on a project on which we've already been working for several years; with Sergiu Hart on another project; and with Hart and Motty Perry on yet another project.

Influence is not limited to joint papers. Innumerable individuals impinge on one, both in person and in what one reads and hears. Prominent among them are one's students, but there are many, many others. Science is one huge cooperative venture. The Nobel Prizes focus attention on important scientific work by focusing on a small number of individuals; but really, any scientific work – including work that merits a Nobel Prize – is the product of many minds.

For the finale, we flash half a century back. Though writing it up took a little longer, my thesis was essentially complete in October of 1954; I remember standing in the shower and being hit with the mathematical idea that enabled its completion. Fifty years later – almost to the day – at 10:00 pm, the phone in my flat rings. My grandson Yakov Rosen, who is in the second year of medical school, is on the line. "Grandpa," he says, "can I pick your brain? We are studying knots. I don't understand the material, and think that our lecturer does not understand it either. For example, what, exactly, are 'linking numbers'?" "Why are you studying knots?" I ask. "What do knots have to do with medicine?" "Well," says Yakov, "sometimes the DNA in a cell gets knotted up. Depending on the characteristics of the knot, this may lead to cancer. So, we have to understand knots."

I was completely bowled over. Fifty years later, the "absolutely useless" – the "purest of the pure" – is taught in the second year of medical school, and my grandson is studying it.

Science is exploration – exploration for the sake of exploration, and for nothing else. We must go where our curiosity leads us, we must go where we want to go. And eventually, it is sure to lead us to the beautiful, the important, and the useful.

For me, life has been – and still is – one tremendous joyride, one magnificent tapestry. There have been bad – very bad – times, like when my son Shlomo was killed and when my wife Esther died. But even these somehow integrate into the magnificent tapestry. In one of his beautiful letters, Shlomo wrote that there can be no good without bad. Both Shlomo and Esther led beautiful, meaningful lives, affected many people, each in his own way.

And there have been a *lot* of very good times. The excitement of research, of groping in the dark and then hitting the light. The satisfaction of teaching, of meeting someone at a party who tells you that the course in complex variables that he heard from you twenty-five years ago was the most beautiful that he *ever* heard. The exhilaration of climbing – seeking and finding foot- and handholds – on an almost vertical rock face. The beauty of a walk in the woods with a four-year-old grandchild, who spots and correctly identifies a tiny wild orchid about which you told him last week. Dancing with your wife at your child's wedding. Unraveling an intricate passage in the Talmud with your eighteen-year-old granddaughter, or with a study partner with whom you have studied for thirty years. Slipping on a "black" (expert) ski slope, tumbling two hundred meters down, and then going back and doing the same slope again – this time without a slip. Cooking a meal and hearing from a guest that the soup was the best she *ever* tasted. Raising a beautiful family. Seeing the flag of Israel fluttering in the wind, right next to that of Sweden, from the roof of the Grand Hotel in Stockholm.

WAR AND PEACE

Prize Lecture[1], December 8, 2005

by

ROBERT J. AUMANN

Center for the Study of Rationality, and Department of Mathematics, The Hebrew University, Jerusalem, Israel.

"Wars and other conflicts are among the main sources of human misery." Thus begins the *Advanced Information* announcement of the 2005 Bank of Sweden Prize in Economic Sciences in Memory of Alfred Nobel, awarded for Game Theory Analysis of Conflict and Cooperation. So it is appropriate to devote this lecture to one of the most pressing and profound issues that confront humanity: that of War and Peace.

I would like to suggest that we should perhaps change direction in our efforts to bring about world peace. Up to now all the effort has been put into resolving specific conflicts: India–Pakistan, North–South Ireland, various African wars, Balkan wars, Russia–Chechnya, Israel–Arab, etc., etc. I'd like to suggest that we should shift emphasis and study war in general.

Let me make a comparison. There are two approaches to cancer. One is clinical. You have, say, breast cancer. What should you do? Surgery? Radiation? Chemotherapy? Which chemotherapy? How much radiation? Do you cut out the lymph nodes? The answers are based on clinical tests, simply on what works best. You treat each case on its own, using your best information. And your aim is to cure the disease, or to ameliorate it, in the specific patient before you.

And, there is another approach. You don't do surgery, you don't do radiation, you don't do chemotherapy, you don't look at statistics, you don't look at the patient at all. You just try to understand what happens in a cancerous cell. Does it have anything to do with the DNA? What happens? What is the process like? *Don't* try to cure it. Just try to *understand* it. You work with mice, not people. You try to make them sick, not cure them.

Louis Pasteur was a physician. It was important to him to treat people, to cure them. But Robert Koch was not a physician, he didn't try to cure people. He just wanted to know how infectious disease works. And eventually, his work became tremendously important in treating and curing disease.

War has been with us ever since the dawn of civilization. Nothing has been more constant in history than war. It's a phenomenon, it's not a series of iso-

[1] A very lightly edited version of the 40-minute lecture actually delivered at the Royal Swedish Academy of Sciences in Stockholm. We are grateful to Professor Nicolaus Tideman for pointing out an error in a previous version.

lated events. The efforts to resolve specific conflicts are certainly laudable, and sometimes they really bear fruit. But there's also another way of going about it – studying war as a general phenomenon, studying its general, defining characteristics, what the common denominators are, what the differences are. Historically, sociologically, psychologically, and – yes – *rationally*. Why does *homo economicus* – rational man – go to war?

What do I mean by "rationality"? It is this:

A person's behavior is ***rational*** *if it is in* ***his*** *best interests, given* ***his*** *information.*

With this definition, can war be rational? Unfortunately, the answer is yes; it can be. In one of the greatest speeches of all time – his second inaugural – Abraham Lincoln said: "Both parties deprecated war; but one would make war rather than let the nation survive; and the other would accept war rather than let it perish. And the war came."

It is a big mistake to say that war is irrational. We take all the ills of the world – wars, strikes, racial discrimination – and dismiss them by calling them irrational. They are not necessarily irrational. Though it hurts, they may be rational. If war is rational, once we understand that it is, we can at least somehow address the problem. If we simply dismiss it as irrational, we can't address the problem.

Many years ago, I was present at a meeting of students at Yale University. Jim Tobin, who later was awarded the Prize in Economic Sciences in Memory of Alfred Nobel, was also there. The discussion was freewheeling, and one question that came up was: Can one sum up economics in one word? Tobin's answer was "yes"; the word is *incentives*. Economics is all about incentives.

So, what I'd like to do is an economic analysis of war. Now this does *not* mean what it sounds like. I'm not talking about how to finance a war, or how to rebuild after a war, or anything like that. I'm talking about the *incentives* that lead to war, and about building incentives that prevent war.

Let me give an example. Economics teaches us that things are not always as they appear. For example, suppose you want to raise revenue from taxes. To do that, obviously you should raise the tax rates, right? No, wrong. You might want to *lower* the tax rates. To give people an incentive to work, or to reduce avoidance and evasion of taxes, or to heat up the economy, or whatever. That's just one example; there are thousands like it. An economy is a game: the incentives of the players interact in complex ways, and lead to surprising, often counter-intuitive results. But as it turns out, the economy really works that way.

So now, let's get back to war, and how *homo economicus* – rational man – fits into the picture. An example, in the spirit of the previous item, is this. You want to prevent war. To do that, obviously you should disarm, lower the level of armaments. Right? No, wrong. You might want to do the exact opposite. In the long years of the cold war between the US and the Soviet Union, what prevented "hot" war was that bombers carrying nuclear weapons were in the air 24 hours a day, 365 days a year. Disarming would have led to war.

The bottom line is – again – that we should start studying war, from all viewpoints, for its own sake. Try to understand what makes it happen. Pure, basic science. *That* may lead, eventually, to peace. The piecemeal, case-based approach has not worked too well up to now.

Now I would like to get to some of my own basic contributions, some of those that were cited by the Prize Committee. Specifically, let's discuss repeated games, and how they relate to war, and to other conflicts, like strikes, and indeed to all interactive situations.

Repeated games model long-term interaction. The theory of repeated games is able to account for phenomena such as altruism, cooperation, trust, loyalty, revenge, threats (self-destructive or otherwise) – phenomena that may at first seem irrational – in terms of the "selfish" utility-maximizing paradigm of game theory and neoclassical economics.

That it "accounts" for such phenomena does not mean that people deliberately choose to take revenge, or to act generously, out of consciously self-serving, rational motives. Rather, over the millennia, people have evolved norms of behavior that are by and large successful, indeed optimal. Such evolution may actually be biological, genetic. Or, it may be "memetic"; this word derives from the word "meme," a term coined by the biologist Richard Dawkins to parallel the term "gene," but to express social, rather than biological, heredity and evolution.

One of the great discoveries of game theory came in the early seventies, when the biologists John Maynard Smith and George Price realized that strategic equilibrium in games and population equilibrium in the living world are defined by the same equations. Evolution – be it genetic or memetic – leads to strategic equilibrium. So what we are saying is that in *repeated* games, strategic equilibrium expresses phenomena such as altruism, cooperation, trust, loyalty, revenge, threats, and so on. Let us see how that works out.

What do I mean by "strategic equilibrium"? Very roughly, the players in a game are said to be in *strategic equilibrium* (or simply *equilibrium*) when their play is *mutually optimal*: when the actions and plans of each player are rational in the given strategic environment – i.e., when each knows the actions and plans of the others.

For formulating and developing the concept of strategic equilibrium, John Nash was awarded the 1994 Prize in Economics Sciences in Memory of Alfred Nobel, on the fiftieth anniversary of the publication of John von Neumann and Oskar Morgenstern's *Theory of Games and Economic Behavior*. Sharing that Prize were John Harsanyi, for formulating and developing the concept of *Bayesian* equilibrium, i.e., strategic equilibrium in games of incomplete information; and Reinhard Selten, for formulating and developing the concept of *perfect* equilibrium, a refinement of Nash's concept, on which we will say more below. Along with the concepts of *correlated* equilibrium (Aumann 1974, 1987), and *strong* equilibrium (Aumann 1959), both of which were cited in the 2005 Prize announcement, the above three fundamental concepts constitute the theoretical cornerstones of noncooperative game theory.

Subsequent to the 1994 prize, two Prizes in Economic Sciences in Memory of Alfred Nobel were awarded for *applications* of these fundamental concepts. The first was in 1996, when William Vickrey was awarded the Prize posthumously for his work on auctions. (Vickrey died between the time of the Prize announcement and that of the ceremony.) The design of auctions and of bidding strategies are among the prime practical applications of game theory; a good – though somewhat dated – survey is Wilson 1992.

The second came this year – 2005. Professor Schelling will, of course, speak and write for himself. As for your humble servant, he received the prize for applying the fundamental equilibrium concepts mentioned above to *repeated* games. That is, suppose you are playing the same game *G*, with the same players, year after year. One can look at this situation as a single big game – the so-called *supergame* of *G*, denoted G^∞ – whose rules are, "play *G* every year." The idea is to apply the above equilibrium concepts to the supergame G^∞, rather than to the one-shot game *G*, and to see what one gets.

The theory of repeated games that emerges from this process is extremely rich and deep (good – though somewhat dated – surveys are Sorin 1992, Zamir 1992, and Forges 1992). In the few minutes that are available to me, I can barely scratch its surface. Let me nevertheless try. I will briefly discuss just one aspect: the *cooperative*. Very roughly, the conclusion is that

Repetition Enables Cooperation.

Let us flesh this out a little. We use the term *cooperative* to describe any possible outcome of a game, as long as no player can *guarantee* a better outcome for himself. It is important to emphasize that in general, a cooperative outcome is *not* in equilibrium; it's the result of an agreement. For example, in the well-known "prisoner's dilemma" game, the outcome in which neither prisoner confesses is a cooperative outcome; it is in neither player's best interests, though it is better for both than the unique equilibrium.

An even simpler example is the following game *H*: There are two players, Rowena and Colin. Rowena must decide whether both she and Colin will receive the same amount – namely 10 – or whether she will receive ten times more, and Colin will receive ten times less. Simultaneously, Colin must decide whether or not to take a punitive action, which will harm both Rowena and himself; if he does so, the division is cancelled, and instead, each player gets nothing. The game matrix is

	Acquiesce	**P**unish
Divide **E**venly	10 10	0 0
Divide **G**reedily	1 100	0 0

The outcome (**E**,**A**), yielding 10 to each player, is a cooperative outcome, as no player can guarantee more for himself; but like in the prisoner's dilemma, it is not achievable in equilibrium.

Why are cooperative outcomes interesting, even though they are not achievable in equilibrium? The reason is that they are achievable by contract – by agreement – in those contexts in which *contracts* are *enforceable.* And there are many such contexts; for example, a national context, with a court system. The Talmud (Avot 3, 2) says,

הוי מתפלל בשלומה של מלכות, שאלמלא מוראה, איש את רעהו חיים בלעו.

"Pray for the welfare of the government, for without its authority, man would swallow man alive." If contracts are enforceable, Rowena and Colin can achieve the cooperative outcome (**E**,**A**) by agreement; if not, (**E**,**A**) is for practical purposes unachievable.

The cooperative theory of games that has grown from these considerations predates the work of Nash by about a decade (von Neumann and Morgenstern 1944). It is very rich and fruitful, and in my opinion, has yielded *the* central insights of game theory. However, we will not discuss these insights here; they are for another Prize in Economic Sciences in Memory of Alfred Nobel, in the future.

What I do wish to discuss here is the relation of cooperative game theory to repeated games. The fundamental insight is that repetition is like an enforcement mechanism, which enables the emergence of cooperative outcomes *in equilibrium* – when everybody is acting in his own best interests.

Intuitively, this is well-known and understood. People are much more cooperative in a long-term relationship. They know that there is a tomorrow, that inappropriate behavior will be punished in the future. A businessman who cheats his customers may make a short-term profit, but he will not stay in business long.

Let's illustrate this with the game H. If the game is played just once, then Rowena is clearly better off by dividing **G**reedily, and Colin by **A**cquiescing. (Indeed, these strategies are *dominant.*) Colin will not like this very much – he is getting nothing – but there is not much that he can do about it. Technically, the *only* equilibrium is (**G**,**A**).

But in the supergame H^∞, there *is* something that Colin can do. He can *threaten* to **P**unish Rowena for ever afterwards if she ever divides **G**reedily. So it will not be worthwhile for her to divide greedily. Indeed, in H^∞ this is actually an equilibrium in the sense of Nash. Rowena's strategy is "play **E** for ever"; Colin's strategy is "play **A** as long as Rowena plays **E**; if she ever plays **G**, play **P** for ever afterwards."

Let's be quite clear about this. What is maintaining the equilibrium in these games is the *threat of punishment.* If you like, call it "MAD" – mutually assured destruction, the motto of the cold war.

One caveat is necessary to make this work. The discount rate must not be too high. Even if it is anything over 10% – if \$1 in a year is worth less than 90 cents today – then cooperation is impossible, because it's still worthwhile for Rowena to be greedy. The reason is that even if Colin punishes her – and himself! – for ever afterwards, then when evaluated today, the entire eternal punishment is worth less than $90, which is all that Rowena gains today by dividing greedily rather than evenly.

I don't mean just the monetary discount rate, what you get in the bank. I mean the personal, subjective discount rate. For repetition to engender cooperation, the players must not be too eager for immediate results. The present, the now, must not be too important. If you want peace now, you may well never get peace. But if you have time – if you can wait – that changes the whole picture; *then* you may get peace now. It's one of those paradoxical, upside-down insights of game theory, and indeed of much of science. Just a week or two ago, I learned that global warming may cause a cooling of Europe, because it may cause a change in the direction of the Gulf Stream. Warming may bring about cooling. Wanting peace now may cause you never to get it – not now, and not in the future. But if you can wait, maybe you will get it now.

The reason is as above: The strategies that achieve cooperation in an equilibrium of the supergame involve punishments in subsequent stages if cooperation is not forthcoming in the current stage. If the discount rates are too high, then the players are more interested in the present than in the future, and a one-time coup now may more than make up for losses in the sequel. This vitiates the threat to punish in future stages.

To summarize: In the supergame H^∞ of the game H, the cooperative outcome (**E,A**) is achievable in equilibrium. This is a special case of a much more general principle, known as the *Folk Theorem*, which says that *any* cooperative outcome of *any* game G is achievable as a strategic equilibrium outcome of its supergame G^∞ – even if that outcome is not an equilibrium outcome of G. Conversely, every strategic equilibrium outcome of G^∞ is a cooperative outcome of G. In brief, for any game G, we have

THE FOLK THEOREM: **The cooperative outcomes of G coincide with the equilibrium outcomes of its supergame G^∞.**

Differently put, repetition acts as an enforcement mechanism: It makes cooperation achievable when it is not achievable in the one-shot game. Of course, the above caveat continues to apply: In order for this to work, the discount rates of all agents must be low; they must not be too interested in the present as compared with the future.

There is another point to be made, and it again relates back to the 1994 Prize. John Nash got the Prize for his development of equilibrium. Reinhard Selten got the Prize for his development of *perfect* equilibrium. Perfect equilibrium means, roughly, that the threat of punishment is *credible;* that *if* you have to go to a punishment, then after you punish, you are still in equilibrium – you do not have an incentive to deviate.

That certainly is *not* the case for the equilibrium we have described in the supergame H^∞ of the game H. If Rowena plays **G** in spite of Colin's threat, then it is *not* in Colin's best interest to punish forever. That raises the question: In the repeated game, can (**E,A**) be maintained not only in strategic equilibrium, but also in *perfect* equilibrium?

The answer is yes. In 1976, Lloyd Shapley – whom I consider to be the greatest game theorist of all time – and I proved what is known as the *Perfect Folk Theorem*; a similar result was established by Ariel Rubinstein, independently and simultaneously. Both results were published only much later (Aumann and Shapley 1994, Rubinstein 1994). The Perfect Folk Theorem says that in the supergame G^∞ of any game G, any cooperative outcome of G is achievable as a *perfect* equilibrium outcome of G^∞ – again, even if that outcome is not an equilibrium outcome of G. The converse of course also holds. In brief, for any game G, we have

THE PERFECT FOLK THEOREM: **The cooperative outcomes of G coincide with the perfect equilibrium outcomes of its supergame G^∞.**

So again, repetition acts as an enforcement mechanism: It makes cooperation achievable when it is not achievable in the one-shot game, even when one replaces strategic equilibrium as the criterion for achievability by the more stringent requirement of *perfect* equilibrium. Again, the caveat about discount rates applies: In order for this to work, the discount rates of all agents must be low; they must not be too interested in the present as compared with the future.

The proof of the Perfect Folk Theorem is quite interesting, and I will illustrate it very sketchily in the game H, for the cooperative outcome (**E,A**). In the first instance, the equilibrium directs playing (**E,A**) all the time. If Rowena deviates by dividing **G**reedily, then Colin punishes her – plays **P**. He does not, however, do this forever, but only until Rowena's deviation becomes unprofitable. This in itself is still not enough, though; there must be something that motivates Colin to carry out the punishment. And here comes the central idea of the proof: If Colin does not punish Rowena, then Rowena must punish Colin – by playing **G** – for not punishing Rowena. Moreover, the process continues – any player who does not carry out a prescribed punishment is punished by the other player for not doing so.

Much of society is held together by this kind of reasoning. If you are stopped by a policeman for speeding, you do not offer him a bribe, because you are afraid that he will turn you in for offering a bribe. But why should he not accept the bribe? Because he is afraid that you will turn him in for accepting it. But why would you turn him in? Because if you don't, he might turn you in for not turning him in. And so on.

This brings us to our last item. Cooperative game theory consists not only of delineating all the possible cooperative outcomes, but also of choosing among them. There are various ways of doing this, but perhaps best known is the notion of *core*, developed by Lloyd Shapley in the early fifties of the last century. An outcome x of a game is said to be in its "core" if no set S of players can *improve* upon it – i.e., assure to each player in S an outcome that is better for him than what he gets at *x*. Inter alia, the concept of core plays a central role in applications of game theory to economics; specifically, the core outcomes of an economy with many individually insignificant agents are the same as the competitive (a.k.a. Walrasian) outcomes – those defined by a system of prices for which the supply of each good matches its demand (see, e.g., Debreu and Scarf 1963, Aumann 1964). Another prominent application of the core is to *matching* markets (see, e.g., Gale and Shapley 1962, Roth and Sotomayor 1990). The core also has many other applications (for surveys, see Anderson 1992, Gabszewicz and Shitovitz 1992, Kannai 1992, Kurz 1994, and Young 1994).

Here again, there is a strong connection with equilibrium in repeated games. When the players in a game are in (strategic) equilibrium, it is not worthwhile for any one of them to deviate to a different strategy. A *strong* equilibrium is defined similarly, except that there it is not worthwhile for any *set* of players to deviate – at least one of the deviating players will not gain from the deviation. We then have the following

THEOREM (AUMANN 1959): **The core outcomes of G coincide with the strong equilibrium outcomes of its supergame G^{∞}.**

In his 1950 thesis, where he developed the notion of strategic equilibrium for which he got the Prize in Economic Sciences in Memory of Alfred Nobel in 1994, John Nash also proposed what has come to be called the *Nash Program* – expressing the notions of cooperative game theory in terms of some appropriately defined noncooperative game; building a bridge between cooperative and noncooperative game theory. The three theorems presented above show that repetition constitutes precisely such a bridge – it is a realization of the Nash Program.

We end with a passage from the prophet Isaiah (2, 2–4):

והיה באחרית הימים, נכון יהיה הר בית יי בראש ההרים, ונישא מגבעות, ונהרו אליו כל הגוים.
והלכו עמים רבים ואמרו, לכו ונעלה אל הר יי, אל בית אלהי יעקב, ויורנו מדרכיו, ונלכה באורחותיו; כי
מציון תצא תורה, ודבר יי מירושלם. ושפט בין הגוים, והוכיח לעמים רבים; וכיתתו חרבותם לאיתים,
וחניתותיהם למזמרות; לא ישא גוי אל גוי חרב, ולא ילמדו עוד מלחמה.

"And it shall come to pass ... that ... many people shall go and say, ... let us go up to the mountain of the Lord, ... and He will teach us of His ways, and we will walk in His paths. ... And He shall judge among the nations, and shall rebuke many people; and they shall beat their swords into ploughshares, and their spears into pruning hooks; nation shall not lift up sword against nation, neither shall they learn war any more."

Isaiah is saying that the nations can beat their swords into ploughshares when there is a central government – a Lord, recognized by all. In the absence of that, one *can* perhaps have peace – no nation lifting up its sword against another. But the swords must continue to be there – they cannot be beaten into ploughshares – and the nations must continue to *learn* war, in order *not* to fight!

REFERENCES

Anderson, R. M., 1992, "The Core in Perfectly Competitive Economies," in Aumann and Hart 1992, 413–457.

Aumann, R. J., 1959, "Acceptable Points in General Cooperative *n*-Person Games," in *Contributions to the Theory of Games IV*, Annals of Mathematics Study 40, edited by A. W. Tucker and R. D. Luce, Princeton: at the University Press, 287–324.

Aumann, R. J., 1964, "Markets with a Continuum of Traders," *Econometrica* 32, 39–50.

Aumann, R. J., 1974, "Subjectivity and Correlation in Randomized Strategies," *Journal of Mathematical Economics* 1, 67–96.

Aumann, R. J., 1987, "Correlated Equilibrium as an Expression of Bayesian Rationality," *Econometrica 55,* 1–18.

Aumann, R. J. and Hart, S. (eds.), 1992, 1994, 2002, *Handbook of Game Theory, with economic applications,* Vols. 1, 2, 3, Elsevier, Amsterdam.

Aumann, R. J. and Shapley, L. S., 1994, "Long-Term Competition: A Game-Theoretic Analysis," in *Essays in Game Theory in Honor of Michael Maschler,* edited by N. Megiddo, Springer, New York, 1–15.

Debreu, G. and Scarf, H., 1963, "A Limit Theorem on the Core of an Economy," *International Economic Review 4,* 235–246.

Forges, F., 1992, "Repeated Games of Incomplete Information: Non-Zero-Sum," in Aumann and Hart 1992, 155–177.

Gabszewicz, J. J. and Shitovitz, B., 1992, "The Core in Imperfectly Competitive Economies," in Aumann and Hart 1992, 459–483.

Gale, D. and Shapley, L. S., 1962, "College Admissions and the Stability of Marriage," *American Mathematical Monthly 69,* 9–15.

Kannai, Y., 1992, "The Core and Balancedness," in Aumann and Hart 1992, 355–395.

Kurz, M., 1994, "Game Theory and Public Economics," in Aumann and Hart 1994, 1153–1192.

Peleg, B., 1992, "Axiomatizations of the Core," in Aumann and Hart 1992, 397–412.

Roth, A. and Sotomayor, M., 1990, *Two-Sided Matching: A Study in Game-Theoretic Modeling and Analysis,* Econometric Society Monograph Series, Cambridge: at the University Press.

Rubinstein, A., 1994, "Equilibrium in Supergames," in *Essays in Game Theory in Honor of Michael Maschler,* edited by N. Megiddo, Springer, New York, 17–28.

Sorin, S., 1992, "Repeated Games with Complete Information," in Aumann and Hart 1992, 71–107.

von Neumann, J., and Morgenstern, O., 1944, *Theory of Games and Economic Behavior,* Princeton: at the University Press.

Wilson, R., 1992, "Strategic Analysis of Auctions," in Aumann and Hart 1992, 227–279.

Young, H. P., 1994, "Cost Allocation," in Aumann and Hart 1994, 1193–1236.

Zamir, S., 1992, "Repeated Games of Incomplete Information: Zero-Sum," in Aumann and Hart 1992, 109–154.

Portrait photo of Robert J. Aumann by photographer D. Porges.

THOMAS C. SCHELLING

I was born April 14, 1921, in Oakland California, spent most of my boyhood in California, with three years in the east and two in the Panama Canal Zone, my father being a naval officer. I attended the University of California, Berkeley (with two years out in Chile), graduating in economics in 1944. After a year and a half as an analyst with the U. S. Bureau of the Budget I attended Harvard University, completing my Ph. D. exams in June of 1948. Appointed a Junior Fellow of the Society of Fellows, I took leave to join the administration of the Marshall Plan, spending one year in Copenhagen and a year and a half in Paris, resigning my fellowship. In November, 1950, I joined the White House Staff of the foreign policy adviser to the President, which in 1951 became the Office of the Director for Mutual Security, the office that managed all foreign aid programs. I left in the fall of 1953 to join the faculty of Yale University.

My experience abroad and in Washington mostly involved negotiations. I was an active participant in negotiating the European Payments Union in 1950; in Washington my responsibilities related to aid negotiations with European governments, primarily in connection with those governments' contributions to the new NATO defense establishment. I had, at Harvard, become interested in bargaining strategy, and my government experience gave me much of the background I needed when later I decided to make bargaining theory my primary theoretical interest.

At Yale I began publishing what I believe the Nobel selection committee considered my contribution to "understanding cooperation and conflict," first an "Essay on Bargaining" in 1956, in the *American Economic Review,* and "Bargaining, Communication, and Limited War" in the inaugural issue of the *Journal of Conflict Resolution,* 1957. Interestingly, these two articles were completed before I had more than a smattering of acquaintance with formal game theory. In 1957 the book, *Games and Decisions* by Howard Raiffa and R. Duncan Luce was published; it was my professional introduction to game theory, and I spent at least a hundred, maybe two hundred, hours with it.

In the spring and summer of 1958 I took my family to London, where I pursued what I considered my concept of game theory in a manuscript – typed by the woman on Charing Cross Road who did all of Agatha Christie's books and plays – and submitted it to the *Journal of Conflict Resolution.* It was so long that that Journal decided to make it a whole issue. I persuaded the editor that a smart way to publicize the new journal would be to give me, without charge, instead of reprints three hundred copies of the journal to send to everyone I could think of. I called my article, "Prospectus for a Reorientation of

Game Theory." I was trying to get game theorists to pay more attention to strategic activities, things like promises and threats, tacit bargaining, the role of communication, tactics of coordination, the design of enforceable contracts and rules, the use of agents, and all the tactics by which individuals or firms or governments committed themselves credibly. I don't think I had any noticeable influence on game theorists, but I did reach sociologists, political scientists, and some economists.

While in London I had made the acquaintance of several scholars and former military officers who were interested in theories of deterrence and limited war. I began to appreciate that the most immediate and important application of the kind of "game theory" I was pursuing was in military foreign policy, especially nuclear weapons policy. I became a close friend of Alastair Buchan, who was just establishing the Institute for Strategic Studies in London, an institute that was to be hugely influential in drawing scholars from all over Western Europe, North America, and Japan to its annual meetings at Oxford, Cambridge, Bonn, and other sites.

I then became the guest of the RAND Corporation, in Santa Monica, California, for twelve months, before settling at Harvard University, which had offered me a position I'd share between the Department of Economics and the Center for International Affairs. At RAND I continued my theoretical work, and went to Washington with a small contingent attached to the staff preparing for a prospective Geneva Convention on Measures to Safeguard Against Surprise Attack. I did not go to Geneva; I did, however, produce two papers. One, "Surprise Attack and Disarmament," explored the concept that the problem of nuclear surprise attack was the problem of the advantage, in case of war, of being the side to start it. Arms control should be oriented toward measures that precluded either side's acquiring a pre-emptive capability, a "first-strike" capability as it was called. And this objective, somewhat paradoxically, entailed arranging for the safety not of populations and industrial assets but of retaliatory nuclear weapons.

At RAND I also developed the idea of a "probabilistic threat," and spelled it out under the title, "The Threat That Leaves Something To Chance." I also, that year at RAND, began drawing on an idea that is sometimes referred to as a "Schelling point," or "focal point," to argue that the only viable convention regarding the use of nuclear weapons would be "no weapons," not some quantitative or qualitative limits. (This idea became the germ of my Nobel Memorial Lecture, forty-five years later.)

Most of the work I have described appeared in 1960 as "*The Strategy of Conflict,*" Harvard University Press.

I then spent thirty-one years at Harvard University, first in the Department of Economics and the Center for International Affairs, then in the Department but also, beginning with its establishment in 1969, in the John F. Kennedy School of Government. For ten years the Center gave me freedom to write and to consult, and I spent much of my time, especially during the summer, doing advisory work for the government.

During my first year at Harvard the Center received a grant, together with the MIT Center for International Studies, to spend on some joint activity. A colleague at MIT and I decided we'd establish a Center for Arms Control, that would meet every three weeks at one or the other faculty clubs for dinner discussion. The summer of 1960 I spent, with a dozen or more colleagues from Harvard and MIT at a "summer study" of arms control, financed by the Twentieth Century Fund. I had arranged to host a young colleague from the Yale graduate school, Morton H. Halperin, for his dissertation work, and took the occasion to make him a rapporteur for the summer study. At the end of the summer, Halperin and I decided to write a book reflecting the consensus the group was developing. We took advantage of the Harvard MIT Center for Arms Control by submitting chapter after chapter as the texts for discussion. The book, *Strategy and Arms Control, 1961,* was finished and available within a couple of weeks of the Kennedy inauguration.

The timing was perfect. Kennedy appointed as his national security adviser a Harvard dean who had participated in the autumn discussions of arms control, and as his White House science adviser an MIT professor who had been one of the group; another member became Deputy Assistance Secretary of Defense for Arms Control, another General Counsel of the State Department. Because of these connections I was appointed chairman of several interagency committees concerned with nuclear weapons policy over the next several years. (One of them brought into being the "hotline" between the Kremlin and the U. S. Government, another initiated the process that led, after a hiatus caused by the Soviet invasion of Czechoslovakia, to the Anti-Ballistic Missile Treaty.)

Partly because I had "connections," I devoted most of my research during the '60s to weapons policy, publishing *Arms and Influence,* Yale University Press, 1977. In the spring of 1970, upon the U. S. invasion of Cambodia, I led a group of Harvard faculty to meet with President Nixon's national security adviser to declare our opposition to the invasion and break relations with the Administration. That ended my connection with the government.

During the seventies and eighties two subjects intrigued me. One resulted from my participation, for seven years, in a committee of the National Academy of Sciences on Substance Abuse and Addictive Behavior. I observed that people who had habits or addictions or delinquencies often attempted, sometimes successfully, sometimes not, to deal with themselves as they might deal with another's misbehavior, attempting, in effect, to "commit" themselves to avoiding the bad behavior or performing the good. Several essays on this topic are in two books of mine, *Choice and Consequence,* 1984 and, just recently, *Strategies of Commitment,* 2006.

The second subject that occupied me in the seventies was the ways that individual behavioral choices could aggregate into social phenomena that were unintended or unexpected. One part of this work involved modeling spatial "segregation," the ways that people who differ conspicuously in binary groups – e.g. blacks and whites, males and females, officers and enlisted personnel, francophones and anglophones – get separated spatially, in residence, in dining halls, at public events. Without knowing it I was pioneering a field of study that later became known as "agent-based computational modeling." Much of this work was published in *Micromotives and Macrobehavior*, 1978.

In 1980 President Carter was to attend a "summit" in Venice. The Chancelor of Germany had submitted, for the agenda, the "carbon dioxide problem." The White House asked the National Academy of Sciences for advice on what to do with that item. I was invited to chair a committee that would do a quick study and prepare advice; I confessed I knew virtually nothing of the subject and was told I could learn most of what was known in the four weeks before the committee would meet. I took the job, I had a superb committee and learned a lot, we did a satisfactory report, and I thought that was the end of an interesting experience.

A few months later the Congress appropriated funds for a longer, more substantial study, and, undoubtedly because I recently chaired a committee on the subject, I was asked to join the Carbon Dioxide Assessment Committee of the National Academy of Sciences. There I spent some fifty days over a two year period with a dozen scientists from the most pertinent disciplines and became an extremely well educated amateur. I wrote the chapter of our report on "policy and welfare implications of climate change."

That subject remains a major interest. Its relevance to my Prize is that mobilizing to do something about prospective global warming and climate change is what I expect to be, during this century, what nuclear arms control was during the century just past, namely an immense challenge to "cooperation amid conflict." My latest thoughts on the subject can be found in the 2006 book mentioned above.

In 1990 I retired from Harvard and accepted appointment as Distinguished University Professor at the University of Maryland, in the Department of Economics and the School of Public Policy. I continued my interest in nuclear weapons policy, climate change, commitment, and terrorism, the latter interest stimulated by another invitation to participate in a committee of the National Academy of Sciences, the National Academy of Engineering, and the Institute of Medicine, the Committee on Science and Engineering for Counterterrorism, two months after September 11, 2001.

As I reflect on my career I am struck with how much of what I am pleased to have accomplished was initiated by good luck and by the initiative of others. During the War, deemed unfit for military service by the Army and the Navy, I landed a superb job in the Bureau of the Budget; with that experience I was admitted to Harvard Graduate School with a teaching fellowship; I was invited to join the Marshall Plan and my boss took me to Copenhagen; from there to Paris and from there to the White House. RAND was by unsolicited invitation. The Kennedy Administration drew colleagues into influential positions and gave me access to senior officials. National Academy of Sciences committees approached me unexpected. I've had all the advantages. And now the Bank of Sweden Prize in Economic Sciences in Memory of Alfred Nobel promises more opportunities.

AN ASTONISHING SIXTY YEARS: THE LEGACY OF HIROSHIMA

Prize Lecture, December 8, 2005

by

THOMAS C. SCHELLING

Department of Economics and School of Public Policy, University of Maryland, College Park, MD 20742, USA.

The most spectacular event of the past half century is one that did not occur. We have enjoyed sixty years without nuclear weapons exploded in anger.

What a stunning achievement – or, if not achievement, what stunning good fortune. In 1960 the British novelist C. P. Snow said on the front page of the New York Times that unless the nuclear powers drastically reduced their nuclear armaments thermonuclear warfare within the decade was a "mathematical certainty." Nobody appeared to think Snow's statement extravagant.

We now have that mathematical certainty compounded more than four times, and no nuclear war. Can we make it through another half dozen decades?

There has never been any doubt about the military effectiveness of nuclear weapons or their potential for terror. A large part of the credit for their not having been used must be due to the "taboo" that Secretary of State Dulles perceived to have attached itself to these weapons as early as 1953, a taboo that the Secretary deplored.

The weapons remain under a curse, a now much heavier curse than the one that bothered Dulles in the early 1950s. These weapons are unique, and a large part of their uniqueness derives from their being *perceived* as unique. We call most of the others "conventional," and that word has two distinct senses. One is "ordinary, familiar, traditional," a word that can be applied to food, clothing, or housing. The more interesting sense of "conventional" is something that arises as if by compact, by agreement, by *convention.* It is simply an established *convention* that nuclear weapons are different.

True, their fantastic scale of destruction dwarfs the conventional weapons. But as early as the end of the Eisenhower administration nuclear weapons could be made smaller in explosive yield than the largest conventional explosives. There were military planners to whom "little" nuclear weapons appeared untainted by the taboo that they thought ought properly to attach only to weapons of a size associated with Hiroshima, or Bikini. But by then nuclear weapons had become a breed apart; size was no excuse from the curse.

This attitude, or convention, or tradition, that took root and grew over these past five decades, is an asset to be treasured. It is not guaranteed to survive; and some possessors or potential possessors of nuclear weapons may not share the convention. How to preserve this inhibition, what kinds of policies or activities may threaten it, how the inhibition may be broken or dissolved, and what institutional arrangements may support or weaken it, deserves serious attention. How the inhibition arose, whether it was inevitable, whether it was the result of careful design, whether luck was involved, and whether we should assess it as robust or vulnerable in the coming decades, is worth examining. Preserving this tradition, and if possible helping to extend it to other countries that may yet acquire nuclear weapons, is as important as extending the Nuclear Non-Proliferation Treaty, now being renegotiated after its first twenty-five years.

The first occasion when these weapons might have been used was early in the Korean war. Americans and South Koreans had retreated to a perimeter around the southern coastal city of Pusan and appeared in danger of being unable either to hold out or to evacuate. The nuclear-weapons issue arose in public discussion in this country and in the British parliament. Clement Atlee flew to Washington to beseech President Truman not to use nuclear weapons in Korea. The visit and its purpose were both public and publicized. The House of Commons, considering itself to have been a partner in the enterprise that produced nuclear weapons, considered it legitimate that Britain have a voice in the American decision.

The successful landing at Inchon mooted the question whether nuclear weapons might have been used if the situation in the Pusan perimeter had become desperate enough. But at least the question of nuclear use had come up, and the upshot was in the negative.

There may be more than enough reasons to explain the non-use at that time in Korea. But I do not recall that an important consideration, for the U.S. government or the U.S. public, was apprehension of the consequences of demonstrating that nuclear weapons were "usable," of preempting the possibility of cultivating a tradition of non-use.

Nuclear weapons again went unused in the disaster brought by the entry of Chinese armies, and were still unused during the bloody war of attrition that accompanied the Panmunjom negotiations. Whether they would have been used, and where and how they might have been used, had the war ground on for many more months, and what the subsequent history would have been had they been used in North Korea or in China at that time is of course speculative. Whether the threat of nuclear weapons, presumably in China rather than on the battlefield, influenced the truce negotiations remains unclear.

McGeorge Bundy's book, *Danger and Survival: Choices About the Bomb in the First Fifty Years* (1), documents the fascinating story of President Eisenhower and Secretary of State Dulles and nuclear weapons. At the National Security Council on February 11, 1953, "Secretary Dulles discussed the moral problem in the inhibitions on the use of the A-bomb … It was his opinion that we should break down this false distinction" (p. 241). I do not know of any analysis of that time within the government of actions that might tend to break down the distinction and what actions or inactions would preserve and strengthen it. But evidently the Secretary believed, and may have taken for granted that the entire National Security Council believed, that the restraints were real even if the distinction was false, and that the restraint was not to be welcomed.

Again on October 7, 1953, Dulles: "Somehow or other we must manage to remove the taboo from the use of these weapons" (p. 249). Just a few weeks later the President approved, in a Basic National Security document, the statement, "In the event of hostilities, the United States will consider nuclear weapons to be as available for use as other munitions" (p. 246). This statement surely has to be read as more rhetorical than factual. Taboos are not easily dispelled by pronouncing them extinct, even in the mind of one who does the pronouncing. Six months later at a restricted NATO meeting the U.S. position was that nuclear weapons "must now be treated as in fact having become conventional" (p. 268). Again, saying so cannot make it so; tacit conventions are sometimes harder to destroy than explicit ones, existing in potentially recalcitrant minds rather than on destructible paper.

According to Bundy, the last public statement in this progress of nuclear weapons toward conventional status occurred during the Quemoy crisis. On March 12, 1955, Eisenhower said, in answer to a question, "In any combat where these things can be used on strictly military targets and for strictly military purposes, I see no reason why they shouldn't be used just exactly as you would use a bullet or anything else" (p. 278). Bundy's judgment, which I share, is that this again was more an exhortation than a policy decision.

Was Ike really ready to use nuclear weapons to defend Quemoy, or Taiwan itself? It turned out he didn't have to. The conspicuous shipment of nuclear artillery to Taiwan was surely intended as a threat. Bluffing would have been risky from Dulles' point of view; leaving nuclear weapons unused while the Chinese conquered Taiwan would have engraved the taboo in granite. At the same time, Quemoy may have appeared to Dulles as a superb opportunity to dispel the taboo. Using short range nuclear weapons in a purely defensive mode, solely against offensive troops, especially at sea or on beachheads devoid of civilians, might have been something that Eisenhower would have been willing to authorize and that European allies would have approved, and nuclear weapons might have proved that they could be used "just exactly as you would use a bullet or anything else." The Chinese did not offer the opportunity.

On the status of nuclear weapons, the Kennedy and Johnson administrations were a sharp contrast to the Eisenhower. There was also a change in roles within the Cabinet. Hardly anybody born after World War II remembers the name of Eisenhower's Secretary of Defense, Charles Wilson. But most who have studied any American history know the name of John Foster Dulles. A bit of research with Bundy's book shows the contrast. In Bundy's index there are 31 references to Dulles, 2 to Charles Wilson. Under Kennedy and Johnson the score is reversed: 42 references to Secretary of Defense Robert McNamara, 12 to Secretary of State Dean Rusk.

The anti-nuclear movement in the Kennedy administration was led from the Pentagon and in 1962 McNamara began his campaign – his and President Kennedy's – to reduce reliance on nuclear defense in Europe by building expensive conventional forces in NATO. During the next couple of years McNamara became associated with the idea that nuclear weapons were not "useable" at all in the sense that Eisenhower and Dulles had intended. Undoubtedly the traumatic October of 1962 contributed to the revulsion against nuclear weapons of some of Kennedy's key advisors and Kennedy himself.

The contrast between the Eisenhower and Kennedy-Johnson attitudes toward nuclear weapons is beautifully summarized in a statement of Johnson's in September 1964. "Make no mistake. There is no such thing as a conventional nuclear weapon. For 19 peril-filled years no nation has loosed the atom against another. To do so now is a political decision of the highest order" (2). That statement disposed of the notion that nuclear weapons were to be judged by their military effectiveness. It disposed of Dulles' "false distinction": "A political decision of the highest order" compared with "as available for use as other munitions."

I am particularly impressed by the "19 peril-filled years." Johnson implied that for 19 years the United States had resisted the temptation to do what Dulles had wanted the United States to be free to do where nuclear weapons were concerned. He implied that the United States, or collectively the United States and other nuclear weapon states, had an investment, accumulated over 19 years, in the non-use of nuclear weapons; and those 19 years of quarantine for nuclear weapons were part of what would make any decision to use those weapons a political one of the highest order.

It is worth a pause here to consider just what might be the literal meaning of "no such thing as a conventional nuclear weapon." Specifically, why couldn't a nuclear bomb no larger than the largest blockbuster of World War II be considered conventional, or a nuclear depth charge of modest explosive power for use against submarines far at sea, or nuclear land mines to halt advancing tanks or to cause landslides in mountain passes? What could be so awful about using three "small" atomic bombs to save the besieged French at Dien Bien Phu as was discussed at the time? What so wrong about using nuclear costal artillery against a communist Chinese invasion flotilla in the Gulf of Taiwan?

There are two answers that this question has received, one mainly instinctive, the other somewhat analytical, but both resting on a belief, or a feeling – a feeling somewhat beyond reach by analysis – that nuclear weapons were simply different, and generically different. The more intuitive response can probably best be formulated, "If you have to ask that question you wouldn't understand the answer." The generic character of everything nuclear was simply – as logicians might call it – a primitive, an axiom; and analysis was as unnecessary as it was futile.

The other, more analytical, response took its argument from legal reasoning, diplomacy, bargaining theory, and theory of training and discipline, including self discipline. This argument emphasized bright lines, slippery slopes, well defined boundaries, and the stuff of which traditions and implicit conventions are made. (The analogy to "one little drink" for a recovering alcoholic was sometimes heard.) But both lines of argument arrived at the same conclusion: nuclear weapons, once introduced into combat, could not, or probably would not, be contained, confined, limited.

Sometimes the argument was explicit that no matter how small the weapons initially used the size of weapons would ineluctably escalate, there being no natural stopping place. Sometimes the argument was that the military needed to be disciplined, and once they were allowed any weapons it would be impossible to stop their escalation.

The "neutron bomb" is illustrative. This is a bomb, or potential bomb, that, because it is very small and because of the materials of which it is constructed, emits "prompt neutrons" that can be lethal at a distance at which blast and thermal radiation are comparatively moderate. As advertised, it kills people without great damage to structures. The issue of producing and deploying this kind of weapon arose during the Carter Administration, evoking an anti-nuclear reaction that caused it to be left on the drawing board. But the same bomb – at least, the same idea – had been the subject of even more intense debate 15 years earlier, and it was there that the argument was honed that was ready to be used again in the 1970s. The argument was simple; and it was surely valid, whether or not it deserved to be decisive. It was that it was important not to blur the distinction – the firebreak, as it was called – between nuclear and conventional weapons; and either because of its low yield or because of its "benign" kind of lethality it was feared, and it was argued, that there would be a strong temptation to use this weapon where nuclears were otherwise not allowed, and that the use of this weapon would erode the threshold, blur the firebreak, pave the way by incremental steps for nuclear escalation.

The argument is not altogether different from that against so-called peaceful nuclear explosion (PNE's). The decisive argument against PNE's was that they would accustom the world to nuclear explosions, undermining the belief that nuclear explosions were inherently evil and reducing the inhibitions on nuclear weapons. The prospect of blasting new river beds in northern Russia or a bypass canal for the waters of the Nile, or harbors in developing countries, generated concern about "legitimizing" nuclear explosions.

A revealing demonstration of this antipathy was in the universal rejection by American arms controllers and energy-policy analysts of the prospect of an ecologically clean source of electrical energy, proposed in the 1970s, that would have detonated tiny thermonuclear bombs in underground caverns to generate steam. I have seen this idea unanimously dismissed without argument, as if the objections were too obvious to require articulation. As far as I could tell the objection was always that even "good" thermonuclear explosions were bad and should be kept that way. (I can imagine President Eisenhower: "In any energy crisis where these things can be used on strictly civilian sites for strictly civilian purposes I see no reason why they shouldn't be used just exactly as you would use a barrel of oil or anything else." And

Dulles: "Somehow or other we must manage to remove the taboo from the use of these clean thermonuclear energy sources.")

But it is important not to think that nuclear weapons alone have this character of being generically different, and independently of quantity or size. Gas was not used in World War II. The Eisenhower-Dulles argument could have applied to gas: "In any combat where these gases can be used on strictly military targets and for strictly military purposes, I see no reason why they shouldn't be used just exactly as you would use a bullet or anything else." But as Supreme Commander of the Allied Expeditionary Forces, General Eisenhower, as far as we know, never proposed any such policy. Maybe if, at the time, he had been put through the exercise he would have convinced himself, not that gas should never be used but that gas was at least different from bullets, and decisions on its use raised new strategic issues. And ten years later he might have recalled that line of thinking when, I think reluctantly, he let his secretary of state urge doing for nuclear weapons what Eisenhower apparently never thought of doing for gas in the European theater.

Some other things have this all-or-none quality in warfare. Nationality is one. The Chinese did not visibly intervene in the Korean war until it was time to intervene in force. American military aid personnel have always been cautioned to avoid appearing to engage in anything that could be construed as combat, the notion being that contamination could not be contained. There was some consideration of American intervention in Indochina at the time of Dien Bien Phu, but not on the ground; and in the air it was thought that reconnaissance would count less as "intervention" than would bombing. There is typically the notion that to provide equipment is much less participatory than to provide military manpower; we arm the Israeli and provide ammunition even in wartime, but so much as a company of American infantry would be perceived as a greater act of participation in the war than $5 billion worth of fuel, ammunition, and spare parts.

I mention all this to suggest that there are perceptual and symbolic phenomena that persist and recur and that help to make the nuclear phenomenon less puzzling. And I find it remarkable how these perceptual constraints and inhibitions cross cultural boundaries. During the Chinese phase of the Korean war the U.S. never bombed airbases in China; the "rules" were that Chinese bombing sorties originated from North Korea, and to abide by the rules Chinese aircraft originating in Manchuria touched wheels down at North Korean airstrips on the way to bombing their American targets. That reminds us that national territory is like nationality: crossing the Yalu, on the ground or in the air, is a qualitative discontinuity. Had General MacArthur succeeded in conquering all of North Korea, even he could not have proposed that penetrating just "a little bit" into China proper wouldn't have mattered much because it was only a little bit.

Still, these qualitative all-or-none kinds of thresholds are often susceptible to undermining. A Dulles who wishes the taboo were not there may not only attempt to get around it when it is important, but may apply ingenuity to dissolving the barrier on occasions when it may not matter much, in anticipation of later opportunities when the barrier would be a genuine embarrassment. Bundy suggests that in discussing the possibility of atomic bombs in defense of Dien Bien Phu Dulles and Admiral Radford, the Chairman of the Joint Chiefs of Staff, had in mind not only the local value in Indochina but the use of Dien Bien Phu in "making the use of atomic bombs internationally acceptable," a purpose that Dulles and Radford shared.

The aversion to nuclear weapons – one might even say the abhorrence of them – can grow in strength and become locked into military doctrine even without being fully appreciated, or even acknowledged. The Kennedy administration launched an aggressive campaign for conventional defenses in Europe on grounds that nuclear weapons certainly should not be used, and probably would not be used, in the event of a war in Europe. Throughout the 1960s the official Soviet line was to deny the possibility of a non-nuclear engagement in Europe. Yet the Soviets spent great amounts of money developing non-nuclear capabilities in Europe, especially aircraft capable of delivering conventional bombs. This expensive capability would have been utterly useless in the event of any war that was bound to become nuclear. It reflects a tacit Soviet acknowledgement that both sides might be capable of non-nuclear war and that both sides had an interest, an interest worth a lot of money, in keeping war non-nuclear – keeping it non-nuclear by having the capability of fighting a non-nuclear war.

Arms control is so often identified with limitations on the possession or deployment of weapons that it is often overlooked that this reciprocated investment in non-nuclear capability was a remarkable instance of unacknowledged but reciprocated arms control. It is not only potential restraint in the use of nuclear weapons; it is investment in a configuration of weapons to make them capable of non-nuclear combat. It reminds us that the inhibitions on "first use" may be powerful without declarations, even powerful while one party refuses to recognize its own participation for what it is.

With the possible exception of the Anti-Ballistic-Missile treaty, this conventional buildup in Europe was the most important east-west arms understanding until the demise of the Soviet Union. It was genuine arms control, even if inexplicit, even if denied – as real as if the two sides had signed a treaty obliging them, in the interest of fending off nuclear war, to put large amounts of treasure and manpower into conventional forces. The investment in restraints on the use of nuclear weapons was real as well as symbolic.

That the Soviets had absorbed this nuclear inhibition was dramatically demonstrated during their protracted campaign in Afghanistan. I never read or heard public discussion about the possibility that the Soviet Union might shatter the tradition of non-use to avoid a costly and humiliating defeat in that primitive country. The inhibitions on use of nuclear weapons are such common knowledge, the attitude is so confidently shared, that not only would the use of nuclear weapons in Afghanistan have been almost universally deplored, it wouldn't even have been thought of.

But part of that may be because President Johnson's nineteen-year nuclear silence had stretched into a fourth and then a fifth decade, and everyone in responsibility was aware that that unbroken tradition was a treasure we held in common. "We have to ask, could that tradition, once broken, have mended itself? Had Truman used nuclear weapons during the Chinese onslaught in Korea, would Nixon have been as impressed in 1970 by the nineteen-year hiatus as Johnson was in 1964? Had Nixon used nuclear weapons, even ever so sparingly, in Viet Nam would the Soviets have eschewed their use in Afghanistan, and Margaret Thatcher in the Falklands? Had Nixon used nuclear weapons in 1969 or 1970, would the Israeli have resisted the temptation against the Egyptian beachheads north of the Suez canal in 1973? "

The answer surely is that we do not know. One possibility is that the horror of Hiroshima and Nagasaki would have repeated itself and the curse would have descended again with even more weight. The other possibility is that, the long silence broken, nuclear weapons would have emerged as militarily effective instruments and, especially used unilaterally against an adversary who had none, a blessing that might have reduced casualties on both sides of the war as some think the bomb on Hiroshima did. Much might have depended on the care with which weapons were confined to military targets or used in demonstrably "defensive" modes.

We were spared from temptation in the Gulf in 1991. Iraq was known to possess, and to have been willing to use, "unconventional" weapons – chemicals. Had chemical weapons been used with devastating effect on U. S. forces the issue of appropriate response would have posed the nuclear question. I am confident that had the president, in that circumstance, deemed it essential to escalate from conventional weapons, battlefield nuclear weapons would have been the military choice. Nuclear weapons are what the Army, Navy, and Air Force are trained and equipped to use; their effects in different kinds of weather and terrain are well understood. The military profession traditionally despises poison. There would have been strong temptation to respond with the kind of unconventional weapon we know best how to use. To have done so would have ended the forty-five peril-filled years. We can hope no president has to face such a "political decision of the highest order." I've no doubt any president would recognize that that was the kind of decision he was facing.

I have devoted this much attention to where we are and how we got here with the status of nuclear weapons in the belief that the development of that status is as important as the development of nuclear arsenals has been. The non proliferation effort, concerned with the development, production, and deployment of nuclear weapons, has been more successful than most authorities can claim to have anticipated; the accumulating weight of tradition against nuclear use I consider no less impressive and no less valuable. We depend on non proliferation efforts to restrain the production and deployment of weapons by more and more countries; we may depend even more on universally shared inhibitions on nuclear use. Preserving those inhibitions and extending them, if we know how, to cultures and national interests that may not currently share those inhibitions will be a crucial part of our nuclear policy.

I quote from an editorial that Alvin M. Weinberg, the distinguished nuclear physicist, wrote on the 40th anniversary of Hiroshima and Nagasaki in the

Bulletin of the Atomic Scientists. After saying that he had always been convinced that both American and Japanese lives were saved by the use of the bomb in Japan, he gives another reason for his belief that Hiroshima (but not Nagasaki) was fortunate. "Are we witnessing a gradual sanctification of Hiroshima – that is, the elevation of the Hiroshima event to the status of a profoundly mystical event, an event ultimately of the same religious force as biblical events? I cannot prove it, but I am convinced that the 40th Anniversary of Hiroshima, with its vast outpouring of concern, its huge demonstrations, its wide media coverage, bears resemblance to the observance of major religious holidays ... This sanctification of Hiroshima is one of the most hopeful developments of the nuclear era."

A crucial question is whether the anti-nuclear instinct so exquisitely expressed by Weinberg is confined to "western" culture. I believe the set of attitudes and expectations about nuclear weapons is more recognizably widespread among the people and the elites of the developed countries; and as we look to North Korea, Iran, or others as potential wielders of nuclear weapons we cannot be sure that they inherit this tradition with any great force. But it is reassuring that in the same way we had no assurance that the leadership of the Soviet Union would inherit the same tradition or participate in cultivating that tradition. Not many of us in the 1950s or 60s would have thought that were the Soviet Union to engage in war, and lose a war, in Afghanistan it would behave there as if nuclear weapons did not exist.

We can be grateful to them for behaving that way in Afghanistan, adding one more to the list of bloody wars in which nuclear weapons were not used. Forty years ago we might have thought that the Soviet leadership would be immune to the spirit of Hiroshima as expressed by Weinberg, immune to the popular revulsion that John Foster Dulles did not share, immune to the overhang of all those peril-filled years that awed President Johnson. In any attempt to extrapolate western nuclear attitudes toward the areas of the world where nuclear proliferation begins to frighten us, the remarkable conformity of Soviet and Western ideology is a reassuring point of departure.

An immediate question is whether we can expect Indian and Pakistani leaders to be adequately in awe of the nuclear weapons they now both possess. There are two helpful possibilities. One is that they share the inhibition – appreciate the taboo – that I have been discussing. The other is that they will recognize, as the United States and the Soviet Union did, that the prospect of nuclear retaliation made any initiation of nuclear war nearly unthinkable.

The instances of non-use of nuclear weapons that I've discussed were, in every case, possible use against a non-possessor. The non-use by the USA and the USSR was differently motivated: the prospect of nuclear retaliation made any initiation appear unwise except in the worst imaginable military emergency, and that kind of military emergency never offered the temptation. The experience of the USA-USSR confrontation may impress Indians and Pakistanis; the greatest risk is that one or the other may confront the kind of military emergency that invites some limited experiment with the weapons, and there is no history to tell us, or to tell them, what happens next.

Most recently there is the concern that Iran and North Korea may acquire, or may already have acquired, some modest number of nuclear explosives. (Libya appears to have withdrawn from contention.) Great diplomatic skill and international cooperation will be required to suppress or discourage their interest in acquiring such weapons. Equally great skill, or greater, will be required to create or enhance the expectations and institutions that inhibit the use of such weapons.

Those nineteen years have stretched to sixty. The taboo that Ike appeared to denigrate, or pretended to denigrate, but that awed President Johnson a decade later, has become a powerful tradition of nearly universal recognition.

The next possessors of nuclear weapons may be Iran, North Korea, or possibly some terrorist bodies. Is there any hope that they will have absorbed the nearly universal inhibition against the use of nuclear weapons, or will at least be inhibited by the recognition that the taboo enjoys widespread acclaim?

Part of the answer will depend on whether the United States recognizes that inhibition, and especially on whether the United States recognizes it as an asset to be cherished, enhanced, and protected or, like John Foster Dulles in Eisenhower's cabinet, believes "somehow or other we must manage to remove the taboo from the use of these weapons."

There is much discussion these days of whether or not "deterrence" has had its day and no longer has much of a role in America's security. There is no Soviet Union to deter; the Russians are more worried about Chechnya than about the United States; the Chinese seem no more interested in military risks over Taiwan than Khrushchev really was over Berlin; and terrorists cannot be deterred anyway – we don't know what they value that we might threaten, or who or where it is.

I expect that we may come to a new respect for deterrence. If Iran should, despite every diplomatic effort or economic pressure to prevent it, acquire a few nuclear weapons, we may discover again what it is like to be the deterred one, not the one doing the deterring. (I consider us – NATO at the time – as having been deterred from intervening in Hungary in 1956 and Czechoslovakia in 1968.) I also consider it crucial that Iran' leaders, civilian and military, learn to think, if they have not already learned to think, in terms of deterrence.

What else can Iran accomplish, except possibly the destruction of its own system, with a few nuclear warheads? Nuclear weapons should be too precious to give away or to sell, to precious to waste killing people when they could, held in reserve, make the United States, or Russia, or any other nation, hesitant to consider military action. What nuclear weapons have been used for, effectively, successfully, for sixty years has not been on the battlefield nor on population targets: they have been used for influence.

What about terrorists? Any organization that gets enough fissile material to make a bomb will require many highly qualified scientists, technologists, machinists, working in seclusion away from families and occupations for months with nothing much to talk about except what their A-bomb might be good for, for whom. They are likely to feel justified, by their contribution, to have some claim on participating in any decisions on the use of the device. (The British Parliament in 1950 considered itself, as partner in the development of the atomic bomb, qualified to advise President Truman on any possible use of the bomb in Korea.)

They will conclude – I hope they will conclude – over weeks of arguing, that the most effective use of the bomb, from a terrorist perspective, will be for influence. Possessing a workable nuclear weapon, if they can demonstrate possession – and I expect they will be able to without actually detonating it – will give them something of the status of a nation. Threatening to use it against military targets, and keeping it intact if the threat is successful, may appeal to them more than expending it in a purely destructive act. Even terrorists may consider destroying large numbers of people as less satisfying than keeping a major nation at bay.

The United States was slow to learn, but learned eventually (1961), that nuclear warheads require exceptionally secure custody – against accident, mischief, theft, sabotage, or a Strangelove-like unauthorized adventure. There is always a dilemma: reward violators of the Nonproliferation Treaty by offering the technology to keep the warheads secure, or withhold the technology and let the weapons be less secure. At least we can try to help educate the new members of the nuclear club to what the United States did not appreciate for its first fifteen years as a nuclear power.

I know of no argument in favor of the Comprehensive Test Ban Treaty, which the Senate rejected in 1999, more powerful than the potential of that treaty to enhance the nearly universal revulsion against nuclear weapons. The symbolic effect of nearly 200 nations ratifying the CTBT, which is nominally only about testing, should add enormously to the convention that nuclear weapons are not to be used and that any nations that does use nuclear weapons will be judged the violator of the legacy of Hiroshima. I never heard that argument made on either side of the debate over the Treaty. When the Treaty is again before the Senate, as I hope it will be, this major potential benefit should not go unrecognized.

The most critical question about nuclear weapons for the United States Government is whether the widespread taboo against nuclear weapons and its inhibition on their use is in our favor or against us. If it is in the American interest, as I believe obvious, advertising a continued dependence on nuclear weapons, i.e. a U. S. readiness to use them, a U. S. need for new nuclear capabilities (and new nuclear tests) – let alone ever using them against an enemy – has to be weighed against the corrosive effect on a nearly universal attitude that has been cultivated through universal abstinence of sixty years.

REFERENCES:

1. Bundy, McGeorge, *Danger and Survival: Choices About the Bomb in the First Fifty Years*, New York, Random House, Inc., 1988.
2. New York Times, September 8, 1964, p. 18.

Portrait photo of Thomas C. Schelling by photographer T. Zadig.